Endangered Birds

Management Techniques
for Preserving Threatened Species

DIANE PIERCE '77 ©

Proceedings of the
Symposium on Management Techniques for
Preserving Endangered Birds

1977
University of Wisconsin-Madison

Supported by
The U.S. Fish and Wildlife Service
The National Audubon Society
The New York Zoological Society
The World Wildlife Fund
The International Council for Bird Preservation

Endangered Birds

Management Techniques
for Preserving Threatened Species

Edited by Stanley A. Temple

The University of Wisconsin Press
Croom Helm Limited

Published in the United States and Canada by
The University of Wisconsin Press
Box 1379, Madison, Wisconsin 53701
ISBN 0-299-07520-6

Published in the United Kingdom and Continent of Europe by
Croom Helm Ltd
2-10 St John's Road, London SW 11
ISBN 0 85664-831-0

First printing 1978
Printed in the United States of America

For Library of Congress and British Library
Cataloging in Publication data see the colophon

Publication of this book has been made possible in part
by a grant from the U.S. Fish and Wildlife Service

Contributors

George W. Archibald
International Crane Foundation
City View Road
Baraboo, Wisconsin 53913

Harry Armbruster
Canadian Wildlife Service
10025 Jasper Avenue
Edmonton, Alberta T5J 1S6

Ursula Banasch
Canadian Wildlife Service
10025 Jasper Avenue
Edmonton, Alberta T5J 1S6

Jonathan Bart
New York Cooperative Wildlife
  Research Unit
Cornell University
Ithaca, New York 14853

Lizzanne J. Beaver
Canadian Wildlife Service
10025 Jasper Avenue
Edmonton, Alberta T5J 1S6

Andrew J. Berger
Department of Zoology
University of Hawaii
Honolulu, Hawaii 96822

Elwood G. Bizeau
Idaho Cooperative Wildlife
  Research Unit
University of Idaho
Moscow, Idaho 83843

G. Vernon Byrd
U.S. Fish and Wildlife Service
Aleutian Islands National Wild-
  life Refuge
Adak, Alaska 98791

Tom J. Cade
Section of Ecology and System-
  atics
Division of Biological Sciences
Cornell University
Ithaca, New York 14853

William G. Conway
New York Zoological Society
Bronx Park
Bronx, New York 10460

Kendall W. Corbin
Bell Museum of Natural History
  and Department of Ecology and
  Behavioral Biology
University of Minnesota
Minneapolis, Minnesota 55455

Carter Denniston
Laboratory of Genetics
University of Wisconsin
Madison, Wisconsin 53706

Steven J. Dobrott
Department of Wildlife Ecology
University of Arizona
Tucson, Arizona 85721

Roderick C. Drewien
Idaho Cooperative Wildlife
  Research Unit
University of Idaho
Moscow, Idaho 83843

David H. Ellis
U.S. Fish and Wildlife Service
Patuxent Wildlife Research Center
Laurel, Maryland 20810

J.A. Douglas Flack
RFD 2
Enosburg, Vermont 05450

Richard W. Fyfe
Canadian Wildlife Service
10025 Jasper Avenue
Edmonton, Alberta T5J 1S6

John G. Goodwin, Jr.
Department of Wildlife Ecology
University of Arizona
Tucson, Arizona 85721

Björn Helander
The Swedish Society for the
  Conservation of Nature
Kungsholms Strand 125
Stockholm, Sweden

Udo Hirsch
Theodor Brauer Strasse 35
Cologne 80, West Germany

Jerome A. Jackson
Department of Zoology
Mississippi State University
Mississippi State, Mississippi
  39762

Janet Kear
The Wildfowl Trust
Martin Mere
Burscough, Ormskirk
Lancashire, England

Cameron B. Kepler
U.S. Fish and Wildlife Service
Haleakala Field Station
Kula, Maui, Hawaii 96790

Warren B. King
International Council for Bird
  Preservation
Smithsonian Institution
Washington, D.C. 20560

Stephen W. Kress
Laboratory of Ornithology
Cornell University
Ithaca, New York 14850

Anne LaBastille
West of the Wind Publications
Big Moose, New York 13331

Thomas E. Lovejoy
World Wildlife Fund
1319 18th Street
Washington, D.C. 20036

David B. Marshall
Endangered Species Program
U.S. Fish and Wildlife Service
Portland, Oregon 97208

Harold F. Mayfield
9235 River Road
Waterville, Ohio 43566

Donald A. McCrimmon, Jr.
National Audubon Society and
Laboratory of Ornithology
Cornell University
Ithaca, New York 14850

Donald V. Merton
New Zealand Wildlife Service
Wellington, New Zealand

Bernd-Ulrich Meyburg
Free University Berlin
Berlin, West Germany

Richard S. Miller
School of Forestry and
 Environmental Studies
Yale University
New Haven, Connecticut 06511

Eugene S. Morton
National Zoological Park
Smithsonian Institution
Washington, D.C. 20009

Holly A.J. Nichols
10611 Mount Boracho Drive
San Antonio, Texas 78213

Ian C.T. Nisbet
Massachusetts Audubon Society
South Great Road
Lincoln, Massachusetts 01773

Richard R. Olendorff
Bureau of Land Management
2800 Cottage Way
Sacramento, California 95825

Richard L. Plunkett
National Audubon Society
950 Third Avenue
New York, New York 10022

Sergej Postupalsky
Department of Wildlife Ecology
University of Wisconsin
Madison, Wisconsin 53706

Keith M. Schreiner
U.S. Fish and Wildlife Service
Washington, D.C. 20240

Ulysses S. Seal
International Species Inventory
 System
Minnesota Zoological Garden
Apple Valley, Minnesota 55124
      and
Veterans Administration Hospital
Minneapolis, Minnesota 55417

Clare J. Senecal
U.S. Fish and Wildlife Service
Washington, D.C. 20240

Noel F.R. Snyder
U.S. Fish and Wildlife Service
Patuxent Wildlife Research Center
Laurel, Maryland 20811

Paul R. Spitzer
Section of Ecology and System-
 atics
Division of Biological Sciences
Cornell University
Ithaca, New York 14853

Paul F. Springer
U.S. Fish and Wildlife Service
Wildlife Research Station
Humboldt State University
Arcata, California 95521

John D. Taapken
U.S. Forest Service
Box 21
Palmer, Puerto Rico 00721

Stanley A. Temple
Department of Wildlife Ecology
University of Wisconsin
Madison, Wisconsin 53706

Sanford R. Wilbur
U.S. Fish and Wildlife Service
California Field Station
Ojai, California 93023

David B. Wingate
Department of Agriculture and
 Fisheries
Box 834
Hamilton 5, Bermuda

Dennis W. Woolington
Department of Wildlife Management
Humboldt State University
Arcata, California 95521

Yoshimaro Yamashina
Yamashina Institute for Ornith-
 ology
8-20 Nampeidai-machi
Shibuya-ku
Tokyo, Japan

William D. Zeedyk
U.S. Forest Service
Box 2417
Washington, D.C. 20013

Lawrence Zeleny
4312 Van Buren Street
University Park
Hyattsville, Maryland 20782

Contents

Preface   *xxi*

PART I: ENDANGERED BIRD PROBLEMS AND

THE CONCEPT OF MANAGING THREATENED SPECIES

1.   The Concept of Managing Endangered Birds   3

   Stanley A. Temple

2.   Endangered Birds of the World and Current Efforts
     toward Managing Them   9

   Warren B. King

3.   The American Government's Programs for Endangered
     Birds   19

   Keith M. Schreiner and Clare J. Senecal

PART II: INCREASING REPRODUCTIVE EFFORT AND

SUCCESS BY REDUCING NEST-SITE LIMITATIONS

4.   Increasing Reproductive Effort and Success by
     Reducing Nest-Site Limitations: A Review   27

        Noel F.R. Snyder

5.   Artificial Nesting Platforms for Ospreys and Bald
     Eagles   35

        Sergej Postupalsky

6.   Puerto Rican Parrots and Nest-Site Scarcity   47

        Noel F.R. Snyder

7.   Nesting Box Programs for Bluebirds and Other
     Passerines   55

        Lawrence Zeleny

8.   Artificial Nest Ledges for Bald Ibises   61

        Udo Hirsch

9.   Improving Oilbird Nesting Ledges in Trinidad   71

        William G. Conway

          PART III: ALLEVIATING PROBLEMS OF COMPETITION,

                  PREDATION, PARASITISM AND DISEASE

10. Alleviating Problems of Competition, Predation,
     Parasitism, and Disease in Endangered Birds   75

        Jerome A. Jackson

11. Brood Parasitism: Reducing Interactions between
     Kirtland's Warblers and Brown-headed Cowbirds   85

        Harold F. Mayfield

12.   Excluding Competitors from Bermuda Petrel
      Nesting Burrows   93

         David B. Wingate

13.   Competition for Cavities and Red-cockaded
      Woodpecker Management   103

         Jerome A. Jackson

14.   Puerto Rican Parrots and Nest Predation by Pearly-
      eyed Thrashers   113

         Noel F.R. Snyder and John D. Taapken

15.   Controlling Introduced Predators and Competitors
      on Islands   121

         Donald V. Merton

PART IV: SUPPLEMENTAL FEEDING AND

MANIPULATION OF FEEDING ECOLOGY

16.   Supplemental Feeding and Manipulation of Feeding
      Ecology of Endangered Birds   131

         George W. Archibald

17.   Supplemental Feeding of California Condors   135

         Sanford R. Wilbur

18.   Winter Feeding Programs for Cranes   141

         George W. Archibald

19.   Feeding White-tailed Sea Eagles in Sweden   149

         Björn Helander

20.   The Feeding of Japanese Crested Ibises   161

         Yoshimaro Yamashina

      PART V: MANIPULATING ASPECTS OF NESTING BIOLOGY

21.   Manipulating the Nesting Biology of Endangered Birds   167

         Tom J. Cade

22.   Osprey Egg and Nestling Transfers: Their Value as
      Ecological Experiments and as Management Procedures   171

         Paul R. Spitzer

23.   Fostering and Cross-fostering of Birds of Prey   183

            *Richard W. Fyfe, Harry Armbruster,
            Ursula Banasch, and Lizzanne J. Beaver*

24.   Sibling Aggression and Cross-fostering of Eagles   195

         Bernd-Ulrich Meyburg

25.   Cross-fostering Whooping Cranes to Sandhill Crane
      Foster Parents   201

            Roderick C. Drewien and Elwood G. Bizeau

      PART VI: CAPTIVE BREEDING OF ENDANGERED BIRDS

26.   Breeding Endangered Birds in Captivity: The Last
      Resort   225

         William G. Conway

27.   Captive Propagation of Whooping Cranes:
      A Behavioral Approach   231

         Cameron B. Kepler

28.   Captive Propagation of Waterfowl   243

         Janet Kear

29.   What Makes Peregrine Falcons Breed in Captivity?   251

Tom J. Cade and Richard W. Fyfe

30.   Captive Breeding Programs for Amazona Parrots   263

Holly A.J. Nichols

PART VII: GENETIC ASPECTS OF

MANAGING DWINDLING BIRD POPULATIONS

31.   Genetic Aspects of Dwindling Populations:
A Review   275

Thomas E. Lovejoy

32.   Small Population Size and Genetic Diversity:
Implications for Endangered Species   281

Carter Denniston

33.   Genetic Diversity in Avian Populations   291

Kendall W. Corbin

34.   The Noah's Ark Problem: Multigeneration Management
of Wild Species in Captivity   303

Ulysses S. Seal

35.   Fitness of Offspring from Captive Populations   315

Andrew J. Berger

PART VIII: REINTRODUCING ENDANGERED BIRDS TO THE WILD

36.   Reintroducing Endangered Birds to the Wild: A Review   323

Richard W. Fyfe

37. Reestablishing Aleutian Canada Geese 331

    Paul F. Springer, G. Vernon Byrd and
    Dennis W. Woolington

38. Reintroduction of Hawaiian Geese 339

    Andrew J. Berger

39. Reintroduction Techniques for Masked Bobwhites 345

    David H. Ellis, Steven J. Dobrott and
    John G. Goodwin, Jr.

40. Reintroducing Birds of Prey to the Wild 355

    Stanley A. Temple

41. Interisland Transfers of New Zealand Black Robins 365

    J.A. Douglas Flack

42. Establishing Atlantic Puffins at a Former Breeding
Site 373

    Stephen W. Kress

43. Reintroducing Recently Extirpated Birds into
a Tropical Forest Preserve 379

    Eugene S. Morton

PART IX: INTEGRATED APPROACHES TO

MANAGEMENT OF ENDANGERED BIRDS

44. Integrated Management of Endangered Birds: A Review 387

    Richard L. Plunkett

45. Management of Giant Pied-billed Grebes on Lake Atitlán 397

    Anne LaBastille

46.   Using the North American Nest Record Card Program
      to Monitor Reproductive Patterns in Raptors   .   403

          Donald A. McCrimmon, Jr. and Jonathan Bart

47.   Population Modeling as an Aid to Designing Management
      Programs   413

          Richard S. Miller

48.   Land Management for the Conservation of Endangered
      Birds   419

          Richard R. Olendorff and William D. Zeedyk

49.   The Recovery Plan Approach to Endangered Species
      Restoration in the United States   429

          David B. Marshall

50.   Manipulating Behavioral Patterns of Endangered
      Birds: A Potential Management Technique   435

          Stanley A. Temple

            PART X: SUMMARY

51.   Concluding Remarks on the Problems of Managing
      Endangered Birds   447

          Ian C.T. Nisbet

Index   453

Illustrations

(following page 200)

PLATE 1. Bald Eagles on nesting platform (photo by S. Postupalsky)

PLATE 2. Dropping an Osprey nest-pole (photo by P. McLain)

PLATE 3. Bald Ibis (photo by U. Hirsch)

PLATE 4. Martin nesting-box (photo by L. Zeleny)

PLATE 5. Bermuda Petrel baffler (photo by Bermuda News Bureau)

PLATE 6. Puerto Rican Parrot (photo by N. Snyder)

PLATE 7. Thrasher-pecked eggs (photo by H. Snyder)

PLATE 8. Thrasher-injured parrot (photo by N. Snyder)

PLATE 9. Nesting boxes (photo N. Snyder)

PLATE 10. Thrasher nest in box (photo by N. Snyder)

PLATE 11. Oilbird on nest (photo by New York Zoological Society)

PLATE 12. Cowbird trap (photo by H. Mayfield)

PLATE 13. Introduced goats (photo by F. Kinsky)

PLATE 14. Red-cockaded woodpecker (photo by J. Jackson)

PLATE 15. Japanese Cranes (photo by G. Archibald)

PLATE 16. California Condors (photo by F. Sibley)

PLATE 17. White-tailed Sea Eagles (photo by B. Helander)

PLATE 18. Osprey eggs (photo by P. Spitzer)

PLATE 19. Lesser Spotted Eagles (photo by B.-U. Meyburg)

PLATE 20. Whooping Crane (photo by R. Drewien)

PLATE 21. Peregrine Falcon (photo by R. Fyfe)

PLATE 22. Whooping Crane chick (photo by U.S. Fish and Wildlife Service)

PLATE 23. Peregrine Falcon eggs (photo by The Peregrine Fund)

PLATE 24. Peregrine Falcon and eggs (photo by The Peregrine Fund)

PLATE 25. Masked Bobwhites (photo by D. Ellis)

PLATE 26. Aleutian Canada Geese (photo by L. Goldman)

PLATE 27. Atlantic Puffins (photo by B. Edinger)

PLATE 28. Captive-produced Peregrine Falcon (photo by P. McLain)

PLATE 29. Giant Pied-billed Grebe (photo by D. Allen)

PLATE 30. Cousin Island Nature Reserve (photo by S. Temple)

PLATE 31. Mauritius Kestrel (photo by R. Chevreau de Montléhu)

Preface

Saving endangered species--particularly endangered birds--has
become the current *cause célèbre* in the field of wildlife conservation. Motivated by both the general heightening of environmental
awareness during the 1960's and the frustrating realization that most
classical wildlife management techniques were less than effective in
stabilizing or increasing the numbers of many rare and endangered
species, wildlife biologists had to seek new solutions to the problems of saving threatened animals. These solutions, of necessity,
had to go far beyond the old standby prescriptions for helping wildlife: legal protection, habitat preservation and education. Instead
it became necessary for biologists to devise highly manipulative procedures that intervened directly into the threatened species' life
cycle at the precise stage where it had proven vulnerable to adverse
environmental pressures. The actual application of such manipulative
techniques has been a fairly recent development--most work having occurred during the past 10 years. Owing to the rapid development and
proliferation of these management techniques, there has been a certain
amount of skepticism and reluctance to accept such procedures as
scientifically sound and justifiable. Nonetheless, the initial results of many pioneering efforts at managing endangered species
have been encouraging.

One reason for skepticism is that most manipulative techniques
that have been employed are "crisis" management procedures. They
often have the potential for preventing an imminent extinction when
all else seems futile, but in the long-run they will not succeed in
securing a safe future for the threatened species unless the environmental problems that placed the species in jeopardy are simultaneously corrected. The manipulative management techniques are not,
therefore, a final solution to conservation problems, but there is
little doubt that they can save species from extinction.

Because contemporary society views endangered species as both evocative and worth saving, much attention has been given to endangered species research in the popular literature. The triumphs and setbacks of such programs have become media events. Nonetheless, there has not been concomitant attention given to the subject in scientific literature. To date, the scholarly treatment of endangered species management has been restricted to a few conferences devoted to specific taxonomic groups or to special techniques such as captive breeding. The only overall coverage of current management efforts for endangered birds has been a semi-popular book.

The management of endangered species is now an established subdiscipline of applied ecology, and as such, it demands scholarly review by the scientific community. To this end, I organized an international symposium on management techniques for preserving endangered birds. The present volume is based on papers presented at this symposium which was jointly sponsored by the International Council for Bird Preservation, the World Wildlife Fund, the National Audubon Society, the New York Zoological Society, and the U.S. Fish and Wildlife Service. The symposium was held at the University of Wisconsin-Madison during 17-20 August 1977.

The symposium offered a unique opportunity for leading scientists from around the world to meet and share their experiences with managing endangered birds. For many of the contributors, this was the first time that they had formally presented their own results. It was also the first time that so many of the leaders in this new field had assembled to review and evaluate their accomplishments. Contributing authors were selected on the basis of their past research on endangered birds or their personal and professional involvement in some aspect of endangered bird management. The individual papers were organized to span the breadth of the field and to explore the depth of specific management programs. The intent was to provide a thorough and balanced coverage of endangered bird management.

As editor of this volume, I wish to express my appreciation to all the people who helped me organize the symposium and assisted me in the preparation of this book. The initial organization of topics and list of potential contributors was improved significantly through the suggestions of William G. Conway, Cameron B. Kepler, Warren B. King, Thomas E. Lovejoy, and Richard L. Plunkett. Helpful suggestions were also received from many of the invited participants. The faculty, staff and students of the Department of Wildlife Ecology assisted me in innumerable ways with the logistics of preparing for and assuring the smooth functioning of the symposium. I am grateful to my colleagues for their help. The College of Agricultural and Life Sciences and the University of Wisconsin-Madison provided a congenial environment for the symposium.

My wife, Barbara, not only typed most of the final manuscript but also helped me with much of the editorial work.

The symposium and the present volume were made possible through the financial and other support provided by the co-sponsoring organizations: the International Council for Bird Preservation, the

World Wildlife Fund, the National Audubon Society, the New York Zoological Society, and the U.S. Fish and Wildlife Service. I wish to
express my appreciation to these organizations and to those organizations that sent participants to the symposium.

Finally, I am grateful to the symposium participants for their
enthusiastic optimism over the prospects for saving endangered birds
through management. The fragile futures of many endangered birds
will increasingly depend on the skill and passion that these scientists have invested in their work.

Stanley A. Temple   *Madison, Wisconsin*
                                                     December 1977

Part I
Endangered Bird Problems and the Concept of Managing Threatened Species

1

The Concept of Managing Endangered Birds

Stanley A. Temple

Today's endangered birds have invariably been placed in jeopardy
as a result of man's purposeful or unwitting alterations of natural
ecosystems. Although there have been many attempts at categorizing
the various causes of endangerment, with respect to the dynamics of
the threatened population, there are but 2 major factors that can
cause a population to decline in numbers:
1. Factors that reduce survivorship in the population (e.g.,
    overharvesting, increased rates of predation, reduction of
    suitable habitat).
2. Factors that reduce fecundity in the population (e.g., com-
    petition for nesting sites, reproductive dysfunctions caused
    by toxic chemicals, reduction of habitats required for breed-
    ing).
When faced with the task of designing a management program to
increase the numbers of an endangered species, the manager must by
some means counteract these 2 detrimental factors with the ultimate
goal of enhancing either the population's survivorship, its fecundity,
or both.
    In a sense, these goals are not so very different from the goals
of the traditional game manager who attempts to increase the "standing crop" of game animals that is available for harvest by hunters
(Leopold, 1933). However, there are some important differences, and
these often have to do with the basic biological characteristics of
the animals involved. Differences resulting from either r selection
or K selection (Pianka, 1970; Hairston et al., 1970) come immediately
to mind. Most managed game species fall into the former category in
which many of the animal's life history characteristics promote or
derive from a high intrinsic rate of growth. Most endangered species
tend to be K-selected species in which efficient use of resources has
been the dominant trait favored by natural selection. As a result,

enhancing fecundity among endangered species may present a challenge that in certain evolutionary respects is opposed by natural selection. A high degree of specialization is also a characteristic trait of K-selected species, and this specificity can often cause difficulties in deciphering the precise factors that limit the population.

As might be expected on the basis of such fundamental differences in the biology of the 2 groups of species, management procedures that are highly effective with r-selected populations do not necessarily work as well with K-selected populations. So it is with game species and endangered species. The old, standard prescriptions for the management of declining game populations--legal protection and habitat preservation--are often less than effective in reversing the downward trends of many of today's endangered species. Nonetheless, until recently, such *laissez-faire* approaches were all we had to offer the threatened species.

One area of great similarity between game management and endangered species management is the desirability for detailed studies of the managed animal's life history and ecology to precede the management attempt. When one considers the tomes of research reports that have been published on game birds, it is not surprising that management of these birds is solidly based in a detailed understanding of the birds' ecology. But, consider the literature that exists on the life history and ecology of most endangered birds. I suspect that the total published work on North American species of endangered birds does not even approach the literature on one North American gamebird, the Ring-necked Pheasant (*Phasianus colchicus*), which is not even an indigenous species! If management of endangered birds is to succeed, we must look forward to investing considerable time, effort and probably money into studying these birds just as game managers have in gamebirds.

Only in the last 10 or 15 years has there been an incentive to study endangered species with a view to developing management procedures. What has emerged as a result of this research is a new approach to management of endangered forms. The first order of business is determining precisely what the species' immediate problems are. Then the goal becomes the design of manipulative approaches that help the species at the precise point where its life style has conflicted with environmental conditions. Often the urgency of the situation means that there is little or no time for controlled experiments, and the manager must learn while working directly with the endangered bird.

The approach that has evolved is one in which the endangered species manager often focuses primary attention not so much on the ultimate causes of a species decline (e.g., habitat alterations, toxic chemicals, competitors, etc.) but on the proximate causes. These proximate causes of endangerment can perhaps be most easily viewed as the symptoms shown by the population in response to ultimate factors. These include poor reproductive success, difficulties in coping with antagonistic species, and difficulties in locating adequate food. Because this strategy places emphasis on treating symptoms, D.R. Zimmerman has coined the term "clinical ornithology" to describe the new approach (Zimmerman, 1975).

This approach to managing endangered species has met with suspicion and criticism from conservation purists who validly stress that we should be devoting our attention toward controlling the ultimate causes of endangerment. They also point out that a successful attempt at helping a species through manipulating proximate factors often detracts from efforts to counter ultimate problems by giving the impression that the endangered species is out of trouble. However, it must also be stressed that in many instances time is a factor working against the endangered species. Alleviating ultimate problems is almost always time consuming, and prompt manipulative interventions can, therefore, "buy time" for the population while its ultimate problems are corrected.

The management of endangered species is clearly not an either-or proposition. The most effective management programs will be those that address both ultimate and proximate causes of endangerment. There is ample evidence that each approach alone is insufficient. For example, while we spent a decade winning the very necessary battle against the ultimate problem of toxic chemicals, we lost an entire population of Peregrine Falcons (*Falco peregrinus*) in the eastern United States (Hickey, 1969). That population might have been saved if interventions had started earlier. However, instead of taking an active approach to solving the proximate problems of the Peregrine Falcon, conservationists literally protected the eastern population of the Peregrine Falcon until it became extinct. In retrospect, many have come to regret that approach (Cade, 1974).

On the other hand, all of the Peregrine Falcons that Tom Cade, Richard Fyfe and their associates have reared in captivity and released to the wild will amount to naught if the environment into which they are released is not free of the toxic chemicals that led to the demise of former populations. There clearly should be room in the conservationist's repertory for both approaches.

Our task at this symposium is to review the progress that has been made in the field of "clinical ornithology" and to evaluate the procedures that have evolved during the pioneering phases of this new approach to endangered bird management. Most techniques have already been proven in the field; some have been more successful than others, but each has unquestionably made some contribution toward saving a bird from extinction.

Some of the manipulative techniques are of general utility and do not really address themselves to single problems, but rather they can be prescribed for a wide variety of proximate factors. Captive breeding of endangered birds is exactly such a technique. It can potentially be used with almost any endangered bird, but in the end, it is so far removed from even the proximate causes of endangerment, let alone the ultimate causes, that it easily becomes a "catch-all" remedy. Nonetheless, after careful consideration is given to other options, captive breeding certainly has its place, especially when wild populations have little immediate hope of improving their reproductive performance or when the progeny of the captive population is used to repopulate vacant portions of the species' range. Captive breeding is perhaps best considered a last resort to which one falls back when all else seems futile. Several reviews of captive breeding as a conservation technique have already been published (Conway, 1967; Bridgewater, 1972; Martin, 1975), and most seem to agree with this evaluation.

Many of the other manipulative techniques are far more specific and attempt to remedy precise proximate problems confronting the endangered population. It is primarily these more specific approaches that we will consider in this symposium.

One aspect of habitat deterioration that is often important in causing declines in bird populations is scarcity of nest sites. This is especially true among those species which are secondary cavity-nesters and for which nest sites are a primary limiting factor even in the best of habitats. In such cases, the endangered species manager must cope with the proximate problem of poor reproductive performance caused either by a shortage of nest sites, by a failure of birds to find the available sites, or by exclusion of the birds from sites by competitors. The provision of additional nest sites, either artificial or improved natural ones, is often the easiest and most immediate solution to this problem. This does not, obviously, reduce the ultimate problem of habitat deterioration or an increased level of competition, but it does permit the species to overcome the proximate problem of poor reproductive performance that resulted from nest site scarcity.

Likewise, reducing pressures resulting from competition, predation, parasitism or disease does not address the ultimate ecological question of how and why the antagonistic species became a problem to the threatened bird. Instead, the approach seeks to alleviate an immediate proximate problem that resulted in reduced fecundity or increased mortality for the endangered population.

Artificial feeding programs are in the same category. Supplementing a threatened species' food supply does not get to the bottom of what went wrong with the bird's natural food supply, but in an immediate context, it attempts to make up for the deficiencies.

Manipulating various aspects of a threatened species' breeding biology by such techniques as transferring eggs and young to maximize reproductive output does not address the ultimate question of why the population is experiencing reproductive difficulties. But these manipulations, as labor-intensive as they may be, do provide a very real way to boost the reproduction of a declining species.

The short-term success of these manipulative procedures hinges importantly on whether or not the technique itself was properly conceived and executed as well as on whether the technique addresses the right proximate problem. This means that the endangered species manager must not only be talented in manipulating the species, but he must also be very familiar with the life history and ecological characteristics of the species he is managing. Certainly, throughout this symposium, it will be clear that the most successful management programs grew out of an intimate knowledge of a threatened species' life history and ecology.

Long-term success at managing an endangered species can depend on a different set of factors. Potential genetic problems that have resulted from a reduced population size and problems of population demography cannot be overlooked. However, the most important factor

that must be taken into account is whether or not concomitant attention has been given to resolving and correcting the ultimate causes of
endangerment. Unless ultimate problems are corrected, the manipulative
procedures that may have saved the species will, in all likelihood,
need to be applied continually in order to keep the species out of
danger. In some instances, such a long-term commitment to intervention may not be objectionable, but in most cases the goal of an
intervention is to finally allow the species to make it on its own
without further active interventions. An intensive intervention is
merely a way of getting the species through a difficult and crucial
period. In the end, this means that the only realistic approach to
endangered bird management is an integrated approach that combines
skillful, well-conceived interventions with amelioration of basic underlying ultimate problems.

As will be clear in the papers given in this symposium, many of
the most successful interventions have been the result of a single,
dedicated individual's commitment to saving a species. Although the
individual researcher may be very familiar with his or her chosen
species and may have the gift--and indeed it is a gift, not an acquired skill--of being able to manipulate that species, rarely can one
person accomplish an integrated approach single-handedly. To provide
the necessary balance, it is important that organizations and agencies
concerned with bird conservation work in concert with the manager,
supporting the manipulations and, at the same time, providing the
larger effort of correcting ultimate problems. All of the organizations that have chosen to support this symposium provide outstanding
examples of how concerned groups can work effectively with individual
researchers to accomplish difficult goals.

Finally, we must take into consideration the magnitude of the
endangered bird problem on a world-wide scale and the limitations,
both in terms of manpower and financial support, under which we must
operate. Manipulative management techniques are almost always labor-
intensive and expensive. In the future, more and more situations are
going to arise where questions of priorities or probability of success
will determine which endangered birds will receive intensive management. Some species are inevitably going to be overlooked and allowed
to slip away, even though an intensive intervention could have saved
them.

As we continue with our management of endangered birds, we should
not rest on our past accomplishments and assume that we have discovered and mastered all of the possible types of manipulations. Twenty
years ago, few conservationists would have been able to predict the
success that we have accomplished to date. It is hoped the coming
decades will see the development of even more effective means of managing endangered birds and the solution of many of the ultimate problems that cause endangerment.

Perhaps, our watchwords as developers of management programs for
endangered birds should be "don't hesitate to try it." Many of the
most successful techniques were once "far out," visionary schemes that
had no shortage of antagonists at the time of their conception. A
confident critic only 5 years ago wrote that "breeding Peregrine Falcons in captivity is a feat so difficult that it cannot possibly re-

populate the wild." It is reassuring to note that it is the endangered species managers and not their critics who can now say, "We told you so."

LITERATURE CITED

Bridgewater, D. 1972. Status of rare and endangered birds in captivity with a general reference to mammals. Zoologica 57:119-125.

Cade, T.J. 1974. Plans for managing the survival of the Peregrine Falcon. Raptor Research Report 2:89-104.

Conway, W.G. 1967. The opportunity for zoos to save vanishing species. Oryx 9:154-160.

Hairston, N.G., D.W. Tinkle and H.M. Wilbur. 1970. Natural selection and the parameters of population growth. J. Wildlife Manage. 34:681-690.

Hickey, J.J. (ed.) 1969. Peregrine Falcon populations: their biology and decline. Univ. of Wisc. Press, Madison.

Leopold, A. 1933. Game management. Charles Scribner's Sons. New York.

Martin, R.D. (ed.) 1975. Breeding endangered species in captivity. Academic Press, London.

Pianka, E.R. 1970. On r and K selection. Amer. Nat. 104:592-597.

Zimmerman, D.R. 1975. To save a bird in peril. Coward, McCann & Geoghegan, Inc., New York. 286p.

2

Endangered Birds of the World and Current Efforts toward Managing Them

Warren B. King

The *Red Data Book* series, published by the International Union for the Conservation of Nature and Natural Resources (IUCN) in Switzerland, is widely regarded as the authoritative, comprehensive compilation of the status of threatened organisms of the world. The volume on birds (Vincent, 1966) was compiled by the International Council for Bird Preservation (ICBP) for IUCN. It was published in 1966, updated through 1971, and is now the most out-of-date of the series, but a complete revision is scheduled to be published toward the end of 1977 or early 1978. While this revision is not yet finished, it is sufficiently complete to permit an assessment of the current geography, ecology, etiology, and management of the endangered birds of the world.

The 1966 *Red Data Book* listed 333 taxa, species or subspecies. The revised *Red Data Book* will contain just over 400 taxa. Ninety-four of those in the original volume will be omitted, largely because new information shows these taxa not to be at risk. Fifteen taxa are now considered to be extinct, but 4, pronounced extinct in the original edition, have been rediscovered. These include Blewitt's Owl (*Athene blewitti*) of India, the Barred-wing Rail (*Rallus poecilopterus*) and the Long-legged Warbler (*Trichocichla rufa*) of Fiji, and the Molokai Thrush (*Phaeornis obscurus rutha*) of Hawaii.

The revised *Red Data Book* on birds will treat about 265 species and 140 subspecies. A number of the species are polytypic, their component subspecies sometimes being treated separately, sometimes together, for the sake of convenience. Of these, 36.9 percent are considered endangered, 17.5 percent vulnerable, 29.2 percent rare, 15.6 percent of indeterminate status but likely to be at serious risk, and 1.0 percent out of danger.

HABITATS OF ENDANGERED BIRDS

Endangered birds occur in a wide variety of habitats, but the majority are found in forests. Some, of course, occur in more than one habitat type, although these are a minority, for most endangered species are either restricted geographically or have specialized habitat requirements. Only 51 taxa occur in two distinct habitat types, three occur in three habitat types, and one, the Peregrine Falcon (*Falco peregrinus*), occurs in several. Forest is a habitat for 64.1 percent of threatened birds; an additional 3.1 percent are found in xeric forest. Wetland is the habitat for 12.7 percent. Grassland accounts for 7.0 percent of habitat for threatened birds. Brush or scrubland habitat accounts for 9.8 percent, while coastline, man-modified lands, mangrove, lakes and rivers, and cliffs each account for less than 5 percent.

CAUSES OR PRESUMED CAUSES OF ENDANGERMENT

The most significant cause of endangerment is habitat destruction, three-quarters of which is in the form of forest destruction. Destruction of habitat can be identified as a cause of endangerment in 65.3 percent of taxa. Hunting is a contributory cause of endangerment in a surprisingly large 24.9 percent of taxa, while human molestation of birds or eggs was noted for 10.6 percent of taxa. Predation has been identified in rather fewer cases (21.5 percent of taxa). Lesser causes of endangerment include competition (9.3 percent), limited habitat (8.6 percent), disease (5.2 percent), environmental pollution (2.8 percent), hybridization (1.4 percent), climatic changes (1.0 percent), and parasitism (1.0 percent). In 5.2 percent of taxa, the causes of endangerment are unknown.

A total of 163 taxa (39.0 percent) are threatened by more than one factor. Of these 17.2 percent are threatened by three factors and 14.1 percent by four factors. Multiple causes of endangerment pose the most serious problem for endangered species' managers. It is not surprising to find that most of the critically endangered species suffer from multiple causes of endangerment. Examples of species threatened by multiple causes include the Puerto Rican Parrot (*Amazona vittata*), which is or was threatened by forest destruction resulting in reduction of total range and a shortage of nest sites, predation on adults by a hawk and on eggs and young by a thrasher, parasitism of chicks by a bot fly, molestation of nests by suppliers of pet birds, shooting of birds, by occasionally severe weather, and the possibility of competition from an introduced congener. The endemic birds of Hawaiian rain forests face threats from forest destruction or deterioration through the spread of exotic vegetation, competition from exotic birds, predation by introduced rats, and avian disease against which they apparently have no immunity. In such cases where several threats exist, it is usually necessary to develop separate management programs to alleviate each of the causes of endangerment.

GEOGRAPHY OF ENDANGERMENT

Island forms exceed continental forms slightly, 53.0 percent
to 47.0 percent. (Large islands like Madagascar, Taiwan, and
Borneo are considered continental, but New Zealand is considered
insular. If all of these are considered insular, island forms
comprise 58.0 percent of endangered taxa.) Among continents,
South America with 58 taxa (27.4 percent of continental taxa) shows
the largest increase since 1966, when 15 taxa were listed. Africa,
including Madagascar, has 42 taxa listed; Middle America has 10
threatened taxa; and North America has 25 taxa listed. Thirty-six
taxa are listed for Southeast Asia; the Asian Palearctic has 18;
Europe has 6, and Australia has 6.

Over half of the threatened taxa on islands are in the Pacific
(130 taxa, 57.0 percent of island taxa), while 62 (27.2 percent) are
from the Atlantic including the Mediterranean and Carribean seas,
and 36 (15.8 percent) are from the Indian Ocean.

CONCENTRATIONS OF ENDANGERED SPECIES

Among continental areas, perhaps the most serious situation
exists along the coast of southeastern Brazil between southern
Bahia and Rio Grande do Sul, where widespread, extensive forest
destruction has resulted in fragmentation of once continuous forest
into a mosaic of small tracts. As a result, 21 species and a subspecies endemic to this area are endangered. Among the most
seriously threatened are the Red-billed Curassow (*Crax blumenbachii*),
restricted to two areas in Espirito Santo totalling 28,000 hectares
and with a total population of about 70 birds, and the Hook-billed
Hermit (*Glaucis dohrnii*) with a population of about 20 birds restricted to one forest of 4,000 hectares. This latter area, pri-
vately owned by a prominent Brazilian industrialist, maintains
populations of 10 endangered taxa of birds, a density unprecedented
elsewhere on earth. Management in southeastern Brazil has consisted
solely of the creation of a few parks or reserves.

Forest destruction along the Cordilleran slopes of Colombia
has resulted in the endangerment of 9 taxa, a number that under-
states the promise of future wholesale endangerment and extinction
as the number of forested tracts is reduced faster than threatened
populations can be identified in them.

In East Africa forest destruction in isolated outlying tracts
of the great Congo forest threatens 3 endemics of the Arabuko-
Sokoke Forest, Kenya; 3 from the Uluguru Mountains, Tanzania; and
4 from the Usambara Mountains, Tanzania. The future of 7 additional
near-endemics in the Usambaras gives cause for concern as well.

The destruction of forests in Madagascar threatens 10 species
and 2 subspecies of humid forests and 4 species and a subspecies
of dry forests. Over 90 percent of Madagascar's forests have been
destroyed, and the process of conversion of forest to grassland is
accelerating as human populations increase. The prognosis for the
future of these species is bleak, for the Malagasy government has

demonstrated little interest in protecting more than token bits of forest. With an attitude of hostility toward outside advice or help in all matters, including conservation, and with increasing provincialization of governmental authority, there is frustratingly little that can be accomplished in the near term on behalf of Madagascar's endangered birds. Trends in forest destruction have already decided their long-term fate.

The number of endangered birds on islands is disproportionately large because of their limited distribution, small populations, and sensitivity to man's activities and introductions. The greatest concentration of insular endangered birds occurs in the Hawaiian Islands. A total of 29 threatened species or subspecies comprise 7 percent of the world's threatened taxa. This total is alarmingly high, yet in historical perspective the situation is worse; 24 taxa from the Hawaiian Islands have become extinct since James Cook's arrival 2 centuries ago. Several additional taxa are about to join this list: the Kauai Akialoa (*Hemignathus procerus*) last seen in 1965; the Kauai O'o (*Moho braccatus*) now down to the last pair or 2; the 2 remaining extant subspecies of the Nukupu'u (*Hemignathus lucidus*); and the Maui subspecies of the Akepa (*Loxops coccinea*).

The situation in New Zealand is scarcely better. Sixteen taxa are listed in the *Red Data Book*. Since 1600, 12 taxa have become extinct, and several additional forms will soon join these. The Laughing Owl (*Sceloglaux albifacies*) and the enigmatic Piopio (*Turnagra capensis*), both of which had subspecies on North and South Islands, have only recently succumbed. The most critical among those still considered extant are the New Zealand Bush Wren (*Xenicus longipes*), the last remaining subspecies of which is now only questionably extant, and the Kokako (*Callaeas cinerea cinerea*) of South Island, for which hope of rediscovery is fading. The spectacular Kakapo (*Strigops habroptilus*), a large nocturnal, flightless, lek-displaying parrot, the sole member of a unique subfamily, was given a reprieve last year when a viable population was discovered in a remote part of Stewart Island.

The Chatham Islands, 800 kilometers east of New Zealand, have 6 endangered forms, including the Chatham Island Black Robin (*Petroica traversi*), perhaps the most endangered bird in the world, at least among those for which information is available. Six additional taxa have become extinct since 1600.

Norfolk and Lord Howe islands, widely separated in the Pacific off the east coast of Australia, share a history of ecological disaster. The latter has 2 endangered taxa, including the Lord Howe Wood Rail (*Tricholimnas sylvestris*) whose population is 20 birds, but 9 taxa have become extinct in historical times. The former island has 4 endangered taxa, all restricted to a 405 hectare patch of forest around Mount Pitt, and 4 have become extinct; 2 of these, a cuckoo-shrike and a starling, have disappeared in the last 2 decades.

In the Indian Ocean, Mauritius has 7 endangered taxa, of which the most critically threatened are the Mauritius Kestrel (*Falco punctatus*) with a population of 15, and the Mauritius Pink Pigeon (*Nesoenas mayeri*) with a population of about 24. Six taxa

have become extinct in historical times, one of which, the Dodo
(*Raphus cucullatus*), has become symbolic of extinction. Rodrigues,
administered by Mauritius, has 2 endangered species, a figure insig-
nificant beside the 8 species that are now extinct.

Réunion has suffered 8 extinctions as well, and 2 additional
species are presently listed in the *Red Data Book*.

Nine taxa are threatened in the Seychelles Islands. Two of
these are among the world's rarest: the Seychelles Magpie-Robin
(*Copsychus sechellarum*) has a population of 34, and the Black Paradise
Flycatcher (*Terpsiphone corvina*) has about 70 birds. Two extinctions
have occurred in the Seychelles in historical times.

In the Atlantic Ocean, the Antilles, as a whole, harbor 39
threatened taxa, but these are not heavily concentrated on any one
island. Eight threatened forms occur on Cuba, 7 on Puerto Rico,
5 on St. Lucia, and lesser numbers occur on several other islands.
Of special note in the Antilles is the threat to 5 species and 2 subspecies of *Amazona* parrots. Thirteen parrots have already become
extinct in the Antilles, although this figure may be inflated considerably because most of these are known only from hearsay evidence
and were lost before specimens could be secured.

MANAGEMENT EFFORTS

Management of endangered species can be either active or passive.
Passive management involves the passage and enforcement of national
legislation or international treaties to protect species from direct
human interference through hunting or molestation. It also involves
the establishment of parks or reserves to protect species' habitat.

Active management involves any of a wide range of manipulative
activities to alter factors causing endangerment. Among traditional
active management procedures are control of predators or competitors,
control of factors detrimental to habitat--for example, herbivore
control--and transplantation of species to healthy habitat. Research
can be considered active management if it is applicable to or shows
the way toward recovery efforts. Captive breeding is also active
management when it is tied to augmentation of wild populations
through a program of reintroduction.

This symposium will treat exhaustively the various active management techniques currently in application. It should go without say-
ing that in all respects passive management is preferable to active
management, if it is adequate for the long-term preservation of
endangered species. The best management is the least management
that is sufficient to permit species to maintain populations viable
over the long term. Active management of a species without the safeguard of existing passive protection is likely in most cases to be
a waste of resources. Only a small percentage of endangered species
will likely be susceptible to active management.

Table 1 shows the number of endangered taxa for which active,
passive, or no management exists in various geographical areas.
The figures reveal the rather inadequate state of current efforts to
manage endangered birds. The table indicates that active programs are

TABLE 1. INCIDENCE AND ADEQUACY OF MANAGEMENT PROGRAMS FOR ENDANGERED BIRDS IN VARIOUS REGIONS

Region	Number of Species Having Management Programs of Indicated Type and Adequacy[a]						
	Active, Adequate	Active, Uncertain	Active, Inadequate	Passive, Adequate	Passive, Uncertain	Passive, Inadequate	None
North America	2	5	4	4	3	6	0
Middle America	1	1	0	0	1	6	1
South America	0	1	0	3	1	45	8
Australia	1	0	0	9	1	5	1
Southeast Asia	0	2	0	2	1	24	7
Palearctic Asia	0	5	1	2	0	7	3
Europe	0	3	1	0	0	2	0
Africa	0	2	1	0	1	8	30
Pacific Ocean	9	5	15	21	2	54	24
Atlantic Ocean	0	3	2	10	2	17	28
Indian Ocean	2	3	3	13	1	8	6
Total	15	30	27	64	13	182	108

[a]Passive programs involve legal protection of a species or its habitat; active programs involve direct human intervention on behalf of a species.

underway for 16 percent of endangered taxa, and that more existing active programs are inadequate than are adequate, while even more have not yet demonstrated their adequacy. Only 18 percent of endangered taxa enjoy adequate management; 28 percent have adequate or questionably adequate management; 25 percent have neither legal protection nor habitat protection. Madagascar accounts for most of the African species without protection. Brazil and Colombia account for most of the South American species without protection or with inadequate protection. Adequate or at least uncertain management has been undertaken for at least half of the endangered species of North America, Europe, and Australia. Most of the adequate management of endangered taxa of the Pacific are accounted for by Hawaiian and New Zealand taxa. Hawaii and New Zealand are the only areas of major concentration of threatened species in which extensive active management occurs.

RESULTS OF MANAGEMENT EFFORTS

     Very few endangered species have been successfully managed to recovery. The population of the Trumpeter Swans (*C. cygnus buccinator*) south of Alaska recovered after hunting was prohibited and a refuge was established, but the Alaska population probably would have been sufficiently large to maintain the species if more southerly populations had been extirpated.
     Captive breeding and subsequent release of well over 1,000 Hawaiian Geese (*Branta sandvicensis*) is often said to have been responsible for that species' recovery, but the field work that will determine whether the wild population will be self-sustaining or will decline abruptly following cessation of release of captive birds is only recently underway.
     The only endangered bird species unequivocally to recover as the direct result of active human intervention is the Saddleback (*Philesturnus carunculatus*) of New Zealand. Both subspecies were resurrected, the South Island form literally at the last possible moment, by translocation to islands without predators or from which predators had been removed. The species is now out of danger, for several island populations of each subspecies have been established and are thriving.
     The New Zealand Wildlife Service has applied the technique of translocation repeatedly, most recently with the Chatham Island Black Robin. The entire breeding population, both pairs, was moved from Little Mangere Island to Mangere Island where thousands of seedlings had been planted to speed revegetation following removal of sheep. Translocation has also been attempted by the New Zealand Wildlife Service on the Kakapo, on the New Zealand Shore Plover (*Thinornis novaeseelandiae*), on the Chatham Island Snipe (*Coenocorypha aucklandica iredalei*), and on the Stewart Island Bush Wren. However, the Kakapo has lived in apparent celibacy for several years on the island to which it was translocated. Translocation has limited applicability elsewhere, but in certain areas, for example in the Seychelles, it holds the best hope for the recovery of certain species. The

Seychelles Brush Warbler (*Bebrornis sechellensis*) of Cousin Island, Seychelles, has increased in abundance tenfold in the last two decades and is now out of danger, although it will remain at risk until it is reestablished on a second island. Passive management of Cousin Island by the ICBP to promote the return of indigenous vegetation was responsible for the species' recovery.

The Turquoise Parakeet (*Neophema pulchella*) and the Western Whipbird (*Psophodes nigrogularis*) of Australia have both recovered sufficently as the result of protection of habitat through establishment of national parks to be considered out of danger.

Several species have shown improved status as the result of active management but are not yet out of danger. Among these are the Whooping Crane (*Grus americana*) and the Aleutian Canada Goose (*Branta canadensis leucopareia*) of North America, the White-naped Crane (*Grus vipio*) and the Hooded Crane (*Grus monacha*) of Asia, the Atitlán Grebe (*Podylimbus gigas*) of Guatemala, the Cahow (*Pterodroma cahow*) of Bermuda, and the Koloa (*Anas wyvilliana*) of Hawaii. Management has arrested declines in several species including the Takahe (*Notornis mantelli*) of New Zealand, the Puerto Rican Parrot of Puerto Rico, the Eastern Ground Parrot (*Pezoporus wallicus wallicus*) and the Noisy Scrubbird (*Atrichornis clamosus*) of Australia, the Seychelles Magpie-Robin, and the Kirtland's Warbler (*Dendroica kirtlandii*) of the United States and the Bahamas.

Recently the New Zealand Wildlife Service attempted the first control program to eliminate a threat to the Forbes' Parakeet (*Cyanoramphus auriceps forbesi*) through hybridization by elimination of all Chatham Island Parakeets (*C. novaeselandiae chathamensis*) in the zone of contact. A similar program might have prevented or delayed the hybridization of the distinct subspecies of the Madagascar Dove (*Streptopelia picturata rostrata*) of the Seychelles with the introduced nominate subspecies on certain outlying islands, but the opportunity has now passed.

The active management techniques presently in use that are applicable to endangered species are expensive, short-term and labor-intensive, and must be viewed realistically as only stopgaps. We have all asked ourselves, "Is it worth the effort?" Most of us have answered affirmatively, for we recognize the continued existence of a species is precious, and extinction is painfully irreversible. There will be no shortage of critically endangered species on which to work this special and newly-conceived magic, but an administrative mechanism must be found to permit application of realistic budgets to the most needy species, and those most likely to respond to treatment, regardless of national boundaries. Future endangered species will come increasingly from the forests of Middle and South America, from Southeast Asia, and from forested Africa. Unless existing schedules can be changed, whole avifaunas will be lost. For example, virtually all the primary forests of Borneo are already contracted for and will be cut by 1995. The significance of specialized techniques of active management pale in the face of massive forest destruction and resultant massive endangerment and extinction. Yet, there will always be species of special significance, amenable to active management, and worth the effort to some of us. We will

need to be increasingly selective in choosing species to manage actively, recognizing management's shortcomings and strengths, and ad-
mitting we are not capable of saving everything.

LITERATURE CITED

Vincent, J. (ed.) 1966. Red Data Book; Vol. 2, Aves. IUCN, Morges,
Switzerland.

3

The American Government's Programs for Endangered Birds

Keith M. Schreiner and Clare J. Senecal

I am honored by the kind invitation to address you on the Endangered Species Program of the U.S. Fish and Wildlife Service. Know-
ing that this symposium's attendants are primarily interested in avian
species, I will try to emphasize our work with birds. Doing this
makes the job easier for me because a substantial segment of our listing efforts, research efforts, recovery plans, and other facets of the
program are directed toward the preservation of birds.

A large part of this symposium will be spent hearing of the progress that has been made with recovery plans for endangered species.
Another part of your time will be involved in sharing management ideas.
In order to help put these discussions in perspective, I will present
background material describing the history and philosophy of the federal Endangered Species Program. And then I will touch briefly on
each of several activities of the program, emphasizing our work with
birds.

Federal wildlife law has been with us for a long time. The
Lacey Act of 1900, the establishment of the refuge system in 1903, and
the passage of the Migratory Bird Protection Act in 1918 are examples
of early legislation. Specific endangered species legislation has
evolved more recently.

The first federal action program for endangered species took the
form of a Rare and Endangered Species Committee, organized by the U.S.
Fish and Wildlife Service. This group published a series of "Red
Books", the first one being published in 1966 (U.S. Department of the
Interior, 1966).

The first legislation passed specifically for endangered species
was the Endangered Species Preservation Act of 1966. This Act provided only for the preservation of higher forms of native endangered
species. It required the Service to prepare and maintain an official
endangered species list. The first list, containing 72 entries, was

published in March of 1967. While the Service was authorized by this Act to expend funds for the management of listed species, there was no federal authority to prohibit taking, trade, or other potentially harmful acts. The Service also was authorized to use Land and Water Conservation Funds to acquire habitat for endangered species. The Office of Endangered Species was established in 1966 to help implement the Act. The first staff consisted of 2 persons.

The research program for endangered species gained momentum in the Service during this period. Essentially, it began in 1965 with an effort to restore the Whooping Crane (*Grus americana*) through captive propagation at Monte Vista National Wildlife Refuge in Colorado. Later, the program shifted to the Patuxent Wildlife Research Center in Laurel, Maryland, where it now provides a facility for research on 9 species in addition to the Whooping Crane.

The 1966 legislation was amended with passage of the Endangered Species Conservation Act of 1969. The Service was thereby given authority to list foreign species and to restrict their import; but there was still no protection for native endangered species, a major shortcoming of both the 1966 and 1969 Acts. The endangered species programs continued their expansion and in 1973 carried a budget of $1.8 million and a staff of 16 in the Office of Endangered Species. The Endangered Species Act of 1973 was signed into law in December of that year.

The 1973 Act is far more comprehensive than the 1969 Act. It reaches all animals, whereas the 1969 Act addressed only vertebrates, mollusks, and crustaceans. It recognizes threatened as well as endangered species, thus establishing authority for protection before the danger of extinction becomes grave. It addresses all plant and animal taxa, whereas the 1969 Act recognized no category below subspecies. The 1973 Act provides for listing and conservation of plants, a provision totally absent from previous legislation. For the first time, native endangered species were provided with real protection backed by tough penalties for violators. The 1973 Act mandates federal employees and agencies to take positive action toward protection of endangered or threatened species wherever found on lands controlled by them. Furthermore, the 1973 Act implemented the Convention on International Trade in Endangered Species of Wild Fauna and Flora and increased our authority for appropriations to a high of $10 million annually.

Fortified now by the 1973 Act, we are strengthening our capability to save the world's heritage of wild plant and animal species and the ecosystems of which they are part and parcel. We are assisted in our task by new concepts of wildlife conservation, and we are urged on by an acute awareness of dwindling nonrenewable wildlife resources.

The goal of the Service's Endangered and Threatened Species Program is "...to stop endemic plant and animal endangerments and extinctions caused by man's influence on wild ecosystems and to restore the species to the point where they are no longer threatened or endangered." This goal states a measurable ultimate objective. If achieved, it will fulfill the purposes of the Act and the purposes of the international agreements meant to save endangered species.

The Service's goal to eliminate endangerment and extinction is limited to that caused by man. The limitation is appropriate, for it would be unwise for the program to attempt the halt extinctions which occur naturally. However, man's involvement is far reaching and sometimes subtle. As a practical consequence, program efforts will apply this limitation with great caution.

The conservation of ecosystems, first used in the 1973 Act, is definitely a primary goal of our program. Saving ecosystems, not individual organisms or individual species, requires cooperation on a wide spectrum. Taking this approach means the intermeshing of many scientific disciplines and efforts. It means the intermeshing of disciplines within the biological sciences themselves. Saving ecosystems means cooperation among and between federal, state and private groups because it cannot be accomplished in any other way. The future of the federal Endangered and Threatened Species Program will work toward an endangered and threatened ecosystem conservation program as time goes on.

Endangered species are just one facet of several programs within the Fish and Wildlife Service. We feel that we have our various divisions and branches meshing well and feeding effectively into each of the Service's programs. The remainder of this paper will show how several offices, divisions, and branches of the Service--Research, Refuges, International Affairs, Law Enforcement, Wildlife Permits, and Endangered Species--all feed into and support the overall Endangered Species Program effort.

Eight specific activities make up the main thrust of the Endangered Species Program. The first of these actions is screening candidate species and conducting status surveys to determine which species should be listed as threatened or endangered. This effort includes carrying out the required steps for listing, delisting, or reclassifying appropriate species. The same process also includes the delineation of critical habitat, a provision under Section 7 of the Act to help perserve the essential habitat of these species.

Since the inception of this program, there have been a number of notable accomplishments. Among them are the official listing of 211 endangered and 1 threatened bird species. This total of 212 listed birds represents nearly a third of the total number of listed species which currently totals 641. Avian species are the largest taxonomic class listed.

Thus far, critical habitat has been determined for only 7 species. Two of these critical habitat designations were for birds--the California Condor (*Gymnogyps californianus*) and the Yellow-shouldered Blackbird (*Agelaius xanthomus*). Many more will follow in the weeks and months ahead.

A second specific action undertaken by the program is enforcing the protection of listed species. Section 9 of the Act prohibits taking, import and export, interstate traffic for commercial purposes, and selling or offering for sale without the proper permit. Implementation of this Section is handled by the Service's Division of Law Enforcement and, indirectly, by the Wildlife Permit Office, which issues permits for the transfer of species for scientific or propagation purposes and other limited and controlled reasons.

During 1975, the Service handled 1,343 investigations under the
Endangered Species Act. In 1976 and the transition quarter, 1,590
investigations were initiated; and during the first 6 months of 1977,
1,134 investigations were initiated. Since the Act became law through
1976 and the transition quarter, criminal prosecutions have resulted
in conviction of 209 individuals with the courts imposing total fines
of $33,619 and 12,500 days of jail sentences. In addition, through
June 30, 1977, 239 civil actions have been concluded with total penalties pending. We have obtained forfeiture of endangered species
items totaling over $90,000 in assessed value.

Protecting the Bald Eagle (*Haliaeetus leucocephalus*) has become
a job requiring more and more time and effort from Law Enforcement
special agents. There has been an apparent increase in the incidence
of illegal shooting of Bald Eagles by farmers and ranchers who view
them as threats to livestock, and by slob gunners who find them to be
tempting targets. In 1976, 33 eagles were taken by shooting; 9 of
these cases resulted in convictions with fines ranging from $100 to
$5,000 and 6 months in jail. Thus far in 1977, 33 eagles have been
taken by shooting. Eight of these cases were prosecuted. Fines
ranged from $300 to $500.

A third effort of the program is the development and implementation of Recovery Plans for the restoration of endangered native
species. This is one of our important and effective endangered species activities. I take great personal pride in this activity because it has the potential for being the salvation of many species
for many years to come, and it was implemented in spite of some
tough initial opposition.

Recovery Plans identify limiting factors, propose corrective
measures, and make recommendations for land acquisition, management
actions, and other efforts essential to restoring the species. Thus
far, 58 official teams have been established to work on 68 endangered
species. Twenty-eight Recovery Plans have already been approved for
implementation. Ten teams have draft plans which are currently being
reviewed. The Recovery Plan concept will be dealt with in other
talks during this symposium and, consequently, I will not pursue it
further in this paper.

Another program thrust is that of enlisting the help of as many
state and territorial fish and wildlife agencies as possible. These
organizations, with their 6,000 plus biologists and their 6,000 plus
enforcement officers and their millions of acres of state controlled
wild plant and animal habitat, have the potential expertise and resources to make or break the national program for endangered species.
To date, 18 states have signed cooperative agreements with us. Fourteen more states are now actively seeking legislation and authoriza-
tion necessary for entering into cooperative agreements.

Signed cooperative agreements make a state eligible for federal
funds, among other things. A total of $2.0 million was appropriated
in 1976 and an additional $4.0 million this year. Of this amount,
$1.6 million has been allotted to 16 states of which about $0.5 million was earmarked especially for the conservation of endangered
birds.

Under the agreements, the states provide one-third of the total cost of a project. In cases where two or more states have a cooperative project, one-fourth of the funds comes from the states. In addition to financial assistance, the agreements establish cooperative law enforcement efforts between federal and state officials, and they permit the states to manage and regulate the taking of endangered and threatened species as long as the mandate of the agreement and other federal laws are not violated.

A fifth effort of the program is managing Service-owned lands to provide maximum benefits for endangered species. We also strive to assist others with the management of non-Service lands where possible and practical. Establishment of Pelican Island Refuge in 1903 was an early recognition that special protection for some threatened wildlife species was needed. Several more refuges were created for the protection of other endangered species. The Key Deer (*Odocoileus virginianus clavium*), Dusky Seaside Sparrow (*Ammospiza maritima nigrescens*), Whooping Crane, Florida Manatee (*Trichechus manatus*) and American Alligator (*Alligator mississippiensis*) were among the species that have benefited. At least 137 National Wildlife Refuges encompass parts of the range of one or more endangered species. Twenty-five avian species are protected and conserved on the National Wildlife Refuge System. Again, avian species are the largest taxonomic class protected. Over one-half of all the endangered species found on refuges are endangered birds.

Section 7 of the 1973 Act mandates, for the first time, responsible actions by all federal agencies to insure protection of endangered and threatened species, and their critical habitat. This mandate, which specifically delineates federal agency responsibilities, is far reaching in effect.

The Service strives to assist other federal land managers through the process of listing the species, delineating its critical habitat and consulting with them on the consequences their planned actions might have on endangered species and their habitats. The concept of requiring responsible environmental considerations in developmental activities was a part of the 1966 Act. Earlier, however, federal authorities were obligated by these provisions to preserve species only so long as it was economically or technically practical. Section 7 of the 1973 Act is much stronger in this requirement.

Recently, the Service conducted a survey of all Section 7 consultations that have been conducted since the passage of the Act in 1973. The survey reveals that an estimated 4,500 consultations have been conducted; 124 of these are formal, documented consultations. One extremely satisfying result of the survey is the fact that irreconcilable conflicts were found in only a very few instances. Generally, statutory conflicts could be resolved through consultation, project-design modification, and other means. This means that Section 7 is working as intended to save endangered species and their habitats. It is unthinkable to change it now because of two or three sensationally reported conflicts that the national news media blew all out of proportion to their true import.

A sixth effort of the Program is conducting research studies and conducting research and surveys to determine the problems confronting endangered species and the management techniques needed for their restoration. The Division of Research operates out of several research centers located in the United States. A good portion of the research done at these centers is done with endangered birds. Over a quarter of a million dollars will be used to fund endangered bird research projects during 1978.

The seventh effort of the program is acquiring as rapidly as possible those lands and waters providing essential habitat for the continued existence of endangered species. The Endangered Species Act of 1973 authorizes the use of Land and Water Conservation Fund monies for acquiring lands to further the conservation of endangered and threatened species. Since 1968, about $30.0 million of these funds have been used to purchase over 24,300 ha of key habitats for endangered and threatened species. During 1976, 1,890 ha were acquired at a cost of $5,134,000. A total of $14.9 million is scheduled for use in 1977. Of this total, $12.9 million will be used to acquire key habitat for endangered birds. Monies proposed for appropriations for 1978 total about $10 million. Most of this total is for endangered bird habitat.

The eighth and final facet of the Endangered Species Program consists of efforts to join and assist foreign countries in wildlife conservation. This action takes several forms. We are expanding a program to train foreign nationals, and we also provide assistance and consultation services when requested to do so. We administer and enforce existing international treaties. We continue to develop new treaties which strive to accomplish the same purposes as provided by the Endangered Species Act.

In addition, we are actively engaged in cooperative endangered species programs with Russia, Spain, Venezuela, Brazil, Mexico, Canada, and Saudi Arabia. Additional programs are being sought with Egypt, Pakistan, and India.

These eight functions describe our program from an activities point of view. This, however, is still an incomplete picture . Dedication, enthusiasm, and hard work are qualities of the Endangered Species Program personnel which are less easy to spell out but nonetheless crucial to the program and deeply appreciated by its supervisors and managers. All of us in the Service feel supported by the many dedicated people everywhere working to implement this Program.

In closing, permit me to thank you for your interest in, support of, and involvement with endangered species.

LITERATURE CITED

U.S. Department of the Interior, Committee on Rare and Endangered
    Wildlife Species. 1966. Rare and Endangered Fish and Wildlife
    of the United States. Bur. of Sport Fisheries and Wildlife,
    Resource Publ. 34. U.S. Gov. Printing Office, Washington, D.C.

Part II
Increasing Reproductive Effort and Success by Reducing Nest-Site Limitations

4

Increasing Reproductive Effort and Success by Reducing Nest-Site Limitations
A Review

Noel F. R. Snyder

The nesting habits of many endangered species of birds are high-ly specialized. Peregrine Falcons (*Falco peregrinus*) and Bald Ibises (*Geronticus eremita*) nest for the most part only on ledges of precip-itous cliffs. Other species, such as the Puerto Rican Parrot (*Amazona vittata*) and the California Condor (*Gymnogyps californianus*) are lim-ited to large natural cavities in trees or cliffs, while still other species, such as the Bald Eagle (*Haliaeetus leucocephalus*) often re-quire relatively tall trees in terrain where such trees may be in lim-ited supply. Regardless of the reasons why species may come to depend on specialized nest sites, it is enough to note here that shortages of such nest sites, along with problems relating to acquisition and con-trol of such nest sites, appear to be among the primary factors limit-ing the abundance of a number of endangered forms.

THE NATURE OF NEST-SITE LIMITATIONS

Nest-site limitations can result from 3 major causes: (1) an in-trinsic scarcity of adequate nest sites relative to other necessary resources, (2) behavioral limitations in the abilities of the species to locate what nest sites may exist, and (3) vulnerability of nest sites to competitors and predators. All 3 factors may act in concert for a given species, but the relative importances of the 3 factors vary considerably from case to case.

Everglade Kites (*Rostrhamus sociabilis*) and Ospreys (*Pandion haliaetus*) are examples of species that apparently are not usually faced with significant interspecific competition for nest sites or with unusually high vulnerability of nests to predators. Nor is there evidence that these species commonly experience difficulties in locat-ing what good nest sites may exist. But both species are often faced with a basic shortage of good quality sites, and both commonly attempt to nest in poor sites (Sykes and Chandler, 1974; Postupalsky and Stackpole, 1974; Reese, 1977). Where there are limited numbers of shrubby trees and snags in good feeding areas, Everglade Kites have often built nests in actively growing clumps of *Typha*, and the nests have often progressively tilted, and nest contents have spilled out. In the case of the Osprey, a shortage of good nest trees in some areas has likewise led to nesting in unstable sites and in sites so close to the water surface that they have been subject to flooding.

Another endangered species that apparently has been stressed by a basic shortage of good nest sites in interaction with food supply problems is the California Condor (Wilbur et al.,1974; S.R. Wilbur, *unpublished data*). Rather than gathering in the historical nesting areas in the breeding season, much of the condor population of recent years has been concentrated in a feeding area far from cliffs, probably because food supplies have been poor in the historical areas. Yet efforts to increase food supplies in the historical breeding range have not so far produced any obvious increase in breeding effort. The alternative of providing artificial nesting sites near the current feeding area has not yet been tried.

The Puerto Rican Parrot is an example of a species that has been suffering from limitations in the abilities of pairs to find what good nest sites do exist, as well as from problems with a basic scarcity of the sites and competition for the sites. In several recent years, certain pairs have failed to locate adequate sites, although there were good unused sites not far from the boundaries of the territories occupied by the pairs. Since the unused sites were located in regions known to have been formerly occupied by nesting parrots, there is no reason to believe that the habitats there were unsuitable for nesting. Apparently behavioral constraints prevented the pairs from seeking nest sites outside of their territories, but why territories can become established and can persist in areas lacking good nest sites remains unclear. In recent years we have had success in getting nonbreeding pairs into production by providing good artificial sites within the territories of the pairs.

Although it is usually very difficult to document cases in which species experience limitations in their abilities to locate existing nest sites, such limitations are not necessarily rare. In a number of Wood Duck (*Aix sponsa*) studies (e.g., Bellrose et al., 1964; Strange et al., 1971), researchers have found unused natural cavities of apparently good quality to be reasonably common, yet the duck populations have responded strongly to the introduction of artificial nest boxes. In most of these studies, it was not clear whether the population increase was a result of greater nest success in the artificial sites than in the natural sites, a result of greater conspicuousness of the artificial sites to the ducks, or a result of both factors. However, in the Bellrose et al. (1964) study, there was no difference in nest success of artificial and natural sites during one period of strong population increase, and the most reasonable explanation for the original lack of occupancy of many of the natural cavities is that the ducks had difficulty finding them.

DETERMINING WHETHER NEST-SITE LIMITATIONS EXIST

In general, the usual method employed to determine if a species is stressed by nest-site limitations is to provide good quality nest sites in the range of the species. In many cases, when this has been done the population has increased enormously, giving good evidence of former nest-site limitations. Examples of such responses to artificial nest sites can be cited for many species, including Ospreys (Postupalsky and Stackpole, 1974; Garber et al., 1974; Reese, 1977), American Kestrels (*Falco sparverius*) (Hamerstrom et al., 1973), Pied Flycatchers (*Ficedula hypoleuca*) (von Haartman, 1971), Wood Ducks (Dreis and Hendrickson, 1952; Bellrose et al., 1964; Grice and Rogers, 1965; Strange et al., 1971; Haramis, 1975), and many others. Care is in order in interpreting the results with some species; provision of nest sites may only cause a shift in the distribution of the population rather than a significant overall increase. If one is not monitoring the entire population, a shift in distribution can be erroneously interpreted as an increase.

In some cases artificial nest sites have not increased the population of a species. Often the failure appears to be an indication that nest sites were not truly a limiting factor and that some other factor, such as food scarcity, was dominant, as has been suggested for some populations of Ospreys (*see* Postupalsky and Stackpole, 1974). In other cases, however, failure may result if the artificial nest sites favor competitors more than the endangered species. We suspect, for example, that the early nest-box program for the Puerto Rican Parrot may have had such an effect. The nest boxes installed were closer in characteristics to ideal thrasher and honeybee boxes than they were to ideal parrot boxes, and essentially all were immediately occupied by thrashers and honeybees while none were occupied by parrots. The net result very likely was increased difficulties for the parrots because of higher densities of competitors. In more recent years, nest sites of high acceptability to parrots and low acceptability to competitors have been developed, and there are now hopes that the parrot population may be starting to show a positive response. Thus, while an increase of a population following establishment of artificial nest sites can give good evidence that the population was formerly limited by nest-site problems, the failure of a population to increase should not necessarily be interpreted to mean the species is free of nest-site limitations.

Typically, the provision of artificial nest sites to species that are limited by nest sites results in large initial increases in the populations to new levels, above which increased numbers of nest sites are decreasingly effective in producing positive responses (*see* von Haartman, 1971). This declining effectiveness can result if some other resource, such as food, now becomes a dominant limiting factor, if disruptive intraspecific strife begins to become important, or if a predation balance is shifted sufficiently. For example, Bellrose et al. (1964) reported a Wood Duck nest-box program in which a great initial increase in the population was followed by greatly increased problems with Raccoon (*Procyon lotor*) predation on nests, which stopped the population increase and initiated a decline. Similarly, competitive

balances may come to a new equilibrium which halts the increase or re-
verses it. In recent years, House Sparrows (*Passer domesticus*) have
become an increasing problem for Bluebird (*Sialia sialis*) nest-box
programs, threatening to undermine the programs in some areas. So far
the only proven solutions to increased House Sparrow occupancy of the
boxes have been the laborious trapping of sparrows and manual destruction of their nests (Zeleny, 1976). Actually, many nest-site competitors are also, in fact, nest predators, and it becomes difficult to
classify these species. Thus, Starlings (*Sturnus vulgaris*), Yellow-
shafted Flickers (*Colaptes auratus*), Pearly-eyed Thrashers (*Margarops
fuscatus*), and Raccoons, all of which may destroy the nest contents of
other hole-nesting species, nest in cavities themselves, and the
predation they practice may often be an integral part of the process
of searching for and gaining nest sites for themselves.

ALLEVIATING NEST-SITE LIMITATIONS

      Techniques to improve nest-site availability need to be adapted
to the specific problems faced by the species in question. Species
with primary problems of simple scarcity of nest sites can sometimes
be helped by nothing more than provision of artificial nest structures
or by improvement of existing natural nest structures without much
regard for nest competitors or predators. For other species, the primary problem may be a scarcity of nest sites plus difficulties in
locating nest sites, and here it may be critical to place artificial
nests in areas where they are sure to be found by the species and to
design structures so they are conspicuous to the species. For species
troubled more by competition for nest sites, the critical challenge is
often to design sites of high acceptability to the threatened species
and low acceptability to the competitors. For hole-nesting species,
this can sometimes be accomplished by accurate control of the size of
the entrance hole in cases where the competing species are larger
than the threatened forms, such as has been done for cases of Bluebird
versus Starlings and Bermuda Petrels (*Pterodroma cahow*) versus Tropicbirds (*Phaethon lepturus*). The problems are much more difficult when
a competitor is smaller in size than the threatened species, as is the
case with Bluebirds versus House Sparrows, and Puerto Rican Parrots
versus Pearly-eyed Thrashers. Still, it is sometimes possible to find
enough differences between the species to exclude the competitors on
the basis of depth or darkness of the site or through special shape of
the site (*see* McGilvrey and Uhler, 1971).
      With some endangered species, nest-site flexibility is sufficient-
ly broad that potentials exist for conquering nest-site problems by
shifting the population to a new kind of nest site free from competition, predation, and scarcity. As Newton (1976) has pointed out, it i
likely that the nest-site preferences of many species are not genetically fixed, and that deviations from the normal nest-site preferences
can become established in the population through imprinting or conditioning processes, if the deviations prove to be successful (*see*
Hildén, 1965). Thus, ground-nesting populations of various falcons
have become naturally established on several occasions, sometimes suc-

cessfully and sometimes not, depending primarily on the density of terrestrial predators. Peregrine Falcons, normally cliff-nesters, have become tree-nesters in some areas; one population in Tennessee used natural cavities in giant trees (Hickey and Anderson, 1969), while another population in Germany regularly used old stick nests of other raptorial birds (Mebs, 1969).

Theoretically, one can hope to shift nest-site preferences of relatively flexible species by such techniques as fostering young of the species into nests of other species which use the favored nest type or by arranging for release of captive-reared stock that have been conditioned to the favored structure or nest-site type. Apparent success in changing nest-site preferences has been achieved in Black Duck (*Anas rubripes*) studies at the Patuxent Wildlife Research Center, where a significant fraction of the wild population shifted over from ground-nesting to nesting in predator-proof elevated cylinders following release of conditioned young (F.B. McGilvrey, *unpublished data*). However, these studies were not continued long enough to establish whether or not the changes in nest-site preferences observed were truly stable.

In many cases, the best overall method of insuring adequate availability of nest sites for secondary cavity-nesting birds lies not in nest-box programs but in fostering forestry practices that provide such nest sites naturally. A number of studies, including our own in Puerto Rico, have now demonstrated conclusively the great importance of large trees of the proper species in producing natural cavity nest sites (*see* Gysel, 1961; Bellrose et al., 1964; Hansen, 1966; Weier, 1966, Prince, 1968; and Haramis, 1975). Differences between tree species in tendencies toward branch breakage and heart rot result in significant differences in the tendency to form cavities. Thus various maples, gums, and sycamores, to name a few species, are generally superior trees in cavity formation, while many conifers, such as spruce, are inferior. There are even more significant differences between various sizes of trees in frequency of cavities. For example, in Luquillo Forest in Puerto Rico, most tree species exhibit a cavity frequency rate of about 1 cavity per 14 trees for trees 30 cm to 60 cm in diameter at breast-height (dbh), rising to a frequency of about 1 cavity per 2 trees for trees over 122 cm dbh. The Palo Colorado (*Cyrilla racemiflora*) has a cavity frequency of 1 cavity per 6 trees for the 30-60 cm dbh class, rising to a frequency of 1 cavity per 2 trees for the 122 cm and over dbh class. The general superiority of this species in cavity formation and the overall abundance of large specimens of this species in Luquillo Forest are unquestionably the major reasons why parrots have nested primarily in it.

Clearly, mature trees of species with high cavity formation rates are of enormous importance to secondary cavity-nesting birds, and forestry practices which select against such trees also select against the bird species dependent on them, not just in a reproductive sense, but also, as Balda (1975) has discussed, in the sense of winter roosting. Although to a limited extent forestry practices that eliminate mature trees can be made consistent with conservation of cavity-nesting species if nest boxes can be simultaneously provided, this solution is of little value for primary cavity-nesting species such as

woodpeckers which are dependent on mature rotting trees not only for
nesting but also for feeding (see Conner et al., 1975). In almost all
respects, it appears to be generally preferable to encourage timber
management practices which allow for the existence of mature trees and
dead trees in at least some compromise fashion.

LITERATURE CITED

Balda, R.P. 1975. The relationship of secondary cavity nesters to
    snag densities in western coniferous forests. Wildlife Habitat
    Technical Bulletin No. 1, 37 p.
Bellrose, F.C., K.L. Johnson, and T.U. Meyers. 1964. Relative value
    of natural cavities and nesting houses for wood ducks. J. Wild-
    life Manage. 28:661-676.
Conner, R.N., R.G. Hooper, H.S. Crawford, and H.S. Mosby. 1975. Wood-
    pecker nesting habitat in cut and uncut woodlands in Virginia.
    J. Wildlife Manage. 39:144-150.
Dreis, R.E., and G.O. Hendrickson. 1952. Wood duck production from
    nest-boxes and natural cavities on the Lake Odessa area, Iowa,
    in 1951. Iowa Bird Life 22:19-22.
Garber, D.P., J.R. Koplin, and J.R. Kahl. 1974. Osprey management on
    the Lassen National Forest, California, p. 119-122. In F.N.
    Hamerstrom, Jr., B.E. Harrel, and R.R. Olendorff (eds.) Manage-
    ment of raptors. Raptor Research Foundation, Raptor Research
    Report No. 2.
Grice, D. and J.P. Rogers. 1965. The wood duck in Massachusetts. Mas-
    sachusetts Div. Fisheries and Game, Boston. 96 p.
Gysel, L.W. 1961. An ecological study of tree cavities and ground bur-
    rows in forest stands. J. Wildlife Manage. 25:12-20.
Hansen, H.L. 1966 (1965). Silvical characteristics of tree species
    and decay processes as related to cavity production, p. 65-69.
    In Wood duck management and research: a symposium. (Wildlife
    Management Institute, Washington, D.C.).
Hamerstrom, F., F.N. Hamerstrom, and J. Hart. 1973. Nest boxes:
    an effective management tool for kestrels. J. Wildlife
    Manage. 37:400-403.
Haramis, G.M. 1975. Wood duck (Aix sponsa) ecology and management
    within the green-timber impoundments at Montezuma National Wild-
    life Refuge. M.S. thesis, Cornell University. 153 p.
Hickey, J.J., and D.W. Anderson. 1969. The peregrine falcon: life
    history and population literature, p. 3-42. In J.J. Hickey (ed.)
    Peregrine Falcon populations. Univ. of Wisconsin Press, Madison.
Hildén, O. 1965. Habitat selection in birds. Ann. Zool. Fenn. 2:53-75.
McGilvrey, F.B., and F.M. Uhler. 1971. A starling-deterrent wood duck
    nest box. J. Wildlife Manage. 35:793-797.
Mebs, T. 1969. Peregrine falcon population trends in West Germany, p.
    193-207. In J.J. Hickey (ed.) Peregrine Falcon populations. Univ.
    of Wisconsin Press, Madison.
Newton, I. 1976. Population limitation in diurnal raptors. Can. Field-
    Naturalist. 90:274-300.

Postupalsky, S., and S.M. Stackpole. 1974. Artificial nesting platform for ospreys in Michigan, p. 105-117. *In* F.N. Hamerstrom, Jr., B. E. Harrel, and R.R. Olendorff (eds.) Management of raptors. Raptor Research Foundation, Raptor Research Report No. 2.

Prince, H.H. 1968. Nest sites used by wood ducks and common goldeneyes in New Brunswick. J. Wildlife Manage. 32:489-500.

Reese, J.G. 1977. Reproductive success of ospreys in central Chesapeake Bay. Auk 94:202-221.

Strange, T.H., Cunningham, E.R., and J.W. Goertz. 1971. Use of nest boxes by wood ducks in Mississippi. J. Wildlife Manage. 35:786-793.

Sykes, P.W., Jr., and R. Chandler. 1974. Use of artificial nest structures by everglade kites. Wilson Bull. 86:282-284.

von Haartman, L. 1971. Population dynamics, p. 391-460. *In* D.S. Farner and J.R. King (eds.) Avian biology. Vol. 1. Academic Press, New York.

Weier, R.W. 1966. A survey of wood duck nest sites on Mingo National Wildlife Refuge in southeast Missouri. p. 91-112. *In* Wood Duck management and research: a symposium. (Wildlife Management Institute, Washington, D.C.)

Wilbur, S.R., W.D. Carrier, and J.C. Borneman. 1974. Supplementary feeding program for California condors. J. Wildlife Manage. 38:343-346.

Zeleny, L. 1976. The bluebird. Indiana University Press, Bloomington, Indiana, 170 p.

5

Artificial Nesting Platforms for Ospreys and Bald Eagles

Sergej Postupalsky

The use of man-made nests of one type or another has become an established management and research tool for a growing number of avian species. Among the birds of prey, the Osprey (*Pandion haliaetus*) is perhaps the foremost, but by no means the only species, which readily accepts artificial nest sites. The use of such structures by the Bald Eagle (*Haliaeetus leucocephalus*), however, appears to be a new development. It is appropriate, therefore, that I discuss work with these two species separately.

USE OF ARTIFICIAL NESTING PLATFORMS BY OSPREYS

While the Osprey is not currently considered endangered in North America, its populations have been depleted in several parts of its breeding range on this continent (Henny, 1977), and by virtue of its position as a terminal link of a long aquatic food chain, it is sensitive to environmental pollutants (Wiemeyer et al., 1975). These developments have led to a growing number of efforts to provide man-made nest sites of various designs for the species. Some of these are described and pictured by Ames and Mersereau (1964), Reese (1970), Rhodes (1972,1977), Kahl (1972), Postupalsky and Stackpole (1974), and Kennedy (1977). Workers in New Jersey have recently devised an efficient method of placing such nest structures in the salt marshes by dropping the poles--like giant darts--from a helicopter (P.D. McLain, *personal communication*).

During the mid-1960's, Michigan's Ospreys were reproducing very poorly and were declining in numbers, giving cause for serious concern about their survival as a breeding species in the state (Postupalsky, 1969). In addition to the effects of the then widely prevalent thin-eggshell syndrome (Hickey and Anderson, 1968; Anderson and Hickey,

1972; Postupalsky, 1977) reproduction was also affected locally by the poor and deteriorating condition of many nest sites. This became especially serious in the 2 principal breeding colonies, on Fletcher Pond and on the Dead Stream Flooding in the northern Lower Peninsula, where Ospreys built their nests on dead trees killed by inundation. Fletcher Pond is a storage reservoir, about 3,000 hectares in area, maintained by a hydroelectric power company. The Dead Stream Flooding is a smaller impoundment established for waterfowl by the Michigan Department of Natural Resources.

Early in 1967, 26 artificial nest platforms were constructed on these 2 impoundments. In following years, additional platforms were erected there and on several other wildlife floodings. The platforms are plywood discs or octagons 0.9 m across, equipped with concentric rows of dowels to keep sticks and other nesting material in place. Most are mounted on 3 steel legs; 8 are placed on existing dead, but still sturdy trees. The platforms, their construction, and the selection of locations are described, and results of the project through 1972 evaluated in an earlier paper (Postupalsky and Stackpole, 1974).

After the 2 initial seasons, between 37 and 43 platforms were available, and between 20 and 29 were occupied by Ospreys each year (Table 1). Altogether, these man-made nests were available 425 platform-years and were occupied 234 times (55 percent) during the 11-year period. This occupancy rate is very close to the 58 percent occupancy reported by Reese (1977) for 285 platforms in tidewater areas of central Chesapeake Bay. In Michigan, a minimum of 227 first clutches were laid, and 4 second clutches were induced by removal of the first clutch soon after its completion. In all, 291 young Ospreys were raised to fledging age on Michigan platforms during 1967-77.

TABLE 1. OCCUPANCY OF ARTIFICIAL NESTING
PLATFORMS BY OSPREYS IN MICHIGAN, 1967-1977

Year	Number of Platforms Available	Number of Platforms Occupied
1967	26	11
1968	31	18
1969	41	20
1970	40	20
1971	42	23
1972	39	24
1973	42	23
1974	43	24
1975	41[a]	22
1976	37[a]	22
1977	43[a]	29

[a]Includes one platform occupied by Bald Eagles.

The platforms have also proven attractive to other birds. Herring Gulls (*Larus argentatus*) nested on tripod platforms on Fletcher Pond at least 6 times and raised young 3 times. Great Horned Owls (*Bubo virginianus*) nested twice on Dead Stream platforms producing 1 and 2 young, respectively. Finally, for the past 3 years, a tripod-type platform was taken over by yet another uninvited, but nevertheless very welcome tenant--the Bald Eagle. I shall return to this later.

Before proceeding with an evaluation of the efficacy of the nesting platforms, I should stress that the Michigan project was initiated as a management measure to help maintain the species in the state; it was not designed as a controlled experiment. This precludes a rigorous analysis of the data and makes difficult a separation of the precise effects of the platforms from other factors that were operating on the population at the same time.

Perhaps the most dramatic effect of the platforms was the reversal of the decline of the Fletcher Pond Osprey colony which grew from 11 pairs in 1966 to 18 pairs in 1972 (Figure 1). This increase was apparently not caused by an influx of birds which had been nesting elsewhere in the region, but rather by new pairs, believed to be breeding for the first time. Banding has shown that at least several individuals occupying previously unused platforms were indeed young adults. Since 1972, the Fletcher Pond population has remained fairly stable, fluctuating between 32 and 38 adults, including up to 2 unmated adults in some years. The pattern of initial increase followed by a leveling off suggests that the population may have reached the carrying capacity of this impoundment and that limiting factors other than nest sites are now operating. At the end of the 1974 breeding season, there were over 60 Ospreys on Fletcher Pond (17 pairs plus 33 fledglings). Nesting mortality increased substantially in the last 2 seasons from an average of 7 percent during 1968-75 to 29 percent for 1976-77. While in 1976 most deaths occurred during a hailstorm in late June, several lines of evidence point to starvation as the dominant mortality factor in 1977.

The Dead Stream colony consisted of 7 pairs until 1964. By 1967, when 6 artificial nests were provided, it had declined to 6 pairs. No increase occurred even though an excess of platforms was available. Only 3 pairs remained during 1972-77. This impoundment has become very weedy during the past 12 years, and shallow, open water areas have been substantially reduced. The Osprey's preferred foraging sites have thus been largely eliminated, reducing the capacity of this flooding to support as many Ospreys as it did in the past.

The productivity, measured as large or fledged young per occupied nest (for this and other definitions see Postupalsky, 1974), on manmade nests taken for the entire period was twice that recorded on natural nests (Table 2). Nearly all occupied platforms and all natural nests considered in Table 2 are in the northern Lower Peninsula of Michigan. The sole exception is one platform in the Upper Peninsula, occupied by Ospreys in 1970-72. Productivity during 1969-70 averaged 0.7 on both platforms and natural nests, an increase over the average of 0.4 for the preceding 3 seasons (Postupalsky, 1977). From 1971 through 1977, however, productivity on platforms averaged 1.4, while it remained low on natural nests, averaging only 0.5 for the

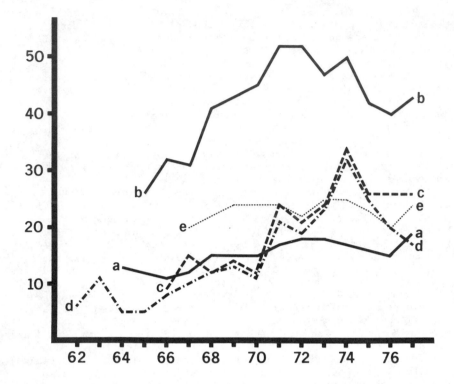

a)   Number of Osprey pairs present in area
b)   Total number of eggs produced by all pairs
c)   Total number of young Ospreys hatched in area
d)   Total number of young Ospreys fledged in area
e)   Number of artificial nesting platforms available;
     platforms were first available in 1967

FIGURE 1.   Trends in Osprey population numbers and reproduction
    in relation to the number of artificial nesting platforms
    provided on Fletcher Pond, Michigan, 1962-1977.

TABLE 2. COMPARISON OF OSPREY PRODUCTIVITY ON NATURAL
NESTS AND ARTIFICIAL PLATFORMS IN MICHIGAN, 1967-1977

	Natural Nests		Platforms	
Year	Number Occupied	No. of Young per Occupied Nest	Number Occupied	No. of Young per Occupied Nest
1967	16	0.5	11	0.9
1968	11	0.7	18	0.7
1969	9	0.7	20	0.7
1970	13	1.0	18	0.7
1971	13	0.7	23	1.4
1972	12	1.0	24	1.0
1973	10	0.2	23	1.4
1974	12	0.3	24	1.8
1975	13	0.6	22	1.8
1976	9	0.4	22	1.6
1977	8	0.5	29	1.2
	126	0.6	234	1.2

same period. The difference in productivity is not entirely attributable to the platforms. First, the data are subject to several
sources of bias (Postupalsky and Stackpole, 1974). The distribution
of platforms and natural nests relative to habitat quality is not
random; platforms were placed selectively in what was believed to be
"prime" habitat and to provide stable nest supports for previously
productive pairs. Few natural nests remain in Lower Michigan, and
most are occupied by pairs with a record of poor nest success due to
causes other than nest blowdowns. Furthermore, beginning about 1970,
productivity has also improved appreciably in the Upper Peninsula,
where the influence of platforms is negligible (Postupalsky and Stackpole, 1974; Postupalsky, 1977). By attracting more young pairs to
good habitat, the man-made nests have served to maximize productivity
which might not have materialized had these birds settled elsewhere
(e.g., in places with good, natural nest sites but poorer fishing).
Garber et al. (1974) reached the same tentative conclusion while trying to explain an increase in breeding pairs and nest success subsequent to the provision of artificial nests and topped trees at Eagle
Lake, California. The same pattern may also account for the dramatic
increase from 4 or 6 pairs to 22 pairs of Ospreys associated with
high productivity within 4 years after man-made nest structures were
made available on an island in Chesapeake Bay (Rhodes, 1972 and 1977).
Mortality of nestlings was greatly reduced on platform nests. Of
328 nestlings hatched on platforms during 1967-77, 34 (10 percent)
died before reaching fledging age. In contrast, the mortality rate in
natural nests during 1965-77 was 34 percent (20 out of 59 young).
While nest blowdowns caused 57 percent of the mortality in natural

nests, this source accounted for only 6 percent of the mortality on platforms. The sole case involved the death of 2 young when a platform on top of a dead stub broke off at the waterline during a storm in late June 1976, the tenth season of its existence. Reduction of losses due to nest blowdowns during the breeding season is an important and direct effect of artificial nests upon productivity.

Results of the Michigan work with man-made Osprey nests and of work done elsewhere show that these structures can be used to accomplish several management objectives:

1. Breeding pairs can be maintained in suitable habitat despite the deterioration of natural nest sites. This applies especially to impoundments where Osprey nest sites are an ephemeral feature. Man-made ponds are subject to successional changes: an initially high fish production, associated with high organic productivity, eventually tends to decline, and shallow areas tend to become choked with rooted vegetation. Generally, nest sites (i.e., dead trees, especially "soft woods") tend to deteriorate faster than the capacity of the pond to produce an abundant and accessible supply of fish. Thus, artificial nests can substantially extend the utilization of these floodings by Ospreys. The importance of impoundments to the species is demonstrated by the fact that in the Lower Peninsula of Michigan, fully 91 percent of the Osprey population nests on Fletcher Pond and on the smaller wildlife floodings.

2. By eliminating the limiting role of nest sites, man-made nests allow the Osprey population to grow up to the level which the available habitat is capable of supporting, as has evidently taken place on Fletcher Pond, the largest Osprey colony in the Great Lakes region. An excess of available nest sites facilitates the recruitment of young individuals into the breeding population, a strategy also used with success by Reese (1970, 1977) and others.

3. Artificial nests can make a substantial contribution to the maintenance of the Osprey population over a larger area by maximizing reproduction. In the Lower Peninsula approximately two-thirds of the breeding population are currently using the platforms and account for 80 percent of the production of young. Individuals fledged from platforms have started to colonize previously unoccupied impoundments.

4. Platforms facilitate certain aspects of Osprey research by making nests structurally stable and more accessible (Postupalsky and Stackpole, 1974). Nesting activity can be monitored more closely, the young examined, weighed, measured and banded, food remains studied, and adults trapped for banding and individual marking. Such work is often impossible in natural nests of uncertain stability. By minimizing losses of natural nests due to storms, which lead to frequent moves by the birds, platforms enable the researcher to follow individual breeding sites from year to year. Ames and Mersereau (1964) used platforms to evaluate the role of tidal flooding and of terrestrial predators in the nest success of Connecticut Ospreys.

USE OF ARTIFICIAL NESTING PLATFORMS BY BALD EAGLES

While the Ospreys' ready acceptance of artificial nest supports is well known, there are but few documented reports of Bald Eagles nesting on man-made structures. Langille (1884) reported a nest with young in the mow of an abandoned barn near the Niagara River. More recently, a land developer made a much publicized effort to build four artificial nests for Bald Eagles displaced by a housing development in Florida (Anon., 1971), but I know of no reports indicating if the birds used these structures. Sherrod et al. (1976) mention a nest built "on the platform of an approach light at the airstrip" on Amchitka Island, Alaska. Finally, Helander (1975) reports 3 man-made nests accepted by the closely related White-tailed Sea Eagle (*H. albicilla*) in Sweden. Here I wish to report recent experiences with 3 artificial eagle nests in Michigan.

Nest 1

A pair of Bald Eagles nesting on a small island in Bond Falls Basin, a storage reservoir in Ontonagon County, produced 16 young from 1961-68. Its nest tree, a Sugar Maple (*Acer saccharum*), was largely dead by 1967 and completely so by the following breeding season. It collapsed in September 1968. The forest in the surrounding area consisted almost wholly of pole-size Aspen (*Populus* sp.) and Jack Pine (*Pinus banksiana*), lacking large trees with a crotch suitable for a nest. Because of their consistent nest success, it was especially desirable to keep this pair breeding in their established breeding area. I selected the largest available tree, a Sugar Maple, located on another island, about 150 m from the former nest site. Its top was cut off about 15 m above ground and an oversize "Osprey platform" (1.5 m diameter) was installed on top of the stub, offset and supported by 6 metal trusses. A collection of sticks was arranged on top to simulate a nest.

The following spring, a lone adult frequented the site, but no nesting attempt took place. In 1970, no eagles were noted on 8 April, but on 16 April one was sitting in incubating posture on the man-made nest. On 17 June, the platform held only an abandoned egg. The egg contained a partially developed embryo, indicating that it had been fertile. No further nesting attempts took place at this breeding site.

Nest 2

On 6 June 1969, J.B. Holt banded 2 eaglets in a nest in a Red Oak (*Quercus rubra*) near Fletcher Pond in Alpena County. On 20 June, Holt and I found that the nest had been blown out of the tree, probably by a storm on 12 June. One of the eaglets, then about 7 weeks old, was standing at the base of a bush about 10 m from the base of the nest tree. It was still being fed and cared for by the adults. Some scattered pin feathers and a leg, still bearing the band, were all that remained of the other eaglet. Given these circumstances, we thought it advisable to get the surviving eaglet off the ground. We obtained a wooden pallet (ca. 0.9 by 1.2 m) of the type used by fork lifts. Holt nailed this structure to the tree about 14 m above ground between the two main branches which had supported the nest, reinforced it with a wooden beam, hauled up some sticks and other nest material, and placed the young eagle on top. The adults continued to care for it, and it fledged successfully. Dunstan and Borth (1970) describe a similar reconstruction of a fallen, active Bald Eagle nest. Later in autumn, the pallet was reinforced with metal struts, a 1.5 m diameter platform with dowels was attached on top, and a stick nest constructed on top of it.

Early the following spring, the eagles built a new nest in another oak about 150 m away and used it each season from 1970-73 and 1975-76, raising a total of 10 young during this period. They nested on the platform unsuccessfully in 1974. The eagles returned to the man-made nest again in 1977 and produced 3 eaglets.

Nest 3

Early in 1969, a tripod-type Osprey nest platform was constructed in a shallow portion of a reservoir in the central Upper Peninsula. A pair of Ospreys used it during 1970-72 and raised 1 young in 1971. The platform then remained vacant for 2 seasons.

On 22 May 1975, during an Osprey nest-checking flight, R.F. Aartila, a Michigan Department of Natural Resources biologist, noted 2 adult Bald Eagles at this platform, one of them apparently incubating. During a later visit on 19 June, U.S. Forest Service workers found what appeared to be an abandoned egg in the nest.

The pair returned to the platform in 1976 and started incubation sometime between 7 and 12 April. The nest contained one egg which evidently never hatched. The female was a young adult.

In 1977, this pair again nested on the platform, this time successfully; there were 2 young, about 3 weeks old, on the platform nest on 25 May. I banded both eaglets on 2 July, and on 21 July both were flying.

Conclusions about Bald Eagles Using Artificial Nests

Altogether, 6 nesting attempts were made by 3 different pairs of Bald Eagles at 3 different artificial nests. Two of these were built especially for eagles; the third was a tripod-type platform intended for Ospreys. Two of these attempts were successful, and 5 eaglets were raised to fledging age. These observations show that: (1) Bald Eagles will initiate nesting activity on suitable man-made nest structures placed within their breeding territory, and (2) new pairs being recruited into the breeding population may be attracted to suitable unoccupied habitat by the provision of appropriate nest supports The existence in the same region of a healthy breeding population reproducing at or above minimum replacement level is a prerequisite for the second situation.

The initial experience with man-made eagle nests in Michigan suggests several potential management applications:

1. Structurally weak natural nests can be replaced by artificial nests to encourage a pair to remain in a productive breeding area which may be lacking adequate nest supports.

2. Nests exposed to excessive human activity (such as roads, campgrounds, boat landings, construction sites or logging operations)

can be removed and rebuilt in a more remote spot within the home range of the pair. Moving the nest a few hundred meters just out of sight of the public may solve the problem. Helander (1975) makes the same suggestion.

3. The provision of man-made nests in suitable, but currently unoccupied habitat may help attract maturing individuals searching for a breeding site. It could be used to encourage the return of breeding Bald Eagles to areas where this species had bred in the past but now only visits in the winter. In the last 5 years, I have noted the reoccupation by eagles of several breeding sites which had been vacant for a decade or longer. Some of the new birds took over and repaired such old nests as remained. One pair built its nest in the same tree from which a nest had been blown out 11 years earlier. In at least 2 sites where no eagle nests remained, the new pairs had taken over Osprey nests--one natural and the platform discussed above. These observations suggest either that suitable nest supports may be limited in some areas, or that the presence of a nest structure may constitute an important stimulus in nest site selection by this species.

The work with artificial eagle nests, along with other recently applied techniques, shows that the Bald Eagle does lend itself to manipulative management. While this comes as no surprise to raptor workers, it needs to be stressed because some conservationists and wildlife managers view the species as intolerant of human presence. They espouse a "hands-off" policy relative to the Bald Eagle, seeking to exclude all human activity and intervention, including research work such as banding, from the breeding areas. This policy will be counterproductive if it is allowed to hamper needed research upon which any sound and knowledgable management program ultimately depends.

ACKNOWLEDGMENTS

My work with Ospreys and Bald Eagles in Michigan was made possible by funding from the National Audubon Society and from Conservation for Survival, founded by Stephen M. Stackpole, who also financed and supervised the construction and maintenance of the artificial nest platforms. The Michigan Department of Natural Resources, U.S. Forest Service, and U.S. Fish and Wildlife Service cooperated with population studies of both species. The Michigan Department of Natural Resources, Alpena Power Company, Upper Peninsula Power Company, and Cleveland Cliffs Iron Company granted permission to place the nest structures on their lands. John B. Holt, Jr., B. Keith Baldwin, Thomas U. Fraser, Thomas V. Heatley, William G. Robichaud, and others assisted in the field. I am very grateful to all these individuals, agencies, and organizations.

LITERATURE CITED

Ames, P.L., and G.S. Mersereau. 1964. Some factors in the decline of the Osprey in Connecticut. Auk 81(2):173-185.
Anderson, D.W., and J.J. Hickey. 1972. Eggshell changes in certain North American birds. Proc. Int. Ornith. Congr. 15:514-540.

Anon. 1971. News briefs: Artificial eagle aeries. Pop. Mechanics
    136(6):40.
Dunstan, T.C., and M. Borth. 1970. Successful reconstruction of
    active Bald Eagle nest. Wilson Bull. 82(3):326-327.
Garber, D.P., J.R. Koplin, and J.R. Kahl. 1974. Osprey management
    on the Lassen National Forest California, p. 119-122. In
    F.N. Hamerstrom, Jr., B.E. Harrell, and R.R. Olendorff (eds.)
    Management of raptors. Raptor Research Foundation, Raptor
    Research Report No. 2.
Helander, B. 1975. Havsörnen i Sverige. Stockholm, Svenska
    Naturskyddsföreningen.
Henny, C.J. 1977. Research, management, and status of the Osprey in
    North America, p. 199-222. In R.D. Chancellor (ed.) World
    conference on birds of prey, Vienna 1975. Report of proceedings.
    International Council for Bird Preservation, London.
Hickey, J.J., and D.W. Anderson. 1968. Chlorinated hydrocarbons and
    eggshell changes in raptorial and fish-eating birds. Science
    162:271-273.
Kahl, J. 1972. Better homes for feathered fishermen. Outdoor Cali-
    fornia 33(3):4-6.
Kennedy, R.S. 1977. The status of the Osprey in tidewater Virginia,
    1970-1971, p. 121-133. In J.C. Ogden (ed.) Transactions of the
    North American Osprey research conference. U.S. Nat. Park Service,
    Trans. and Proc. Ser., No. 2.
Langille, J.H. 1884. Our birds in their haunts. S.E. Cassino and Co.,
    Boston.
Postupalsky, S. 1969. The status of the Osprey in Michigan in 1965.
    p. 338-340, In J.J. Hickey (ed.) Peregrine Falcon populations:
    their biology and decline. Univ. of Wisconsin Press, Madison.
Postupalsky, S. 1974. Raptor reproductive success: some problems
    with methods, criteria, and terminology, p. 21-31. In F.N.
    Hamerstrom, Jr., B.E. Harrell, and R.R. Olendorff (eds.)
    Management of raptors. Raptor Research Foundation, Raptor Re-
    search Report No. 2.
Postupalsky, S. 1977. Status of the Osprey in Michigan. p. 153-165.
    In J.C. Ogden (ed.) Transactions of the North American Osprey
    research conference. U.S. Nat. Park Service, Trans. and Proc.
    Ser., No. 2.
Postupalsky, S., and S.M. Stackpole. 1974. Artificial nesting plat-
    forms for Ospreys in Michigan, p. 105-117. In F.N. Hamerstrom,
    Jr., B.E. Harrell, and R.R. Olendorff (eds.) Management of
    raptors. Raptor Research Foundation, Raptor Research Report No. 2.
Reese, J.G. 1970. Reproduction in a Chesapeake Bay Osprey population.
    Auk 87(4):747-759.
Reese, J.G. 1977. Reproductive success of Ospreys in central Chesapeak
    Bay. Auk 94(2):202-221.
Rhodes, L.I. 1972. Success of Osprey nest structures at Martin Nation-
    al Wildlife Refuge. J. Wildlife Manage. 36(4):1296-1299.
Rhodes, L.I. 1977. An Osprey population aided by nest structures,
    p. 77-83. In J.C. Ogden (ed.) Transactions of the North American
    Osprey research conference. U.S. Nat. Park Service, Trans. and
    Proc. Ser., No. 2.

Sherrod, S.K., C.M. White, and F.S.L. Williamson. 1976. Biology of the Bald Eagle on Amchitka Island, Alaska. Living Bird 15:143-182.

Wiemeyer, S.N., P.R. Spitzer, W.C. Krantz, T.G. Lamont, and E. Cromartie. 1975. Effects of environmental pollutants on Connecticut and Maryland Ospreys. J. Wildlife Manage. 39(1): 124-139.

6

Puerto Rican Parrots and Nest-Site Scarcity

Noel F. R. Snyder

With a total wild population averaging under 20 individuals for the last 10 years, the Puerto Rican Parrot (*Amazona vittata*) is one of the most critically endangered species of bird in the world. The species was once abundant throughout the main island of Puerto Rico, and also occurred on several of the offshore islands. But even as early as 1911-12, when Wetmore conducted his year-long study of the avifauna of the island (Wetmore, 1927), the range of the parrots had already been reduced to just 4 local regions of the main island. There were 2 western populations in rugged regions of limestone hills (Rio Abajo and Guajataca) and 2 eastern populations in high elevation rain forest (Carite and Luquillo Forests). A small flock found by Wetmore in the Mameyes Swamp just north of Luquillo Forest may only have been a subpopulation of the Luquillo Forest population. By 1930, the 2 western populations had been extirpated, and by 1940 the only remaining population was the Luquillo Forest population.

A number of factors have led to the endangerment of the species. The island of Puerto Rico was nearly deforested by about 1910 to 1920 (*see* Murphy, 1916), and since the parrots nest primarily in natural cavities in large trees, this deforestation must have been a major cause of the historical decline. In addition, the species was shot for food in many areas and was routinely taken into captivity essentially everywhere. The process of robbing nests for young often involved destruction of nest sites, thus providing a two-fold stress on the populations.

Luquillo Forest, the remaining home of the species, has been a National Forest since 1918. Now known officially as the Caribbean National Forest, it presently encompasses some 11,000 hectares of mountainous woodland. Because of land acquisitions, the forest is now actually more than double the area it was early in the century, and for the most part, it has not been extensively cut. About

2,000 hectares of the forest are believed to be virgin.

Despite the protected status and overall improvement of its habitat in recent years, the parrot population in Luquillo Forest has continued to decline. In Table 1, I present minimum population figures from the time of the first study of the parrots by Rodriguez-Vidal (1959) to the present. The Endangered Species Program of the U.S. Fish and Wildlife Service in collaboration with the U.S. Forest Service, the World Wildlife Fund, and the Commonwealth Government began an intensive effort to save the parrot in late 1968. By then, the total wild population had been reduced to approximately 24 individuals, and the decline continued until about 1971. Since 1971, the population has been fluctuating between about 15 and 20 individuals. There has been no clear recovery as yet, but the decline has leveled off.

The causes of decline in Luquillo Forest have been somewhat different from the causes of the historical decline outside the forest. To be sure, illegal shooting and nest robbing have continued to some extent in recent decades, but other problems have assumed dominance. In particular, the parrots have been stressed by predation from exceedingly dense populations of Red-tailed Hawks (*Buteo jamaicensis*), by poor nesting success due to occupancy of inadequate nest sites, parasitism of young by bot fly maggots (*Philornis pici*), and destruction of eggs and young by Pearly-eyed Thrashers (*Magarops fuscatus*); and, strangely enough, by a failure of a significant fraction of the potential breeders to attempt breeding because of a scarcity of nest sites. In this paper, I will concentrate on problems of nest-site scarcity and quality. The impact of Pearly-eyed Thrashers, which causes significant reductions in parrot breeding success, will be con-

TABLE 1. MINIMUM POPULATION COUNTS OF PUERTO RICAN
PARROTS IN THE LUQUILLO MOUNTAINS, 1954-1977

Year	Minimum Number of Parrots Counted during Indicated Month
1954	200 (Nov.)
1955	200 (Oct.)
1963	130 (May)
1966	70 (Dec.)
1968	24 (Nov.)
1969	22 (Apr.)
1970	20 (Jan.)
1971	16 (Jan.)
1972	14 (Feb.), 16 (Oct.)
1973	16 (Feb.), 19 (May)
1974	16 (Apr.), 17 (June)
1975	14 (Mar.), 19 (May)
1976	17 (Mar.), 22 (June)
1977	18 (Mar.), 18 (July)

sidered separately (N.F.R. Snyder and J. Taapken, Ch. 14, *this volume*).

THE AVAILABILITY OF GOOD NEST SITES

It was not immediately obvious that a scarcity of good nest sites might be depressing parrot reproduction when intensive studies of the parrot were begun by C.B. Kepler in 1968. It was clear that reproduction overall was very poor, but the apparent abundance of natural cavities in Palo Colorados (*Cyrilla racemiflora*) and the extremely reduced size of the parrot population in relation to what nest sites were presumably available seemed to rule out nest-site scarcity as a major cause of the population decline. Nevertheless, Kepler did install a number of artificial nest boxes in 3 traditional parrot nesting areas in 1969 in hopes that they might be of some benefit to the population. These boxes were not adopted by parrots, although they were used extensively by honeybees and Pearly-eyed Thrashers.

We believe now that the failure of parrots to adopt the early nest boxes may have been due, at least in part, to the relatively small size of the boxes, but at the time, the fact that parrots did not use them further reinforced suspicions that nest sites were not a problem. It was only during 1971, the last year of Kepler's studies in Puerto Rico, that the first clear evidence of nest-site problems surfaced. One of 2 pairs of parrots found nesting in that year adopted a miserably-wet nest hole and quite clearly failed because of an inability to hatch eggs in the site.

Kepler left the parrot program in late 1971, and no intensive studies were made in the breeding season of 1972. Intensive studies were resumed in late 1972, and in the 1973 breeding season, we finally began to accumulate considerable evidence of nest site problems. In 1973, one pair adopted a nest tree that was completely hollow to the ground, open at the base, and had no flat internal substrate on which eggs might have rested. Not surprisingly, the pair failed to reproduce in 1973. We found this nest site only when we began systematic climbing of Palo Colorados in the pair's territory late in the breeding season. An abundance of freshly-moulted parrot feathers inside the hole and massive chewing on the vines in front of the entrance left no doubt they had adopted this site. Although we immediately installed an artificial bottom in the hole below the entrance, it was apparently already too late in the breeding season for egg-laying. We have no evidence that the pair ever returned to the site. Systematic climbing of all other large trees in the territory revealed no clearly usable natural cavities. Many cavities were located, but all were too small or too wet to be practical nest sites. The present nesting areas of the parrots sometimes receive as much as 500 cm of rain in a year, and it is an unusual cavity that is dry at the bottom.

Hopes were high that in 1974 the same pair of parrots would return to the hollow tree with the artificial bottom and become a producing pair of parrots. Instead, the pair shifted its territory and challenged another pair of parrots further down the valley for its nesting site. Neither of the 2 pairs laid eggs, and they battled

viciously over the nest site until late in the breeding season when
first the female of the invading pair lost one eye and then the male
of the defending pair disappeared, probably the victim of predation.
Shortly afterwards, the remaining two-eyed female re-paired with the
male of the invading pair, but this new pair produced no eggs in 1974.

When we first saw the conflict over the nest site developing, we
immediately provided several artificial nest sites near the nest hole,
but neither pair paid any attention to the artificial sites. Apparently, both pairs were already committed to the natural site.

Another pair, first found in 1973, gave equally strong evidence
of reproduction suppressed by a scarcity of good nest sites. We located no nest for the pair during the breeding season of 1973; after the
breeding season, we began systematically climbing trees to determine
if there were potential nest sites in the area. We found only 1 reasonably good cavity, near the center of the territory of the pair, but
it was so close to the ground--only 3 meters high--that we wondered if
it was an acceptable site.

We do not know if the pair laid eggs in the hole in 1973, but we
suspect they did not because of observations made at the site in 1974.
In 1974, the pair, clearly checking other cavities in the area, was
several times observed checking the site in question. On arrival, the
male immediately dropped down from the lower canopy to the hole and
began the usual wailing of a nest inspection, going in and out of the
hole without hesitation. The female, in contrast, remained in the
lower canopy, apparently reluctant to descend so close to the ground,
and we never once saw her enter the hole. The pair did not completely
adopt this or any other site in 1974 and presumably laid no eggs.

It appeared that the 3 m high hole was too low for the female
but not too low for the male, so in the fall of 1974 we mounted an
artificial-log nest site 3 m higher up on the very same stub. The
pair returned again in 1975, and although the male showed some initial
interest in the lower hole, the female took an immediate interest in
the 6 m hole. The male soon switched his attentions to conform.

Unfortunately, between 1974 and 1975, the female had broken her
left leg and was having great difficulty getting in and out of the
upper hole. In an effort to ease her difficulties, we partially filled in the hole so that it was only about 60 cm deep. In view of
subsequent events, this was probably a mistake.

The day she began egg-laying, the female first entered the upper
hole several times, then surprisingly she descended to the lower hole
and struggled inside--the first time we had ever seen her enter the
lower hole in several weeks of observation. Here she laid her first
egg. She incubated the egg until the first evening, then abandoned
the nest. Subsequently, she made a few brief visits to the nest, but
she laid no additional eggs and never resumed steady incubation.

As we now interpret these events, we think that neither hole
was fully satisfactory for the female. Perhaps she did not lay in the
upper hole because it was too shallow and bright inside to be toler-
able for the actual egg-laying process, but perhaps the hole was
otherwise stimulating enough to get her to the point of egg-laying.
It is important to note that the entrance of the upper hole was relatively large and that sunlight was streaming into the hole at the time

of egg-laying. The lower hole was a much darker cavity inside. Perhaps she abandoned the egg in the lower hole for the same apparent reason she had originally rejected the hole--its proximity to the ground.

Support for these interpretations has come from events of the 1976 and 1977 breeding seasons. In late 1975, we deepened the upper nest site to about 90 cm and half-closed-off its entrance, making the interior much darker. In the 1976 breeding season, the pair again adopted the upper hole, and this time they persisted in laying a full clutch of 3 eggs in the hole and fledging 3 young successfully. Likewise, the pair again nested successfully in the upper hole in 1977, although the site had now been deepened even further to 150 cm.

In sum, it appears that only 3 out of 5 potential breeding pairs of parrots laid eggs in 1973 and only 2 out of 5 laid in 1974, or an average loss of 50 percent of the potential reproductive effort--all attributable to nest-site problems. Since 1975, on the other hand, a number of pairs have adopted artificially-created nest sites, and all potential breeding pairs have apparently laid eggs each year. As of 1976 and 1977, all parrot pairs were occupying either artificially created or rehabilitated nest sites. Most of the artificial nest sites adopted were originally poor-quality natural cavities that we modified into superior holes by preventing entry of water and by deepening and darkening the interiors.

REPRODUCTIVE LOSSES DUE TO ADOPTION OF POOR-QUALITY NEST HOLES

Reproductive losses have been caused not only by a failure of many pairs to lay eggs, but also by the adoption of poor-quality sites, especially wet cavities, by other pairs. As mentioned earlier, one site adopted by parrots in 1971 almost surely failed because the nest was soaking wet on the inside. Since that time, there have been 5 additional cases of parrots adopting holes with mud bottoms. It was possible to prevent failures of some of these nests by incubating the eggs artificially and then replacing young in the holes. In other cases, new dry bottoms were placed repeatedly in the cavities throughout the breeding season. While their eggs are incubated artificially, female Puerto Rican parrots can be readily maintained sitting on plaster-of-paris dummy eggs, even when these eggs become coated with a layer of mud.

AN ASSESSMENT OF CAVITY ABUNDANCE IN THE RANGE OF THE PARROT

Because of the evident difficulty the parrots have been having in finding good nest sites, we began a direct, systematic checking of all large trees in some 27.5 ha encompassing the 4 recently active parrot nesting and roosting areas. In this tree survey, only 7 natural cavities (approximately 1 per 4 ha) we found to be clearly of good quality for parrot nesting, using the criteria of depth, internal diameter, dryness, and height from the ground derived from known successful parrot nests. The distribution of these good, natural cavities is not uniform among the 4 recent nesting areas, and, in fact, 2 of the nesting areas now lack clearly usable natural nest sites, although they have been supplied with good artificial ones.

One of the puzzling aspects of the distribution of good, natural sites has been the discovery that, for both pairs of parrots that settled on territories lacking good cavities in 1973, there were good cavities available within a few hundred meters of the territory boundaries. Yet, both pairs remained within their territories through the breeding season rather than moving to the areas possessing good cavities. In one of the two cases, a good site not far from the territory boundary was actually a former successful parrot nest, so it is difficult to argue that the area containing the site might have been inadequate in some subtle way for parrot nesting.

Thus, the failure of some pairs to settle on good nest sites has depended on more than the overall scarcity of nest sites, as some good sites have been remaining unused. While in recent years parrots have nested successfully in artificial sites, it appears that this has been achieved only because we knew exactly where to provide sites from watching the territorial behavior of the birds. Territoriality in the parrots apparently functions primarily, if not exclusively, to protect nest sites, while feeding areas are generally outside the territories. It, therefore, seems doubtful that the extreme conservatism seen in occupancy of territories could relate to food resource considerations. What the adaptive value of the extreme conservatism might be is not clear, but it does seem clear that the lack of flexibility in finding existing natural cavities has been significantly depressing reproductive effort.

Since it is known that parrot nesting activities have been concentrated in the very same nesting areas for decades and that the parrot population was formerly many times larger than it is now, one is led to suspect that either more nest sites were available in the past or that the parrot population was not a self-sustaining one in the past.

There are a number of grounds for suspecting that the present availability of good nest sites may be poorer than in the past:

1. Until about 1950, Palo Colorados were legally felled to make charcoal in 3 of the 5 nesting valleys then active.
2. Many of the large Palo Colorados in the 2 western nesting areas have died and fallen in recent decades, possibly a result of severe hurricanes in 1928 and 1932.
3. Some parrot nest holes have been destroyed by people harvesting young parrots.
4. Many good-quality holes have been destroyed by people robbing natural honeybee hives.

The extent of legal cutting of Palo Colorados in the nesting areas was apparently quite limited, and we doubt that this was a major factor. Of the remaining factors, we suspect that the tree-cutting to rob honeybee hives may have been the most important. While it is unlikely that parrots would nest in a hole simultaneously occupied by honeybees, it is known that cavity preferences of these 2 species overlap considerably, and it is also known that honeybee hives are not immortal and that parrots have used holes formerly occupied by the bees. Judging from interviews, many people used to roam the forest in search of hives, and harvesting almost invariably involved the felling of trees. Many individuals have commented that hives are much less common now than formerly. Moreover, in our systematic coverage of trees in the parrot nesting areas, we have come across several cavity-bearing trees that had clearly been chopped down either for honeybees or to obtain parrot nestlings. Thus, selective destruction of honeybee trees could have had an important influence on availability of nest sites for parrots. If, indeed, the availability of good nest sites may have been considerably better in the past, it is possible that the anomalous situation seen in recent years, when pairs adopted territories lacking good nest sites, might rarely have arisen.

ACKNOWLEDGMENTS

   The recent efforts to conserve and study the Puerto Rican Parrots have been truly cooperative, involving critical observations and support from many individuals and organizations. Special acknowledgment should be made to Frank Wadsworth, Director of the Institute of Tropical Forestry in Rio Piedras, Puerto Rico, and to Ray Erickson, Assistant Director for Endangered Wildlife Research of the Patuxent Wildlife Research Center, for their roles in initiating the research program and for their continuing support and guidance of efforts on behalf of the species. Forest Service personnel who have been involved in field studies of the parrot are Mike Lennartz, Howard Smith, Helen Snyder, John Taapken, Dwight Smith, James Wiley, Jesse Grantham, Carlos Delannoy, and Jose Rivera. Commonwealth of Puerto Rico personnel participating in the field studies have been Herb Raffaele and Mitch Fram. Fish and Wildlife Service contributors have been Cam Kepler, Noel Snyder and James Wiley, who is currently in charge of the field effort. In addition, the parrot program has received important voluntary assistance from numerous private citizens, most notably Beth Wiley, Kay Kepler, and Donna Taapken, who have donated uncounted hours of their time in various aspects of the studies. Financial support for the studies has come primarily from the U.S. Forest Service and the U.S. Fish and Wildlife Service, with important additional support coming from the World Wildlife Fund and the Commonwealth of Puerto Rico.

LITERATURE CITED

Murphy, L.S. 1916. Forests of Porto Rico, past, present, and future.
     U.S.D.A. Bull. No. 354. 99 p.
Rodriguez-Vidal, J.S. 1959. Puerto Rican Parrot Study. Dept. of Agri.
     and Commerce Monogr. No. 1. 15 p.
Wetmore, A. 1927. The birds of Porto Rico and the Virgin Islands.
     N.Y. Acad. of Sci. Scientific Survey of Porto Rico and the
     Virgin Islands, Vol. 9. 222p.

7

Nesting Box Programs for Bluebirds and Other Passerines

Lawrence Zeleny

During the long process of evolution, certain passerine birds have become specialized for building their nests in cavities, generally in the trunks or large branches of dead or dying trees. Most of these birds use natural cavities formed by the process of decay or those that have been excavated by woodpeckers. A few of the cavity-nesting passerines are capable of excavating their own nesting cavities.

In general, the cavity-nesting habit has been advantageous to those species that have adopted it. Their eggs and nestlings, as well as the brooding adults, are better protected from the weather and from most predators than is the case with species that nest in more open locations. For this reason, the nesting success of cavity nesters is usually somewhat higher than that of other birds. In addition, the young of cavity nesters usually remain in the nest a few days longer than those of open nesters, presumably because they need to be stronger and more fully developed to scramble up to and out of the entrance of the cavity. They are then usually able to fly well enough to keep off the ground and are, therefore, more likely to survive the crucial first day or two after fledging, the most hazardous period in the lives of nearly all altricial birds.

Several North American cavity nesting passerines have been under increasingly severe pressure in modern times mainly as a result of: (1) habitat destruction with a consequent reduction of suitable nesting cavities, and (2) competition for nesting sites from more aggressive exotic species.

BLUEBIRDS

Bluebirds, especially the Eastern Bluebird (*Sialia sialis*), have suffered drastic population losses over the past 50 years. It is

generally believed, however, that these birds increased considerably
in numbers during the years when the country was being settled. Partial clearing of the forests for agricultural and other purposes resulted in the more open type of habitat favorable to bluebirds. With
the continued advance of civilization, however, and the more intensive
use of land for human pursuits, bluebird habitat suffered accordingly.
Dead trees in the more open areas favored by bluebirds are now usually
destroyed, and the dead branches of living trees are commonly removed.
This trend has been greatly accelerated by the advent of the portable
power saw which makes it easy to cut away dead branches and whole
trees. At the same time, wooden fence posts, which in decaying provided numerous nesting cavities for bluebirds, have been largely sup-
planted by metal posts that offer no nesting sites. And, in many parts
of the country, small farms with a mixture of wood lots, hedgerows,
pastures, and orchards, that in earlier times offered good and varied
habitat for wildlife, have given way to huge commercial farms devoted
to monoculture. The natural habitats of bluebirds and many other species have been virtually eliminated from such farms.

Perhaps the greatest single cause of the decline in the bluebird
population is the overwhelming competition for cavity nesting sites
between the bluebirds and the introduced House Sparrow (*Passer domesticus*) and Starling (*Sturnus vulgaris*). Both of the latter species
were introduced to North America during the late part of the last century and invaded much of the continent in a remarkably short time,
becoming the predominant species in many areas. Both are basically
cavity-nesting birds, but since they do not depend exclusively on
cavities for nesting, a shortage of cavities does not seem to limit
their numbers appreciably.

Initially, both House Sparrows and Starlings nested mainly in
cities and towns where they gradually made it almost impossible for
bluebirds to nest. Later, population pressure caused these foreign
birds to expand their territories into rural areas where they again
found favorable living conditions. Even in rural areas, however,
House Sparrows tend to remain close to human habitations. But,
Starlings have gradually pushed farther and farther into the remote regions of the country, usually preferring essentially the same
type of habitat required by the bluebirds.

Bluebirds can sometimes, but not often, compete successfully with
House Sparrows for nesting cavities, but they can rarely, if ever,
compete with Starlings for any cavity that the Starlings can enter.
So, wherever Starlings are abundant during the nesting season, bluebirds disappear almost completely, except perhaps in those rare locations where there are more than enough cavities to meet the needs of
all the local Starlings.

Bluebirds of all three species readily accept nesting boxes
mounted in suitable bluebird habitat. With an entrance hole of the
right size, these boxes are Starling-proof, so the most serious enemy
of nesting bluebirds is easily controlled in any nesting box program.
Nearly any kind of nesting box that bluebirds can enter may be accepted by these birds, but for the most satisfactory results adherence
to certain general principles of construction is important.

Wood is generally the most satisfactory material for nesting boxes. Almost any kind of wood may be used, but western red cedar, redwood, and exterior grade plywood are particularly good because of their superior weathering qualities. Boards not less than 19 mm thick are recommended to provide adequate insulation (Zeleny, 1968).

The most critical dimension of a bluebird nesting box is the diameter of the entrance hole. To provide easy access for bluebirds and, at the same time, to exclude Starlings effectively, the entrance hole should be not less than 36 mm and not more than 40 mm in diameter, 38 mm being the commonly recommended diameter (Zeleny, 1969).

The bottom of the entrance hole should be at least 15 cm above the floor on the inside of the nesting box. Lesser depths increase the danger of attacks by Starlings which will reach through the entrance, if they can, and break the bluebird eggs or kill nestlings. Greater depths, up to 25 cm, are recommended in areas where Raccoon (*Procyon lotor*) predation is a serious problem (Zeleny, 1976).

The inside dimensions of the floor of the nesting box should be at least 10 x 10 cm. This provides adequate room for Eastern Bluebirds. Mountain Bluebirds (*Sialia currocoides*) and Western Bluebirds (*Sialia mexicana*) sometimes have larger broods and hence may benefit from a somewhat larger floor of up to about 13 x 13 cm.

Nesting boxes should have drainage holes in the floor and openings for ventilation just below the roof. The roof should overhang the entrance hole to protect the nest from rain. Boxes should be easy to open from the top or one side for observation and cleaning. Detailed instructions for making both top-opening and side-opening nesting boxes are given by Zeleny (1976).

Nesting boxes are best mounted on posts or poles one meter or more above the ground. They may face in any direction but preferably toward and within 15 or 20 m of a low tree, shrub, or fence to which the young birds can fly at the time of fledging. The boxes should be placed in rural areas or in the outermost fringes of small towns or suburban developments. Because of the territorial behavior of bluebirds during the nesting season, little is gained by spacing the boxes closer together than about 90 m. Open areas with scattered trees provide the best bluebird habitat, particularly if the areas are relatively free of underbrush and tall growing grass or weeds. Pastures, golf courses, country cemetaries, large lawns, and abandoned orchards where insecticides are no longer used are often favorite bluebird haunts.

Threats from climbing predators, such as Raccoons, Skunks (*Mephitis mephitis*), Opossums (*Didelphis marsupialis*), and domestic cats that are able to reach through the nesting box entrance, can usually be reduced by the extra deep nesting boxes already mentioned. These and other climbing mammalian predators can also usually be kept out of nesting boxes by mounting them on smooth metal poles and keeping the poles heavily coated with soft automobile grease during the nesting season. Snakes will often climb greased poles, but preliminary experiments by Geitgey (*personal communication*) indicate that ground hot red pepper applied liberally to the greased poles may thwart snakes.

House Sparrows usually present the greatest problem in efforts to provide bluebirds with nesting sites. Partial control can be accom-

plished by frequent monitoring of the nesting boxes, daily if possible,
and removing the sparrow nests; by trapping the sparrows; and by mounting the boxes as far as possible from buildings and at a height of not
more than about 1 m. Some success has also been obtained by using nesting boxes made from discarded gallon-size plastic jugs (Zeleny, 1976).
These jugs must be treated with 2 or more coats of light-colored paint
to prevent overheating. These jugs are often used by bluebirds, although they prefer wooden boxes, but they seem to be rejected by House
Sparrows. Bauldry (*personal communication*) is using open-top wooden
nesting boxes covered with hardware cloth. He reports that bluebirds
readily accept these boxes but that House Sparrows use them only infrequently.

Since early colonial times in the United States, the bluebird has
probably been cherished more than any other bird for its beauty, its
song, and its appealing nature. It always has been a symbol of love
and happiness and, in the north, the true harbinger of spring. The
bluebird has been mentioned more often than any other bird in American
poetry and in the lyrics of our popular songs. Yet, today few people
under 30 years of age have ever seen a bluebird.

Public concern over the plight of the bluebird has increased remarkably in recent years. The establishment of "bluebird trails"--
lines of from several to thousands of nesting boxes--by individuals
and organizations is becoming an increasingly popular and often highly
effective conservation effort. Both the concept and the name "bluebird trail" were originated some forty years ago by the late Dr. T.E.
Musselman of Quincy, Illinois, one of the leading pioneers in the
bluebird conservation movement.

The world's longest and probably most productive bluebird trail
was originated by the late Dr. John Lane and his wife, Nora, of Brandon, Manitoba who organized the Brandon Junior Birders primarily for
that purpose in 1959. With the cooperation of other individuals and
groups of dedicated workers, the original trail has now been greatly
expanded and extends from Winnipeg, Manitoba to Denholm, Saskatchewan,
about 965 km to the west. The trail with its numerous side trails covers a total distance of more than 3,200 km and consists of about 7,000
nesting boxes from which more than 8,000 young bluebirds (mostly Mountain Bluebirds) and approximately 15,000 young Tree Swallows (*Irido-
procne bicolor*) were fledged in 1976. The history of this mammoth project has been outlined by Dr. C. Stuart Houston, one of its principal
operators (Houston, 1977).

An exceptionally complete and valuable scientific study of the
behavior of the Eastern Bluebird during the breeding season and of
the factors influencing breeding success has been conducted by Pinkowski (1975). A thorough study of this important work is recommended to anyone contemplating any serious, large-scale bluebird conservation program.

It appears that bluebirds of all 3 species are well on their way
to complete dependence on man's help for their survival. This help
cannot be supplied by professional ornithologists alone, but they can
and must help supply the guidelines. Broad public participation by
thousands of dedicated individuals and organizations is necessary for
success. Public response during the past few years has been hearten-

ing, and hundreds of people have attested to the delight and satisfaction they have obtained through the operation of successful bluebird trails.

THE PURPLE MARTIN

The Purple Martin (*Progne subis*), the largest of our swallows, originally nested in tree cavities, but only occasionally does such nesting occur today. Over a long period of years, this bird has in most localities gradually become almost completely dependent on man-made structures for nesting sites. People have always taken a great fancy to Purple Martins because of their delightful vocalizations, their fascinating aerial acrobatics, and their apparent propensity for close association with man. Martins consume huge quantities of flying insects and are believed by many observers to provide an effective control for mosquitoes, although scientific evidence for this seems to be lacking (Kale, 1968).

Even before the advent of the white man in America, Indians were said to have attracted martins to their camps by hanging hollowed-out gourds on poles. This practice persists to some extent today. Gourds for martins were later largely replaced by wooden multi-compartment nest boxes. These are sometimes very elaborate structures, containing as many as several hundred compartments (or rooms) for the colonial-nesting martins. But, after the House Sparrow and Starling spread across the country, these martin houses were so often occupied by one or the other of these exotic species that interest in attracting martins declined. The task of lowering these massive houses or climbing up them to evict the sparrows or Starlings was discouraging.

More recently, light-weight, factory-made aluminum, as well as plastic, martin houses have been developed. Most of these have several important advantages over wooden structures. They are equipped with special metal poles that permit them to be lowered very easily for cleaning, observation, and the removal of sparrow or Starling nests. They are also equipped with guard rails to prevent the nestlings from falling from the house before they are ready to fly. Starlings usually avoid these houses presumably because they dislike their bright interiors. Because of these advantages, these modern martin houses have caused a resurgence of interest in supplying houses for martins, and the species is benefiting accordingly.

CRESTED FLYCATCHERS

Of the North American Flycatchers, only those of the genus *Myiarchus* are cavity nesters. The Great Crested Flycatcher (*M. crinitus*) of the eastern half of the United States frequently must compete with Starlings for nesting cavities, and, like the bluebird, it is no match for the Starling in competition over a nesting site. The flycatcher's only effective defense--a defense not shared by the bluebird--is to abandon the semi-open areas it formerly inhabited in favor of more heavily wooded areas where Starlings do not often nest. Thus, this bird, whose haunting calls delighted so many people near their homes in earlier times, is no longer found commonly close to most human habitations.

The slightly smaller Ash-throated Flycatcher (*M. cinerascens*) of the western United States readily uses the standard bluebird nesting box according to Prescott (*personal communication*), but it has generally been considered impossible to construct Starling-proof nesting boxes for Great Crested Flycatchers because the commonly recommended 51 mm diameter hole for the flycatchers (U.S. Department of the Interior, 1969) is easily entered by Starlings. I have received several reports, however, of flycatchers successfully using bluebird nesting boxes. Careful investigation showed that in all such cases, the diameters of the entrance holes were at least 40 mm rather than the 38 mm recommended for bluebirds. Earlier, Zeleny (1969) had shown that the minimum size hole that Starlings can enter is approximately 41 mm. Thus, there may be a possibility of designing Starling-proof nesting boxes for Great Crested Flycatchers. Further investigation of this possibility is needed.

LITERATURE CITED

Houston, C. 1977. The prairie bluebird trail. Nature Canada 6(2):3-9.

Kale, H. 1968. The relationship of purple martins to mosquito control. Auk 85(4):654-661.

Pinkowski, B. 1975. A comparative study of the behavioral and breeding ecology of the Eastern Bluebird (*Sialia sialis*). Ph.D. Thesis Wayne State Univ., 471p.

U.S. Dept. of the Interior. 1969. Homes for birds. U.S. Fish and Wildlife Serv., Conservation Bull. 14. 18 p.

Zeleny. L. 1968. Bluebird nesting box temperatures. Atlantic Naturalist 23(4):214-218.

Zeleny, L. 1969. Starlings versus native cavity nesting birds. Atlantic Naturalist 24(3):158-161.

Zeleny, L. 1976. The bluebird--how you can help its fight for survival. 170 p. Indiana Univ. Press, Bloomington.

8

Artificial Nest Ledges
for Bald Ibises

Udo Hirsch

In 1555, the Swiss physician and naturalist, Conrad Gesner, described a bird which he named the "Waldrapp" (*Corvus silvaticus*). He not only gave an accurate description of this bird and its breeding habits, but he also commented favorably on its gastronomical qualities (Gesner, 1555). Several edicts were issued during the 16th and 17th centuries, making the capture of young Waldrapps punishable. In spite of this, however, the continued capture of birds as well as the increased cultivation of the Alpine region and, possibly, climatic changes within that region, were responsible for the extinction of the Waldrapp in Europe by the mid-17th century.

In 1825, two Crested Ibises were collected near the Red Sea; identical specimens were captured in Algeria and Morocco shortly thereafter. In 1879, a breeding colony of these birds was discovered in Bireçik on the Euphrates, Turkey; this was followed by the discovery of several additional colonies in Syria. It was not until 1897 that it was established that Gesner's "Waldrapp" and the North African and Asian Crested Ibis were, in fact, the same bird, which is now named the Bald Ibis (*Geronticus eremita*). As a result, specimens of skins, eggs and young birds became in great demand throughout Europe, and the hunting of the ibises by the local populations caused their extinction in both Syria and Algeria.

In Turkey, on the other hand, the bird was protected by the local people. Their reason for this was that they believed that when Noah landed his ark on Mount Ararat, he set free 3 different birds: a dove, as a symbol of peace; a swallow to symbolize the new era; and a black ibis called "Abu Mengel" (sickle beak) representing fertility. Noah and his sons followed this ibis which led them to a small house in a river valley. Translated into Turkish, "a small house" becomes "bir evçik", and this became the name of a small town, Bireçik, on the Euphrates River. Abu Mengel came to be regarded as God's messenger who guided the pilgrims on their long way to Mecca during June of each year and during February returned with them to Bireçik where his arrival was then duly celebrated.

By 1900, the Turkish ibis population was the last breeding population in Asia. In 1911, Weigold (1912,1913) reported having observed about 1,000 Bald Ibises nesting on the rocks along the Euphrates River and also on rocks above the town of Bireçik. However, in 1962 this number was reported by Kumerloeve (1962) to have been reduced to only 120 pairs above the town. The breeding sites along the Euphrates had been wholly deserted. When I arrived at Bireçik during 1971, the situation had deteriorated even further.

In reporting on what I found and what has been attempted to rectify this situation, I must emphasize that the conservation measures taken could not be tested in advance and that one had to learn as one went along. This, of course, is not an unusual feature of endangered species management. Consequently, I shall describe the progress of this project as it occurred in time, rather than attempt to classify it retrospectively in terms of the constituents of the total problem.

OBSERVATIONS AND CONSERVATION WORK IN 1971

When I first visited Bireçik in June 1971, there were only 12 pairs of Bald Ibises left out of a total of 71 birds which had arrived earlier that spring. All of the nesting birds were clustered on one nesting rock above the town. These 12 pairs had produced 11 offspring who were just about ready to leave their nests. The houses surrounding the nesting site on the rock represented a disturbance factor, and I suspect that the pairs that had lost their brood had left just before my arrival.

OBSERVATIONS AND CONSERVATION WORK IN 1972

In order to investigate the decline of the Bald Ibis population more fully, I again visited Bireçik during 4-16 May 1972. I found that local interest in these birds had declined, and the traditional religious celebrations, for instance, had not taken place for the past 15 years.

Photographs taken during 1964 showed that the breeding ledge on the rock was then 60-80 cm wide, and mostly shaded by an overhanging rock. Since then, new houses had been built above the breeding ledge, causing rubble and domestic waste to fall down upon the site. Also, a substantial part of the overhanging rock broke off and fell onto the ledge. By 1972, the breeding ledge had been reduced to a width of only 20-30 cm. Moreover, it was now sloping.

Below the ledge, existing houses had been extended upward, and new houses had been added. In some cases, the roofs now reached the actual level of the breeding sites of the birds.

During my visit, I counted 23 breeding pairs and 10 additional individuals. By 14 May, all eggs had hatched, and 64 young birds had been added to the population, but parent birds were frequently forced to leave their nests and young due to rubbish being thrown down from above or human disturbance from below. Between 5-16 May, 19 young birds perished, 11 of these as a result of falling from their nests when their parents were panicked by disturbance. Another 3 fell down from the narrow ledge while being fed. The remaining 5 young birds were found dead lying near their nests; the cause of their death was unknown. In the end, apparently only 6-8 young ibises fledged during June.

In order to prevent the extinction of the Bireçik Bald Ibis population, I concluded that the following measures would need to be taken:

1. Widening of the existing breeding ledge to at least 80 cm and creating additional ledges,
2. Preventing rubbish from being thrown down from above,
3. Protecting the site from other human disturbances,
4. Observing the site during the breeding season to gather additional data,
5. Identifying the birds' preferred feeding areas and studying the effect of insecticides,
6. Reviving the traditional ibis celebrations by the local people to engender local concern for the birds' welfare.

OBSERVATIONS AND CONSERVATION WORK IN 1973

I arrived back at Bireçik in early January. The ibises were expected to return from their unknown wintering grounds by mid-February, and the work on improving the breeding ledge had to be completed by that time. For several weeks, stone masons prepared the 37 m long ledge: it had to be cleaned and widened to a width of 80-120 cm. In addition, a new ledge, to create further breeding places, was being hewn into a nearby rock face. This new ledge was only about 30 cm deep when the first ibises arrived in Bireçik.

As speed was now of the essence, we had to improvise. Some iron bars were driven into the rock to support a wooden platform of 30 cm depth, thus giving the new ledge a total depth of 60 cm. In addition, a wall was built to a height of 180 cm to protect the site from rubbish thrown down from the houses above.

A total of 72 ibises were counted on their arrival. These formed 26 pairs, leaving 20 unmated birds. Twenty-two pairs produced eggs, and out of a total of about 75 eggs, 21 young birds finally hatched.

Description of the Renovated Nesting Ledges

The overall breeding ledge runs in a north-south direction and consists of 6 distinct sections, each with its own characteristics and attending problems.

Ledge 1. This ledge is 5 m long and approximately 50 cm deep. It is a completely natural ledge at the northern end of the rock. The danger of rock slides prevented the widening of this ledge. There was considerable disturbance from the houses below. This ledge was occupied by 4 pairs who produced 14 eggs. Three young birds finally fledged; the total loss was 78 percent.

Ledge 2. This is the newly created ledge, previously referred to. It is an artificial wooden ledge, 13 m long, subjected to only slight disturbance from some flat-roofed houses below. This ledge was initially occupied by 4 pairs who produced 15 eggs. A total of 8 young birds finally fledged; the total loss was 47 percent. At a later stage, this group was joined by an additional 4 pairs; although these also built nests, they produced no eggs.

Ledge 3. This is a ledge measuring 4 x 1 m. It was cleaned and then left in its natural state. No birds nested here. There was alot of disturbance from the houses above the ledge.

Ledge 4. This 5 m long ledge was widened to a depth of 120 cm. It is adjoined by a plateau with a surface area of approximately 10 square meters. There was some disturbance from the houses situated above this area. The ledge was occupied by 5 pairs who produced 18 eggs. A total of 7 young birds finally fledged; the total loss was 60 percent. The greater width of this ledge allowed the birds to build their nests in double rows, but this resulted in frequent territorial fights that damaged eggs and injured nestlings. The plateau was not used by the birds, and I was thus able to build my observation post there, within 250 cm of the nearest nest.

Ledge 5. This is a small ledge, just large enough to accommodate 2 nest sites, both of which were occupied. A further 2 pairs also bred on the rock, just above this ledge. There were disturbances from the houses underneath. The 4 pairs produced 14 eggs, resulting in 3 young birds. The total loss was 78 percent.

Ledge 6. The entire length of this 10 m ledge was widened to a depth of at least 80 cm. The roofs of the houses underneath reached right up to the ledge. Five pairs produced 14 eggs, but no young birds survived. The total loss was 100 percent.

The 2 main observed causes for these losses were: outside disturbances from nearby houses causing the birds to fly away in panic and, thus, upset both eggs and chicks; and the resulting prolonged exposure of the eggs to the direct radiation of the sun. I also found a total of 12 young birds lying dead in the immediate vicinity of their nests; the cause of these deaths was unknown.

LOCAL CONDITIONS

When Kumerloeve visited Bireçik during 1953, he was allowed to spend only 1 day there, due to restrictions on the movement of foreigners east of the Euphrates River. Although these restrictions had officially been lifted prior to my visit to Bireçik in 1971, the hostile attitude of the local people forced me to leave 3 days after my arrival. The human population had grown considerably over the past few years, mainly due to immigration of semi-nomads from the east of the country. A tight family life, combined with orthodox religious customs, an aversion to strangers and, paradoxically, a strongly developed sense of hospitality, are the main characteristics of the people of Bireçik. When staying there for some length of time, it is, therefore, essential to recognize these attitudes and to adapt accordingly.

For instance, the women of Bireçik are not allowed to go unveiled outside their homes or outside the tight circle of their family and close
friends. Thus, when I found that I needed to position myself on some
20 rooftops in order to observe ibis nests, I first had to become close
friends with each family concerned so as not to break any rules regarding the observation of women without veils.

Also, in order to enlist the support and commitment of the people
living nearest to the nest sites, a sheep was sacrificed and its meat
distributed to the residents. The acceptance of this gift signified
their moral support of the project and avoided many arguments which
otherwise would have ensued during later stages of the work. These 2
examples, out of many, may serve to illustrate how the implementation
of a conservation program may not always depend solely on measures
derived from subject-related biological knowledge.

By involving the local people in the project through discussions,
the presentation of slide shows and inviting them to explain their
religious beliefs, I was able to create a new level of interest which
resulted, for the first time after 15 years, in a local ibis festival
being held on 19 February 1973. To what extent my appearance amongst
the ibises, high up against the rock face, may have contributed toward
the local people's newly revived religious fervor, I am unable to
judge. Television, newspapers and other media throughout Turkey contributed in promoting further general interest in the fate of the
ibises of Bireçik.

Feeding Areas and Toxic Chemicals

The birds inhabiting ledges 1-2 obtained their food, mainly insects, from river banks and other uncultivated areas north of Bireçik;
the birds from ledges 5 and 6 went south of Bireçik to feed in marsh-
lands and cultivated areas. Some insight into the possibility of
toxic chemical threats to the ibises may be obtained by reference to
the lists of insecticides sold officially in the Bireçik area (T.
Gürpinar, *personal communication*); these include sales of 20,000 kg
of DDT alone during one season. However, according to T. Gürpinar,
the actual amount used in the region was at least 4 times greater.
During 1972, one egg and one chick from this area were analysed and
found to contain 1.8 ppm DDE and 0.4 ppm DDE, respectively (Parslow,
1973). These findings were not, of course, conclusive, but in 1976,
results of an analysis of some 30 eggs and chicks, collected in 1973,
became known. These showed an average contamination of 10.5 ppm DDE.

Without being given a reason, I was expelled from Turkey on 26
June 1973. I understand that the ibises left Bireçik on 29 June,
together with 21 young birds.

OBSERVATIONS AND CONSERVATION WORK IN 1974 AND 1975

Despite several requests, the Turkish Government declined to state
its reason for my expulsion which, therefore, remained in force. As a
result, I was unable to work with the Bireçik ibis population during
these years. Instead, I spent some time examining the 21 captive

ibises at the Basel Zoo, Switzerland, and I formulated a system by
which the age of individual birds can be established (Hirsch, 1976).
I also visited the Bald Ibis colonies of Morocco and estimated their
total population at some 600 birds, as compared to a 1940 population
of about 1,500 birds. Ibises nested only in holes or ledges that received less than 4.5 hours of direct sunlight per day.

OBSERVATIONS AND CONSERVATION WORK IN 1976

     In order to gather further data on the relationship between the
ages and the breeding habits of Bald Ibises, I studied an additional
67 captive birds in various European zoos. I found that Bald Ibises
would breed for the first time when 3 years old, but only if stimulate
by older companions. In other conditions, these birds are not known
to breed until their sixth year. The Basel Zoo was the first zoo to
receive Bald Ibises; between 1949 and 1954, they obtained a total of
38 one-year-old birds of which 3 are still alive at an age of 24 years
old. Normally, young ibises do not return to their colonies to breed
until they are 6 years old. Photographic records made during 1973
enabled me, at this stage, to determine retrospectively the age composition of the Bireçik ibis population. Of the total population of 72
birds, 4 were aged 12-14 years, 4 were aged 16-20 years, and the remaining 64 birds were 20 years or older.

SUMMARY OF RECENT TRENDS AND FUTURE PROBLEMS FOR IBISES

     On the basis of the information collected so far, it is possible
to chart the decline of the Bireçik Bald Ibis population (Table 1).
During the period 1911-1954, records suggest an average annual population of about 1,300 individual birds. Then, during 1956-1959, a
bridge across the Euphrates River was built in Bireçik leading to an
intensified cultivation of the river valley. As a result, the use of
insecticides increased sharply; this was further enhanced by malaria
and locust control programs during the same period. Local residents
remember having seen "hundreds of dead ibises" during one season at
about this time; also, during the next few years, many birds were reported found dead. This suggests a causal connection between the increased use of insecticides and the decreasing number of birds.
Later, in 1965, Warncke (1965) reported having found an unusually high
percentage of infertile eggs in this area. I have already mentioned
that samples collected in 1973 showed a high level of contamination
(10.5 ppm DDE). As we have already seen, only 120 pairs nested in
Bireçik during 1962. This number was reduced to 65 pairs by 1964.
Although a few more were counted in 1965, a further decline has taken
place; at the last count, in 1977, there were only 13 pairs in Bireçik
     In this connection, it is worth noting that the birds which
survived the period of heavy insecticide use from 1956-1959 were effected by poison; they did not produce any offspring for some years to
come. This created an imbalance in the age structure of the population, a situation which was further aggravated by poor reproductive

TABLE 1.   ESTIMATES OF THE BALD IBIS POPULATION NESTING
AT BIREÇIK, TURKEY, 1911-1977.

Year	Total No. of Ibises	No. of Pairs	No. of Fledglings	Sources of Data
1911	ca. 1,000	--[a]	--[a]	Weigold (1912, 1913)
1953	ca. 1,300	--[a]	--[a]	Kumerloeve (1958)
1954	--[a]	600-800	--[a]	Kumerloeve (1958)
1961	--[a]	ca. 200	--[a]	Kumerloeve (1962)
1962	ca. 250	ca. 120	--[a]	Kumerloeve (1962)
1964	130	65	65	Kumerloeve (1965)
1965	--[a]	ca. 75	70	Kumerloeve (1965)
1965	--[a]	100	--[a]	Warncke (1965)
1967	--[a]	45-48	--[a]	Kumerloeve (1969)
1968	96	45-46	--[a]	Kumerloeve (1969)
1969	78	37-39	--[a]	Kumerloeve (1969)
1971	70	12	11	Hirsch (1976)
1972	56	23	6-8	Hirsch (1976)
1973	72	22	21	Hirsch (1976)
1974	60	25	64	A. Gürpinar (*pers. comm.*)
1975	54	25	36	A. Gürpinar (*pers. comm.*)
1976	39	13	17	A. Gürpinar (*pers. comm.*)
1977	34	13	17	G. Sahin (*pers. comm.*)

[a]No data available.

success caused by human disturbance. Although extensive improvements
made to the nesting ledges during 1973, together with the subsequent
guarding of the birds during the breeding season and the reintroduction of the traditional veneration of ibises by the people of Bireçik, have resulted in increased reproductive success, the number of
existing breeding pairs will, of course, continue to decline, at
least until recent cohorts of young birds have reached breeding age.
The question, however, is how many young birds will survive to return
to Bireçik at 6 years of age. Another question is whether there will
be enough older birds left at that time to stimulate the younger ones
into breeding. The last question is how the remaining birds might
cope with the effects of the Keban dam project which, upon its completion, will bring about the cultivation of areas now being used as
feeding grounds by the ibises.

AN EVALUATION OF THE VALUE OF ARTIFICIAL NEST LEDGES

In 1973, lack of time prevented me from carrying out all of the
envisioned modifications to the nesting ledges, especially Ledge 2
which was finally constructed partially of wood. Nonetheless, this

TABLE 2.   NUMBER OF BALD IBISES USING THE ARTIFICIAL
NESTING LEDGE, 1973-1977

Year	No. of Pairs in Colony	No. of Pairs Using Artificial Ledge
1973	22	4
1974	25	13
1975	25	13
1976	13	11
1977	13	12

artificial ledge attracted an increasing proportion of the nesting
birds during the following years (Table 2). I believe the following
explanations account for these rather remarkable results:
1. The addition of the wooden platform in combination with a
    newly-created rock overhang provided a much improved pro-
    tection from outside disturbances.
2. The total depth of the ledge (60 cm) prevented the birds
    from building their nests in double rows (as on Ledge 4),
    while the straight 13 m length allowed them to space their
    nests approximately 80 cm apart. This, in turn, prevented
    the outbreak of territorial conflicts and disturbances from
    neighboring birds with their consequent harm to eggs and
    young birds.
3. In conformity with observations made in Morocco during 1975,
    the Bald Ibises of Bireçik also appeared to prefer a minimum
    exposure to direct sunlight. Whereas all the other ledges
    received up to 7-9 hours of continuous sunshine, Ledge 2
    received only about 5 hours.
    Although it would seem that this artificial ledge has made some
contribution towards the ibises' comfort and, possibly, hopes of short
term survival, it is clear that much more needs to be done if the
extinction of the Asian Bald Ibis is to be prevented. Unless the environmental problems that placed the species in jeopardy can be
avoided in the future, there can be no hope for their ultimate survival. Although theoretically possible, a final solution will not, in
my opinion, be reached as it will be in conflict with social and
economic objectives of a higher governmental priority. We may, therefore, only hope that the lessons learned from the research that has
taken place will be of some use in promoting the survival of the Moroc
can Bald Ibises whose chances of survival are better. The Bireçik
Bald Ibis population has, sadly, nearly reached the end of its road.

ACKNOWLEDGMENTS

    This project received financial support from the World Wildlife

Fund. I would like to acknowledge my grateful thanks to Dorothy and Ger Rietman who have been more than helpful in both translating my article into English and shaping it in a more rational form than I would otherwise have achieved.

LITERATURE CITED

Gesner, C. 1555. Historiae Animalium, Liber 3. Chr. Froschauer, Zürich.
Hirsch, U. 1976. Beobachtungen am Waldrapp (*Geronticus eremita*) in Marokko und Versuch zur Bestimmung der Alterszusammensetzung von Brutkolonien; Orn. Beob. 73:225-235.
Kumerloeve, H. 1956. Beim Waldrapp am Euphrat. Kosmos 52:350-354.
Kumerloeve, H. 1958. Von der Kolonie des Waldrapps *Geronticus eremita* bei Birecik am Euphrat. Beitr. Vogelk. 6:189-202.
Kumerloeve, H. 1962. Zur Geschichte der Waldrapp-Kolonie in Birecik am oberen Euphrat. Journ. f. Ornith. 103:389-398.
Kumerloeve, H. 1965. Zur Situation der Waldrappkolonie *Geronticus eremita* (L. 1758) in Birecik am Euphrat. Die Vogelwelt 86:42-48.
Kumerloeve, H. 1969a. Situation de la colonie d`Ibis chevelus *Geronticus eremita* à Birecik en 1968 et 1969. Alauda 37:260-261.
Kumerloeve, H. 1969b. Vom Waldrapp, *Geronticus eremita*, dem einstigen Brutvogel der Alpen. Jb. Ver. Z. Schutz d. Alpenpfl. u. Tiere München 34:132-138.
Parslow, J.L.F. 1973. Organochlorine insecticide residues and food remains in a Bald Ibis (*Geronticus eremita*) chick from Birecik, Turkey. Bull. British Ornithologists' Club. 93(4):163-166.
Warncke, K. 1965. Beitrag zur Vogelwelt der Türkei. Vogelwelt 86:1.
Weigold, H. 1912. Ein Monat Ornithologie in den Wüsten und Kulturoasen Nordwestmesopotamiens und Innersyriens. Journ. f. Ornith. 60:249-297, 365-410.
Weigold, H. 1913. Ein Monat Ornithologie in den Wüsten und Kulturoasen Nordwestmesopotamiens und Innersyriens. Journ. f. Ornith. 61:1-40.

9

Improving Oilbird Nesting Ledges in Trinidad

William G. Conway

In 1967-68, artificial nesting ledges were constructed at the nesting site of a precariously small colony of Oilbirds (*Steatornis caripensis*) in Dunston Cave at the Asa Wright Nature Center in Trinidad. The colony's size appeared limited by the 15 or 16 suitable nest sites available. Since that time, the cave's population has increased from 25-30 birds to 102±2 birds.

Oilbirds are the largest and strangest of the family Caprimulgidae. Found only in Trinidad and northern South America, they are restricted to a few caves for nesting and roosting. Unlike all other members of their order, they feed exclusively upon fruits. Most of what we know of their biology is a result of the studies in Trinidad by David W. Snow, then of the New York Zoological Society (Snow, 1961; 1962). From 1957 through 1962, Snow studied *Steatornis* intensively, especially at Dunston Cave. In Trinidad, the Oilbird's population was estimated by Snow as 1,460±500. My familiarity with the species comes from a dozen visits to Trinidad between 1959 and 1971, the first to Dunston Cave under the guidance of Snow. Because Oilbirds nest and roost only in caves, they are exceptionally vulnerable to poaching. Trinidadians consider them good eating, especially the fat, oily chicks. The nesting cycle is unusually long. Incubation requires about 33 days, and the nestlings do not fledge until they are 88 to 125 days old. The high fat and low protein content of the bird's diet is thought to contribute to the lengthy nestling period. In Trinidad, Oilbirds feed primarily upon palm fruits, about 60 percent from a single species of oil palm *(Euterpe langloisii)* and the remainder from a limited number of palms and fruits of the Burseraceae and Lauraceae.

Several of Trinidad's caves formerly inhabited by Oilbirds are now abandoned. Whether this is entirely due to poaching or not is unclear. In some of the remaining caves, the density of non-nesting birds suggests that a lack of suitable nesting sites is a limiting factor upon population. Snow, however, has expressed concern about food supply in an environment where forest destruction is proceeding rapidly. Little is known about the species' foraging requirements.

In the hope that lack of nesting sites was the limiting factor in tiny Dunston Cave, the late Trinidad naturalist John Dunston constructed additional ledges of concrete. The results seem to support his hypothesis for this site, but the population in Dunston Cave is and always has been so small that Snow's fear that food supply is a more crucial limiting factor cannot be set aside. No one has studied Dunston Cave intensively since Snow's investigations were concluded 15 years ago. At that time, he found that 25 or 30 birds were usually present and that the 15 or 16 suitable nest sites produced 60 fledglings from 68 nesting attempts from 1957 through 1961.

Following the construction of additional nesting ledges by Dunston in the late 1960's under a World Wildlife Fund grant, Richard ffrench was able to report in 1975, that 60-80 birds were present and 28-32 nest sites were active (Jackson, 1975). J. Copeland reports (*personal communication*) that 102±2 birds were present in 1977 and that 43 nests were active, 22 on natural ledges and 21 on artificial ledges. While the relative importance of nest site and food supply is unresolved, it appears that this peripheral colony has been aided by provision of artificial nest sites.

LITERATURE CITED

Jackson, P. (ed.). 1975. Trinidad. World Wildlife Fund Yearbook (1974-74):260.

Snow, D.W. 1961. The natural history of the oilbird, *Steatornis caripensis*, in Trinidad, W.I. Part 1. Zoologica 46:27-48.

Snow, D.W. 1962. The natural history of the oilbird, *Steatornis caripensis*, in Trinidad, W.I. Part 2. Zoologica 47:199-221.

Part III
Alleviating Problems of Competition, Predation, Parasitism, and Disease

10

Alleviating Problems
of Competition, Predation, Parasitism,
and Disease in Endangered Birds
A Review

Jerome A. Jackson

Tales of endangerment and extinction of many forms of birds around the world have been the subjects of an increasing number of popular books, movies, and television programs. The stories are now familiar; perhaps their abundance is a result of increasing environmental awareness, perhaps a result of dramatic increases in numbers of threatened species, perhaps a little of both. Habitat destruction has been labelled as the major threat to many species. Historical accounts of past centuries dwell on the slaughter of species by men whose foresight did not keep up with technology. But the greatest losses to date can be attributed to the rats that stole passage from port to port around the globe and to the cats, dogs, mongooses, and weasels that were set free to control the rats. Also destructive were pigs, rabbits, sheep, goats and other livestock and exotic herbivores left free on islands around the world as provender for the next ship to call. Lethal, but not as obvious, and perhaps underestimated, were avian diseases transmitted from imported birds to susceptible native birds by stowaway arthropods. Figure 1 estimates the number of avian extinctions caused by different agents.

Predation, competition for food and a place to live, disease, and parasites are the old reliable dealers in extinction. They are still with us, only recently joined by man-made chemicals and mechanized habitat destruction. In this paper I will briefly review some of the problems of predation, competition, parasitism, and disease that are facing endangered birds today. Next I will describe some of the efforts being made to counter these problems. Then I will make some predictions of problems of this nature that wildlife will likely be facing in the future. Finally, I will suggest lines of attack that endangered species managers might take to head off these problems and to restore some endangered forms to a non-endangered status.

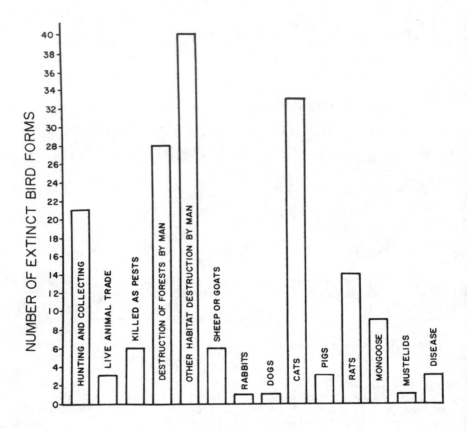

FIGURE 1.   Relative importance of causes of avian extinctions since
1600; data are summarized from Ziswiler (1967).

THE PROBLEMS RECOGNIZED TODAY

     Most of the recognized problems of predation, competition,
parasitism, and disease are faced by endangered birds on islands.
The Hawaiian and New Zealand avifaunas have suffered the greatest
losses in terms of forms already extinct, and they have the most
forms in jeopardy today (Berger, 1972a, Goodwin, 1972; Williams,
1974).   Rats, cats, mongooses, and pigs still take their toll of
species that evolved in the absence of mammalian predators.   Sheep,
goats, other domestic livestock and exotic herbivores still destroy
island habitats necessary for survival of some unique forms.

Introduced diseases and parasites wreak havoc among populations with
no resistance.
The predators that I have mentioned already are the most ubiquitous
threats, but others are serious threats to some species. Introduced
Arctic Foxes (*Alopex lagopus*) have eliminated the Aleutian Canada
Goose (*Branta canadensis leucopareia*) from most of the islands on
which it nested (Cottam, 1962; Jones, 1963). White-tailed Tropicbirds
(*Phaethon lepturus*) are a major threat to the Cahow (*Pterodroma cahow*)
as a result of predation on Cahow chicks (Wingate, 1961). The Pearly-
eyed Thrasher (*Margarops fuscatus*) destroys the eggs and young and
usurps the nest cavities of at least 2 endangered species, the Puerto
Rican Parrot (*Amazona vittata*) (Marshall et al., 1975; Snyder, 1976),
and the Yellow-shouldered Blackbird (*Agelaius xanthomus*) (Post and
Wiley, 1976). Red-tailed Hawks (*Buteo jamaicensis*) are also a problem
for the Puerto Rican Parrot (Snyder, 1976). Eggs of the Mauritius
Kestrel (*Falco punctatus*), which had a total population reported as
6 in 1974, are reported to be regularly taken by introduced macaque
monkeys (*Macaca irus*) (Temple, 1974). Gulls have been reported as
predators of the eggs and young of the New Zealand Shore Plover
(*Thinornis novaeseelandiae*), the Audouin's Gull (*Larus audouinii*),
and other threatened species (Fisher et al., 1969; Bruyns, 1958).
Native crows were once reported to take up to one-third of the chicks
of the Short-tailed Albatross (*Diomedea albatrus*) (Greenway, 1958)
though more recent accounts report increases in the albatross population and make no mention of problems with predators (Marshall et al.,
1975). Another native crow may be preying on nestlings of the Cloven-
feathered Dove (*Drepanoptila holosericea*) (Vincent, 1966). Marshall
et al. (1975) reported that most nesting attempts of the Everglade
Kite (*Rostrhamus sociabilis plumbeus*) were failing in December 1974
primarily due to predators which had access to nests as a result of
low water levels. One apparent predator on nestling Everglade Kites,
the Boat-tailed Grackle (*Cassidix major*), doesn't have to wait for low
water (Vincent, 1966). A rather unusual predator on birds, the Largemouth Bass (*Micropterus salmoides*) is causing problems for the Atitlán
Grebe *(Podilymbus gigas)* (LaBastille, 1974). Stranger still, perhaps,
an ant species which appeared on Norfolk Island during World War II
may kill nestlings of the endangered Scarlet-breasted Robin (*Petroica
multicolor multicolor*) (Vincent, 1966). Introduced Cattle Egrets
(*Bulbulcus ibis*) are suspected of preying on some of the few remaining
Seychelles Magpie-robins (*Copsychus seychellarum*) (Vincent, 1966).
Finally, the Seychelles White-eye (*Zosterops modesta*) may be dis-
appearing as a result of predation by both introduced rats and Barn
Owls (*Tyto alba*) introduced to control the rats (Vincent, 1966).
     Competition between species is less easy to document and is
easiest to identify when the competition is direct interference
rather than differential exploitation of a resource (Jaeger, 1974).
It is not surprising, therefore, that the identified cases of competition with endangered species involve primarily competition for
nest sites between cavity-nesting species. Examples include: nest-
site competition between introduced Barn Owls and both the Seychelles
Kestrel (*Falco araea*) and the Seychelles Owl (*Otus insularis*) (Fisher
et al., 1969); between Pearly-eyed Thrashers and the endangered

Puerto Rican Parrot and Yellow-shouldered Blackbird (Marshall et al., 1975; Post and Wiley, 1976); between several cavity nesting bird, mammal, and reptile species and the Red-cockaded Woodpecker (*Dendrocopos borealis*) (Jackson, Ch. 13, *this volume*); between White-tailed Tropicbirds and Cahows (Wingate, 1961); and between Starlings (*Sturnus vulgaris*) and the West Indies Red-bellied Woodpecker (*Centurus superciliaris bahamensis*) (Vincent, 1966). Competition for food resources is difficult to identify, but some possible cases include competition between the Seychelles Magpie-Robin and an introduced Indian House Mynah (*Acridotheres tristis*) (Dawson, 1965), between the Hawaiian Nukupu'u (*Hemignathus lucidus*) and an introduced white-eye (*Zosterops japonica*) (Vincent, 1966), and between the Everglade Kite and both the Limpkin (*Aramus guarauna*) and the Boat-tailed Grackle (Snyder and Snyder, 1969

Diseases and parasites are always a threat to any population but are often difficult to detect and identify; they can be disasterous to small isolated populations of endangered species. The following are a few examples. Warner (1968) and Berger (1972*b*) discuss the problems of introduced diseases and their effects on the Hawaiian avifauna. Fowl pox has been found in 18.7 percent of a large sample of Yellow-shouldered Blackbirds (Post and Wiley, 1976). Parasitic insects have been reported as a problem for Short-tailed Albatrosses (Greenway, 1958). The Puerto Rican Parrot reportedly has some problem with warble flies (Marshall et al., 1975). Parasitic nematodes may further endanger the Japanese Crested Ibis (*Nipponia nippon*) (Simon and Geroudet, 1970). Brown Pelicans (*Pelecanus occidentalis*) on the Texas coast have suffered total nestling losses to tick infestations (King et al., 1977). Endangered raptors in Mexico and the southwestern U.S. may lose nestlings to the Mexican Chicken Bug (*Haemotosiphon inodorus*) (Platt, 1975).

Brood parasitism as a threat to endangered species has now been documented for at least 3 endangered birds. Parasitism of the Kirtland's Warbler (*Dendroica kirtlandii*) by the Brown-headed Cowbird (*Molothrus ater*) is now a classic case (Mayfield, 1960, 1977). More recently, the Shiny Cowbird (*M. bonariensis*) has been identified as a primary factor in the decline of the Yellow-shouldered Blackbird (Post and Wiley, 1976) and the Barbados Yellow Warbler (*Dendroica petechia petechia*) (Vincent, 1966). Another possible case involves parasitism of Saddlebacks (*Philesturnus carunculatus*) by Shining Cuckoos (*Chalcites lucidus lucidus*) (Atkinson and Campbell, 1966).

In examining the case histories of each of the species just mentioned, the influence of man was always obvious. If man did not introduce the problem species, he altered the habitat such that it was possible for that species to invade naturally, or he altered the habitat to a point where the new endangered species was forced into a less suitable environment where it had to deal with what has now become a problem species. For example, the Brown-headed Cowbird invaded the range of the Kirtland's Warbler only after human destruction of the native forest (Mayfield, 1977). Expansion of the Shiny Cowbird's range is a similar story (Grayce, 1957; Post and Wiley, 1976). The Cahow was forced from its best nesting habitat by human developments and predation by rats into less optimal habitat that was already occupied by the White-tailed Tropicbird (Wingate, 1961). Thus, what has been identified as a threat from predators or competitors could more justifiably be labelled a threat resulting from habitat destruction by man.

PRESENT MANAGEMENT TO ALLEVIATE THE PROBLEMS

The approaches to dealing with these problems of endangered species have varied tremendously and have had equally variable results. For many species the problems have only been identified and nothing has been done (Vincent, 1966). For others, single individual conservationists have taken up the banner for a species. Most recently some governments--notably that of New Zealand, the United States, Canada, and a few others--have funded serious endangered species programs.

Examples of some of the management approaches taken include the following:

1. Shooting of predators has been a widespread approach that has been a stopgap measure for many programs but usually with short-lived gains unless combined with other control measures (King et al., 1976).

2. David Wingate and others have capitalized on the size differences between the Cahow and the larger White-tailed Tropicbird and have created a baffle which lets a Cahow enter a nest burrow but keeps the White-tailed Tropicbird out (Zimmerman, 1975).

3. Similarly, workers in Puerto Rico learned that Pearly-eyed Thrashers prefer much shallower nests than those that the Puerto Rican Parrot will use. By providing deep nesting boxes for the parrots and nearby shallower boxes for the thrasher, they have found that the thrashers will not only use the shallower nest box, but will keep other thrashers from the area as a result of territorial behavior (Marshall et al., 1975).

4. Poisoning has been a part of predator control programs for several endangered species such as the Hawaiian Goose (*Branta sandvicensis*) (Elder and Woodside, 1958) and the Aleutian Canada Goose (King et al., 1976). However, such programs carry with them the danger of killing non-target species and generally contaminating the environment (King et al., 1976).

5. Trapping and removal of cowbirds has been a very successful program on behalf of the Kirtland's Warbler (Mayfield, 1977), and it has been proposed as a possible measure for controlling the cowbird threat to some Yellow-headed Blackbird populations (Post and Wiley, 1976).

6. Construction of artificial nest sites for endangered species and/or their competitors has eased nest site competition for the Puerto Rican Parrot (Marshall et al., 1975); the Yellow-shouldered Blackbird (Post and Wiley, 1976); the Cahow (Wingate, 1961); and the Red-cockaded Woodpecker (J. Jackson, Ch. 13, *this volume*). Artificial nest boxes are undoubtedly responsible for the present populations of birds such as Purple Martins (*Progne subis*) (Jackson

and Tate, 1974) and Eastern Bluebirds (*Sialia sialis*) (Zeleny, 1976).
These species, without such help, would today almost certainly be on
endangered species' lists as a result of habitat destruction and
competition from Starlings and House Sparrows (*Passer domesticus*).
In the same category--though usually resulting from less forethought--
construction of spoil islands by dredging operations has created new
nesting sites for some endangered or rare seabirds such as Brown
Pelicans (*Pelecanus occidentalis*) (Williams and Martin, 1970).
Artificial nest structures have also played a dramatic role in the
comeback of some threatened Osprey (*Pandion halieetus*) populations,
possibly reducing competition for some old nest sites and lessening
chances of predation (Postupalsky and Stackpole, 1974).
    7. A unique approach to saving endangered New Zealand birds
from introduced mammalian predators has been the transfer of
populations to islands without predators (Rearden, 1977). This has
been credited with saving at least one form, the South Island Saddleback (*Philesturnus carunculatus carunculatus*) from certain extinction
(Merton, 1973; Zimmerman, 1975).
    8. Use of trained dogs has facilitated cat eradication programs
on many South Pacific islands (*see* D.V. Merton, Ch. 15, *this volume*).
    9. Strict import-export regulations have undoubtedly been
successful in preventing introductions of some diseases, parasites,
and potential problem species (Courtenay and Robins, 1975; Leeper,
1975).

PREDICTION OF PROBLEMS TO COME

    The events of the past few centuries that have resulted in the
large-scale extinctions and present endangerment of island forms will
also begin to take their toll of continental species. Many of our
wildlife species are being relegated to man-made islands which will
make them vulnerable to rapid population declines and extinction.
These man-made islands are not surrounded by water, but by the
biotic deserts of our culture. A view from an airplane window
on a transcontinental flight clearly reveals the archipelago-like
remnants of the extensive forests that we once had. Not only have
the forests been fragmented (MacClintock et al., 1977), but their very
structure has been changed. Monocultures replace natural diversity,
and young even-age stands replace multi-age forests. The bird
species to go first will include those requiring large home ranges,
those that belong to mature ecosystems--particularly old forest
ecosystems, those species with traditional breeding areas, and
those with poor dispersal capabilities. Cavity nesters will face
more and more competition with Starlings and House Sparrows as
human populations impinge on the remaining forest areas. Species
with small geographic distributions, such as some western woodpeckers, may be particularly susceptible to such competition.
    Other exotic species may cause problems for native birds.
Some already are. For example, I have records of competition
between Purple Martins and Budgerigars (*Melopsittacus undulatus*)

for cavities in a martin house in St. Petersburg, Florida. In spite of more stringent laws (Leeper, 1975), I predict that we will continue to have difficulty with new exotics and new introduced diseases and parasites. There are just too many weak places in our system--beginning with the expertise of customs agents in identifying species--to make the laws failsafe.

FUTURE MANAGEMENT FOR ENDANGERED SPECIES

Future approaches to dealing with problems of competition, predation, parasitism, and disease will undoubtedly include many of the techniques in use today. While many are effective, their effectiveness could usually be enhanced by additional funding. For many problems, we now know that more than one approach may offer at least a partial solution to difficulties. Consideration and funding needs to be given to well-organized, integrated approaches involving multiple techniques. Perhaps then, some problems which have seemed hopeless might become solvable. For example, eradication of rats from any but the smallest islands has been considered an impossibility. The recent development of chemosterilants (e.g., Balser, 1964; Gwynn and Kurtz, 1970; Gwynn, 1972) and genetically sterile males in a strain of *Rattus norvegicus* (Christensen, 1974; Landreth et al., 1976) provides us with some new tools. Island rat populations would offer perfect opportunities to test the efficacy of using such developments as control measures for natural populations. A combination of chemosterilants and/or genetically sterile males, live-trapping, and selective removal of non-sterile rats would seem a new, but as yet untried, ray of hope. Other rat control techniques might also be incorporated into an eradication program: use of dogs, hunting, introduction of unisex populations of rat predators, and careful use of poisons might be feasible. Some populations of rats have apparently developed immunity to the rodenticide Warfarin (Greaves et al., 1976); perhaps this immunity could be bred into the sterile male strain which could then be used in connection with an extensive poisoning campaign.

Results of some other recent studies may offer promise for some control of species which compete for nest sites of cavity-nesting endangered species. Leisler (1977) has demonstrated that at least for some passerines, the size of a nest box may influence the clutch size of the birds nesting in it. With proper study, it may be possible to tailor nest box size to maximize reproduction of endangered species and minimize reproduction of their competitors.

In reviewing the literature for this paper, it has been obvious that there is a tremendous need for basic life history information on many endangered species, their predators, competitors, and parasites. Much of the information available to endangered species managers is old, descriptive, unquantified, and often inadequately documented. We desperately need a return to the study of natural history, but this time it needs to be quantitative and thorough. Unfortunately, proposals for basic life history studies are generally not viewed favorably by many funding agencies. Perhaps a re-evaluation of funding priorities, in light of needs of endangered species, is in order.

Finally, I feel that for many endangered species the hue and cry for their salvation is rather hollow--we offer as an excuse for species which have declined to extinction that we just did not know what to do. Nonsense. Hamerstrom and Hamerstrom (1961), in commenting on the decline of the Attwater's Prairie Chicken (*Tympanuchus cupido attwater*, have beautifully identified the status and remedy for many of our endan ered species problems--including those of predation, competition, parasitism, and disease:

> "The solution lies in habitat management--in giving back, in some small measure, what has been taken away. If the Attmater's Prairie Chicken is finally lost it will not be through lack of knowledge of what to do, but through lack of doing. What needs to be done has been known for 20 years."

ACKNOWLEDGMENTS

I thank Bette J. Shardien for help in preparing this manuscript and editing the final draft. Preparation of the manuscript was made possible by a research contract to me from the Energy Research and Development Administration for endangered species research at the Savannah River Plant, S.C.

LITERATURE CITED

Atkinson, I.A.E. and D. J. Campbell. 1966. Habitat factors affecting Saddlebacks on Hen Island. Proc. New Zealand Ecol. Soc. 13:35-40.
Balser, D.S. 1964. Management of predator populations with antifertility agents. J. Wildl. Manage. 28:352-358.
Berger, A.J. 1972a. Hawaiian birds, 1972. Wilson Bull. 84:212-222.
Berger, A.J. 1972b Hawaiian Birdlife. The University Press of Hawaii, Honolulu.
Bruyns, M.F.M. 1958. The Herring Gull problem in the Netherlands. Int. Council Bird Preserv. Bull. 7:103-107.
Christensen, M.T. 1974. Comparative aggressive behavior of wild and genetically sterile Norway rats, *Rattus norvegicus*. M.Sc. Thesis. Univ. of Oklahoma, Norman.
Cottam, C. 1962. Report of research committee. Int. Assoc. Game, Fish, and Conserv. Commissioners 52:83-98.
Courtney, W.R., Jr. and C.R. Robins. 1975. Exotic organisms: An unsolved, complex problem. BioScience 25:306-313.
Dawson, P.G. 1965. Bristol University Seychelles Expedition. Part 6. Frigate, home of the Magpie Robin. Animals (London) 7(19):520-522
Elder, W.H. and D.H. Woodside. 1958. Biology and management of the Hawaiian Goose. North Am. Wildl. Conf., Trans. 23:198-215.
Fisher, J., N. Simon, and J. Vincent. 1969. Wildlife in danger. Viking Press, New York.

Goodwin, H.A. 1972. Endangered and extinct wildlife of Hawaii. Elepaio 33:14-16.

Grayce, R.L. 1957. Range extensions in Puerto Rico. Auk 74:106.

Greaves, J.H., B.D. Renniston, and R. Redfern. 1976. Resistance of the Ship Rat, *Rattus rattus*, L. to Warfarin. J. Stored Prod. Res. 12: 65-70.

Greenway, J.C., Jr. 1958. Extinct and vanishing birds of the world. Am. Committee for Int. Wild Life Protection, New York. Spec. Publ. No. 13.

Gwynn, G.W. 1972. Field trial of a chemosterilant in wild Norway rats. J. Wildl. Manage. 36:823-828.

Gwynn, G.W. and S.M. Kurtz. 1970. Acceptability and efficiency of an antifertility agent in wild Norway rats. J. Wildl. Manage. 34: 514-519.

Hamerstrom, F. and F. Hamerstrom. 1961. Status and problems of North American grouse. Wilson Bull. 73:284-294.

Jackson, J.A. and J. Tate, Jr. 1974. An analysis of nest box use by Purple Martins, House Sparrows, and Starlings in eastern North America. Wilson Bull. 86:435-449.

Jaeger, R.G. 1974. Competitive exclusion: Comments on survival and extinctions of species. BioScience 24:33-39.

Jones, R.D., Jr. 1963. Buldir Island, site of a remnant breeding population of Aleutian Canada Geese. Wildfowl Trust, 14th Annual Report 1961-62.

King, K.A., D.R. Blankinship, R.T. Paul, and R.C.A. Rice. 1977. Ticks as a factor in the 1975 nesting failure of Texas Brown Pelicans. Wilson Bull. 89:157-158.

King, W.B., G.V. Byrd, J.J. Hickey, C.B. Kepler, W. Post, H.A. Raffaele, P.F. Springer, H.F. Snyder, C.M. White, and J.W. Wiley. 1976. Report of the committee on conservation 1975-1976. Auk 93(4 suppl.): 1-19.

LaBastille, A. 1974. Ecology and management of the Atitlán Grebe. Lake Atitlán, Guatemala. Wildl. Monogr. 37:1-66.

Landreth, H.F., M.T. Christensen, L.J. Bussjaeger, A.J. Stanley, and J.E. Allison. 1976. Influence of genetically sterile males on fecundity of Norway rats. Biol. Reproduction 15:390-395.

Leeper, E.M. 1975. FWS announces new rules for animal importation. BioScience 25:337-338.

Leisler, B. 1977. The influence of nest-box area on clutch size in some hole-nesting passerines. Ibis 119:207-211.

MacClintock, L., R.F. Whitcomb, and B.L. Whitcomb. 1977. Island biogeography and "habitat islands" of eastern forest. II. Evidence for the value of corridors and minimization of isolation in preservation of biotic diversity. Amer. Birds 31:6-12.

Marshall, D.B., A. Baldridge, J.C. Bartonek, W. Ling, O.T. Owre, R.J. Robel, and J.M. Scott. 1975. Report of the committee on conservation. Auk 92(4, suppl.):1-16.

Mayfield, H.F. 1960. The Kirtland's Warbler. Cranbrook Institute Sci. Bull. No. 40.

Mayfield, H. 1977. Brown-headed Cowbird: Agent of extermination? Amer. Birds 31:107-113.

Merton, D.V. 1973. Conservation of the Saddleback. Wildlife--A Review. No. 4:13-23.

Platt, S.W. 1975. The Mexican chicken bug as a source of raptor mortality. Wilson Bull. 87:557.

Post, W. and J.W. Wiley. 1976. The Yellow-shouldered Blackbird--present and future. Amer. Birds 30:13-20.

Postupalsky, S. and S.M. Stackpole. 1974. Artificial nesting platforms for Ospreys in Michigan. Raptor Research Report 2:105-117.

Rearden, J. 1977. Rare birds, bold men. Int. Wildl. 7:4-11.

Simon, N. and P. Geroudet. 1970. Last survivors. World Publ. Co., New York.

Snyder, N.F.R. 1976. Status of efforts to prevent extinction of the Puerto Rican Parrot (*Amazona vittata*). Abstract No. 46, Abstracts of American Ornithologists' Union meeting, Haverford, Pa.

Snyder, N.F.R. and H.A. Snyder. 1969. A comparative study of mollusc predation by Limpkins, Everglade Kites, and Boat-tailed Grackles. Living Bird 8:177-223.

Temple, S.A. 1974. Wildlife in Mauritius today. Oryx 12(5):584-590.

Vincent, J. (ed.) 1966. Red Data Book. Vol. 2, Aves. IUCN, Morges, Switzerland.

Warner, R.E. 1968. The role of introduced diseases in the extinction of the endemic Hawaiian avifauna. Condor 70:101-120.

Williams, G.R. 1974. Birds. New Zealand Dept. of Internal Affairs. Wildlife Publ. No. 162.

Williams, L.E., Jr. and L.L. Martin. 1970. Nesting populations of Brown Pelicans in Florida. Southeastern Assoc. of Game and Fish Commissioners Proc. 24:154-169.

Wingate, D.B. 1961. Present status of the Bermuda Petrel (Cahow). Linnean News Letter 15(4):1-3.

Zeleny, L. 1976. The bluebird. Indiana University Press, Bloomington.

Zimmerman, D.R. 1975. To save a bird in peril. Coward, McCann & Geoghegan, Inc., New York.

Ziswiler, V. 1967. Extinct and vanishing animals. Springer-Verlag, New York.

11

Brood Parasitism
Reducing Interactions between Kirtland's Warblers and Brown-headed Cowbirds

Harold F. Mayfield

Since its discovery as a migrant near Cleveland, Ohio, in 1851, the Kirtland's Warbler *(Dendroica kirtlandii)* has always been considered a rare bird. At various times people have called it America's rarest songbird. Its wintering ground in the Bahama Islands was discovered in 1879, and if we may judge from the frequency with which collectors found it there, its peak population within historic times occurred in the 1880's and 1890's.

At about that time two significant developments occurred on the nesting ground, one beneficial and temporary, the other detrimental and permanent. First, the pinelands of northern Michigan were lumbered rapidly, and the practices of the loggers led to vast fires that created an unprecedented amount of habitat for the nesting warblers. Second, as agriculture crept northward and the farmers cleared the hardwood forests from much of the southern Great Lakes region, the Brown-headed Cowbird *(Molothrus ater)* extended its range from the grasslands of the Midwest up into northern Michigan. This brood parasite, which lays its eggs in nests of other birds, found the Kirtland's Warbler the perfect host. It steadily grew in numbers and took an increasingly heavy toll up to the present time when control of cowbirds was instituted (Mayfield, 1977).

An appraisal of the true numbers of Kirtland's Warblers did not become possible until 1903 when the nesting ground was discovered in northern lower Michigan. At that time, before organized fighting of forest fires, the population might have been a few thousands of birds. Today a fairly accurate census is feasible because of our knowledge of the bird's requirements and behavior. In breeding season the pairs occupy small territories, and the males are loud and persistent singers. The habitat is highly distinctive. The nesting bird lives only among young pines the size of Christmas trees, growing densely enough to form thickets. The ground cover

must be low but ample to conceal the nests, which are imbedded in the
ground. Nests are built on pervious soils that do not flood during
rainstorms. The right forest stage occurs naturally about 8 years
after forest fire, where regrowth consists mainly of Jack Pines
(Pinus banksiana). Fortunately, the warbler will accept plantations
of pines also if the tracts are extensive. Although the Jack Pine
ranges from British Columbia to Nova Scotia and from the Great Lakes
to the arctic, all the necessary conditions apparently come together
only on the sandy plains of a small part of Michigan. All nests found
to date have been on one soil type, Grayling Sand, and 90 percent of
them have been located in the drainage of one stream, the Au Sable
River (Mayfield, 1960).

The first census was taken in 1951, probably the first complete
count of an entire songbird species in the world (Mayfield, 1953).
This census and the second one, a decade later, showed the population
remaining essentially stable at about 500 singing males. Since females
are believed to be approximately equal in numbers, the total population
of adults was about 1,000 (Mayfield, 1962). Field studies in the 1940's
and 1950's caused me to doubt the species was maintaining itself, but my
dire predictions were not confirmed until the third census in 1971, when
the count dropped 60 percent to about 400 birds (Mayfield, 1973a).

Alarmed by this decline, John Byelich of the Michigan Department
of Natural Resources and G. William Irvine of the Huron-Manistee
National Forests, called together a group of interested people in
November 1971. These included members of the Kirtland's Warbler
Committee of the Michigan Audubon Society, originally established
in 1956 to advise the agencies. Many possibilities were discussed,
including attention to problems on the wintering ground and censuses
every year on the nesting ground, but discussion centered on preservation efforts that could be started immediately. Control of cowbirds
promised instant results; whereas improvement of habitat would not
benefit the warblers for years.

Concern about the cowbird was not new. Its effect on the warblers
was well-documented, and means of control had been explored. The cowbird causes damage at every stage of the nesting process. First, it
removes from the nest about as many of the host's eggs as it lays of
its own. It usually accomplishes this unnoticed because the action
is synchronized with the host's egg-laying, a time when nests are not
ordinarily attended. Next, since the cowbird is usually larger than
the host, its egg gets more than its share of the heat from the
incubating host, thereby reducing the hatching success of the other
eggs. Finally, cowbirds hatch two or three days ahead of the host
young, and by virtue of their larger size and maturity, they trample
nestlings of the host species. At the time of Kirtland's Warbler
hatching, cowbird nestlings already in the nest weigh about five
times as much as the warbler nestlings and are much stronger and
more active.

In my field studies of the 1940's and 1950's, I found about 55
percent of Kirtland's Warbler nests parasitized by cowbirds, and
losses from this cause alone reduced production of young by 36
percent (Mayfield, 1961). Parasitism rates climbed in the 1960's,
exceeding 70 percent in some years (Walkinshaw, 1972). The effect

of increased parasitism was disproportionately severe; as more nests were parasitized, increasing numbers of nests contained two or more cowbird eggs each (Mayfield, 1965). In small host species, two or more cowbird eggs in a nest are almost always lethal to the entire host brood. In one 1966 sample, 83 percent of the nests received cowbird eggs, and only 2 warblers fledged from the group of 29 nests (Cuthbert and Radabaugh, *personal communication*).

The effect of the cowbird is particularly insidious because its effect on any one host is not density-dependent. Utilizing various hosts at all times and not dependent on any one, the cowbird pressure does not relent even though the host population is reduced toward extinction.

The decline in population revealed by the 1971 census called for emergency measures. A way to meet the cowbird problem had been pointed out by N. Cuthbert and B. Radabaugh. They found that cowbirds could be trapped efficiently and that the warblers produced many more young when protected from cowbirds. So, in 1972 trapping of cowbirds began on the warbler's major nesting areas. From the outset, the project was a cooperative effort. The Michigan Audubon Society provided the materials, the Michigan Department of Natural Resources constructed the traps, and the U. S. Fish and Wildlife Service and the U. S. Forest Service attended the traps.

The traps used in this program are generally known as "blackbird traps." Basically, they are rectangular cages of chickenwire netting (5 m square and 2 m high). The walls and ceiling are made of 1-inch mesh wire except for the entrance way, which is about 1 X ½ m in area and floored with 2-inch mesh wire, recessed about ½ m into the center of the ceiling. Here the birds enter but cannot find their way out. Sunflower seeds provide food for captured birds, but the prime attraction is the voices and movement of cowbirds left in the trap at all times. These decoys attract cowbirds from considerable distances, and one trap of this kind effectively removes cowbirds within a radius of more than 1 km, while capturing relatively few birds of other species. Cowbirds are removed daily and dispatched quickly. Other species are released, except for Blue Jays (*Cyanocitta cristata*), which are known predators on Kirtland's Warbler eggs and young, and these are transported 160 km and released (Shake and Mattsson, 1975). Trapping begins about 1 May and continues until about 15 July. Between 15 and 38 traps have captured from 3,100 to 4,300 cowbirds each year after the first, when coverage was not complete and the catch was somewhat smaller. In 6 years of trapping, a total of 17,529 cowbirds have been removed.

Fortunately for preservation efforts, nearly all the present nesting areas are on public lands. Beginning in 1957, the Michigan Department of Natural Resources set aside three tracts of 4 square miles (surveyor's sections) each, 3,100 ha in all, to be managed for the benefit of Kirtland's Warblers. In 1962 the U. S. Forest Service followed suit, setting aside about 1,700 ha in the Huron National Forest (Radtke and Byelich, 1963; Mayfield, 1963). These areas are all in the center of the nesting range. When the population shrank in the 1960's, it collapsed back into this central portion of its range, where the bird remained as densely distributed as before.

Nearly half the nesting warblers now are on lands dedicated to their management.
The success of cowbird control has been phenomenal. Parasitism of nests has been reduced to negligible levels, and the production of young has been higher than that reported for any other North American warbler. This experience has laid to rest any doubts about the fecundity of the species. Continuing field work by Walkinshaw and Faust (1975) and their associates have monitored the effect of the program from the start. Working mainly in two nesting areas, they have gathered data on about 15 percent of all warbler nests through the period 1972-1977. Among the nearly 200 studied warbler nests, the parasitism rate has usually been below 5 percent. The mean number of warbler eggs was about 4.6 per nest, and the mean number of fledglings was almost 3 per nest. However, enough pairs produced two broods in one season to raise the production slightly above 4 fledglings per pair per year. This is a remarkably high yield for a warbler, most of which produce only one brood per summer. Previously, before the cowbirds were controlled, the production had been less than 1 per pair per year.

The cowbird control program has accomplished its goal. It took a burden off the nesting warblers, allowing them to approach more nearly their full breeding potential. Yet, for the last 7 years the adult population has continued to teeter along at about 200 singing males (pairs) as follows: 1971 (201), 1972 (200), 1973 (216), 1974 (167), 1975 (179), 1976 (200), 1977 (219) (Mayfield, 1972, 1973a, 1973b, 1975; Ryel, 1976, 1977). We take some comfort from the steady increase of the last three years, but we find more assurance in the evidence that we have arrested the disastrous decline of the previous decade. Had the former low production of young continued and the same survival rate persisted, the species would be close to extinction today.

We have no completely satisfactory hypothesis to account for the slow recovery of the species. Since the adults consistently show a rate of return from one June to the next of 65 percent of the previous year's count, we deduce a survival rate of less than 20 percent for the first year of life. We do not identify enough yearlings to measure their mortality and survival directly, but it is clear the detrimental factor, whatever it may be, bears mainly on birds in their first year of life.

The mystery has prompted the following speculations: Possibly, the amount of ideal nesting habitat is not sufficient for an expanded population, although to our eyes the nesting birds do not seem crowded. Possibly, the loss of fledglings is severe in the postbreeding period on the nesting ground, although our scanty field observations during this stage have not revealed evidence of high mortality. Possibly migration has been particularly hazardous in recent years, although we are not aware of unusual hurricane patterns on the migration route, and the danger of pesticides along the way in the southeastern states seems to be subsiding. Possibly, competition for food and space with other North American migrants and endemic birds in the wintering region limits the species, although conditions in the Bahama Islands appear to

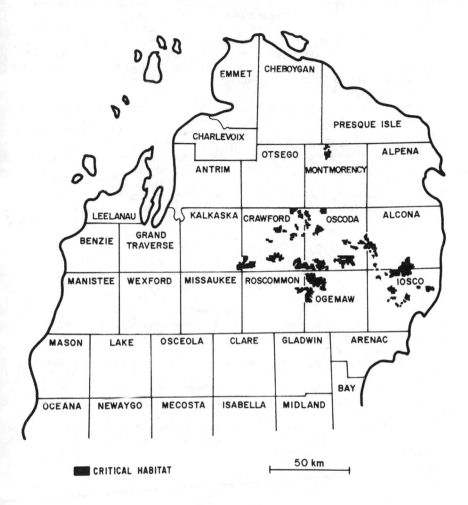

FIGURE 1. Critical habitat for the Kirtland's Warbler exists in the indicated portions of 8 counties in northern Lower Michigan. (Map prepared by Michigan Dept. of Natural Resources).

have changed little in recent centuries. Possibly, the extremely
reduced nesting range of the present decade presents a difficult
target for inexperienced birds making their first flight northward
in May. In 1977, an unmated singing male of unknown age remained
for several weeks in the sandy pinelands of northern Ontario about
550 km northeast of its normal summer range. Perhaps other burned-
over pinelands temporarily attract wandering individuals. Such strays
would seldom be noticed. The answers to all these questions call for
further research.

What does the future hold? The Endangered Species Act of 1973
came onto the scene after the steps described were under way. However, this legislation formalized and mobilized public concern at an
official level. Already it has provided means for closing areas to
visitors and for providing guide service to bird watchers, hundreds
of whom visit the region each June and July to see this rare bird.

The Recovery Team led by John Byelich submitted a Recovery Plan
in the spring of 1976. It was one of the first such plans completed
under the new federal system. Its stated goal was to raise the popula
tion on the nesting ground to 1,000 pairs. A cornerstone of the Plan
was the proposal to manage 55,000 ha of national and state forest
lands for the benefit of the warbler, recognizing that only about one-
fourth of it would be in the growth stage utilized by Kirtland's
Warblers at any one time. Lands that have potential for nesting sites
have been designated "critical habitat," and these probably mark out
fairly completely the future range of the species (Figure 1). These
areas meet 7 criteria covering soil type, Jack Pine forest, previous
occupation by nesting warblers, large contiguous forest tracts, public
ownership, low economic value, and level topography.

How long we must continue the cowbird removal program remains to
be seen. The fact that cowbirds in the warbler's range use the nests
of other host species much less frequently than Kirtland's Warblers
suggests that some cowbirds may have imprinted to some extent on this
host. When these individuals are removed, the pressure on the warbler
may be brought down, at least temporarily, to levels that do not pose
a threat. It is also possible that a new means of repelling or re-
straining cowbird activity may be discovered. Meanwhile, the emergenc
measures described here remain in effect.

LITERATURE CITED

Mayfield, H.F. 1953. A census of the Kirtland's Warbler. Auk 70:17-20.
Mayfield, H.F. 1960. The Kirtland's Warbler. Cranbrook Inst. Sci.,
    Bloomfield Hills, Mich.
Mayfield, H.F. 1961. Cowbird parasitism and the population of the
    Kirtland's Warbler. Evolution 15:174-179.
Mayfield, H.F. 1962. 1961 decennial census of the Kirtland's Warbler.
    Auk 79:173-182.
Mayfield, H.F. 1963. Establishment of preserves for the Kirtland's
    Warbler in the state and national forests of Michigan. Wilson
    Bull. 75:216-220.

Mayfield, H.F. 1965. Chance distribution of cowbird eggs. Condor 67:257-263.
Mayfield, H.F. 1972. Third decennial census of Kirtland's Warbler. Auk 89:263-268.
Mayfield, H.F. 1973a. Census of Kirtland's Warbler in 1972. Auk 90: 684-685.
Mayfield, H.F. 1973b. Kirtland's Warbler census, 1973. American Birds 27:950-952.
Mayfield, H.F. 1975. The numbers of Kirtland's Warblers. Jack-Pine Warbler 53:39-47.
Mayfield, H.F. 1977. Brown-headed Cowbird: agent of extermination? American Birds 31:107-113.
Radtke, R. and J. Byelich. 1963. Kirtland's Warbler management. Wilson Bull. 75:208-215.
Ryel, L.A. 1976. The 1975 census of Kirtland's Warblers. Jack-Pine Warbler 54:2-6.
Ryel, L.A. 1977. The Kirtland's Warbler in 1976. American Birds (*In press*).
Shake, W.F. and J.P. Mattsson. 1975. Three years of cowbird control: an effort to save the Kirtland's Warbler. Jack-Pine Warbler 53: 48-53.
Walkinshaw, L.H. 1972. Kirtland's Warbler--endangered. American Birds 26:3-9.
Walkinshaw, L.H. and W.R. Faust. 1975. 1974 Kirtland's Warbler nesting success in northern Crawford County, Michigan. Jack-Pine Warbler 53:54-58.

12

Excluding Competitors from Bermuda Petrel Nesting Burrows

David B. Wingate

The rediscovery of the Bermuda Petrel or Cahow (*Pterodroma cahow*) on its breeding grounds in 1951 (Murphy and Mowbray, 1951) was an exciting ornithological event. The history of this bird and especially the remarkable chain of events leading up to its rediscovery have been extensively reviewed in a number of scientific and popular articles (Verrill, 1901, 1902; Nichols and Mowbray, 1916; Beebe, 1935; Murphy and Mowbray, 1951; Wingate, 1964; Rogin, 1968; Zimmerman, 1973). Although Murphy and Mowbray were not actually the first to rediscover the Cahow, their expedition was significant because they were the first to find living birds on their breeding grounds. This discovery made it possible to launch a conservation program for the species.

Murphy correctly recognized that the key to the Cahow's survival was the existence of a few tiny offshore islands which had managed to remain free from human disturbance and the larger introduced mammalian predators (pigs, dogs and cats) since human colonization began on Bermuda in the late 16th century. Accordingly, emphasis was given during the initial stages of the conservation program to the control of rats, primarily *Rattus rattus*, which frequently colonize the islets by swimming from the Bermuda mainland. These were successfully eliminated by the use of the anti-coagulant poison, warfarin, a technique which has been used routinely ever since.

But mammalian predators, as it turned out, were no longer the primary factor limiting the Cahow population. Early in March of 1951, just after the single eggs in some of the Cahow burrows had successfully hatched, disaster struck. March is the month when the still common White-tailed Tropicbirds (*Phaethon lepturus*) return to breed on Bermuda. Within 10 days they had taken over all of the Cahow nest sites with the inevitable result that the Cahow chicks were killed. Ten years were to pass before a solution to this

problem was fully implemented, but in the meantime, it became
abundantly clear that the survival of the Cahow on the relatively
predator-free offshore islets had been possible only at the expense
of its displacement from optimal to marginal breeding habitat, where
nest-site competition with tropicbirds became a critical limiting
factor.

Fossil evidence (Schufeldt, 1916, 1922; Wetmore, 1962) clearly
shows that the Cahow nested abundantly throughout the main islands
of Bermuda, even well inland in burrows under the forest floor.
Likewise, the earliest historic accounts (see Lefroy, 1877-1879)
describe the Cahow as nesting in soil burrows on Coopers Island
like "conyes in a warren." Soil deep enough for petrel burrows
does not occur on the smallest offshore islands of Bermuda where
the Cahow now breeds; erosion caused by extreme exposure to wind
and salt spray and the burrowing activities of the abundant land
crab Gecarcinus laterallus has stripped the soil from the islands.
Consequently, the Cahows have been forced to nest in the natural
erosion-crevices of the aeolian limestone sea-cliffs which are the
optimal breeding sites of the tropicbird (Gross, 1912). This might
not have mattered except that the breeding seasons of the two species
overlap (Table 1). When the adult tropicbirds return to breed in
early March, the Cahow chicks have just hatched, and they are left
alone during the day while the adults forage at sea. Being no match
for the aggressive tropicbirds, chicks are quickly killed and kicked
to one side. As soon as the magnitude of this problem was realized,
the impetus of the conservation program was redirected in search of
a solution.

DEVELOPMENT OF THE BAFFLER

In 1954 Richard Thorsell was employed under a New York Zoological
Society (NYZS) grant to work on the Cahow project with Louis Mowbray
(Thorsell, unpublished data). Their first step was to eliminate the
tropicbirds which were already occupying the Cahow nest sites. This
stop-gap measure was invaluable in buying time for further research
because both tropicbirds and Cahows return to the same nest sites
year after year and because recolonization of vacant nest sites by
new birds is generally a slow process. However, this was unpopular
from a public relations point-of-view because the tropicbird is much
beloved as Bermuda's national bird. The alternative approach was
to try and take advantage of the differences in daily activity
cycles of the two species--Cahows are nocturnal whereas tropicbirds
are diurnal on the breeding grounds. The idea was to block the Cahow
burrows at dawn and re-open them just before sunset. But, this meant
that all islets had to be visited twice daily from March until mid-
June. The prevalance of gales, particularly in the early part of
the season, made this virtually impossible. An attempt by Thorsell
to use this method on just one island in 1954 ended in failure within a week.

At this point, Richard Pough suggested a solution based on the
size difference between the Cahow and the tropicbirds. His idea was

TABLE 1. MANAGEMENT PROCEDURES IN RELATION TO THE BREEDING CALENDARS OF CAHOWS AND TROPICBIRDS

	Breeding Calendar (Pterodroma cahow)	Sequence of Management Activities	Breeding Calendar (Phaethon lepturus)	
OCT	NO BIRDS PRESENT / RETURN	OPEN BURROWS, REMOVE BAFFLERS, SET OUT RAT POISON, PROVIDE EXTRA NESTING MATERIAL	LATE NESTING (FEW BIRDS)	OCT
NOV	COURTSHIP		NO BIRDS PRESENT	NOV
DEC	DEPART / EXODUS	REMOVE STONES AND OTHER HARD OBJECTS FROM NESTS. PROVIDE MORE NESTING MATERIALS		DEC
JAN	EGG LAYING / INCUBATION	SET OUT MORE RAT POISON		JAN
FEB	HATCHING			FEB
MAR		INSTALL BAFFLERS AND CHECK THEM TWICE WEEKLY UNTIL CAHOWS DEPART	MAIN RETURN	MAR
APR	FLEDGING		MAIN COURTSHIP / MAIN LAYING	APR
MAY	DEPARTURE		MAIN INCUBATION	MAY
JUN	NO BIRDS PRESENT	BLOCK BURROWS, REPAIR ANY ERODED BURROWS, BUILD ADDITIONAL BURROWS	MAIN HATCHING / MAIN FLEDGING PERIOD	JUN
JUL			MAIN DEPARTURE	JUL
AUG				AUG
SEP			LATE NESTING (FEW BIRDS)	SEP

-95-

to design a nest "baffler" that would allow Cahows to enter burrows but exclude tropicbirds in the same way that a properly constructed bluebird nest-box excludes Starlings (*Sturnus vulgaris*). Tropicbirds are larger, weighing an average of 400 g compared to the 250 g weight of an adult Cahow. Thorsell developed the prototype baffler by measuring the size and shape of the hole produced when Cahows pushed through a thin layer of sand placed at the burrow entrance. He also experimented with live tropicbirds to determine the minimum-sized hole through which they would escape from a box. He quickly determined that an elliptical hole (127 mm x 57 mm) was optimal. However, the margin of error was small. Holes 127 mm x 54 mm were too small for most Cahows, and holes of 127 mm x 64 mm were negotiable by most tropicbirds. Thorsell installed bafflers of this optimum size in 5 burrows on 2 islets before terminating his research in April 1955.

There followed a hiatus of 3 years during which no further progress was made, owing to administrative failings of the kind that Zimmerman (1975) has so clearly identified as a limiting factor to be reckoned with in any endangered species management program.

My own involvement with the conservation program began under Mowbray's direction with NYZS funds in 1957 and continued until 1966, at which time I took over the program as head of the Bermuda government's conservation division. I have continued to work in this capacity ever since.

My first task in 1958 was to repeat Thorsell's experiments to determine the optimum dimensions for a baffler. The fact that I obtained identical results is significant, because I was not aware of Thorsell's unpublished report at the time. My only new finding was that the baffler worked reliably only when both adults of a pre-established tropicbird pair in a Cahow nest site had been eliminated. This was because pre-established tropicbirds had such a strong site tenacity that they persisted in their attempts to force a way through a baffler until they finally succeeded.

Elimination of the tropicbirds was accomplished by blocking the effected nest sites at dawn and re-opening them at sunset beginning in early March and continuing until footprints or other evidence confirmed that adult tropicbirds had returned and were trying to enter. A watch was then posted on every subsequent day until both members of the pair could be caught and killed as they landed at the entrance. This task was especially difficult because it either required camping on the islets for several days at a time or being prepared to land on them twice daily irregardless of the weather. During major storms the only way to get ashore is by swimming between the boat and the islet.

Elimination of pre-established tropicbirds and installation of bafflers was finally completed by late spring of 1961. There have been no further recorded instances of Cahow chick mortality from tropicbirds since that date.

The annual sequence of events in the baffler program is outlined in Table 1. The only disadvantage of the program is the necessity for frequent checking (every 2-4 days) to ensure that the bafflers do not work loose or become obstructed. Although there have been no problems to date, the mere possibility that a baffler could become blocked makes these time-consuming routine checks essential.

Meanwhile in the period 1958 to 1961, I began turning my attention to the puzzling question of how the Cahow had managed to survive at all, let alone for three and a half centuries. All but one of the 8 nest sites known prior to 1960 were subject to nest-site competition, and those which could be examined closely contained literally generations of Cahow chick bones indicating that this competition had been going on for ages. The first clue came with the revelation of the Cahow's extreme longevity. Most pairs discovered in 1951 were still returning in 1960, and one is now known to have survived for 16 years. Thus, the replacement time for each new generation spanned many years, and comparatively few new generations of offspring had been required to keep the population going since the crises of human colonization made nest-site competition a limiting factor. The second clue came from an examination of nest-visitation patterns. Because tropicbirds are strictly diurnal and Cahows are strictly nocturnal, adults of the two species rarely meet. By the time the tropicbirds had laid and were remaining in the nest site overnight to incubate, the adult Cahows, after finding their chicks killed, had long since abandoned the sites. Thus, spared from a direct confrontation which would favor the larger tropicbird, they were able to return to try again and again in subsequent years. There was always the slim chance that in some years the higher mortality rate of tropicbirds might result in a burrow becoming vacant for a season, enabling the Cahow pair to occasionally rear a chick.

These findings were still inadequate to explain how the Cahows survived over a time span of centuries. I could only conclude that some additional nest sites, not subject to tropicbird competition, remained undiscovered. Early in 1960 I began an intensive search for new nest sites, making use of new information which had been obtained from observations of the Cahow's breeding biology (Palmer, 1962). Ironically, most earlier searches had been conducted during December when the adults were at sea on their pre-egg-laying exodus which averages 40 days. I knew that the best time to search was in late January and February when the aerial courtship activities of nest-seeking pairs are at a peak and established pairs leave a maximum number of clues such as excrement and freshly picked nest material. By 1961 I had finally found what I was looking for. No less than 11 new nesting pairs were located of which 8 were free from tropicbird nest-site competition. Two other competition-free sites have been colonized by new pairs since that time.

Of the 10 competition-free nest sites now known, 5 are in very deep crevices or caves with sufficiently large interiors to enable the Cahows to nest beyond reach of the tropicbirds; at least 2 have "natural baffler" entrances which are too small to be attractive to tropicbirds; and 3 are in locations which make them accessible to Cahows but not to tropicbirds because of crucial differences in the nest-prospecting behavior of the 2 species. Cahows, like most petrels, are able to walk like a duck, are good climbers and are capable of vertical takeoffs into the wind. Thus, they do most of their nest prospecting on the ground, often exploring deep under

vegetation and climbing sloping limbs into the canopy for takeoff.
Tropicbirds, on the other hand, have short tarsi and are only able
to push themselves along the ground with the help of wings and beak.
They are poor climbers--sometimes getting wings caught in crevices
or branches with fatal results--and are barely capable of taking-
off from level, unobstructed ground. For these reasons they do all
of their nest prospecting on the wing and, with rare exceptions,
only colonize those cliff holes and crevices which they can see
from the air and land at directly. It was these differences in
nest-prospecting behavior which resulted in the original breeding
niche separation of the majority of Cahows and tropicbirds before
human colonization of Bermuda.

Discovery of the additional competition-free nest sites was
the final step which permitted reasonable explanation of the Cahow's
survival. But, with less than half of the pairs capable of fledging young successfully, it was apparent that the population had been
declining steadily ever since nest-site competition first became a
limiting factor early in the 17th century. Examination of the recent
Cahow bone deposits on the Castle Harbour Islands and a careful
review of the more recent historical reports, (e.g., F.T. Hall,
unpublished data; and verbal accounts by some Nonsuch Island care-
takers and fishermen) has enabled me to estimate that the rate of
this decline was approximately 50 percent every 30 years. Thus,
in 1906 when Mowbray collected the type specimen on Castle Island
(where Cahows no longer breed), the population may have numbered
on the order of 70 nesting pairs. One thing is certain; the rediscovery and conservation measures came only in the nick of time to
offer any hope of a recovery. By 1965 the momentum of decline would
probably have become irreversible, following the pattern of the
Bermuda population of Audubon's Shearwater (*Puffinus l'herminieri*)
which has collapsed from 8 known pairs in 1951 to 1 in 1977 despite
conservation measures.

ARTIFICIAL BURROWS

After the development of the baffler, the next logical step in
the conservation program was to provide additional nesting sites.
A few artificial burrows had already been dug into the cliff faces
adjacent to occupied burrows between 1954 and 1960. The fact that
3 of these were almost immediately occupied clearly demonstrated
that availability of suitable nest sites was already a limiting
factor. The primary reason for this shortage was, of course, lack
of soil for burrowing, but further observations on the breeding
biology now revealed 3 other contributing reasons: 1) the Cahow
will only accept holes and crevices which are sufficiently deep or
curved so that the actual nest is dark (i.e., the occupied sites
ranged in depth from 1 m curved to 4 m straight); 2) the holes must
have sufficient level ground at their entrances to enable the birds
to walk about and collect nest material at night; and 3) because
social facilitation has been shown to be important in the establishment of new procellariform nest colonies, new pairs will only

colonize in close proximity to already-established pairs. This third
factor has effectively limited the choice of nesting sites to the
0.86 ha of rocky islets on which the breeding population is presently
confined and where not more than 35 natural holes that meet the Cahows
rather exacting requirements exist. Considering that at least 25 of
these holes were also subject to nest-site competition with tropicbirds when first discovered, the effective number of safe nesting
sites was 10, and all of these were, in fact, already occupied or
being visited by Cahows. Quite clearly, if the population was to
increase, new nesting burrows would have to be provided. Moreover,
these burrows would have to be both safe from tropicbirds and in
close proximity to the existing Cahow nest sites.

In 1964 I began building artificial burrows of a new type (Figure 1) which could be located on the level tops of the islands amongst
vegetation where tropicbirds were less likely to use them. These
burrows are of the typical petrel "plunge-hole type" which Cahows
would dig themselves if the soil were deep enough. In effect, they
are designed to recreate artificially the original breeding niche
separation of the two species. They are constructed by digging
trenches into the rock and roofing them over with concrete poured
onto a wire form. One additional feature is the provision of a
removable lid over the nest-chamber to facilitate nest observation.
Thirteen of these plunge-hole burrows have so far been constructed,
and 2 of these were occupied within 3 years of construction. The
fact that more have not been occupied merely reflects the present

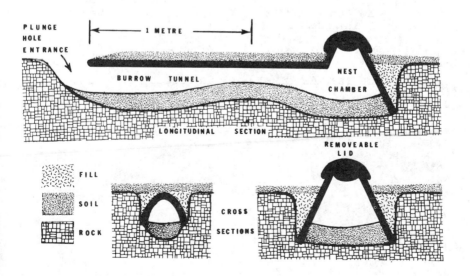

FIGURE 1. Details of the construction of artificial "plunge-hole"
burrows for Cahows.

low rate of recruitment in the population. The number of artificial burrows of all types created to date is 20, of which 9 have been occupied by Cahows. Of those 9, all but the two plunge-hole burrows are potentially subject to tropicbird interference and thus still require bafflers.

The status of each Cahow nest site, with respect to tropicbird competition, has been known since 1962, and the history of breeding success in each has also been recorded since that date. These records made it possible for us to measure the success of the conservation program quantitatively. Table 2 compares the actual breeding success in "safe nest sites" with that in artificial burrows and burrows requiring baffler protection from tropicbirds. From this, it is apparent that the production of young has been effectively tripled since 1961. This dramatic increase in the number of young fledged undoubtedly accounts for the gradual recovery of the breeding population from 18 pairs in 1962 to 26 pairs in 1977, despite the advent of new problems which have effected breeding success (*see* Wurster and Wingate, 1968; Wingate et al., *unpublished data*). If this increase continues, there is no reason

TABLE 2. A COMPARISON OF BREEDING SUCCESS OF CAHOWS THAT NEST IN NATURAL NEST SITES THAT ARE SAFE FROM COMPETITORS WITH SUCCESS OF CAHOWS THAT NEST IN ARTIFICIAL BURROWS OR SITES PROTECTED BY BAFFLERS

	Natural Sites That Are Safe from Competitors		Artificial Burrows and Sites Protected by Bafflers	
Year	No. of Nests Observed	No. of Chicks Fledged	No. of Nests Observed	No. of Chicks Fledged
1962	8	5	10	3
1963	8	4	9	4
1964	8	2	9	5
1965	8	4	10	4
1966	8	1	13	5
1967	9	4	12	4
1968	9	2	15	6
1969	7	1(+1)	15	4
1970	7	1	17	6
1971	8	4	16	9
1972	8	3(+1)	18	12
1973	8	3	17	9
1974	7	9	18	8
1975	7	2	18	9
1976	7	4	19	7
Totals		49(+2)		104

why it can not be sustained by the construction of more artificial plunge-hole burrows.

EXPANSION OF SUITABLE BREEDING HABITAT

One unique advantage of the artificial plunge-hole burrows is that they can be constructed anywhere and duplicated as required until the entire surface of an island is covered with them. Indeed, I have calculated that several hundred could be constructed on the Cahow's present breeding islets alone, making it potentially possible to build up the population to the point where it might be able to colonize the larger neighboring islands where the soil cover is sufficient for the birds to dig their own burrows. It was in anticipation of this population growth that the larger islands (totaling 10.8 ha) were recommended as additional bird sanctuaries in 1961. Now that they are part of the national park, they are being maintained free of mammalian predators, including rats, and it is estimated that they could support a naturally-burrowing population of more than 1,000 Cahow pairs.

ACKNOWLEDGMENTS

The Cahow conservation program has been funded by grants from the New York Zoological Society from 1951 to the present. I would particularly like to thank New York Zoological Society trustees, Childs Frick, H. Clay Frick, and Nixon Griffis, for their close involvement and support. The Bermuda Government's support began in 1951 with the declaration of the known breeding islets as bird sanctuaries under the provisions of The Bermuda Protection of Birds Act, 1949. Later, in 1961, the larger Castle Harbour Islands, including 6.2 ha Nonsuch Island, were declared sanctuaries. In 1966, the Bermuda government established a conservation division within the Ministry of Agriculture and Fisheries, under which I am now employed as Conservation Officer. The Castle Harbor Islands are now managed as Nature Reserves under the provisions of the Protection of Birds Act of 1976. Finally, I would like to acknowledge the important contributions of Louis S. Mowbray, Richard Thorsell, and Richard Pough during the difficult early days of the project when crucial decisions had to be made on the basis of fragmentary information.

LITERATURE CITED

Beebe, W. 1935. Rediscovery of the Bermuda Cahow. Bull. New York Zool. Soc. 38(6):187-190.

Gross, A.O. 1912. Observations on the yellow-billed tropicbird (*Phaethon americanus* Grant) at the Bermuda Islands. Auk 29: 49-71.

Lefroy, J.H. 1877-1879. Memorials of the discovery and early settle-
     ment of the Bermudas or Somers Islands 1515-1652. Compiled from
     the Colonial Records and other original sources. Vol. 1 and 2.
     Longmans, Green, and Co., London.
Murphy, R.C. and L.S. Mowbray. 1951. New light on the Cahow (*Ptero-
     droma cahow*). Auk 68:266-280.
Nichols, J.T. and L.L. Mowbray. 1916. Two new forms of petrels from
     the Bermudas. Auk 33:194-195.
Palmer, R.S. 1962. Handbook of Birds, Vol. 1. Yale Univ. Press, New
     Haven and London.
Rogin, G. 1968. There are problems when man plays God. Sports Illus-
     trated 4 Nov. 1968:78-90.
Schufeldt, R.W. 1916. The bird caves of the Bermudas and their former
     inhabitants. Ibis 10(4):623-635.
Schufeldt, R.W. 1922. A comparative study of some subfossil remains
     of birds from Bermuda, including the 'Cahow'. Ann. Carnegie
     Mus. 13 (1918-1922):333-418.
Wetmore, A. 1962. Notes on fossil and subfossil birds. Smithsonian
     Mus. Collections 145(2):15-17.
Wingate,D.B. 1964. John Tavernier Bartram, Naturalist of 19th
     century Bermuda. The Bermuda Hist. Quart. 21(4).
Wurster, C.F. and D.B. Wingate. 1968. DDT residues and declining
     reproduction in the Bermuda Petrel. Science 159(3181):979-981.
Verrill, A.E. 1901. The story of the cahow. The mysterious extinct
     bird of the Bermudas. Pop. Sci. Monthly 60:22-30.
Verrill, A.E. 1902. The 'Cahow' of the Bermudas, an extinct bird.
     Ann. Mag. Nat. Hist. 7(9):26-31.
Zimmerman, D.R. 1973. 'No longer extinct' N.Y. Times Mag., 2 Dec.
Zimmerman, D.R. 1975. To save a bird in peril. Coward, McCann &
     Geoghegan, Inc., N.Y. 286p.

13

Competition for Cavities
and Red-cockaded Woodpecker Management

Jerome A. Jackson

Lightning-started fires are frequent in the southern coastal plain and have been a feature of evolutionary importance to the area (Komarek, 1972, 1973; Jackson, 1971). The southern pines are fire-climax species (Harper, 1962); without fire, hardwoods quickly shade the forest floor and inhibit pine regeneration. The Red-cockaded Woodpecker (*Dendrocopos borealis*) is also a fire-climax species, having evolved with and become dependent on pines (Jackson, 1971). Unlike most woodpeckers which excavate nests in dead trees or limbs, the Red-cockaded Woodpecker has adapted to the periodically burned southern pine forests by nesting only in mature living pines--the most fireproof of potential nest trees.

The difficulty of excavating a cavity in a living tree--often taking months or years to complete (Baker, 1971; Jackson, 1976a)--is offset by the persistence of the cavity. One cavity on Noxubee National Wildlife Refuge, Mississippi, has been used periodically for over 20 years (B. Webster, *personal communication*), and some cavities that were opened by egg collectors early in this century on the Francis Marion National Forest in South Carolina still persist (T. Beckett, *personal communication*). Such persistence, while of obvious value to the Red-cockaded Woodpecker, also increases the potential value of the cavity for use by other cavity nesting species. Several workers have documented the use of Red-cockaded Woodpecker cavities by other cavity nesting birds, mammals, reptiles, amphibians, and arthropods (e.g., Dennis, 1971a,b; Beckett, 1971; Baker, 1971; Kilham, 1977). In this paper, I will discuss interspecific competition for cavities in Red-cockaded Woodpecker colonies, the relationship of cavity-tree dispersion to interspecific competition, and management which will minimize the competition.

STUDY AREAS AND METHODS

From 1970 through 1977, I studied Red-cockaded Woodpeckers throughout their range and will here present data from several southeastern states. Most of my data, however, are from 3 areas: (1) Noxubee National Wildlife Refuge in Oktibbeha, Winston, and Noxubee counties, Mississippi; (2) Fort Benning, Chattahoochee County, Georgia; and (3) the Savannah River Plant (SRP) in Aiken and Barnwell counties, South Carolina. At and near Noxubee Refuge, I worked at 52 colony sites, 17 of which are active colonies; the remaining colonies have been abandoned by Red-cockaded Woodpeckers. At each colony, I evaluated the status of each cavity (see Jackson, 1977a,b) as active (in use by Red-cockaded Woodpeckers), inactive (abandoned by Red-cockaded Woodpeckers), or as a cavity start. Many cavity starts are never completed, others may be worked on intermittently over a period of years before a cavity is completed.

Between 1970 and 1973, I measured with a rule graduated to 1 mm the horizontal and vertical diameter of the entrance of 534 of the cavities and cavity starts at Noxubee Refuge. Because of a characteristic upward slope of the floor of the cavity entrance, horizontal diameter of the entrance is likely the best indicator of the body size limit of animals capable of entering the cavity; only horizontal diameter data will be presented here.

In addition to measuring cavities, I tallied the frequency of cavity use by other species and especially noted the frequency of cavity enlargement by Pileated Woodpeckers (*Dryocopus pileatus*). Pileated-enlarged cavities are readily identified by their large size (horizontal diameter about 100 mm) and their elongate shape.

RESULTS AND DISCUSSION

Entrance Diameters of Red-cockaded Woodpecker Cavities

Figure 1 illustrates the distribution of entrance sizes of active and inactive cavities and cavity starts. Mean horizontal diameters and standard deviations were 70.6 $\pm$ 19.2 mm, 94.5 $\pm$ 23.2 mm, and 57.1 $\pm$ 18.0 mm, respectively. Each mean is significantly different from the others (*t*-tests, $p < 0.05$). The significant difference between cavity starts and active cavities reflects the fact that: many of the cavity starts were barely initiated and enlargement of the entrance diameter takes place gradually as the cavity is excavated deeper; and many of the active cavities had been enlarged by Red-headed or Red-bellied woodpeckers (*Melanerpes erythrocephalus* and *Centurus carolinus*). Red-bellied Woodpeckers are so common on Noxubee Refuge that few Red-cockaded Woodpecker cavities likely escape at least some enlargement. Neither Red-headed nor Red-bellied woodpeckers are capable of entering a Red-cockaded Woodpecker cavity without first enlarging it. As an example, on 19 July 1974 a juvenile Red-bellied Woodpecker attempted to enter an active, unenlarged Red-cockaded Woodpecker cavity; it could get its head in, but could not squeeze its shoulders through the entrance though it tried hard. By the spring of 1975, the cavity had

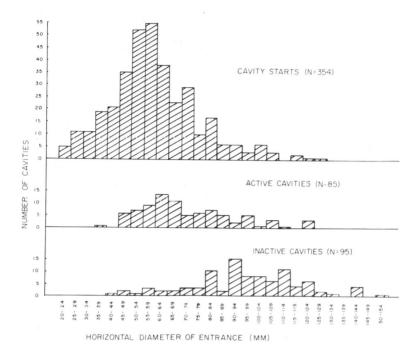

FIGURE 1.   Variation in the horizontal diameter of Red-cockaded
Woodpecker cavity entrances.

been enlarged and was used as a nest cavity by a pair of Red-bellied
Woodpeckers.

The significantly larger size of inactive cavities reflects
the fact that at least 66 (69 percent) had been enlarged to some
extent by Pileated Woodpeckers. Reexamination in 1976 and 1977 of
the largest cavity starts and active cavities that were measured between 1970 and 1973 supports the conclusion that enlargement by Pileated Woodpeckers leads to cavity abandonment by Red-cockaded Woodpeckers: none of the 25 largest cavity starts were completed as
cavities by Red-cockaded Woodpeckers, and all of the 27 largest active cavities were abandoned by Red-cockaded Woodpeckers.

There are 2 major reasons for abandonment of Pileated-enlarged
cavities by Red-cockaded Woodpeckers:

1. Enlarged cavities frequently fill with rain water; most
    woodpeckers excavate their cavities on the underside of a
    limb or sloping trunk, and the cavities are thus protected
    from the weather (Jackson, 1976a). Southern pines grow
    straight, and a cavity excavated in the trunk might be expec-
    ted to lack protection from wind-blown rain. Red-cockaded

Woodpeckers achieve protection by excavating their entrance
upward before starting down.   Enlargement by a Pileated Woodpecker, however, opens the cavity to weather.
2. Most avian and mammalian predators could not take a Red-
cockaded Woodpecker from an unenlarged cavity.   Cavity enlargement inevitably leaves a roosting bird more vulnerable
to predation.   At Noxubee Refuge, I found a chewed Red-
cockaded Woodpecker wing at a tree with a Pileated-enlarged
cavity that a Red-cockaded Woodpecker had occasionally roosted in.

Use of Red-cockaded Woodpecker Cavities by Other Species

I have found several other species using Red-cockaded Woodpecker
cavities for roosts or nests.   Table 1 lists the species and frequency
of encounters.   For each cavity, I counted each species only once for
each calendar year, regardless of the number of times the species was
seen in the cavity.
Red-bellied Woodpeckers, in addition to being the most frequent
cavity usurpers, in 2 instances nested in the only active cavity in 2
different colonies on Noxubee Refuge.   They likely prevented the clans
from nesting and may have caused abandonment of both colonies.   Use of

TABLE 1.   FREQUENCY OF USE OF RED-COCKADED WOODPECKER
CAVITIES BY OTHER ANIMALS

Species	Number of Encounters
Red-bellied Woodpecker (*Centurus carolinus*)	26
Flying Squirrel (*Glaucomys volans*)	18
Red-headed Woodpecker (*Melanerpes erythrocephalus*)	8
Tufted Titmouse (*Parus bicolor*)	6
Starling (*Sturnus vulgaris*)	6
Great Crested Flycatcher (*Myiarchis crinitus*)	4
Common Flicker (*Colaptes auratus*)	4
Pileated Woodpecker (*Dryocopus pileatus*)	3
Wood Duck (*Aix sponsa*)	3
Gray Rat Snake (*Elaphe obsoleta*)	3
Brown-headed Nuthatch (*Sitta pusilla*)	2
Eastern Bluebird (*Sialia sialis*)	2
Broad-headed Skink (*Eumeces laticeps*)	2
Gray Tree Frog (*Hyla chrysoscelis*)	2
Fox Squirrel (*Sciurus niger*)	1
Gray Squirrel (*Sciurus caroliniensi*)	1
Screech Owl (*Otus asio*)	1
Five-lined Skink (*Eumeces fasciatus*)	1
Honey Bee (*Apis melifera*)	1

a Red-bellied-enlarged cavity for nesting by Red-cockaded Woodpeckers exposes that nest to predators that could not enter a normal Red-cockaded cavity. Such predators include the Red-bellied Woodpecker. On 28 May 1971, I saw a male Red-bellied Woodpecker pull a nestling Red-cockaded Woodpecker from a nest at Noxubee Refuge. In another colony at Noxubee Refuge, Red-cockaded and Red-bellied woodpeckers had nests with young of approximately the same age in cavities that were 1.4 m apart in the same tree. Both of those cavities had been enlarged by Red-bellied Woodpeckers. A predator took the young from both nests when the young were about 9 days old.

All of the cavity-related problems that Red-bellied Woodpeckers can cause for Red-cockaded Woodpeckers can also be caused by Red-headed Woodpeckers. In addition, Red-headed Woodpeckers are often extremely antagonistic near their foraging perches. This species forages extensively by flycatching (Jackson, 1976b) and often uses a perch in a dead tree as the "home base" for its flycatching. In Mississippi, Georgia, and South Carolina, I have often observed a Red-headed Woodpecker using a dead tree or dead limb near a Red-cockaded Woodpecker cavity tree and harassing Red-cockaded Woodpeckers that came into view--including birds attempting to go to roost in the cavity. At one cavity in Georgia, a Red-cockaded Woodpecker abandoned its roost after being harassed on 2 consecutive days by a Red-headed Woodpecker that was foraging from a dead tree 20 m away.

Flying squirrels are common and persistent occupants of Red-cockaded Woodpecker cavities. They are capable of using cavities that have not been enlarged and do not seem to be hindered by the sticky flow of gum on active cavity trees. I have never observed direct interactions between flying squirrels and Red-cockaded Woodpeckers but have found cavities alternately used by these squirrels on successive nights. Flying squirrels fill the cavity with nesting material, but the Red-cockaded Woodpecker quickly removes it. In other cases, flying squirrels have continuously occupied an inactive cavity--for at least 5 years at one Noxubee Refuge colony. Aside from nesting in Red-cockaded cavities, flying squirrels are also known to eat bird eggs (Hoffmeister and Mohr, 1957) and even adult woodpeckers (Stoddard, 1920) and are, thus, potential predators at active Red-cockaded Woodpecker nests.

Starlings may not be able to enter normal Red-cockaded Woodpecker cavities, but they can and do enter cavities that have been enlarged by Red-bellied or Red-headed woodpeckers. The Starling could be a serious cavity competitor and egg and nestling predator for Red-cockaded Woodpeckers as it is for other hole-nesting species (e.g., Flentge, 1940). Thus far, fortunately, I have only encountered Starlings as cavity competitors in colonies near human habitations.

Pileated Woodpecker use of Red-cockaded Woodpecker cavities is something of an enigma. This species very commonly enlarges cavities, rendering them unsuitable for use by Red-cockaded Woodpeckers. However, Pileated Woodpeckers rarely use the cavities they have enlarged. I found Pileated Woodpeckers roosting in enlarged Red-cockaded cavities but never nesting. Similarly, while 40 percent of the Red-cockaded Woodpecker cavities Dennis (1971) examined were enlarged by Pileated Woodpeckers, he found no evidence of Pileated Woodpeckers roosting or nesting in them. Dennis did cite a personal communication from E. McDaniel to the effect that McDaniel had observed 1 or 2 Pileated Woodpecker nests in Red-cockaded Woodpecker cavities in Texas.

While most of the remaining species are regularly found in Red-cockaded Woodpecker colonies, their use of Red-cockaded Woodpecker cavities is generally of incidental nature and unlikely to result in colony abandonment. Several are only capable of using the cavities after they have been enlarged by Pileated Woodpeckers. Some species will nest in nest boxes, and providing these will alleviate some competition for the Red-cockaded cavities. For example, from 1970 through 1975, Eastern Bluebirds and Tufted Titmice nested in Red-cockaded Woodpecker cavities in a colony on Noxubee Refuge. In 1976, nest boxes were placed in this colony, and these species have since used only the nest boxes.

Cavity Enlargement by Pileated Woodpeckers

Hoyt (1957) and Conner et al. (1975) have found that Pileated Woodpeckers typically nest near water. In Virginia, Conner et al. found no Pileated Woodpecker nests farther than 150 m from water. If this association between Pileated Woodpeckers and habitat near water is generally true, one might expect that Red-cockaded Woodpecker colonies near water would have a greater problem with Pileated Woodpeckers than would colonies at drier sites. To test this hypothesis, I compared the frequency of Pileated-enlarged Red-cockaded cavities in colonies within approximately 150 m of permanent water to those in colonies that are more than 150 m from permanent water (Table 2). I did not measure the distance to water, but from maps, field notes, and recollection of the sites, I felt justified in assigning the colonies to one or the other category. All such assignments were made prior to examination of the data on cavity enlargement. The trend is clear: the frequency of Pileated Woodpecker enlargement of cavities is higher in colonies near water. Chi square analysis of the sample totals rejects the hypothesis that there is no difference between the "near water" and "away from water" colony sets (χ^2 = 30.7; p < .001). A pair-

TABLE 2. FREQUENCY OF CAVITY ENLARGEMENT BY PILEATED
WOODPECKERS IN RELATION TO LOCATION OF COLONY

Distance to Water	No. of Colonies	No. of Cavities	No. of Pileated-enlarged Cavities	Percent Pileated-enlarged Cavities
Within 150 m	54	354	130	37.6
More than 150 m	31	228	37	16.2

ed *t*-test (one-tailed) comparing the arcsine-transformed percentages for locations with colonies in both sets also indicates a significant increase in Pileated enlargement of cavities in wet areas ($t=2.43$; $p < .05$).

When there are few potential replacement cavity trees available for Red-cockaded Woodpeckers, Pileated enlargement of cavities could result in colony abandonment. Indeed, at 2 abandoned Red-cockaded Woodpecker colonies on Noxubee Refuge, every cavity has been enlarged by Pileated Woodpeckers. Because of this cavity enlargement, the optimum colony site for Red-cockaded Woodpeckers may be the upland drier sites. Despite this, many colonies are located in wetter areas. It is easier to harvest trees on the drier sites, and, as a result of differential harvesting of timber and differential growth rates of trees on wet and dry sites, Red-cockaded Woodpeckers may be forced into areas where they face greater competition.

Cavity Tree Dispersion and Competition for Cavities

Red-cockaded Woodpeckers are unusual in that they live in social groups called clans (Jackson and Thompson, 1971) and may have home ranges of 80 ha or more (Beckett, 1974; Skorupa and McFarlane, 1976). In contrast, woodpeckers such as the Red-headed Woodpecker and Red-bellied Woodpecker generally have home ranges of less than 12 ha (Fitch, 1958). A clan of Red-cockaded Woodpeckers may include up to 8-10 individuals, but there is never more than one breeding pair per colony. Several of the clan members may help in caring for the young. A colony may include from 1 to over 30 cavity trees that are usually clustered in a small area of the clan's home range (Figure 2). The cavities are used as roosts throughout the year, and one cavity is used as the nest.

The clustering of cavity trees facilitates social interactions of clan members and may be a product of the species' social system, but it may also be adaptive in reducing competition for cavities in an environment where adequate nest sites for cavity nesters are scarce. Dispersion of individuals of the other cavity nesting birds is maintained by territoriality; for example, one would not expect more than 1 pair of Red-bellied Woodpeckers per 12 ha. If Red-cockaded Woodpecker cavities were widely dispersed (*see* Figure 2), each cavity owner might have to defend his cavity against individuals of several of the species included in Table 1. Collectively, the clan members would be defending their cavities against far more competing individuals than would be the case if the cavity trees were clumped and the competing species limited their own numbers in the colony site by territoriality (*see* Figure 2). Removal of potential replacement cavity trees within a colony site may force Red-cockaded Woodpeckers to excavate cavities in widely scattered trees. The resulting increased competition could cause colony abandonment. Scattered cavity trees within a younger forest are characteristic of many of the abandoned colonies I have observed throughout the southeast. Hence, it seems likely that many former Red-cockaded Woodpecker colonies existed in situations that increased the frequency of competitive interactions and placed the woodpeckers at a disadvantage.

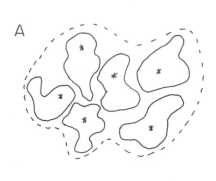
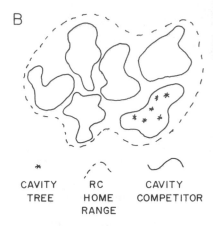

FIGURE 2. Two hypothetical home ranges of a Red-cockaded Woodpecker
    clan (dotted lines) and 6 pairs of Red-bellied Woodpeckers (solid
    lines). In "A", Red-cockaded Woodpecker cavity trees are dis-
    persed, and the clan must compete with 6 pairs of Red-bellied
    Woodpeckers. In "B", Red-cockaded Woodpecker cavity trees are
    clumped, and the clan competes with only 1 pair of Red-bellied
    Woodpeckers.

Management Suggestions for Alleviating Competition

    As a result of the foregoing observations, I have the following
4 recommendations for management which could alleviate competition for
Red-cockaded Woodpecker cavities:
    1. Leave all Red-cockaded Woodpecker cavity trees and potential
        cavity trees in or near a colony site. Abandoned cavity
        trees still have value for Red-cockaded Woodpeckers in that
        they may reduce competition for active cavities.
    2. Leave dead trees within and near the colony site that are
        potential cavity sites for other hole-nesting birds. In
        some cases, it may be advisable to remove a dead tree or to
        prune a dead limb from a tree if it has become the perch
        site for a Red-headed Woodpecker that is unduly harassing a
        clan. Controlling the dispersion of potential cavity sites
        and foraging perches should benefit Red-cockaded Woodpeckers.
    3. In harvesting timber around a colony site, link the colony
        site to an upland or drier forest area when possible rather
        than to a moist area or to an area contiguous with a perma-
        nent body of water. This may make the colony less vulnerable
        to cavity enlargement by Pileated Woodpeckers.
    4. If practical, provide nest boxes of varying sizes in and near
        the colony site. These can reduce use of Red-cockaded Wood-
        pecker cavities by species such as Eastern Bluebirds, Caro-
        lina Chickadees, Tufted Titmice, Screech Owls, Wood Ducks,
        Gray Squirrels, Fox Squirrels, and Flying Squirrels and ease

the competition for Red-cockaded cavities among those species which will not use nest boxes.

ACKNOWLEDGMENTS

This research was supported by grants or contracts from the National Science Foundation (grant GB 33984); the International Council for Bird Preservation; the Southeastern Forest Experiment Station, Clemson, South Carolina; the U.S. Army Corps of Engineers, Savannah District; and the Energy Research and Development Administration. Many students assisted in various aspects of my work over the past 7 years; I am grateful to all. Bette Schardien and Patricia Ramey read the manuscript and provided helpful suggestions. David Werschkul assisted with statistical computations. Finally, I appreciate the cooperation of personnel at Noxubee National Wildlife Refuge; Ft. Benning, Georgia; the Savannah River Ecology Laboratory; and the U.S. Forest Service at the Savannah River Plant and elsewhere.

LITERATURE CITED

Baker, W.W. 1971. Progress report on life history studies of the Red-cockaded Woodpecker at Tall Timbers Research Station, p. 44-59. *In* R.L. Thompson (ed.), The Ecology and Management of the Red-cockaded Woodpecker. Bureau of Sport Fisheries and Wildlife and Tall Timbers Research Station, Tallahassee, Florida.
Beckett, T.A., III. 1971. A summary of Red-cockaded Woodpecker observations in South Carolina, p. 87-95. *In* R.L. Thompson (ed.), The Ecology and Management of the Red-cockaded Woodpecker. Bureau of Sport Fisheries and Wildlife and Tall Timbers Research Station, Tallahassee, Florida.
Beckett, T.A., III. 1974. Habitat acreage requirements of the Red-cockaded Woodpecker. EBBA News 37:3-7.
Conner, R.N., R.G. Hooper, H.S. Crawford, and H.S. Mosby. 1975. Woodpecker nesting habitat in cut and uncut woodlands in Virginia. J. Wildlife Manage. 39:144-150.
Dennis, J.V. 1971a. Utilization of pine resin by the Red-cockaded Woodpecker and its effectiveness in protecting roosting and nest sites, p. 78-86. *In* R.L. Thompson (ed.), The Ecology and Management of the Red-cockaded Woodpecker. Bureau of Sport Fisheries and Wildlife and Tall Timbers Research Station, Tallahassee, Florida.
Dennis, J.V. 1971b. Species using Red-cockaded Woodpecker holes in northeastern South Carolina. Bird-Banding 42:79-87.
Fitch, H.S. 1958. Home ranges, territories, and seasonal movements of vertebrates of the Natural History Reservation. Univ. Kans. Publ. Mus. Nat. Hist. 11(3):63-326.
Flentge, L.G. 1940. The European Starling--friend or foe? Audubon Bull. 1940(34):1-6.
Harper, R.M. 1962. Historical notes on the relation of fire to forests. p. 11-29. Proc. Tall Timbers Fire Ecol. Conf., No. 1.

Hoffmeister, D.F. and C.O. Mohr. 1957. Fieldbook of Illinois mammals.
    Manual 4. Natural History Survey Division, Urbana, Illinois.
Hoyt, S.F. 1957. The ecology of the Pileated Woodpecker. Ecology 38:
    246-256.
Jackson, J.A. 1971. The evolution, taxonomy, distribution, past
    populations and current status of the Red-cockaded Woodpecker.
    p. 4-29. In R.L. Thompson (ed.), The Ecology and Management of
    the Red-cockaded Woodpecker. Bureau of Sport Fisheries and Wild-
    life and Tall Timbers Research Station, Tallahassee, Florida.
Jackson, J.A. 1976a. How to determine the status of a woodpecker nest.
    Living Bird 15:205-221.
Jackson, J.A. 1976b. A comparison of some aspects of the breeding
    ecology of Red-headed and Red-bellied woodpeckers in Kansas.
    Condor 78:67-76.
Jackson, J.A. 1977a. Red-cockaded Woodpeckers and pine red heart dis-
    ease. Auk 94:160-163.
Jackson, J.A. 1977b. Determination of the status of Red-cockaded Wood-
    pecker colonies. J. Wildlife Manage. 41:448-452.
Jackson, J.A. and R.L. Thompson. 1971. A glossary of terms used in
    association with the Red-cockaded Woodpecker, p. 187-188. In
    R.L. Thompson (ed.), The Ecology and Management of the Red-cock-
    aded Woodpecker. Bureau of Sport Fisheries and Wildlife and Tall
    Timbers Research Station, Tallahassee, Florida.
Kilham, L. 1977. Nest-site differences between Red-headed and Red-
    bellied woodpeckers in South Carolina. Wilson Bull. 89:164-165.
Komarek, E.V. 1972. Ancient fires. p. 219-240. Proc. Tall Timbers
    Fire Ecol. Conf. No. 11.
Komarek, E.V. 1973. Introduction to lightning ecology. p. 421-427.
    Proc. Tall Timbers Fire Ecol. Conf., No. 12.
Skorupa, J.P. and R.W. McFarlane. 1976. Seasonal variation in forag-
    ing territory of Red-cockaded Woodpeckers. Wilson Bull. 88:
    662-665.
Stoddard, H.L. 1920. The flying squirrel as a bird killer. J. Mammal.
    1:95-96.

14

Puerto Rican Parrots and Nest Predation by Pearly-eyed Thrashers

Noel F. R. Snyder and John D. Taapken

One usually thinks of hole-nesting birds, especially large, hole-nesting birds, as enjoying considerable freedom from nest predation. Their nest success rates consistently outscore the nest success rates of open-nesters, and generally average 60 percent or greater, even in the tropics (*see* Skutch, 1976). The abysmally poor nest success recorded historically for the endangered Puerto Rican Parrot (*Amazona vittata*) presents a sharp contrast to the usual situation. In the years prior to 1973, no more than 11 to 26 percent of the pairs laying eggs were successful in fledging young. Poor nest success of the parrot has been traced to 3 major factors: (1) adoption of sub-standard nest sites (especially wet holes), (2) loss of adults during the breeding season, and (3) direct loss of nest contents to various nest predators.

Historically, a variety of nest predators, including man, Red-tailed Hawks (*Buteo jamaicensis*), Puerto Rican Boas (*Epicrates inornatus*), and feral cats (*Felis catus*) have threatened the safety of parrot nests. But, by far the most important of the nest predators in the last few years has been another species of hole-nesting bird, the Pearly-eyed Thrasher (*Margarops fuscatus*). Almost all recent breeding pairs of parrots have been harassed vigorously by thrashers, and efforts to save the parrot from extinction have been slanted heavily toward developing effective and practical means of countering the threat posed by this species.

HISTORY OF THE CONFRONTATION BETWEEN PARROTS AND THRASHERS

The Pearly-eyed Thrasher is an aggressive mimid of basically Lesser Antillean distribution, although it reaches as far west as the southern Bahamas and Beata Island off southern Hispaniola. The thrasher was a very rare species in Puerto Rico at the turn of the century, but its numbers were clearly increasing by the 1930's (Wetmore, 1927; Danforth, 1931). It has now become one of the most abundant passerines on the island in many habitat types.

Judging from interviews with residents of the region, the thrasher was nearly non-existent in upper Luquillo Forest prior to about 1950. The species increased greatly in abundance there during the 1950's and early 1960's, but the increase has apparently levelled off since then. Thrashers are presently most common in well-developed stands of Palo Colorado (*Cyrilla racemiflora*), exactly the habitat in which the remaining Puerto Rican Parrots still nest. Probably both bird species are concentrated in Palo Colorado forest because this forest type possesses a higher frequency of natural cavities than other zones of the forest. In any event, the recent invasion of upper Luquillo Forest by thrashers has presented the parrots with a stress that they did not formerly have to withstand.

INTERACTIONS BETWEEN PARROTS AND THRASHERS

Parrots are dominant over thrashers in head-on interactions, and significant risk for the parrots develops only when they leave the vicinity of their nests, as they often do. At such times, thrashers, which are apparently seeking nest sites for themselves, can enter the parrot nests, and when they happen upon unattended eggs or small young, they quickly respond with attacks.

We have witnessed 2 such attacks. In the first case, a thrasher entered a nest just 5 minutes after the female parrot had flown from the hole. It grabbed one egg and flew off with it in its bill. In the second case, a thrasher dragged a young parrot weighing almost as much as itself--approximately 90 grams--up to the entrance of a nest. Fortunately, we were able to frighten off the thrasher at this point, and the chick rolled back down to the nest bottom. Despite a nasty gash on its neck, the chick recovered and later fledged. Apparently, once parrot chicks reach about 200 grams in weight (approximately 3 weeks of age) they are no longer vulnerable to thrasher attacks, as we have seen several cases of thrashers entering and quickly leaving holes containing chicks this size.

Strong circumstantial evidence suggests that thrashers caused 5 nesting failures of parrots in the years just prior to 1973, a massive effect considering the low numbers of parrots at the time. Since 1969, the parrot population has generally been below 20 individuals, and usually only 2 or 3 pairs have attempted nesting each year.

EFFORTS TO COUNTER THE THRASHER

Efforts to counter the Pearly-eyed Thrasher have proceeded on several fronts.

Direct Guarding of Parrot Nests

Since 1973 we have attempted, as far as manpower has permitted, to guard all parrot nests through early vulnerable stages of breeding. Blinds overlooking the nests have been equipped with pellet guns, and thrashers attempting to enter unattended parrot nests have been shot out or at least frightened away from the holes whenever possible. This direct method has been successful in preventing most thrasher predation, although, as discussed above, there have been 2 cases in which thrashers have entered parrot nests unseen and have attacked eggs and young. Nevertheless, no parrot nests have failed because of thrashers since 1973, and the total loss attributable to thrashers has been just one egg. We feel quite sure that at least 2, very likely 4, and possibly as many as 6 parrot nests that have been successful during this period would have been lost to thrasher predation in the absence of direct guarding.

Artificial Incubation of Parrot Eggs

Another technique we have used has been artificial incubation of parrot eggs taken from the wild. Dummy parrot eggs made from plaster-of-paris have been substituted into nests to keep them active, and when chicks have hatched at the field station, they have been hand-raised for a few days, then replaced in the nests. We handled 1 chick in this way in 1974, 6 chicks from 3 nests in 1975, and 5 chicks from 2 nests in 1976. Parrots have always tolerated the switches from real eggs to plaster eggs to young (up to a week old) without obvious distress. However, we have twice seen incipient desertion when delays of more than about a week after the hatching date were made before young were returned to the holes.

The placement of plaster eggs in parrot nests has allowed us to curtail constant guarding of the nests in question and permitted us to concentrate our efforts on other nesting pairs. One nest of 1975 clearly demonstrated the value of the technique. All 3 plaster eggs left in the hole ended up heavily pitted, presumably by blows of the bills of thrashers, and the nest would surely have failed had the real eggs been left in the hole.

Nest-Box Experiments

It has always appeared that the best solution to the thrasher problem might be to design a nest structure acceptable to parrots but unacceptable to thrashers. Since thrashers are smaller than parrots, they can enter any size hole that the parrots can enter; so at the outset, there did not appear to be any potential for excluding thrashers from parrot nests by manipulating the size of entrance holes. However, we became interested to learn if there might be some differences between the parrots and the thrashers in depth preferences and tolerances. In 1974, 1975, and 1976 we carried out a series of nest-box experiments with the thrashers, and in 1975 and 1976 we began some modifications of parrot nest sites on the basis of these experiments. The results have been very encouraging.

In 1974, three different nest-box types were installed at 160 m intervals along Route 191 through upper Luquillo Forest to test depth preferences of thrashers. Two of the 3 designs were choice boxes, that is rectangular boxes open at one end mounted side by side and differing only in depth. One of the 2 designs allowed thrashers to choose between depths of 30 cm and 90 cm, and the other design allowed thrashers to choose between depths of 90 cm and 150 cm. For each design, half the choice boxes had the deeper choice on the right side and half had the deeper choice on the left to detect any possible right-left biases of the thrashers. Both designs were mounted on 35 degree slants from horizontal in tree crotches at least 5 m from the ground.

Results of the experiments with the 2 choice box designs were clear. Eleven of the twenty 30-90 cm choice boxes were occupied by thrashers, and in every case, thrashers chose the 90 cm side in which to construct nests. For the 90-150 cm choice boxes, 16 out of 21 were occupied, and of these, 12 choices were of the 90 cm side. However, in 3 of the 4 choices of the 150 cm side, the actual nests were wedged only part way down inside, at depths ranging from 60 cm to 107 cm. In the fourth case, no nest was actually built, and only a few sticks were distributed down the 150 cm long side. Thus, both designs gave strong evidence that thrashers prefer to nest at depths of approximately 90 cm when choices are available. No left-right biases were detected.

The same depth preference was demonstrated in the third type of box tested in 1974. This design was a single rectangular box 150 cm in length mounted horizontally in tree crotches. For this design, the thrashers were not given any alternative boxes in the vicinity, but they were, of course, free to place their nests at any depth up to 150 cm from the entrance, since the boxes were mounted horizontally. Nests were built in 4 of the 10 boxes in the field, and nest depths ranged from 60 cm to 90 cm for 3 of the 4. The fourth nest was placed at a depth of 142 cm. Two other boxes had some sticks placed in them, but no actual nests were constructed. In one of the 2 cases, sticks were scattered the entire length of the box, and in the other case, a few sticks were found between 122 and 150 cm in depth.

Thus, the horizontal box design, like the choice boxes, gave evidence that thrashers prefer nest depths of about 90 cm, although, of course, these experiments were not designed to test whether this depth preference was a true depth preference or perhaps a light-intensity preference, nor were they designed to reveal depth limits that thrashers might tolerate. In 5 cases, once the thrashers had chosen the 90 cm side of a 90-150 cm choice box, we then blocked off the 90 cm side to see if they might switch to the 150 cm side, and in all 5 cases, the thrashers did switch to the deeper side. In 3 of the 5 cases, the new nests were wedged part way down the boxes at depths of about 76 cm, but in 2 cases, nests were placed right at the bottoms of the 150 cm boxes. Thus, it was clear that even 150 cm depth is not too deep for use by thrashers, at least when no other alternatives are available.

In 1975, we experimented with 2 more box types designed to test depth preferences and tolerances of thrashers. One of these designs was a vertically mounted box 168 cm deep, and the other was a choice box structure, also vertically mounted, but in this case 122 cm deep. One half of the choice box was painted flat black on the inside, the other was left natural, light-colored wood. All the boxes tested in 1975 replaced boxes that had housed active thrasher pairs in 1974. Thus, we could reasonably assume that the habitats were adequate for thrashers and that failure of thrashers to occupy a box could be an indication of lack of tolerance for the structure itself. When only 1 out of 6 of the 168 cm deep vertical boxes was adopted by thrashers, we concluded that this depth might be approaching a depth limit for the thrashers. However, further experiments in 1976 have clearly shown that this was an incorrect interpretation, as will be discussed below.

Eight of the 11 dark-light choice boxes were occupied by thrashers; in 5 cases the dark side was chosen, and in 3 cases the light side was chosen, indicating no significant preferences. Since the 122 cm depth was greater than the 90 cm depth preference demonstrated for the species in 1974, and since the dark sides of the light-dark choice boxes were considerably darker in the interior than the interiors of the 90 cm deep boxes chosen by thrashers in 1974, this result suggests that the species may have a true depth preference rather than a light-intensity preference in nesting.

In 1976, we installed 9 vertical boxes that were 229 cm deep in thrasher territories that had been occupied in previous years. All of these boxes were used to some extent by thrashers, although complete nests were built in only 6 of the boxes; in the other boxes, thrashers merely added amounts of loose sticks. Thus the 168 cm deep vertical boxes tested in 1975 were clearly not close to the depth tolerances of the thrashers, and even 229 cm does not represent a depth limit. Our hopes for defeating the thrashers simply on the basis of cavity depth were not greatly encouraged by these results.

Nevertheless, another series of nest box experiments which we had been pursuing simultaneously in 1974, 1975, and 1976 has given much more hopeful results. In these experiments, we have tested thrasher acceptance of various boxes in which the bottoms were not visible from the entrances because of 45-degree-angle bends at various distances from the entrances. In 1974 we tested 8 angle boxes in which the entrance section sloped down to a vertical section 38 cm in from the entrance, and in which the bottom vertical section was 50 cm deep. Four of the 8 boxes were occupied by thrashers, and it is interesting that the nests were all built on piles of sticks about 30 cm high, which resulted in the nests themselves being placed approximately at the level of the bends in the boxes.

Deeper versions of the same box design were tested in 1975 with essentially similar results. All 4 boxes installed in the field were used by thrashers, and nests were again built on tops of loose masses of sticks bringing them up approximately to the level of the bends of the boxes.

In 1976, two additional angle box designs were tested which differed from the designs tested in 1974 and 1975 in that the entrance sections were vertical in orientation, and the angle bends came off at the bottoms of the vertical sections. For one design, the angle section came off at a depth of 86 cm from the entrance, and for the other design the angle section came off at a depth of 124 cm. We put sawdust and plaster-of-paris dummy parrot eggs in the bottoms of these boxes to assess whether thrashers might descend to the bottoms and attack the eggs. As in other experiments of 1975 and 1976, these boxes were installed replacing nest boxes that had held active thrasher pairs in previous years.

Thrashers built nests in 3 of the 5 shallow vertical-angle boxes. In 2 cases, the nests were built on loose piles of sticks 46 cm and 61 cm deep, and the plaster eggs were not blemished with peck marks. In the third case, the thrasher pair had constructed its nest on the very bottom of the nest box and did peck one of the plaster eggs. One other of the shallow vertical-angle boxes was used by thrashers, but use amounted to only a few unarranged sticks at the bottom, and plaster eggs were not damaged in this box. The lack of damage to eggs in all but one box in which a nest had been built on the bottom and the loose nature of foundation sticks in the other boxes strongly suggested that the thrashers were generally dropping sticks into the boxes from the entrances rather than carrying them down into the boxes.

Similar results were obtained for the deep vertical-angle boxes. For this design, complete thrasher nests were built in 5 of the 6 boxes installed, and in all 5 cases, the nests were built on huge piles of loose sticks, and plaster eggs were left unpecked at the bottoms of the boxes. The heights of the piles of sticks in these boxes ranged from 90 cm to just under the nest entrances. Thus, it appears clear that a deep vertical structure with bottom not visible from the entrance is a structure into which thrashers will not readily descend. While thrashers did use these structures for nesting, the manner of use suggested that parrot nests of similar design might receive considerable protection of their contents from thrasher depredations.

Alternative Nest Sites for Thrashers

Meanwhile, a completely different nest-box approach to the thrasher problem was being tested at active parrot nests of 1974, 1975, and 1976. We provided alternative nest boxes for thrashers in the immediate vicinity of parrot nests to see if this might reduce the frequency with which thrashers might attempt to enter the parrot nests. In 1974 two parrot nests were equipped with thrasher boxes 4 m and 2 m away from the entrances, respectively, and developments were watched intensively from blinds. In both cases, thrashers did adopt the alternative structures, and thrasher activity at parrot nests was relatively infrequent. Once thrashers were settled in the alternative sites, they rarely visited the parrot nests and did a fairly efficient job of excluding other thrashers prospecting for nest sites, thus giving significant protection to the parrot nests, although protection was by no means 100 percent. Like the deep, angled nest-box design, the technique of providing alternative nest sites for thrashers next to parrot nests appeared to be a useful one, but it was not a complete solution to the problem in itself.

Nevertheless, it appeared that a safe and practical solution to

the thrasher problem might be obtained by combining the protection offered by the territorial-exclusion effect of thrashers nesting in
boxes close to parrot nests with the reluctance of thrashers to descend
into deep holes with bottoms not visible from the entrances. The possibility of combining the 2 effects received partial testing at 2 parrot nests of 1976. In the fall of 1975, one parrot nest was deepened
from 90 cm to 150 cm and was provided with an internal baffle blocking the view of the bottom from the entrance. In addition, the entrance was half closed off so the amount of light entering the hole
was considerably reduced, and an alternative thrasher box was mounted
4 m from the entrance of the parrot nest. When the parrot pair returned in the breeding season of 1976, they accepted the modifications
of their site and proceeded to lay eggs on schedule. As hoped, thrashers occupied the alternative nest box. Constant observations early in
the breeding season revealed that the parrot nest was checked practically every day by the resident thrasher pair, but the checking did
not proceed beyond the point of the thrashers peering into the nest
from the vines in front of the entrance. In fact, we never once observed the thrashers landing on the lip of the parrot nest, and it appeared that the view from the vines was sufficiently discouraging to
them that they were not motivated to further investigations.

In previous years, this same nest site, then only 90 cm deep and
much brighter on the inside, had been subjected to intense thrasher
pressure. Both in 1971 and 1972, there was evidence that thrashers
destroyed the parrot eggs, and in 1973 we shot a total of 26 thrashers
at the entrance of the hole during the breeding season. Although provision of an alternative thrasher box on the same tree in 1974 and
1975 had reduced the frequency of thrasher inspections, these inspections still involved the thrashers landing on the nest entrance and
descending within the cavity. In 1976, the combination of the alternative thrasher box and the deeper and darker nest hole with the bottom not visible from the entrance seemed to render the nest perfectly
safe from thrashers.

The other parrot nest tested in 1976 with the combined technique
described above was not deepened as much as we would have liked, and
it ended up only 122 cm deep and still relatively bright inside.
Nevertheless, this nest site received very little attention from
thrashers during the breeding season, and plaster eggs left in the
hole during the incubation period were unmarked by blows of thrasher
bills. The plaster eggs left in the same hole the year before, when
the hole was only 90 cm deep and lacked a baffle obscuring the bottom,
had been extensively damaged. Thus, even though this site was not
modified as much as we would have liked, it still was much safer from
thrasher predation in 1976 than in 1975.

Obviously, the 2 nests modified for the 1976 breeding season represented an insufficient sample to prove conclusively the value of the
combined technique, although results were encouraging. During the
summer of 1976, extensive modifications were made to all active and
recently active parrot nests to make them as deep as possible and to
make the bottoms invisible from the entrances. Thrasher boxes were
provided adjacent to each nest. In 1977, all 3 nesting pairs of parrots occupied the modified structures, and there was no significant

thrasher pressure on any of the parrot sites during the breeding season. Thus, the thrasher problem now appears to be under control to
the extent that parrots can be persuaded to adopt the deep and dark
artificial structures. Considerable circumstantial evidence suggests
that the parrots may actually prefer such structures when they are
available, and we are cautiously optimistic that there may be no
further thrasher difficulties for the parrots in the years ahead.

ACKNOWLEDGMENTS

The recent efforts to conserve and study the Puerto Rican Parrot
have been truly cooperative, involving critical observations and support from many individuals and organizations. Special acknowledgment
should be made to Frank Wadsworth, Director of the Institute of Tropical Forestry in Rio Piedras, Puerto Rico, and to Ray Erickson, Assistant Director for Endangered Wildlife Research of the Patuxent Wildlife Research Center, for their roles in initiating the research program and for their continuing support and guidance of efforts on behalf of the species. Forest Service personnel who have been involved
in field studies of the parrot are Mike Lennartz, Howard Smith, Helen
Snyder, John Taapken, Dwight Smith, James Wiley, Jesse Grantham,
Carlos Delannoy, and José Rivera. Commonwealth of Puerto Rico personnel participating in the field studies have been Herb Raffaele and
Mitch Fram. Fish and Wildlife Service contributors have been Cam
Kepler, Noel Snyder, and James Wiley, who is currently in charge of
the field effort. In addition, the parrot program has received important voluntary assistance from numerous private citizens, most
notably Beth Wiley, Kay Kepler, and Donna Taapken, who have donated
uncounted hours of their time in various aspects of the studies.
Financial support has come primarily from the U.S. Forest Service and
the U.S. Fish and Wildlife Service, with important additional support
coming from the World Wildlife Fund and the Commonwealth of Puerto
Rico.

LITERATURE CITED

Danforth, S.T. 1931. Puerto Rican ornithological records. J. Dept. Ag.
    Puerto Rico 15(1):33-106.
Skutch, A.F. 1976. Parent birds and their young. Univ. of Texas Press,
    Austin.
Wetmore, A. 1927. The birds of Porto Rico and the Virgin Islands.
    N.Y. Acad. of Sci. Scientific Survey of Porto Rico and the
    Virgin Islands, Vol. 9. 222p.

15

Controlling Introduced Predators and Competitors on Islands

Donald V. Merton

"Islands are a link with a land and biota of the past, a
measure of how we are conserving our biota at present, and
a key to a more varied landscape for mankind in the future."
(Atkinson and Bell, 1973)

Until the present century, the remoteness and inaccessability of
most the the world's half million islands served to effectively isolate
them as sanctuaries for animals and plants. Now it is recognized that
man's most devastating effect upon island biotas--especially those of
isolated oceanic islands that lacked indigenous land mammals--has resulted from his deliberate or accidental introduction of alien animals,
particularly mammals. Mayr (1965) has estimated that whereas less
than 20 percent of all birds are island forms, more than 90 percent of
those which have become extinct in historical times were island
species. Islands constitute less than 7 percent of the earth's surface, yet 53 percent of the world's endangered bird species are island
forms (W.B. King, Ch. 2, this volume).

The spread of alien mammals to islands is a continuing and growing problem (Bourne, 1975). For instance, in 1976 alone, at least 2
New Zealand islands were colonised by alien animals, and mongooses
(Herpestes auropunctatus) reached Kauai, the last major mongoose-free
Hawaiian Island (C.B. Kepler, personal communication). An effective
policy of education and management is vital in order to offset this
erosion of the immensely valuable biological resource which islands
represent.

New Zealand, an archipelago comprised of 3 large and approximately 700 offshore and outlying islands in the southwest Pacific Ocean
between latitudes 29°S and 53°S, provides an ideal testing ground for
island management techniques (Williams, 1977). Its biogeographical
history is similar to that of some other isolated oceanic islands. A

very long period of geographical isolation and the absence of land mammals (other than bats) has, as emphasized by McDowell (1969), resulted in the evolution of an unusual avifauna, the older elements of which are often characterized by flightlessness and sensitivity to the impact of human settlement.

With the introduction of mammals, which followed human settlement, the various elements of the indigenous fauna inhabiting the 3 main islands were greatly effected. On the other hand, many of the smaller islands escaped the major influences of man and, as a result, support biological communities that approach, to varying degrees, those which formerly occurred on the main islands. These less-modified islands now play a major role in conservation management, and most have been declared biological reserves with entry strictly controlled.

The New Zealand Wildlife Service (NZWS), the national wildlife conservation agency, has, in recent years, expended much of its limited resources in the rehabilitation of endangered fauna, of which the region has more than its share. According to the *Red Data Book* (Vincent, 1966), 333 endangered bird taxa exist throughout the world. Of these, 32 or almost 10 percent are from New Zealand and its outlying islands--a greater density of endangered birds than exists in any other comparable region. Of the 112 land-, coastal-, and fresh-water-inhabiting endemic birds present in 1800, 15 percent are now extinct, and 30 percent are designated rare and endangered. Twenty-six of the latter bird species are presently the subjects of increasingly successful conservation management that includes both classical and contrived techniques.

Whereas the causes of extinctions on the main islands of New Zealand are by no means clear-cut, there is no doubt as to the causes on some offshore and outlying islands. On many, the impact of introduced mammals has induced widespread ecological changes and eliminated indigenous plant and animal species. Furthermore, whereas eradication of alien mammals from the major islands is generally not feasible, their elimination from smaller coastal and oceanic islands is often practicable.

INTRODUCED PREDATORS

Rodents

Rats are the most widespread alien mammals inhabiting islands in the New Zealand region; they have colonised no fewer than 43 biologically-important islands (Atkinson, 1977). They are not only efficient predators but often compete with indigenous island animals. Circumstantial evidence implicates them as limiting the distribution and population densities of some indigenous reptiles (Crook, 1973; Whitaker, 1973) and birds, especially the breeding distribution of smaller species of petrels and shearwaters (Merton, 1970b; Imber, 1975; Atkinson, 1977).

On the other hand, some avifaunas of oceanic islands seem little affected by introduced rats. For instance, Christmas Island (135 km^2) in the Indian Ocean was until 1897 inhabited by 2 indigenous rats and a shrew. By 1908, *Rattus rattus* had colonised the island and replaced the indigenous rodents (Gibson-Hill, 1947). Although *R. norvegicus* and *R. exulans* have since colonised the island as well, the avifauna, which includes 9 endemic forms (which have evolved with rats), appears unaffected, and no losses have occurred.

Three species of rat occur in the New Zealand region, and each has distinctive habits that affect the kinds of animals most frequently preyed upon. *R. rattus* is arboreal and preys upon perching birds, their eggs and young; *R. norvegicus* is terrestrial and preys upon breeding seabirds and ground birds, their eggs and young; and *R. exulans* is somewhat intermediate, preying upon breeding seabirds and forest birds, but taking fewer species than either of the European rats (Atkinson, 1977).

Big South Cape Island (about 930 ha) off Southwest Cape, Stewart Island, is one of the most recent biologically-important New Zealand islands to have been colonised by rats, in this instance *R. rattus* (Bell, 1977). The colonising rat population irrupted in 1963-64 and caused the loss of the local population of an indigenous bat and 6 bird species, 3 of which occurred nowhere else. There are no methods known for eliminating rats from an island of this size. Warfarin poison, protected from birds in bait boxes, was used in an attempt to "buy time" while efforts were made to transfer threatened species to other islands. The effort was successful with one species, the South Island Saddleback (*Philesturnus c. carunculatus*) (Merton, 1975).

Rats can sometimes be eliminated from very small islands, and Maria Island (2 ha) in the Hauraki Gulf of northern New Zealand is an example. Following an invasion of this island by *R. norvegicus* in the early 1960's, a warfarin poisoning campaign was initiated, and the rats were exterminated (Merton, *unpublished data*). Plans are underway by the NZWS to eliminate rats from a larger island using a combination of techniques, including the introduction and subsequent removal of a single-sex population of Stoats (*Mustela erminea*) as suggested by Fitzgerald (1977).

Feral Cats

Fifteen biologically-important islands in the New Zealand region have been colonised by domestic cats (*Felis catus*); these predators are implicated in the extinction of at least 6 endemic New Zealand birds, as well as some 70 local extinctions.

Elimination of feral cat populations is feasible, at least from relatively small islands; cats have been removed from 4 New Zealand islands ranging in area from 40 to 2,000 ha.

Cats became feral on Little Barrier Island (2,800 ha) in the Hauraki Gulf about 1880 and are responsible for the local extinction of 7 bird species (Turbott, 1947). One other species, the Black Petrel (*Procellaria parkinsoni*), is approaching extinction due to predation by cats on adults and young (Imber, 1975). During recent years, trapping of cats just prior to the fledging period has permitted a greater number of young birds to reach independence. However, the NZWS has recently begun a large-scale and long-term program of cat extermination using a combination of viral disease, trapping, poisoning, and hunting with dogs.

Cats became established on Herekopare Island (40 ha) off Stewart Island sometime between 1925 and 1931. In 1943, the petrel breeding population there was estimated by Richdale (1943) to have been reduced from some 400,000 birds to "a few thousand." Cats were eliminated by the NZWS through trapping and dogging in 1970, and already some displaced species are recolonising the island.

Following the establishment of a lighthouse station on Cuvier Island (200 ha) in the outer Hauraki Gulf in 1889, cats and goats became feral. Goats soon destroyed the island's forest and scrub vegetation, and cats contributed to the local extinction of at least 5 species of birds. Between 1960 and 1968, the NZWS eliminated the goats by shooting and the cats by trapping. Two bird species lost from the island have been successfully reintroduced, and 2 others are recolonising naturally (Merton, 1970a). A key factor in the cat eradication campaign was the tendency of cats to seek forest openings on warm, dry ridges in order to sun themselves. We exploited this behavioral trait by concentrating the light-weight gin-traps, which used raw fish and canned cat food as baits, in these places. Trapping and shooting of cats over the whole of this extensively cliffed island would have been a formidable task.

Mustelids

In the New Zealand region, colonisation by Stoats is limited to the 2 main islands and larger, rodent-inhabited islands, up to about 2 km from shore. Presumably, food supplies on smaller, rodent-free islands are inadequate to sustain permanent Stoat populations. The impact of Stoats upon island ecosystems is confused by the presence of rodents, but without exception, indigenous birdlife has been depleted by introduced mustelids. Reinfestation from the adjacent mainland is inevitable and renders long-term extermination impracticable. Ferrets (*Mustela putorius*) and weasels (*M. nivalis*) are restricted to the 2 main islands where eradication is not feasible.

Predatory Birds

The Weka or Wood-hen (*Gallirallus australis*), a large, flightless rail endemic to the main islands of New Zealand, was introduced by sealers, whalers, and muttonbirders (petrel harvesters) to at least 25 islands--mainly in the vicinity of Stewart Island--often with disasterous ecological consequences. The omnivorous Weka will prey upon small petrels, as well as upon the eggs and young of ground-nesting species. Weka populations on islands, unlike those on the mainland, often reach high densities and deplete indigenous birdlife. The species has, therefore, been eliminated from 3 islands, and eradication is proceeding on an additional 3.

Wekas on Maud Island (250 ha) in the Marlborough Sounds have been exterminated during the past 6 years through trapping, dogging, and shooting; tape recordings of Weka calls have been used as an attractant. Maud Island is now being managed as an "open aviary" for en-

dangered birds (Merton, 1976). One alien mammal, however, is being
retained on this island; controlled grazing by sheep is being used to
maintain some open grassland amidst scrub and forested areas. This
creates a greater diversity of habitat types for the management of a
variety of endangered species.

INTRODUCED MAMMALIAN COMPETITORS

Goats, rabbits, deer, pigs, Australian Brush-tailed Possums
(*Trichosurus vulpecula*), and feral sheep and cattle have, in varying
combinations, colonised islands in the New Zealand region. Atkinson
and Bell (1973) have described the major, direct impact these animals
have had upon indigenous plant communities of some islands. These
animals have also had a considerable indirect influence upon indigenous animal communities. For instance, goats introduced to Macauley
Island (300 ha) in the Kermadec Group some time before 1836 had by
1887 transformed the indigenous scrub-forest association there to
close-cropped eroding grassland. By the late 1960's when the population of over 3,000 animals was eliminated by shooting, virtually no
woody vegetation remained, and arboreal birdlife was virtually absent
(Williams and Rudge, 1969). Woody vegetation--including some species
which had long vanished--is now regenerating, and birdlife has already
shown a marked recovery.

Goats and cats became established on Raoul Island (2,900 ha) in
the Kermadec Group in the mid-19th century, and Norway Rats reached
the island in 1921. Nine species of birds, some of which bred in vast
numbers, have been lost, and 3 others are in greatly reduced numbers.
However, most still abound on neighboring mammal-free islands (Merton,
1970*b*). The NZWS, assisted by the New Zealand Forest Service, has
undertaken an extermination program involving the shooting, poisoning,
and dogging of goats, and the trapping, poisoning, and dogging of cats.

Feral pigs are particularly destructive to breeding petrels and
other seabirds, as well as to some invertebrate populations and plant
communities. For this reason, they have been eradicated from 2 biologically-important islands in the New Zealand region. Hunting by
trained dog packs and poisoning appear to be the most effective means
of control.

Deer populations (mainly *Cervus elaphus* and *Odocoileus virginianus*) are restricted to inshore islands where reinfestation from the
adjacent mainland renders eradication impracticable.

The removal of large browsing and grazing mammals from major islands can be achieved by subdivision of the area with fences, creating
a series of smaller "islands" from which the animals can be systematically removed. Sheep were eradicated by this means from one half of
Campbell Island (11,000 ha) in New Zealand's subantarctic zone; this
was part of an experiment started in 1970 to determine the effect of
sheep upon albatross breeding colonies there. The United States National Park Service is employing the same principle with success in
the eradication of goats from Hawaii Volcanoes National Park on the
island of Hawaii. Regeneration in one small goat-exclosure on this
island was dominated by a previously undescribed leguminous plant.

The removal of high-density populations of browsing animals from islands may result in the invasion of sparsely vegetated ground by aggressive pioneer weed species such as has occurred on Motunau Islet (3.6 ha) off the east coast of the South Island, New Zealand (Taylor, 1968). Since the removal of rabbits in 1962, a persistent growth of African Boxthorn (*Lycium ferocissimum*) has necessitated periodic control of this weed. However, with the regeneration of a dense covering of coastal scrub and forest, this problem will probably cease to exist. This situation illustrates why follow-up inspections and management must be regarded as an integral part of any eradication program.

Progress in the elimination and control of introduced vertebrate predators and competitors on New Zealand islands is summarized in Table 1.

SOME GENERALIZATIONS

In conclusion, it is possible to make some generalizations about the problems of exotic animals on islands:

1. Any proposal to eliminate an alien animal population from an island must be considered on its own merits and be justifiable on biological grounds. Due consideration must be given to all likely ecological consequences.

2. No animal or plant--endangered or otherwise--should be introduced to a "pristine" island ecosystem unless such action is vital to the survival of that species and no practical alternative exists. The impact of such an introduction may place a unique natural ecosystem at risk.

3. Some alien mammal populations on islands are, in their own right, of scientific interest. However, such values must not be per-

TABLE 1.   INTRODUCED VERTEBRATE PREDATORS AND COMPETITORS WHICH HAVE BEEN ELIMINATED FROM NEW ZEALAND ISLANDS

Introduced Species	No. of Islands on Which Species Has Been Eliminated	No. of Islands with Extermination Programs in Progress
Rat (*Rattus norvegicus*)	1	1
Cat (*Felis catus*)	4	2
Goat (*Capra hircus*)	7	2
Pig (*Sus scrofa*)	2	2
Rabbit (*Oryctolagus cuniculus*)	3	0
Sheep (*Ovis aries*)	3 and part of 3	0
Cattle (*Bos tauris*)	part of 2	0
Weka (*Gallirallus australis*)	3	3

mitted to overshadow conservation requirements of indigenous animals, plants, and communities.

4. The loss of some non-target animals is justifiable provided such losses do not jeopardize the survival of indigenous species or communities, and no long-term ecological damage results.

5. Sound planning, including biological, political, social, financial, and logistic considerations, is crucial. Furthermore, field operations must always be preceded by thoughtfully-presented public relations programs in order to enlist public support and reduce emotional and misinformed criticism.

6. Eradication of alien animals, even from relatively small islands, is invariably a difficult and exacting task. All available resources and all ecologically-acceptable means of extermination should be used.

7. Success often depends entirely upon the extent to which project personnel are dedicated to the objective of total extermination; for an eradication project is as much a psychological challenge as it may be a physical and biological achievement. The last few animals are invariably wary and extremely difficult to eliminate, and without total commitment to the ultimate goal by hunters--and financiers--the cause is likely to be lost at this juncture.

ACKNOWLEDGMENTS

I am indebted to I.A.E. Atkinson, G.R. Williams, and B.D. Bell for criticism of an earlier draft of this paper.

LITERATURE CITED

Atkinson, I.A.E. 1977. Evidence for effects of rodents on the vertebrate wildlife of New Zealand Islands. *In* Rodents in New Zealand island and mainland reserves. New Zeal. Dept. Lands and Surv. Information Ser. No. 3

Atkinson, I.A.E. and B.D. Bell. 1973. Offshore and Outlying Islands, p. 372-392. *In* G.R. Williams (ed.) The Natural History of New Zealand. Reed Ltd., Wellington.

Bell, B.D. 1977. The Big South Cape Island rat irruption. *In* Rodents in New Zealand island and mainland reserves. New Zeal. Dept. Lands and Surv. Information Ser. No. 3.

Bourne, W.R.P. 1975. Mammals on islands. New Scientist 165: 422-425.

Crook, I.C. 1973. The tuatara, *Sphenodon punctatus* (Gray), on islands with & without populations of the Polynesian rat *Rattus exulans* (Peale). Proc. New Zeal. Ecol. Soc., 20:115-120.

Fitzgerald, B.M. 1977. A proposal for biological control. *In* Rodents in New Zealand island and mainland reserves. New Zeal. Dept. Lands and Surv. Information Ser. No. 3.

Gibson-Hill, C.A. 1947. A note on the mammals of Christmas Island. Bull. Raffles Mus. 18:166-167.

Imber, M.J. 1975. Petrels and predators. Bull. Int. Council Bird
    Preserv. 2:260-263.
Mayr, E. 1965. Avifauna: Turnover on islands. Science. 150:1587-1588.
McDowell, R.M. 1969. Extinction and endemism in New Zealand landbirds.
    Tuatara. 17(1):1-12.
Merton, D.V. 1970a. The rehabilitation of Cuvier Island, p. 5-8. *In*
    Wildlife 1970 - A Review. New Zeal. Wildlife Service.
Merton, D.V. 1970b. Kermadec Island expedition reports: a general ac-
    count of birdlife. Notornis 17(3):147-199.
Merton, D.V. 1975. The Saddleback: its status and conservation, p.
    61-74. *In* R.D. Martin (ed.) Breeding Endangered Species in
    Captivity. Academic Press, New York. 420p.
Merton, D.V. 1976. Kakapo on Maud Island. Wildlife - A Review. New
    Zeal. Wildlife Service. 7:30-35.
Richdale, L.E. 1943. Whero: Island of seabirds. Wildlife in New
    Zeal. 3. Otago Daily Times & Witness Newspapers, Dunedin, New
    Zeal.
Taylor, R.H. 1968. Introduced mammals and islands: priorities for
    conservation and research. Proc. New Zeal. Ecol. Soc. 15:61-67.
Turbott, E.G. 1947. Birds of Little Barrier Island. New Zeal. Bird
    Notes 2(5):98.
Vincent, J. (ed.) 1966. Red Data Book; Vol. 2, Aves. IUCN, Morges,
    Switzerland.
Whitaker, A.H. 1973. Lizard populations on islands with and without
    Polynesian rats, *Rattus exulans* (Peale). Proc. New Zeal. Ecol.
    Soc. 20:121-130.
Williams, G.R. and M.R. Rudge. 1969. A population study of feral
    goats (*Capra hircus* L.) from Macauley Island, New Zealand.
    Proc. New Zeal. Ecol. Soc. 16:17-28.
Williams, G.R. 1977. Marooning - a technique for saving threatened
    species from extinction. Int. Zoo Yearbook 17:102-106.

Part IV
Supplemental Feeding
and Manipulation of Feeding Ecology

16

Supplemental Feeding and Manipulation of Feeding Ecology of Endangered Birds
A Review

George W. Archibald

Artificial feeding programs have been provided for threatened
populations of swans, cranes, vultures, condors, eagles, and ibises
to supplement or replace natural food resources that are limited or
eliminated and to provide noncontaminated food when the natural food
is polluted. Perhaps the best example of a supplemental feeding
program that clearly aided the recovery of an endangered bird is the
case of the Trumpeter Swan (*Cygnus cygnus buccinator*). This swan was
once widely distributed over prairie marshes of central North America
(i.e., the inland population) and on wetlands in northern British
Columbia and southeast Alaska (i.e., the Pacific population). The
Pacific population has apparently always remained stable at about
several thousand birds, whereas the inland population was almost
extirpated by habitat destruction, egg-collecting, and hunting.
Swan pelts brought a good price, and the inland population was ruth-
lessly slaughtered on its breeding grounds and on its winter haunts
in southeastern United States (Banko, 1960).

By the 1930's, only two small groups within the inland population
survived: a group of perhaps 100 that bred near Grand Prairie in
western Alberta and that migrated to Wyoming and a locally migratory
group that bred in what is now Red Rock Lakes National Wildlife Refuge,
Montana. This Rocky Mountain population bred on vast marshes around
lakes and moved in autumn to open areas of water associated with hot
springs in the same region. The remote distribution of the Alberta
and Montana swans is perhaps the foremost factor responsible for the
survival of the inland population.

In 1936, the Montana swans numbered about 15 pairs. They were
easily counted on their winter habitat where they fed on submersed
aquatic vegetation. The main mortality to the swans occurred in late
winter when severe cold constricted the area of open water at the hot
springs and, thus, the availability of food. Game managers concluded

that winter food was the limiting factor to population increase. Grain was scattered in the water during particularly cold weather from 1936 to present with a corresponding increase in the swan numbers to about 600 birds by the mid-1950's (Fjetland, 1974). Food in winter was clearly the pre-1936 limiting factor to swan increase. Availability of nesting habitat is assumed to be the controlling factor during the last two decades for the number of breeding pairs has remained stable, but their productivity has declined to maintain a stable population.

Man's management of the dwindling population of Trumpeter Swans through protection of the birds and their habitats and the provision of supplemental food in late winter stands as a conservation monument to the cause of endangered species management. Likewise, in Japan and England, wintering populations of Whooper Swans (*Cygnus cygnus cygnus*) and Bewick Swans (*Cygnus atratus*) have been provided supplemental food, programs that likewise resulted in the increase in swan numbers (Scott, 1972).

Since 1958, White-naped Cranes (*Grus vipio*) and Hooded Cranes (*Grus monacha*) have been provided with grain at feeding stations on their wintering grounds in Japan. A similar program for the Japanese Crane (*Grus japonensis*) began in 1952. Since feeding began the numbers of all 3 species have increased dramatically. When feeding began almost 20 years ago, there were only about 60 White-naped Cranes and 700 Hooded Cranes surviving; the populations have since grown to about 700 and 3,000 birds, respectively. They continue to increase apparently because neither breeding habitat on mainland Asia nor winter food in Japan is limiting. Unlike the White-naped and Hooded Cranes that migrate to Japan in autumn, the Japanese Crane is sedentary in south-eastern Hokkaido, moving in autumn from marshes where they breed to fresh water streams that remain open through winter because they are fed by hot springs. In 1952, there were only 30 Japanese Cranes in Hokkaido, remnants of a former population that once bred over much of Hokkaido and northern Honshu and which presumably migrated to now-developed areas of southern Japan. The winter feeding program began in 1952 because of the unusually harsh winter and has continued to present at some 20 feeding stations. The crane numbers increased to about 200 birds in the late 1960s and remained stable in subsequent years, presumably because of the high mortality of birds, particularly young cranes, through collision with electric power lines. In recent years, many of the marshes used by cranes during the breeding season have been developed.

Although swans and cranes are highly territorial on their breeding grounds in spring and summer, they readily congregate into flocks in fall and winter, if food is abundant. This tendency to flock and to readily accept grains in the non-breeding period has made the supplemental feeding programs particularly applicable to the conservation of winter populations of these birds. Carrion feeders such as vultures will gather in flocks at a carcass in both the breeding and nonbreeding season, making the potential for artificial feeding even more applicable to scavengers than to the cranes and swans. In Israel and Spain populations of the Griffon Vulture (*Gyps fulvus*) have declined because of the widespread use of pesticides (Mendelssohn

1972; and Zimmerman, 1975). Uncontaminated carcasses provided at one feeding station in the Negev desert, Israel have been readily used by a colony of Griffon Vultures, and their numbers have increased since artificial feeding began. A second feeding station located near the Dead Sea in a region where Griffon Vultures are migrants, was visited regularly by the vultures with the result that three pairs started a breeding colony about one kilometer away from the feeding station (Mendelssohn, *personal communication*). Similarly, in Spain this species has benefitted by artificial feeding (Zimmerman, 1975), demonstrating that in densely populated countries like Israel and Spain where large wilderness areas are difficult to conserve, artificial feeding programs may eventually be the only way to maintain wild populations of scavengers.

Feeding stations have likewise been established for the White-tailed Sea Eagle (*Haliaeetus albicilla*) in Sweden and the acutely-endangered California Condor (*Gymnogypus californianus*) because of poor productivity related to pesticide contamination and possibly because of food scarcity, particularly for immatures. Since feeding began in Sweden in 1971, the survival rate of subadult sea eagles has increased, but the nesting success has remained constant indicating either the breeders are not using the noncontaminated food or the contaminants have not yet been eliminated from their bodies.

The California Condor artificial feeding program has been operative since 1974, and again subadults appear to benefit most from the feeding, while there is no apparent improvement in the nesting success.

The Japanese Crested Ibis (*Nipponia nippon*) has been reduced to only 9 birds in Japan because of mercury poisoning from pesticides spread on the rice paddies in which the ibises feed. A small population survived in a high-altitude area of forest and farmland on Sado Island, an area that is now protected as an ibis sanctuary. Two pairs of ibises usually nest there each spring. A feeding station in the reserve has helped to keep the breeding pairs within the clean environment of the reserve and away from the polluted agricultural fields in the nearby lowlands. Although food is clean and abundant at the feeding station in the reserve, the tendency for the immatures to disperse overweighs their tendency to remain in the natal area, and they are contaminated in the lowlands.

CONCLUSION

The operation of supplemental feeding programs is recommended for endangered species of birds only when the natural food resource is limited or eliminated and/or when natural food sources are contaminated. Attracting wild birds to and maintaining them at artificial feeding stations detracts from the natural behavior of the species; however under the above conditions, the conservationist is left with few alternatives. Perhaps the greatest potential risks involved in an artificial feeding program are the increased potential for disease that results from concentrating the birds in a small area and the chance of birds becoming tame which might place the birds in jeopardy in other areas where people are less conservation-minded. Fortunately neither disease nor tameness have become problems associated with endangered species feeding stations to date.

Aside from the direct value of feeding stations to the birds, the programs offer excellent opportunities for public education. Interpretive centers can usually be constructed near the feeding stations; this permits the general public to see the birds at close range and learn about their needs. Birds are easily captured at the feeding station through use of oral tranquilizers or nets, practices that allow researchers to readily mark the birds and better understand their biology and thus their conservation.

LITERATURE CITED

Banko, W.E. 1960. The trumpeter swan. North American Fauna, Number 63, United States Fish and Wildlife Service, Washington, D.C. 214 p.

Fjetland, C.A. 1974. Trumpeter swan management in the National Wildlife Refuge System, p. 136-241. *In* Transactions of the 39th North American Wildlife and Natural Resources Cenference, Wildlife Management Institute, Washington, D.C.

Mendelssohn, H. 1972. The impact of pesticides on bird life in Israel ICBP Bulletin, 11:75-104.

Zimmerman, D. 1975. To save a bird in peril. Coward, McCann & Geoghegan, New York. 286p.

17

Supplemental Feeding
of California Condors

Sanford R. Wilbur

The California Condor (*Gymnogyps californianus*) has been almost completely dependent on man's livestock for its food supply since the decline of the large mammal fauna of California after 1850. The disappearance of Tule Elk (*Cervus nannodes*) and Pronghorn Antelope (*Antilocarpa americana*) from the southern portions of the state and public use and development of the coastline that decreased the opportunity for condors to feed on carcasses of marine mammals, have resulted in dead cattle and sheep assuming even greater importance as a food supply. By the 1940's, following a major decline in sheep numbers in California, cattle had become the principal food of the condor (Koford, 1953).

Dependence on a single-item diet now appears to be causing problems for the condor population because livestock carcasses are becoming less available to condors. The amount of foraging habitat has diminished as urbanization, industry, and intensified agriculture replace livestock use on California rangelands. Yearlong grazing operations have in part given way to seasonal influxes of "stocker" cattle that are kept on the range for only a few months, then moved to stockyards for finishing. Improved nutrition and medication have generally contributed to a lower livestock mortality rate, and greater effort to remove cattle from the range for sanitary reasons has resulted in fewer carcasses left for scavengers. The combined result has been a marked decrease in potential condor food. The greatest decrease has occurred in close proximity to the principal condor nesting areas in Ventura and Los Angeles Counties. Since 1968, production in the California Condor population has been significantly depressed (Wilbur et al., 1972; Wilbur, 1976), and it seemed likely that the diminished food supply was a contributing factor.

A small-scale condor feeding program was in operation from February 1971 through May 1973 in the Sespe Condor Sanctuary, Los

Padres National Forest, California (Wilbur et al., 1974). During that time, 83 animal carcasses, primarily Mule Deer (*Odocoileus hemionus*), were provided for the condors. Condors definitely fed on 47 of these, and probably fed on some of the others. During that time, production of condors in the sanctuary increased somewhat over previous years. As there seemed to be no major biological or operational problems involved in the feeding program, and as there were preliminary signs that feeding might be enhancing the nesting environment, the program was expanded in 1974.

METHODS AND RESULTS

From 31 May 1974 to 5 April 1977, 246 animal carcasses were distributed at 10 sites in the Sespe Condor Sanctuary and adjacent Hopper Mountain National Wildlife Refuge. Most carcasses were domestic goats, but sheep, cattle, and Mule Deer were also used. The objective was to set out 2 carcasses per week throughout the year. Some variation occurred due to temporary shortages of carcasses or inability to reach feeding sites during inclement weather, but the only long interruption in the program was from 20 July 1975 to 31 October 1975.

Before January 1976, use of a carcass by condors was verified by direct observation or by examining animal sign at the carcasses (feathers, tracks, excrement, and condition of the carcass). After 7 January 1976, surveillance cameras (time-lapse movie cameras) monitored use of the feeding sites during daylight hours.

The feeding record is fairly clear for 183 of the 246 carcasses. California Condors definitely fed on 38 (21 percent) of these and may have fed on 18 others, so that condors probably used 56 (31 percent) of the carcasses. Usually, 1 to 3 condors were at the feeding site simultaneously; occasional groups of up to 8 condors occurred. In most cases, condors were not the primary users of the carcasses but shared them with Golden Eagles (*Aquila chrysaetos*), Turkey Vultures (*Cathartes aura*), Ravens (*Corvus corax*), or Coyotes (*Canis latrans*). Black Bears (*Ursus americanus*) were occasional visitors to the feeding sites.

Condors occurred at feeding sites most frequently from November through April, with January being the month of most intensive use (19 percent of total condor records). Approximately 20 percent of the visits by condors occurred from May through July; there was no apparent use from August through October. Only a limited number of carcasses were made available during the latter period, so the seasonal distribution of use may be somewhat distorted. However, feeding opportunity was approximately equal during the other 9 months of the year. The pattern of visits to the feeding stations coincides with the historical records of condors being most abundant in and near the Sespe Condor Sanctuary in winter and spring, with lesser numbers occurring in summer and fall (Koford, 1953; Wilbur et al., 1972).

Direct operational costs of the feeding program have been approximately $5,000 per year. This includes salaries, transportation costs, and purchase and storage of animal carcasses. Costs of monitoring the sites with cameras has been approximately $500.00 per year.

DISCUSSION

The objective of the condor feeding program has been to supplement an apparently much-diminished food supply in the vicinity of condor nesting sites. More specifically, we hoped to accomplish one or more of the following:

1. To make it possible for breeding birds to spend less time foraging and more time attending the nest, thereby increasing the likelihood of a successful nesting attempt.

2. To make it possible for more breeding pairs to simultaneously use the nesting habitat of the Sespe Condor Sanctuary, by increasing the food supply and by distributing food so as to reduce the effects of intraspecific competition at carcasses. It seems likely that one pair of dominant condors can effectively keep other pairs and individuals from feeding and, therefore, breeding in the area if carcasses are scarce.

3. To make it possible for immature condors to become independent of parents at an earlier age, thereby permitting the adults to breed more frequently. Condors normally do not breed every year because they must feed their young well into the year following fledging. However, this is apparently because the young birds cannot compete with older condors at carcasses, rather than because young birds are incapable of feeding by themselves. It was hoped that providing carcasses would give the young birds a chance to feed without social pressures from dominant adults.

4. To help maintain a tradition of condors using the historical nesting areas. Since at least the 1930's, condors have reached peak numbers in the nesting areas in winter. In spring, most nonbreeding birds emigrated to outlying roosting and feeding areas, leaving the nesting areas to breeding condors. This emigration was probably beneficial because it reduced food competition and reduced the likelihood of nesting condors being disturbed by nonbreeding birds. A tendency to congregate in large flocks and move back into the nesting areas in the fall facilitated pair formation and maintained contact between the birds and the most suitable nesting habitat. In recent years, perhaps because of diminished food supplies near the main nesting area, movements in and out of the nesting habitats have decreased, and nonbreeding birds are spending more time in areas of good food supply but limited nesting habitat. Restoring the food supply in nesting areas was seen as a possible way to restore traditional patterns of seasonal movement, or at least keeping the tradition from breaking down entirely.

Condor use of the Sespe Condor Sanctuary has not increased during the past 3 years; in fact, it appears to be decreasing. This may partially explain why over 50 percent of carcasses distributed in 1971-1973 were used by condors, but only 20-30 percent were used in recent years. The increase in reproduction noted during the 1971-1973 period has not continued; only 2 young are thought to have been produced in the past 4 years by pairs nesting within foraging distance of the feeding sites. Obviously, supplemental feeding, as practiced to date, has not resulted in a major recovery in the condor population.

On the other hand, condors are using the feeding areas regularly. Subadult birds (those less than 6 years old) have been present in approximately one-half of all condor feeding observations, so the feeding may be helping to preserve traditional ties with the nesting area. Also, condors less than one year old have been seen feeding by themselves on several occasions. Although increased reproduction by individual pairs has not yet been seen in this area since feeding began, early ʳdependence of young is the first step.

Looking to the future, there appear to be several alternatives. We could assume that the relatively light use of feeding stations indicates that condors do not need or do not want the food provided and terminate the project. We could continue to feed at approximately the same rate but relocate feeding stations in areas where condors would be more likely to find and use them; or we could increase both the amount of feed and the distribution of feeding sites in an all-out-effort to aid the failing population.

California Condor reproduction since 1968 has been 50 percent or less of what is needed to stabilize the population; and numbers are declining. Even if supplemental feeding benefits only a few birds, terminating the project might reduce the likelihood of saving the species. Continuing the present program would likely benefit some birds, but relocating food sites might be more satisfactory. Sites currently in use are frequented by condors, but the locations appear to be away from the primary flight lines to and from nesting areas. Perhaps other sites to the north and east of present sites would receive more use. Other potential sites are more difficult to reach with carcasses, and the time and effort involved in the program would be greatly increased.

I think the best alternative is to expand the program. We have increased the food supply locally by supplemental feeding, but in general, condor food has decreased in the regions most frequented by breeding birds. In various species, food shortage has been thought to:

1. completely arrest breeding of all or part of the population (Drury, 1960; Kahl, 1964; Houston, 1971);
2. cause deferred breeding beyond normal minimum reproductive age (Ashmore, 1971; Houston, 1971; Palmer, 1972);
3. increase intervals between breeding (Jonkel and Cowan, 1971);
4. decrease adult fertility (Klein, 1970; King, 1973); and
5. increase juvenile mortality (Klein, 1970).

A number of these effects are possible within the condor population. Additionally, food shortage may indirectly affect condors by causing them to congregate in fewer areas and in larger groups, increasing their vulnerability to shooting and other man-caused mortality. Finally, chemical pesticides stored in body fats may be mobilized during periods of food stress and released in the body in harmful doses (Stickel, 1975). An expanded feeding program, providing more carcasses at more locations, would be more likely to alleviate any of the above conditions than would the current program. However, it would require developing new sources of animal carcasses, which are already difficult to acquire. Nevertheless, I think it is warranted at this critical time in the California Condor's existence.

Food shortages are often cited as a problem for scavenging birds (de la Fuente, 1964; Houston, 1971; Hiraldo, 1974; Jarvis et al., 1974), and feeding stations have been developed in several countries, apparently with desired results (Iribarren, 1971; Zimmerman, 1975; Bijleveld, 1974). Wildlife managers whose experiences with feeding programs are limited to winter feeding of gallinaceous birds or deer may rightly question the need for and desirability of such programs for most species. However, for wildlife that has lost its traditional food source, supplemental feeding becomes a legitimate and possibly essential technique.

ACKNOWLEDGMENTS

Michael D. Silbernagle, U.S. Fish and Wildlife Service, has been responsible for carrying out most of the operational aspects of the condor feeding the past two years. John C. Borneman (National Audubon Society) has helped with the feeding and monitoring of use, and he and W. Dean Carrier (U. S. Forest Service) worked with me in developing the feeding program. Acquisition and storage of carcasses has been a cooperative program of the U. S. Fish and Wildlife Service and California Department of Fish and Game.

LITERATURE CITED

Ashmole, N. 1971. Seabird ecology and the marine environment, p. 223-286. *In* D. Farner and J. King (eds.) Avian Biology, Vol. I. Academic Press, New York.

Bijleveld, M. 1974. Birds of prey in Europe. MacMillan Press Ltd., London. 263p.

de la Fuente, F. 1964. Status of predatory birds in Spain, p. 120-123. *In* Proc. Working Conf. on Birds of Prey and Owls. 10-12 April 1964, Caen, France, International Council for Bird Preservation.

Drury, W. 1960. Breeding activities of long-tailed jaeger, herring gull and arctic tern on Bylot Island, Northwest Territories, Canada. Bird-Banding 21(2):63-79.

Hiraldo, F. 1974. Colonias de cria y censo de los buitres negros (*Aegypius monachus*) en Espana. Naturalia Hispanica 2:1-31.

Houston, D. 1971. The ecology of Serengeti vultures. Ph.D. Thesis. Trinity College, Oxford Univ., England. 193 p.

Iribarren, J. 1971. Birds of prey conservation programme in northern Spain. World Wildlife Fund Yearbook (1970-71):495.

Jarvis, M., W. Siegfried and M. Currie. 1974. Conservation of the Cape vulture in the Cape Province. J. South African Wildlife Manage. Assoc. 4(1):29-34.

Jonkel, C. and I. Cowan. 1971. The black bear in the spruce-fir forest. Wildlife Monogr. 27:1-57.

Kahl, M. 1964. Food ecology of the wood stork (*Mycteria americana*) in Florida. Ecol. Monogr. 34:97-117.

King, J. 1973. Energetics of reproduction in birds, p. 78-107. *In* D. Farner (ed.) Breeding biology of birds. Natl. Acad. Sci., Wash. D.C.

Klein, D. 1970. Food selection by North American deer and their response to overutilization of preferred plant species, p. 25-46. *In* A. Watson (ed.) Animal populations in relation to their food resources. Blackwell Sci. Publs., Oxford and Edinburgh.

Koford, C. 1953. The California condor. Natl. Audubon Soc. Res. Rep. No. 4, 154 p.

Palmer, R. 1972. Patterns of molting, p. 65-102. *In* D. Farner and J. King (eds.) Avian biology, Volume III. Academic Press, New York.

Stickel, W. 1975. Some effects of pollutants in terrestrial ecosystems, p. 25-69. *In* A. McIntyre and C. Mills (eds.) Ecological toxicology research. Plenum Publ. Corp., New York.

Wilbur, S. 1976. Status of the California Condor, 1972-1975. Amer. Birds 30(4):789-790.

Wilbur, S., W. Carrier and J. Borneman. 1974. Supplemental feeding program for California condors. J. Wildlife Manage. 38(2):343-346.

Wilbur, S., W. Carrier, J. Borneman and R. Mallette. 1972. Distribution and numbers of the California condor, 1966-1971. Amer. Birds 26(5):819-823.

Zimmerman, D. 1975. To save a bird in peril. Coward, McCann and Geoghegan, Inc., New York. 286 p.

18

Winter Feeding Programs for Cranes

George W. Archibald

Cranes are monogamous, long-lived, slow-reproducing birds with two distinct phases to their annual cycles: a breeding period and a non-breeding period. During the breeding period that lasts from 3 to 5 months, each pair rigorously defends a shallow wetland territory ranging in size from several to many hundreds of hectares. Within this territory, they construct a platform nest, lay 2 eggs, and usually rear a single chick. After the precocial chicks fledge at about 3 months of age, cranes abandon their territories, join other crane families and non-breeders and move to wintering areas where they are often encountered in large flocks in areas of food abundance.

Each of the 5 critically-endangered species of cranes--the White-naped Crane (*Grus vipio*), the Hooded Crane (*Grus monacha*), the Japanese Crane (*Grus japonensis*), the Whooping Crane (*Grus americana*), and the Siberian Crane (*Grus leucogeranus*)--has been reduced to low numbers primarily because of the destruction of winter habitats which, being at southern latitudes, coincide with areas of dense human populations. However, since cranes have a tendency to flock at areas of food abundance during the non-breeding period, artificial feeding programs have greatly benefited populations of White-naped, Hooded, and Japanese cranes wintering in Japan, and feeding stations are now being started for Japanese and White-naped cranes in South Korea. Although feeding programs are not provided for Whooping and Siberian cranes, such practices might be useful should their natural winter wetlands be polluted or developed.

FEEDING PROGRAMS FOR THE WHITE-NAPED CRANE

The White-naped Crane breeds in forest-steppe areas of north-

eastern Mongolia and narrow riparian marshes in northern China and
southeastern USSR (Cheng, 1976; Shibaev, 1975). In autumn, they migrate to the Yangtze River basin in the People's Republic of China, to
the Korean peninsula and to Kyushu, Japan (Archibald, 1973). Information is not available on numbers of cranes in China or North Korea, but
Chinese officials consider the species as uncommon. Almost 2,000
White-naped Cranes winter in the Republic of Korea where they feed on
natural food resources. A population of about 700 birds winter in
Japan where they are maintained at a feeding station since the natural
feeding habitat for the species has been developed.

In South Korea, most of the White-naped Cranes gather on the Han
River estuary between Seoul and the Demilitarized Zone (DMZ) which
separates the two Koreas at the 38th parallel (Archibald, 1975). The
entire Han River estuary, 10 kilometers south of the DMZ, has been
fenced and mined, inadvertently making about 40 square kilometers of
tidal salt marsh a sanctuary for wildlife. A sedge (*Scirpus maritimus*)
constitutes the predominant vegetation of the upper littoral zone.
Wintering White-naped Cranes on the Han River estuary feed almost exclusively on the tubers of this sedge, and presumably they formerly
fed on the same plant in other areas of the eastern Asian coast. Unfortunately, lowlands are in great demand for agricultural development
in densely populated and predominantly mountainous east Asia. The
upper tidal marshes have been diked, drained, and cultivated. With the
deterioration of coastal wetlands came the steady decline in wintering
populations of White-naped Cranes. Fortunately, the South Korean
Government has protected the Han River estuary sedge marshes as a Natural Monument in view of the importance to the cranes that are likewise a Natural Monument. In addition, small numbers of White-naped
Cranes are feeding on grains at artificial feeding stations established for Japanese Cranes near and in the DMZ.

Presumably because of habitat development, but also because of
hunting, particularly by United States occupation forces after World
War II, the Japanese population of White-naped Cranes dropped to a low
of 45 birds in 1958 (Nishida, 1969). Realizing the cranes were becoming exceedingly rare, the Japanese Government supported artificial
feeding of the remnant flock near Izumi, Kyushu, in 1958, and the
program has continued to date. Because of protection and artificial
feeding, the cranes gradually increased each winter at the feeding
station to a current population of about 700 birds (Kuroiwa, 1977)
(Table 1).

In 1972, I studied the White-naped Cranes at Izumi, and I found
the upper tidal marshes that supported small communities of sedge were
in the final stages of deterioration as a result of land-reclamation
programs. However, cranes still flew to the drying marshes after
visiting at the feeding station. When I returned to the area in 1975,
the marshes were gone; the area was in agricultural use and not frequented by the White-naped Cranes. Were it not for artificial feeding, the Japanese population of White-naped Cranes would likely have
disappeared several decades ago.

TABLE 1. NUMBERS OF CRANES AT WINTER FEEDING STATIONS IN JAPAN

Year	Japanese Cranes	White-naped Cranes	Hooded Cranes
1952	33[a]		
1953	42		
1954	52		
1955	61		
1956	61		
1957	92		
1958	125		
1959	139	45[a]	357[a]
1960	172	60	376
1961	175	71	723
1962	184	96	811
1963	147	45	1,053
1964	154	121	1,127
1965	172	129	1,442
1966	170	181	1,447
1967	200	221	1,450
1968	171	203	1,452
1969	212	233	1,562
1970	179	257	2,072
1971	147	287	2,023
1972	222	401	2,256
1973	233	449	2,793
1974	253	582	2,157
1975	194	781	2,367
1976	220	732	2,701

[a]Year in which feeding program was initiated.

FEEDING PROGRAMS FOR THE HOODED CRANE

Unlike the other species of endangered cranes that depend on
aquatic habitats in winter, the Hooded Crane is an upland bird that
feeds on a variety of animal and plant foods in areas of dense agricultural development (Archibald, 1974). Habitat destruction is not
likely the reason for this rare species' decline to about 350 birds
wintering in Japan in 1958, but rather the main cause seems to be
hunting. Unlike the larger and more beautiful cranes such as the
Japanese and White-naped Cranes, the small and plain Hooded Cranes received less protection from the ruling classes in feudal times and
were often hunted. Cranes become extremely wary if disturbed, and
perhaps hunting and wariness eventually resulted in the restriction of
Hooded Cranes to 2 wintering areas in Japan: a mountain valley near
Yashiro on Honshu; and the Izumi Valley, Kyushu (Kawamura, 1975),
where populations of about 100 and 3,000 birds, respectively, winter
from November through March.

The Hooded Cranes near Izumi roost at night with the White-naped
Cranes near the feeding station, but at dawn, most of the Hooded Cranes
fly to upland feeding sites in mixed farming areas throughout the valley, rather than remaining on the lowland rice paddies where the feeding station is located. However, several hundred Hooded Cranes, predominantly non-breeding birds, do feed with the White-naped Cranes at
the feeding stations. In Whooping Cranes, a large mortality appears
to occur among non-breeding birds between the time they leave their
parents and breed (Erickson, 1974). Perhaps similar mortality occurs
in immature Hooded Cranes; if so, the use of the feeding station by
immatures, in addition to providing protection from hunting, may have
in part been responsible for the increase of Hooded Cranes near Izumi
from 350 birds in 1958 to about 3,000 birds today (Table 1).

FEEDING PROGRAMS FOR THE JAPANESE CRANE

The Japanese Crane was once distributed as a breeding resident in
Hokkaido and perhaps northern Honshu, Japan, and throughout the northeast regions of the People's Republic of China as far west as eastern
Mongolia, and north to the wetlands bordering the Amur and Ussuri rivers in southeastern Siberia (Masatomi and Kitagawa, 1974; Cheng, 1976)
The mainland population was migratory to southern China, the Korean peninsula, and perhaps to southern Japan, while the birds that nested in
Japan presumably were those seen in winter in southern Honshu. A
half-century ago, the species was recorded in Yokohama, a region that
is now a densely populated suburban area of Tokyo (Y. Yamashina, *personal communication*).
Prior to the Meiji Restoration of 1868, the Japanese Crane was
afforded protection by the ruling classes. Only highest nobility
were allowed to hunt the species with their falcons. Technology
was not available to drain the wetlands, and the cranes were abundant.
After the Meiji Restoration, came the right for all people to hunt the
cranes, the machinery to dredge marshes to produce more food for a
growing human population, and the decline of cranes throughout the
archipelago.
The species was believed extirpated from Japan as a breeding bird
until 1924 when about 30 cranes were found in southeastern Hokkaido,
particularly on or near the Kushiro marsh (Inoue, 1976). Just as the
Trumpeter Swans (*C. cygnus buccinator*) are believed to have survived
in the Red Rock Lakes area of Montana because they both bred and winte-
ed in the region, the Japanese Cranes in remote southeastern Hokkaido
survived. Rather than migrating, the small southeastern Hokkaido
group moved locally in autumn from their breeding marshes to streams
kept open through winter via the action of hot springs. The population apparently remained stable and unstudied until 1952, a year of
unusual cold when many of the streams froze, isolating the cranes from
their aquatic animal food. Local people were concerned that the
cranes were starving, so they scattered grains on the snow near the
former feeding areas of the cranes. The cranes accepted the food, and
the tradition of feeding the Japanese Cranes in Hokkaido began. Crane
feeding has been continued to the present with a resulting increase in

the population from 30 to about 200 birds (Table 1). The cranes are
fed at 29 feeding stations funded by the Japanese Government. In winter, the cranes are readily approached and appreciated by an admiring
general public. The Japanese people take great pride in their aid to
this acutely threatened bird. The Hokkaido population has remained
stable during the past decade, presumably because almost 10 percent of
the population, particularly young birds, are killed each winter by
colliding with electric power lines near the feeding stations. Breeding habitats are also limiting, and many of the areas used as nesting
territories by the Japanese Cranes are in the throes of development
(Archibald, 1972).

The remnants of the mainland population of Japanese Cranes breed
along the Sino-Soviet border and winter on the Korean DMZ (Archibald,
1972). Unknown numbers of cranes survive in Mongolia, China, and
North Korea; however, the Chinese report that the species is very
rare in the wild. About 150 birds are believed to nest in regions
along the Ussuri River in the Soviet southeast (Shibaev, 1975), and
approximately 60 birds were counted near and in the Korean DMZ in
the winter of 1974-1975. Just as in Japan, in Korea the natural wetlands needed by the cranes have been developed. Today the remnant
population wintering in Korea feeds on invertebrates, particularly
sea worms, along tidal channels north of Inchon and along fresh water
streams associated with hot springs in the DMZ. In 1974 a feeding
station was established for the Japanese Cranes in the DMZ, and in
subsequent years 2 more feeding programs have been conducted just
south of the DMZ. The cranes readily accept the food, and their survival rate in winter is believed to have improved. The winter counts
indicate an increase from about 40 birds in 1974 to 60 in 1977, although the increase may be attributed to movements of birds wintering
in North Korea to the feeding stations.

FEEDING PROGRAMS FOR THE WHOOPING CRANES

Whooping Cranes wintering on the Aransas National Wildlife
Refuge disperse as pairs, family groups, and small non-breeding groups
over brackish-water marshes bordering the intercoastal canal that
transects the southern portion of the refuge (Allen, 1952). Each
group remains on, and sometimes defends against the intrusion of other
Whooping Cranes, an area of marsh approximately 162 ha in size. An
experiment was conducted to determine if Whooping Cranes could be attracted to a feeding station where grain was provided in abundance on
dry ground (Shields, 1969). The cranes soon discovered the grain, and
most of the population gathered at the site. Feeding was discontinued
for fear of transmission of a disease to the entire species population
which was then congregated on one small plot of ground.

The wetlands used by wintering Whooping Cranes are surrounded by
developed areas. Winter feeding stations may be one means of mitigating the problem of winter food for a potentially larger Whooping Crane
population which may eventually be limited by winter habitat. In addition, tankers filled with toxic chemicals daily pass through the
Aransas National Wildlife Refuge on the intercoastal canal. Should the

contents of one of these tankers spill and the marshes used by the
cranes become contaminated, the establishing of a feeding station in a
dry, secure area and the flushing of cranes from the marshes toward
the station might save the crane population from decimation.

FEEDING PROGRAMS FOR THE SIBERIAN CRANE

The Siberian Crane has been reduced to fewer than 360 individuals;
a remnant eastern population of about 300 birds winters along the
Yangtze River basin, and a western population of about 50 birds winters
at the Keoladeo Ghana Bird Sanctuary, India. The western population
depends almost exclusively on large expanses of shallow water supporting dense communities of several species of sedges whose tubers com-
pose the diet of the cranes (Sauey, 1976). During years of high
water, the cranes disperse in pairs, families, and other small groups
to many areas of available habitat within the sanctuary. However,
during winters when the water level is low, the cranes congregate in
flocks at the few remaining ponds in the region. Siberian Cranes
have never been recorded feeding in upland habitats in India, and
their dependence on wetlands is considered to be the major factor contributing to the demise of the species, particularly since these wetlands are easily drained and occur in areas of dense human habitation.
Should the remaining wetlands be lost to development, the Siberian
Crane may become extinct.
Occasionally, a young Siberian Crane loses its parents somewhere
along the 3,100 km migration route from Yakutia to central China
and ends up with the White-naped Cranes at the feeding station in
Kyushu, Japan (Kuroiwa, 1977). Presumably, these immature cranes feed
on grain at the feeding stations with the White-naped Cranes, for little wetland habitat remains in the region. This tendency of vagrant
Siberian Cranes to feed in upland areas with other cranes in Japan and
the flocking behavior of Siberian Cranes in India in winter in years
of low water indicate that dry-ground feeding stations might be used
by Siberian Cranes should their natural wetland habitat dry out through
either natural or man-induced causes.

DISCUSSION

Feeding programs for cranes in Japan have been responsible for
the continued existence of the White-naped Crane as a winter migrant
to Japan and have been the cause for an increase in the numbers of
both White-naped and Japanese Cranes; the feeding has perhaps benefited the Hooded Crane as well. However, a crane that is dependent on a
feeding station is, in a certain esthetic sense, not equivalent to a
crane existing independently in its natural habitat. In addition,
congregations of cranes at a permanent feeding spot pose a potential
risk of disease.
Nonetheless, cranes at a feeding station are preferable to having
no cranes at all. Were it not for the feeding station, the White-
naped Cranes undoubtedly would no longer winter in Japan, since the

natural habitat of the species has been destroyed. Two hundred Japanese Cranes at feeding stations is perhaps preferable to 30 cranes at the hot springs. Approximately 8 percent of the population dies annually through collision with electric power lines, and a population of 200 can better withstand such unnatural mortality than 30 birds. In addition, development has been so rampant in Hokkaido that perhaps the hot springs areas formerly used by cranes will be developed. If feeding was discontinued, the remaining natural habitat might not be able to support even 30 birds. In addition, the Japanese Cranes have become much tamer since artificial feeding began in 1952, making them more accommodating of human disturbance, a trait that has undoubtedly benefited their survival in Hokkaido where the human population and development are increasing rapidly.

As for the risk of disease, there has never been an outbreak of a communicable disease at either a crane feeding station in Japan or at migration staging areas which concentrate enormous numbers of cranes in other parts of the world. Feeding stations in Hokkaido and Korea are on frozen ground, and the pathogen risk is therefore reduced. White-naped and Hooded Cranes roost and are fed on rice paddies in southern Japan that rarely freeze and that contain open water. In 1972, about 10 dead Hooded Cranes were found at the roost. However, pesticide contamination and outright poisoning by farmers that resented Hooded Crane crop-depredations were responsible for the observed mortality. Cranes are hardy birds adapted to spending their migration and winter period in large concentrations together with enormous numbers of other aquatic birds. Congregations of cranes at a dry-ground feeding station where fresh, clean grain is provided daily in amounts not exceeding consumption likely poses little disease risk.

The conservation of cranes is also related to the preservation of breeding habitat, particularly since each pair requires a breeding territory that sometimes includes as many as several square kilometers of wetland. Territory size is related to food availability, visual isolation from other cranes, and population density. It might be reasoned that if feeding stations were started on or near the breeding areas, food pressure might be reduced and with it the need for large territories. Thus, the same area might then be able to support more breeding pairs. However, several pairs of Japanese Cranes are fed throughout the breeding season by farmers living beside the marshes, and these cranes continue to defend territories equal in size to territories defended by pairs that are not fed in spring and summer. Apparently, food scarcity may increase the territory needs of a pair, but food abundance at artificial feeding stations does not result in the concession of territory space to other pairs. Artificial feeding of cranes during the breeding season is of nebulous value since growing crane chicks require aquatic food sources, particularly animal food to support their rapid growth.

Although purists may be appalled at seeing a flock of cranes fed at an artificial feeding station, the general public in Japan is delighted by the opportunity to watch the cranes from their automobiles or from towers, shops, and even hotels built beside the fields on which the cranes are fed. Accommodations for tourists at the feeding stations and the tameness of the cranes combine to please the public, and each winter thousands of people visit the stations.   The ultimate survival of cranes and other wildlife depends on human values.   The feeding stations have created a positive incentive among the Japanese people to help cranes and wildlife in general.   As human populations continue to increase in areas supporting winter populations of cranes, feeding stations may provide the only practical means of maintaining the cranes.

LITERATURE CITED

Allen, R.P. 1952. The Whooping Crane. National Audubon Society Res. Report No. 3. 246 p.

Archibald, G.W. 1972. Tancho conservation report. Yacho Bull. 312: 450-464.

Archibald, G.W. 1973. Cranes over Kyushu. Animal Kingdom 76(6):17-21.

Archibald, G.W. 1974. Misty morning in crane country. Animal Kingdom 77(2):19-24.

Archibald, G.W. 1975. Cranes over Panmunjom. Int. Wildlife 5(5):18-21.

Cheng, T. 1976. Birds of China. Academia Sinica, Peking. 1218p.

Erickson, R. 1974. Report on Whooping Crane research and management. Int. Council for Bird Preserv. 16 World Conference, Canberra, 7 p.

Inoue, M. 1974. History of Tancho. Oji Institute for Forest Tree Improvement, Kuriyama, Hokkaido, Japan.

Kawamura, N. 1975. Studies of the Hooded Crane at Yashiro, Yama-gouchi: Its roosting behavior. Misc. Reports of the Yamashina Institute for Ornithology 7(5):550-561.

Kuroiwa, S. 1977. The Gyudebook to Cranes in Izumi, Areseki Feeding Station, Areseki, Kagoshima-ken, Japan. 15 p.

Masatomi, H. and T. Kitagawa. 1974. Bionomics and sociology of Tancho or the Japanese crane, *Grus japonensis*, I. Distribution, habitat and outline of annual cycle. J. Fac. Sci. Hokkaido, Univ. Ser. Zool. 19(3):777-802.

Nishida, S. 1969. Social construction of the cranes in Izumi District. Rep. Moju. Comm. High School, Kagoshima-ken, Japan. 6 p.

Sauey, R. 1976. The behavior of Siberian Cranes wintering in India. p. 326-342. *In* J.C. Lewis (ed.) Proc. Int. Crane Workshop. Oklahoma State Univ. Publ. & Printing, Stillwater, Oklahoma.

Shibaev, Y.V. 1975. On migrations of cranes in South Primorye. p. 254-262. *In* Proceedings of Ornithological Studies in the Soviet Far East, Institute of Biology and Pedology, Far East Science Centre, Academy of Sciences of the USSR, Vladivostok.

Shields, R.H. and E.L. Benham. 1969. Farm crops as food supplement for Whooping Cranes. J. Wildlife Manage. 33(4):811-817.

19

Feeding White-tailed Sea Eagles in Sweden

Björn Helander

Sweden's White-tailed Sea Eagles (*Haliaeetus albicilla*) breed in two separate areas: along the Baltic coast from the county of Smaland north to the county of Vasterbotten, and in parts of Lapland. Reports of poor reproductive success from parts of the Baltic breeding range caused the Swedish Society for the Conservation of Nature (SNF) to start an inventory of the present distribution of breeding eagles and their nest success in 1964. The results were alarming, and the surveys were continued, leading in 1971 to the start of Project Sea Eagle. The project consists of the following main parts:

1. yearly surveys to determine nest success,
2. studies on choice of prey,
3. analyses of environmental pollutants in eagles and prey species,
4. protection of breeding-areas,
5. feeding with uncontaminated meat during autumn and winter.

The project is sponsored by the World Wildlife Fund (WWF), by the National Environment Protection Board (SNV), by private foundations, and by private donations. Expenditures during 1977 are estimated at $40,000, not including the cost of biocide analyses (covered by the Swedish Museum of Natural History) and protection of habitat (mainly covered by the SNV).

POPULATION ESTIMATES AND NEST SUCCESS

The Swedish Baltic population is estimated at about 60 breeding pairs. An average of about 40 pairs have been checked annually for nest success (i.e., percent of all occupied nests that produce young). Breeding success has been poor, averaging 22 percent nest success and 0.25 young produced per occupied nest during 1970-75. A slow decrease has taken place both in breeding success and in the number of pairs

breeding since 1964 (Helander, 1975).
    The Lapland population is estimated to be at least 20 breeding
pairs. Data on nest success are sparse and scattered over the years,
but the breeding results seem to be considerably better than in the
Baltic population. During 1964-75, 67 percent of 50 attempts were
successful (Helander, 1975), and in 1976 the nest success of 10 pairs
was 60 percent.

THREATS TO THE SWEDISH SEA EAGLES

    The following are the main factors behind the decline of Sweden's
sea eagle populations:
    1. Contamination with environmental pollutants affects sea eagles
        the same way it effects other predatory birds. Baltic sea
        eagles and their eggs contain high levels of pollutants,
        mainly PCB's, DDE and mercury, while the few analyses from
        Lapland eagles show much lower values (Jensen et al., 1969;
        Olsson et al., 1972; Helander, 1975).
    2. Loss of habitat is a serious problem along the Baltic coast
        and an increasing problem in Lapland. Timber cutting,
        building of summer homes, industrial developments, roads
        and power lines are the most important factors causing
        reductions of suitable habitat.
    3. Human disturbances resulting in nest failure seem to be an
        increasing problem largely attributed to the increased use
        of snow-scooters in Lapland. Disturbances have been a
        problem for many years on the Baltic coast, although its
        effects are often difficult to evaluate since even undisturbed
        pairs fail to hatch their eggs--the heavy contamination with
        pollutants is most probably a much more serious problem.
    4. Illegal persecution is still a problem in Lapland; along
        the Baltic the attitude towards the eagles is generally more
        positive, but occasional shootings still occur.

MEASURES REQUIRED FOR SURVIVAL

    It is unlikely that the Baltic sea eagle population will be
able to maintain itself at its present reproductive rate. The outlook
for the Lapland population is perhaps better, but more data are needed.
Sprunt et al. (1973) estimated the reproductive rate required to maintain stable populations of the Bald Eagle (*Haliaeetus leucocephalus*)
to be at least 50 percent nest success and at least 0.7 young produced
per occupied nest. The Baltic sea eagle's reproductive rate of about
0.3 young per pair would require that 67 percent of the young reach
maturity and have an average life span of at least 15 years (Helander,
1975).
.   The long-term survival of the sea eagle in Sweden will depend on
the continuing availability of suitable breeding areas and natural,
healthy food. The most important conservation measures presently
needed are minimizing the use of and pollution with toxic chemicals

on an international basis, and protecting enough areas of suitable breeding habitat from exploitation.

Legal protection of breeding areas as nature reserves, general restrictions of forestry in eagle areas, and when necessary, protection from disturbances by establishing bird sanctuaries are the protective measures used. The SNF is continually in contact with the Provincial Governor's Offices and the SNV concerning land-use planning. In Lapland, guarding of a few nests was undertaken during 1976 and 1977 to prevent illegal persecution.

The pollution of the Baltic Sea presents serious problems. The narrow and shallow connections with the Atlantic Ocean limit water exchange. The Baltic Sea is rather cold, with a resulting low biological activity. These factors tend to promote the accumulation of persistent pollutants in the ecosystem. Even if future pollution of the Baltic Sea can be limited, the effects of the pollutants already in the ecosystem will probably persist for many years. Sea eagles feed mainly on fish and water birds which are often highly contaminated with pollutants (Olsson et al., 1972; Helander, 1975; Koivasaari et al., 1976).

In addition to protection of habitat and control of pollutants, it seems necessary to increase the recruitment of new individuals into the Baltic sea eagle population. Alternatives for achieving this are: increasing reproduction, decreasing mortality, and artificially transplanting fertile eggs or young. Two young Norwegian sea eagles were released in Sweden in 1967 (Berglund, 1967), and in 1976 one West German eaglet was successfully transplanted to a nest already containing one nestling (Helander, 1976a). The Swedish authorities have not yet decided whether to take up captive breeding of sea eagles. The only long-term possibility for a sufficient improvement in nest success seems to lie in a drastic reduction of chemical pollution. Presently, the only way to reduce the eagles' intake of pollutants is to feed them uncontaminated meat as a substitute for their contaminated natural prey. Mortality could be decreased through public education to minimize illegal persecution, and by artificial feeding to increase survival during the winter.

WINTER HABITS AND NATURAL MORTALITY

Adult sea eagle pairs along the Baltic Sea normally stay in their breeding territories throughout the year. The juvenile birds normally leave their natal areas during October and fly southwards (*see* Figure 1). There is evidence that sea eagles from other areas migrate to the southern half of Sweden during autumn and winter. Banded Finnish juveniles have been recovered in south-east Sweden (*see* Figure 1), and there are observations of eagles coming from the Aaland Archipelago to Sweden. Norwegian sea eagles seem to spend the winter mainly along the Norwegian coast (Willgohs, *personal communication*). There is one recovery in western Sweden of a banded Norwegian specimen (Figure 1).

The winter habits of sea eagles in Swedish Lapland are not precisely known. Observations during the winter indicate that at least some adults stay the whole year, while young birds leave in autumn.

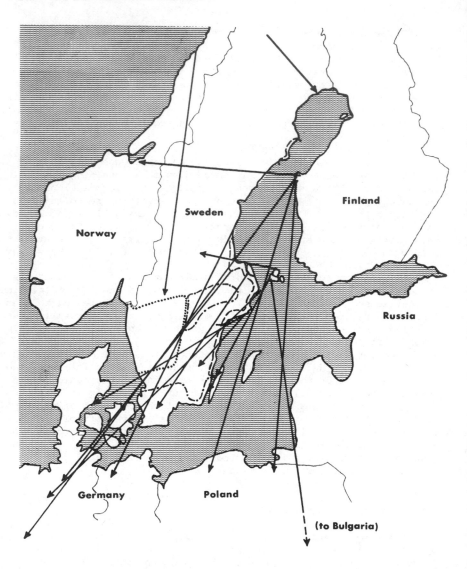

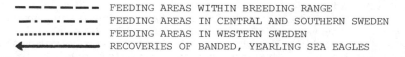

------------ FEEDING AREAS WITHIN BREEDING RANGE
—·—·—·—·— FEEDING AREAS IN CENTRAL AND SOUTHERN SWEDEN
················ FEEDING AREAS IN WESTERN SWEDEN
◄———————— RECOVERIES OF BANDED, YEARLING SEA EAGLES

FIGURE 1.   Recoveries of White-tailed Sea Eagles banded as nestlings
    and recovered in their first year and the distribution of eagle
    feeding areas.

There are few observations of migrating sea eagles in northern Sweden, and some may go unnoticed over the fjelds to the Norwegian coast. Figure 1 shows one recovery of a banded Lapland juvenile that had moved to the southeast. The need for more data on migration from different areas led the SNF to initiate a color-banding program in North Europe in 1976.

Of 14 dead sea eagles, all banded as nestlings between 1946-1965, 11 (79 percent) were immature (Helander, 1975). Seven of the birds were yearlings, all of them found during the months October through April. Of 29 unbanded birds (10 adults, 5 subadults between 1-4 years old, and 14 juveniles) found dead during 1950 through 1960, all except 2 adults had died during October-April. These figures indicate a high mortality in juveniles, and a considerably higher mortality in all age classes during the winter months compared to the summer.

THE FEEDING PROGRAM FOR SEA EAGLES

Especially during the winter, sea eagles as well as Golden Eagles (*Aquila chrysaetos*) readily feed on carrion. Feeding carcasses to eagles has been used by sportsmen to keep eagles from preying on game species and was also used during the 19th century in order to shoot eagles. The SNF decided to start a feeding program as part of the sea eagle project; this was done with two main purposes in mind: to reduce mortality during the winter; and to minimize the influence of toxic pollutants on adults, thus helping to increase nest-success.

The feeding takes place from October or November through March. Continued feeding during the spring has been tried, but it was unsuccessful. When the ice breaks in the spring, the eagles seem to prefer live prey to the carrion. Feeding with live prey (i.e., by constructing fish pools within the breeding territories) has not been tried.

There are two reasons for starting the feeding early during the autumn: to attract migrating young birds, thus making them stay within the country; and to feed the adults for as much of the year as possible with uncontaminated meat. Both goals have been achieved; adults often start to feed as soon as food is brought out in their territories in October, and yearlings may even stay in their natal area the whole winter if feeding is started before they would normally leave. Limiting migratory movements and restricting the eagles to selected areas with continuous food supplies should enhance their survival.

The feeding program, in general, is organized by the SNF. Local ornithological societies are operating several of the feeding stations, while others are run by single ornithologists. In western Sweden, local ornithologists in 1972 formed a special working group that now organizes about 25 feeding stations there (Hagborg and Ahlgren, 1976).

Most of the work is done on a voluntary basis, but feeding within some nature reserves and bird sanctuaries is performed or supported by the County Forestry Boards. The number of feeding places and amounts of food are given in Table 1, and their approximate distribution is shown in Figure 1.

The total cost for the feeding project is hard to estimate. Much of the work is voluntary; some of the travel costs are covered by the

TABLE 1.   NUMBER OF SEA EAGLE FEEDING STATIONS AND
TONS OF FOOD PROVIDED, 1971-1977

| | Feeding Stations and Tons of Food: | | | |
Year	Within the Breeding Range[a]	In Central and Southern Sweden[a]	In Western Sweden[a]	Total[a]
1971-72	30 (6.2)	28 (10.0)	3 (2.8)	62 (19.0)
1972-73	28 (6.6)	18 (8.6)	9 (9.6)	55 (24.8)
1973-74	21 (10.5)	20 (11.5)	13 (8.3)	54 (30.3)
1974-75	28 (18.2)	21 (12.3)	15 (12.0)	64 (42.5)
1975-76	43 (27.7)	32 (25.4)	20 (20.5)	95 (73.6)
1976-77	42 (29.0)	28 (24.3)	26 (28.4)	96 (81.7)

[a]Number of feeding stations (tons of food provided).

volunteers themselves; and a large part of the food is obtained free
of charge. Expenditures for administration, travel, equipment and
food during 1976-1977 was approximately $10,000.

FOOD AND FEEDING STATIONS

The food used is of two categories: slaughterhouse offal consisting mainly of embryos, throats, lungs and intestines from domestic
cattle and pigs; and whole animals, mainly dead domestic pigs and
calves or car-killed Roe Deer (*Capreolus capreolus*) and Moose (*Alces
alces*). The slaughterhouse offal is obtained from slaughterhouses
usually against payment, and whole animals are obtained, usually free
of charge, from slaughterhouses, farmers, or local hunting organizations.

The domestic animals used for food are mainly killed by stress
(e.g., fighting or heart-failures) or by accident (e.g. transport
kills). Diseased carcasses are not used. Animals treated with anti-
biotics are avoided or used only after a stipulated period. The food
chosen has very low concentrations of pollutants. The eagles' normal
prey has 10 to several 100 times more DDT and PCBs than was found in
samples of pig meat (Helander, 1975).

The feeding stations are located in areas with little human activity during autumn-winter. The carrion is placed so that the eagle
have a clear view all around. Examples of suitable places used in
Sweden are frozen lakes or bays of the sea, open fields, bogs, frozen
marshes, and open shorelands. Access to solitary trees, forests or
rocks suitable for roosting in the vicinity are favorable.

Whole carcasses are generally more suitable for feeding than
pieces of slaughterhouse offal which can easily be picked up and
carried away by crows and ravens. About 100 kg of slaughterhouse offal can be consumed in a day or two, whereas a 100 kg pig carcass may
last a week in the same place. Whole carcasses are fixed to the

ground to prevent foxes from dragging them away when partly eaten. In a few cases, platforms have been built to prevent foxes from reaching the carcasses. The amount of food consumed per day, of course, depends on the number of animals being fed and varies a great deal from one place to another. Food should be available continuously to prevent dispersal of the birds.

The sanitary aspects of feeding eagles have been covered in guidelines issued by the SNV. They state that the feeding stations must be cleaned of food remnants after each season; regulations on choice of food and suitable feeding places are also included.

EFFECTS OF THE FEEDING PROGRAM

Feeders are instructed to regularly check the numbers and ages of the eagles at their feeding stations. Reports are sent to the SNF after the end of each season. Data from the most important feeding stations within the breeding range and in central and southern Sweden have been used to study the average number of immature eagles per station from 1971-1972 through 1976-1977. Most of the stations in the central and southern areas are located in southern Sweden. To exclude double counts of birds, a minimum number is taken from one defined period during the season. Through the exclusion of reports from stations visited occasionally by eagles or reports where data on ages are missing, the counts are based on about 40 percent of the total number of feeding stations in the 2 areas each year. The number of stations where counts have been made remains approximately the same each year. For each season, the number of young birds per station is tabulated (Table 2).

TABLE 2.　NUMBERS OF IMMATURE SEA EAGLES AT FEEDING STATIONS
WHERE COUNTS HAVE BEEN MADE, 1971-1977

Locations	1971 -72	1972 -73	1973 -74	1974 -75	1975 -76	1976 -77
Within Breeding Range:						
No. of Stations	11	12	7	13	16	14
No. of Immatures	2	4	1	5	10	12
Immatures/Station	0.18	0.33	0.14	0.39	0.63	0.86
Cent. and S. Sweden:						
No. of Stations	10	8	10	9	11	12
No. of Immatures	14	7	11	21	29	31
Immatures/Station	1.40	0.88	1.10	2.33	2.65	2.58
Total:						
No. of Stations	21	20	17	22	27	26
No. of Immatures	16	11	12	26	39	43
Immatures/Station	0.76	0.55	0.71	1.18	1.44	1.65

The figures in Table 2 indicate an increase in the mean number of young birds per feeding station from the 1972-1973 season to 1976-1977. The number of feeding stations is approximately constant with a few more during the latter half of the period. An increased number of feeding stations could theoretically lead to "competition" between the stations for eagles, which would lead to a decrease in the number of birds per station even if the total number of birds visiting stations remained constant. Since the number of birds per station does, in fact, increase, the data in Table 2 lead to the conclusion that the number of young eagles has increased at these feeding stations in Sweden. This could indicate either an increase in the total number of young in Sweden during winter or an increased use of the stations over the years by a constant number of resident young. Birds that have found feeding stations one year could possibly be more inclined to return there during following winters. It can not presently be established whether this is contributing to the observed increase in birds at the stations. Even if it does contribute, it is unlikely to be responsible for the entire increase. The general opinion among ornithologists in Sweden seems to be that the number of young eagles during winter has increased.

An increased number of sea eagles during winter in Sweden could be due to either improved nest success, increased survival of young, or an increase in the number of birds that stay through the winter instead of leaving the country. One of the purposes of the feeding program is to attract more young birds and make them stay. Because the number of feeding stations where counts have been made are approximately the same each season, there is no reason why a progressively larger portion of the immatures should stay at these particular feeding stations, unless there has been an increase in survival or nest success.

The breeding success of Swedish sea eagles is checked by the SNF with voluntary help from selected ornithologists. The criteria of nest success follow the standards given by Postupalsky (1974). The nest success and productivity for an average of 39 pairs per year during 1964-1977 are given in Figure 2.

The production of young eagles in Sweden and Finland has been fairly stable during the 1970's (Helander, 1976b; Joutsamo and Kiovusaari, 1976). Figure 2 shows the nest success and productivity of the Swedish Baltic population. Data from northeastern Europe are scarce: productivity in Estonia is low and seems to have decreased during the past decade (Randla, *personal communication*), and the number of eagles migrating through Finland seems to have decreased considerably (Bergman, *personal communication*). Unless there has been an unnoticed, progressive increase in production in areas that influence the number of eagles in Sweden during winter, the increased number of young at the Swedish feeding stations indicates increased survival during the 1970's. This presupposes that the increase is caused by immatures older than one year. All subadult age classes are combined in one category in the present data, and reliable statistics are lacking on the distribution of yearlings versus older immatures. The color-banding program will hopefully give information on this point in subsequent years. Since White-tailed Sea Eagles have adult plumage in

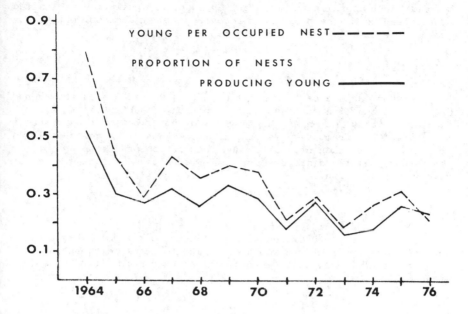

FIGURE 2.   Nest success and productivity of the White-tailed Sea
Eagle population along the Swedish Baltic coast, 1964-1976.

their fifth year, increased survival with a constant rate of reproduction would lead to an increase in the number of immatures during
4 years, after which the number should stabilize.   The data in Table
2 suggest that this may be the case, although observations will have
to continue for more seasons before conclusions can be drawn.
        Nest success for the Baltic population as a whole has not in-
creased during the 1970's (Figure 2).   This could mean either that
the feeding has no improving effect on nest success or that it has
halted a further decline that would otherwise have taken place.   Nest
success of 12 pairs fed continually during the winters of 1968-1974
tends to be better during 1969-1977 than in the remaining pairs in the
population, in which nest success has decreased.   However, there are
only a few instances where pairs which were fed actually increased
their nest success.   One pair, unsuccessful during 1965-1968, has had
4 successful breedings out of 6 attempts since feeding was started in
their territory in late 1968.   Another pair, unsuccessful for several
years, has raised young for the last 3 years since feeding was introduced in late 1974.   In a few other pairs, the improvement in nest
success is less evident.   Sea eagles are large and rather inactive
raptors with a comparatively slow metabolism.   Artificial feeding during half of the year is apparently not sufficient to reduce contamination with pollutants enough for a general improvement in nest success.
However, feeding may help to maintain productivity in some pairs,

possibly less contaminated than the average. If pollution is limited, winter feeding may help hasten a recovery in nest success, but at present the effects seem to be limited.

CONCLUSIONS

The Swedish sea eagle population of the Baltic Sea is threatened by poor reproductive success and destruction of habitat. Artificial feeding probably increases the survival of young but must nevertheless be regarded as a temporary measure that does not solve the underlying problems. Protection of habitat and restriction of the spread of persistent pollutants are essential if Sweden's sea eagles are to survive in the long run.

ACKNOWLEDGMENTS

The SNF wishes to express its gratitude to all voluntary bodies supporting the project. I would also like to thank Torbjörn Fagerström for useful viewpoints in evaluating the results of the feeding program.

LITERATURE CITED

Berglund, B. 1967. Havsörnen tillbaka vid Vänern. Sveriges Natur
    No. 1, (in Swedish).
Hagborg, K. and C.G. Ahlgren. 1976. ÖRN-72 verksamhet i västsverige
    1972-1975 (in Swedish).
Helander, B. 1975. Havsörnen i Sverige (English summary: The White-
    tailed Sea Eagle in Sweden). Report on the sea eagle project, is-
    sued by the SNF.
Helander, B. 1976a. Sea eagle adoption in Sweden. SNF Newsletter
    16 August.
Helander, B. 1976b. The White-tailed Sea Eagle-Swedish Report. Pro-
    ceedings from the World Wildlife Fund Sea Eagle Symposium, Nor-
    way, Sept. 1976.
Jensen, S., A.G. Johnels, M. Olsson and G. Otterlind. 1969. DDT and
    PCB in marine animals from Swedish waters. Nature 224(5216):247-
    250.
Joutsamo, E. and J. Koivusaari. 1976. White-tailed Eagle in Finland
    1970-1976. Proceedings from the World Wildlife Fund Sea Eagle
    Symposium, Norway, Sept. 1976.
Koivasaari, J., I. Nuuja, R. Palokangas, and M.-L. Hattula. 1976.
    Chlorinated hydrocarbons and total mercury in the prey of the
    White-tailed Eagle (Haliaeetus albicilla L.) in the Quarken
    Straits of the Gulf of Bothnia, Finland. Bull. of Environmental
    Contamination and Toxicol. 15(2):235-241.
Olsson, M., S. Jensen, A.G. Johnels and T. Westermark. 1972. Miljög-
    iftshalter i havsörn och sjöfågel. Rapport till Statens natur-
    vårdsverk. 25 February (in Swedish).

Postupalsky, S. 1974. Raptor reproductive success: some problems with methods, criteria and terminology, p. 21-31. *In* Hamerstrom, F.N., B.E. Harrell and R.R. Olendorff (eds.). Management of Raptors. Raptor Research Report No. 2.

Sprunt, A. IV., W.B. Robertson, Jr., S. Postupalsky, R.J. Hensel, C.E. Knoder and F.J. Ligas. 1973. Comparative productivity of six bald eagle populations. Transactions of the North American Wildlife and Natural Resources Conference. 38:96-106.

20

The Feeding of Japanese Crested Ibises

Yoshimaro Yamashina

Japanese Crested Ibises (*Nipponia nippon*) have long been protected in Japan, and since the species was designated as a Special Natural Monument in 1952, they were placed under special protection. After the 1950's, in Japan, large quantities of organic mercury compounds were applied to paddy fields in order to protect the rice from rice blast disease. Also, BHC and other related agricultural chemicals were used as pesticides. Consequently, many Japanese Crested Ibises died from these toxic chemicals, and even those that escaped direct mortality from the poisons lost their ability to breed. An analysis of the dead bodies of Japanese Crested Ibises found in the field at this time revealed high concentrations of mercury not only from the viscera and fat but even from bones. By the 1960's, Japanese Crested Ibises were totally exterminated in Ishikawa prefecture.

Japanese Crested Ibises on Sado Island living on the lowlands were also exterminated, but those that lived in the forests and fed in the streams and ponds of the highlands were less severely influenced by the pesticide and managed to survive the disaster. Yet, in 1960, only 4 birds were counted on the island. Since nearly 100 birds used to live on Sado Island in 1930's, the population had obviously suffered a drastic decline. Even though a few Japanese Crested Ibises were able to survive the latter half of the 1960's breeding in the highland forests of Sado Island, the population remained in danger for in autumn the young birds often fed in paddy fields in the lowlands.

Generally, the foods of the wild Japanese Crested Ibis are as follows:
1. Freshwater fish:
      Oriental weatherfish (*Misgurnus anguillicaudatus*)
      Crucian carp (*Carassius carassius*)
      Catfish (*Parasilurus asotus*)

2. Amphibians:
        Frogs: exclusive of Green frog (*Rhacophorus viridis*)
        Newt (*Cynops pyrrhogaster*)
        Salamander (*Hynobius nigrescens*)
3. Crustaceans:
        River crab (*Potamon dehaani*)
        Crawfish (*Cambaroides japonicus*)
4. Insects:
        Water-scavenger beetles (*Hydrophilus acuminatus*)
        Japanese diving beetles (*Cybister japonicus*)
        Crickets: exclusive of Grasshoppers (*Acridioidea* sp).
        Larva of beetles
5. Freshwater Molluscs:
        Mud snail (*Viviparus japonica*)
        Freshwater mussel (*Cristaria plicata*)
    Most of the creatures stated above can be found in the paddy fiel
of flatlands and near by brooks, ponds and swamps, except for the rive
crabs and salamanders that mainly inhabit ponds, swamps, and torrents
of highlands. In captivity, healthy Japanese Crested Ibises eat a
total of 300-500 g of food per day.

SUPPLEMENTAL FEEDING OF IBISES ON SADO ISLAND

    The Japanese Government has purchased 1000 hectares of ibis habi-
tat on Sado Island and has established the *Nipponia nippon* Protection
Centre in the heart of it. Through the support of the Japanese Gover
ment and the World Wildlife Fund, shallow ponds were constructed with
the protected area in order to establish Oriental Weatherfish and oth
aquatic animals that are the primary food of wild ibises. Facilities
for heating the ponds were also provided in order to keep the ponds
from freezing up in winter. Decoy birds of the same shape, color and
size as *Nipponia nippon* were made with styrofoam and set up around
the ponds to attract wild ibises. In a short time, several wild
ibises began to feed around the facilities. Now, they can be observe
at close range from the buildings at the Protection Centre; this made
it much easier to conduct research on the habits of *Nipponia nippon*.
    However, no matter how much food is scattered in the ponds, the
ibises only come to feed there from December to April; they continue
to feed in natural ponds and disused paddy fields in the mountain are
near their breeding ground during other seasons. From April to June,
they frequent feeding grounds near their nests. From July to September, they disperse throughout the habitat, and in this season, the
young birds go down to the lowlands to feed in the paddy fields. In
October and November, those birds that do not come to the Protection
Centre continue to feed in the disused paddy fields in the mountains.
    Because of the tendency of the ibises to disperse to widely-
separated areas, feeding places were also constructed in abandoned
paddy fields at several other locations. If abandoned paddy fields
are left unattended, they soon fill in with weeds and become unsuitable as *Nipponia* foraging habitat. Although they may not be used for
growing rice, it is necessary to continue cultivating the abandoned

paddies in order to keep them in a condition acceptable to foraging ibises.

Perhaps as the result of management, 2 chicks were produced in 1972, another 2 in 1973, and another 2 in 1974. All fledged successfully into the wild. The total number of the birds increased to 15 in the autumn of 1974.

However, since 1975, although ibises nested every year, they have not fledged young, and according to the 1975 census, the Sado Island population had decreased to only 8.

All the persons concerned for the welfare of the ibises were observing the remaining wild Japanese Crested Ibises with great expectations. On 4 May 1977, one pair was observed incubating eggs in the forest of Shigarasawa. Then on 14 May, another pair was found to be incubating eggs in the Koyabasawa forest. Observers kept a close watch over these nests and waited for the eggs to hatch. However, on 31 May, the eggs of the first pair were found broken under the nest, and on 1 June, the eggs of the second pair were also found smashed under the nest. Neither pair of ibises attempted to renest.

Close examination of the egg shells found under the nests showed that the thickness of the egg shells was normal (0.189-0.315 mm). Some of the egg contents showed a positive occult blood reaction, indicating that the eggs had been fertile. Also, small holes were found on some of the larger fragments of the egg shells that seemed to have been made by the beak of some small bird. From all these facts, the following explanation seems likely. The eggs were initially damaged by jays (*Garrulus glandarius*) that breed close to the ibis nests. As a result, embryos stopped developing at an early stage, and the parents abandoned the eggs. If the ibises should lay eggs again in 1978, there is a plan to remove the eggs, artificially incubate them, and hatch them in captivity. The young could then be returned to their parents.

DIET OF CAPTIVE JAPANESE CRESTED IBISES

In 1965, young ibises were caught on Sado Island and taken into captivity in hopes that they would breed. The main purpose of this early captive breeding attempt was to prevent mercury poisoning of the young ibises that had come down to the lowland during the autumn. Although the Oriental Weatherfish was used as the main food for the ibises because these fish can be obtained easily, it was later found that these fish were highly contaminated with mercury. Therefore, it was decided that sea fish--Sandfish (*Arctoscopus japonicus*) and Wall-eye Pollock (*Theragra chalcogramma*)--would be used for they were readily available but were not contaminated with mercury. The captive ibises were very fond of these sea fishes, when the fish were chopped in small pieces. Nevertheless, one captive Japanese Crested Ibis died suddenly. The autopsy indicated that a nematode (*Anisakis*) that depends upon sea fish as its intermediate host, had torn the veins of the wall of the ibises stomach, causing excessive hemorrhage and then death. From 1966 to 1968, 5 captive Japanese Crested Ibises died of the same cause. Clearly, sea fish was not a suitable food for the birds.   Therefore, I began using the ibis diet successfully developed at the Basel Zoo, Switzerland.

Uneo Zoo in Tokyo immediately asked a supplier in Japan to prepare the Basel Zoo ibis diet.   But, because mutton was then very difficult to obtain in Japan, they substituted chopped Saurel (*Trachurus japonicus*) for the mutton.   The resulting food was given to other species of ibis as an experiment, and the results seemed satisfactory. On Sado Island, the diet of the captive ibises at the Protection Centre was changed from the fish diet to the Basel Zoo formulas, only whalemeat was substituted for mutton.   At first, the ibises did not seem to like this food, but eventually they began to eat it.   Then suddenly lack of appetite and emesis inflicted the birds, and 3 of them died.   On autopsy, it was found that there was a hemorrhage in the liver and intestines.

In order to determine whether this problem was caused by the new diet, experiments were conducted at Ueno, Tama, and Inokashira Zoos. The Basel ibis diet mixed with mutton or horsemeat was given to 20 ibises of the species *Threskiornis melanocephala* and *Eudocimus ruber*, and the Basel ibis diet mixed with whalemeat was given to another group of 8 ibises.   The birds fed with the diet containing mutton or horsemeat remained healthy, but those that were fed with the whalemeat soon became weak.   Whalemeat is clearly not an acceptable addition to the ibises' diet.

From these experiments, it was concluded that the following foods were the most satisfactory for captive *Nipponia*.

1.   For staple food, mutton (which is now being imported from New Zealand) mixed with other items in the Basel Zoo's ibis diet.
2.   For subsidiary food, artificially-bred Oriental Weatherfish, unpolluted with pesticide, are given.   Also, young mice, mealworms, boiled eggs, and crickets are given from time to time.

Thus, at the end of the experiment, a single remaining *Nipponia nippon* in the flight cage of the Protection Centre in Sado has lived in fine condition since 1971 while being fed the above-mentioned assorted foods.

ACKNOWLEDGMENTS

First, I would like to express my gratitude to the Education Committee of Niigata prefecture for offering me the detailed data on *Nipponia nippon* on Sado Island.   Also, my sincere thanks to the members of the Subcommittee for the Protection of *Nipponia nippon* of Ueno, Tama, and Inokashira Zoos, who have collaborated in the basic experiments on the breeding of *Nipponia nippon*.

I am further indebted to Miss Yoriko Iwase, Yamashina Institute for Ornithology, and Dr. George W. Archibald, International Crane Foundation, for translating this manuscript.

Part V
Manipulating Aspects of Nesting Biology

21

Manipulating the Nesting Biology of Endangered Birds

A Review

Tom J. Cade

In various of his writings, Niko Tinbergen has confessed to a penchant for dabbling experimentally with animals in nature. Not content merely to sit in an observation hide and watch his gulls, he has often been compelled to intervene in their lives by testing them in various systematic ways to learn how they react. Experimenting in nature it is called. Among European field naturalists, the habit can be traced at least as far back as the French amateur entomologist, Jean Henri Fabre, who in a series of ingenious tests in the 19th century demonstrated the unreasoning automaticity of insect behavior. A survey of the literature of the last 30 years shows that quite a few field workers with an ethological bent have shared Tingergen's enthusiasm for playing "tricks" on animals in the out-of-doors. While most of these studies have been carried out as exercises in "pure science," the wildlife manager may, nevertheless, discover some useful manipulations that can serve their more practical concerns for increasing the numbers of dwindling wildlife populations.

Manipulative techniques are very much at the fore of our practices in managing endangered species these days, and while this session of papers deals with nesting biology, I suggest that we ought always to look more broadly--as indeed we are doing at this conference--and consider the possible use of manipulative interventions in any phase of the life cycle of an animal, or plant, if there is a reasonable likelihood that such tampering will promote the survival of the species in question.

Briefly, what are some of the possibilities that involve manipulation of nesting biology?

I have not been able to discover who did the first cross-fostering experiment with birds. It was probably Aristotle or Frederick II of Hohenstaufen or somebody like one of them--both were great manipulators. But certainly the German ethologists were doing some exploratory

experiments along these lines in the 1930's. One particularly instructive experiment involved placing the eggs of the tree-nesting Mew Gull
(*Larus canus*) into the nests of the Black-headed Gull (*Larus ridibundus*)
which breeds colonially in marshes. On reaching sexual maturity, some
of the cross-fostered Mew Gulls returned to their hatching and rearing
location and formed a colony of half a dozen pairs within the Black-
headed Gull colony in the reeds (Schuz, 1940). While some details of
this experiment are unclear, the results are interesting from two
standpoints. First, the Mew Gulls adopted an entirely new kind of
habitat for nesting, and secondly they evidently recognized each other
as mates and were not seriously imprinted on their foster parent specie
although this latter conclusion was not carefully verified.

The more recent experiment conducted by Harris (1970) on Herring
Gulls (*Larus argentatus*) and Lesser Black-backed Gulls (*Larus fuscus*)
nesting on islands off the coast of Wales cautions us that generalizations about the effects of cross-fostering on subsequent habits are
not to be made easily. He planted large numbers of Herring Gull eggs
into pure colonies of Lesser Black-backs and vice versa, resulting over
a 3-year period in a sample of 496 cross-fostered Herring Gulls and
389 Lesser Black-backed Gulls. The Herring Gull is non-migratory in
Britain, whereas the Lesser Black-backed Gull migrates to the coasts
of Spain, Portugal, and Morocco for the winter. The cross-fostered
Herring Gulls adopted the migratory habits of their parents, but the
cross-fostered Lesser Black-backed Gulls did not become sedentary; the
also migrated normally. It would have been impossible to predict this
result ahead of time, I believe. Harris's work shows us what some of
the unanticipated consequences of cross-fostering can be. From the
standpoint of our concerns, a more serious consequence of his experiment is that many of the cross-fostered gulls that survived to breeding age mated with members of their foster species—almost all of the
females did so, about half of the males—and the result has been extensive hybridization in the gull colonies.

Cross-fostering is a technique that has great potential for extend
ing the range of an endangered species into new areas or for re-estab-
lishing populations in vacant areas of a former range, where a suitable
foster species exists. It may also be a way of changing the habits and
habitat preferences of some species—of creating new lifestyles that
are more adaptive to the conditions of our present world than the old
ways of living are. I view the current attempt to establish a population of Whooping Cranes (*Grus americana*) on new range by cross-fosteri
as the forerunner of many such manipulations that will be necessary
for species in the future. But, depending on the species, cross-
fostering can also result in maladaptive behaviors, and sexual imprinting on the foster parent species is certainly one of the most serious
of these. Unfortunately, since many of our endangered bird species
are slow to reach sexual maturity, it often takes several years to
know the outcome of cross-fostering in terms of adult sexual response,
and therefore we cannot afford to put all our eggs in one basket, so
to speak. There certainly are going to be important species differences with respect to the problem of sexual imprinting. Personally,
I have stronger reservations about cross-fostering a precocial species
like the Whooping Crane than I do about cross-fostering an altricial

species such as the Peregrine Falcon (*Falco peregrinus*), and I will be interested to learn what our speakers have to say about this problem.

Fostering the eggs or young from one population to parents in another population of the same species has been less frequently tried than cross-fostering, probably because the results are not as interesting in terms of behavior, reproductive isolating mechanisms, hybridization, or related problems that ethologists can test in the field by cross-fostering. For critically endangered species of birds, however, fostering appears to be a safe and effective way to increase the reproductivity of local, poorly reproducing populations and to tide them over the period required to correct whatever factors may be responsible for the reduced intrinsic production of young, whether it be the effects of DDE on eggshells or something else.

Particularly when fostering can be combined with "egg removal" to increase the total reproductive output of local breeding populations, I think we have a combination of methods that can make a significant difference to the survival and increase of endangered species. The Peregrine program of the Canadian Wildlife Service and the Peregrine Fund program have both been involved in these sorts of manipulations. Richard Fyfe is going to tell you about his very impressive Canadian results; I want briefly to summarize the results of some work carried out this year in Colorado and New Mexico, a joint effort of the U.S. Fish and Wildlife Service, Bureau of Land Management, Forest Service, Colorado Division of Wildlife, New Mexico Fish and Game Commission, and the Peregrine Fund. In doing so, I want to make a point.

I will make the point first. It is all well and good to show technical success with these manipulations. It is great to know that a pair of wild Peregrine Falcons will recycle and lay a second set of fertile eggs after the first has been removed, and that the wild parents will accept fostered young and rear them successfully, even in larger than normal broods. We take pride in the fact that we can hatch a higher percentage of wild falcon eggs in our incubators than the birds themselves do at the eyries. So what? We need to have some base lines for judging how much better off the population is for having been subjected to our manipulations than it would be if left alone. Too often in our work we do not have such a comparison to offer our critics.

This year the Rocky Mountain-Southwestern Peregrine Falcon Recovery Team obtained permission to remove eggs from Peregrine Falcon eyries in Colorado and New Mexico for hatching in incubators and to return the hatched young and captive-produced young to the wild parents. This experiment involved 9 pairs. Their first clutches totaled 27 eggs, of which 3 were infertile, one addled, and 6 were cracked, pitted or so thin-shelled that they obviously would not have survived to hatching. A maximum of 17 eggs might have hatched if left in the nests. If half of these hatchlings had survived to flying age--a generous allowance--the total production of the 9 pairs would have been 8 or 9 young, about one per laying pair. We can use this calculation as one base for comparison with the results from manipulation. Or we can take the average production of young from Colorado eyries and use that figure. The 9 pairs would then have produced about 5 young.

We obtained a total of 35 eggs from these 9 pairs for incubation (two laid second clutches). Of the 17 eggs judged to be hatchable, we hatched 10; of 14 eggs judged to be unhatchable, by gluing the shells where pitted, sealing cracks with wax, or sanding down shells of eggs that were not evaporating fast enough, we were able to hatch 5. Thirteen young survived from the wild eggs. By adding our captive produced young to the pool, we were able to return a total of 20 young to the 9 wild pairs. Seventeen of them fledged. We doubled or quadrupled the number of young that probably would have been produce by this population if left to their own devices, but a truly herculean effort was ne ·3sary to achieve this result. Ask Jim Enderson, Jerry Craig, Dan Berger, Bill Burnham, and Bill Heinrich who climbed up and down those 9 cliffs so many times.

Aggression between siblings, or the "Cain and Abel struggle," is a special reproductive problem that occurs in the nests of certain eagles, cranes, and some other large birds. By devising methods for preventing the death of Abel, it is possible to double the reproductive rate of a severely endangered species such as the Spanish Imperial Eagle (*Aquila heliaca*), as we shall shortly hear.

Other possibilities for manipulating the breeding biology of species will no doubt be realized as needs arise. The Sage Grouse (*Centrocercus urophasianus*) is not yet an endangered species, but if the strip-miners in Montana, Wyoming, and Colorado have their way, it could become one. Already an enterprising young man named Ed Pitcher is trying to develop a way to get the grouse to shift their traditional leks off mining properties to safer ground where the sage brush will remain. He has had some initial reactions from hens and young males to silhouettes of strutting grouse in association with playbacks of recorded vocalizations that are promising.

The ingenuity of endangered-species biologists will be put to the test repeatedly in the closing decades of the 20th century. While the preservation of natural habitat should remain our primary concern, as many species approach critically low numbers, creative manipulation of their populations may save some, especially if individuals can be induced to adopt new ways of living and reproducing in an altered environment.

LITERATURE CITED

Harris, M.P. 1970. Abnormal migration and hybridization of *Larus argentatus* and *L. fuscus* after interspecies fostering experiments. Ibis 112:448-498.

Schuz, E. 1940. Bericht der Vogelwarte Rossitten der Kaiser Wilhelm-Gessellschaft zur Forderung der Wissenschafter (April 1938 bis June 1940). Vogelzug 11:109-120.

22

Osprey Egg and Nestling Transfers
Their Value as Ecological Experiments and as Management Procedures

Paul R. Spitzer

By the year 1968, the tremendous reproductive failure and population decline of Ospreys (*Pandion haliaetus*) nesting in the Connecticut River estuary and the surrounding Long Island Sound region had been well documented (Ames and Mersereau, 1964; Ames, 1966; Peterson, 1969). It was known that the hatching rate was less than 20 percent in some areas, with many eggs containing dead embryos. Eggs were heavily contaminated with DDE, a stable breakdown product of the organochlorine pesticide DDT, but the role of DDE in hatching failure was still unproven.

During the previous decade, Ames, Peterson, and several cooperators had erected predator-proof nesting structures in an attempt to increase reproductive success. These were readily accepted by the Ospreys, but reproduction did not improve markedly.

In 1968 and 1969, eggs from Maryland Ospreys with a history of relatively good hatching rate and lower DDE contamination were placed in Connecticut Osprey nests as an experiment to assess the role of external influences on the viability of the eggs. These might have included abnormal incubation behavior in adults contaminated by pollutants or human disturbance during the incubation period.

EGG-TRANSFER EQUIPMENT AND TRANSPORT METHODS

Eggs were transported in a suitcase lined with soft upholstery foam. Each egg was placed in a depression in the foam; the area over the eggs was covered with a sheet of styrofoam. Holes through the styrofoam and between each individual egg depression allowed air circulation. Two hot water bottles filled with hot tapwater were attached to the inside of the suitcase lid; they rested on the styrofoam sheet when the suitcase was closed. The temperature inside the

case was held between 29 and 36° C and was monitored with a thermo-
meter inserted through a hole in the case lid. Eggs were moved by
boat, airplane, and car and spent from 6 to more than 30 hours in
transit (see Wiemeyer et al., 1975).

RESULTS OF EGG AND NESTLING TRANSFERS

Maryland eggs placed in Connecticut nests in 1968 and 1969
hatched at rates comparable to the source areas, supporting the
hypothesis that their lower DDE contamination was the reason for
higher viability (Wiemeyer et al., 1975).

As a further test of the Connecticut habitat, nestlings from 3
to 30 days of age were collected in Maryland and moved to Connecticut
to create broods of 2 and 3 young, which were typical of the pre-DDT
era. These provided an additional test of adult behavior and of
food availability. Between 1968 and 1970, 45 out of 53 Maryland
young (85 percent) introduced in these experiments fledged successfully, suggesting that adult behavior and food availability were
adequate. It is worth mentioning that shipments of young of
various ages occasionally required redistributing nest contents on the
receiving end to create broods of uniform age. At least 2 pairs of
birds had 2 young 3 to 4 weeks old replaced with 3 young 1-week old,
without apparent ill effects.

In 1973, another transfer of eggs from Chesapeake Bay was carried out, this time to nests on Orient Point and Gardiners Island,
New York. Up to hatching, the results paralleled the work of previous
years. Ten of 12 eggs placed on Gardiners Island hatched, resulting
in initial broods of 3,3,2, and 2 young. Six of 11 eggs placed on
Orient Point hatched, resulting in 2 initial broods of 3 young. The
74 percent hatching rate of these eggs was typical of their site of
origin. The 2 broods of 3 young on Orient Point went on to fledge
successfully. However, the young on Gardiners Island began to disappear shortly after hatching, sometimes being found dead in the nest.
The 4 broods resulting from transferred eggs were reduced by this process to 0,1,2, and 1 young, respectively. Similar brood size reduction was occurring among native broods on Gardiners Island, such
that the 15 nests successful that year fledged only 18 young or 1.2 pe
successful nest. No broods of 3 young were fledged.

The results of the egg transfer experiment on Gardiners Island
provided support for my hypothesis that reproductive success on the
island has been limited in some recent years by food availability and
limited much more severely than in surrounding breeding areas which
have a more diverse feeding habitat. The Connecticut coast and Orient
Point nest sites are included in those surrounding areas. Fledging
success of young hatched from eggs transferred to these areas and
Gardiners Island are compared in Table 1. An 8-year comparison of
mean brood sizes on Gardiners Island and surrounding areas is given
in Table 2.

Field observations made after the nestling transfer experiments
provide a better understanding of the causes of brood size reduction
and support the food-limitation hypothesis. In June and July of 1973,

TABLE 1. PERCENTAGE OF TRANSFERRED OSPREY EGGS THAT
PRODUCED FLEDGLINGS IN THREE AREAS

Location and Year	No. of Eggs Hatched	No. of Young Fledged	Percent of Eggs Producing Fledglings
Gardiners Island, 1973	10	4	40
Orient Point, 1973	6	6	100
Connecticut Coast, 1968 and 1969	20	16	80

male Ospreys on Gardiners Island were frequently flying 6 to 12 km
to hunt over salt marsh creeks, tidal flats and shallow cove habitats
lacking around the island--while most Orient Point and Connecticut
males had some or all of these habitats within sight of the nest. At
such hunting distances, energetic limitations were probably coming
into effect. Also, the percentage of successful dives--in which a
fish is caught--was below 50 percent in the distant feeding areas,
and fish taken were generally smaller than 20 cm, enhancing the limitation.

Frequent checks of transferred young allowed calculation of the
male Osprey's "attendance rate". If he appeared during the course of
a nest check, which involved a climb to the site and usually took 10
to 20 minutes, he was considered "in attendance". On Gardiners Island, this rate was lower than at other nestling introduction sites
(Table 3).

TABLE 2. COMPARISON OF MEAN BROOD SIZES FLEDGED BY OSPREYS
NESTING ON GARDINERS ISLAND AND IN SURROUNDING AREAS

Year	Mean Brood Size for:	
	Gardiners Island	Surrounding Areas
1969	1.50	1.63
1970	1.79	1.71
1971	1.60	2.20
1972	1.25	2.07
1973	1.20	1.53
1974	1.44	1.94
1975	1.33	1.72
1976	1.86	1.97

TABLE 3. NEST ATTENDANCE RATES OF MALE OSPREYS DURING
THE NESTLING PERIOD IN THREE AREAS

Location and Year	No. of Times Investigator Visited Nests	No. of Times Males Were Present	Attendance Rates of Males (%)
Gardiners Island, 1973	80	58	73
Orient Point, 1973	45	41	91
Connecticut, 1968 & 1969	56	48	86

These supporting observations are included here for 2 reasons:
1. To emphasize the importance of collecting related data while doing a transfer of eggs or nestlings.
2. Because many rare and endangered species are in a habitat which is marginal for them in some way, and an introduction experiment can bring that out.

Any egg or nestling transfer should be regarded as a "bioassay" of the environment. The ecological question "Why is the species declining or no longer present here?" must be constantly asked. Detailed and continuous field work is necessary because limiting conditions may occur at certain times or for short periods. This may be the case with the Brown Pelican (*Pelecanus occidentalis*) in Louisiana, near the outflow of the Mississippi River where it formerly bred in abundance. Young pelicans have been reintroduced from Florida and have survived to begin breeding, but it is suspected that occasional large flushes of the organochlorine pesticide, Endrin, used extensively upriver, poison large numbers of the introduced birds.

RETURN OF TRANSFERRED OSPREYS AT BREEDING AGE

In terms of gene flow, the fledging of a group of Ospreys 560 km northeast of their birthplace was not a severe alteration of normal patterns. A small percentage of northeastern coastal Ospreys typically breed 100 km or more from where they fledge, as reported in Table 4. One bird which fledged in Chesapeake Bay bred at Orient Point, transporting her genes in a manner comparable to the experimental transfer.

In the years 1968-1970, 45 transferred fledglings augmented roughly 200 native young that fledged between New York and Boston. The nestlings transferred in 1968 were marked with yellow plastic legbands. The 20 nestlings transferred in 1969 were each marked with one red leg-band of this type and a short orange "jess" made of polyvinyl chloride and sealed with a small rivet on the other leg. The 11 nestlings transferred in 1970 received single red leg-bands made of a

TABLE 4. LONG-DISTANCE MOVEMENTS OF NORTHEASTERN COASTAL OSPREYS
BANDED AS NESTLINGS AND TRAPPED AS BREEDING ADULTS

Fledging Site	Breeding Site	Distance Moved (km)
Gardiners Is., N.Y.	Martha's Vineyard, Mass.	120
Old Lyme, Conn.	Westport, Mass.	115
Stone Harbor, N.J.	Shelter Island, N.Y.	296
Mechanicsville, Md.	Avalon, N.J.	192
St. Michaels, Md.	Orient, N.Y.	520

superior plastic called DARVIC and twice as wide as those used previously. Also, all transferred nestlings were banded with U.S. Fish
and Wildlife Service aluminum bands. The long, pale, unfeathered
legs of the Osprey aided greatly in subsequent detection of these
color markers.

In 1971, a casual search for returning marked Ospreys began with
no success. In 1972 and 1973, the search was intense, and a Questar
field-model telescope was used. This instrument combines high magni-
fication and high resolution, and accurate checks could often be made
from 300 m or more. At ranges of 25-30 m, it was often possible to
read numbers on the U.S. Fish and Wildlife Service aluminum-bands
which are 5 mm high.

In 1972, 216 out of 252 (86 percent) of the breeding Ospreys
between New York and Boston were checked for bands. If one considers
only those breeding within 32 km of a site where transferred young
had fledged, the proportion of birds checked rises to 168 out of 182
(92 percent). In 1973, the check was almost as thorough.

The results are detailed in Table 5. Seven birds are known to
have returned to the area, at least 4 of them bred at least once, and
at least 3 were involved in a successful breeding effort, which can
be considered a test of an organism's fitness. The distribution of
ages at first breeding is comparable to a sample of 20 native young
observed breeding at sites where they did not breed the previous year.
Ten or 50 percent were 4 or 5 years old. Ten of the native birds
were females and had moved a mean distance of 26.2 km from their
fledging site (a range of 8-120 km), and 10 were males which had moved
a mean distance of 9.8 km (a range of 0.5-36.8 km). The 4 transferred
females were 19, 25-29, 22-27, and 26 km, respectively, from the site
of introduction, and the 2 males were 8 and 10 km away. Thus, their
dispersal is similar to native birds.

A more precise evaluation of the transferred-fledglings return,
especially the actual number which survived and returned to breed, was
hindered by 3 factors.

    1. Most of the color bands and jesses attached to transferred-
        fledglings' legs were lost by the time they were 3 or 4 years
        old. In the years 1971-1973, 11 birds with only a U.S. Fish

TABLE 5.   HISTORY OF SEVEN OSPREYS THAT WERE TRANSFERRED AS EGGS
           OR NESTLINGS FROM MARYLAND TO CONNECTICUT DURING 1968-
           1970 AND THEN RETURNED TO THE LONG ISLAND SOUND REGION
           IN 1972-1973

Fledging Location	Condition at Rediscovery	Location of Rediscovery	Subsequent History
1. Trumbull Airport, Groton, Conn.	Male, 3 yrs old, breeding, nest failed	Fishers Is., N.Y.; 10 km from fledging site	Bred successfully for next 4 yrs
2. Great Is., Old Lyme, Conn.	Female, 4 yrs old, breeding, nest failed	Shelter Is., N.Y.; 19 km from fledging site	Bred successfully when 5 yrs old
3. Between Mystic & Old Lyme, Conn.	Female, 3 yrs old, not breeding	Gardiners Is. N.Y.; 25 km from fledging site	Unknown
4. Between Mystic & Old Lyme, Conn.	Female, 3 yrs old, breeding, nest failed	Gardiners Is. N.Y.; 22 km from fledging site	Unknown
5. Great Is., Old Lyme, Conn.	Female, 3 yrs old, not breeding	Gardiners Is. N.Y.; 26 km from fledging site	Bred successfully when 5 yrs old
6. Brainard Is., Niantic, Conn.	Male, 5 yrs old, found dead	Niantic Bay, Conn.; 8 km from fledging site	None
7. Great Is., Old Lyme, Conn.	? sex, 3 yrs old, found dead near active nest	Stonington, Conn.; 35 km from fledging site	None

and Wildlife Service aluminum band were sighted for the first time at nests between New York and Boston, and some of these were probably transferred birds.

2. About half of all returning young do not breed until 4 or 5 years of age, and this was not known at the time of the most extensive search for returnees in 1972.

3. For reasons as yet unknown and not revealed in the fledging rates of transferred young, the Connecticut River estuary breeding-habitat (centered on Great Island, Old Lyme, Connecticut) is no longer strongly attractive to new breeders. Although 29 out of 45 (64 percent) of the transferred young fledged there, none ever returned, to my knowledge. In 1977 when 3 new pairs, presumably native birds, nested within 24 km of the estuary on the Connecticut coast, all chose other areas abandoned 10 to 20 years ago rather than the estuary itself. It may be that some local prey species are unpalatable due to lingering pollution of various kinds. Shipments of White Perch (*Morone americana*), an important prey species commercially gill-netted in the estuary, have been rejected at New York City fish markets because they tasted like fuel oil.

In summary, the available data suggest that the age at first breeding, dispersal, and survivorship of transferred young was comparable to that of native young.

REASONS FOR SUCCESS WITH TRANSFER EXPERIMENTS

Both the transfer of nestlings and the subsequent search for returns were greatly facilitated by particular characteristics of the Osprey and the region:

1. The Osprey spends a long period at the nest. The pair is usually present 2 or 3 weeks before laying; completion of the clutch takes 6 to 11 days; the incubation period is 35 to 41 days; and nestlings do not fledge until they are 7 or 8 weeks old.

2. No effort is made to conceal the nest, which is a large mass of sticks, often placed high in a dead tree or on a power pole, and seldom hard to find.

3. The birds have considerable tolerance of human activity in the vicinity of the nest, including frequent checks of its contents.

4. Ospreys breeding between New York and Boston nest within a few kilometers of the coast, very often within sight of salt water. Proceeding inland, one must go at least 200 km north before encountering the first few breeding Ospreys. To the west, there is a gap of about 96 km between breeding Ospreys in Long Island and coastal New Jersey. To the east and north, there is a gap of at least 144 km between nests in southern Massachusetts and those on the Maine coast. Thus, Ospreys in this area can be considered a discrete population. Because there is so little wild and inaccessible habitat in this area,

and the region is so well surveyed by naturalists, virtually
every Osprey nest can be found. This allows a thorough
search for return of a small experimental sample of young
transferred into the population.

EFFECT OF TRANSFERRED YOUNG ON SIZE OF BREEDING POPULATION

Because of the discrete nature of this population and the collection of data on total number of active nests (i.e., those in which
eggs are laid) and their reproductive outcome since 1969, it is possible to examine the relationship between population size and previous
reproduction. This requires 2 assumptions:
1. Emigration and immigration rates of young to and from surrounding breeding areas are roughly equal and fairly low,
   perhaps 5-15 percent of the young fledged in any given year.
   This assumption is supported by the mass of banding data accumulated on northeastern coastal Ospreys.
2. Roughly 50 percent of first-time breeders are 3 years
   of age, 25 percent are 4, and 25 percent are 5. This
   estimate is drawn from data on age at first breeding of 20
   native young (P. Spitzer, *unpublished data*) that returned
   to breed in the region.
One effect of this variation in age of first breeding is to
smooth out the effect of annual fluctuations in Osprey productivity
(i.e., total young fledged (Y) per total active nests (N), or mean
young per active nest) on recruitment rate. To estimate the
reproductive rate effecting recruitment of new breeders in any
given year, I combined the data from 3 to 5 years ago, giving
double weight to the 3-year old group. The "recruitment productivity for the year t" is given in the following equation:

$$R_t = (2Y_{t-3} + Y_{t-4} + Y_{t-5}) / (2N_{t-3} + N_{t-4} + N_{t-5})$$

First, I constructed a table of productivity in the years 1969-
1977, calculated with and without transferred young (Table 6). This
shows the effect of transferred young on total productivity in any
given year. The increase ranged from 5 to 35 percent. Then, I used
this data to calculate the recruitment productivity (R) for the years
1974-1977, which I compared to the change in population size (Table 7).
The comparison suggests that the reproductive rate which will
stabilize this population at its current density is about 0.7 to
0.8 young per active nest. In 4 of the 5 years transfers were
made, the productivity was close to, within, or above that range
(Table 6). At the same time, native reproduction was increasing
due to declining DDE contamination. The rates recorded in 1969-1972
may be as much as twice those of the early and middle 1960's. These
effects combined to keep the population close to a stable level after
1971. The one exception is the year 1975. Three years before, native
reproduction slumped a bit to 0.568 young per active nest, and there
were no transfers of eggs or young. Although the better reproduction--

TABLE 6. OSPREY PRODUCTIVITY BETWEEN NEW YORK CITY AND BOSTON, 1968-1977

Year	Active Nests with Known Outcome (N)	Native Young Fledged	Transferred Young Fledged	Native Young per Active Nest	Total Young per Active Nest (Y/N)	Percent Increase in (Y/N) due to Tranferred Young
1968			14			
1969	127	67	20	0.528	0.685	30
1970	129	79	16[a]	0.612	0.736	20
1971	117	75	4	0.641	0.675	5
1972	118	67	0	0.568	0.568	0
1973	114	88	10	0.772	0.860	11
1974	115	102	0	0.887	0.887	0
1975	107	92	0	0.860	0.860	0
1976	109	147	0	1.350	1.350	0
1977	115	119	0	1.030	1.030	0

[a]Includes 5 young transferred to Massachusetts from Maryland by J. and G. Fernandez.

TABLE 7.   OSPREY POPULATION SIZE AND PREVIOUS PRODUCTIVITY BETWEEN
NEW YORK CITY AND BOSTON, 1970-1977

Year (t)	Annual Percent Change in No. of Active Nests	Recruitment Productivity (R_t)	Year on which Active Nest Count is Based[a]
1970	-10.8		1969
1971	-10.3, -10.5		1969, 1970
1972	-2.5		1970
1973	-2.6		1970
1974	-1.8	0.694	1970
1975	-6.3, -6.9	0.639	1970, 1974
1976	+0.9	0.740	1974
1977	+8.3	0.799	1974

[a]The survey was enlarged in 1970 and 1974 when more nests became
known and accessible.

including transfers--of the 2 previous years lifted recruitment
productivity to 0.639, the population still declined by 6 to 7
percent in 1975.

CONCLUSIONS

Given a transport technique that did not reduce egg viability,
a convenient source of eggs whose hatching rate was reasonably high
and predictable, and a convenient source of nestlings, the experiments
provided a powerful tool for examining the ecological limitations on
Osprey reproduction at the times and places in which they were carried
out.   The loss of transferred Maryland young through brood size reduction on Gardiners Island in 1973, identical to what was happening
to native broods there, supports the hypothesis that low food availability was causing death of nestlings.

Considered as a management technique, transfers of eggs and nestlings do not alter the ecological conditions leading to reproductive
failure, and thus in a constant (DDT-polluted) environment, they would
have to be carried out annually on a large scale to maintain a stable
population.   The data on returns and recent population stability
suggest this would work.   If a more "natural" factor, such as reduced food availability, had been limiting reproduction throughout
the region, they would have had less effect, as demonstrated by
the Gardiners Island situation.   Also, the genetic fitness of
transfers taking place over long distances, particularly with
species of lower mobility, would have to be considered.

The transfers required considerable inputs of money, detailed
human organization, and fossil-fuel energy and could in many ways be
considered a "technological," energy-intensive solution, relying on

cars, boats, airplanes, styrofoam-lined egg transport cases, and hot water bottles. Ironically, as solutions through human organization and applied technology, they became the kind of task our society already performs fairly well and accepts; consequently, the operation received considerable attention and enthusiasm. The opportunity to "go on the offensive" and approach a problem with a new method was psychologically attractive. However, the ultimate problems of organochlorine pesticide use and habitat preservation were not directly affected by the technique.

Alternatives to organochlorines are being found through technology and human organization, particularly in the more developed nations, but the question of habitat preservation for species of no obvious economic value to man remains the ultimate one world-wide. Research is constantly examining scientific rationales for habitat preservation, but in many cases such preservation will continue to depend on subjective human value systems.

To conclude on a positive note, the transfers did affect human values. A major benefit of the work was indirect, educational, and political, in that it dramatized the Osprey's plight and generated interest in reducing the DDT contamination that had led to reproductive failure. Greater interest in protection of coastal feeding and nesting habitat was also encouraged at private, municipal, state, and federal levels.

ACKNOWLEDGMENTS

Thanks are due to many people and organizations for the cooperation that made this project possible. During the 1968 and 1969 field seasons, I was an employee of the Patuxent Wildlife Research Center, U.S. Fish and Wildlife Service, Laurel, Maryland. William Krantz and Stanley Wiemeyer carried out collection and transport of Maryland eggs and young in those years. In subsequent years, Mitchell Byrd and Stanley Wiemeyer assisted in collection of eggs and young in their study areas. Russ Kinné and Herman Kitchen flew eggs north in their airplanes. Robert Hernández and James Johnston assisted with field work in southern New England and eastern Long Island. Robert D.L. Gardiner and Alexandra Goelet provided access to Gardiners Island. Jerry Callis provided access to Plum Island, N.Y., and Daniel Daly to the Mashomack Preserve on Shelter Island. Tom Cade, Joseph Hickey, Eugene Knoder, Austin Platt, and especially David Zimmerman provided advice and inspiration at various stages of the work. Finally, the research would not have been possible without grants from the National Audubon Society, the Deerfield Foundation, the Northeast Utilities Company, and a National Science Foundation Research Traineeship.

I am grateful to those who have generously supplied population data from Osprey breeding areas they observe. They include Josephine and Gilbert Fernandez in Westport, Massachusetts; Robert Bierregaard on Martha's Vineyard; Eloise Saunders in Rhode Island; Thomas Hoehn in Connecticut; Edwin Horning on Fishers Island; Christopher McKeever on the south fork of Long Island; and Dennis Puleson on the south shore of Long Island. Alan Poole has helped with the survey since

1974 and took it over in 1977. The research has been supported in recent years by the Carolyn Foundation, New York Zoological Society, Mashomack Foundation, N.Y. State Department of Environmental Conservation, and the Northeast Utilities Company.

LITERATURE CITED

Ames, P.L. 1966. DDT residues in the eggs of the osprey in the northeastern United States and their relation to nesting success. J. of Applied Ecology 3 (Suppl.): 87-97.

Ames, P.L. and G.S. Mersereau. 1964. Some factors in the decline of the osprey in Connecticut. Auk 81:173-185.

Peterson, R.T. 1969. Population trends of ospreys in the northeastern United States. *In* Hickey, J.J. (ed.), Peregrine Falcon Populations: Their Biology and Decline, University of Wisconsin Press, Madison.

Wiemeyer, S.N., P.R. Spitzer, W.C. Krantz, T.G. Lamont, and E. Cromartie. 1975. Effects of environmental pollutants on Connecticut and Maryland Ospreys. J. of Wildlife Manage. 39(1):124-139.

23

Fostering and Cross-fostering of Birds of Prey

Richard W. Fyfe, Harry Armbruster,
Ursula Banasch, and Lizzanne J. Beaver

The 1965 International Conference on Peregrine Falcon Populations held in Madison, Wisconsin (Hickey, 1969) has stimulated considerable research on North American birds of prey. Particular emphasis has been placed on population surveys and investigations of factors influencing populations. In addition, an outgrowth of this research has been a series of management-oriented projects including captive-breeding and reintroduction. It is largely in these areas that extensive experimental manipulations of raptor eggs and/or young have been carried out. In particular, specific problems relating to captive breeding and reintroduction have led to experimental manipulations in which eggs or young of one species have been fostered (i.e., reared by other parents of the same species) or cross-fostered (i.e., reared by parents of another species).

Recent manipulations of raptor eggs and nestlings are not without precedent; extensive manipulations of Peregrine Falcon (*Falco peregrinus*) clutches were carried out early in this century when egg collecting was in vogue (Nethersoll-Thompson, 1931). In contrast, manipulation of nestling raptors and the use of foster parents appears to be a relatively recent development. Perhaps the first exchange of eggs or young between falcon species was carried out by falconers in Colorado in 1962 when eggs and nestlings were deliberately exchanged between Peregrine Falcon and Prairie Falcon (*Falco mexicanus*) aeries to foil nest-raiding falconers (M. Person, *personal communication*). The first attempt at fostering young falcons was apparently accidental when Beebe (1967) observed captive adult Peregrine Falcons attempting to feed newly captured young located in an adjacent room. Indeed, when the door was opened, the adult pair proceeded to feed and defend their newly adopted brood of 10 young birds.

More recent manipulations of falcon eggs and young have generally been attempts to enhance production through double-clutching and/or the fostering or cross-fostering of eggs or young.

EGG MANIPULATIONS AND DOUBLE-CLUTCHING

In 1965, the Canadian Wildlife Service undertook a program of raptor-population surveys and pesticide-residue monitoring. Birds of prey were likely indicators of residues in food chains, and the Prairie Falcon was chosen as an indicator species of toxic chemical residues in western-Canadian terrestrial ecosystems. Beginning in 1967, random sampling of Prairie Falcon eggs was carried out annually in the prairie region; however, in subsequent years, concern was expressed over the possibility that this sampling was causing decreased productivity in some Prairie Falcon populations. Therefore, in 1972 we investigated the fostering of eggs as a method of normalizing production. In that year we manipulated eggs in selected areas where data on current egg-laying dates were available. We began by removing, from individual pairs being sampled for pesticide residues, full clutches with known periods of incubation. These pairs were then left to renest, and the eggs in their first clutches were substituted for those collected from other pairs with similar breeding phenologies. After performing these initial manipulations to enhance production, we also carried out experimental egg transfers, specifically, altering clutch sizes and incubation periods of wild Prairie Falcons.

Many of our early attempts at breeding Peregrine and Prairie Falcons in captivity were characterized by what appeared to be normal courtship followed by pair-bond formation, nest-site selection and, to our disappointment, production of unfertilized eggs. At that time, we believed asynchrony between mates was the main problem, and we theorized that synchrony might be achieved either by allowing the adults to lay second or third clutches or by allowing them to rear young, thereby completing the breeding cycle. Consequently, our initial attempts at double- or triple-clutching and manipulations of young through fostering and cross-fostering were carried out to synchronize pairs of captive adults or to carry these unsuccessful pairs through a complete breeding cycle. Since the literature strongly suggested that Peregrine Falcons renest readily (Nethersoll-Thompson, 1931), we decided to remove the full clutches of infertile eggs from the nests of captive birds. To ensure renesting, we deliberately removed the eggs in the first and second clutches immediately following the completion of each clutch. Most pairs readily recycled, and 2 weeks later a replacement clutch was begun. The adults were allowed to incubate the last clutch for the normal incubation period; then small nestling falcons or buteos were substituted for the eggs, and the adults were given the opportunity to raise these young and complete their breeding cycle.

Once we were successfully breeding falcons in captivity, double- and triple-clutching became the primary method of increasing production. However, Peregrine Falcons from northern latitudes do not normally renest, and we soon found that captive birds held at the latitude of our breeding facility in Wainwright, Alberta did not always produce third clutches, as was often the case at other breeding stations at lower latitudes. Therefore, to maximize production, our alternate strategy has been sequential egg-removal (i.e., simply removing each egg as it is laid) until 8 to 10 eggs have been removed from a given pair. Subsequent eggs are then left in the nests, and the pairs complete and incubate a normal clutch of 3 or 4 eggs.

Double-clutching or sequential egg-removal does create an additional problem in that eggs which have been removed must either be stored for extended periods, artificially incubated, or cross-fostered to other incubating falcons or domestic chickens. Since there is some hazard involved in lengthy storage and full-term artificial incubation, most breeders have opted for initial fostering or cross-fostering of eggs followed by a final period of artificial incubation and hatching. The hatched young are then hand-fed for 3 to 10 days, whereupon they are placed with new foster parents and raised to fledging. The manipulation of eggs and young in this manner is now a standard procedure, and it is perhaps worth noting that, with few exceptions, the eggs and young are seldom returned to the natural parents.

A further complication which arises in captive breeding is that normal incubation periods are frequently prolonged. Also, because of the increased number of young produced, we have had to experimentally foster young birds to the captive parents in a wide variety of situations. For example, the eggs under incubating adults are frequently taken and replaced with young of ages up to about 3 weeks; sometimes broods containing 4- to 5-week old young are taken from adults, and in their place, new broods of 3- to 4-day old young are substituted. In order to achieve maximum production in fostering situations in captivity and in the wild, we have been forced to attempt a variety of manipulations. However, we have also attempted a variety of manipulations simply to determine the feasibility of fostering as a management technique.

FOSTERING

In 1972 we attempted deliberate double-clutching and fostering with the only pair of *anatum* Peregrine Falcons known to remain south of the boreal forest and east of the Rocky Mountains. On the day following the completion of their first clutch, one of the 4 eggs was found dented. Eggshell thinning or aberrant parental behavior were apparently responsible, so we removed the clutch and placed it under an incubating wild Prairie Falcon a few kilometers away. Sixteen days later, these eggs were transferred to captive Peregrine Falcons in the breeding facility.

The entire clutch was taken to force the wild Peregrine Falcons to renest. We hoped that the female would lose some of her burden of chemical residues through laying the first clutch and that this would, in turn, increase shell thickness and decrease the potential for aberrant behavior in the second clutch. It was also our intention to increase production through double-clutching so that young produced from the first clutch could be added to the captive-breeding stock and so that the adults could recycle and produce young which would remain in the wild.

In 1974, all of the 13 known Peregrine Falcon nesting sites in northern Alberta were checked, but only 4 were occupied, and one pair had failed to lay eggs. Since this northern population was clearly showing the familiar pattern of other declining Peregrine Falcon populations, we decided to try to maintain this remnant population through increased production, utilizing techniques of double-clutching and fostering to increase brood size and fledging success. In cooperation with the Alberta Fish and Game Branch, we were allowed to remove the first clutches from 2 of the 3 remaining pairs. The 2 clutches of 4 eggs each were then taken to our captive breeding center at Wainwright, Alberta where they were artificially incubated. After the expected two-week interval, the 2 wild pairs renested, and they were allowed to incubate their second clutches.

Encouraged by this successful double-clutching, we then attempted our first fostering of young to these same 2 pairs of wild Peregrine Falcons in 1974. This was a very straight-forward operation; we simply combined the broods that were produced from the second clutches, placed them into one nest, and then substituted 3 young which had been raised at Wainwright in the second nest.

In 1975, only 3 of the 13 known sites in northern Alberta were occupied, and one of the 3 pairs failed to nest or was unsuccessful. In mid-May, the first clutches of 4 eggs each were removed from the 2 remaining pairs and were artificially incubated at Wainwright. Unfortunately, no young were hatched from these eggs. Further problems were encountered when only one of the 2 pairs renested and produced 3 young. In an attempt to maximize production, we removed these 3 young when they were 2 weeks old and, in their place, substituted 6 captive-produced young which were 4 to 5 weeks old. All 6 fostered young fledged.

In 1976, pairs of Peregrine Falcons occupied 6 of the known sites. Four of these pairs received foster young varying in age from 2 to 4 1/2 weeks. In one instance, we replaced a single 8-day old chick with 4 chicks that were 4 1/2 weeks old.

In 1977, 7 of the known sites were occupied. Five first clutches were collected and taken to Wainwright for incubation. After the birds renested, we again gave foster young to 3 of the wild pairs. One pair with newly hatched young was given eggs to hatch; another pair received 3 young 3 1/2 weeks old as a replacement for 3-day old young; still another received 3 young 3 1/2 weeks old as replacements for nearly-full-term unhatched eggs. All of these manipulations which are summarized in Table 1 have been closely observed so that the fostered young could be rescued if they were not adopted successfully.

CROSS-FOSTERING

Whereas supplementing production of wild pairs through double-clutching and the fostering of captive-raised young seems fairly straight forward, we have had to ask ourselves what methods might be suitable in areas where there are no longer remnant breeding populations. One potential solution is to use the falconers' technique of hacking (see S.A. Temple, Ch. 40, *this volume*). Alternatively, it

TABLE 1. RESULTS OF FOSTERING EGGS AND YOUNG TO WILD PEREGRINE AND PRAIRIE FALCONS

Year	Species	Fate of First Clutch	Results of Renesting	Additional Young or Eggs Fostered	Outcome of Nesting
1973	Prairie Falcon	destroyed[b]	cold eggs	4 yng (3 wks old)	4 yng fledged
1974	Peregrine	taken[a]	2 pipped eggs[a]	3 yng (3 wks old)	3 yng fledged
1974	Peregrine	taken[a]	2 pipped eggs	2 pipped eggs	3 yng fledged
1975	Peregrine	taken[a]	no renesting	3 yng (4-5 wks old)	yng rejected
1975	Peregrine	taken[a]	3 yng (10 days old)[a]	6 yng (4-5 wks old)	6 yng fledged
1976	Peregrine	left	—	2 yng (2 wks old)	yng killed[b]
1976	Peregrine	left	—	5 yng (4-5 wks old)	5 yng fledged
1976	Peregrine	destroyed[b]	1 yng (8 days old)[a]	6 yng (3-4 wks old)	6 yng fledged
1977	Peregrine	left	2 yng (2 wks old)	4 yng (4-5 wks old)	4 yng fledged
1977	Peregrine	taken[a]	3 eggs[a]	3 yng (2-3 wks old)	5 yng fledged
1977	Peregrine	taken[a]	2 yng (3 days old)[a]	3 yng (3-4 wks old)	3 yng fledged
1977	Peregrine	taken[a]	1 yng (3 days old)	2 yng (3 days old)	yng killed[b]
				2 eggs (well-dev.)	4 yng fledged

[a] Eggs or young transferred to another nest or taken into captivity.
[b] Eggs or young apparently killed by a predator.

should be possible to cross-foster captive-produced Peregrine Falcons
to wild parents of different species. Such an approach immediately
raises a number of questions having to do with feasibility and inappropriate sexual imprinting. Since we already had some experiences in
cross-fostering young Prairie Falcons and buteos to Peregrine Falcons
and in cross-fostering young buteos to Prairie Falcons, we decided that
we would attempt to cross-foster young falcons to buteos. In our first
attempt in 1972, we exchanged 4 five-day old Prairie Falcons for unhatched eggs and newly hatched young in 2 nests of cliff-nesting Ferruginous Hawks (*Buteo regalis*). These nests were specifically selected because of their cliff location and because the Ferruginous Hawk
and Prairie Falcon both feed extensively on Richardson's Ground
Squirrel (*Spermophilus richardsonii*). Two years later, our second attempt at cross-fostering young falcons to buteos was carried out
further north in central Alberta. In this experiment, we exchanged 13
2-week old Prairie Falcons for unhatched eggs or newly hatched young
Red-tailed Hawks (*Buteo jamaicensis*) and Swainson's Hawks (*Buteo
swainsoni*) in tree nests. Our aim was specifically to determine if
falcons could be raised in tree nests by buteos feeding on a somewhat
different prey than is normal for Prairie Falcons. These nests were
located in isolated clumps of trees just north of the normal range of
the Prairie Falcon; this permitted easy observations of the cross-
fostered young in an area where large falcons are seldom seen and
where a somewhat different range of prey was available. All of these
cross-fostering manipulations are summarized in Table 2.

RESULTS OF FOSTERING AND CROSS-FOSTERING EXPERIMENTS

    To date we have kept data on 13 attempts at deliberate double-
clutching in wild Prairie Falcons and on 9 attempts at deliberate
double-clutching in wild Peregrine Falcons. It is of interest to
note that our results for both species parallel the early results of
Nethersoll-Thompson (1931). Roughly 66 percent of the birds renested,
and in all but one instance, the second clutches contained one egg
less than the original clutch. Although our data are limited, they
suggest that first- and second-year female Peregrine and Prairie
Falcons seldom renest and that birds which lose eggs that are well
advanced in incubation are less likely to renest. However, these gen-
eralities are not always true; we have also recorded instances of 2-
year old birds renesting in the wild and one instance of a pair renesting after the loss of newly hatched young.
    In captivity, fostering and cross-fostering of Peregrine and
Prairie Falcon eggs to incubating Gyrfalcons (*Falco rusticolus*),
Prairie Falcons and Peregrine Falcons has, in general, been very successful. Of an estimated 100 manipulations, on only 2 occasions have
we had eggs rejected by the foster parents. In one instance, a pair
of our captive Peregrine Falcons repeatedly rejected eggs with different pigmentation than those that they had already been incubating. In the second instance, one pair of wild Peregrine Falcons expelled 2 chicken eggs which were dyed the same color as but were
noticably larger than their own. This pair later accepted 2 well-

TABLE 2. RESULTS OF CROSS-FOSTERING RAPTOR EGGS AND YOUNG

Year	Foster Parent Species	Original Nest Contents[a]	Eggs or young Cross-fostered	Outcome of Cross-fostering
1972	Prairie Falcon	3 eggs	3 Peregrine eggs	Eggs incubated for 16 days then taken into captivity, 2 yng reared
1972	Ferruginous Hawk	5 yng (1-2 days old)	3 yng Prairie Falcons (4-5 days old)	1 yng died, 2 fledged (1 recaptured and bred in captivity)
1972	Ferruginous Hawk	1 egg	2 yng Prairie Falcons (4-5 days old)	2 yng fledged
1972	Prairie Falcon	3 eggs	5 yng Ferruginous Hawks (1-2 days old)	yng fell from cliff at different ages
1974	Red-tailed Hawk	2 eggs	3 yng Prairie Falcons (2 wks old)	1 yng killed in storm, 2 fledged
1974	Red-tailed Hawk	3 eggs	3 yng Prairie Falcons (2 wks old)	3 yng fledged
1974	Red-tailed Hawk	2 yng (1 wk old)	5 yng Prairie Falcons (2 wks old)	5 yng apparently fledged
1974	Swainson's Hawk	3 eggs	5 yng Prairie Falcons (2 wks old)	1 yng killed, 4 fledged

[a] Eggs or young transferred to other nests.

-189-

advanced Peregrine Falcon eggs which were not their own and hatched
them successfully. In addition, we have also had one example of
desertion of a clutch of Peregrine Falcon eggs cross-fostered to a
captive pair of Prairie Falcons. Our only explanation for this desertion is that the male of this pair did not become involved in incubation.

Following our initial successes in fostering Prairie Falcon eggs
and young to non-productive pairs of captive Peregrine Falcons, we
carried out our first attempt at fostering young Peregrine Falcons to
captive birds. This came about as a result of the double-clutching
and fostering of the eggs from wild Peregrine Falcons in 1972. Their
4 eggs, after being incubated 16 days under a wild Prairie Falcon,
were then moved and fostered to a pair of captive Peregrine Falcons.
Two of the 3 good eggs were hatched and successfully raised by the
captive falcons.

In 1974 we made our next attempt at double-clutching wild Peregrine Falcons. Of the 8 eggs in the 2 clutches we collected, 5 were
fertile, and 3 young were hatched and raised to approximately 3 weeks
of age. During this interval, the 2 wild pairs relaid second clutches
of 3 eggs each; 4 of these were fertile, and 3 young hatched. These
newly hatched young were then placed in one aerie, and 3 older young
were fostered to the second pair. Both broods were accepted, and all
6 young fledged successfully.

In 1975 we again collected from wild Peregrine Falcons a total of
8 eggs from 2 clutches. Of these, 4 were fertile; however, that year
we varied our artificial incubation procedures, and all of the fertile
eggs were lost. To further complicate the situation, only one of the
2 wild pairs nested, and they hatched 3 young. We had successfully
raised several young Peregrine Falcons at Wainright, and we decided to
foster 6 of these young to the wild birds. However, the pair which
had failed to renest refused to accept any young. As a result, all 6
young were fostered to, and subsequently fledged by, the other pair.

Double-clutching was not attempted in 1976. However, the number
of breeding pairs in the northern Alberta Peregrine Falcon population
increased from 3 to 6, and we were able to foster 15 captive-produced
young to these wild pairs to supplement the 14 young they had already
hatched. Of these 29 nestlings, 6 were killed by predators, 2 died,
2 were taken for the captive-breeding project, and 19 fledged.

During 1977, seven pairs of Peregrine Falcons occupied territories in northern Alberta, and 5 of these were double-clutched. A total
of 17 eggs was collected; 15 of these hatched, and 4 of the 5 pairs
renested and produced 6 young. One additional pair produced 2 young,
and the pairs were given 9 foster young produced in captivity. At
the time of this symposium, one of the broods has been lost to Great
Horned Owls (Bubo virginianus), one nestling died, and 13 young have
fledged. Results of all our fostering attempts with wild Peregrine
and Prairie Falcons are summarized in Table 1.

In the cross-fostering experiments between Prairie Falcons
and buteos, all but 3 of the young Prairie Falcons fledged. Of the 3
which died, one was killed by an unknown predator, the second died of
exposure during a severe thunderstorm, and another simply disappeared.
One of the females that was fostered by Ferruginous Hawks in 1972 was

captured and placed in the breeding project where she bred once in 1974 with a conspecific mate. We have only a few observations of the other cross-fostered Prairie Falcons. We have one banding recovery from one of the young which was killed by an automobile several months after fledging. We had 5 separate observations of Prairie Falcons in the release area in 1975, and we observed one Prairie Falcon near a tree nest site in 1976. No Prairie Falcons were seen in the area in 1977. Results of all our cross-fostering attempts are summarized in Table 2.

The objective of all these manipulations is to increase the production of young in an endangered population. While it is often difficult to prove, where manipulations have occurred, one is tempted to interpret any increase in the population as the result of manipulations. Such a case is the establishment of 2 new Prairie Falcon aeries along the North Saskatchewan River in 1977. These sites are well north of the normal range for this species in Alberta, but both are within 30 km of the area where young falcons were cross-fostered to buteos. However, we have not been able to trap the adults and are, therefore, unable to say whether they are some of our cross-fostered young. Similarly, our first, and only, record of Prairie Falcons utilizing a Ferruginous Hawk cliff nest-site occurred within 13 km of the cliff nest where Prairie Falcons were cross-fostered to Ferruginous Hawks. This nest was also occupied the following year, but again we failed to catch either member of the pair to confirm that they might be cross-fostered birds.

Even more tantalizing is the current--though admittedly slight--recovery of the breeding Peregrine Falcon population in the area where we have been fostering young since 1974 (Figure 1). The number of occupied territories has now increased from 3 to 7; the seventh is a territory previously occupied only once since 1966. We have been able to ascertain that several of the breeding birds in this population are banded, and, of course, we have hopes that some of our fostered young are, in fact, contributing to this apparent recovery.

Although these observations suggest strongly that our manipulations have led to additions to wild breeding populations, we still had no actual proof until August 1 of this year when we were able to read and photograph the number P21 on the black-and-white color-band of a breeding female Peregrine Falcon at an Alberta nest site. Our records showed that band P21 had been placed on a female in the brood of 6 young that had been fostered in 1975 at an aerie approximately 10 km away. This female had been produced by captive parents at Wainwright in 1975. In her first breeding attempt, this 2-year old female has laid 2 clutches; 6 of the 7 eggs were fertile, and she has, in turn, fledged 3 fostered young to the wild. She is the first captive-produced Peregrine Falcon known to have bred in the wild.

CONCLUSIONS

On the strength of our results to date, we are satisfied that fostering and cross-fostering of eggs between the large falcons is a reasonable and reliable management technique. Our data also indicate

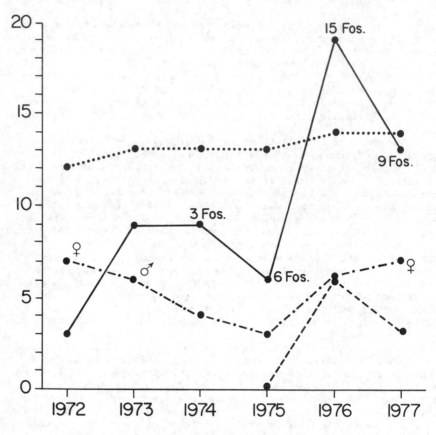

●······· Total know territories in and adjacent to study area

●—·—·— Pairs on territory, ♂or ♀= lone bird on territory.

●——— Young fledged. Fos.= fostered from Wainwright

●———— Young known lost to predators prior to fledging

FIGURE 1. Data on occupancy of breeding territories and production of young by Peregrine Falcons in northern Alberta, 1972-1977.

that adult Peregrine Falcons, Prairie Falcons, and Gyrfalcons, as well as Ferruginous, Red-tailed and Swainson's Hawks readily adopt eggs or young of other raptor species. We have had few rejections of eggs and no rejection of young in either fostering or cross-fostering situations. Except for cases of natural mortality due to predation, weather, etc., all of the fostered or cross-fostered young have fledged satisfactorily. At least some of these young have subsequently entered wild breeding populations.

ACKNOWLEDGMENTS

We are indebted to the many persons who have assisted in the release program and to Phil Trefry and all of his able technicians who have been responsible for data compilation and Peregrine Falcon production at Wainwright. We also would like to acknowledge the assistance and full cooperation of the Alberta Fish and Wildlife Branch which has been so closely involved in this project.

LITERATURE CITED

Beebe, F.L. 1967. Experiments in the husbandry of the peregrine. Raptor Research News 1(4):61-86.
Hickey, J.J. (ed.) 1969. Peregrine Falcon populations; their biology and decline. Univ. of Wisconsin Press, Madison. 596 p.
Nethersole-Thompson, D. 1931. Observations on the peregrine falcon (*Falco peregrinus peregrinus*). Oologists' Record 11(4):73-80.

24

Sibling Aggression and Cross-fostering of Eagles

Bernd-Ulrich Meyburg

In many species of raptors that lay clutches containing more than 1 egg, fewer chicks leave the nest than are initially hatched. In some species of eagles, like the Lesser Spotted Eagle (*Aquila pomarina*) and the Verreaux's Eagle (*A. verreauxi*), the number of chicks is reduced by half during the first weeks following hatching; two chicks are hatched in most aeries but never, or hardly ever, do both young eagles fledge successfully. For various reasons the presence of the older chick (C-1) brings about the death of its younger nestmate (C-2). The same phenomenon is found in some other species of large birds.

Since 1964, I had considered trying to increase the reproductive rate of such eagles by preventing the premature death of the smaller chick. The Lesser Spotted Eagle seemed the most suitable subject for my first attempts since, compared with all other European raptors, it is the one most effected by this natural nestling mortality. Neither Wendland (1959) nor Golodushko (1961) in over 50 and 35 cases, respectively, had been able to establish that 2 young eagles ever left the same nest. In the case of the Golden Eagle (*A. chrysaetos*), on the other hand, the second chick survives in about 1 in 4 nests, and in the African Hawk-eagle and Bonelli's Eagle (*Hieraetus fasciatus*), C-2 survives in about 1 in 5 cases (Brown, 1976a).

The success of my subsequent experiments was achieved only because I first acquired a precise knowledge of the events that normally lead to the death of C-2; this is why I propose to go into this in some detail and why the few attempts made by others--which have not been published--failed. According to Wendland (1959) who had studied this question most closely, the death of C-2 is caused by C-1's drive to continually squat on its younger sibling, thus preventing it from being fed and crushing it. I, therefore, assumed that this drive which, according to Wendland, is unique in the animal world, would soon subside after it had achieved its purpose with the death of C-2, just as a young cuckoo's drive to push every other object out of the nest ceases after a few days. I felt that it would be relatively easy to prevent the death of C-2 by one of 2 methods: by the temporary removal of one of the 2 chicks from the aerie or by exchanging chicks from several aeries so that 2 of the same size were always together. But, the behavioral sequence described by Wendland was not observed. Rather, if I placed 2 young eagles together, they immediately began to peck at each other fiercely. In every case, the fight ended quickly, even when the chicks were of equal size. The loser crouched down and hardly dared to stir, for at the slightest movement the other chick immediately attacked it with its beak. Frequently attacks occurred for no apparent reason. This so intimidated the weaker chick that, even in captivity, it could not be induced to eat as long as the dominant chick was in sight. The same thing happened at nests in the wild. If I placed 2 chicks together, I always had to remove the subordinate one the following day because it retreated to the edge of the aerie and received no food. This repeatedly observed behavior, which must be regarded as the main cause of C-2's death, I termed "acceptance of intimidation" (Meyburg, 1974). Even at the age of 3 weeks, one young eagle starved when I did not remove him in time after an attack by a dominant nestmate.

In order to understand this behavior more precisely, I tried to observe from a hide the events at the nest from the hatching of C-2 until its death; this was the first time this has ever been done in the case of the Lesser Spotted Eagle (Meyburg, 1974). Rowe (1947) provided the only previous observations of this type. There are no such reports for even the extremely well-studied Golden Eagle. In the meantime, such observations have been described in only 2 other cases, the African Hawk-eagle (Meyburg, 1974) and Verreaux's Eagle (Gargett, *personal communication*). I therefore feel it is appropriate to enlarge on this.

At one Lesser Spotted Eagle nest I observed in 1971, C-2 seemed quite weak immediately after hatching and apparently took no nourishment during its short life of about 1 day. Nevertheless, had C-1 been removed, C-2 would probably have been reared.

In 1974 I was again able to make further observations at 2 aeries. At the first nest, C-1 hatched early on 13 June and weighed 64 g. On the morning of 14 June, C-2 began to hatch and emerged the next day during the afternoon, 60 hours after its sibling; it weighed 58 g. During the days that followed, close observations were carried out from a hide some 80 m away. On 16 June, during one feeding both chicks received about the same number of pieces of meat; the female brooded the remainder of the time. On 17 June, during the first feeding, C-2 did not wake up until 12 minutes had passed and even then made no real effort to be fed. At the end of this feeding, it was attacked fiercely by C-1 but offered no resistance. During a second feeding, C-1 received 14 pieces of meat; C-2 did not look at the adult female, who offered food to C-1 first, but constantly pecked towards the head of C-1, who pecked back now and again. At the end of the feeding, the female seemed quite helpless when confronted with the aggression between her chicks. On 18 June, during the first feeding, C-1 received 19 pieces of meat, C-2 only 1. The female constantly offered food to C-1 first, even though it cried less than its sibling. The feeding ended despite the fact that C-2 was still begging loudly. Compared with the older chick, C-2's begging was rather non-directional, and at first it even turned its back towards the female. During a second feeding, C-1 appeared to have no appetite at all, did not beg, and ate only 1 piece of meat. C-2 received at least 12 pieces and constantly pecked towards C-1 who took no notice. Although C-1 showed no interest, the tendency of the female to give this chick precedence was unmistakable. On 19 June, after I reached the hide, C-1 attacked C-2 vigorously before the arrival of the female. At the first feeding, C-1 was given 38 pieces of meat. C-2 made no attempt to take part in the feeding, at the end of which it was again fiercely attacked by its older sibling. Later, C-1 again pecked at the weakling when the female ceased brooding briefly. During the second feeding, again only C-1 ate, consuming 14 pieces of food. C-1 now weighed 128 g, its sibling only 46 g, 12 g less than it did after hatching. On 20 June, as the female stood up in order to commence feeding, C-1 immediately attacked its sibling, which did not move. On 21 June, the female brooded during the entire observation period. On 23 June there was no trace of C-2. C-1 weighed 266g.

I assume that this case is fairly typical of events at most aeries. C-2 is quite viable, but because it is less adroit and tenacious--due to hatching later--it is severely disadvantaged at feeding times, a situation aggravated by the fact that the female pays less attention to C-2 than C-1. In the case of the African Hawk-eagle observed in 1971, the behavior of the female was identical. How long C-2 survives appears to depend primarily on the interval between hatching of the 2 chicks.

On 6 July 1974 a second Lesser Spotted Eagle aerie was found containing 2 chicks whose age, on the basis of weight and feather development, was estimated at 3 weeks. Never before had I seen a Lesser Spotted Eagle aerie in which C-2 had survived so long, since it usually dies during the first week. From 7-10 July, I observed this nest and found that the arrival of a parent bird at the nest, with or without prey, frequently triggered C-1's attacks on its sibling which, at the first peck, invariably fled--often crying loudly--to the edge of the aerie often climbing onto the branch bearing the nest. The branch was very thick and almost horizontal; this was probably a factor in C-2's survival. There it remained motionless, with wings hanging and head drooping. C-2 had apparently come to associate the arrival of the adult bird with aggressive behavior on the part of C-1. Consequently, C-2 always retreated to the edge of the aerie when an adult arrived even if C-1 did not react in any way. Attacks by C-1 were not restricted to feeding times; they also took place when C-1 had a completely full crop and was no longer interested in food. Sometimes C-1 would pursue its sibling to the edge of the nest, causing C-2 to flee to the opposite side. However, the arrival of an adult and feeding made C-1 particularly aggressive. In such situations, C-2 then stood with its back to the middle of the nest, begging loudly but not even daring to look at the adult. C-2 was so intimidated that at times the adult female could not feed it, even though she bent over the chick, exerting herself and displaying aston-

ishing patience in order to offer it pieces of meat.   Thus, on 8 July
the female fed a mouse to C-1 on one side of the nest, after which she
moved to a second mouse in the middle of the aerie, tore a piece of
meat from it and took it to C-2 on the opposite side.   But, although
begging loudly, C-2 did not dare to take it, whereupon the female
crossed the nest and gave it to C-1.   After this had been repeated
several times, she finally seized the mouse and carried it to C-1.
Sometimes she even had to climb half-way under the edge of the aerie
in order to feed C-2.

The events at this aerie entirely confirmed my earlier conclusions
(Meyburg, 1970, 1974) that "acceptance of intimidation" is decisive in
causing the death of Ç-2 when this has not already been brought about
by factors such as smaller size at hatching, later hatching and the
resultant lack of adroitness and tenacity in taking the pieces of meat
offered, or neglect on the part of the female.

On 14 July, C-2 fell out of the aerie.   C-1 had already been fed
and attacked C-2, which was already sitting on the edge of the nest;
then C-2 fled to the other side and fell from the aerie, surviving the
fall from a height of 12.4 m without injury.   During the preceding 6
days it had gained only 10 g in weight.   After the fall, it was reared in captivity for a time and by 4 August weighed 1205 g.   Even then
it did not dare to eat as long as the other young eagles also being
reared in captivity were in sight.

Brown (1976a) refers to the fact that the true evolutionary value
of the inter-sibling strife has never been satisfactorily explained.
Brown et al. (unpublished data) refute my hypothesis (Meyburg, 1974)
that the second egg acts as a kind of "reserve," ensuring that at
least 1 eaglet will hatch and that one will fledge with certainty.
They have shown that for African eagles, species that normally lay 2
eggs do not have a significantly better reproductive success than those
that normally lay one egg. In fact, there is some evidence that one-
egg clutches do better than two-egg clutches despite the second egg in
the nest.   Brown (1976b) does not offer an alternative theory, according to which species like the Lesser Spotted and the Verreaux's Eagle,
may have formerly reared both chicks (Wendland, 1958).   In the course
of time, again for reasons we do not know, such a reproductive rate
was no longer necessary, and thus a form of birth control was adopted
which is, so to speak, an intermediate stage leading to the one-egg
clutch.   This theory is supported by the known fact that, as a rule,
the second egg is smaller.

TECHNIQUES FOR PREVENTING THE DEATH OF C-2

These observations suggest that it might be possible to essentially double the reproductive rate of the Lesser Spotted Eagl by preventing the death of second chicks.   The technique I have developed is as
follows: one of the newly-hatched chicks or one of the eggs--which is
then hatched in an incubator--must be removed and placed in the nest
of another raptor--a Common Buzzard (Buteo buteo) or Black Kite
(Milvus migrans).   The young eagle is reared by the foster-parents.
The chicks of the foster parents must be placed in other nests of the

species containing only a few chicks. About one week before it is due to leave the nest, the young eagle must be returned to a nest of one of its own species where there is another nestling of approximately the same age. If no suitable foster parents are available, the young eagle may be hand-reared, but in such cases, it is advisable to periodically place the chick back in the nest and take its nestmate for hand-rearing. In this way, each of the two nestlings is alternately in captivity or in the nest. Soon after being returned to the aerie, hand-reared birds behave towards humans as if they had never had any contact with them. Both methods were used successfully on 11 occasions. Once, a Lesser Spotted Eagle reared by a pair of Black Kites left the nest before we could return it to its parents. Whereas Lesser Spotted Eagle parents apparently care for their young for at least one month after the young leave the nest, the Black Kites abandoned the fledgling eagle as soon as it left the nest. It is, therefore, essential that cross-fostered eagles be returned to their natural parents before fledging.

The investigations carried out in 1968-1977 in eastern Slovakia, where Lesser Spotted Eagles are still relatively numerous, served to demonstrate that increasing the reproductive rate by this method is practicable. Its application on a larger scale would be highly desirable, particularly in areas where eagle populations are decreasing.

TECHNIQUES USED WITH SPANISH IMPERIAL EAGLES

In 1971 I began a study of the Spanish Imperial Eagle (*Aquila heliaca adalberti*) in collaboration with my wife and J.G. Heydt. In the very first brood I was able to observe, the smallest of 3 nestlings disappeared at the age of 3 weeks. I therefore decided to make a particularly thorough study of this problem of natural nestling mortality and its prevention, for this eagle is regarded as the most endangered of the birds breeding in Europe. It is listed in the *Red Data Book* of the IUCN and many other publications.

So far it has been possible to locate the nests of about a quarter of the estimated total population of 50-60 pairs, and from 1971-1977 we monitored the number of chicks hatched in 37 broods in central Spain: over the 7-year period, 6 clutches were infertile, and no young were hatched; 10 broods contained single nestlings; 4 broods contained 2 nestlings; 12 broods contained 3 nestlings; and 5 broods contained 4 nestlings. It became apparent that up to 4 chicks could be reared, but in many broods the last chicks to hatch did not survive. Over the years, distinct differences between individual pairs began to emerge. For example, over 7 years, one pair hatched 3 young 5 times, 2 young once, and 1 young once. In two years when 3 chicks remained in the aerie, the smallest disappeared at the age of about 3 weeks, therefore in 3 subsequent years, the smallest chick was removed. All the remaining chicks left the nest successfully. Since the literature contained no reports of 3 young Spanish Imperial Eagles ever fledging from the same nest, in all cases where broods consisted of more than 2 nestlings, we removed the last chicks to hatch. In all, 14 chicks were removed and transferred to other nests containing either infertile eggs or only a single chick of the same size. During the first few days after a transfer, we watched closely to make sure that the chick was accepted, especially when the aerie had contained only infertile eggs. If there was already one chick in the nest, we monitored the development of both chicks closely, since it would appear that some pairs are unable to rear 2 chicks. Another technique is to rear the youngest chick in captivity for a few weeks and return it to its own nest as soon as it has caught up with its sibling(s). This method has, so far, been used only once. In 1973, a pair which had 2 chicks lost the youngest within a fortnight. This pair hatched 2 chicks again in 1977, and the youngest was found in a weak condition on the edge of the aerie. It was removed and returned again after a few weeks. Which of these two methods is to be applied can be decided only according to the circumstances of each individual case.

ACKNOWLEDGMENTS

     In my field work I was supported by a number of people, and here I should like to express my sincere thanks, in particular, to Jesús Garzón Heydt, Dr. Ján Svehlik, Dr. Ladislav Simák and my wife. Dr. Leslie H. Brown, Valerie Gargett and Peter Steyn allowed me to see the drafts of their papers, and Margaret Cain translated the text into English. Mrs. V. Gargett also kindly read the manuscript and made helpful suggestions.

LITERATURE CITED

Brown, L. 1976a. Eagles of the World. David & Charles, Newton Abbot.
Brown, L. 1976b. Birds of Prey, their biology and ecology. Hamlyn, London.
Golodushko, B.Z. 1961. On the food relations in the birds of prey of the Bialowieza Forest reserve. Fauna i Ekologiya Nazemnykh Pozvonochnykh Belorussii Minsk: 112-132 (in Russian).
Meyburg, B.-U. 1970. Zur Biologie des Schreiadlers (Aquila pomarina). Jb. Dt. Falkenorden 69:32-66.
Meyburg, B.-U. 1974. Sibling aggression and mortality among nestling eagles. Ibis 116:224-228.
Rowe, E.G. 1947. The breeding biology of Aquila verreauxi Lesson. Ibis 89:387-410; 576-606.
Wendland, V. 1958. Der Schreiadler. Falke 5:6-13.
Wendland, V. 1959. Schreiadler (Aquila pomarina) und Schelladler (A. clanga). Neue Brehm-Bücherei, No. 236. A. Ziemsen Verlag, Wittenberg Lutherstadt.

PLATE 1. Artificial nesting platforms, such as this one in central Upper Michigan, have been readily adopted by Ospreys. Recently Bald Eagles have also used these structures (*see* Postupalsky, Ch. 5, *this volume*). The photograph shows two nestling Bald Eagles on a nesting platform in 1977. Nesting success often improves on these stable structures which can be placed in habitats that are ideal but lack adequate nesting sites.

PLATE 2. Erecting artificial nesting platforms for Ospreys can be difficult in marshy habitats. An ingenious solution to the problem of setting nest poles in coastal salt-marshes is to drop the poles--like giant darts--from a helicopter hovering above the desired site.

PLATE 3. By 1977 the only Bald
Ibis colony in Asia had dwindled
to 34 birds because of chemical
pollutants and excessive disturbance at the nesting cliffs. Existing nest ledges for these
ibises have been improved and
new artificial ledges have been
created. Ibises enjoyed improved
nesting success on these new
ledges (*see* Hirsch, Ch. 8, *this
volume*).

PLATE 4. Artificial nesting
boxes for passerine birds--
such as this nesting box for
Purple Martins--can be very
useful in managing birds whose
nest-sites have become scarce
or whose competitors usurp
available nests. Successful
nesting box programs have
probably helped keep North
American bluebirds off the
endangered species list (*see*
Zeleny, Ch. 7, *this volume*).

PLATE 5 (above). In marginal habitats, competition with White-tailed Tropicbirds can cause Bermuda Petrels to abandon their nesting burrows. To prevent tropicbirds from entering petrel nests, a "baffler" was designed that allowed petrels to enter easily but excluded the larger tropicbirds (*see* Wingate, Ch. 12, *this volume*). The photograph shows a tropicbird incubating just above a petrel burrow protected with a wooden "baffler."

PLATE 6 (left). Puerto Rican Parrots face a scarcity of nest sites. Constructing artificial nest cavities in parrot nesting territories can alleviate this problem (*see* Snyder, Ch. 6, *this volume*). In the photograph, a female parrot perches outside an artificial cavity in which she nested.

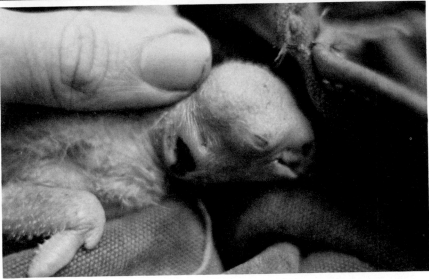

PLATES 7-8. Puerto Rican Parrots frequently failed in their reproductive efforts because Pearly-eyed Thrashers forced them to
abandon their nesting cavities, destroyed their eggs, or killed
nestlings (*see* Snyder and Taapken, Ch. 14, *this volume*). Plaster
eggs placed in parrot nests became pitted from the pecks of
thrashers; real eggs would have been broken by such treatment.
Occasionally, thrashers attack small parrot nestlings. The
photograph shows one which received a large gash from a thrasher's beak.

PLATES 9-10. Artificial nesting boxes were designed to provide Puerto Rican Parrots with nests that Pearly-eyed Thrashers would not disturb or to provide thrashers with alternate nest sites so they would not harass parrots. Many designs were tested: A) 30-90 cm choice box, B) 90-150 cm choice box, C) 150 cm horizontal box, D) 168 cm vertical box, E) 122 cm light-dark choice box, F) 229 cm vertical box, G) shallow angle box, H) deep angle box, I) shallow vertical-angle box, J) deep vertical-angle box. Parrots were safest in deep, dark boxes into which thrashers were reluctant to descend. Occasionally, thrashers would attempt to fill deep boxes with sticks to raise the level of their nest. The nest box in the photograph contained 3 plaster eggs that parrots were incubating when thrashers filled the box with sticks.

PLATE 11. Oilbirds are limited both in geographic distribution and in numbers by the availability of caves with suitable nesting ledges. The creation of artificial nesting ledges in a cave in Trinidad allowed the oilbird population nesting there to increase from 25-30 to 100-105 individuals in 10 years (*see* Conway, Ch. 9, *this volume*).

PLATE 12. Before 1972, Brown-headed Cowbirds parasitized about 70% of all Kirtland's Warbler nests and caused a reduction in fecundity to about 1 young per pair each year. Since then, cowbirds have been removed from the warbler nesting area using traps like the one illustrated. About 4,000 cowbirds are removed each year; parasitism rates have dropped to below 5% while production has risen to about 4 young per pair each year (*see* Mayfield, Ch. 11, *this volume*).

PLATE 13. Man has introduced many exotic species to islands around the world, and most introductions have been disastrous to endemic island faunas. The New Zealand Wildlife Service has carried out highly effective programs to remove exotic animals, such as goats, from islands, thus allowing the island's natural communities to recover (*see* Merton, Ch. 15, *this volume*).

PLATE 14. Red-cockaded Woodpeckers excavate nesting and roosting cavities only in large, living pine trees; older trees suitable for such cavities are now often in short supply. Alteration of cavities by other woodpeckers can cause abandonment, and a number of other cavity-nesting species can usurp sites. Careful management of areas used by Red-cockaded Woodpeckers can help alleviate the impact of competitors (*see* Jackson, Ch. 13, *this volume*).

PLATE 15. A flock of Japanese Cranes congregates at a winter
feeding station in southeastern Hokkaido, Japan. Apparently
in response to this winter feeding program, the number of
Japanese Cranes visiting the feeding station has increased
from 33 in 1952 to 220 in 1976. Similar increases have also
been recorded in Hooded Cranes and White-naped Cranes which
also visit winter feeding stations (*see* Archibald, Ch. 18,
this volume).

PLATE 16. California Condors have probably been faced with a
decreasing supply of carrion since the Pleistocene Epoch.
Shortages of carrion in the range of the remnant condor population prompted a supplemental feeding program. Condors
used about 31 percent of the carcasses placed at the feeding
stations within the condor's range between 1974 and 1977 (*see*
Wilbur, Ch. 17, *this volume*). The photograph shows 3 California Condors congregated at a feeding station.

PLATE 17. Like most predatory birds, White-tailed Sea Eagles
in Sweden have suffered population declines because of toxic
chemicals in their natural food chain. Providing wintering
eagles with uncontaminated food, such as slaughterhouse offal,
can limit the eagles' intake of contaminated prey and can encourage them to remain within the breeding range during the
winter. Swedish sea eagles have shown improved reproductive
success and survivorship since winter feeding programs began
(*see* Helander, Ch. 19, *this volume*).

PLATE 18. A styrofoam-lined suitcase warmed with hot-water bottles
served as the transport case in
which Osprey eggs from nests in
Maryland were successfully transferred to the nests of failing
Osprey populations in New England.
Osprey eggs and young transferred
from Maryland to New England between 1968 and 1973 accounted for
a demonstrable increase in recruitment in the failing populations
and helped prevent further declines
in the region (*see* Spitzer, Ch. 22,
this volume).

PLATE 19. Some birds of prey that lay 2 eggs fledge only a single young, even if both eggs hatch. The oldest nestling causes the death of the younger nestling in what has been called the "Cain and Abel struggle." The photograph shows the smaller nestling in a Lesser Spotted Eagle aerie cowering at the edge of the nest after being intimidated by its older sibling. By preventing the death of the smaller nestling, it is possible to effectively double the fecundity of each pair (*see* Meyburg, Ch. 24, *this volume*).

PLATE 20. Beginning in 1975, eggs from Whooping Crane nests in Wood Buffalo National Park or eggs produced by captive cranes have been cross-fostered to Sandhill Cranes nesting at Grays Lake, Idaho. Sandhill Cranes successfully adopted and reared the young Whooping Cranes which migrated with their foster parents to New Mexico. The photograph shows a 2-year old, cross-fostered Whooping Crane among a flock of Sandhill Cranes. It is hoped that cross-fostered cranes will form the nucleus of a new Whooping Crane population what will nest in Idaho and winter in New Mexico.

PLATE 21. Fostering captive-produced Peregrine Falcons to wild parents is an appealing way to bolster wild populations and return captive-produced birds to the wild. The nestling Peregrine Falcon wearing the color band P21 (shown here just before being fostered to wild parents) was produced in captivity and adopted by wild parents in Alberta in 1975. In 1977, as a 2-year old bird, this female mated and bred near the place where she was raised. Thus, she became the first captive-bred Peregrine Falcon known to have become established as a breeding bird in a wild population (see Fyfe et al., Ch. 23, this volume).

PLATE 22. Beginning in 1967, second eggs in the nests of wild Whooping Cranes were removed and hatched in captivity. The cranes that hatched from these eggs formed the nucleus of a captive breeding program. Because cranes do not mature until 5 years of age, success at captive propagation had to wait until the young cranes matured. In 1975, a 7-year old bird laid the first eggs; in 1977, 4 captive pairs produced 22 eggs, and Whooping Crane chicks (such as the one in the photograph) were reared successfully (see Kepler, Ch. 27, this volume).

PLATE 23. Wild Peregrine Falcons in western North America still lay thin-shelled eggs that break before hatching. By removing thin-shelled eggs from wild pairs and carefully incubating them artificially, it is possible to hatch a far greater percentage of the eggs than the falcons could in their eyrie. In 1977, 35 eggs were taken from the wild, and 15 of these hatched--at least twice as many as would have hatched in the wild (*see* Cade, Ch. 21, *this volume*).

PLATE 24. Domestic propagation of Peregrine Falcons and many other large raptors is now an accomplished fact. In 1977, the two largest Peregrine Falcon breeding programs in North America held 39 laying females, such as the one in the photograph, that produced a total of 345 eggs (*see* Cade and Fyfe, Ch. 29, *this volume*). One hundred twenty-nine young Peregrine Falcons were hatched in 1977, and most of them were released to the wild.

PLATE 25. Efforts to restock Masked Bobwhites into their former range in Arizona have involved several techniques, all designed to give pen-reared birds experience in the wild before final release (*see* Ellis et al., Ch. 39, *this volume*). One of the most useful procedures is fostering of young, pen-reared quail to experienced foster parents. The photograph shows a Texas Bobwhite foster parent leading an adopted brood of Masked Bobwhite chicks away from a release box.

PLATE 26. Aleutian Canada Geese that have been reared in captivity and released on fox-free islands in the Aleutians do not know the long migratory route to the traditional wintering grounds in California. Experienced wild geese are caught during their flightless molting period and placed with the pen-reared juveniles. When the experienced birds can fly, they act as "guide birds" and lead the flock of young geese on the traditional migratory route (*see* Springer et al., Ch. 37, *this volume*).

PLATE 27. Reestablishing Atlantic Puffins at an abandoned breeding island involved the artificial rearing of 347 puffin chicks which were then fledged from the island. To encourage released birds to return to the island when they matured, carved decoys were placed on conspicuous rocks around the island. In 1977, the first of the released birds returned to the island (*see* Kress, Ch. 42, *this volume*). The photograph shows a returning, banded puffin perched amongst four decoys.

PLATE 28. Since 1974, a total of 101 captive-produced Peregrine Falcons have been returned to the wilds of the eastern United States by using a modification of the falconry technique of "hacking." Survival of these birds has been comparable to that of normal, wild birds, and in 1977 at least 10 birds over 1-year old returned to the sites where they had been hacked (*see* Temple, Ch. 40, *this volume*). The photograph shows a 2-year old male that returned to and established as his territory the man-made tower where he was hacked in coastal New Jersey.

PLATE 29. The Giant Pied-billed Grebe is endemic to Lake Atitlán, Guatemala where it is threatened by introduced predatory fish, habitat destruction, and poaching. The integrated management program for the grebe includes: education programs, protection by wardens, habitat management, creation of a sanctuary, and research on the birds' ecology (*see* LaBastille, Ch. 45, *this volume*).

PLATE 30. Cousin Island in the Seychelles Archipelago of the Indian Ocean has 2 endangered birds and is an important seabird breeding station. Since it was made a nature reserve in 1968, the island's avifauna has been managed on an integrated basis that includes: public education, habitat management, protection by wardens, and research (*see* Plunkett, Ch. 44, *this volume*).

PLATE 31. With a total population of 6, the Mauritius Kestrel was
in 1973 the rarest bird in the world. In 1974 a "tradition shift"
occurred in the population, and one pair of birds nested on a
cliff rather than in a tree cavity. The cliff site was safe from
predators, and the pair raised young which became imprinted on
cliff nesting-sites and bred on cliffs when they matured. By 1977
the population had tripled because of the reproductive success
which resulted from the new tradition. Forcing endangered birds to
make adaptive tradition shifts may be a potential management
technique (Temple, Ch. 50, *this volume*).

25

Cross-fostering Whooping Cranes to Sandhill Crane Foster Parents

Roderick C. Drewien and Elwood G. Bizeau

In May 1975, officials of the Canadian Wildlife Service (CWS) and United States Fish and Wildlife Service (USFWS) began a cooperative experiment to reintroduce Whooping Cranes (*Grus americana*) into the Rocky Mountain region of the United States. The reintroduction technique involved collecting wild Whooping Crane eggs in Wood Buffalo National Park, Northwest Territories, Canada, transporting them to Grays Lake National Wildlife Refuge, Idaho, and placing them into the nests of Greater Sandhill Cranes (*Grus canadensis tabida*). The proposal to utilize Sandhill Cranes as foster parents to hatch, rear and reintroduce these Whooping Cranes into the wild was originated in the 1950's by Fred E. Bard, former director of the Saskatchewan Museum of Natural History.

International concern over the status of Whooping Cranes in the 1950's and early 1960's prompted research on wild cranes. The future of the Whooping Crane was believed by some people to depend upon acquiring captive stock and propagating offspring that could be released back into the wild to augment the only wild flock or to start new flocks. Procedures for successful collection and transportation of eggs and various aspects of crane propagation were tested on Sandhill Cranes at Patuxent Wildlife Research Center, Laurel, Maryland (Erickson, 1976).

After analyzing winter population counts of Whooping Cranes made at the Aransas National Wildlife Refuge from 1938-1960, Erickson postulated that one egg might be taken from each Whooping Crane clutch of 2 eggs with little impact on the welfare of the wild population since Whooping Crane families rarely included 2 young on the wintering grounds. Studies conducted by the CWS on the nesting grounds in Wood Buffalo National Park between 1954 and 1965 confirmed that Whooping Cranes normally lay 2-egg clutches, but only 1 young usually survives (Novakowski, 1966).

Success in egg collection and propagation studies at Patuxent and findings from nesting-ground studies in Canada prompted the CWS and USFWS to collect wild Whooping Crane eggs in 1967. Egg collections were made in 4 of the years through 1974. Whooping Cranes raised from these eggs formed the nucleus of the captive flock currently maintained at Patuxent. Details and results of egg collection, transportation, and propagation are described elsewhere (Erickson, 1976; Kuyt, 1976a; Kepler, 1976; Ch. 27, *this volume*).

In 1969, we initiated studies of Greater Sandhill Cranes nesting in southeastern Idaho and adjacent states. Our research involved intensive studies of their nesting biology at Grays Lake National Wildlife Refuge, Idaho (Drewien, 1973, *unpublished data*), and their seasonal movements and activities throughout the Rocky Mountain region (Drewien and Bizeau, 1974). Considerable data on the nesting biology and seasonal movements of individual crane families were obtained after capturing and color-marking over 700 cranes between 1969 and 1974. Responses of nesting pairs to manipulative experiments--such as removing 1 egg and extending or reducing the normal incubation period--were noted. Individual families showed predictable, seasonal movement patterns in successive years. Pairs used the same breeding territories annually, gathered at the same migration staging-areas, and generally used the same wintering areas. Young raised by specific pairs tended to adopt the seasonal movements of their parents. Virtually all young Sandhill Cranes remained within the geographic range occupied by the population.

These findings indicated that Greater Sandhill Cranes nesting at Grays Lake Refuge could well serve as potential foster parents for Whooping Cranes. Further justifications were:

1. The 8,900 ha Grays Lake Marsh represents one of the best Sandhill Crane breeding habitats in North America; some 250 pairs nest there annually.

2. Studies between 1969 and 1974 showed that the nesting success of over 400 nests ranged annually from 78-92 percent.

3. Nesting chronology of the high altitude (1,946 m) marsh between 1969-1974 was similar to the nesting chronology of Whooping Cranes in Canada (Novakowski, 1966).

4. Pesticide contamination did not seem to be a hazard; analysis of Sandhill Cranes at Grays Lake revealed very low residues of organochlorines and heavy metals (Mullins, 1974).

5. There are many national and state wildlife refuges on the summer areas, along the migration route, and in the winter areas used by the Rocky Mountain populations of Greater Sandhill Cranes. These would presumably be used by cross-fostered Whooping Cranes and afford them added protection.

6. The geographic range utilized by the Rocky Mountain population of Greater Sandhill Cranes is on the western periphery of the historical range of the Whooping Crane (Allen, 1952).

Cross-fostering Whooping Cranes to Sandhill Cranes, as proposed by Fred Bard, appeared to have merit. The 2 species have many similarities including: monogamous pair-bonds that probably last for life; a tendency to use the same breeding territories each year; normal clutches consisting of 2 eggs; eggs that are similar in size, shape, and coloration; incubation periods of about 30 days; young that are very similar in appearance at hatching; maintenance of family units; young that accompany parents for approximately the first 9 months of life; use of traditional geographic ranges through association with parents; and an omnivorous diet.

Ecological, ethological, and physical differences do exist between the 2 species. Whooping Cranes tend to be more carnivorous, solitary, and occupy a more aquatic niche on both the wintering and breeding grounds. Ethological differences in displays and calls exist (Allen, 1952; Walkinshaw, 1973; Archibald, 1976; Erickson, 1976). Biologists familiar with cranes believe these species-specific differences are sufficient to prevent hybrid matings between cross-fostered Whooping Cranes and foster parent species (G. Archibald, R. Erickson, C. Kepler, C. Littlefield, *personal communications*). The final answer, however, can only be determined by actual experiments in the field.

The Sandhill Crane foster-parent experiment at Grays Lake Refuge was designed to evaluate the technique of cross-fostering Whooping Cranes to Sandhill Cranes. If the technique proved feasible, then it could be used to reintroduce Whooping Cranes into the Rocky Mountain region and eventually to other suitable areas in North America. This paper describes the progress of the cross-fostering experiments from May 1975 through August 1977.

PROCEDURES

Selection of Sandhill Crane Foster Parents

We selected foster parents which had histories of high hatching and fledging rates, nested in areas that were relatively free from human disturbance, and had been previously observed wintering at the Bosque del Apache National Wildlife Refuge, New Mexico. A sufficient number of foster parent pairs were selected annually to accomodate Whooping Crane eggs scheduled to arrive at Grays Lake Refuge. Additional pairs were also selected to serve as reserve candidates.

Transportation of Whooping Crane Eggs to Grays Lake Refuge

Procedures for egg-pickup, handling, and transportation followed those successfully employed in previous egg-pickups (Kuyt, 1976a, Erickson, 1976). Eggs were transported in specially designed containers from the nesting grounds to the CWS laboratory in nearby Fort Smith and kept overnight in an incubator. Eggs were transported from Fort Smith to Idaho Falls, Idaho, by chartered aircraft. From Idaho Falls, eggs were taken to Grays Lake Refuge by helicopter. Eggs were transported by airboat, amphibicus vehicle or helicopter to the general location of each preselected nest and then hand-carried to nests.

Eggs obtained from the captive Whooping Crane flock maintained at Patuxent Wildlife Research Center were transported by commercial airlines to Pocatello, Idaho, or Jackson, Wyoming. The eggs were hand-carried and attended by USFWS personnel. Eggs were then transported to Grays Lake Refuge and distributed to Sandhill Crane nests.

An incubator was maintained at Grays Lake Refuge and was set at the proper temperature and humidity for crane eggs. The incubator was used to temporarily store Whooping Crane eggs if they arrived during inclement weather and to keep Sandhill Crane eggs removed during the experiment. All Sandhill Crane eggs removed during the experiment were sent either to Patuxent Wildlife Research Center or to the International Crane Foundation, Baraboo, Wisconsin, for use in research programs.

Whooping Crane Egg Substitution and Hatching Success

Egg substitutions involved removing the entire clutch of 2 Sandhill Crane eggs from each foster-parent nest and replacing it with a single Whooping Crane egg. Our previous experiments showed that during the first 10 days of incubation Sandhill Cranes were more likely to desert nests after losing 1 egg than they were later in the incubation period. Consequently, the manner in which each clutch was removed depended on how long it had been incubated.

Pairs which had been incubating clutches for 2 weeks or longer had single eggs removed prior to the arrival of Whooping Crane eggs. This was done to eliminate any pair which might respond adversely to the loss of 1 egg by deserting their nest.

Single eggs were not removed from those pairs which had recently initiated incubation. Instead, a Whooping Crane egg was substituted for 1 egg, and the second egg was left in the nest. The Sandhill Crane eggs left in nests were removed either later during incubation or 24-36 hours after the Whooping Crane egg hatched.

Each Whooping Crane egg was marked individually when it was removed from its nest in Canada or Maryland. This enabled us to follow the fate of individual eggs and to provide comparisons with clutchmates left in nests in Canada and data on fertility of specific birds in Maryland. The foster parents were disturbed as little as possible during incubation. Nests were only visited (1) after foster parents had terminated incubation, (2) late in incubation to remove any Sandhill Crane eggs left in nests, and (3) after anticipated hatching dates.

E. Kuyt monitored progress of hatching at Wood Buffalo National Park and informed us when specific eggs were hatched. We then checked the success of the corresponding clutch-mates at Grays Lake Refuge. Laying dates of all eggs received from Maryland were known, and by adding 30 days for incubation, anticipated hatching dates were obtained. Nests were usually visited 24-36 hours after the anticipated hatching dates. Unhatched eggs were collected and shipped to Patuxent Wildlife Research Center for analyses.

Banding and Color-marking

During August of each year, we attempted to capture, band, and color-mark flightless, young Whooping Cranes which were either run-down and caught with a net or captured with the aid of a helicopter. All captured young were banded with USFWS leg-bands and individually color-marked with colored-plastic leg-bands.

Monitoring Movements and Activities

Activities and movements of cross-fostered Whooping Cranes were monitored on summer areas, along the spring and fall migration routes, and on winter areas. Information was recorded on feeding activities, social interactions with other cranes, behavior, and daily and seasonal movements and activities.

RESULTS AND DISCUSSION

Habitat Conditions at Grays Lake Refuge, 1975-1977

Habitat conditions at Grays Lake Marsh varied during the 3 years when the cross-fostering experiments took place (Table 1). The 1975 nesting season was abnormally late due to deep snow and unseasonably cold weather. Nesting chronology in 1976 was about 1 week later than normal, compared to the period 1969-1975. There was little late spring and summer precipitation in 1976, and natural foods for young cranes appeared limited. Only runoff into the marsh from above-average winter snowpacks probably prevented the 1976 brood-rearing season from being extremely poor. Spring water levels in the marsh in 1977 were the lowest in 43 years. In 1977, about 15 percent of the Sandhill Cranes breeding at Grays Lake failed to nest, apparently because of the drought.

Productivity of Sandhill Cranes reflected annual variations in habitat conditions. During 1970-1974, young cranes accounted for an average of 11.2 percent of the fall population at Grays Lake, and mean brood size was 1.35 young. During 1975-1977, annual Sandhill Crane productivity was below this previous 5-year average (Table 1). Sandhill Crane productivity in 1976 and 1977 was the lowest recorded since we began our studies at Grays Lake in 1969.

Arrival of Whooping Crane Eggs and Egg Substitution

Forty-five Whooping Crane eggs were transported from Canada to Grays Lake from 1975-1977. An additional 16 eggs produced by captive Whooping Cranes were sent to Grays Lake in 1976 and 1977. Information about the eggs is presented in Table 2.

All but 2 eggs were placed in Sandhill Crane nests the day they arrived. Inclement weather prevented us from putting the 2 exceptional eggs directly into Sandhill Crane nests, and the 2 eggs were kept in an incubator and placed in nests the following day.

Each year only 36-38 hours elapsed between the time the first egg was picked up in Wood Buffalo National Park and the last egg was placed in a Sandhill Crane nest at Grays Lake Refuge. All except 2 eggs received from Maryland were in Sandhill Crane nests within 14 hours of the time they were removed from incubators at Patuxent.

TABLE 1. HABITAT CHARACTERISTICS AND SANDHILL CRANE POPULATION STATISTICS AT GRAYS LAKE
NATIONAL WILDLIFE REFUGE, IDAHO (1975-1977)

Characteristic or Statistic	1975	1976	1977
1. Snowpack on nearby mountains (1 April)[a]	153 cm (above normal)	166 cm (above normal)	71 cm (below normal)
2. Spring-summer water levels in the marsh	good-excellant	good-fair, very low in late summer	very low, 80-90% of marsh dry
3. Summer precipitation	below normal	drought	drought
4. Peak of crane egg-laying	20-25 May	10-24 May	22-30 May
5. Weather during crane nesting period	cold and wet until mid-May	fair except for snow 10-15 June	warm in April, cold 15-30 May
6. Percent young cranes in fall population	9.9 (n=959)	7.3 (n=981)	7.1 (n=1,043)
7. Mean brood size in fall population	1.31 (n=120)	1.23 (n=86)	1.14 (n=76)

[a]Data collected by Soil Conservation Service on Samsen Ranch (2,134 m) near Grays Lake; data show trends only (for example, in 1975 there were heavy snows during late April and May).

TABLE 2. FATE OF WHOOPING CRANE EGGS TAKEN FROM WOOD BUFFALO NATIONAL PARK OR PATUXENT WILDLIFE RESEARCH CENTER AND CROSS-FOSTERED TO GREATER SANDHILL CRANES AT GRAYS LAKE NATIONAL WILDLIFE REFUGE

Source and Statistic	1975	1976	1977[a]	Total
A. Eggs from Canada				
date received	29 May	20 May	21 May	–
hatching dates	3 June–	23 May–	22 May–	–
	10 June	7 June	2 June	
eggs received	14	15	16	45
eggs addled or infertile	3	0	1	4
eggs lost to predators	2	4	0	6
eggs deserted	0	0	0	0
eggs hatched	9	11	15	35
young alive at 30 days	7	7	9	23
young alive at 60 days	6	5	6	17
young fledged	5	4	4	13
young alive at 6 months	4	3	–	7
young alive at 1 year	4	2	–	6
young alive at 2 years	3	–	–	3
B. Eggs from Maryland				
date received	–	16 June	7 & 25 May	–
hatching dates	–	–	11 May–	–
			17 June	
eggs received	–	2	14	16
eggs addled or infertile	–	1	5	6
eggs lost to predators	–	1	1	2
eggs deserted	–	0	3	3
eggs hatched	–	0	5	5
young alive at 30 days	–	0	1	1
young alive at 60 days	–	0	1	1
young fledged	–	0	0	0

[a]Data through August, 1977.

Incubation and Hatching Success of Whooping Crane Eggs

Of 45 eggs received from Canada, 35 successfully hatched; 6 were lost to nest predators; and 4 were addled or infertile (Table 2). Sign observed at nests where eggs were destroyed by predators indicated that Coyotes (*Canis latrans*) were responsible for the loss of at least 3 eggs, and a fourth egg appeared to have been destroyed by Ravens (*Corvus corax*). At 2 other nests, it was impossible to ascertain the type of predation, although Coyotes were suspected.

The 4 eggs which failed to hatch were laid by 2 pairs that had known histories of poor hatching success and productivity (E. Kuyt, *personal communication*). Two of 3 infertile eggs received in 1975 (Table 2) were obtained from an unusual 3-egg clutch, all eggs from which proved to be infertile (Kuyt, 1976*b*). The remaining egg which failed to hatch in 1975 was from a clutch in which the egg left in the nest in Canada proved to be infertile (E. Kuyt, *personal communication*). In 1977, the entire clutch of 2 eggs from the pair with the poorest productivity record was sent to Grays Lake while an egg from another nest with excellent fertility history was substituted in its place. At Grays Lake, one egg failed to hatch; the second egg hatched, but the chick soon vanished. The data indicate that the failure of 4 eggs to hatch at Grays Lake was apparently related to inherent problems associated with 2 specific breeding pairs and not to handling or transporting of eggs.

Hatching dates for eggs received from Canada are given in Table 2. These data show that the Whooping Cranes initiated nesting 1-2 weeks earlier in 1975 and 1976 than Sandhill Cranes at Grays Lake Refuge. The 2 species exhibited similar nesting chronologies in 1977.

Sixteen eggs were received from Patuxent Wildlife Research Center, 2 in 1976 and 14 in 1977. Of these, 5 eggs hatched; 6 were addled or infertile; 3 were deserted during snowstorms; and 2 were lost to nest predators (Table 2).

Although Greater Sandhill Cranes have an incubation period of about 30 days (Drewien, 1973), many pairs in 1975 and 1976 incubated eggs only 12-20 days before young Whooping Cranes hatched. Foster-parent pairs readily accepted young regardless of duration of incubation period. Only 3 pairs incubated eggs beyond 40 days; these included 2 pairs with addled or infertile eggs and 1 pair which hatched an egg from Maryland which had been laid very late in the season. The pair with the successful egg incubated 49-50 days; whereas, infertile eggs were removed from the other 2 pairs after they had incubated 42-43 days and 45 days, respectively.

Sandhill Crane Foster Parents and Whooping Crane Young

Foster parents readily adopted the young Whooping Cranes which accepted and remained with their foster parents. Activities and interactions between foster parents and young Whooping Cranes appeared similar to what we have observed among normal Sandhill Crane families.

Activity patterns of foster-parent families were essentially identical to those which we have observed among Sandhill Crane families at Grays Lake (Drewien, 1973). All families confined most of their daily activities to their respective territories which ranged in size from about 9-25 ha. However, both foster-parent families and normal Sandhill Crane families temporarily left their respective territories in 1976 and 1977 to search for food. Drought conditions appeared to reduce availability of natural foods. Foster-parent families occupy-ing territories within 1.5 km of refuge grainfields frequently walked to the nearest fields to forage.

Due to drought conditions in 1976 and 1977, supplemental foods--including barley, wheat, or corn and specially-formulated pellets pro-vided by Patuxent Wildlife Research Center--were placed in 11 foster-parent territories. All 11 families utilized them on an almost daily basis.

The drought was so severe in August 1977 that water was pumped into a refuge stock pond. Two foster-parent families utilized this artificial water supply. All water dried up on 1 foster-parent ter-ritory in August, and a water trough was placed on the area. The family drank daily from the supplemental water source.

In 1975, some problems arose between foster-parent families and cattle that were grazing on portions of the refuge. On several oc-casions, cattle chased and harassed foster-parent families. On other occasions, foster-parent families avoided portions of their territories when large numbers of cattle were present. Several Whooping Crane chicks experienced difficulty traversing certain barbed-wire fences. As a result, after 1975, cattle were eliminated from areas used by foster-parent families, and problem fences were modified or eliminated. Observations in 1976 and 1977 indicated that these adjustments mini-mized some of the hazards observed in 1975.

Capturing, Banding, and Color-marking Young Whooping Cranes

In 1975, all young were captured by running them down and net-ting them. In 1976, 2 young were captured by this method, but several others evaded us in more inaccessible areas of the marsh. As a result, a helicopter was utilized to assist in locating and capturing the re-maining uncaptured young in 1976 and all young in 1977.

Fourteen young Whooping Cranes were captured: 5 in 1975, 4 in 1976, and 5 in 1977. Two additional young, known to be alive when banding operations were in progress, eluded us--1 in 1975 and 1 in 1977. In 1977, one late-hatched young was too small to color-mark when it was captured, and it was released unmarked. It was to be caught and banded at a later date, but it vanished before this was ac-complished.

No problems were encountered in capturing, handling, or releasing the young Whooping Cranes. All foster parents rejoined their banded and color-marked young shortly after they were released. We observed no unusual behaviors in any young or their foster parents after fami-lies reunited.

Survival of Young to Fledging

Thirteen of the 35 young Whooping Cranes that hatched from Can-adian eggs reached fledging age (Table 2). The percentage of young

which fledged from successfully hatched eggs varied annually but declined progressively from a high of 55.6 percent in 1975 to 36.4 percent in 1976 to a low of 22.2 percent in 1977. The annual decline in
the percentage of young that fledged paralleled declines in water
levels, general habitat conditions, and Sandhill Crane production at
Grays Lake Marsh during the 3-year period (Table 1).

Nesting Sandhill Crane pairs, incubating their own eggs on territories adjacent to foster parents, were monitored each year. The
percentage of Sandhill Crane young fledged from successfully hatched
eggs was 61.9 percent in 1975, 40.0 percent in 1976, and 34.3 percent
in 1977. Fledging success followed the same trend observed among
foster-parent pairs but was somewhat higher overall.

Twenty-two young, hatched from Canadian eggs (Table 2), were lost
because of various undetermined reasons. Most mortality occurred during the first 30 days after hatching (Table 2). Losses catagorized by
30-day periods were: 12 young (54.5 percent) from 1-30 days, 6 young
(27.3 percent) from 31-60 days, and 4 young (18.2 percent) from 61
days to fledging.

Inclement weather--in the form of rain, hail, snow, and freezing
temperatures--appeared to contribute to the loss of at least 5 young
between 1975-1977. Four of 5 young had been observed just before
storms but were missing immediately afterwards. These chicks were 7-
17 days old when they disappeared and would have been susceptible to
exposure at this age.

Two young, 1 in 1976 and 1 in 1977, disappeared shortly after
hatching. The 2 young originated from pairs in Wood Buffalo Park
with poor reproductive histories (E. Kuyt, *personal communication*).
One chick, found dead within 15 m of the nest, was sent to Patuxent
Wildlife Research Center and autopsied by J. Carpenter. The apparent
cause of death was pneumonia. Carpenter speculated that the natural
mother of this bird could be carrying some infection that is affecting her eggs and chicks.

Fifteen other chicks vanished during the 3-year period, but the
causes of mortality were unknown. Poor habitat conditions and limited
food supplies caused by the drought in 1976 and 1977 were probably a
major factor contributing to losses.

Predation by Coyotes was believed to be responsible for losses of
some young. Coyotes were observed all 3 summers in areas occupied by
some foster-parent families. In 1976, 26 crane nests, including 3
that contained Whooping Crane eggs, were destroyed along a 4-km section of marsh shoreline in less than 1 week. Prior to egg transfers
in 1977, 12 Coyotes were removed from the marsh by USFWS Animal Damage Control Agents. Nonetheless, the loss of an unknown number of
young in 1977 was believed to be caused by Coyotes which traversed
much of the nearly dry marsh in areas utilized by foster-parent families.

None of the 5 young hatched from eggs received from Patuxent Wildlife Research Center in 1977 fledged (Table 2). Four of the 5 young
disappeared during the first 30 days after hatching. Two vanished
during a severe snowstorm in mid-May, and the remaining 2 were lost to
unknown causes. The last chick vanished when it was 74 days old; evi-

dence indicated that Coyotes were responsible for the loss.

Staging for Fall Migration and Departure from Grays Lake

After the young Whooping Cranes fledged, foster-parent families vacated their territories and slowly joined post-breeding flocks of Sandhill Cranes. Most families left their territories during mid-September when young were 102-107 days old.

Foster-parent families joined the Sandhill Crane flocks when they migrated from Grays Lake. In 1975, 5 foster-parent families migrated between 8-22 October, and in 1976, 4 families departed between 3-14 October (Table 3). The fall migration chronologies of 9 foster-parent families in 1975 and 1976 are presented in Table 3.

Seven of 9 foster-parent families migrating from Grays Lake were relocated in the San Luis Valley, Colorado (Figure 1 and Table 4). The valley is the principal spring-fall stopover area for migrating Greater Sandhill Cranes in the Rocky Mountain region (Drewien and Bizeau, 1974; Lewis, 1977). Most cranes concentrate on and in the vicinity of the Monte Vista National Wildlife Refuge or near the Rio Grande from Monte Vista to Alamosa and south to Lasauces.

The 7 foster-parent families were located in the San Luis Valley 1 1/4 to 5 days after migrating from Grays Lake. The most rapid migration involved a foster-parent family that left Grays Lake at 1030 hours, 8 October 1975, and was sighted 30 1/2 hours later near Monte Vista Refuge some 775 km southeast of Grays Lake. In 1975, one juvenile was never positively sighted again after departing from Grays Lake. In 1976, another juvenile migrated from Grays Lake to the wintering grounds in New Mexico in 5.5 days and was never seen in the San Luis Valley. The day following its departure from Grays Lake, this bird was sighted some 340 km southeast along the Green River near Jensen, Utah (Figure 1) (H. Troester, *personal communication*).

Sandhill Cranes that stop at the San Luis Valley during the fall usually migrate to winter areas in the middle Rio Grande Valley, New Mexico (Figure 1). In 1975, 4 foster-parent families were first observed on winter areas between 25 October - 1 December; whereas, in 1976, 3 families were first observed from 10 October - 6 November (Table 4). Migration time of individual foster-parent families between Grays Lake and winter areas varied from 15 1/2 - 46 days in 1975 and 5 1/2 - 32 days in 1976. The distance from Grays Lake to the Bosque del Apache Refuge, New Mexico, via the San Luis Valley, is some 1,200 km.

Foster-parent Families on Winter Areas in New Mexico

Seven of 9 foster-parent families, including 4 in 1975 and 3 in 1976, which migrated from Grays Lake were located on winter areas in the middle Rio Grande Valley, New Mexico. Five families arrived and remained at the Bosque del Apache Refuge (Figure 1). The other 2 families wintered north of the refuge, 1 near Los Lunas on private lands and the second at the Bernardo Waterfowl Management Area operated by the New Mexico Department of Game and Fish. All winter areas are within the principal winter range traditionally used by the Rocky Mountain

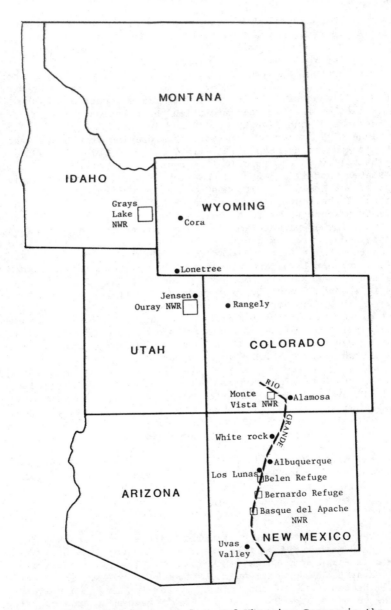

FIGURE 1. Areas used by cross-fostered Whooping Cranes in the Rocky Mountain region between June 1975 and July 1977.

TABLE 3. FALL AND SPRING MIGRATION CHRONOLOGIES OF 9 FOSTER-PARENT FAMILIES AND 3 SUBADULT WHOOPING CRANES THAT HAD BEEN REARED BY GREATER SANDHILL CRANES, OCTOBER 1975 THROUGH MAY 1977

Migration Period	Foster-parent Families		Subadults
	1975-1976	1976-1977	1976-1977
A. Fall Migration			
1. departure from Idaho or summer area[a]	8-22 Oct.	3-14 Oct.	28 Sept.- 3 Oct.
2. presence in San Luis Valley, Colorado	9 Oct.- 20 Nov.	6 Oct.- 31 Oct.	5 Oct.- 14 Nov.
3. first seen on winter areas in New Mexico	25 Oct.- 1 Dec.	10 Oct.- 6 Nov.	16 Nov.- 21 Nov.
B. Spring Migration			
1. departure from New Mexico	15-22 Feb.	21 Feb.- 3 April	20 Feb.- 4 March
2. presence in San Luis Valley, Colorado	17 Feb.- 12 May	28 Feb.- 8 April	21 Feb.- 8 April
3. first seen on summer areas	2-11 June, 21 July[b]	10-25 April[c]	11 April- 2 May

[a] Summer distribution of 3 subadults in 1976 included 1 in Idaho, 1 in Montana, and 1 in Utah; departure dates for subadults are from these respective areas.

[b] Dates 2 Whooping Cranes were seen on their respective summer areas in Idaho and Utah.

[c] For summer areas in Idaho and Wyoming.

-213-

population of Greater Sandhill Cranes (Drewien and Bizeau, 1974; Lewis, 1977). All 7 pairs of foster parents maintained normal family bonds with juvenile Whooping Cranes during the winter in New Mexico.

Interactions occurred between Sandhill Cranes and juvenile Whooping Cranes on winter areas and along the migration route. Sandhill Cranes, other than foster parents, occasionally harassed juveniles by chasing and pecking at them. Many interactions occurred in feeding situations where competition over food existed. Interactions also occurred in roosts and at midday loafing sites.

Most harassment was mild. Foster parents instinctively attempted to protect juveniles and often chased transgressing Sandhill Cranes away. The result of these harassment activities was that some foster-parent families often remained near edges of flocks and became somewhat more solitary than normal Sandhill Crane families.

There appeared to be a relationship between physical development of individual juveniles and their respective social status as measured by their response in interactions with Sandhill Cranes (Table 4). The aggressive and dominant juveniles were also the largest birds, and they acquired adult plumage characteristics more rapidly. In contrast, juveniles which lost more encounters than they won were smaller, and they possessed more juvenile plumage during the same time period.

Spring Migration and Foster-parent Family Break-up

Between 15-22 February 1976, 4 foster-parent families migrated

TABLE 4.   NUMBER AND OUTCOME OF OBSERVED ENCOUNTERS BETWEEN WHOOPING CRANES AND SANDHILL CRANES ON WINTER AREAS IN NEW MEXICO, 1975-1977

Whooping Crane Identification Number[a]	No. of Encounters		% of Encounters Won	
	1975-1976	1976-1977	1975-1976	1976-1977
Hatched in 1975				
75-1	64	138	84	98
75-4	29	202	81	92.5
75-7	59	69	48	61
75-12	24	--[b]	12.5	--[b]
Hatched in 1976				
76-7	--	57	--	86
76-15	--	26	--	46
76-16	--	42	--	73

[a]Identification numbers assigned to eggs by E. Kuyt.
[b]This bird had disappeared by winter 1976-1977.

from winter areas and were located in the San Luis Valley, Colorado, by 1 March. In 1977, 3 foster-parent families migrated from the Bosque del Apache Refuge between 30 January and 16 February. However, all 3 foster-parent families stopped some 80 km north at the Belen Refuge operated by the New Mexico Game and Fish Department, rather than migrating directly to Colorado. One foster-parent family migrated on 21 February, but by 28 February, 2 juveniles remained at the Belen Refuge and were no longer with their foster parents. It was not determined whether the 2 juveniles voluntarily separated from their foster parents or if they became accidentally separated in the large flocks. Each juvenile joined flocks of Sandhill Cranes and migrated on 1 and 5 March, respectively.

The juvenile departing on 1 March was located in the San Luis Valley on 5 March and had located and rejoined its foster parents by late March. The juvenile migrating on 5 March reappeared 80 km south at the Bosque del Apache Refuge and remained until 7 March when it again migrated with Sandhill Cranes. The juvenile was located some 150 km southwest in the Uvas Valley, New Mexico, with 16 Lesser Sandhill Cranes (*G. c. canadensis*) and 1 juvenile Greater Sandhill Crane. The flock left the area on 3 April. This juvenile Whooping Crane was located in late April with a flock of nonbreeding Greater Sandhill Cranes on their summer area near Cora, Wyoming (Figure 1).

The 6 foster-parent pairs which arrived in the San Luis Valley, Colorado, remained through early April in both years. All 6 foster-parent pairs migrated from the valley between 4-10 April. Three juveniles remained behind when their foster parents migrated, while 3 other juveniles departed with their foster parents. Only 1 juvenile,

TABLE 5. SUMMER LOCATIONS OF 6 SUBADULT (1-2 YEARS OLD) WHOOPING CRANES IN THE ROCKY MOUNTAIN REGION DURING 1976 AND 1977

Whooping Crane Identification Number	Summer Location in:	
	1976	1977
Hatched in 1975		
75-1	30 km S. of Grays Lake	Grays Lake Refuge
75-4	near Melville, Mont.	Grays Lake Refuge
75-7	Ouray Refuge & near Jensen, Utah	near Ouray Refuge
Hatched in 1976		
76-7	--	near Cora, Wyoming
76-15[a]	--	Grays Lake Refuge
76-16	--	near Lonetree, Wyoming

[a]Bird found dead near Lonetree, Wyoming, on 29 May 1977.

however, accompanied its foster parents on the entire return trip to
Grays Lake; the other 2 juveniles separated from their foster parents
along the migration route. All 7 foster-parent pairs were located on
their respective breeding territories at Grays Lake between 10-18 April.

The only foster-parent family which completed the return migration intact arrived at Grays Lake on 10 April 1977. This family left
the San Luis Valley on 6 April and was observed at Ouray Refuge, Utah
(Figure 1) on the morning of 7 April (H. Troester, *personal communication*). The family remained together through 16 April, although both
parents, especially the male, were observed chasing the juvenile Whooping Crane off the territory on 4 occasions. On 17 April, the juvenile
left the territory and joined a flock of nonbreeding Sandhill Cranes
utilizing an area about 0.5 km from the territory.

In summary, juvenile Whooping Cranes separated from their foster
parents between 28 February and 16 April. The separation of juvenile
Whooping Cranes from their foster-parents tended to follow family-
breakup patterns we have observed in normal Sandhill Crane families
except that most Sandhill Cranes accompany their parents to the summer
grounds and usually separate in mid-April.

Summer Distribution and Activities of Subadult Whooping Cranes

Six juvenile Whooping Cranes were sighted on summer areas in 1976
and 1977. All 6 remained for the summer in areas where they were
first observed between 10 April to 21-23 July (Table 5). Summer locations and periods of occupancy are shown in Table 5 and Figure 1.

Summer areas occupied in 1977 by 3 subadults (more than 1-year
old) which hatched in 1975 and returned for their second summer varied
somewhat from areas they occupied during their first summer. One bird
spent both summers in the vicinity of Ouray Refuge, Utah. The other 2
subadults, however, summered at Grays Lake in 1977 and did not return
to their 1976 summer areas (Table 5). Distances between first and
second summer locations were 30-35 km for the subadult summering in
Idaho both years and some 325 km for the bird summering in Montana in
1976 and Idaho in 1977 (Table 5). All summer areas occupied by subadults (except for the Utah location) are within the known summer
range of the Rocky Mountain population of Greater Sandhill Cranes
(Drewien and Bizeau, 1974; Lewis, 1977).

All 1-year old subadults except for the bird in Utah summered in
company with nonbreeding Sandhill Cranes. The Whooping Crane in Utah
summered by itself. Summer activity patterns of 1-year old Whooping
Cranes were similar to activities of nonbreeding Sandhill Cranes of
the same age. However, we have never observed subadult Sandhill Cranes
to spend the entire winter summer alone as did the Whooping Crane in
Utah.

Two-year old Whooping Cranes at Grays Lake in 1977 tended to remain alone and did not socialize with Sandhill Cranes as often as the
1-year old Whooping Cranes did. The bird in Utah for its second summer
was solitary, as no Sandhill Cranes remained in the area. The 2 two-
year olds at Grays Lake were observed by themselves in 90.5 percent of
the sightings from the time of their arrival through 31 August. In
contrast, the 1-year olds at Grays Lake were with Sandhill Cranes in

67.9 percent of the sightings during the same time period.

Feeding activities of 1-year old Whooping Cranes, except for the bird in Utah, were similar to those of the Sandhill Cranes with which they associated. All foraged in natural areas, mainly meadows, and the 4 subadults also fed in nearby grainfields. Feeding sites were recorded for the 1-year old at Grays Lake. Of 76 sightings, 60.5 percent were in natural areas, and 39.5 percent were in agricultural fields. Feeding activities of 2-year olds at Grays Lake were confined mainly to natural areas; 92 percent of the sightings were in such sites through August 1977.

Three 1-year olds migrated from their respective summer areas in 1976 between 29 September and 3 October (Tables 3 and 5). The 2 subadults in Montana and Idaho arrived in the San Luis Valley, Colorado, by 5 October. Both migrated from the valley on 14 November and arrived in New Mexico on 16-17 November where they wintered.

The third subadult left its summer area near Ouray Refuge, Utah, on 28 September but only moved northeast a short distance to the vicinity of Jensen, Utah (Figure 1). In the Jensen area, it joined Sandhill Cranes which had stopped during the fall migration. This subadult migrated with Sandhill Cranes on 12 November and arrived in New Mexico on 21 November (Tables 3 and 5).

Distribution and Activities of Subadults on Winter Areas in New Mexico, 1976-1977

Three subadults returned to winter in the middle Rio Grande Valley, New Mexico, where they originally wintered with their foster parents as juveniles. The 3 subadults arrived between 16-21 November 1976; 2 returned to the Bosque del Apache Refuge and 1 to the Bernardo State Waterfowl Management Area (Figure 1). Two subadults moved on several occasions to different Sandhill Crane wintering locations in the valley between Los Lunas and the Bosque del Apache Refuge (Figure 1). One subadult remained at the Bosque del Apache Refuge throughout the winter period.

The 3 subadults which returned to the winter grounds adopted activity patterns similar to the Sandhill Cranes. They roosted nightly in communal roosts and normally foraged and loafed with Sandhill Crane flocks. Subadults never permanently associated with any particular individual or flock. Instead, they behaved as individuals and exhibited no social bonds to other cranes; they only temporarily joined Sandhill Cranes which happened to be in the vicinity.

All 3 subadults were involved in interactions with Sandhill Cranes. The 2 subadults which were the most aggressive juveniles the previous winter were also the most dominant as subadults (Table 4). These 2 subadults frequently drove Sandhill Cranes away and took over choice feeding sites. The third subadult was not as aggressive or as socially dominant as the other 2 subadults. Although it won 61 percent of its encounters with Sandhill Cranes (Table 4), it frequently avoided mixing and tended to remain at edges of flocks or some distance from other cranes while feeding.

Subadults migrated from New Mexico between 20 February and 4 March (Table 3) and were located in the San Luis Valley, Colorado, between 21

February and 10 March. Subadults remained in the San Luis Valley
until migrating on 6-8 April 1977 to summer areas in Idaho and Utah
(Tables 3 and 5).

Losses of Juvenile Whooping Cranes

Nine juvenile Whooping Cranes fledged and migrated with their
foster parents in 1975 and 1976. By August 1977, only 5 of these
birds were known to be alive (Table 2). Of 4 Whooping Cranes which
disappeared, 2 died; whereas, the status of the remaining 2 individuals is uncertain.
      Two of the 4 juveniles that migrated from Grays Lake in 1976
died during their first year. One juvenile was observed flying into
a barbed wire fence at Monte Vista Refuge on 7 October 1976. The
bird died on 10 October from injuries sustained in the collision. The
second juvenile was found dead on 29 May 1977 along a road near Lonetree, Uinta County, Wyoming (Figure 1 and Table 5). Necropsy results
provided by the National Fish and Wildlife Health Laboratory, Madison,
Wisconsin, indicated the bird died from impact injuries.
      Two other Whooping Cranes which migrated from Grays Lake in Octo-
ber 1975 have disappeared. One bird spent the winter of 1975-1976
at the Bosque del Apache Refuge and was last observed on 10 May 1976
in the San Luis Valley, Colorado. The second Whooping Crane migrated
from Grays Lake on 22 October 1975 but has never been positively
sighted since that date. A juvenile Whooping Crane with a flock of
Sandhill Cranes was observed in flight over the Bosque del Apache
Refuge on 31 October 1975, and it may have been the missing juvenile.
None of the 4 other juveniles was in that location at that date. In
early October 1976, an adult Whooping Crane was reported during a 3-
day period between Los Lunas and Bernardo, New Mexico (Figure 1), but
it disappeared possibly to an unknown winter location in Mexico.
These and other reports suggest that at least 1 of the 2 missing Whooping Cranes may still be alive.

Interactions Between Cross-fostered Whooping Cranes

Several interactions occurred between cross-fostered Whooping
Cranes during 1977 which suggest they are capable of finding and
recognizing each other. In early April, 2 subadults, hatched in 1975,
were observed together on several occasions in the San Luis Valley,
Colorado. On 8 April, the 2 subadults migrated together from the valley with a flock of Sandhill Cranes (M. Nail, *personal communication*).
However, they separated during migration as 1 bird summered in Utah
and the other in Idaho.
      Between 1-6 April, another subadult, hatched in 1975, associated
with a foster-parent family in the San Luis Valley. The subadult joined the Sandhill Crane flock with which the foster-parent family associated and was observed displaying to the juvenile Whooping Crane.
Sandhill Cranes near the displaying subadult moved away, whereas, the
juvenile Whooping Crane remained near it (P. Feiger, *personal communication*). The subadult and foster-parent family migrated from the valley in the same flock on 6 April.

The family arrived at Grays Lake on 10 April and the subadult on 11 April. The 2 Whooping Cranes frequented areas about 4 km apart and were only sighted together on 2 occasions. In both instances, the subadult displayed and vocalized when near the juvenile. The juvenile exhibited only a mild response to the displays and, on one occasion, danced briefly with the subadult. The 2 Whooping Cranes were not observed together during the remainder of the summer.

In late July, this same subadult started frequenting an area adjacent to a pair of foster parents rearing a Whooping Crane chick. The subadult persisted in approaching the family on their territory, and the male Sandhill Crane always chased the subadult away. The subadult never exhibited aggression towards the foster parents when chased. Instead, it retreated and then slowly approached the family again. Much of the time, the subadult followed the family but remained 10-100 m from them. This behavior continued until late August when the foster parents allowed the subadult to temporarily join them on several occasions. The subadult displayed to the chick, but the chick did not show any interest in the subadult. The subadult continued to remain near or with the family through the end of August.

CONCLUSIONS

These results demonstrate that cross-fostering is a viable technique for reintroducing Whooping Cranes into a new geographic area. Many questions raised prior to the initiation of the Sandhill Crane foster-parent experiments have been answered. Whooping Crane eggs can be successfully transported from Canada and Maryland to Idaho and substituted into nests of Sandhill Cranes. Greater Sandhill Cranes selected as foster parents will accept and hatch Whooping Crane eggs and rear the young. Foster parents do accept cross-fostered Whooping Cranes as their own young. Cross-fostered Whooping Cranes accept their foster parents, and normal family bonds are maintained. Foster-parent families have successfully migrated to pre-selected wintering areas in the middle Rio Grande Valley, New Mexico, and have returned to the San Luis Valley, Colorado, each spring before most juvenile Whooping Cranes separated from their foster parents. To date, all introduced Whooping Cranes known to have survived have remained within the geographic range occupied by the Rocky Mountain population of Greater Sandhill Cranes.

The ability of Whooping Cranes to adapt successfully to the diet and daily and seasonal activities of the foster-parent species was of major importance. Whooping Cranes normally occupy a more aquatic niche than do Sandhill Cranes, especially on the wintering grounds where much of their food consists of invertebrates (Allen, 1952; Blankinship, 1976). Whooping Cranes reared by Sandhill Crane foster parents have demonstrated an ability to adapt and survive using grain crops as a principal food source during much of the year. The acceptance and apparent suitability of such agricultural crops as food for Whooping Cranes greatly expands the potential areas to which the birds could be reintroduced.

Flightless young were successfully captured, banded, and color-marked, and considerable biological data have been gathered on the individual birds. Although we are able to monitor cross-fostered Whooping Cranes on a year-around basis, we will be unable to adequately assess progress of some facets of the experiment due to lack of basic biological knowledge of wild Whooping Cranes. For example, it is not known at what age wild Whooping Cranes normally first start pairing or nesting. This and other information are needed to provide a standard to better evaluate progress of reintroduction and captive-rearing programs. In 1977, the CWS initiated a banding and color-marking program of young Whooping Cranes in Wood Buffalo National Park, and much needed biological information will be forthcoming in the near future.

A major problem encountered in the cross-fostering experiment has been the excessive mortality of young prior to fledging. It was unfortunate that in 2 of 3 seasons drought conditions prevailed during the brood-rearing seasons and caused much of the mortality. Problems caused by dry conditions and low water-levels were aggrevated by the presence of Coyotes which travelled freely in marsh areas where they normally do not occur. It has been demonstrated at Malheur National Wildlife Refuge, Oregon, that in years when predator control was practiced, Sandhill Crane nesting and fledging success increased (Littlefield, 1976). A more intensive control program is planned for crane-nesting areas at Grays Lake.

Cross-fostered Whooping Cranes frequented areas in Idaho, Colorado, Utah, and New Mexico where waterfowl hunting occurs annually. To minimize the possibility of accidental shooting, an intensive publicity program was initiated to inform and caution hunters about the presence of Whooping Cranes in specific areas. Also, USFWS law enforcement personnel increased their patrols and hunter contacts, especially on the winter area in New Mexico. Results to date have been excellent, and no Whooping Cranes have been shot.

Interactions between cross-fostered Whooping Cranes during the spring 1977 were encouraging and suggested that the cranes are capable of locating and identifying each other even when amongst thousands of Sandhill Cranes. Subadult Whooping Cranes, after separating from their foster parents have, so far, not shown any social or sexual interests towards individual Sandhill Cranes.

Several questions concerning the experiment still remain unanswered. Will Whooping Cranes form pair bonds with each other or attempt to pair with Sandhill Cranes? If species-specific pairing occurs, can Whooping Cranes successfully nest and rear young in the new environment into which they have been introduced? Since Whooping Cranes are not believed to reach sexual maturity until 5 or 6 years old, the answers to these questions--and, thus, the ultimate success of the experiment--will remain unknown for several more years.

ACKNOWLEDGMENTS

We are grateful to the many people with the USFWS and the CWS who made this experiment possible. Approval and endorsement of the experiment was received from the Central and Pacific Flyways Waterfowl Council, the Whooping Crane Conservation Association, and the National Audubon Society. We especially acknowledge the effort, cooperation, and enthusiastic support provided by personnel of the CWS, particularly E. Kuyt. Special thanks are due R. Erickson at Patuxent Wildlife Research Center for providing much assistance and information. For help of many kinds during the study, we thank the following employees of the USFWS: N. Argy, K. Banning, C. Bryant, D. Call, P. Feiger, C. Kepler, E. Loth, R. Madsen, M. Nail, G. Nunn and staff, R. Rigby, M. Sheldon, K. Shreiner, D. Solt, R. Stoor, H. Troester, J. Voelzer, and G. Zahm and personnel at the following National Wildlife Refuges: Grays Lake, Ouray, Monte Vista, Alamosa, and Bosque del Apache. We commend the USFWS law enforcement personnel for their surveillance of Whooping Cranes in Idaho, Colorado, Utah and New Mexico. Information and assistance in the project were provided by personnel of state game departments in Idaho, Utah, Colorado, and Wyoming. We thank personnel of the New Mexico Department of Game and Fish for assistance of many kinds and for monitoring Whooping Cranes when present on state refuges at Belen and Bernardo. Thanks are due E. Knoeder of the National Audubon Society for kindly allowing us to accompany him on aerial surveys of crane wintering areas in northern Mexico. We appreciate the assistance of many interested citizens who provided information on sightings of Whooping Cranes throughout the Rocky Mountain region. A number of land owners temporarily hosted Whooping Cranes, and they made considerable effort to enhance the safety and welfare of the birds while on their land. We especially acknowledge the interest expressed by the following ranchers: M. Trunrud, Jr. and D. Holman of Melville, Montana; J. Fendak of Cora, Wyoming; and P. & M. Edeal of Los Lunas, New Mexico. The project was funded by the Office of Endangered Species, USFWS.

LITERATURE CITED

Allen, R.P. 1952. The Whooping Crane. National Audubon Society Res. Rep. No. 3. 246p.

Archibald, G.W. 1976. Crane taxonomy as revealed by the unison call, p. 225-251. *In* J.C. Lewis (ed.) Proceedings of the international crane workshop. Oklahoma State Univ. Publ. & Printing, Stillwater.

Blankinship, D.R. 1976. Studies of Whooping Cranes on the wintering grounds, p. 197-206. *In* J.C. Lewis (ed.) Proceedings of the international crane workshop. Oklahoma State Univ. Publ. & Printing, Stillwater.

Drewien, R.C. 1973. Ecology of Rocky Mountain Greater Sandhill Cranes. Ph.D. Thesis. Univ. of Idaho, Moscow. 152p.

Drewien, R.C. and E.G. Bizeau. 1974. Status and distribution of Greater Sandhill Cranes in the Rocky Mountains. J. Wildlife Manage. 38:720-742.

Erickson, R.C. 1976. Whooping Crane studies at Patuxent Wildlife Research Center, p. 166-171. *In* J.C. Lewis (ed.) Proceedings of the international crane workshop. Oklahoma State Univ. Publ. & Printing, Stillwater.

Kepler, C.B. 1976. Dominance and dominance-related behavior in the
    Whooping Crane, p. 177-196. *In* J.C. Lewis (ed.) Proceedings of
    the international crane workshop. Oklahoma State Univ. Publ. &
    Printing, Stillwater.
Kuyt, E. 1976*a*. Whooping Cranes: the long road back. Nature Canada
    52:2-9.
Kuyt, E. 1976*b*. Recent clutch size data for Whooping Cranes, including
    a 3-egg clutch. Blue Jay 34(2):82-83.
Lewis, J.C. 1977. Sandhill Cranes (*Grus canadensis*), p. 5-43. *In* G.C.
    Sanderson (ed.) Management of migratory shore and upland game-
    birds in North America. Int. Association of Fish and Game
    Agencies, Washington, D.C. 358p.
Littlefield, C.D. 1976. Productivity of Greater Sandhill Cranes on
    Malheur National Wildlife Refuge, Oregon, p. 86-92. *In* J.C. Lewis
    (ed.) Proceedings of the international crane workshop. Oklahoma
    State Univ. Publ. & Printing, Stillwater.
Mullins, W.H. 1974. Summer food habits, chemical contaminants, and
    distribution of the Greater Sandhill Crane. M.S. Thesis. Univ.
    of Idaho, Moscow. 34p.
Novakowski, N.S. 1966. Whooping Crane population dynamics on the
    nesting ground, Wood Buffalo National Park, Northwest Territories
    Canada. Canadian Wildlife Service Res. Rep. No. 1.
Walkinshaw, L.H. 1973. Cranes of the World. Winchester Press, New
    York. 370p.

Part VI
Captive Breeding of Endangered Birds

26

Breeding Endangered Birds in Captivity
The Last Resort

William G. Conway

The potential of captive propagation to be of aid in avian conservation is often considered questionable. It is a last resort.
The purpose of this review and the papers that follow is to give the
question perspective and to provide illustrations of breeding endangered
birds in captivity and its problems.

Propagating endangered birds in captivity has the potential to
fulfill three main roles: the preservation of a gene bank of a
reduced or vanished species; the development of techniques to aid
the management of rare birds; and the advancement of public education. Despite the fact that nearly one-twelfth of all the species of
birds have been bred in captivity during the past two years, the
technique is beset with obstacles and the concept with detractors.
Many of the obstacles are economic and organizational, but others
are biological. Some may arise from a lack of understanding of the
differences between captive and wild populations. Unfortunately,
however, captive propagation is the only stock in the conservationist's portfolio that stands between an inexorably increasing number
of endangered species and extinction in the face of man's accelerating
destruction of habitat.

Thus far, captive propagation has made few contributions to the
preservation of endangered birds. Instead of support from government
and private conservation organizations, there has been wholesale
discouragement. Even the federal government's own attempts to
propagate failing native species have been plagued with irregular
support and regular criticism. Also, government agencies have
interpreted and now administer certain endangered species and agricultural legislation so as to hinder some worthwhile propagation
programs. Several private conservation groups continue to call for
the abolition of all captive animal collections and studies, along
with many other kinds of intensive wild animal management. Thus,

the fledgling state of captive bird propagation is no accident.
In 1909, William Beebe and Lee S. Crandall listed 82 species of
wild birds which were known to have been bred at least once by American
zoos or private aviculturists up until that time (Beebe and Crandall,
1909). By 1917, Crandall was able to enlarge the list to 149 species
of 15 orders (Crandall, 1917). Almost half were either gallinaceous
birds or waterfowl, but the Carolina Parakeet (*Conuropsis carolinensis*)
and the Passenger Pigeon (*Ectopistes migratorius*) were both included.
In the 1975 *International Zoo Yearbook* census, it was reported that
over 820 species and subspecies of birds were bred throughout the
world. Twenty-two orders were represented including 32 species or subspecies designated rare or endangered by the IUCN (Olney, 1977). Ten
years previously, the breeding of 584 forms was noted including 20
designated rare by IUCN (Jarvis, 1967). The lists are revealing in
what they do not show as well as in what they do (Table 1).

No loons, one grebe, no procellariform birds, only one capri-
mulgiform, no swifts or hummingbirds and no trogons are commonly
bred. Species belonging to these groups are seldom kept in captivity, and several pose difficult care problems. Unless techniques
for their care are soon developed, captive propagation cannot be
considered in their management.

Until recently, only a few species of wild birds had been bred
for more than one generation in captivity, for there was little economic incentive for long-term breeding. Now that multi-generation
propagation is being attained with many orders, the care and biological complexities of long-term management are increasing concern about
the differential responses of the captive propagules of various
species to inbreeding, photoperiod, nutrition, imprinting and so
forth.

If aviculture can be realistically supported and scientifically
advanced, the roles for captive breeding include providing gene banks
from which birds may be re-introduced into nature. Where inbred wild
propagules are confined in areas too small to sustain genetically
viable populations, they may be aided by infusions from captive
stocks. Supportive stocking is a recognized, if often misused,
technique in game fish, bird and mammal management. Another obvious
gene bank function is the preservation of species whose habitat has
vanished in nature. Whether or not the lost environment may be
reconstituted at some time in the future, the educational value of
captive populations has important implications for conservation as
a whole and is another role for endangered species propagation.

Conservationists may discover that zoo and aquarium programs
of public education and recreation will be the strongest economic
support for the continued survival of some species. Zoo attendance
far surpasses that of all professional baseball, football and basket-
ball games combined and can be far better used to promote conservation
than presently. It is interesting to reflect that the international
drive to reduce whaling did not gain broad support until aquariums
began exhibiting live whales and dolphins. Evidently, it is alright
to slaughter distant and unknown creatures, no matter how marvelous,
but not when they are relatives of "Shamu," "Bubbles" or "Flipper,"
those endearing creatures which shake flippers with you.

TABLE 1. NUMBER OF AVIAN SPECIES REPORTEDLY BRED IN CAPTIVITY
DURING THE YEARS 1965 AND 1975

Order	No. of Species Bred during:	
	1965[a]	1975[b]
Sphe023nisciformes	6	5
Struthioniformes	1	2
Rheiformes	1	2
Casuariiformes	2	2
Apterygiformes	1	1
Tinamiformes	2	8
Gaviiformes	0	0
Podicipediformes	1	0
Procellariiformes	0	0
Pelecaniformes	5	4
Ciconiiformes	29	36
Anseriformes	132	159
Falconiformes	10	27
Galliformes	95	94
Gruiformes	28	45
Charadriiformes	20	40
Columbiformes	52	67
Psittaciformes	84	128
Cuculiformes	2	12
Strigiformes	17	25
Caprimulgiformes	0	1
Apodiformes	0	0
Coliiformes	2	1
Trogoniformes	0	0
Coraciiformes	4	17
Piciformes	3	10
Passeriformes	87	137
Totals	584	823

[a]Data from Jarvis (1967).
[b]Data from Olney (1977).

Finally, captive propagation programs should serve the heuristic purpose of stimulating the development of techniques which may be used to succor faltering species in nature; a science of avicultural conservation. Most of the techniques which have created so much interest in this meeting, such as artificial insemination, egg transfer, artificial incubation, and cross-fostering, long have been used in zoological parks or the poultry industry. Although the difference between birds in nature and birds in captivity is frequently alluded to, aviculture of wild birds is not dignified by a single course in any university.

If better captive breeding is to be a tool in conservation, we must recognize the usual differences between captive and wild populations. For example, adult zoo animals, on average, live far longer than their wild counterparts. In nature, annual adult mortality in various gallinaceous birds and ducks ranges from 40-60 percent and 10 percent in one studied species of penguin (Lack, 1954). These rates are unaffected by age, in nature, up to a time when extremely few are left alive. By contrast, at the New York Zoological Park, annual adult mortality in gallinaceous birds and ducks is less than 7 percent, in various shorebirds and gulls, about 7.6 percent and about 5 percent in penguins.

The survivorship curves for most wild birds show extremely high early mortality in comparison with that of captive birds. Young and aged animals in captivity are protected from nature's rigorous selective pressures with the result that the average age of zoo breeding groups tends to become much older than that of wild bird populations.

Long-term captive populations, like small wild populations, may suffer from inbreeding, inadvertent selection and reduced genetic variability. For example, the length of the intestines and caeca in Red Grouse (*Lagopus lagopus*) has been measured in a captive population (Moss, 1972). Over several generations, birds kept upon a pelleted ration showed a substantial decrease in the length of the small intestine and the caeca compared with wild birds. This may not have been of genetic origin, of course, and it is not known whether it is rapidly reversable in birds forced to eat heather in the wild instead of pelleted rations. But, in most captive breeding programs man not only controls diet, climate and space but also access to mates, and the timing and frequency of reproductive opportunity.

While one task of the bird propagator is to minimize unnatural selection pressures, there are a few mitigating factors inherent in most modern breeding programs which may help to preserve much of a species' original genetic composition. The effective rate of the turnover of generations, hence the opportunity for selective processes to exert pressure upon the genotype is likely to be far more rapid in short-lived natural populations than in long-lived captive flocks. Nor should it be forgotten that many wild populations are now being subjected to unnatural pressures. Whether or not the successful Whooping Crane (*Grus americana*) of the future is one that avoids migrating, many wild animals are beginning to face a genetic diminution comparable to that imposed upon captive groups, as their populations become smaller and more isolated. Of course, in captivity there is more likelihood of genetic drift without attendant survival value because of the amelioration of living conditions. But, the excessive survival of young and longevity, by nature's standards, should protract the maintenance of original genotype in well-run programs.

Captive parents may have the opportunity of passing on their genes in more combinations to more young for a greater number of breedings than would occur in nature. This situation, too, can enhance the retention of original genetic variability in a captive, as opposed to a wild, population of comparable size. However, the excessive reproductive success of a few individuals in captivity can reduce variability of captive flocks unless carefully checked. Nevertheless, where a population is relatively free of deleterious genetic traits, its unexpressed genetic potential may permit it to do very well. The genetically pauperate population of the Northern Elephant Seal (*Mirounga angustirostris*) has increased from about 20 animals to more than 30,000 in 80 years, despite a period of great modification of its favored coasts (Bonnel and Selander, 1974).

Although conservation's need for captive breeding programs is demonstrable, and many of the necessary techniques have been developed, there remains an unanswered question, "Who will breed and maintain endangered birds?"

Zoos provide the obvious answer to such an expensive long-term commitment, but all zoos are largely dependent upon gate receipts, donors and local politicians for their support. Their programs must not only be sound biologically but also compel broad public interest. Moreover, zoos are not committed to birds alone, and all the zoo animal areas in the world would fit within the Borough of Brooklyn. Specialized propagation facilities such as Baraboo's International Crane Foundation, Cornell's Peregrine Fund, and Great Britain's Jersey Wildlife Preservation Trust or comparatively huge Wildfowl Trust may make significant contributions towards the preservation of the few species upon which they concentrate, but it seems unlikely that many more organizations like these can survive successfully in a world of dollars and cents. Private aviculturists, especially in the United States and Great Britain, often maintain the most important collections of rare waterfowl, pheasants, pigeons and psittacines. Unfortunately, most do not properly monitor their collections, and these can appear and disappear with the usual transience of personal concerns. It behooves conservationists interested in bird propagation to contact such people, learn from them and attempt to bring them within the mainstream of avian preservation efforts. It is important to insure that captive populations of rare birds are not lost because of death of their owners, or a change in the direction of their interests.

Government agencies, usually in the form of state game departments, have had a long and proprietary interest in the propagation of birds. Thousands of waterfowl and hundreds of thousands of exotic quail, pheasants and partridges have been bred for game introductions (Bohl and Bump, 1970). Only recently, however, has the United States government moved beyond game birds with the advent of federal programs at Patuxent Wildlife Research Center. While there are individual bright spots, facilities for propagating rare birds are largely uncoordinated, except for recent efforts in zoos. There are, as yet, no significant stud books in avian propagation and no agreed-upon record system except among the members of Zoo East. Not even the most simple age-sex models have been constructed for birds held in captivity--to say nothing of the more complex population models required to minimize inbreeding in captivity (Conway, 1974). In this respect, aviculture lags behind the breeding of some wild mammals.

Endangered bird propagation has been discouraged in the past for fear that it would divert scarce resources from preserving species in nature. Ultimately, however, we must ask ourselves whether having a species in captivity is better than not having it at all; whether preserving even a gradually changing representation of some of the earth's biological diversity is not, of itself, worthwhile?

At best, choosing the few species for which captive facilities can be provided will be depressing. Surely the ultimate objective of aviculturists should be a science of bird husbandry so proficient that any propagule from any species can be bred at will. Unhappily, the supporting economics of wild animal propagation are no more secure than those of any other elaborate technique of wild animal conservation. If there are to be many long-term, coordinated, repository programs, they will require a new kind of national commitment to the care of endangered species.

For captive propagation of vanishing animals to fulfill its promise, it must become more than a last resort. There must be an evolution in man's perception of animal captivity away from the stereotypic notion of incarceration and towards a concept of ultimate responsibility, of guardianship and care.

LITERATURE CITED

Beebe, C.W. and L.S. Crandall. 1909. Wild birds bred in captivity in the eastern United States. Zool. Soc. Bull. 36:580-583.

Bohl, W.H. and G. Bump. 1970. Summary of foreign game bird liberations 1960 to 1968 and propagation 1966 to 1968. U.S. Dept. of the Interior, Special Scientific Report--Wildlife No. 130.

Bonnel, M.L. and R.K. Selander. 1974. Elephant seals: genetic variation and near extinction. Science 184:908-909.

Conway, W.G. 1974. Animal management models and long-term captive propagation, p. 141-148. In 1974 AAZPA Conference Proceedings.

Crandall, L.S. 1917. Wild birds bred in captivity in the United States. Zool. Soc. Bull. 20(1):1447-1449.

Jarvis, C. (ed.) 1967. Birds bred in captivity. Int. Zoo Yearbook 7:326-347.

Lack, D. 1954. The natural regulation of animal numbers. Clarendon Press, Oxford.

Moss, R. 1972. Effects of captivity on gut length in red grouse. J. Wildlife Manage. 36:99-104.

Olney, P.J.S. (ed.) 1977. Birds bred in captivity and multiple generation births 1975. Int. Zoo Yearbook 17:260-296.

27

Captive Propagation of Whooping Cranes
A Behavioral Approach

Cameron B. Kepler

The Whooping Crane (*Grus americana*) has probably received more attention than any other endangered bird; Aransas National Wildlife Refuge was established in 1937, primarily to protect it, and conservation agencies since then have stimulated such concern for Whooping Cranes that the species is a symbol for wildlife conservation in North America. Studies of the single flock on its wintering (Allen, 1952; Blankinship, 1976) and breeding (Novakowski, 1966; Kuyt, 1976) grounds have expanded our understanding of the needs of the species in the wild, although much remains to be learned from individually marked birds. The wild population, although protected, showed such a slow population increase in the decades following the establishment of Aransas (26 birds in 1940, 31 in 1950, 36 in 1960) that concerned biologists in the late 1950's vigorously discussed what was then a highly controversial management proposal: breeding the species in captivity. In 1961 an experimental program was begun with captive Sandhill Cranes (*Grus canadensis*), and by 1967 research was sufficiently advanced that a Whooping Crane program was initiated at Patuxent Wildlife Research Center with the taking of one egg from each of 6 two-egg clutches in Wood Buffalo National Park, Canada (Erickson, 1976). In 1967 and the following years, 50 eggs were taken from the wild (Table 1); chicks hatched from them have formed the nucleus of the Patuxent flock. The main goals of the program were to maintain birds in captivity in case of catastrophic loss to the wild flock (48 birds in 1967), to produce offspring for release to the wild, to foster research on captives, and if possible to provide mates for unpaired Whooping Cranes in other institutions. Today there are over 120 Whooping Cranes in the world, and all of the above goals are being met. The program is helping in a dramatic way to provide a secure future for these magnificent birds. In this paper, I discuss some of the practical behavioral approaches to rearing, maintaining, and breeding Whoop-

TABLE 1. THE FATE OF ALL WHOOPING CRANE EGGS BROUGHT TO PATUXENT
FROM WOOD BUFFALO NATIONAL PARK, CANADA[a]

	Number of Eggs:		Number of Birds Lost in:	
Year	Taken	Hatched	First 6 Months	Adult Plumage
1967	6	6	2	2
1968	10	10	3	2
1969	10	7	2	1
1971	11	9	6	0
1974	13	9	5	0
Total	50	41	18	5

[a]In addition to birds hatched from these eggs, the Patuxent flock
includes a male found injured in Wood Buffalo National Park, a
female on loan to ICF, and 3 captive-produced birds.

ing Cranes that I helped develop at Patuxent from 1973 to 1977. Additional aspects of the program have been discussed by Carpenter et
al. (1976), Erickson (1975, 1976), and Kepler (1976).

REARING WHOOPING CRANE CHICKS

The Patuxent flock was derived from eggs taken from wild nests,
so the program was first concerned with hatching, housing, and rearing
young birds. Although Sandhill Cranes had been successfully raised
(Erickson, 1975), Whooping Cranes proved more difficult; of 23 Whooping Cranes lost in 11 years, 18 (78 percent) died within 6 months, the
majority in their first month (Table 1). Mortality stemmed primarily
from leg abnormalities and bacterial infection. Sandhill Cranes reared with or adjacent to Whooping Cranes failed to develop leg problems
and, although carrying the pathogens that killed Whooping Cranes,
rarely showed symptoms of disease. In 1976 we reared 3 healthy *G.
americana* x *G. canadensis tabida* hybrids without incident while a
single Whooping Crane suffered from enteritis, a rotated leg, and
attendant complications. This and many similar experiences with
Whooping Cranes and other species highlights one of the "rules" of
captive breeding programs: it is more difficult to breed and rear
endangered species than it is to breed and rear their closely related
non-endangered congeners.

Leg abnormalities appeared in chicks when rapid weight gains
placed excessive stress on their legs. . Too little food, however, increased their susceptibility to disease. Successful growth may depend
on a delicate balance between the quality and quantity of food and the

amount of leg-strengthening exercises. Other possible contributing factors include incubation temperature and humidity, hatching and rearing substrate, and stress from inter- and intra-specific aggression from penmates (*see* Erickson, 1975). One of my first concerns involved the disease and leg stress problems as they related to food consumption and exercise in crane chicks.

Initiation of Feeding in Crane Chicks

In 1974 we hatched 9 Whooping Cranes: 5 died within the first month, the other 4 became seriously ill. Although an excellent starter diet was available (Erickson, 1975), many chicks failed to recognize it as food. In the past these reluctant eaters had been routinely hand-fed with moist canned dog food. Increasing amounts of starter mash were mixed with the dog food until the chicks learned to feed from this mixture; they then transferred to starter mash alone. Although this system worked, there were 2 major problems. First, the chicks often failed to receive a well-balanced diet because: they ate too much dog food and not enough mash; the dog food stuck to their bills, making ingestion difficult; and the chicks waited for the keepers to feed them, ignoring available food even though hungry. Secondly, inter-chick aggression (when several chicks are raised together), positively correlated with hunger (Quale, 1976), resulted from the problems listed above, and also developed when chicks pecked at food adhering to each other's bills. Clearly we needed a new way to induce early feeding by chicks.

In the wild, adult cranes present to their chicks small food items held in the bill. This was a starting point for an experiment with Sandhill Cranes. In 1974, I selected 5 chicks less than 60 hours old and tested their responsiveness to colored dowels. Each chick was placed in a black box, and a randomized sequence of 7 differently colored dowels (12 mm diameter x 20 cm long) was presented to it at eye level. The number of pecks delivered at each dowel in a 30-second period was tallied, beginning with the first peck, which was not counted. Three-minute rest periods followed each test; rest and test periods alternated until all colors had been presented. The 5 chicks delivered 1,162 pecks in 11 tests (Figure 1). Although red evoked the greatest response, the results were biased because the chicks were taken from standard rearing pens in which water had been placed in red bowls (an attempt in 1975 to test Sandhill Cranes hatched and reared 24 hours in darkness failed because the chicks were unresponsive).

After this experiment, I used red dowels to test 11 additional Sandhill Cranes. Chicks less than 24 hours old were separated into 2 pens. In each group, the 3 first-hatched birds were presented with red dowels waved above, or slightly immersed in, crane starter mash. Dowels were initially held directly in front of the chicks and were moved toward food dishes when chicks began following them. All test chicks eagerly pecked the dowel, the force of their strokes carrying their bills into the mash, which they ingested; all chicks learned to feed in less than one hour. In each pen the last-hatched chicks—5 in all—were never exposed to hand-manipulated dowels. Dowels were placed upright in food dishes; all chicks learned to feed at their base,

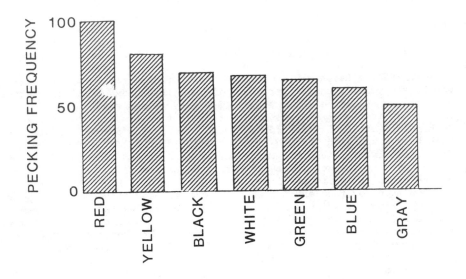

FIGURE 1. Color preferences, measured as pecking responses, of 5
    Sandhill Crane chicks less than 60 hours old. Total number of
    pecks was 1,162; number of pecks at red was 237 (= 100 on the
    graph).

stimulated by them and the feeding behavior of the other cranes.
This is now a standard procedure, both at Patuxent and at the
International Crane Foundation (ICF). Most cranes feed from the
dowel within 1 or 2 short training sessions, although Whooping Cranes
learn more slowly than Sandhill Cranes. Red dowels suspended slightly
above the food are more stimulatory than stationary ones and can be
swung to attract reluctant eaters. Thus, most chicks now ingest high
quality starter mash as soon as they are ready to feed (1 to 3 days
after hatching) and show decreased inter-chick aggression.
    Leg problems still occur with Whooping Cranes, but not Sandhill
Cranes, and although increased exercise has helped, it has not solved
them. At ICF, where chicks are reared singly, G. Archibald (*personal
communication*) discovered that their occasional leg abnormalities develop when chicks gain more than 20 percent of their body weight per
day: food is routinely withheld from these rapidly growing chicks. We
anticipate that leg difficulties will soon yield to further research
and to an integration of management techniques developed at Patuxent
and ICF.

MAINTAINING WHOOPING CRANES

Typically, cranes in most institutions are rendered flightless and housed in adjacent, open-topped pens, and at first Patuxent used this design for Sandhill Cranes (Erickson, 1975). Adjacent breeding pairs, however, fight through fences and may jump over them to attack neighboring birds. Carpenter et al. (1976) found that 30 percent of the 135 cases of Sandhill Crane mortality at Patuxent (1966 to 1975) resulted from trauma, mostly due to intraspecific aggression between adjacent pairs. Similarly, one third of the early losses at ICF resulted from this cause. It was imperative to redesign our facilities for rare cranes.

In late 1973, we built 4 large pens for Whooping Cranes. These facilities measure 17 x 55 m and contain a 17 x 17 m sub-unit in which the birds are held during the breeding season, when they are subjected to photoperiodic manipulation. All pairs are visually isolated but can hear, and are stimulated by, adjacent pairs. Three of the pens are further separated by walkways that decrease the opportunity for birds to jump a fence and enter an adjacent pen. The facilities provide more than adequate space for normal reproductive behavior, and in 1977, three of our 4 productive pairs lived in them.

In 1974 we developed a series of double-unit pens for Mississippi Sandhill Cranes (*G. canadensis pulla*). Each pen is divided into two 9 x 18 m compartments, only one of which is occupied at any given time. A row of such pens allows pairs to occupy a compartment flanked by empty units, thereby creating a visual territory, free of birds, 3 times as large as the unit occupied. Since using this design, there have been no losses caused by interpair aggression, and nervous behavior, evidenced by pacing along the fence, has been nearly eliminated. The empty compartments are ideal for introducing potential mates or crane chicks to adult pairs in adoption experiments. Each year all cranes are moved to their adjacent units, and this has greatly improved sanitation by limiting the accumulation of feces and spilled food. In 1976 four comparable pens were built for Whooping Cranes. Because Whooping Cranes require more space, each unit measured 15 x 18 m. Two pairs were moved into these units in late 1976.

Erickson (1975) has discussed the pen rotation system used for young, non-breeding birds, including the characteristics of group pens in which first-year birds reside until pair formation. While groups of Sandhill Cranes will form pairs when confined to relatively large, open pens, flocks of Whooping Cranes are more reluctant to do so and may form dominance hierarchies instead (Kepler, 1976). We now provide flocks of young Whooping Cranes with as many sources of food and water as there are potential pairs. In this way, pairs can form and defend resources without keeping other birds from food or water. Pairs or potential pairs are taken from these enclosures to breeding units when they are about 2 years old.

BREEDING WHOOPING CRANES

A successful breeding program for any species is critically

dependent upon providing compatible heterosexual pairs with adequate
food, space, and nesting requirements. This, in turn, depends upon a
thorough understanding of the species. How does one sex monomorphic
species; what constitutes compatibility; and what are the species'
essential requirements for food, shelter, and successful reproduction?
With Whooping Cranes, as with many other endangered species, success
is often the hard-won fruit of several seasons and the insights of
many biologists. It is still as much art as science, and patience is
an essential antidote to disappointment.

Behavioral Sexing

Whooping Cranes are monomorphic, and although males are normally
larger than females, measurements overlap; early attempts to sex the
species using physical characteristics were unsuccessful. In 1973, I
noticed that the 4 dominant Whooping Cranes in a hierarchy of 9 birds
produced a form of the "Unison Call" that was distinct, both visually
and vocally, from that given by the 5 subordinate individuals (Kepler,
1976). Since males of most species are dominant over females, this
suggested sexual diethism for the display, a supposition supported
further by the vocal behavior of Sandhill Cranes of known sex at Patuxent and by concurrent research on other crane species by Archibald
(1976). Thus, by late 1973, we had discovered a technique for sexing
Whooping Cranes that is 100 percent accurate. The adult form of this
call, described for Whooping Cranes and other crane species by Archibald (1976), is first given by birds about 18 months old and coincides
with an increase in aggressive behavior. Both sexes "Unison Call"
regularly by the time they are 2 years old, when pairs are selected
and placed in breeding pens.

Forming Compatible Pairs

In late 1973, I isolated 4 pairs from the flock of 9 adults and,
in late 1975, selected 2 more new pairs. These birds were all at
least 4 years old when placed together. In the fall of 1976, I formed a final 2 pairs from 4 birds hatched in 1974 and placed them in new
breeding facilities; they could become productive by 1979. Whenever
possible, pair members have shown attachments to each other when held
in a flock or share some characteristics that make their successful
reproduction probable. To date, members of each pair have originated
from different breeding territories in Wood Buffalo National Park.

Identifying heterosexual pairs had been achieved by late 1973,
but the Whooping Cranes soon provided us with new challenges. It is
not enough to place males and females together, even though they appear compatible, for there is enough individual variation that some
birds will not mate with their partners. Each bird must be treated as
an individual, and this requires long and constant observation to determine its idiosynchrasies and to identify and correct behavioral
problems when they develop. This has also been found in other crane
species (G. Archibald, *personal communication*) as well as with unre-
lated taxa such as the Peregrine Falcon (*Falco peregrinus*) (T. Cade,
personal communication). We identified dominance relationships and

sexual incompatibility as 2 important variables affecting reproductive performance in our Whooping Cranes. Since we are dealing with very small samples, several examples will illustrate their effects.

Dominance. A pair of Whooping Cranes hatched in 1967 had been held together for 8 years, yet no copulation attempts were observed, nor did the female (R-18) show normal reproductive behavior. She was not subordinate to her mate (R-19) and shared such typically male behaviors as defending their territory with high-intensity "Unison Calls." These birds had been penned with another male Whooping Crane (WT-271) for 27 days in 1968. W-271 had been dominant, and R-18 paired with him. R-19 was submissive to this pair. WT-271 died during a thunderstorm on 4 November 1968, and R-18 and R-19 remained together thereafter. It appears that R-18's dominance to R-19 during the 27-day period effectively inhibited their reproductive behavior during the entire 8 years. The female never gave the submissive postures necessary to induce copulation, although the birds thrived together, showing no overt aggression. We separated this pair after the 1975 breeding season, placing the female with another male, but she attacked him and had to be removed. Since we lacked other suitable males, we paired her on 10 February 1976 with "Crip", a large male at the San Antonio Zoo whose former mate had died on 16 June 1971. Our strategy was to encourage "Crip" to assume rapid dominance over R-18, so she was placed in his pen immediately after her transcontinental flight in a dim box. "Crip" asserted dominance, and we now hope that this aggressive female will become productive. Her mate, R-19, was placed with a 1971-hatched female late in 1975, and she produced eggs within 5 months.

Dominance can affect reproductive behavior in other ways. One pair selected from the flock of 9 birds was composed of the highest ranking male (RR) and the highest ranking female (YY). In their second breeding season (1975), they produced 3 eggs and have laid each year since, their breeding behavior enhanced by their dominant positions in the hierarchy. Although the other 3 pairs formed at the same time were held in identical pens, they did not breed in 1975 or 1976. The lowest ranking bird (YR), an excessively submissive female, showed no reproductive behavior when courted by her mate from 1974 to 1976. She was placed with a new male in July 1976 but still failed to develop normal courtship behavior; she may have been irreversibly affected by her 3 years as the subordinate flock member.

Sexual Incompatibility. The lowest ranked female (YR) had been paired to the second-ranked male (RY). He was one of our most sexually active males, courting his unresponsive mate every day during each breeding season. The female (YB) of another pair gave precopulatory displays to her totally uninterested mate, a 1971-hatched male with a deformed leg, more regularly than any other female. In July 1976 we exchanged females between the 2 pairs. YB immediately gave a "Wing-spreading Display" (*see* Masatomi and Kitagawa, 1975), a pre-copulatory posture, to appease her new mate, and they soon danced. In 1977, YB laid her first egg on 18 March, earlier than any other bird, including experienced breeders, and she produced 9 eggs, more than the combined Patuxent total for the previous 2 years. As expected, the reciprocal pair remained unproductive.

The Physical Environment

Each season 4 Whooping Crane pairs are exposed to photoperiods simulating conditions in Wood Buffalo National Park. Extra light is added before dawn to provide 16 hours of daylight, beginning in mid-February, and this is increased 3 percent per week until they receive 22 hours daily, equivalent to 21 June on the breeding grounds. Our first pair to breed in 1975 and 3 of our 4 producing pairs in 1977 received artificial light. Although we lack the data to state that photosimulation is necessary, pairs receiving light have laid earlier and produced more eggs (average of 5 per pair) than the single pair laying without light (average of 3.5 per pair). Photostimulated pairs lay earlier in the spring and have more time to produce clutches before the hot Maryland summer halts egg production.

Each pair produced eggs earlier in its second productive year than in its first, and the pair that began laying in 1975 had laid sooner each year (first egg dates, 1975-1977, were 18 April, 4 April, and 20 March, respectively), a phenomenon known in the wild for such diverse species as Kittiwake Gulls (*Rissa tridactyla*) (Coulson, 1966) and Blue-faced Boobies (*Sula dactylatra*) (Kepler, 1969).

Artificial Insemination

Although egg-laying pairs court regularly and attempt to mount, no successful copulations have been seen. The tenotomized males have trouble mounting and balancing, and the females, perhaps responding to this, prematurely abort copulation attempts by displaying aggresively, normal post-copulatory b avior. Because of this, all productive females are artificially inseminated twice weekly. Of 22 eggs laid in 1977, 12 (55 percent) are known to have been fertile. Artificially inseminated Sandhill Cranes at Patuxent average 80 percent fertility.

Manipulating Egg Production

Crane eggs are routinely collected when laid. In 1977, one Whooping Crane pair produced a total of 9 eggs in 5 clutches, and Sandhill Cranes have yielded up to 17 eggs per season. I wished to understand more about this indeterminate laying, so in 1976 conducted an experiment with Sandhill Cranes. I divided 22 producing pairs into 2 groups. Eggs were immediately removed from the controls, as in 1975, but they were taken from the experimentals only after a 2-egg clutch was completed (if only 1 egg was laid, it was collected 3 days after laying). The results failed to refute the null hypothesis of no differences between the groups, although the controls did lay more eggs (70 versus 59). However, if production per pair was compared between 1975 and 1976, the experimentals showed a significant reduction in egg production (81 to 54) while the controls did not (68 to 59). It thus remains the policy at Patuxent and ICF to collect all eggs daily.

DISCUSSION OF PATUXENT'S BREEDING PROGRAM

Whooping Cranes are long-lived birds with relatively slow reproductive development that apparently pair for life under natural conditions. Their primary territorial vocalization, the "Unison Call,
appears at age 18 to 24 months, but we have not obtained semen before
males are 4 years, nor eggs before females are 5. Although Sandhill
Cranes may rarely produce eggs when 2 years old, it is unlikely that
the more slowly-developing Whooping Cranes will lay fertile eggs before their fourth year. Thus, a captive program that forms a breeding
flock from eggs must expect to wait at least 5 years before regular
egg production can begin. In birds such as condors, this delay could
well exceed 10 years. Since endangered species programs are highly
visible and attract emotional attention, interested laymen should be
apprised of the anticipated biological delays inherent in species with
deferred maturity.

Egg production began in 1975 when a 7-year-old female laid 3 eggs
18 months after she had been paired. The number of pairs held, the
number breeding, and total egg production increased annually in the
following breeding seasons (Table 2). Our first eggs were placed
under wild Sandhill Cranes at Grays Lake National Wildlife Refuge, Idaho, in 1976 (*see* Drewien and Bizeau, Ch. 25, *this volume*). This cross-
fostering program will continue in future years since Patuxent's main
goal is to establish wild populations from the offspring of its captive
flock. Because egg and chick mortality are high at Gray's Lake (80
percent), Patuxent will continue to experiment with the release of
sub-adult cranes raised in captivity; releasing young Sandhill Cranes
reared in large enclosures by their parents has shown encouraging preliminary results.

In addition to the 9 pairs at Patuxent, 2 pairs are held elsewhere: R-18 was sent to San Antonio, and we loaned an additional female to ICF on 15 April 1976. Six days later she was joined by a

TABLE 2. DEVELOPMENT OF THE WHOOPING CRANE BREEDING PROGRAM AT
PATUXENT WILDLIFE RESEARCH CENTER

Year	No. of Pairs	No. of Breeding Pairs	No. of Eggs Produced	No. of Eggs Returned to the Wild[a]
1968-1973	1	0	0	0
1974	5	0	0	0
1975	7	1	3	0
1976	7	2	5	2
1977	9	4	22	14

[a]Eggs placed in wild Sandhill Crane nests at Grays Lake National
Wildlife Refuge.

bachelor male loaned to ICF from the Audubon Park Zoo, New Orleans. The female had become imprinted on humans at San Antonio and was unproductive at Patuxent. Archibald (*personal communication*) worked intensively with her, living in her pen for extended periods, and she produced her first egg in 1977. Because the male produced poor semen, Whooping Crane semen was flown to ICF from Patuxent to cover further eggs, but the female did not produce a second clutch.

In summary, there are now 11 pairs of captive Whooping Cranes in the world: 5 pairs produced 23 eggs in 1977, 40 percent of the world's production. For comparison, the 17 wild pairs laid 34 eggs. A total of 30 eggs, 16 from wild nests in Canada, 14 from Patuxent, were sent to the cross-fostering experiment at Grays Lake. In the 11 years since Patuxent's program began, the wild flock has increased from 48 to 69 birds and has shown no adverse population trends resulting from taking eggs from nests in Wood Buffalo National Park. This program, like its counterparts with the Peregrine Falcon, is demonstrating that captive propagation has a vital role to play in the management of some endangered species.

ACKNOWLEDGMENTS

I am grateful to the many members of the U.S. Fish and Wildlife Service and Canadian Wildlife Service who helped initiate and maintain the Whooping Crane project at Patuxent. Ray Erickson and his staff at Patuxent, particularly J. Carpenter, E. Cowan, G. Gee, J. Serafin, and B. Williams, have provided constant support. I also thank G. Archibald, R. Drewien, and E. Kuyt for their productive exchange of ideas and for demonstrating that biologists from different institutions and nations can work harmoniously together to help secure the future of an endangered bird.

LITERATURE CITED

Allen, R.P. 1952. The Whooping Crane. Nat. Aud. Soc. Res. Rep. 3. 246p.
Archibald, G.W. 1976. Crane taxonomy as revealed by the unison call, p. 225-251. *In* J.C. Lewis (ed.) Proc. Int. Crane Workshop. Oklahoma State Univ. Publ. & Printing, Stillwater, Oklahoma.
Blankinship, D.R. 1976. Studies of Whooping Cranes on the wintering grounds, p. 197-206. *In* J.C. Lewis (ed.) Proc. Int. Crane Workshop. Oklahoma State Univ. Publ. & Printing, Stillwater, Oklahoma.
Carpenter, J.W., L.N. Locke, and J.C. Miller. 1976. Mortality in captive Sandhill Cranes at the Patuxent Wildlife Research Center, 1966-1975, p. 268-283. *In* J.C. Lewis (ed.) Proc. Int. Crane Workshop. Oklahoma State Univ. Publ. & Printing, Stillwater, Oklahoma.
Coulson, J.C. 1966. The influence of the pair-bond and age on the breeding biology of the Kittiwake Gull *Rissa tridactyla*. J. Anim. Ecol. 35:269-279.
Erickson, R.C. 1975. Captive breeding of Whooping Cranes at the Patuxent Wildlife Research Center, p. 99-114. *In* R.D. Martin (ed.) Breeding endangered species in captivity. Academic Press, N.Y.

Erickson, R.C. 1976. Whooping Crane studies at the Patuxent Wildlife Research Center, p. 166-176. *In* J.C. Lewis (ed.) Proc. Int. Crane Workshop. Oklahoma State Univ. Publ. & Printing, Stillwater, Oklahoma.

Kepler, C.B. 1969. Breeding biology of the Blue-faced Booby *Sula dactylatra personata* on Green Island, Kure Atoll. Publ. Nuttall Orn. Club 8:1-97.

Kepler, C.B. 1976. Dominance and dominance-related behavior in the Whooping Crane, p. 177-196. *In* J.C. Lewis (ed.) Proc. Int. Crane Workshop. Oklahoma State Univ. Publ. & Printing, Stillwater, Oklahoma.

Kuyt, E. 1976. Whooping Cranes: the long road back. Nature Canada 5(2):2-9.

Masatomi, H. and T. Kitagawa. 1975. Bionomics and sociology of Tancho or the Japanese Crane, (*Grus japonensis*) II. Ethogram. J. Fac. Sci., Hokkaido Univ. Series VI. Zoology 19:834-878.

Novakowski, N.S. 1966. Whooping Crane population dynamics on the nesting grounds, Wood Buffalo National Park, Northwest Territories, Canada. Can. Wildlife Serv. Rep. Ser. 1:1-19.

Quale, T.R. 1976. Interchick aggression in Sandhill Cranes, p. 263-267. *In* J.C. Lewis (ed.) Proc. Int. Crane Workshop. Oklahoma State Univ. Publ. & Printing, Stillwater, Oklahoma.

28

Captive Propagation of Waterfowl

Janet Kear

Captive breeding programs for waterfowl have been in existence longer, have involved a wider variety of species and have had, probably, greater success than those for any other animal group. Indeed, at least four species were taken into captivity and domesticated in prehistoric times. Much management expertise has been accumulated, and avicultural techniques are well established. Because waterfowl breed readily even when pinioned, captivity does not necessitate a cage, and access to large areas of water and land is possible, thus giving conditions not too dissimilar to those in the wild.

Reintroduction of captive-bred waterfowl into the wild is also not new, as Allen (1975) makes clear in his useful review. Programs for rearing birds for release, mainly to produce a surplus for hunting, have been in operation since the 1920's. Introduction for the purpose of reinforcing the numbers of the wild species in decline seems to be as old. An early example involved the North American Wood Duck (*Aix sponsa*); Ripley (1973) claims that it was saved as a wild species by the release of 2,579 birds in the 1920's and 30's from Litchfield, Connecticut. Captive stock was imported from Belgium, and eventually, banding returns indicated that Litchfield birds had reached 15 states and Ontario and had formed the nuclei of breeding colonies from South Carolina to Massachusetts. In this case, the provision of a large number of artificial nest boxes was probably as important as the release of captive-bred ducks and a hunting ban from 1918 to 1941.

This short paper cannot review all current waterfowl projects, but will focus on recent observations made mostly at the Wildfowl Trust, which was founded by Sir Peter Scott at Slimbridge in 1946 and includes in its objectives saving rare species by captive breeding. Some 120 of the 147 species of waterfowl have bred there in the last 30 years (Table 1).

TABLE 1.   SPECIES OF WATERFOWL THAT HAVE BRED AT THE WILDFOWL TRUST

Anseranas semipalmata	*C. rubidiceps*	*A. clypeata*
Dendrocygna guttata	*C. picta*	*Calonetta leucophrys*
D. eytoni	*Cereopsis novae-hollandiae*	*Somateria mollissima*
D. arcuta	*Tachyeres brachypterus*	*S. spectabilis*
D. bicolor	*Lophonetta specularoides*	*S. fischeri*
D. arborea	*Anas specularis*	*Netta rufina*
D. viduata	*A. angustirostris*	*N. peposaca*
D. autumnalis	*A. capensis*	*N. erythrophthalma*
Coscoroba coscoroba	*A. punctata*	*Aythya valisineria*
Cygnus atratus	*A. versicolor*	*A. ferina*
C. olor	*A. erythrorhyncha*	*A. americana*
C. melanocoryphus	*A. bahamensis*	*A. nyroca*
C. columbianus	*A. georgica*	*A. baeri*
C. cygnus	*A. acuta*	*A. australis*
Anser cygnoides	*A. flavirostris*	*A. novae-seelandiae*
A. fabalis	*A. crecca*	*A. collaris*
A. brachyrhynchus	*A. formosa*	*A. fuligula*
A. albifrons	*A. falcata*	*A. affinis*
A. erythropus	*A. gibberifrons*	*A. marila*
A. anser	*A. castanea*	*Amazonetta brasiliensis*
A. indicus	*A. aucklandica*	*Chenonetta jubata*
A. canagicus	*A. platyrhynchos*	*Aix galericulata*
A. caerulescens	*A. wyvilliana*	*A. sponsa*
A. rossii	*A. rubipes*	*Sarkidiornis melanotos*
Branta canadensis	*A. poecilorhyncha*	*Pteronetta hartlaubi*
B. sandvicensis	*A. superciliosa*	*Cairina scutulata*
B. leucopsis	*A. luzonica*	*C. moschata*
B. bernicla	*A. undulata*	*Bucephala islandica*
B. ruficollis	*A. sparsa*	*B. clangula*
Tadorna ferruginea	*A. strepera*	*B. albeola*
T. cana	*A. penelope*	*Mergus albellus*
T. tadornoides	*A. americana*	*M. cucullatus*
T. variegata	*A. sibilatrix*	*M. serrator*
T. radjah	*A. discors*	*M. merganser*
T. tadorna	*A. cyanoptera*	*Oxyura leucocephala*
Alopochen aegyptiacus	*A. querquedula*	*O. jamaicensis*
Neochen jubatus	*A. platalea*	*O. vittata*
Cyanochen cyanopterus	*A. smithi*	*O. maccoa*
Chloephaga melanoptera		*Heteronetta atricapilla*
C. poliocephala		

RELATIONSHIP BETWEEN LATITUDE AND BREEDING SEASON

The dates, and hence photoperiods, on which captive waterfowl begin laying are fairly consistent from year to year and can be related directly to the latitude of the natural breeding range; temperate species start to breed before Arctic ones (Murton and Kear, 1973). This study of egg-laying seasons also reveals two kinds of responses. In one, egg-laying begins in the spring when daylengths reach a stimulatory level and continues until the corresponding daylength in fall is reached; that is, the breeding season extends symmetrically on either side of the summer solstice. Murton and Kear (*in press*) regard this as the "primitive-type" response, typical of those species that have evolved in or radiated from the tropics; examples include all whistling ducks (*Dendrocygna* sp.), the White-backed Duck (*Thalassornis leuconotus*), Hartlaub's Duck (*Cairina hartlaubi*) and the Ringed Teal (*Anas leucophrys*). The second kind of response is characterized by egg-laying occurring only during the first half of the year and ceasing before midsummer when the moult begins. Examples of this "temperate type" response are provided by the true geese, the sheldgeese, nearly all the shelducks, and Mandarin (*Aix galericulata*), Wood Duck, White-winged Wood Duck (*Cairina scutulata*), all *Aythya* and the Seaducks.

Knowledge that such differences occur is useful, not only because it contributes to our understanding of the evolution of breeding cycles and zoogeography, but because it suggests that the aviculturist can advance and extend the laying seasons of certain species by manipulating the photoperiods they receive. It seems sensible to extend the photoperiods of high Arctic birds that seldom breed in temperate-zone zoos. It may be no coincidence that, so far, all successful waterfowl introductions of captive-bred birds have involved fairly low latitude breeders (*see* Kear, 1975): even the Aleutian Canada Goose (*Branta canadensis leucopareia*) comes from no further north than 52°32'N (i.e., from Buldir Island), roughly the same latitude as Slimbridge.

RELATIONSHIP BETWEEN LATITUDE AND GROWTH RATES OF YOUNG WATERFOWL

Latitude will also effect the development of young birds. Wurdinger (1975) has shown how the rate of growth of various captive geese, kept under identical rearing conditions, is species-specific and correlated with the latitude of origin, in the same way as are the egg-laying cycles of these same geese (Murton and Kear, 1973). In general, waterfowl from the tropics grow slower than those from temperate zones, while those from polar regions grow fastest of all. The significance of this to the aviculturist is that it is possible to "overfeed" the naturally slow growing ones with modern high-protein/high-energy commercial diets. Bandy legs and slipped wings are quite frequently seen in young captive waterfowl from low latitudes given illumination at night, little exercise and abundant food (Kear, 1973).

RELATIONSHIP BETWEEN LIGHT INTENSITY AND BREEDING

The actual light intensity may be important also. The rare, forest-living White-winged Wood Duck appears not to breed on open ponds but needs to have light levels reduced in a shady pen before it will display and nest (Mackenzie and Kear, 1976).

NESTING SITES USED BY CAPTIVE WATERFOWL

Successful avicultural techniques are frequently established from a study of the bird in the wild. For instance, many female stifftails (*Oxyura* sp.) lay in the abandoned nests of rails such as coots (*Fulica* sp.), and it was only after the provision of such empty coot nests that 3 stifftail species laid for the first time in captivity at Slimbridge (*see* Matthews and Evans, 1974). The Black-headed Duck (*Heteronetta atricapilla*) does not build its own nest at all and needs the presence of "active" nests of other birds. Those at Slimbridge laid in 1977--again for the first time in captivity--in the nests of Rosybills (*Aythya peposaca*), a common sympatric South American species (M.R. Lubbock, *personal communication*).

It is normal practice in captivity for waterfowl eggs to be removed from the nest and incubated and hatched elsewhere. This ensures their safety from predators, guards against desertion, and encourages the production of repeat clutches--birds with extended "primitive-type" egg-laying seasons may produce as many as 5. But, the captive bird will not distinguish between the loss of its eggs to humans and true predation. In studies of wild waterfowl, it is an almost invariable finding that a female does not return to renest at a site from which she has lost her eggs. In a pen of limited size, therefore, the captive female may give up laying if her eggs are continually removed from all the obvious nesting sites. This applies particularly to swans and geese for which suitable sites in any pen are limited. Therefore, in the case of the Whistling Swan (*Cygnus c. columbianus*) which laid for the first time at Slimbridge in 1976, the bird was allowed to hatch and rear 1 of the 2 fertile eggs. In 1977, she laid in the same nest from which the eggs were removed; she then renested at the far end of the pen and was allowed to hatch this second clutch. Similarly in 1976, a breeding female of yet another swan species (*Coscoroba coscoroba*) was given a single Barnacle Goose (*Branta leucoptera*) egg to rear--which she did without trouble. In 1977, she laid two clutches in the same pen and successfully reared the second. The same principle was applied to the wild-caught White-headed Duck (*Oxyura leucocephala*). The first bird to lay in 1974 was allowed to hatch one of her own eggs (in an old coot nest), and the rest were artificially reared. Interestingly, a number of these second generation incubator-hatched females laid their eggs, not in coot nests, but in small boxes on the ground. This suggests some early imprinting on the hatching site may have occurred; that is, the first stifftails to lay may themselves have been hatched in coot nests.

INCUBATION AND HATCHING OF EGGS FROM CAPTIVE WATERFOWL

In our experience, no commercial incubator gives reliably good results with waterfowl eggs; in particular, the largest species and those with long incubation periods are difficult to incubate artificially. A usual procedure at the Wildfowl Turst is to put eggs under a broody domestic hen for the first 10 days, and then to complete the process in an incubator. The United Kingdom Science Research Council has for the last 3 years been financing an investigation of the natural nest. A fiberglass egg has been developed that contains electronic sensors capable of monitoring the position and temperature at six points on the shell, the humidity at the blunt pole, and the incidence of light (i.e., whether the incubating parent is sitting or standing) and radios this information to a recorder up to 1 km away. First results (P.W. Howey, personal communication) have shown 2 features in which artificial and natural incubation differ: initially, the female brings the egg to incubating temperature only slowly over the first 24 hours, and there is as much as 6-7°C temperature gradient between the top and bottom of a swan or goose egg.

I have already mentioned the value to the parent of hatching young if she is to continue to produce eggs during her captive life. It is probable that parent-reared offspring also have advantages, especially if birds are intended for release, since parent-imprinting will produce an animal that behaves more "naturally" than a hand-reared one, and the competition imposed by the presence of brothers and sisters tends to eliminate any weak specimens.

INBREEDING CAPTIVE WATERFOWL POPULATIONS

Genetic "weakness" due to inbreeding is a likely problem in any species that is rare and reduced in numbers. It seems impossible to distinguish, without records kept over many years, those that are harbouring deleterious recessive genes--which inbreeding will manifest--and those that are not. The Laysan Teal (*Anas platyrhynchos laysanensis*) and New Zealand Scaup (*Aythya novaeseelandiae*) have both bred successfully at the Wildfowl Trust for many generations after starting with a tiny number of "founder" individuals. Other species-- the Hawaiian Goose (*Branta sandvicensis*) and the New Zealand Brown Teal (*Anas aucklandica*), for instance--have shown a loss of viability in a similar period of time; in particular, male infertility has become common. Outbreeding with wild-taken birds (usually collected as a clutch of eggs, hatched and hand-reared in captivity) may be essential for long-term maintenance of these species. The Hawaiian Goose project in England, which started with 3 already inbred birds, has had 4 new wild males introduced during the 26 years and 10 generations that the scheme has been running. Individual male breeding performance was found to be associated with the numbers and mobility of their sperm. Infertile ganders had few sperm, many of which were damaged and immobile. Collection and examination of semen could be a useful technique in other propagation projects.

DISEASE IN CAPTIVE WATERFOWL POPULATIONS

Captivity in temperate zoos may be conducive to high levels of disease in pinioned waterfowl. The necessity for reducing light levels for the White-winged Wood Duck has already been mentioned; unfortunately, the species is particularly susceptible to avian tuberculosis, and this bacillus is resistant to most treatments except ultra-violet radiation, normally introduced through sunlight (Mackenzie and Kear, 1976). The two requirements seem incompatible, and over 85 percent of our White-winged Wood Ducks die of tuberculosis.

Other disease problems arise from the fact that waterfowl in general, but particularly salt-water ducks, are susceptible to fungal infections, such as aspergillosis and candidiasis. A new prophylactic drug which contains mycostatin may be effective against aspergillosis and is being investigated as a fumigant for young birds. We have so far established that is is ineffective once a bird has started showing clinical symptoms of aspergillosis. We are also currently testing 2 types of antibiotic navel spray that may help prevent yolk-sac infections in newly-hatched--especially incubator-hatched--young. Both Aureomycin and Chloromycetin have proven successful for this purpose.

Two further disease conditions apparently occur only when susceptible waterfowl are moved from their natural environment to temperate, low-latitude rural zoos. Over a dozen Hawaiian Geese bred in England--but so far no other waterfowl species--have suffered from a debilitating condition that appears to be avian pox (Kear and Brown, 1976; Kear, 1977). It is suggested that few endemic Hawaiian birds have any resistance to pox (Warner, 1968) and that since the introduction of continental songbirds and blood-sucking mosquitoes, many native birds are restricted to altitudes above which the mosquito fails to survive. Are English mosquitoes spreading pox to these geese? It does seem possible.

Finally, *Cladosporum herbarum*, a common "sooty mould" on the leaves of trees attacked by green-flies, has been found to act as a pathogen on the plumage of captive flamingos of Andean origin (Beer and Kear, 1973). The fungus forms fruiting bodies within the feather and weakens the structure so that the outer portion breaks off. The mould is slow growing, and its development ceases at 30°C. Because of this, only the flamingo's outer feathers away from its body heat are affected. The scapulars of a captive flock can, however, be totally frayed, and the birds become wet and dingy. No other waterfowl have been affected by this condition, perhaps because their preen gland oil is fungistatic, but obviously, flamingos originating from the windswept, treeless Andes, have no similar resistance.

ACKNOWLEDGMENTS

I am grateful to S.E.M. Goodall for help in the preparation of this paper, and to M.R. Lubbock and P.W. Howey for use of their unpublished information.

LITERATURE CITED

Allen, J.W. 1975. Introduction of Max McGraw Wildlife Foundation mallard ducks into Oklahoma and evaluation of their survival and adaption. Unpublished Doctor of Ed. thesis, Oklahoma State U.

Beer, J.W. and J. Kear. 1973. Fungal infections of the plumage in flamingos. Aviculture Mag. 79:163-164.

Kear, J. 1973. Notes on the nutrition of young waterfowl with special reference to slipped wing. Int. Zoo Yearbook 13:97-100.

Kear, J. 1975. Breeding endangered waterfowl as an aid to their survival, p. 43-60. *In* R.D. Martin (ed.) Breeding Endangered Species in Captivity. Academic Press, New York. 420p.

Kear, J. 1977. The problems of breeding endangered species in captivity. Int. Zoo Yearbook 17:5-14.

Kear, J. and M. Brown. 1976. A pox-like condition in the Hawaiian Goose. Int. Zoo Yearbook 16:133-134.

Mackenzie, M.J.S. and J. Kear. 1976. The white-winged wood duck. Wildfowl 27:5-17.

Matthews, G.V.T. and M.E. Evans. 1974. On the behavior of the white-headed duck with especial reference to breeding. Wildfowl 25:56-66.

Murton, R.K. and J. Kear. 1973. The nature and evolution of the photoperiodic control of reproduction in certain wildfowl (Anatidae). J. Reprod. Fert. (Suppl.) 19:67-84.

Murton, R.K. and J. Kear. 1978. Photoperiodism in waterfowl: phasing of breeding cycles and zoogeography. J. Zool. (*in press*).

Ripley, D.S. 1973. Saving the wood duck *Aix sponsa* through captive breeding. Int. Zoo Yearbook 13:55-58.

Warner, R.E. 1968. The role of introduced diseases in the extinction of the endemic Hawaiian avifauna. Condor 70:101-20.

Wurdinger, I. 1975. Vergleichend morphologische Untersuchungen zur Jugendentwidklung von *Ander-* und *Branta-* Arten. J. Orn., Lpz. 116:65-86.

29

What Makes Peregrine Falcons Breed in Captivity?

Tom J. Cade and Richard W. Fyfe

What makes Peregrine Falcons (*Falco peregrinus*) breed in captivity? One of our teenage sons gave a quick answer: "Falcon breeders do!" In fact, his answer may not be far from the best that we can offer. To put the question in a more analyzable form: Why do some Peregrine Falcons breed in captivity, while others do not? That is an important practical question for the falcon breeder, because less than half of all the Peregrine Falcons that have been paired for propagation have reproduced successfully by their own devices. It also has some interesting implications for theories about how factors associated with captivity modify the normal functions of a wild bird. When we began our work on propagating these falcons, we had expected that by comparing the treatment of Peregrine Falcons that reproduce successfully in captivity with the treatment of those that do not we would eventually be able to identify a set of conditions best designed to promote reproduction. After 7 years, we are somewhat embarrassed to have to confess that we still do not know for sure what does make Peregrine Falcons breed in captivity; but we have some ideas.

Our purpose here is to consider some variables that may influence the probability that a Peregrine Falcon will breed in captivity. Since we feel the most important of these variables are associated with the "psycho-physiological condition" of the birds themselves, we pay particular attention to the variations in how the birds have been handled and treated prior to breeding age or to pair-formation. The effects of such variations have to be evaluated, however, in the larger context of a comparison between the methods and results of our 2 breeding programs, the one headquartered at Cornell University and called The Peregrine Fund, and the other operated by the Canadian Wildlife Service (CWS) at Camp Wainwright, Alberta.

Such a comparison also offers the opportunity to evaluate the capability of large institutional operations to produce enough Peregrine Falcons for significant restoration of wild populations.

Both of our programs and facilities have been well described elsewhere (Cade and Temple, 1977; Cade et al. *in press*; Fyfe, 1975; Fyfe, 1976), and we only need to call attention to certain differences that may have a bearing on our results in breeding Peregrine Falcons. Briefly, both programs started in 1970. Today the Peregrine Fund, Incorporated has lofts located not only at Cornell University, but also in Pennsylvania, Colorado, and New Mexico, with a total capacity for housing about 80 pairs of falcons. We currently have more than 130 Peregrine Falcons in these facilities, including both wild-caught and captive-produced individuals. The Canadian program began in temporary quarters located on Fyfe's farm near Edmonton and moved into its present facilities in 1973. The Canadian facility has a capacity to house more than 36 pairs of raptors, and currently there are 27 pens each with a pair of Peregrine Falcons.

The CWS facility is located almost at 53° N latitude, in a region that experiences severely cold subarctic winters and a relatively short breeding season, whereas the Peregrine Fund facilities are located between latitudes of 43° and 35° N, in regions where winters are less severe and suitable conditions for initiating breeding extend from late February into June. These climatic and geographic differences have dictated certain differences in methods and management. For example, in Canada the mates are separated during severe winters, primarily to avoid problems of competition for food, while mates usually remain together throughout the year in the Peregrine Fund program. Because of the longer breeding season in the more southern latitudes, egg production is usually increased by the removal of completed clutches, whereas in the Canadian program it has proved to be more productive to extend the first clutch by the removal of individual eggs as each is laid.

Housing for the breeding pairs is radically different between the two programs. The Canadian facility consists of outdoor pens, most of which are walled in with open tops by snow fencing; the basic unit for a pair of Peregrine Falcons measures 5 x 10 x 5 m high. The Peregrine Fund facilities consist largely of enclosed chambers with only one end open to the outside; a majority of the units for a breeding pair measure 3 x 6 m in area and range from 4.3 to 5.5 m high. Falcons in the Canadian program only experience the natural cycle of photoperiodic changes at the Wainwright latitude, whereas some pairs in the Peregrine Fund program have been subjected to artificially lengthened days in the late winter and spring, particularly for pairs originating from boreal and arctic latitudes (*see* Weaver and Cade, 1974).

Cade and Temple (1977) have already analyzed some results of earlier attempts to propagate Peregrine Falcons, and one of their conclusions is that falcons taken into captivity as nestlings are much more likely to reproduce as adults than are wild falcons trapped as flying immatures or adults. From a total of 27 pairs in which one or both mates had been taken as a post-nestling, only 2 pairs had been successful in producing fertile eggs and young up to 1975; in both cases, one of the mates had been taken as a nestling. In only one case was the wild-caught bird a fully adult male (Waller, 1962); the other case involves Jim Enderson's Peregrine Falcon, "Lil," which was trapped in her first August, only about 2 months out of the nest. She began laying in her eighth year, and during 8 years of reproduction she has laid a total of 95 eggs, at least 27 of which have been fertile from natural mating. More recently the CWS program has had experience with 2 males captured in the immediate post-nestling period while still at the aerie and still dependent upon their parents for food; both have proved to be first-rate mates in captivity. These 3 Peregrine Falcons captured as flying "juveniles" have responded reproductively in captivity more like birds taken as nestlings, and they raise an interesting question about how old a wild Peregrine Falcon has to be before it becomes difficult to breed in confinement. The determining period must be prior to fall migration, for Peregrine Falcons caught in passage have proved to be very difficult.

Three additional cases of successful reproduction in captivity by wild-caught adult and passage Peregrine Falcons are now known. In Australia, an injured adult male has fertilized 2 clutches of eggs from a 3-year old female, presumably taken as a nestling (Robinson, 1977), and the Melbourne Zoo has a pair of injured adults that successfully produced 3 young in 1976 while on public display (C.M. White, *personal communication*). A very tame and constantly handled pair of passage Peregrine Falcons also produced young by natural mating in Italy last year (F. Pratesi, *personal communication*). It may be significant that all successfully reproducing birds caught as wild adults or on passage have either been injured in some way and, in a sense, forced to accept captivity or have been exceptionally tame birds conditioned to constant, close contact with man.

Not all Peregrine Falcons taken as nestlings breed in captivity either. In some cases improper social imprinting or other early conditioning experiences associated with human keepers are certainly involved. In other cases, in which the young falcons have been reared with a minimum of contact with human beings, the birds appear to be unduly nervous or stressed by confinement, especially during the breeding season, and they may be experiencing some sort of interference in the normal functioning of their sex hormones from abnormally high, stress-induced titers of adrenal cortical steroids (Scharrer, 1966). There must be a wide range of variations in the psychophysiological condition of captive Peregrine Falcons from the completely tame, human-imprinted falcon that fully accepts its handler as a social companion and is never stressed by captivity, to the unhandled, untamed bird that only reacts toward human beings with fear and never accepts confinement with sufficient equanimity to permit normal function of its endocrine system. Somewhere between these extremes of behavior and physiology lies a narrower range of internal conditions within which successful reproduction can occur between conspecific mates in captivity.

The task of the falcon breeder is to discover those environmental conditions and social circumstances that promote the development of sexual competence in his birds. In Tables 1 and 2, for males and females, respectively, we present some results that attempt to identify variables of captive life that either increase or decrease the probability of successful mating and reproduction in our Peregrine Falcons.

Continuing our consideration of age as a variable, it is obvious

TABLE 1. SEXUAL PERFORMANCE OF MALE PEREGRINE FALCONS IN RELATION TO VARIABLES IN THEIR CAPTIVE LIFE

Variable of Captivity	No. of Breeders		No. of Non-breeders		No. that Mate and/or Court with Man	
	Peregrine Fund	CWS	Peregrine Fund	CWS	Peregrine Fund	CWS
1. Taken as Downy Chick	13	0	8	0	1	0
2. Taken as Feathered Nestling	1	5	3	2	0	0
3. Taken as Flying Juvenile	0	2	0	2	0	0
4. Produced in Captivity	0	0	9	1	2	0
5. Not Handled or Tamed after Rearing	3	7	13(7)[a]	4(1)	0	0
6. Handled and Tamed Initially	11	0	6(2)	2	3(2)	0
7. Raised in Brood by Adults	1	5	9(7)	2(1)	0	0
8. Raised in Brood by Man	13[b]	2[c]	8	3[c]	0	0
9. Isolated from Conspecifics until after Fledging	0	0	3(2)	0	3(2)	0
10. Housed with Mate or Con-specific before Breeding	14	7	19(9)	5(1)	(2)	0
11. Separated from Conspecifics one or more Years	0	0	1	0	1	0
Total Number	14	7	20(9)	5(1)	3(2)	0

[a]Parenthetical numbers give subtotals for captive-produced birds.
[b]Includes two fed by a puppet.
[c]Minimum contact with man; never hand-fed.

from Tables 1 and 2 that the Peregrine Fund program has dealt mainly
with downy nestlings taken from hatching up to about 3 weeks of age,
while the CWS program has mainly involved work with older birds taken
as feathered nestlings or flying juveniles from 4 to 6 or more weeks
old. Both downy young and feathered nestlings--males and females--can
develop into reproductively competent adults. In the Peregrine Fund
sample of males, omitting one that was deliberately imprinted on man,
13 out of 21 downy young became capable of copulation with females and
fertilizing their eggs, while only one out of 4 feathered nestlings
has done so. By contrast, in the CWS program, 7 out of 11 advanced
juvenile males have become fully competent breeders. In the Peregrine
Fund sample of 25 females, taken as downies, 12 copulate and produce
fertile eggs, 9 others lay eggs regularly in the presence of a mate
and probably would copulate with a competent male, while only 4 are
non-layers. One is imprinted on humans and lays eggs in the absence
of a conspecific mate. The CWS program also has 2 females taken as
downies that copulate and lay fertile eggs. None of 5 feathered
nestlings copulate as adults in the Peregrine Fund program, but 3 of
them do lay eggs, and it is likely that at least these 3 would mate
with the right males. Again, the Canadian experience is different.
Four out of 9 females copulate and lay fertile eggs, and 4 others lay
in the presence of a mate. Only one is nonproductive. Differences
in the way our birds have been handled, or differences in the size and
other physical variables of our breeding units, may account for our
different results with birds taken as feathered nestlings. While we
can conclude that no age of removal from the wild, from the day of
hatching to flying juvenile, precludes the development of full sexual
performance in captivity, we still cannot identify an optimum age for
removal that results in the highest percentage of sexually competent
birds.

Also, it is too soon to be certain about the effects on breeding
of factors that may be intrinsic to our F_1 generation of Peregrine
Falcons produced in captivity because the oldest are only 4 years old,
barely of breeding age. Most of our captive-produced falcons have
been treated the same way in our 2 programs: handled to a minimum
extent by humans, fledged in the chambers with parent falcons, and
housed during the first year or more of life in groups of all males or
all females before pairing. Table 3 compares the age of first breeding in captivity for wild-caught Peregrine Falcons and captive-produced ones. Wild-caught males typically come into breeding condition
in captivity at 3 to 4 years of age. None of 10 four-year old males
produced in captivity has copulated and fertilized eggs naturally,
although we have obtained viable semen from most of them for artificial insemination. The CWS program does have one male, hatched in
captivity from a wild egg, that mated at 4 years; also John Campbell (*personal communication*) in Alberta has a pair of F_1 Peregrine
Falcons copulating at 3 years of age. These males are either slower
to mature sexually than their wild-caught counterparts, or else their
treatment in captivity has not been conducive to sexual development.
Only time will give the answer.

The females present a rather different picture. The wild-caught
ones may begin laying as early as 2 years but more usually at 3 or 4

TABLE 2.   SEXUAL PERFORMANCE OF FEMALE PEREGRINE FALCONS IN RELATION
            FEMALES FOUR OR MORE YEARS OLD)

Type of Sexual Performance and Program	No. Taken as Downy Chicks	No. Taken as Feathered Nestlings	Produced in Captivity	No. Not Handled or Tamed
1. Courts with Male				
Peregrine Fund	14	4	9	14(9)[a]
CWS	2	8	3	11(3)
2. Solicits Copulation				
Peregrine Fund	13	3	4	8(4)
CWS	2	6	2	9(2)
3. Lays Fertile Eggs after Copulating				
Peregrine Fund	12	0	1	2(1)
CWS	2	4	1	7(1)
4. Lays Eggs (some Fertile by A.I.)				
Peregrine Fund	9	3	8	6(4)
CWS	0	4	2	5(2)
5. Lays without con- specific Mate				
Peregrine Fund	1[b]	0	1	0
CWS	1	1	0	1
6. Non-laying				
Peregrine Fund	4	2	4	8(4)
CWS	0	1	0	0
7. Incubate Normally				
Peregrine Fund	14	3	3	7(3)
CWS	2	7	3	11(3)
8. Rears Young				
Peregrine Fund	10	3	0	2
CWS	2	6	1	7(1)
9. Mates and/or courts with human beings				
Peregrine Fund	1	0	1	0
CWS	0	0	0	0

[a]Parenthetical numbers give subtotals for captive-produced birds.
[b]First clutch only; subsequently this bird has laid with a mate.

TO VARIABLES OF CAPTIVITY (INCLUDES ALL LAYING FEMALES AND OTHER

Handled and Tamed	Raised by Adults	Raised by Humans	Isolated from Conspecifics Until Flying	With Con-specific prior to Breeding	Total Number of Birds
13	(9)	17	1	27(9)	27(9)
2	6(3)	4	3	12(3)	13(3)
13	(4)	15	1	20(4)	20(4)
0	4(2)	3	2	9(2)	9(2)
10	(1)	12	0	13(1)	13(1)
0	2(1)	4	1	7(1)	7(1)
10(2)	(5)	10	1	19(7)	20(8)
1	4(2)	1	3(1)	6(2)	6(2)
2(1)	0	0	2(1)	2(1)	2(1)
1	1	1	0	2	2
5	4	4	1	8(4)	10
1	0	0	1	0	1
13	(3)	16	1	20(3)	20(3)
1	5(3)	4	3	11(3)	12(3)
8	0	11	1	12	13
1	4(1)	4	2	8(1)	9(1)
2(1)	0	0	2(1)	2(1)	2(1)
0	0	0	0	0	0

TABLE 3.   AGE OF FIRST COMPLETE REPRODUCTIVE PERFORMANCE BY CAPTIVE
PEREGRINE FALCONS FROM DIFFERENT SOURCES

Behavior and Background of Birds	Age in Years							
	2	3	4	5	6	7	8	9
1. First Copulation by Males								
No. Wild-caught	0	5	9[a]	3[b]	2	3	0	0
No. Captive-produced	0	0	0	-	-	-	-	-
2. First Egg-laying by Females								
No. Wild-caught	2	10	12	4	1	0	0	1
No. Captive-produced	4	6	0[c]	-	-	-	-	-

[a]Ten potential birds are not breeding.
[b]Dashes indicate no birds of that age available for comparison.
[c]Four potential birds are not breeding.

years of age. Four captive-produced birds began laying in their
second year, and 6 in their third year; but none of 4 potential females laid in their fourth year, possibly because of inadequate stim-
ulation from their mates. As indicated in Table 2, so far only 2 of
these females have produced fertile eggs from copulation with their
mates, but this low figure results primarily from the incompetence of
the males.

Because of concerns expressed about improper imprinting in the
early 1970's, we devised various ways of rearing nestlings with a
minimum amount of social contact with human beings (Fyfe, 1976). It
seems increasingly clear, however, that serious imprinting on humans
only occurs when young falcons are reared in isolation from conspecifics up to flying age and beyond. The varying degrees and expressions
of aberrant sexual behavior in adult life are determined by the
bird's subsequent history. Falcons that are not handled in later life
and are left alone much of the time usually do not respond sexually
either to conspecifics or man, or do so incompletely. Others that
have close association with a conspecific soon after an early period
of rearing in isolation may show some degree of sexual response to
both conspecifics and to man in later life, and a few become reproductively competent with a conspecific mate, although usually continuing to show response to man as well. Fully developed sexual responses
to a human companion usually depend upon continued close contacts and
handling over the years with the human acting as a surrogate mate during the breeding season.

There is much current interest in the use of birds imprinted on
man for the captive propagation of endangered species (Gee and Temple,
1978). The "cooperative method" of artificial insemination (Berry,

1972) has been used with both imprinted male and female Peregrine Falcons; however, there is not much advantage in using imprinted females, since most female Peregrine Falcons will lay eggs in captivity and, if necessary, can be artificially inseminated by the standard poultry technique of everting the oviduct through the cloaca and mechanically injecting a quantity of semen directly into the genital tract. Males are different. Obtaining good quantities of high quality semen by the massage technique used with poultry is often difficult. As Grier (1973) showed with Golden Eagles (*Aquila chrysaetos*), the advantages of obtaining semen from an imprinted male that copulates with a human companion are: the large volume of high quality semen produced per ejaculate, and the ability to obtain daily or twice daily samples over an extended period of time. One of Jim Enderson's male Peregrine Falcons at the Colorado facility of the Peregrine Fund is an imprinted bird and has been trained to copulate with a special hat. This bird remained in reproductive condition for 3 months this year and provided the semen for many artificial inseminations. Since so many of our laying females lack competent males, artificial insemination is necessary to fertilize their eggs; it is well worth the effort to keep a few imprinted males in each breeding program to service these females.

Further examination of the figures in Tables 1 and 2 shows that a wide range of different methods of rearing and handling young falcons prior to pairing can result in the development of birds that reproduce successfully, but the same methods also result in failure for others. The 8 best breeding males in the Peregrine Fund program can be characterized in the following way: 7 were taken as downy young, one as a feathered nestling; all were reared in a brood by human beings; all were handled and tamed initially, and some were flown in falconry one or more years; all were kept with conspecifics or mates prior to breeding age. By contrast, 6 of the 7 copulating males in the Canadian program share the following features: 4 were taken as feathered nestlings, 2 as flying juveniles; none were tamed or handled after rearing; 5 were raised in a brood with adult falcons, 2 were raised in a brood by humans; all were housed for 2 years with other males prior to pairing. The 13 most productive females in the Peregrine Fund program can be described as follows: one was taken as a flying juvenile; the others were all taken as downy young; all were handled and tamed initially, and some were flown in falconry for one or more years; 11 were raised in broods by humans, one by wild adults, and one was reared in isolation from conspecifics from about two and a half weeks old to flying but was in sight of other Peregrine Falcons after that time; all were housed with a mate or conspecific or were tethered in sight of other Peregrine Falcons prior to breeding age. Of the 7 best females in the Canadian program, 6 were taken as feathered nestlings, one as a downy; none were handled or tamed after rearing; 2 were raised in a brood by humans but with minimum contact with the human feeder; and 2 were raised in a brood with adults; all were housed in groups with other females prior to pairing. Obviously there is more than one way to rear Peregrine Falcons for breeding in captivity!

The one requirement that seems most necessary for the development of full reproductive competence in captivity is close association with

TABLE 4. SUMMARY OF REPRODUCTION BY PEREGRINE FALCONS IN CAPTIVE BREEDING PROGRAMS

Reproductive Variable	The Peregrine Fund Program					Canadian Wildlife Service		
	1973	1974	1975	1976	1977	1975	1976	1977
Number of Laying Females	4	6	11	25	29	8	9	10
Total Eggs Laid	41	59	109	191	239	72	100	106
Number of Fertile Eggs	26	34	44	112	139	28	52	51
Number of Eggs Hatched	22	24	27	83	111	19	43	41
Number of Young Raised	20	23	26	69	91	18	41	38
Total Eggs/Laying Females	10.0	9.8	9.9	7.6	8.2	9.0	11.1	10.6
Fertile Eggs/Laying Females	6.5	5.7	4.0	4.5	4.8	3.5	5.8	5.1
Young Raised/Laying Females	5.0	3.8	2.4	2.8	3.1	2.3	4.6	3.8

siblings during nestling life and possibly beyond. Whether reared by
adult falcons or by human beings, such birds are more likely to mate
successfully than falcons which are reared in isolation from conspecifics or which have minimum contacts in early life with members of
their own species.

Table 4 shows the history of production in our breeding programs.
The total number of young Peregrine Falcons produced has increased
steadily each year but not quite at the rate first predicted (Cade,
1973). Despite the fact that we can increase the number of eggs laid
per female to an average of about 10 per year by pulling eggs as they
are laid or by removing clutches, it has proved difficult to obtain
a rate of fertilization higher than about 50 percent. There are 2
reasons. We have more females that have come into laying condition
than we have males that copulate; and artificial insemination is not
as effective in fertilizing falcon eggs as natural mating is. Consequently, we have not been able to sustain the rate of 5 young produced per laying female that we achieved the first year. Even so,
the production of sufficient numbers of domestically raised falcons
will not be a limiting factor on recovery programs for the Peregrine
Falcon in North America, so long as support to carry on with mass
breeding continues to be forthcoming.

The progagation of falcons remains an art. Whether it will ever
achieve the status of a science is doubtful, although much interesting scientific information accumulates as a result of breeding falcons
in captivity. After 7 years of working with these birds, we have come
to the conclusion that propagating Peregrine Falcons will never become
easy or routine. Each pair is a special case, requiring much trial
and error experimentation and intuitive insight by the breeder to
bring the mates into reproductive condition. All these procedures are
time consuming and laborious, and consequently the propagation of
falcons on a large scale will always be a costly undertaking.

Dillon Ripley in his foreward to David Zimmerman's book *To Save
A Bird in Peril* (Zimmerman, 1975) has identified the essential elements
in the success of our breeding programs. They relate to people--to
"green thumb" people, as Ripley calls them--"who have an innate skill
which probably can never be learned and certainly has nothing to do
with the possession of a higher educational degree." And finally, "A
sense of kinship with nature and a single-mindedness of purpose appear
to be the touchstones of success in this work." We have been privi-
leged to have working with us a number of people who have these attributes: Jim Weaver, Phil Trefry, and Bill Burnham come most immediately to mind. They and a few others like them are the ones who
make Peregrine Falcons breed in captivity.

Literature Cited

Berry, R.B. 1972. Reproduction by artificial insemination in captive
American goshawks. J. Wildlife Manage. 36:1283-1288.
Cade, T.J. (ed.) 1973. The Peregrine Fund Newsletter. No. 1:1-6.

Cade, T.J. and S.A. Temple. 1977. The Cornell University falcon pro-
    gramme. p. 353-369. *In* R.D. Chancellor (ed.), Report on Proceed-
    ings. World Conference on Birds of Prey, Vienna 1975. Interna-
    tional Council for Bird Preservation.
Cade, T.J., J.D. Weaver, J.B. Platt, and W.A. Burnham. 1977. The
    propagation of large falcons in captivity. Raptor Research (*in
    press*).
Fyfe, R. 1975. Breeding peregrine and prairie falcons in captivity.
    p. 133-144. *In* R.D. Martin (ed.), Breeding endangered species in
    captivity. Academic Press, London.
Fyfe, R. 1976. Rationale and success of the Canadian Wildlife Service
    peregrine breeding project. Canadian Field-Naturalist 90(3):
    308-319.
Gee, G. and S.A. Temple. 1978. Artificial insemination for breeding
    nondomestic birds in captivity. *In* Artificial insemination of
    nondomestic animals. Symp. Zool. Soc. London (*in press*).
Grier, J.W. 1973. Techniques and results of artificial insemination
    with golden eagles. Raptor Research 7(1):1-12.
Robinson, J. 1977. News from home and abroad. South Australia--1976.
    The Falconer 6(5):243-244.
Scharrer, E. 1966. Principles of neuroendocrine integration. Res.
    Publ. Asso. Res. Nerv. Ment. Dis. 43:1-33.
Waller, R. 1962. Der wilde Falk ist mein Gesell. Verlag J. Neumann-
    Neudamn, Melsungen. 320p.
Weaver, J.D. and T.J. Cade. 1974. Special report on the falcon breed-
    ing program at Cornell University (RRF BPIE No. 90). Hawk Chalk
    13(1):31-43.
Zimmerman, D.R. 1975. To save a bird in peril. Coward, McCann &
    Geoghegan, Inc., New York. 286p.

30

Captive Breeding Programs for *Amazona* Parrots

Holly A. J. Nichols

Captive breeding programs for Amazon parrots are ironically in their infancy. During the last 100 years, many of the species have been bred in captivity. Of the 27 species, I am aware of 14, as listed in Table 1, having been bred in captivity. Many of them--the more common ones--are, of course, bred frequently. I have also indicated those species for which I am aware of serious captive efforts being undertaken. To some extent, my definition of a serious captive effort is arbitrary; however, it requires a timely, sustained, dedicated, altruistic, well-financed effort, the likes of which we have yet to see for any of the species. I have also indicated species for which I suspect captive efforts should be initiated.

The most intensive and impressive attempt to date is, of course, the U.S. Department of the Interior's program for the Puerto Rican Parrot (*Amazona vittata*). From my distant vantage point, it would seem that because of factors so difficult to control in the wild, the survival of this most threatened of all Amazons depends on the success of the captive program. This program, however, seems to be hindered initially by an imbalanced sex ratio: one known male and 7 females out of a total of 14 birds. The solution to this problem may require artificial insemination techniques, never before used with parrots. I am somewhat wary of the long-term effect of such techniques. My most serious fear, however, is that this courageous, exemplary project will be an example of a project initiated too late.

Running a far second to the well organized *A. vittata* program are the programs for the St. Vincent Amazon (*A. guildingii*). It is, of course, no accident that so many have sought to carry the captive breeding banner for this commercially valuable species. Furthermore, of the Lesser Antillean Amazons, *A. guildingii* has been relatively available to collectors. The species is available because it is the most common of the Lesser Antillean species and because Vincentians

TABLE 1.   A SURVEY OF CAPTIVE BREEDING PROGRAMS FOR AMAZON PARROTS

Species	Has Bred in Captivity	Captive Breeding Program Already Exists	Captive Breeding Program Needed
A. aestiva	X		
A. agilis			X
A. albifrons	X		
A. amazonica	X		
A. arausiaca[a]		X	
A. autumnalis	X		
A. barbadensis			X
A. brasiliensis[a]	X		X
A. collaria	X		
A. d. dufresniana			X
A. d. rhodocorytha			X
A. farinosa			
A. festiva			
A. finschi	X		
A. guildingii[a]	X	X	
A. imperialis[a]		X	
A. l. leucocephala	X		
A. l. palmarum			
A. l. caymanensis	X	X	
A. l. hesterna[a]	X	X	
A. l. bahamensis[a]			X
A. mercenaria			
A. o. ochrocephala	X		
A. o. tresmariae			X
A. pretrei[a]			X
A. tucumana			X
A. ventralis	X		
A. versicolor[a]		X	
A. vinacea	X		X
A. viridigenalis	X		
A. vittata[a]		X	
A. xantholora			
A. xanthops			X

[a]Species listed as endangered in the *Red Data Book* (Vincent, 1966).

more often collect them as pets rather than shooting them.

In most respects, programs for *A. guildingii* present a classic example of everything wrong with captive breeding. Before this species was first bred in captivity, 25 specimens had died in zoo collections, and at least a similar number died in private collections. Many of the specimens had been wing shot, a technique which kills perhaps 10 to 20 times as many parrots as are caught. Many of them died alone or with a partner of the wrong sex, even though a potential mate may have been only a few hours away.

Historically, the St. Vincent Government has been sensitive to the strain pet collectors, zoos, and aviculturists have put on the wild population. It has been illegal to export *A. guildingii* without a permit since 1920. However, about 50 percent of the specimens now in zoo collections were either confiscated during illegal exportation attempts or were, in fact, illegally exported. The percentage is about the same for private collections. Although it is now illegal without a permit to import endangered species into countries that have signed the International Treaty on Trade in Endangered Species of Wild Flora and Fauna, as one Texan who is now trying to arrange the importation of 2 *A. guildingii* says, "Do you really think custom agents could recognize a St. Vincent Parrot?"

In each of the past 4 years I have tried to convince officials on St. Vincent to apprehend smugglers. In 1973 I estimated that each year 30 to 40 are lost to collectors; this includes nestlings taken for pets or export and adults shot. If the total population is 450, this is a significant pressure. Last year the San Diego Zoo was offered 2 *A. guildingii*--dyed green to look like common Yellow-headed Amazons (*A. ochrocephala*) for easy passage through customs--for $2,000 each. The price was cheap, but San Diego turned them down. I am sure they are somewhere in the U.S. now. One lady brought a St. Vincent Amazon through Miami with forged export papers. This year a Trinidadian is exporting several smuggled St. Vincent Amazons to the U.S. and England for further shipment to a Swiss aviculturist. There are a few politicians in St. Vincent who feel that the government should either sell parrots to anyone who wants them or heavily tax their export. I fear that if present restrictions are relaxed the St. Vincent Parrot population will quickly rise in captivity and be totally decimated in the wild.

The St. Vincent government has followed the somewhat unusual course of allowing legal exportation of their parrots to several different locations but usually no more than 4 birds to any single project. This policy has resulted partially from political expediency and pressure and partially from a desire to avoid making those almost impossible guesses as to which projects will be able to have a successful productive program. However, as might be expected, the policy has tended to exacerbate male-female imbalances and to permanently isolate many birds. Although such decisions are politically awkward and difficult for local government officials with little avicultural experience, I think it would be best for the government to encourage only 1 or 2 tightly controlled programs.

In the U.S. there are 2 legal collections: my own and the Houston Zoo's. We both lack females. I am sure we will cooperate in the future, and as a direct result of our communication and cooperation we will eventually succeed.

Of the 8 *A. guildingii* in the United Kingdom, 2 are singles, 2 are mismatched, and 4 are apparently properly paired.

I have a reliable report that a pair of *A. guildingii* in another European collection produced eggs this year, but the owners are appar-

ently remaining silent, perhaps because of the illegality of their
collection.

The largest collection of *A. guildingii* is on Barbados. The
owner of these birds is completely uncooperative. He will not allow
his birds to be registered in a studbook; he does not publish; he will
not allow many people to visit him; and he no longer reports to the
St. Vincent Government about his work. I am too close to this problem
to comment further.

Fortunately for the species, *A. guildingii* does not seem to be
threatened with extinction in the wild during this century--at least
while Earle Kirby and a few other Vincentians are active in protecting their wild parrots.

The Imperial Amazon (*A. imperialis*), the giant of the genus, is
an example of another problem. There is no doubt that this species
has experienced a tremendous population decline during the last 25
years. I estimate the current population to be approximately 150
individuals. Although the species will undoubtedly survive in the
wild on the island of Dominica, a captive program should be established now while the attempt will have a minimal effect on the wild
population. Obtaining specimens, however, in the one way I consider
acceptable--taking nestlings--is practically impossible. The remaining birds are sparsely distributed over some of the world's roughest
terrain on Morne Diablotin. That terrain is also inhabited by revolu-
tionaries who have murdered visitors in the past.

The other Dominican species, the Red-necked Amazon (*A. arausiaca*),
has a population of about 350 birds, but is rapidly declining. I am
initiating a captive breeding program for this species.

Next to the Puerto Rican Amazon, the St. Lucia Amazon (*A. versicolor*) may be the most seriously endangered species in the genus. I
estimate the current population to be 125 individuals. There are now
8 specimens at the Jersey Wildlife Preservation Trust (JWPT), including 3 pairs of nestlings and 1 bird on loan from the Bermuda Zoo. I
am certain this will be the last chance aviculture has with the species
One isolated specimen in England--illegally exported from St. Lucia
7 years ago--is now for sale for 2,000 pounds. The price is cheap,
but I think JWPT has some ethical reservations about buying an illegal bird for a conservation project.

Rev. R. Noegel of Florida has been working with subspecies of
the Cuban Amazon (*A. leucocephala*) for many years. Although he does
have some *A. l. leucocephala,* his most important work to date has been
with *A. l. caymanensis.* Some of his pairs have been very productive.
Noegel keeps his birds in relatively small pens but is well aware of
the threat of obesity in such situations and carefully controls the
diet of his birds. Noegel describes his *A. l. caymanensis* as "climbers not fliers," at least when compared with his *A. l. hesterna.* R.
Low (*personal communication*) has made a similar statement about Amazons "spending more time climbing than flying--making a large aviary
unnecessary." Nonetheless, I feel strongly that captive Amazons, when
given a chance, will develop into strong fliers; such exercise can
only be good for birds. My own *A. l. caymanensis* fly frequently in
their 9-m long flight cages.

Last year a Florida dealer imported 12 *A. l. caymanensis.* It

is interesting to note that although the birds came through a U.S.
Department of Agriculture quarantine station and were properly
identified, neither customs agents nor U.S. Department of Agriculture
personnel seemed to note that the species at that time was on the
U.S. Department of the Interior endangered list and required a special
import permit. There are now approximately 45 specimens of *A. l. caymanensis* in avicultural collections.

Noegel has 6 young *A. l. hesterna* which is perhaps the most
seriously threatened of all the *A. leucocephala* subspecies. There
are probably no specimens of *A. l. bahamensis* now in captivity. On
the basis of his past success, Noegel would probably be the best
person to attempt breeding this rare subspecies. However, current
regulations are so complex and delaying as to frustrate even this
well-qualified private aviculturist.

One other Caribbean species which probably now needs more attention in the wild and a captive breeding program is the smallest member
of the genus, the Black-billed Amazon (*A. agilis*). This species is
not now considered endangered, and Noegel has just obtained 4. I
think it highly unlikely that he will have any lasting success with
only 4. The only other *A. agilis* I know of in captivity is a single
bird at the London Zoo.

I believe one island subspecies of the Yellow-headed Amazon (*A.
ochrocephala tresmariae*) should be considered for possible captive
breeding. I know of no recent reports from Tres Marias Island, and
with so many *A. ochrocephala* bred in captivity, it would, indeed, be
unfortunate not to have an effort made for this well-marked subspecies.

The Vinaceous Amazon (*A. vinacea*) is on the endangered list, but
it is not uncommon in captivity. During recent years, I would guess
that at least 200 were imported into the U.S., and probably as many
were imported into the U.K. The specimens, many of which are pets,
are widely scattered. Although many zoos and aviculturists have one
or two pairs, no one is attempting a serious breeding program or maintaining a studbook. I know of one person who imported 10 of these
birds. A few weeks after going through U.S. Department of Agriculture quarantine, 6 of them died. Although this is perhaps not an
entirely typical quarantine experience, it is an example of what can
happen and explains why I will not import an endangered species
through a U.S. Department of Agriculture station.

Several endangered Brazilian Amazons, including the Red-tailed
Amazon (*A. brasiliensis*), the Blue-cheeked Amazon (*A. dufresniana
rhodocorytha*), the Red-spectacled Amazon (*A. pretrei*), and perhaps
the Yellow-faced Amazon (*A. xanthops*) need both study in the wild
and captive breeding programs. In Brazil, it is officially forbid-
den to keep in captivity any Brazilian bird, but many people keep
the Amazons, and the illegal markets are very strong. H. Sick (*personal communication*) reports that *A. brasiliensis* is the rarest of
all Brazilian Amazons. Perhaps it is at least as threatened as *A.
versicolor* of St. Lucia. Certainly if anyone ever attempts to legally begin captive breeding programs for these species, it will have to
be the Brazilian Government itself or one of the large zoological societies. The Brazilian Government has a very rigid policy of prohibiting the export of parrots. This export seems to be effective; I

know of no specimen of these species outside of Brazil, except for one *A. d. rhodocorytha* in a private collection.

Although I do not know the precise status of the Yellow-shoulder-ed Amazon (*A. barbadensis*) on the mainland, I suspect a captive breeding program for the species would be appropriate. R. Low has recently gathered 5 specimens, borrowing one from the London Zoo and 2 from 2 private aviculturists.

I should briefly note 3 of the more common species for which there are stable breeding programs. The San Diego Zoo has been experimenting with Orange-winged Amazons (*A. amazonica*). Noegel now has 5 Yellow-billed Amazons (*A. collaria*). There are specimens of Hispaniolan Amazons (*A. ventralis*) in several institutional collections.

To review what I believe are the essential components of a successful conservation program, first a captive program for Amazons must be legal. I think it would be impossible to sustain a long-term program outside the law in a way which would benefit the species. Illegally obtained birds often end up isolated or mismatched even though the owner starts with the best of intentions. I have personally witnessed the effect of illegally taking birds from the wild, illegal exporting, shipping, and importing. I have seen the effect on a wild population of the demand created by a smuggler offering $1,000--or even in one case $10,000--for birds in their native valley. Captive breeding is not an appropriate management technique if it is the cause of an Amazon's final demise in the wild. All too frequently, eager aviculturists far from the birds in the wild have no idea about the effect of their activities. I do not think a truly endangered species can endure our purchasing specimens that were taken illegally from the wild or our tolerating those who do.

Unfortunately, those who illegally import Amazons into the U.S. now have one argument in favor of their actions. Currently the approval of 7 government agencies is needed to import an endangered parrot into the U.S. The delay can take up to 9 months or longer, even when all the forms are filled out properly, all questions answered, and the importer qualified. Few people are willing to go to such trouble unless the birds are already known to be in captivity awaiting exportation. What happens to the parrots during the long process? Usually, the zoo representative or private aviculturist is not with them, and they are held under substandard conditions. The regulations designed to protect the endangered species in captivity are so delaying as to actually put the birds in jeopardy, and for the first time the illegal importer can argue that with his speed and flexibility he is actually doing what is best for the species.

A successful program must be centered around an aviculturist who is experienced with the genus. I know of some wealthy people who wanted to begin their Amazon experience with *A. guildingii*.

I strongly believe that the aviculturist who will breed the birds should be directly involved in obtaining the specimens from the wild, exporting them, and quarantining them. If the birds are so rare as to justify a breeding program, then they are important enough to be followed closely by the aviculturist from the moment they are taken from the wild.

I believe whenever we are considering or initiating a captive breeding program for an Amazon, a survey and study of the species in the wild is indicated. Such a study is necessary to justify the expense of the captive breeding program. Such a study may help the avicultural effort and may also reveal factors contributing to the population decline which can be addressed through local conservation measures. Ideally, a study of the wild population should involve both an aviculturist and a field biologist.

The converse is also true. If a field biologist is making a study of the species in the wild, there are now enough qualified Amazon aviculturists that it would be a waste of energy and funds not to consider simultaneously capturing specimens for a captive breeding program.

In many parts of South America and occasionally in the Caribbean, there is or has been a rapid destruction of forests. This can result in a large, adult population of Amazons that has no place to nest. In such circumstances, it may be best to attempt to capture adults for a captive breeding program, even though adults frequently have trouble adapting to captivity. Where there is no lack of suitable habitat, however, I believe the only acceptable way to obtain captives is to take young nestlings.

The question inevitably arises as to whether the captive breeding program is to take place in the species' native country or elsewhere. In my limited experience, there are no easy answers, but I would guess the answer must ultimately be decided by where the appropriately qualified, dedicated, altruistic, and well-financed aviculturist is located. I believe it is impossible to establish an acceptable program in a small country without the type of financing that has been invested in the *A. vittata* program.

A captive breeding program for an endangered Amazon requires the eventual holding of at least a dozen, perhaps more, specimens. Unfortunately, very few zoos or private aviculturists will maintain such a collection of one species, most preferring to keep diversified collections.

A serious captive breeding effort requires some type of international registry and studbook for the species. As serious a threat as burglary is, and as concerned about revealing the source of their birds as many owners are, a truly endangered species is not aided by those aviculturists who isolate their birds and will not cooperate in lending agreements.

Forshaw (1973) has written: "Zoos and government institutions have a public responsibility and it is possible to ensure that at all times the purpose for which the birds are held in captivity, namely preservation of the species, always remains the primary objective. On the other hand, private individuals claim that birds obtained by them are their property, a claim that is probably right and legally defensible but one that is totally alien to the objectives pursued." I wish things were so simple. My own experience with Amazons has reminded me that zoos and government institutions are merely collections of individuals and share with private aviculturists the potential for good or bad aviculture, cooperation or greed. Many zoos are concerned about the stability and uncooperativeness of private aviculturists. Many private aviculturists are bitter about zoos' inability to specialize, to act quickly, and to emphasize what is best for the animals.

One of the most difficult challenges with Amazon parrots is sex idenfification. Some aviculturists with considerable experience have been able to identify males as having wider upper mandibles, more curvature to the upper mandibles and especially more prominent foreheads. If you have a dozen birds to compare, this technique is perhaps feasible, but having made a few embarrassing mistakes myself, I know I cannot rely on foreheads. Recently more promising techniques have been developed: electron scanning of blood smears, chromosomal analysis, estrogen/androgen ratios in feces, and laproscopy. Trusting intuitive guesses is no longer appropriate.

Half of the problem of producing young is keeping adult mortality low. Amazons are relatively hardy birds, yet they are still susceptible to a variety of illnesses and seem to have a curiosity which sometimes gets them into trouble. Careful pen construction is necessary. I have seen many Amazons die from pulmonary infections when housed in cages that did not offer sufficient shelter from wind and rain.

Through the years, diets inadequate in greens and too high in fat have probably killed more captive Amazons than anything else. Probably many diets, including those relying heavily on sunflower seeds and peanuts, contain too much fat. Some breeders are feeding "monkey chow" or pigeon pellets, but the quantity of these foods must also be limited. It is virtually impossible to give too many greens or too many fresh tree limbs.

A captive breeding program must produce not only young birds but also publications. There are important observations to be made on every rare Amazon. Every aviculturist caring for these birds has the responsibility of being familiar with the literature on the species under his care and of adding to that literature.

What is the role of captive breeding in the preservation of endangered Amazons? Captive breeding programs are expensive, there are many problems associated with captive breeding, and no Amazon breeding program has clearly been a success to date. If local conservation measures can insure preservation of a species in the wild, then such measures are clearly preferable to captive breeding. However, where rapid destruction of habitat--frequently combined with the pressures of hunting, captive trade, natural predators, and hurricanes--results in a rapidly declining Amazon population, captive breeding programs may be necessary. It is possible that *A. l. hesterna*, *A. vittata*, *A. versicolor*, and *A. brasiliensis* are in this category. Amazons in the second category may also have rapidly declining populations, but there are reasons to hope that the Amazon's habitat will not be totally destroyed. *A. arausiaca, A. guildingii, A. l. bahamensis* and *A. vinacea* may be in this second category. However, captive programs are also appropriate for these species, at least on a temporary basis, both as insurance and because these species may still be vulnerable in the wild. The *A. guildingii* population was severely decimated by an 1898 hurricane and a 1902 volcanic eruption. It is now very possible the species could not survive another such catastrophe. If we are optimistic, we could hope that the remaining Puerto Rican forests will not be destroyed during the next century and that the pressures *A. vittata* faces in the wild can eventually be controlled by measures Snyder (Ch. 6, *this volume*) has discussed. If we are very optimistic, we could hope St. Lucian hunters will stop shooting parrots and that the remaining virgin forest on the island will be promptly protected from lumbering. Captive breeding programs at least offer the hope of survival in a world where alternatives are becoming increasingly remote for all species.

I have chosen not to discuss in detail such important aspects of captive breeding programs as nest boxes, pen size, sexing, stress, and fertility because these are not, at this time, the major hurdles of most programs. The major hurdles usually involve properly obtaining stock, cooperating and sustaining the required effort. These are the human problems which we must master before seeing further progress in captive breeding programs for Amazons.

ACKNOWLEDGMENTS

I thank George Smith, Rosemary Low, Arthur Risser, Ramond Noegel, Helmut Sick, Noel Snyder, Don Bruning, David Jeggo, and John Fleming for making suggestions about the text and my husband for compiling the material while I was in the field.

LITERATURE CITED

Forshaw, J.M. 1973. Parrots of the world. Doubleday & Co., Garden City, N.Y. 584p.
Vincent, T. (ed.) 1966. Red Data Book, Vol. 2--Aves. Inter. Union for Conservation of Nature and Nat. Resources. Morges, Switzerland.

Part VII
Genetic Aspects
of Managing Dwindling Bird Populations

31

Genetic Aspects
of Dwindling Populations
A Review

Thomas E. Lovejoy

The genetics of dwindling populations constitutes one of the two most important scientific questions with fundamental relevance to conservation; the second is the minimum critical size or area of ecosystems (Lovejoy and Oren, *unpublished data*), both of which will ultimately prove to be very intimately intertwined. I will confine my remarks primarily to the genetic problems confronting diminishing and small populations and will not deal with the strong selection pressures man is exerting on populations--as in the classic case of industrial melanism and its reversal, or as must be going on to a great, but unmeasured extent, with toxic substances.

Rare species and endangered species are nothing new. Some species are always rare in the course of their existence. Others become rare on their way to natural extinction. Consequently, the genetics of diminishing populations is really a central, if neglected, problem in biology. Today, rare species are rising in number, and because of endangerment by man, the fraction of the total biota they constitute is growing rapidly. I suppose, to look at the bright side, this provides greater opportunity to understand the problem, and that, in turn, will aid us in addressing the growing conservation problem.

We know that inbreeding problems occur in the barnyard, in zoological gardens, even in people. We also know of cases where it is not a problem with small populations. To the pessimist, we can always cite examples of tiny populations that do not have special problems or populations in which variation *per se* is not of apparent advantage in nature (e.g., Selander and Kaufman, 1973; Selander and Hudson, 1976) and refer to what must be a very large number of successful colonizations by species which obviously started off as very small inocula or propagules. But it is important not to cite colonizing species too glibly, for I can think of no instance, at least for vertebrates, in which the entire history of colonization attempts over a reasonably long period has been properly chronicled. This leaves us in no position to say with any certainty what percentage of colonization attempts were successful and what proportion of the unsuccessful ones may have been attributable to genetic problems. We do know, for example, that the successful introduction of the Starling (*Sturnus vulgaris*) into North America was preceded by unsuccessful attempts, but I am not aware of any good analysis of the causes of those failures.

The crucial question becomes whether we can discern any patterns in populations reduced to small numbers and forced through a "genetic bottleneck" or whether genetic problems occur unpredictably on a case by case, or species by species, basis. Approaching this in simple fashion, let us start with a reasonably large population in which every gene exists as one or two to several kinds of alleles (e.g., we could have several colors of eyes or feathers). Then let us analyze what happens if the population is reduced to a single breeding pair from which a larger population can hopefully be derived.

Obviously, no more than 4 alleles for any gene can survive that reduction--two for each pair of chromosomes of the two individuals. This results in a reduction in the total genetic variation of the species and generally eliminates rarer alleles more than it does abundant ones. But this is a "grab bag" process, and the genetic composition of the resulting population cannot be predicted. This reduction with its random aspects is called "the founder effect" and is very important in our considerations, perhaps more than authors such as Nei et al. (1975) or Soulé (*unpublished data*) have suggested.

Those authors have been more concerned with the genetic drift or inbreeding that follows in the generations after a genetic bottleneck, when opportunities to mate with genetically similar individuals are considerably greater than with genetically different individuals. For a number of generations, the number and proportion of genetically uniform or homozygous individuals grows until an equilibrium is reached, after which mutation slowly introduces new alleles, greater variation and a rising proportion of heterozygotes into the population. An interesting case of drift in a wild population involves not a bird but the Elephant Seal (*Mirounga angustirostris*). The northern population today shows a much greater homozygosity than the southern population presumably because of having hit a population low of 20 in the late 19th century (Bonnell and Selander, 1974).

Almost every species carries a number of deleterious alleles in the population. These can vary in their effect; some are lethal while others cause only minor reductions in the fitness of an individual. The sum of such genes is termed genetic load. Since some species have been shown by Lewontin and Hubby (1966) to carry loads greater than they should be able to bear, it is clear that we do not fully understand genetic load or its function. Often these alleles are rare and infrequently expressed in the homozygous state in a large population, but occasionally such alleles will end up in the handful of alleles in the few surviving pairs of a small population. Trouble can arise in such situations because inbreeding leads to homozygous expression of the deleterious genes.

Do the problems of genetic load or drift occur more often in some kinds of small populations than others? If two species, one with a high reproductive rate and one with a low rate,

have equal genetic loads and are reduced to populations of single
breeding pairs, the species with the higher reproductive rate will
have its genetic variation reduced less and be less likely to encounter
problems from genetic load, simply because the greater number of zy-
gotes and offspring produced in the life span of the pair will take a
larger sample of the parental genetic variation. William Conway's
point (Ch. 26, *this volume*) that captive birds have greater life spans,
greater reproductive productivity and thus great genetic variability
follows this same principle. It constitutes an interesting positive
aspect to captive propagation. Nei et al. (1975) concentrated on the
events that follow a genetic bottleneck and demonstrated that inbreeding occurs to a lesser extent and lasts a shorter time when reproductive rates are higher. This is because faster population growth potentially leads to a higher absolute level of mutations and thus to
restoration of genetic variation to the population. This, in turn,
provides favorable alleles which can be selected for and spread
through the population. With higher reproductive rates and population
growth also comes an increase in various position effects in the course
of recombination.

This tells us we can expect more problems with long-lived, slow
reproducing, so called K-selected species (i.e., those selected to
maintain stable populations near a carrying capacity, K) than those
with high reproductive rates or r-selected species (i.e., selected
to have high reproductive rates to compensate for substantial fluctuations in population size). This immediately says that K-selected
species have a situation of double jeopardy, an inability to recover
quickly from a population reduction coupled with a greater likelihood
of attendant genetic problems. It is then even less surprising that
endangered species tend to be K-selected and obvious that they should
get the greater share of conservation attention, as well as receive it
earlier in their decline. This also says something about colonizing
species--for dispersing species tend to be r-selected--and further
carries implications for island biogeography as well as for minimum
critical size of ecosystems and reserve management. The chances of
the cockroach inheriting the earth or the house sparrow the wind seem
even greater.

One might ask if this implies island species might be better
suited to captive breeding than continental ones. It is important
in this context to note that, although colonizing species tend to be
r-selected, island evolution may often lead to K-selected forms. This
overall trend from r-selected to K-selected forms is really an integral
part of taxon cycles. Whether island species that frequently encounter
problems of small population size have evolved any special genetic
mechanisms is not known and, as far as I know, not particularly likely
from what we currently know of population genetics. They may, however, carry reduced genetic loads by virtue of having gone through
more frequent bottlenecks.

Social structures and mating systems have important bearings on
the genetic problems of dwindling populations. Polygamous mating systems and, indeed, territoriality can exclude some individuals from
breeding, thus reducing the effective breeding population below the
total adult population. For example, Berwick (*unpublished data*) an-

alysed the problem of inbreeding in the Rock Creek, Montana herd of
Bighorn Sheep (*Ovis canadensis*) and pointed out that the effective
breeding population in 1968 was only 6 out of the total group of 12.
This population had gone through more than one bottleneck and morpho-
logically showed effects of inbreeding. Subsequent introduction of 35
sheep from elsewhere has brought the population in 1977 to about 75
noticeably more robust animals.

Genetic swamping, where the distinct genetic composition of one
species is swallowed up by hybridization by another--while probably a
relatively pleasant, if not pleasureful, form of extinction--has not
really been assessed in importance or extent in nature (Ripley and
Lovejoy, 1978). The best known case in this country is the swamping
of the Red Wolf (*Canis niger*) by the Coyote (*Canis latrans*). W.B.
King (Ch. 2, *this volume*) has reported a similar threat to the Forbes'
Parakeet (*Cyanoramphus auriceps forbesi*) of New Zealand's Chatham
Islands by the Chatham Island Parakeet (*C. novaezelandia chathamensis*). It would appear that many of these examples are triggered by
man-induced habitat changes, but in any case, this is obviously a
greater problem for a small population than a large one.

It is interesting to tarry for a moment to consider what genetic
load may actually mean. In a recent examination of *Drosophila* populations, Powell has suggested a somewhat new form of an older idea,
namely that these genes may often represent fine tuning to the environment (Powell, 1971; Taylor and Powell, 1977). In other words, these
genes are only deleterious and can only be considered to constitute
load when the individual is outside the environment type for which it
is adapted. The extent to which this may apply for vertebrates is
difficult to determine, but before brushing it aside, it is important
to remember that local adaptation is more common than once thought.
In that light, the many local forms of widespread species described by
the taxonomic "splitters" might have represented something of this
sort.

There are two known species where the entire population probably
comes not only from a single pair but actually from a single mating,
namely the Golden Hamster (*Mesocricetus auratus*) and the Laysan Teal
(*Anas laysanensis*) (Ely and Clapp, 1973). That both are *r*-selected
species is intriguing, but it would be a mistake to make too much of
this. It does raise an interesting question, in that both seem to
have come through the genetic roulette of the founder effect with virtually no genetic load. Does this mean then that isolated blood lines
should be encouraged in small populations in the hope of similarly
lucky outcomes (i.e., that we should deliberately be pushing species
through genetic bottlenecks)? Or is maximizing interbreeding of the
remaining survivors still the best policy? Or could one devise a
balanced program of both approaches? These questions must be answered
on a case by case basis, and the answers depend on the frequency of
all alleles and of deleterious ones, information which really is not
available. Denniston (Ch. 32, *this volume*) suggests a strategy of
developing several homozygous lines but for different alleles. Our
knowledge of the genome, however, is almost invariably fragementary;
even total knowledge would not give us the ability to predict which
alleles we could fix in those blood lines.

Probably the best answer for now is to maximize interbreeding, but it really points up the need for more information and research. There is a need for more zoos to follow the example of the few which keep proper records such as Seal (Ch. 34, *this volume*) describes. Long isolated herds such as the Fallow Deer (*Dama dama*) of Magdalen College, Oxford can provide helpful data. And perhaps zoos should consider experimental programs on the topic with some of the more prolific species--but hopefully not just *r*-selected ones.

Our own species is not likely to face genetic bottlenecks in the future because isolation of human populations is continually and increasingly being broken down. So, to the skeptic, this topic may appear esoteric and trivial, but there is a larger need for a better understanding of the problem, in terms of a hopefully wiser management of the planet.

ACKNOWLEDGMENTS

The author acknowledges the help and contributions of Steven Berwick, Robert E. Cook, Caryl P. Haskins, G. Evelyn Hutchinson, Donald Kaufman, Warren B. King, Richard S. Miller, Eugene S. Morton, Pamela Parker, Jeffrey Powell, Robert E. Ricklefs, and Michael Soulé.

LITERATURE CITED

Bonnell, M.L. and R.K. Selander. 1974. Elephant seals; genetic variation and near extinction. Science 184:908-909.
Ely, C.A. and R.B. Clapp. 1973. The natural history of Laysan Island, northwest Hawaiian Islands. Atoll Res. Bull. 171:1-361.
Lewontin, R.C. and J.L. Hubby. 1966. A molecular approach to the study of genic heterozygosity in natural populations. II. Amount of variation and degree of heterozygosity in natural populations of *Drosophila pseudoobscura*. Genetics 54:595-609.
Nei, M., T. Maruyama and R. Chakraborty. 1975. The bottleneck effect and genetic variability in populations. Evolution 29:1-10.
Powell, J. 1971. Genetic polymorphisms in varied environments. Science 174:1035-1036.
Ripley, S.D. and T.E. Lovejoy. 1978. Threatened and endangered species, Ch. 23. *In* H. Brokaw (ed.) Wildlife and America. U.S. Government Printing Office, Washington, D.C. (*in press*).
Selander, R.K. and R.O. Hudson. 1976. Annual population structure under close inbreeding: the land snail *Rumina* in southern France. Amer. Naturalist 110:695-718.
Selander, R.K. and D. Kaufman. 1973. Self-fertilization and genetic population structure in a colonizing land snail. Proc. Nat. Acad. Sci. 70:1186-1190.
Taylor, C. and J. Powell. 1977. Microgeographic differentiation of chromosomal and enzyme polymorphism in *Drosophila persimilis*. Genetics 85:681-695.

32

Small Population Size and Genetic Diversity
Implications for Endangered Species

Carter Denniston

I was asked by Professor Temple to review the genetic implications of being a small population. As a population of size one who is likely to go extinct within the next 30 years, I am eminently qualified. However, there are many ways of looking at this problem, so that my review will, of necessity, be quite selective. Much of the genetic thinking on this subject tends to be mathematical, and sometimes the mathematics is rather heavy. I shall try to spare you that aspect of the field by limiting my remarks to results, some well known and some, I think, new.

Figure 1 provides an organization for this discussion; consider the population bottleneck. The population is reduced in numbers, sometimes quite suddenly (the reduction phase), it hovers at the brink of extinction for a while (the endangered phase), then recovers (the recovery phase). This symposium is concerned with populations which have entered the endangered phase, incipient extinctions--or we might say more optimistically, "hopeful bottlenecks."

Let us now discuss what is happening to genetic diversity during each of the 3 phases of a bottleneck. We will measure genetic diversity in 2 ways: as a variance and as the average number of alleles remaining at a typical locus.

THE REDUCTION PHASE

A few years ago, in the hills behind Santa Barbara, I caught sight of a magnificent specimen of the California Condor (*Gymnogyps californianus*). It paused for a moment directly above and then continued on to the southeast. I knew that there were few of these mighty birds left and realized that there was the remote possibility that I was seeing the last one. I considered the possibility that the

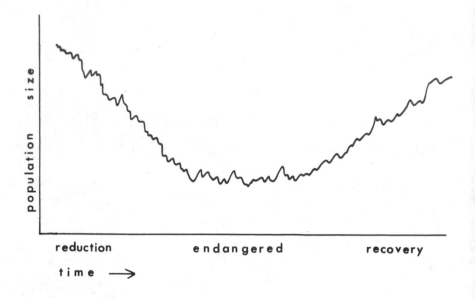

FIGURE 1.   The population bottleneck.

entire population of this dying species was reduced to this single individual and that I then succeeded in reconstituting a population from
it (ignoring, for the moment, bothersome details imposed by the neces-
sities of sexual reproduction). How much of the original genetic
variability could be preserved? Although the question is not altogether precise, I think an appropriate, imprecise answer is one-half.
One-half of the genetic variance of a population is, in a sense, locked up in a single individual.

More exactly, if a large randomly mating diploid population is
reduced to N individuals and then increases back up to a large population again without intervening gene frequency change, the expected
proportion of gene frequency variance remaining is:

$$1 - 1/2N$$

As one can see in Table 1, even as few as 10 individuals contain
within them the bulk of genetic diversity in their population. In
Table 1, genetic diversity is measured as a variance, and this leads
to a rather optimistic view of the effect of small population size.
But rare genes, by virtue of their rareness, do not contribute much to
genetic variance. Consequently, loss of rare, possibly important,
genes are counted hardly at all in these calculations.

Consider a diploid locus segregating m alleles with frequencies
P_1, P_2, P_3...P_m in a large random mating population. Suppose the
population is suddenly reduced to N individuals. Let n be the number

TABLE 1.   PROPORTION OF GENETIC VARIANCE REMAINING
IN SMALL POPULATIONS

No. of Individuals in Population (N)	Proportion of Genetic Variance Retained (1-1/2N)
1	1/2
2	3/4
4	7/8
10	19/20
50	99/100
100	199/200

of alleles remaining out of the m.   Then the expected value of n is:

$$E(n) = m - \sum_j (1 - p_j)^{2N}$$

with variance:

$$V(n) = \sum_j (1 - p_j)^{2N}\{1 - \sum_j (1 - p_j)^{2N}\} + \sum_{i \neq j}(1 - p_i - p_j)^{2N}$$

For $N = 50$, $m = 4$:

p_1	p_2	p_3	p_4	$E(n)$
.70	.10	.10	.10	3.999
.82	.06	.06	.06	3.994
.85	.05	.05	.05	3.982
.88	.04	.04	.04	3.949
.91	.03	.03	.03	3.857
.94	.02	.02	.02	3.602
.97	.01	.01	.01	2.902

By considering the average number of alleles remaining after a sudden reduction in population size rather than the genetic variance, we get a somewhat different view of the effect of small size on genetic diversity.   If a population is reduced to 50 individuals and the original population was segregating four alleles at a locus, one common (i.e., frequency of 0.97) and 3 relatively rare; on the average, one of the alleles at this locus will be lost in the population crash.

My remarks up to this point have been directed to the reduction phase of the bottleneck.   The models were somewhat artificial, of course, in that I have assumed a precipitous drop in population size rather than a gradual one.   Consequently, the conclusions were a bit optimistic.

THE ENDANGERED PHASE

Now let us turn to the endangered phase of the bottleneck, during which the population is being held to a rather small number.   What is happening to the genetic variance and the average number of alleles during this phase?

If the population size, N, is constant and the endangered phase lasts t generations, the genetic variance, V_t, will be further reduced to $(1 - 1/2N)^t$ of its original value.   For example, if N=50 and t=10, the variance is reduced by 10 percent.   Some examples for other population sizes are shown in Table 2.

If the population number fluctuates during this phase, as it is bound to do, a reasonable approximation is obtained by substituting in the above expression the harmonic mean of N over the interval.

What about the actual number of alleles present?   We can extend our previous analysis as follows.   Suppose a population of size N enters the endangered phase with m alleles at a locus with frequencies $p_1, p_2, \ldots p_m$.   We wish to know the expected number of alleles out of the original m remaining after t generations of random genetic drift.

Let n(t) be the number of alleles remaining at generation t.   We can write:

$$n(t) = \sum_j^m a(j,t)$$

where a(j,t) = 1, if allele j is still present at generation t and a(j,t) = 0 otherwise.   What we want is the expected value of n(t), which is:

$$E(n(t)) = E\Sigma\, a(j,t) = \sum E a(j,t).$$

TABLE 2.   LOSS OF GENETIC VARIANCE IN POPULATIONS OF CONSTANT SIZE OVER 10 GENERATIONS

Population Size (N)	Genetic Variance $(1-1/2N)^{10}$
10	0.60
20	0.78
30	0.85
50	0.90
100	0.95
1,000	0.99

But the expected value of a(j,t) is simply the probability that the jth allele is still present in the population after t generations (this argument was suggested to me by William Engels). This quantity is known from diffusion theory (*see* Crow and Kimura, 1970). Thus we have, where the probability that the jth allele has been lost by generation t is $f(p_j,0,t)$,

$$Ea(j,t) = 1 - f(p_j,0,t)$$

$$= 1 - f(1-p_j,1,t)$$

$$= 1 - (1-p_j) - \sum_{i=1}^{\infty} (2i+1)p_j(1-p_j)F(i+2,1-i,2,1-p_j)(-1)^i e^{-\frac{i(i+1)t}{4N}}$$

So, summing over j, we get

$$E(n(t)) = 1 - \sum_{j}^{m} \sum_{i}^{\infty} (2i+1)p_j(1-p_j)F(i+2,1-i,2,1-p_j)(-1)^i e^{-\frac{i(i+1)t}{4N}}$$

In these equations, F( ) is the hypergeometric function. We can look directly at one special case. As t goes to infinity, the sum goes to zero and so the expected number of alleles remaining is one, as expected.

This is somewhat difficult to evaluate because of the infinite sum, but an exact answer now exists derived without the use of diffusion theory from the work of Khazanie and McKean (1966).

Table 3 shows some results using this alternative theory for a population of size of 6. We see, for example, that were a population of 6 individuals to start out with 12 alleles of equal frequencies and drift for 4 generations, only 4 of these alleles would be left on the average. Obviously, rare alleles are at great risk of being lost quickly when the population is small.

So from the crude analysis above, we may take as given that any population said to be endangered has already suffered a degredation of its genetic diversity, especially the loss of rare alleles. We can do nothing about that. Our concern is to prevent, as much as is possible and practical, further loss of genetic variability.

THE RECOVERY PHASE

Finally, let us turn to the recovery phase. I have a proposal to make to you which bears looking into and which, I think, you may find counter-intuitive.

When a population is small, as we have seen, it means that the sample of gemetes which form the next generation is small. As you all know, a small sample may well not be representative of the parent population from which it was drawn. In the case we are considering, the offspring are in reality only a sample of the gametes of their

TABLE 3.   THE EXPECTED NUMBER OF ALLELES AFTER t GENERATIONS OF
DRIFT IN A POPULATION OF 6 INDIVIDUALS GIVEN 3 DIFFERENT
STARTING FREQUENCIES

No. of Generations	Number of Alleles When:		
	$m=2$, $p_1=p_2=1/2$	$m=4$, $p_j=1/4$	$m=12$, $p_j=1/12$
0	2.00	4.00	12.00
1	1.99	3.87	7.78
2	1.99	3.55	5.88
3	1.95	3.22	4.80
4	1.91	2.94	4.08
8	1.67	2.18	2.64
12	1.48	1.77	2.04
16	1.34	1.52	1.68
20	1.24	1.36	1.44
56	1.01	1.02	1.02
∞	1.00	1.00	1.00

parents who, in turn, are a sample of all of the individuals born
to the previous generation. If the sample is not a representative
one, the gene frequencies in the new generation may differ considerably from those in the parental population. The gene frequencies
will have "drifted" randomly, hence the designation "random genetic
drift."

One way of measuring the potency of random genetic drift is by
the variance in gene frequency change from one generation to the
next. If this variance is large, the drift is an important factor.
In an ideal diploid population of size N--by ideal I mean one of
constant size, a binomial progeny distribution and no selection,
migration or mutation--the variance in the change of gene frequency
is $V_{\delta p} = p(1 - p)/2N$. Of course, in a real population, one that is
not ideal, this equation will not be true. Yet, whatever $V_{\delta p}$ actually is in the real population, we may set it equal to $p(1 - p)/2N_e$,
where N_e is called the variance effective number (Wright, 1969).
N_e is the size of an ideal population undergoing the same amount of
random genetic drift as is our real population subject to all of its
nonidealness and is defined as:

$$N_e = p(1 - p)/2V_{\delta p}.$$

If individuals are contributing differing numbers of gametes,
k_1, k_2, ... to the next generation, then:

$$V_{\delta p} = \left[\frac{p(1-p)}{2N\bar{k}}\right]\left(\frac{N}{N-1}\right)\frac{V_k}{\bar{k}}(1+f) + (1-f)$$

so we get:

$$N_e = \frac{N\bar{k}}{\left(\dfrac{N}{N-1}\right)\dfrac{V_k}{\bar{k}}(1+f) + (1-f)}$$

where $\bar{k}$ and V_k are the mean and variance of the k's, p is the gene frequency, N is the actual population size and f is the inbreeding coefficient (Kimura and Crow, 1963).

In an ideal population, $\bar{k} = (N/(N-1))V_k = 2$ and $f = -1/(2N-1)$ giving $N_e = N$, as it should. Actually, two sampling processes contribute to V_{δ_p} in the above formula: 1) segregation of gametes in heterozygotes, and 2) the unequal numbers of progeny from parent to parent as measured by V_k.

Now I would like to make my counter-intuitive proposal. Suppose we are managing a population in the recovery phase and wish to reduce the drift variance as much as possible. Is there any way to do it? Yes, there are two possible approaches. One is to eliminate hetero-zygotes and therefore eliminate their contribution to the drift. This can sometimes be done by breaking up the total population into a series of independent, completely inbred (f=1) lines. Of course, if a substantial fraction of the original genetic variability is to be preserved, a large number of lines will be needed. Another problem is that the effects of inbreeding depression may make the maintenance of such lines difficult or impossible depending on the sensitivity of the particular species to inbreeding.

The other approach is to reduce the sizes of the bigger families so as to reduce V_k. That this would actually increase N_e (reduce $V_{\delta p}$) is not at first blush obvious. By eliminating offspring, one would be reducing the actual size of the population and so the net effect may well be to increase $V_{\delta p}$. Also one would only consider such a scheme if the population has sufficient reproductive capacity to sustain growth despite such intervention. The assumption here is that V_k is primarily the result of chance factors and not selec-tion; this seems to be a reasonable assumption for a small population.

Suppose we removed progeny from the population in the following manner: Remove individuals from the largest family until it has been reduced to the size of the second largest family, then remove alternatively from both families until they are reduced to the size of the third largest family, and so on. This will certainly reduce V_k, but will it increase N_e? The answer is Yes, sometimes. For example, consider a monogamous population consisting of 15 families contributing 0, 0, 1, 1, 1, 1, 1, 6, 6, 7, 7, 7, 7, 8 and 9 progeny, respectively. Here $\bar{k}$ is 4.13 and V_k is 11.55. In Table 4, we see the effect of applying our culling procedure. N_e does, indeed,

TABLE 4.   THE EFFECT ON EFFECTIVE POPULATION NUMBER OF CULLING
PROGENY FROM LARGER FAMILIES IN A MONOGAMOUS POPULATION OF
15 FAMILIES CONTRIBUTING 0,0,1,1,1,1,1,6,6,7,7,7,7,8, AND 9
OFFSPRING, RESPECTIVELY

No. Culled	Mean No. Progeny ($\bar{k}$)	Variance No. Progeny (V_k)	Effective Population Number (N_e) for Indicated Value of (f)				
			-0.04	0.00	0.10	0.20	0.30
0	4.13	11.55	33.22	32.68	31.20	29.85	28.62
1	4.07	10.92	33.63	33.10	31.65	30.32	29.10
2	4.00	10.43	33.79	33.27	31.85	30.55	29.35
3	3.93	9.92	34.00	33.50	32.11	30.83	29.65
4	3.87	9.55	33.92	33.43	32.07	30.81	29.66
5	3.80	9.17	33.88	33.40	32.07	30.84	29.71
6	3.73	8.78	33.88	33.41	32.12	30.92	29.81
7	3.67	8.38	33.94	33.48	32.22	31.05	29.96
8	3.60	7.97	34.04	33.60	32.38	31.24	30.18
9	3.53	7.55	34.21	33.79	32.60	31.50	30.47
10	3.47	7.27	34.01	33.59	32.44	31.37	30.37
11	3.40	6.97	33.84	33.44	32.33	31.28	30.31
12	3.33	6.67	33.72	33.33	32.26	31.25	30.30
13	3.27	6.35	33.65	33.28	32.25	31.28	30.36
14	3.20	6.03	33.64	33.29	32.30	31.37	30.49
15	3.13	5.70	33.70	33.36	32.42	31.53	30.69
16	3.07	5.35	33.83	33.51	32.63	31.79	30.99
17	3.00	5.00	34.04	33.75	32.93	32.14	31.40
18	2.93	4.78	33.74	33.46	32.68	31.93	31.22
19	2.87	4.55	33.49	33.23	32.49	31.79	31.11
20	2.80	4.32	33.31	33.06	32.37	31.71	31.08
21	2.73	4.07	33.19	32.96	32.33	31.72	31.13
22	2.67	3.81	33.14	32.94	32.37	31.82	31.29
23	2.60	3.54	33.19	33.01	32.52	32.03	31.56
24	2.53	3.27	33.34	33.20	32.78	32.38	31.98
25	2.47	2.98	33.62	33.51	33.19	32.89	32.59
26	2.40	2.43	33.14	33.05	32.78	32.52	32.26
27	2.33	2.67	32.75	32.67	32.45	32.24	32.03
28	2.27	2.50	32.42	32.37	32.21	32.06	31.91
29	2.20	2.32	32.19	32.17	32.08	32.00	31.92
30	2.13	2.12	32.07	32.07	32.08	32.09	32.09
31	2.07	1.92	32.07	32.11	32.23	32.34	32.46
32	2.00	1.72	32.22	32.31	32.56	32.81	33.07
33	1.93	1.50	32.56	32.71	33.13	33.56	34.01
34	1.87	1.41	31.76	31.91	32.36	32.82	33.30
35	1.80	1.32	31.05	31.21	31.71	32.22	32.74
36	1.73	1.21	30.44	30.63	31.18	31.76	32.36
37	1.67	1.10	29.96	30.17	30.81	31.48	32.17
38	1.60	0.97	29.62	29.87	30.62	31.40	32.23
39	1.53	0.84	29.45	29.74	30.64	31.60	32.61
40	1.47	0.70	29.49	29.85	30.96	32.15	33.43

increase, reaching a maximum after removing 9 individuals from the larger families in the case f=0. We also see that the effect depends on the level of nonrandom mating as measured by f. James (1962) and Latter (1959) provide for a deeper discussion of this general problem of maintaining a population with minimum drift.

ACKNOWLEDGMENTS

I wish to thank Professor James F. Crow for his careful reading and helpful comments. William Engels suggested certain ideas that I have presented. This is paper number 2190 from the Genetics Laboratory, University of Wisconsin, sponsored by the National Institutes of Health (Grant GM 15422-09).

LITERATURE CITED

Crow, J.F. and M. Kimura. 1970. An Introduction to Population Genetics Theory. Harper and Row.

James, J.W. 1962. The spread of genes in randomly mating control populations. Genet. Res. Camb. (1962) 3:1-10.

Khazanie, R.G. and H.E. McKean. 1966. A Mendelian Markov process with binomial transition probabilities. Biometrika 53:37-48.

Kimura, M. and J.F. Crow. 1963. The measurement of effective population number. Evolution 17:279-288.

Latter, B.D.H. 1959. Genetic sampling in a random mating population of constant size and sex ratio. Australian J. Biol. Sci. 12: 500-505.

Wright, S. 1969. Evolution and the Genetics of Populations: Vol. 2 The Theory of Gene Frequencies. Univ. of Chicago Press.

33

Genetic Diversity in Avian Populations

Kendall W. Corbin

The feasibility of reintroducing a species to an area following local extinction depends on many factors including the genetic constitution of those individuals being introduced. Several biochemical methods are in use for the determination of genetic variability in natural populations, but only the technique of starch-gel electrophoresis has been used to examine the variability at loci in bird populations. A review and synthesis of such studies will be the subject of this paper.

For various reasons, few studies of protein polymorphism in bird populations have been designed specifically for the purpose of determining the extent of genetic diversity in those populations. Rather, such studies were undertaken as a means of answering other questions of biological interest. Nevertheless, the published data do provide a basis for estimating the extent of genetic variability in avian populations.

The first study of allozymic variation in natural--in contrast to domestic--populations of birds was that of Bush (1967), which examined ontogenetic differences of a few blood proteins of the House Sparrow (*Passer domesticus*). Three years later, Sibley and Corbin (1970) presented preliminary data dealing with the allelic variation at 16 loci of several species-pairs of birds that hybridize throughout the Great Plains of North America. Nottebohm and Selander (1972) attempted to find a correlation between song dialects in the Rufous-collared Sparrow (*Zonotrichia capensis*) and variation in allelic frequencies at various enzyme loci. From 1966 to 1972 several other authors dealt with protein polymorphism in bird populations, but they examined only 1 to 3 loci (Stratil and Valenta, 1966; Brush 1968, 1970; Bush et al., 1970; Ferguson, 1971; Brush and Scott, 1972). Such studies thus cannot yield much information about overall heterogeneity in natural populations. Corbin et al. (1974) examined the extent of protein polymorphism in two congeneric species of birds indigenous to the lowlands of Papua-New Guinea and the Bismark Archipelago. These species were the Metallic Starling (*Aplonis metallica*) and the Singing Starling (*Aplonis cantoroides*). Baker (1974, 1975) and Handford and Nottebohm (1976) again examined the question of whether local populations of the genus *Zonotrichia*, which have different song dialects, also differ significantly in the allelic frequencies of selected enzyme loci. Manwell and Baker (1975) used electrophoretic techniques to study pair fidelity and genetic variability in three Australian birds. Smith and Zimmerman (1976) studied the allelic variation of several genera of blackbirds (Family Icteridae) to reconstruct their evolutionary relationships. Corbin, Sibley and Ferguson (*unpublished data*) carried out an analysis of hybrid and parental populations of the Baltimore and Bullock's Orioles (*Icterus g. galbula* and *I. g. bullockii*) to examine genetic changes associated with the process of speciation in birds. Barrowclough and Corbin (*unpublished data*) determined the extent of genetic variation at 31 enzyme loci of several species of wood warblers of the genera *Dendroica*, *Vermivora*, *Seiurus* and *Setophaga* to determine their evolutionary relationships.

HETEROZYGOSITY AND GENETIC DISTANCE

A measure of the level of heterozygosity in a local population is normally obtained from allozyme data in either of two ways. If every individual is scored for each of the loci studied, then the exact heterozygosity value can be calculated. It is equal to the mean of the individual heterozygosities, averaged over all individuals sampled. More recently, the level of heterozygosity has been based on allelic frequency data following the method of calculation proposed by Nei (1975). In such cases, the heterozygosity for a single locus (*h*) is defined as $1 - \Sigma X_i^2$, where X_i is the frequency of the ith allele at a locus. The average heterozygosity (*H*) is the mean of *h* over all loci studied.

An underlying assumption in the use of Nei's measure of heterozygosity (*H*) is that the individuals sampled are members of a randomly mating population. However, pooled samples from separate inbred populations will give erroneously high values of *H*. For a majority of avian populations sampled, the assumption of random mating appears to be reasonable. The measure of heterozygosity (*H*) will therefore be used in this paper to summarize much of the allozyme frequency data published to date for birds. Studies that examined fewer than 14 loci and those that sampled only a few individuals of a species have been excluded.

Table 1 presents the average heterozygosities (*H*) for each of 12 species of birds. Subspecific values are included if available. For those studies in which more than one population of a species was sampled, *H* was first calculated using the allelic frequencies for the respective populations, and the resulting values of *H* were then averaged In calculating *H*, assumptions about the homology of alleles sometimes had to be made when such homologies were not explicitly described and

TABLE 1.   MEAN HETEROZYGOSITIES (H) IN SEVERAL AVIAN SPECIES[a]

Species	No. of Loci, No. of Genomes	H ± SE	Reference
Aplonis metallica	18, 712	0.0466±0.0019[b]	Corbin et al. (1974)
Aplonis cantoroides	18, 216	0.0135±0.0054[b]	Corbin et al. (1974)
Zonotrichia leucophrys oriantha	19, 155	0.0474±0.0057[b]	Baker (1975)
Zonotrichia leucophrys nuttalli	19, 293	0.0950±0.0020[b]	Baker (1975)
Zonotrichia capensis	14, 390	0.0986±0.0090[b]	Handford and Nettebohm (1976)
Icterus galbula galbula	19, 300	0.0714±0.0020[b]	Corbin et al. (*in press*)
Icterus galbula bullockii	19, 132	0.0731±0.0001[b]	Corbin et al. (*in press*)
Vermivora ruficapilla	31, 44	0.1226±0.0335	Barrowclough and Corbin (*unpublished data*)
Dendroica coronata	31, 70	0.1214±0.0310	"
Dendroica palmarum	31, 24	0.1335±0.0385	"
Seiurus noveboracensis	31, 48	0.1577±0.0391	"
Passer domesticus	15, ∼50	0.1070±0.0440	Manwell and Baker (1975)
Hirundo tahitica	15, ∼40	0.0710±0.0490	"
Petrochelidon ariel	15, ∼60	0.0750±0.0410	"

[a] Calculated using the method of Nei (1975).
[b] H is the mean value averaged over several populations.

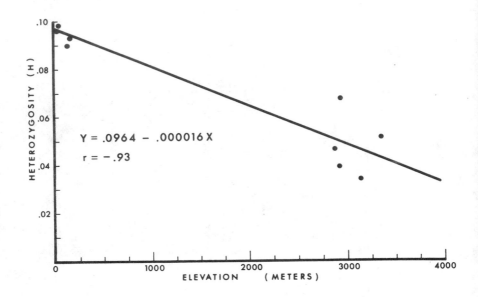

FIGURE 1.   Average heterozygosity (*H*) in populations of White-crowned
Sparrows as a function of the elevation of the locality
where the population breeds.

identified by an author. I have assumed that if an allele is fixed in
one position, it is homologous to the most frequent allele in adjacent
or next closest populations.

The question of variability in marginal populations versus central
populations of a species may be approached by comparing the average
heterozygosities (*H*) of the respective areas. None of the studies
cited in Table 1 were designed to measure such differences, but the
data for the White-crowned Sparrow (*Zonotrichia leucophrys*) are striking when reanalyzed with this question in mind. In his second study
of this species, Baker (1975) sampled populations not only of different song dialects but also at altitudinal extremes for the distribution of this species. Average heterozygosities (*H*) were calculated
from Baker's (1975) data on allelic frequencies and the resulting
values of *H* were regressed against the elevation of the sample site.
The results are shown in Figure 1. The regression of *H* against
elevation is highly significant: (a = 0.0964, b = -0.000016 ± 0.000002,
t_7 = -6.966, $p<0.001$).

Two indices of genetic distance between taxa have been devised
specifically for use with allelic frequency data. These are Rogers'
index (*S*) which measures the mean geometric distance between allelic

frequency vectors over all loci (Rogers, 1972) and Nei's normalized
genetic identity (*I*) of alleles between two populations, subspecies,
or species (Nei, 1972). The latter index will be used here.

The normalized genetic identity of alleles between two populations at the *j*th locus is defined as:

$$I_j = (\Sigma X_i Y_i) / (\sqrt{\Sigma X_i^2 \Sigma Y_i^2})$$

where X_i and Y_i are estimates of the frequencies of the ith allele in
population X and Y respectively. The overall genetic identity between
populations X and Y is:

$$I = J_{xy} / \sqrt{J_x J_y}$$

where J_x, J_y and J_{xy} are the arithmetic means over all loci of the
Σx_i^2, Σy_i^2 and $\Sigma x_i y_i$, respectively. The genetic distance (*D*) between
populations X and Y is estimated as $-\ln I$ (Nei, 1972).

Calculations of *I* rest upon one's ability to recognize homologous
alleles in the populations being compared. The more distantly related
pairs are to one another, the more likely it is that non-homologous
alleles will be assumed, incorrectly, to be homologous. For the
separate populations of a species and for closely related species it
is probable that allozymes in identical positions after electrophoresis are, indeed, homologous. However, recent detailed electrophoretic
and genetic analyses of the variation at enzyme loci have revealed
that substantial genetic variation goes undetected if one relies
solely upon electrophoretic information to detect that variability
(Singh et al., 1976). The values of *I* and *D* presented below were
calculated from data obtained prior to the recognition of this potential source of error. Consequently it is possible that populations,
subspecies etc. may appear to be somewhat more closely related than
they in fact are. However, a similar bias exists for each of the
studies cited, including those of non-avian species.

Table 2 presents the normalized genetic identity (*I*) and genetic
distance (*D*) for a variety of comparisons between birds at different
taxonomic levels. Table 3 provides a comparison of *D* among different
taxa for several classes of vertebrates and for *Drosophila*.

DISCUSSION

The data presented in Figure 1 and Tables 1-3 provide some
evidence that may have significant implications for endangered
species of birds. To focus attention on the issues involved, two
questions are posed. First, how different genetically are individuals of a species that are members of different local populations
or different subspecies? Second, is there evidence that natural
selection acts differentially on marginal or isolated populations

TABLE 2.   GENETIC DISTANCES AMONG AND BETWEEN DIFFERENT TAXONOMIC
           DISTANCE (D) WERE CALCULATED USING THE METHOD OF NEI (1972)

Taxa Compared	$I \pm$ SE
1. Among Local Populations:	
Aplonis metallic (15)[a]	0.9968±0.0009
Aplonis cantoroides (4)[a]	0.9968±0.0011
Zonotrichia leucophrys nuttalli (2)[a]	0.9961
Zonotrichia leucophrys nuttalli	0.9983±0.0006
Zonotrichia leucophrys oriantha (5)[a]	0.9955±0.0015
Zonotrichia capensis (5)[a]	0.9956±0.0011
Icterus g. galbula (6)[a]	0.9976±0.0010
Icterus g. bullockii (2)[a]	0.9992
Mean	0.9969±0.0004
2. Between Subspecies:	
Aplonis m. metallica vs.	0.9974±0.0004
A. m. nitida	
Aplonis m. metallica vs.	0.9883±0.0023
A. m. purpureiceps	
Aplonis m. nitida vs.	0.9934±0.0009
A. m. purpureiceps	
Zonotrichia leucophrys oriantha vs.	0.9911±0.0009
Z. l. nuttalli	
Icterus g. galbula vs.	0.9968±0.0004
I. g. bullockii	
Mean	0.9934±0.0017
3. Between Sibling Species:	
Aplonis metallica vs.	0.9657
A. cantoroides	
Sturnella magna vs.	0.9886
S. neglecta	
4. Among Species Within a Genus:	
Within 3 genera of Parulids (10)[b]	0.9060±0.0100
5. Between Genera Within a Family:	
7 species, 6 genera, Icteridae (21)[c]	0.7970±0.0250
15 species, 9 genera, Parulidae (95)[c]	0.8320±0.0090
6. Between Families:	
Coeribidae vs. Parulidae (15)[d]	0.8110±0.0100

[a]Number of populations sampled.
[b]Number of pairwise comparisons within genera.
[c]Number of pairwise comparisons between genera.
[d]Number of pairwise comparisons between species of families.

LEVELS OF BIRDS. NORMALIZED GENETIC IDENTITY (*I*) AND GENETIC

D ± SE	Reference
0.0026±0.0006	Corbin et al. (1974)
0.0026±0.0008	Corbin et al. (1974)
0.0039	Baker (1974)
0.0017±0.0006	Baker (1975)
0.0045±0.0015	Baker (1975)
0.0044±0.0011	Handford and Nottebohm (1976)
0.0024±0.0010	Corbin et al. (*in press*)
0.0008	Corbin et al. (*in press*)
0.0029±0.0004	
0.0026±0.0004	Corbin et al. (1974)
0.0118±0.0024	Corbin et al. (1974)
0.0066±0.0009	Corbin et al. (1974)
0.0089±0.0009	Baker (1975)
0.0032±0.0004	Corbin et al. (*in press*)
0.0066±0.0017	
0.0349	Corbin et al. (1974)
0.0115	Smith and Zimmerman (1976)
0.100 ± 0.011	Barrowclough and Corbin (*unpubl. data*)
0.248 ± 0.031	Smith and Zimmerman (1976)
0.179 ± 0.007	Barrowclough and Corbin (*unpubl. data*)
0.210 ± 0.012	Barrowclough and Corbin (*unpubl. data*)

versus central populations of a species?

The answer to the first question is critical to alternative strategies for managing endangered species. This is particularly true of programs involving the reintroduction of species following local extinctions. Presumably each local population is at or approaching an adaptive peak for the constellation of genes that comprise its gene pool. On the one hand, the introduction of individuals carrying maladaptive genes for a given area is not likely to be a productive strategy in a management program. On the other hand, if the genes possessed by an individual, drawn at random from a given local population of the species, are likely to be identical to those of individuals from other local populations, then it is probable that reintroductions will be successful.

The Nei index of normalized genetic identity (I) provides a measure of the probability that any two sets of genes drawn at random from different populations are identical. The value of I would be equal to 1.0 if the two sets of genes are identical and equal to zero if they are completely different.

An examination of Tables 2 and 3 reveals a somewhat surprising relationship for birds in comparison to those for other vertebrates. In comparison to mammals, salamanders and fish, local populations of birds are approximately an order of magnitude more similar to each other, as measured by I or D. Subspecies of birds are about 100 times more similar to each other than are subspecies of mammals, salamanders and fish. Indeed, genera of birds are about as genetically similar to one another as are subspecies of these other vertebrate classes!

It is likely that coadapted gene pools of birds differ somewhat among geographic areas. However, the genetic identity data suggest that for management purposes the origin of individuals being used to repopulate areas following local extinctions need not be a major concern of the program. Although it would be prudent to reintroduce individuals from areas that are similar ecologically, it now appears that, for birds, potential genetic differences will not present so great a problem as is the case for other classes of vertebrates.

A note of caution is in order here. Approximately half of the species of birds of the world are members of the order Passeriformes. All of the species listed in Table 2 are passeriforms; thus, the data may not be representative of the class Aves. However, preliminary data for three families of the Order Procellariiformes (albatroses, petrels and shearwaters) are consistent with the results in Table 2 (Corbin and Barrowclough, *unpublished data*). That is, families and genera of procellariids are as genetically similar to one another as are families and genera of passerines.

Regarding the second question posed above, there is presumptive evidence, in the form of Figure 1, that marginal populations of birds may be less variable than central populations. For the White-crowned Sparrow it is plausible that high altitude populations are indeed at ecological limits, and thus marginal, for the distribution of the species. Although it is possible that the significantly lower levels of heterozygosity in the populations at high elevation are due to higher levels of inbreeding, this appears unlikely since populations of *Zonotrichia capensis* at high elevation also show reduced hetero-

TABLE 3. GENETIC DISTANCES BETWEEN DIFFERENT TAXONOMIC LEVELS

	Genetic Distance Between:						
Taxa	Local Populations	Subspecies	Sibling Species	Species	Genera	Families	References
Drosophila	0.0280	0.230	0.740	1.056	–	–	Ayala (1975)
Sunfish	0.0200	0.174	–	0.616	–	–	Avise and Smith (1974a,b)
Minnows	0.0310	–	–	–	0.528	–	Avise (1976)
Salamanders	0.0510	0.174	–	0.462	1.170	–	Hedgecock (1974) Hedgecock and Ayala (1974)
Mammals	0.0560	0.219	–	–	–	–	Ayala (1975)
Birds							
Aplonis	0.0026	0.007	0.035	–	–	–	Corbin et al. (1974)
Zonotrichia	0.0035	0.009	–	–	–	–	Baker (1975) Handford and Nottebohm (1976)
Icteridae	0.0016	0.003	0.042	–	0.248	–	Corbin et al. (*unpubl. data*) Smith and Zimmerman (1976)
Parulidae	–	0.003	–	0.100	0.179	0.210	Barrowclough and Corbin (*unpublished data*)

zygosity. The differences in *Z. capensis* are not quite significant however.

Taking another tack, if the outermost islands of the Bismarck Archipelago are in some way ecologically marginal for *Aplonis metallica*, then there is again a suggestion of reduced heterozygosity in the outermost islands versus mainland Papua-New Guinea. From Table 2 we also learn that the outermost islands inhabited by *A. metallica purpureiceps* are the most distinct genetically in comparison to the Papua-New Guinea populations comprised of *A. m. metallica*.

Finally, the question of structure in avian populations should be addressed briefly. In spite of their similarity in terms of genetic distance (D), the Baltimore Oriole and Bullock's Oriole ($D = 0.0032 \pm 0.0004$, Table 2) are sufficiently distinct, genetically, to maintain sympatry in some areas (Corbin and Sibley, 1977). Levels of heterozygosity for *Vermivora ruficapilla* ($H = 0.1226 \pm 0.0335$), *Dendroica coronata* ($H = 0.1214 \pm 0.0310$), *Dendroica palmarum* ($H = 0.1335 \pm 0.0385$) and *Seiurus noveboracensis* ($H = 0.1577 \pm 0.0391$), as calculated from allelic frequency data, are much higher than actual, observed heterozygosities (Barrowclough and Corbin, *unpublished data*). This suggests that birds collected during migration come from local populations having different constellations of alleles. A similar relationship has been observed in procellariids (Corbin and Barrowclough, *unpublished data*).

The conclusions to be drawn concerning genetic diversity in populations of passerine birds are therefore somewhat contradictory under certain conditions. Local populations and subspecies of song birds appear to be more similar genetically than are comparable taxonomic levels of other vertebrate classes. But there is evidence that structural differences exist and that marginal populations, in particular, may have been selected differentially. This means that endangered marginal populations may have lower levels of variability and, therefore, be more susceptible to perturbations of their environment. By contrast, individuals from central populations should be better colonizers because they may be somewhat more heterozygous on average while possessing many of the same alleles held in marginal populations.

LITERATURE CITED

Avise, J.C. 1976. Genetic differentiation during speciation, p. 106-12 *In* F.J. Ayala, (ed.). Molecular Evolution. Sinauer Assoc., Inc., Sunderland, Mass.

Avise, J.C., and M.H. Smith. 1974*a*. Biochemical genetics of sunfish. I. Geographic variation and subspecific intergradation in the bluegill, *Lepomis macrochirus*. Evolution 28:42-56.

Avise, J.C., and M.H. Smith. 1974*b*. Biochemical genetics of sunfish. II. Genic similarity between hybridizing species. Amer. Natur. 108:458-472.

Ayala, F.J. 1975. Genetic differentiation during the speciation process, p. 1-78. *In* T. Dobzhansky, M.K. Hecht, and W.C. Steere (eds.). Evolutionary Biology. Vol. 8. Plenum Press, New York.

Baker, M.C. 1974. Genetic structure of two populations of white-crowned sparrows with different song dialects. Condor 76:351-356.

Baker, M.C. 1975. Song dialects and genetic differences in white-crowned sparrows (*Zonotrichia leucophrys*). Evolution 29:226-241.

Brush, A.H. 1968. Conalbumin variation in populations of the Red-winged Blackbird, *Agelaius phoeniceus*. Comp. Biochem. Physiol. 25:159-168.

Brush, A.H. 1970. An electrophoretic study of egg whites from three blackbird species. Univ. Conn. Occ. Papers 1:243-264.

Brush, A.H., and A.F. Scott. 1972. Development of protein polymorphisms in Red-wing Blackbirds. J. Embrol. Exp. Morphol. 28:481-489.

Bush, F.M. 1967. Developmental and populational variation in electrophoretic properties of dehydrogenases, hydrolases and other blood proteins of the House Sparrow, *Passer domesticus*. Comp. Biochem. Physiol. 22:273-287.

Bush, F.M., J.R. Price, and J.I. Townsend. 1970. Plasma esterases, their definitions and status as isozymes in the House Sparrow. Int. J. Biochem. 1:85-107.

Corbin, K.W. and C.G. Sibley. 1977. Rapid evolution in orioles of the genus *Icterus*. Condor 79:335-342.

Corbin, K.W., C.G. Sibley, A. Ferguson, A.C. Wilson, A.H. Brush, and J.E. Ahlquist. 1974. Genetic polymorphism in New Guinea starlings of the genus *Aplonis*. Condor 76:307-318.

Ferguson, A. 1971. Geographic and species variation in transferrin and ovotransferrin polymorphism in the Columbidae. Comp. Biochem. Physiol. 38B:477-486.

Handford, P. and F. Nottebohm. 1976. Allozymic and morphological variation in population samples of rufous-collared sparrow, *Zonotrichia capensis*, in relation to vocal dialects. Evolution 30:802-817.

Hedgecock, D. 1974. Protein variation and evolution in the genus *Taricha* (Salamandridae). Ph.D. dissertation, Univ. of Calif., Davis.

Hedgecock, D., and F.J. Ayala. 1974. Evolutionary divergence in the genus *Taricha* (Salamandridae). Copeia 1974:738-747.

Manwell, C., and C.M.A. Baker. 1975. Molecular genetics of avian proteins XIII. Protein polymorphism in three species of Australian passerines. Austral. J. Biol. Sci. 28:545-557.

Nei, M. 1972. Genetic distance between populations. Amer. Natur. 106:283-292.

Nei, M. 1975. Molecular Population Genetics and Evolution. North-Holland, Amsterdam.

Nottebohm, F., and R.K. Selander. 1972. Vocal dialects and gene frequencies in the Chingolo Sparrow (*Zonotrichia capensis*). Condor 74:137-143.

Rogers, J.S. 1972. Measures of genetic similarity and genetic distance. Univ. Texas Publ. 7213:145-153.

Sibley, C.G., and K.W. Corbin. 1970. Ornithological field studies in the Great Plains and Nova Scotia. Discovery 6:3-6.

Singh, R.S., R.C. Lewontin, and A.A. Felton. 1976. Genetic heterozygosity within electrophoretic "alleles" of xanthine dehydro-
genase in *Drosophila pseudoobscura*. Genetics 84:609-629.
Smith, J.K., and E.G. Zimmerman. 1976. Biochemical genetics and
evolution of North American blackbirds, Family Icteridae.
Comp. Biochem. Physiol. 53B:319-324.
Stratil, A., and M. Valenta. 1966. Protein polymorphism of egg white
and yolk in geese and ducks. Folia Biol. Praha 12:307-309.

34

The Noah's Ark Problem
Multigeneration Management
of Wild Species in Captivity

Ulysses S. Seal

Noah was instructed to construct an ark and bring aboard representatives of all the creatures of the earth, the skies, and the waters to provide a nucleus of survival during the floods. At the conclusion of the floods, the instructions received were "Be fruitful, and multiply, and replenish the earth." The ark was stocked with 7 pairs of each species. This early wisdom in collecting a significant gene-pool reflects, I am sure, the animal husbandry skills of Noah's society.

Modern-day zoos and aviculturists are faced with the responsibility of developing and maintaining self-sustaining populations of captive wild species and, in selected instances, of providing the only reservoir for species on the verge of extinction or already extinct in the wild. To accomplish these goals, it is necessary to develop policies for genetic and demographic management of the gene pools over multiple generations, to collect data and share it, to continue work on development of methods for enhancement of reproduction, and finally to develop policies and methods for managing problems of surplus production.

Collecting and reporting of appropriate census, vital statistics, and pedigree data on zoo animals (including mammals, birds, and shortly reptiles and amphibians) are being partially accomplished by the International Species Inventory System (ISIS) program of the American Association of Zoological Parks and Aquariums (AAZPA), American Association of Zoo Veterinarians (AAZV), and United States Department of the Interior(USDI). Inclusion of gene-pool management concepts as part of a comprehensive breeding policy and breeding management philosophy are sorely needed. Enhancement of reproduction is being accomplished by development of innovative management techniques, behavioral and field studies, and in selected cases through the use of artificial insemination and hormonal manipulation. The problem of managing surplus has become acute for some species, including several species on the endangered list with annual production so overwhelming that the carrying capacity of zoos is saturated. However, no coordinated policy has been formulated on a national basis to provide genetic and demographic guidelines for breeding any species.

ROLES OF THE MODERN ZOO

The multiple and expanding roles of the modern zoo have been given thoughtful discussion by people interested in the role of captive animals as a part of man's cultural and biological heritage. The roles of the modern zoo are generally agreed to include recreation, education, conservation and research. It is simple to demonstrate in an analysis of these functions that they can be strongly interrelated and that if they are being performed effectively by a given zoo, it will be reflected in their personnel organization and budgetary expenditures. The primary concerns of this paper are in the area of conservation. The topics include:
1. The roles of zoos
2. Components and rationale of breeding programs
3. A summary of our thinking on problems of long-term genetic and demographic management of captive gene pools.

Conservation

The participation of zoos in current conservation efforts may be considered in terms of 4 aspects. The first and primary effort is in terms of education or increasing public awareness through education programs, graphics, design of exhibits, publicity, and gaining participation in local programs. These efforts require personnel and budgetary commitments.

Secondly, design of exhibits and holding facilities are being oriented toward breeding of individual species. This includes a gradual reduction in numbers of species being exhibited by individual zoos and an increase in the numbers of each of the individual species. The current design of exhibits with emphasis on habitat relationships, as well as zoogeographic distribution, provides a sharp contrast to the past image of zoo animals in sterile environments or caged bathrooms.

Thirdly, as research centers, zoos can provide a major contribution to the needed data base for efforts to increase the likelihood of survival of endangered or threatened species in their native habitat. Thus, it is possible to describe many features of a species' life history from careful studies in captivity. Indeed, it is far more likely that we will develop the information necessary for many species from captive animals than from studies in the wild simply because of the limitations of people, time, and money. Utilization of adequate record-keeping techniques, allotment of staff time and liasons with researchers at local universities or elsewhere will do much to hasten this process.

Finally, the breeding programs of zoos can also make a direct contribution to the conservation effort. This includes total captive production of animals for exhibit purposes and the actual preservation of a limited number of seriously endangered species or subspecies.

Breeding Programs

The breeding programs of zoos may be considered in terms of 2 objectives. The first would be that of developing self-sustaining, captive populations from which animals may be drawn for exhibit purposes which may be used to provide further information concerning the life history of the respective species. The other objective would be conservation and perhaps actual preservation of species or gene pools whose continued existence in the wild is doubtful or which are actually on the verge of extinction. It is in this capacity that the zoos might be a modern days' Noah's Ark. They would then be faced with the Biblical admonition to "Be fruitful, and multiply, and replenish the earth."

Since the reasons for developing self-sustaining, captive populations can be very different, it is important to consider the genetic strategies by which these different goals might be accomplished. It is possible to selectively breed a zoo-domesticated stock of a given species which is well-suited to captive life but completely unsuited to an existence in its original or any wild habitat. In those cases where it is clearly unnecessary to provide a reservoir of a gene pool for preservation of the species, this strategy might be employed. However, this choice should be clearly recognized and documented since such selectively inbred strains in all probability will not provide an accurate representation of the species either for life history studies or development of data suitable for management of the species in the wild. They also run a high risk of loss of vigor, reduced viability, growth rate, fertility, and extinction.

The other major strategy is to attempt to maintain as much of the genetic variability present in the wild gene-pool as possible. This strategy requires a deliberate policy of avoiding inbreeding (Figure 1) and demographic management of the gene pool to establish a stable population. It should include consideration of such variables as the number of generations over which the population may have to be sustained; what will be the age- and sex-composition of the over-all breeding population; age and sex specific fecundity and survivorship; how large a stable population is required on the basis of known features of the life history; carrying capacity of the zoos; surplus requirements and the practicality of developing controlled breeding or mating arrangements. Both of these strategies require accurate record keeping and explicit formulation of the breeding policy to be followed with agreement by all parties concerned.

The components of conservation-oriented, long-term breeding programs would include:

1. Zoos and other institutionalized facilities or formal, private collaborators which can provide long-term maintenance and management. Aspects of zoo management include exhibit design, development of holding facilities, development of auxiliary breeding facilities, breeding loans, development of breeding techniques, and data collec-

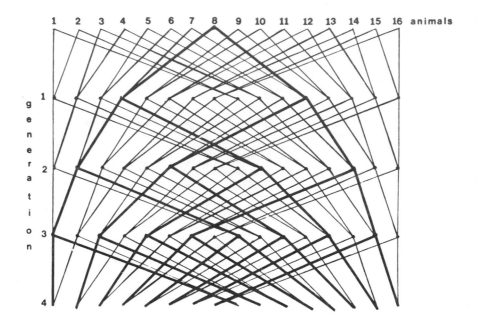

FIGURE 1.   Scheme for maximum avoidance of inbreeding in a stationary
   population of 16 individuals composed of 8 males and 8 females,
   each of whom contribute 1 individual to the next generation.
   From Flesness (1977).

tion.
   2.   An available gene-pool is required.   Thus, it is desirable to
have animals of known origins and pedigrees traceable back to wild-
caught animals.   The number of animals should be chosen on the basis
of the breeding strategy, if possible.   The age and sex structure
should be defined.   Explicit definitions of the need for introduction
of new wild stock should be made in terms of breeding strategy and
breeding management programs with a view to maintaining some defined
level of genetic variability in the population.
   3.   Data collection and sharing are vital elements of a deliberate breeding program.   The ISIS program of the AAZPA can provide census and vital statistics data for breeding programs.   It can also provide demographic projections, pedigrees, studbooks, and the data for
analysis of breeding relationships within the captive population, including calculation of inbreeding coefficients.   Additional components
of the life history analysis are being developed within the ISIS
framework; these will include baseline laboratory data in the "Physio-
logical Norms Program" in collaboration with the AAZV.

Seal: *The Noah's Ark Problem* 307

4. Finally, management of breeding and reproduction are an essential component of this effort. This includes successful breeding
with sufficient frequency to provide for survival and sustaining the
numbers required. Management of reproduction will include both enhancement and limitation of reproduction. Enhancement, where not attainable by management and behavioral manipulation, might include
development of techniques for artificial insemination, estrus synchro-
nization and induction of ovulation. The control of reproduction also
implies that reductions in the number of offspring produced may be desirable, especially when the emphasis is on selectively removing particular individuals by one of several strategies. The costs of such
programs need evaluation, and consideration must be given to the possibility of marketing surplus production for exhibit or other acceptable purposes. This would provide assistance for the establishment of
breeding centers with adequate carrying capacities.

Genetic and Demographic Management of Captive Populations

Computer-based demographic programs for analyzing studbook records, such as those kept by ISIS, have been developed (Foose, 1977;
Seal et al., 1977). The proper use of this tool for captive management programs requires the formulation of a model for each species
based upon the following kinds of information.
1. An estimate of the carrying capacities of the captive breeding groups should be made. This estimate might include, in addition
to sheer physical limitations, considerations of logistic, genetic,
demographic, and conservation criteria. This estimated population
size would then be considered an optimum determined by multiple criteria.
2. The need for surplus animals should be evaluated giving consideration to the needs for replacing animals, providing animals for
exhibit in nonbreeding center institutions, utilizing animals for
research projects that contribute to further understanding of life
history of the species, or other appropriately defined needs. The
size of the existing population, relative to the optimum size of the
population and the need for surplus animals will determine the desired
growth rate of the population.
3. The fecundity and survivorship by age and sex classes must be
determined or estimated. It is particularly important for relatively
long-lived species to have adequate data on the first-year survivorship and the average annual adult survivorship (Figure 2). These 2
characteristics of a species then determine the average number of offspring per parent necessary to maintain a stationary population. This
means that accurate reporting of mortality data is essential in order
to develop a sound demographic plan. Mortality data, especially during the neonatal period or the first year of life, are also absolutely
essential for detection of detrimental inbreeding effects. The failure to recognize inbreeding effects, in most cases, can be attributed
to the lack of adequate records, not to the overall success of random
or inbred breeding programs.
4. The age and sex structure of the existing population must be
known. This information combined with fertility and survivorship data

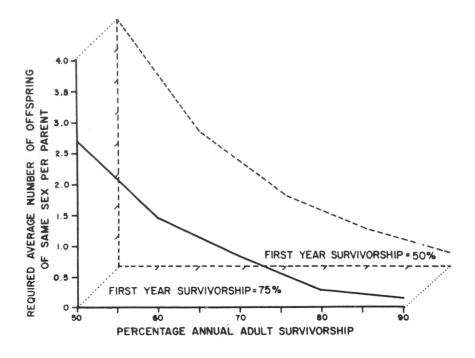

FIGURE 2. Interaction of first-year and adult survivorship to
determine the number of offspring of the same sex per parent
required to maintain a stationary population. From Foose (1977).

may then be utilized to predict the demographic structure of the population. One may then test the effects of various culling or selective removal strategies. Sex and age data also makes it possible to
compare actual performance with expectations and thereby allow the
detection of deviations which might signal unsuspected problems.
      5. An explicit plan should be devised, tested and agreed upon
for moving from the current population to the desired stationary or
stable population. This plan should then be examined carefully,
utilizing stochastic methods to predict fluctuations that might occur in the population. Stated differently, one should be aware of the
likelihood of significant deviations from the stationary population as
the result of random or chance factors and the likelihood that extinction might occur. It is possible to fail despite all best efforts.
      6. This same model and the resulting projections can be utilized
to formulate a strategy for planned reintroductions into the wild of
animals from the captive populations. It might also be used to assist
in the initial management of these wild populations and guide data
collection to assess the success of the reintroduction plan.
      Genetic management of captive populations to provide the maximum

preservation of heterozygosity can be accomplished more effectively
with a deliberate breeding plan rather than the current random efforts
(Flesness, 1977). Our analysis of 3 currently available studbooks indicates that inbreeding has occurred at about 10 times the rate necessary with the available populations. There is evidence of significant
detrimental effects occurring with this inbreeding. The guidelines
for a maximally efficient genetic management program include 3 considerations.

   1. The effective population size will determine the rate of loss
of genetic diversity per generation (Figure 3). The smaller the population, the more rapid the loss of diversity through the generations.
However, it will be noted that a population as small as 64 adults
would allow maintenance of about 65 percent of the original heterozygosity or diversity present in the starting population after 100
generations. It therefore becomes of considerable importance to consider the factors which affect the effective population size in relation to the actual adult animal population in captivity.

   2. Two factors are of primary importance in determining the size
of the effective population, given the use of a maximum avoidance of
inbreeding scheme as shown in Figure 1. These 2 factors can be ad-
justed to give an effective population size equal to twice the number
of adults in the population so that, for example, an effective size of
64 can be achieved with only 32 adults. First, there should be an
equal contribution by all members of the population to the next generation. That is, family size should be equal between all members, or
no animal is bred in preference to another. This is contrary to virtually all current zoo or avicultural practices. There is a strong
and understandable tendency to favor animals that fare well in captivity and breed readily; this clearly promotes selection for inbred and
captive-adapted strains. It also results in a very rapid loss of
genetic diversity. Great care should be taken to randomize the selection of offspring from the pool available from a given pairing so that
selection based on more or less unconscious preferences also does not
occur. Breeding to types should be rigorously avoided. If the population is at the stationary size, then each parent would contribute
one offspring to the next generation. If it is desired to increase
the size of the existing population, then the proportional number of
offspring might be increased to a larger number by the addition of
the same number of offspring from each of the parents. It is desirable to effect the increase in population size from the current population to the desired population size as rapidly, and in as few
generations, as possible. The second feature of the breeding program
is that there should be an equal number of males and females within
the breeding population (Figure 4). Deviation from this equal sex
ratio in terms of production of young for the next breeding generation
will rapidly lead to the loss of genetic diversity. Many species have
special social/behavioral requirements that do not make such an ar-
rangement possible in terms of the managed social groups. This, of
course, is true of herd animals characterized by a dominant male and
a number of breeding females. However, it is possible to rotate males
each year and not use the same male as the breeder for the group year
after year, as has been done for the Przewalski's Horse (*Equus prze-*

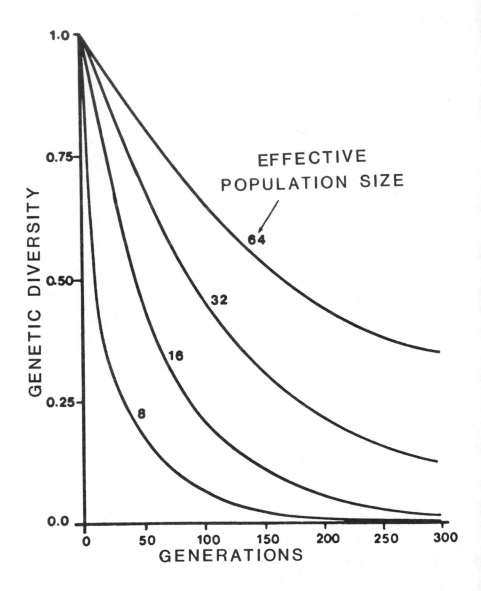

FIGURE 3.   The rate of loss of genetic diversity per generation as
   a function of effective population size. From Flesness (1977).

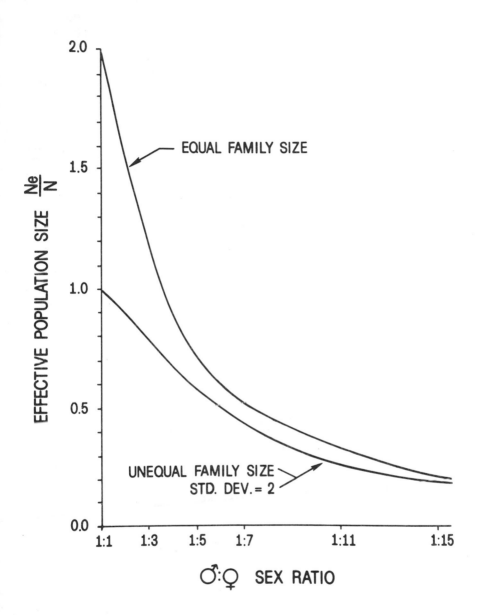

FIGURE 4. The effects of family size and sex ratio on the effective population size of breeding populations. From Flesness (*unpublished data*).

walskii), for example. It is this specific practice with the horse
that has resulted in a nearly 10-fold greater rate of inbreeding than
was necessary. The impact of these 2 factors upon effective population size may be illustrated by the observation that a population of
16 animals with a 1:1 sex ratio, equal family size, and bred according
to the maximum avoidance of inbreeding scheme will preserve as much
genetic diversity as a randomly mating population of 128 animals with
a 1:5 sex ratio and a standard deviation of 1.4 for family size. This
is an 8-fold decrease in efficiency.

   3. The maximum avoidance of inbreeding scheme (Figure 1) devised
many years ago by Wright (1921) can be used for any size population
and is designed to insure that each individual contributes approximately equally to the next generation, thereby holding inbreeding to
an absolute minimum. Another way to maintain or preserve genetic diversity by the apparent reverse of this strategy is also possible.
This would involve establishing perhaps 8 inbred lines. Each of these
lines would include 4 to 8 adults which would themselves be bred according to the maximum avoidance of inbreeding approach, but with the
limited number of animals, each line would become inbred quickly.
Single groups of 2 run a very high risk of more rapid extinction.
However, even groups of this size run a 95 percent risk of extinction
within 20 generations. Those that survived would preserve indefinitely approximately 90 percent of the genetic diversity of a single wild
animal. Then, at some time in the future, individuals from each of
the inbred lines could be crossed to recreate a variable population
representing the original population. This approach, although theoretically possible, is far more risky and would require far more individual animals to establish. This approach might, however, be used
for segments of the population that for some reason are not able to
contribute to the gene pool of the larger population.

   The necessary guidelines and tools are now available to construct
rational genetic and demographic programs for management of captive
wild species. It remains only to decide that it is worth the effort.

ACKNOWLEDGMENTS

   The work described in this paper is the result of collaborative
efforts with D. Makey, D. Bridgwater, L. Simmons, N. Flesness, and T.
Foose in the development of the ISIS program. The heroic data and
systems management efforts of Linda Murtfeldt, Kim Hastings and Jan
Olsen have assured the functioning of this program.

LITERATURE CITED

Flesness, N.R. 1977. Gene pool conservation and computer analysis.
     Inter. Zoo Yearbook 17:77-81.
Foose, T.J. 1977. Demographic models for management of captive popula-
     tions. Inter. Zoo Yearbook 17:70-76.

Seal, U.S., D.G. Makey, D. Bridgwater, L. Simmons and L. Murtfeldt. 1977. ISIS: A computerised record system for the management of wild animals in captivity. Inter. Zoo Yearbook 17:68-70.

Wright, S. 1921. Systems of mating. II. The effects of inbreeding on the genetic composition of a population. Genetics 6:124-143.

35

Fitness of Offspring from Captive Populations

Andrew J. Berger

As a generalization, it seems reasonable to suggest that captive propagation with the intent of saving endangered and threatened species should be viewed as an action of last resort. I say this because biologists no longer think in terms of a single species of plant or animal, but rather of the total ecosystem of which the plants and animals are integral parts. Unless one can preserve the ecosystem in which an animal evolved, it may be futile to release captive-reared birds.

Many bird species that are classified as "endangered" are species that are ecologically intolerant. They cannot, like the Starling (*Sturnus vulgaris*) in North America and the Japanese White-eye (*Zosterops japanica*) in Hawaii, adapt to a wide variety of ecological environments. For intolerant species such as Kirtland's Warbler (*Dendroica kirtlandii*) the preservation and/or improvement of suitable habitat is essential; for this warbler, a drastic reduction of the population of the parasitic Brown-headed Cowbird (*Molothrus ater*) also seems essential.

In most parts of the world, however, great and continuing effort is required to save wild areas, and such efforts have been in vain in all too many countries. Consequently, we are forced to resort to captive rearing programs in our efforts to save species and their gene pools.

That a number of species can be propagated in captivity is now well known. What has not yet been demonstrated with certainty is whether we really can prevent the extinction of an endangered species or subspecies merely by releasing pen-reared birds. The odds are, of course, that we cannot assume success with such a limited approach. One function of this symposium is to investigate the manifold problems involved both in captive breeding programs and in the release of pen-reared birds. Indeed, we know very little about the answers

to the problems I will outline. What I can do, primarily, is to
point to questions, many of which can be answered only by those
investigators who will study the pen-reared birds that they will
release into natural habitats in the years to come.

GENERAL PROBLEMS

Hawaiian birds constitute more than half of all birds listed
by the U. S. Department of the Interior as threatened or endangered
in the United States. Because I live in Hawaii, my ideas are influenced by conditions on those remote islands. Nevertheless, certain
general factors certainly apply in developing propagation programs
for most, if not all, endangered species.

The Genetic Stock

To be most effective, rearing programs must begin before the
size of the wild population has dropped so low that the gene pool
becomes deficient. Little seems to be known about critical population numbers in wild birds. We do know that excessive inbreeding
over a 30-year period in a captive population of the Hawaiian Goose
(*Branta sandvicensis*) seriously affected sperm production in the
ganders, but not the fecundity of the geese. In this instance,
the breeding stock was derived from 2 pairs of birds that had been
captive since 1918. Not until wild stock was added to the breeding
population did fertility and hatchability of fertile eggs rise to
reasonable levels.

Location of Propagation Facilities

Because of economy and convenience, it would seem best to raise
captive birds as close as possible to the intended release site. It
might seem logical to raise them in climatic zones similar to those
inhabited by the wild population. Most programs are so recent,
however, that little information is available on the possible
influence of environmental factors on pen-reared birds in relation
to their reproductive behavior after release in their natural habitat.
In its native habitat on the island of Hawaii (20° N. latitude),
the Hawaiian Goose begins to nest during the early winter (November
in the wild; as early as September in captivity), when daylengths
are decreasing; the shortest daylength at this latitude is 10.8
hours. By contrast, at the Wildfowl Trust in England (52° N), the
birds usually begin to lay in February, when daylength is about 9.5
hours. Janet Kear wrote to me that, in a pen where floodlights
burned until midnight in winter, "Nene moulted in January (three
months early) and failed to breed at all." Unfortunately, we do
not know how the Slimbridge birds adapt when released on the island
of Maui in the Hawaiian Islands.
Ray C. Erickson wrote to me that Masked Bobwhite (*Colinus
virginianus ridgwayi*) that were kept at Patuxent Wildlife Research
Center adopted the breeding phenology of the Eastern Bobwhite

(*C. v. virginianus*) in Maryland; when the offsrping were taken to southern Arizona, however, they nested in late summer, the usual time for the southwestern populations. Similarly, individuals of two subspecies of Sandhill Crane (*Grus canadensis pratensis* and *G. c. pulla*) were hatched at Patuxent from eggs collected in Florida and Mississippi; when mature, these birds nested much later under the natural photoperiod at Patuxent than did the parent populations in Florida and Mississippi.

Thus, it is clear that birds can be induced to breed under different conditions of climate and photoperiod than occur in the native habitat of the species. What is not yet clear is how success-ful are the pen-reared birds in producing young when released in their native habitat. In any event, each species presents a unique set of problems.

Diseases and Parasites

Although perhaps of more critical importance when dealing with island species, care should be taken to prevent the contamination of captive breeding stocks by parasites and diseases that are foreign to the wild populations of the species. This, of course, is easier said than done, and the problems increase greatly where a variety of propagation programs are underway at the same facility. Reasons for releasing parasite-free birds into the wild population are obvious.

Imprinting

Every ornithologist is aware of the phenomonon of imprinting, especially in those precocial species that have been used experi-mentally. It is true that imprinted geese or ducks that have directed all of their attentions to a human keeper for many months may, when mature, mate successfully with their own kind and raise young in captivity. It is questionable, however, how adequately such birds could adapt in the wild environment. In comparing the breeding behavior of wild and captive Gyrfalcons (*Falco rusticolus*), Joseph B. Platt (*personal communication*) pointed to "the overriding necessity of two factors for successful captive breeding: proper rearing so that imprinting on humans does not occur and a pair bond in which the female is dominant over the male."

I should mention that we know next to nothing about the nature of imprinting in most altricial species, even though hand-raised passerine birds sometimes appear to imprint on humans. Therefore, people working in captive-rearing programs must keep imprinting behavior in mind. Passerine birds that are hand-raised from the nestling stage may survive when given their freedom, but we have few examples of such birds (Berger, 1966*a*).

THE HAWAIIAN GOOSE

The propagation program for the Hawaiian Goose is now in its twenty-eighth year. This program has demonstrated clearly that it

is not sufficient simply to release annually 50 or more pen-reared
birds into the native habitat in order to save a species. Following
are some of the problems encountered after the release of these geese.

Feather Pulling

It has been the practice to cut the primary flight feathers in
order to minimize injuries while immature birds are maintained at
the breeding facility at Pohakuloa, Hawaii. The stubs of these
feathers then are pulled out when the birds are placed in the release pens on the sanctuaries. When all is well, the birds grow a
new set of flight feathers in about 6 weeks and then can fly from
the pens. Sometimes, however, feather growth is abnormal after
plucking, and as many as 24 percent of the birds either have impaired
flying ability or cannot fly at all. A large number of these birds
sustain permanently damaged wing feathers so that the birds have to
be returned to captivity. Brailing (tying the bird's hand to the
forearm) of young birds for only 8 days also resulted in impaired
flying ability.

Tameness

Island birds are noted for their tameness in comparison with
continental species, but problems may arise when any pen-reared
birds are released in the wild. Again, I refer to experiences with
Hawaiian Geese. One group of 5 recently released geese flew to
Puako at sea level; these birds were captured and returned to the
Keauhou sanctuary on 8 June 1976. Several months later, the same
birds were found in a State park, about 90 km from the release site.
Other geese have been recovered at distances up to 80 km from their
release site. Moreover, these birds often turn up in inhabited
areas, such as a sugarcane plantation, a papaya farm, near small
towns, and along main roads. The birds were tame enough that
several were caught by teenagers; others were captured with throw
nets. It does not seem likely that such birds can be an effective
addition to the wild population.

Homing

The homing abilities of the Hawaiian Goose have not been studied,
but there have been some notable examples of birds returning to the
breeding pens at Pohakuloa. A goose was released at Haleakala Crater
on Maui in 1962, and a gander in 1968. These two birds were discovered in the Kahuku sanctuary on Hawaii during the 1972-1973 breeding
season. Other geese raised at Pohakuloa and released on Maui in
1966 and 1969 were found on Hawaii during the breeding season of
1970. One goose returned to Pohakuloa twice after being released
in the Keauhou sanctuary on Hawaii. She was then released at the
Paliku site on Maui, but again returned to Pohakuloa after a flight
of about 112 km from Maui to Hawaii; this bird was given to the
Honolulu Zoo.

Aberrant Birds

Genetic aberrations turn up in some progeny. Hawaiian Geese sometimes hatch with a condition called "hairy down." These goslings survive in captivity and develop what appears to be normal adult plumage. Personnel of the State Division of Fish and Game reported in 1965 that 3 such birds were unable to adapt to the release pens and had to be returned to Pohakuloa, each of the birds in "an emaciated condition." Another goose developed "weakened legs" while in the release pen and had to be killed because a cure could not be found. Other birds with tremors and similar neurological signs have died or been unable to leave the release pens. "Hairy down" is a recessive character, and the frequency of such characters increases with an increase in inbreeding.

Predators

One must assume that the techniques used in propagating birds for release will not "hinder" whatever innate responses to predators are found in the different bird species. The problem presumably is not serious for continental species. There are no endemic mammalian predators in the Hawaiian Islands, but the introduced predators have been a serious threat to all ground nesting Hawaiian birds. It seems certain, for example, that the extinction of the Hawaiian Duck (*Anas wyvilliana*) on all islands except Kauai during this century was due to the presence of the Mongoose (*Herpestes auropunctatus*) on all islands except for Kauai. Other predators that eat eggs, downy young, and flightless adults are rats and feral pigs, dogs, and cats, common introduced predators on islands throughout the world. Predator control (by using poisoned goat meat), therefore, is an important part of the Nene release program; baits are placed around the release pens before Nene are released; and baits also are used in the vicinity of active nests during the breeding season.

Competition for Food

It is ironic that some introduced game birds may be competing for the same foods eaten by the Hawaiian Geese. The best evidence comes from crop examinations of Wild Turkeys (*Mealeagris gallopavo*) on Hawaii.

Adverse Weather

Severe weather can cause the desertion of nests or the death of goslings. For example, 64.7 cm of rain fell at the Maui release site between 4-10 December 1968, and hail plus 91.4 cm of rain fell during a 3-day period ending on 1 February 1969. Eggs hatched in only 2 of 14 nests, and 3 of 5 goslings later were found dead. Luck, as well as careful planning, therefore, may be essential for the reproduction of released birds.

SUMMARY STATEMENT

Endangered bird species run the gamut from pelicans to passerines. We will need refined techniques in order to rear many of these species in captivity (Berger, 1966b; 1968). Moreover, because the stated goal is to remove species from the endangered species list, we must accomplish more than the successful propagation of birds in captivity. We must add to the wild populations captive-raised birds that will be successful in reproducing into succeeding generations. To achieve this goal, basic biological studies must be conducted both before and after the birds are released.

We must have available the information that can be obtained only by conducting intensive studies of the annual cycle of each species. Such studies must include details of breeding biology, food habits, and limiting factors for the species. Such information is now available for very few species, and for a number of species on the endangered list, the nest and eggs have not even been described.

Artificial nest sites have been used successfully with eagles and ospreys. Nest sites may be limiting for other species. For example, we have learned recently that two endemic species of endangered Hawaiian birds appear to be cavity nesters. One reason for the drastic reduction in the populations of these birds, therefore, may have been the destruction of virgin forests with their very large, old trees that contained nesting cavities; by contrast, the younger trees now found in these forests rarely have cavities that are suitable for hole nesters. Thus, a failure to determine the limiting factor (or factors) could doom the entire effort to save a species. Zimmerman (1975) has discussed other techniques used with several endangered species.

It also is essential to conduct intensive studies after the release of captive birds in order to observe the behavior of the birds and to discover any problems that they may be having. The failure to conduct such studies of the wild populations of the Hawaiian Goose has led to the present uncertainties as to the effectiveness of this release program.

LITERATURE CITED

Berger, A.J. 1966a. Survival in the wild of hand-reared passerine birds. Condor 68(3):304-405.
Berger, A.J. 1966b. Experience with insectivorous birds in captivity. Jack-Pine Warbler 44(2):65-73.
Berger, A.J. 1968. Behavior of hand-raised Kirtland's Warblers. Living Bird 7:103-116.
Zimmerman, D.R. 1975. To Save a Bird in Peril. Coward, McCann & Geoghegan, Inc. New York, 286 p.

Part VIII
Reintroducing Endangered Birds to the Wild

36

Reintroducing Endangered Birds to the Wild
A Review

Richard W. Fyfe

I feel that I must begin this review by stating that I have been unable to locate a single example of a self-sustaining wild population that resulted from the reintroduction of an endangered bird back into its original habitat. The closest example seems to be the successful translocation of New Zealand's endangered Saddleback (*Philesturnus carunculatus rufusater*) from North Island to the previously unoccupied Middle Chicken Island (Merton, 1973, 1975). However, this is actually an example of an introduction into new habitat rather than a reintroduction into previously occupied habitat. Another example involves the apparently successful reintroductions of the rare, but not endangered, Eagle Owl (*Bubo bubo*) into portions of its European range where it had been extirpated (Wayre, 1975). The much heralded reintroductions of Hawaiian Geese (*Branta sandvicensis*) have not yet clearly led to the successful establishment of wild breeding populations (Kear, 1975; A. Berger, Ch. 38, *this volume*). Other reintroduction programs for endangered birds are still in their early phases, and their success cannot be properly evaluated at this time.

Hence, if I were to take the title of this paper literally, my review could end here, thereby providing the shortest paper of the symposium! However, taking a somewhat more liberal view of the question of reintroductions, I find that there are numerous examples of successful introductions and reintroductions of non-endangered birds that can provide a valuable framework for a discussion of reintroducing endangered species.

There are at least 3 different situations that have relevance to the problems of reintroductions.

1. The colonization of a remote oceanic island by landbirds provides a natural example of the same types of biological problems inherent in reintroductions. A small number of individuals form the initial propagule that arrives in a new habitat. If they reproduce

successfully, a new population may be derived from them. By examining the characteristics of successful propagules, we can gain some insight into the possible traits that would favor a successful reintroduction.

2. Throughout history, man has introduced exotic birds into the regions of the world he has settled. Fortunately, many of man's introductions of exotic birds have failed, but those that succeeded and resulted in new populations probably hold some clues about the necessary requirements for a successful reintroduction.

3. Restocking of gamebirds after local populations have been depleted or even extirpated through overharvesting is a standard technique in game management (Bump, 1951). Once again the experience that game managers have gained during these restocking operations can have a bearing on the question of reintroducing endangered species.

LESSONS FROM SUCCESSFUL ISLAND COLONISTS

The study of island zoogeography has recently been a very popular endeavor among avian ecologists (e.g., Diamond, 1973; Lack, 1976). From our point of view, such ecological studies of island birds have revealed what we might call an optimal strategy that most consistently leads to the successful establishment of a population on an island after an initial propagule has arrived. Presumably, these same strategies would be useful in reintroduction programs. At least 3 biological traits appear to be characteristic of successful island colonists: 1) having a high reproductive rate that permits the initial founding population to rapidly increase in size, 2) being an ecological generalist so that the progagule can readily adapt to a fairly wide range of environmental conditions, and 3) being gregarious--especially forming flocks--so that the small number of initial colonists will not have difficulty finding each other for mating.

LESSONS FROM INTRODUCTIONS OF EXOTIC BIRDS

There have been remarkably few reviews of the histories of introductions of exotic birds. Those case histories that have been catalogued are usually the most successful introductions, but little if anything is ever recorded about the introductions that have failed. Hence, we have a very biased set of data to examine. If we examine the successful cases that have been documented in reviews such as Laycock (1966), we find that there are a number of common features: 1) repeated introductions of relatively large numbers of birds were usually necessary to build up the initial populations, 2) the birds involved usually had high reproductive rates, were ecological generalists, and were gregarious--just like successful island colonists; and 3) the environments into which the exotics were released usually contained few effective predators or competitors so that there was little resistance to population growth. Some outstanding examples of successful introductions of exotics occurred in North America. Starlings (*Sturnus vulgaris*), House Sparrows (*Passer domesticus*) and Rock Doves (*Columba livia*) have reached all corners of the continent after being released initially in cities on the East Coast.

LESSONS FROM THE STOCKING OF GAMEBIRDS

Since the stocking of gamebirds, unlike the introduction of exotics, is usually carried out as an organized and well-documented exercise, we have a great wealth of data on successes and failures. There are numerous examples we could cite, but some of the best are: the Ring-necked Pheasant (*Phasianus colchicus*) in North America, the Wild Turkey (*Meleagris gallopavo*) in North America, the Capercaillie (*Tetrao urogallus*) in Scotland, the Canada Goose (*Branta canadensis*) in New Zealand, and the Coturnix Quail (*Coturnix coturnix*) in North America. It is interesting to note that all these gamebirds are gregarious and possess high reproductive rates.

Ring-necked Pheasant

The successful establishment of the Ring-necked Pheasant as an exotic gamebird in North America is a classic (Laycock, 1966). After many failures--some dating back to 1730--the pheasant was finally introduced successfully in 1882 in Portland, Oregon. It has been stocked in all parts of North America since then. In areas where conditions are suitable, pheasants have established self-sustaining populations that can even stand being harvested. In other areas, the continued existence of pheasants in the wild has depended on repeated restocking of birds because the wild populations are not self-sustaining. The main lessons are that large numbers of birds and repeated restocking were required and that in only a few optimal situations did self-sustaining populations result.

Wild Turkey

The Wild Turkey underwent a great population decline and range contraction in response to overhunting, habitat change, and the loss of its staple food to chestnut blight. Restocking, careful management, and habitat improvement have brought the turkey back to much of its former range, and these efforts have been reviewed at length by turkey specialists (e.g., Hewitt, 1967; Sanderson, 1973). There are special lessons to be learned from these efforts. The type of stock that is released influences the success of the stocking. Usually experienced, wild-caught birds do better than inexperienced, pen-reared birds. Also, habitat improvements and protection must coincide with the initial releases in a region.

Capercaillie

After being extirpated in the British Isles, the Capercaillie was successfully restocked in Scotland during the last century (Harvie-Brown, 1879; Rennie, 1950). Paralleling the restocking of turkeys, success was achieved by restocking wild-caught Capercaillie, by providing suitable habitat, and by protecting the initial restocked populations from hunting pressures and predation.

Canada Goose

The Canada Goose was introduced into New Zealand several times beginning in 1876. It became firmly established in the wild only after a 1905-release of 48 wild-caught geese (Clark, 1949). By 1950 the goose population had become a pest, competing with sheep for green grass and grazing in grain fields. Once again, repeated introductions and wild-caught birds were necessary before a self-sustaining wild population was established.

Coturnix Quail

The Coturnix Quail provides an example of a gamebird stocking program that failed. Beginning in 1875, and continuing until 1956, thousands of quail were released in North America, but all attempts failed (Laycock, 1966). Despite their adaptability in Europe and Asia, their high reproductive rate, and the lavish attention that game managers bestowed on them, quail succumbed to predators and their instinctive tendency to migrate took them into unsuitable habitats. The North American environment clearly was not suitable for Coturnix Quail, and no matter how many were released, what their prior background was, or where they were placed, there was no chance for success.

THE PROSPECTS FOR REINTRODUCING ENDANGERED BIRDS

Based on the information on successful introductions and reintroductions of exotic birds and gamebirds and on the types of birds that successfully colonize islands, the reintroduction of endangered species presents many obstacles. The best candidates for successful reintroductions have high reproductive rates, are ecological generalists, and are gregarious flocking species. Many endangered species are characterized by low reproductive rates, highly specialized ecological requirements, and solitary social organizations. Most successful introductions of non-endangered birds have required repeated releases of large numbers of birds, whereas most endangered species are so rare that existing populations are neither numerous nor productive enough to provide an abundant stock for release in empty portions of the species' range. It appears from all indications that the reintroduction of endangered species into the wild will be a very difficult task.

REQUIREMENTS FOR A SUCCESSFUL REINTRODUCTION OF AN ENDANGERED BIRD

Despite all the apparent odds against reintroductions of endangered birds, there are several approaches that may increase the likelihood of success. When dealing with endangered birds, managers do not have large numbers to work with; hence great emphasis must be placed

on enhancing the survivorship and reproductive success of a few
individuals. This requires a considerable investment of time and
effort. Some of the prerequisites for a successful reintroduction
of an endangered bird are summarized below.

Prior Identification of the Species' Requirements

It is essential that the endangered species manager identify
the critical limiting factors for the species being reintroduced.
An understanding of these factors permits the manager to minimize
their effects on the released birds. For example, as we shall soon
learn, prior studies of a species' requirements and limiting factors
have played a major role in the reintroduction programs for Aleutian
Canada Geese (*Branta canadensis leucopareia*) (P. Springer et al., Ch.
37, *this volume*), the Black Robins (*Petroica traversi*) (J. Flack,
Ch. 41, *this volume*). In both of these programs, the habitat into
which the birds were reintroduced was improved by either eliminating
predators and competitors or improving the condition of the vegetation.

Concentrating Releases to Promote Mating

When dealing with small numbers of released birds, it is essential to locate the birds so that they can easily find each other for
mating. Concentrating all releases in one restricted area can accomplish this goal for solitary species; releasing social units or flocks
can be used for gregarious species; and taking advantage of behavioral
mechanisms such as imprinting and site tenacity can promote success.
Each of the various reintroduction programs we shall learn about in
this symposium has used some special technique for helping released
birds find each other.

Minimizing Mortality in Released Birds

Excessive mortality during the initial period after release is
characteristic of many introductions, especially where large numbers
of birds are released so that the losses are not critical to the
success of the program. Once again, the reintroduction of small
numbers of endangered birds makes such losses unacceptable; special
efforts must be made to ensure the survival of each individual. For
example, legal protection from hunting has helped improve the survival
of Aleutian Canada Geese (P. Springer et al., Ch. 37, *this volume*), and
radio-tracking of released falcons has helped managers to rescue
released birds from accidents (S. Temple, Ch. 40, *this volume*).

Releasing Birds that are Fit for the Wild

It is important to select birds with genetic traits and behavioral
backgrounds that will enhance their survival in the environment where
they are released. Usually release stock should be as close as possible to wild birds in genetic traits. For this reason, birds kept
for many generations in captivity are less desirable than birds taken

directly from the wild or only a few generations removed from wild stock. Berger (Ch. 38, *this volume*) explains how problems of this type affected the Hawaiian Goose reintroduction program. Insuring that birds have the essential behavioral requirements for existence in the wild is just as important. When it is impossible to release experienced birds, releasing inexperienced birds gradually so as to allow them time to make behavioral adjustments results in the best survivorship. Ellis et al. (Ch. 39, *this volume*) used intensive training procedures to improve the condition of released quail. Temple (Ch. 40, *this volume*) and Kress (Ch. 42, *this volume*) point out the advantages of releasing young fledglings that are primed psychologically and physiologically for rapidly acquiring traits that enhance survival.

Monitoring the Survival of Released Birds

Releasing birds--and then not subsequently making a careful assessment of their survivorship--can lead to repetition of mistakes in future releases (e.g., A. Berger, Ch. 38, *this volume*). Careful follow-up work to determine where, when, and how the released birds have encountered problems is essential for perfecting release procedures. The use of marked birds is described by Temple (Ch. 40, *this volume*), Kress (Ch. 42, *this volume*), Morton (Ch. 43, *this volume*), and Springer et al. (Ch. 57, *this volume*). Follow-up census work and checks for reproduction are also essential parts of a reintroduction program.

CONCLUSIONS ON REINTRODUCING ENDANGERED BIRDS

Although presenting many obstacles, the reintroduction of endangered birds back into their natural geographic range can be accomplished as long as several demanding prerequisites are met. Because of the small numbers that are usually involved in endangered species reintroductions, it is necessary for the endangered species manager to take special measures to insure the survival of released individuals. This often demands that the manager must work intimately with the released birds during the crucial early stages of their existence in the wild. Intensive efforts at this early stage can make the crucial difference in survivorship to breeding age. Once the reintroduced birds have become successful breeders, additional reintroductions, continued protection, and management may be necessary before they become a self-sustaining wild population, which is the goal of any reintroduction program.

LITERATURE CITED

Bump, G. 1951. Game introductions: where, when, and how. Trans. North Am. Wildl. Conf. 5:409-420.
Clark, A.H. 1949. The invasion of New Zealand by people, plants, and animals. Rutgers Univ. Press, New Brunswick, N.J.

Diamond, J. 1973. Distributional ecology of New Guinea birds. Science 179:759-769.

Harvie-Brown, J.A. 1879. The capercaillie in Scotland. Edinburgh, Scotland. 189 p.

Hewitt, O.H. (ed.) 1967. The wild turkey and its management. The Wildlife Society, Washington, D.C. 589p.

Kear, J. 1975. Returning the Hawaiian Goose to the wild, p. 115-124. *In* R.D. Martin (ed.). Breeding Endangered Species in Captivity. Academic Press, London. 419 p.

Lack, D. 1976. Island biology illustrated by the land birds of Jamaica. Univ. of California Press, Berkeley. 445 p.

Laycock, G. 1966. The alien animals: the story of imported wildlife. The Natural History Press, Garden City, N.Y. 240 p.

Merton, D.V. 1973. Conservation of the saddleback. Wildlife--A review 4:13-23.

Merton, D.V. 1975. The saddleback: its status and conservation, p. 61-74. *In* R.D. Martin (ed.). Breeding Endangered Species in Captivity. Academic Press, London. 419 p.

Rennie, T.D. 1950. The history and distribution of the Capercaillie in Scotland. Scot. Naturalist 62:9-87.

Sanderson, G.C. and H.C. Schultz (eds.). 1973. Wild turkey management: current problems and progress. Univ. of Missouri Press, Columbia. 355 p.

Wayre, P. 1975. Conservation of Eagle Owls and other raptors through captive breeding and return to the wild, p. 125-132. *In* R.D. Martin (ed.). Breeding Endangered Species in Captivity. Academic Press, London. 419 p.

37

Reestablishing Aleutian Canada Geese

Paul F. Springer, G. Vernon Byrd,
and Dennis W. Woolington

The Aleutian Canada Goose (*Branta canadensis leucopareia*) is a small subspecies of Canada Goose distinguished by a white neck-ring at the base of the black neck. Once it bred in the thousands (Turner, 1886) on the outer two-thirds of the Aleutian Islands (Figure 1) from the Islands of Four Mountains group (Jochelson, 1933) west to the Commander (Stejneger, 1883) and Kuril Islands (Snow, 1897) of the Soviet Union. It was said to winter south to California and Japan (Delacour, 1951). Today the total known spring population is about 1,150, and the geese nest only on Buldir Island, a 1,990 ha speck of volcanic rock in the western Aleutians. Although hunting on the breeding, migration, and wintering grounds (Turner, 1886; Grinnell et al., 1918) as well as habitat modification have probably played a role in reducing the number of birds, the principal factor has undoubtedly been predation by Arctic Foxes (*Alopex lagopus*) introduced to the Aleutians for fur-farming purposes during the century from about 1836 (Tikhmenev, 1861) to about 1930 (R.D. Jones, *personal communication*). Because it is isolated and lacks a good harbor, Buldir was spared this fate (Jones, 1963).

THE RECOVERY PROGRAM FOR ALEUTIAN CANADA GEESE

The program to reestablish the Aleutian Canada Goose was actually started nearly 30 years ago by the Aleutian Islands National Wildlife Refuge. However, it was not until a few years ago, especially after the U.S. Fish and Wildlife Service appointed a Recovery Team in 1975, that the program was broadened and accelerated. The recovery program has as its goal the restoration of the Aleutian Canada Goose to a secure status within its historical range. There are 4 parts to the program (Byrd and Springer, 1976):

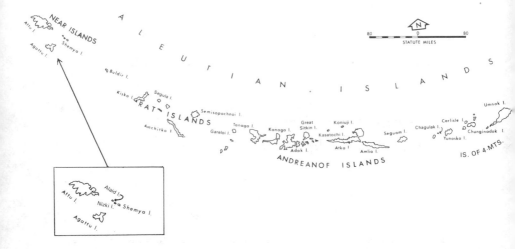

FIGURE 1.   The breeding range of the Aleutian Canada Goose in the
outer two-thirds of the Aleutian Islands.

1.   Removing foxes from goose breeding islands
2.   Captive breeding of geese
3.   Reintroducing captive-reared geese
4.   Studying and protecting wild geese

Removing Foxes from Goose Breeding Islands

The first part of the program involves eliminating the introduced
foxes from former goose-nesting islands. The recovery team feels that
if 50 self-sustaining, breeding pairs of geese can be reestablished on
2 major islands or island groups, the birds would repopulate these release sites and could be safely designated a threatened species rather
than endangered. If similar success could be achieved on a third island, it is believed the birds would be sufficiently secure that they
could be removed from the threatened category.
Accordingly, 3 sites, separated to reduce the danger of local
disasters such as earthquakes and tidal waves, have been selected.
These are: Agattu Island (22,480 ha) with nearby Nizki Island (690 ha)
and Alaid Island (590 ha) in the Near Island group, Amchitka Island
(29,560 ha) in the Rat Island group, and Kanaga Island (37,130 ha) in
the Andreanof Island group. Agattu was selected because it was nearly
fox-free and, historically, had possibly the greatest density of nesting geese. Foxes had been exterminated on Amchitka, and the island
has support and aircraft-landing facilities built by the Atomic Energy
Commission. Kanaga is a large island in the middle of the Aleutian

chain and was a known goose breeding area.

The first efforts to eliminate foxes began on Amchitka in 1949 when Robert D. Jones, Jr., the first resident manager of the Aleutian Islands National Wildlife Refuge, and his staff poisoned foxes with strychnine or Compound 1080. Continuation of this program coupled with trapping and shooting was effective in eliminating all foxes from the island by 1965 (R.D. Jones, *personal communication*).

Amchitka had no native land mammals which might be affected by the poisoning program, and baits were kept small to prevent birds from detecting them. No noticeable reductions in Glaucous-winged Gulls (*Larus glaucescens*) was noted, but the numbers of Bald Eagles (*Haliaeetus leucocephalus*) and Common Ravens (*Corvus corax*) were reduced. The eagle population recovered quickly (Kenyon, 1961), but the ravens required a longer time.

On Agattu, poisoned bait was applied aerially in 1964, and this was followed with ground control through 1970. It was thought that no foxes remained, but in 1974 foxes were found. The population was estimated to be less than 100. Guns and traps were used to exterminate the remaining foxes because the use of chemical toxicants for predator control on federal lands had been prohibited in 1972. By the spring of 1977, all foxes were thought to have been eradicated, but special permission was obtained to use M-44 cyanide devices through the summer to ensure that no animals remained. When the devices were removed in August, none had been discharged, but one set of fresh fox tracks was found. An environmental statement has been prepared on the use of chemical toxicants for fox control on Agattu.

On Nizki and Alaid Islands, ground control programs were conducted from 1969 through 1976, and no foxes remained. Fox control was initiated on Kanaga in 1977.

Captive Breeding of Geese

The second part of the program is the production of birds in captivity for later release on fox-free islands. In 1963, 18 goslings were taken from Buldir, where breeding birds had been discovered during the previous year (Jones, 1963). These captive birds were held at the Monte Vista National Wildlife Refuge in Colorado until 1966, when 8 of the birds were transported to the newly established Endangered Species Research Program facility in Laurel, Maryland. This flock was supplemented with additions of 21 goslings from Buldir in 1972 and 20 in 1975. The birds bred in captivity at Patuxent, and altogether about 381 geese have been reared to 3 months of age or older from 1966 through 1977.

In 1976, a second propagation facility was established on Amchitka with birds from Patuxent and birds that had been sent from Patuxent to the Northern Prairie Wildlife Research Center in Jamestown, North Dakota. In that year, 26 goslings were raised on Amchitka from eggs taken from wild nests on Buldir; in 1977, a total of 56 goslings were produced by the captive flock on Amchitka. An annual production of 100 birds at Patuxent and 100 at Amchitka has been set as a goal for 1978. All of these captive-reared birds will be used for restocking purposes.

Reintroducing Captive-reared Geese

The third part of the program is to release captive-reared geese on fox-free islands in the Aleutians and to monitor their fate.

The first reintroduction attempt occurred in May 1971 when 75 free-flying, 1-, 2-, and 3-year old birds were released on Amchitka. Some of the birds were killed by Bald Eagles, but most apparently left the island shortly after release and were never seen again.

In March 1974, 41 wing-clipped, 2- and 3-year old birds were sent to Attu Island at the west end of the Aleutians and held there until early May when they were released on Agattu. Prior to the release, it was discovered, as previously mentioned, that foxes were still present on the island. Since the number of foxes appeared to be relatively low, the birds were released as planned. Of the 16 females and 25 males, 4 pairs nested, and 2 successfully hatched 5 young. The other geese remained in a group near the release site all summer. Only 1 bird was killed, possibly by a fox.

In order to guide the birds to the wintering grounds, 9 flightless, molting, wild geese were brought to Agattu from Buldir and released in August with the captive-reared birds. The flock departed on September 4 in an easterly direction. Three of the captive-reared birds are known to have reached the wintering ground on the northern California coast. One, apparently a lone bird, was shot on December 16 near Crescent City in Del Norte County (Figure 2), and another was reported seen twice the following March with the wild flock near the same location. The third was found dead in January in Mendocino County. In addition, one of the guide birds was shot out of a flock of 8-10 birds just outside the San Luis National Wildlife Refuge in Merced County on December 21. Unfortunately, no further confirmed records of the released birds have been obtained at Agattu, at Buldir, or on the migration route and wintering grounds.

In 1976, 20 wing-clipped geese were released on Amchitka in May, and an additional 10 free-flying geese were released in September. All but one of these were 3-year old birds. Three wild, adult geese from Buldir were added to the fall group. Again, eagle predation was a problem. In the spring release, at least 2 birds were killed by eagles, and 3 birds rejoined the captive flock after being harassed by eagles; the rest of the birds were not seen after the second day of release. Eight of the fall-released birds also disappeared. Of these, 3, including 1 wild guide-bird, were known to have been killed by eagles. The remaining 5 birds were trapped and placed back with the captive flock after they displayed no inclination to migrate.

Study and Protection of Wild Geese

The final part of the recovery program involves studying the population size, biology, and ecology of the wild geese on their breeding, migration, and wintering grounds and insuring their protection.

During the summers of 1974-77, the breeding biology of the geese was studied on Buldir. Most of the birds nest on steep sea slopes in tall vegetation and lay an average of 5.6 eggs in late May and early

FIGURE 2. Locations in northern California of recoveries or sightings of Aleutian Canada Geese and of areas closed to Canada Goose hunting.

June. Incubation lasts 27-28 days, and nesting success is about 90 percent. At fledging, the average brood size is about 4. A stratified, random sampling of the island revealed an estimated 167 breeding pairs in 1977.

Canada Geese are hunted widely, and Aleutian Canada Geese are difficult to distinguish in the field from other subspecies. Banding has been used to trace the movements of the birds and appraise mortality factors. During the summers of 1974-76, a total of 327 molting adults or flightless young were caught on Buldir and banded with monel and colored-plastic leg-bands. In addition, in the spring of 1976 and 1977, 55 and 158 birds, respectively, were trapped with cannon nets at Crescent City. These were banded and marked with either colored-plastic leg-bands or neck-collars. Hunters recovered 9 of the banded birds in the Sacramento and San Joaquin Valleys during the 1974-75 hunting season. In addition, 4 unbanded birds identified as Aleutian Canada Geese were shot in Humboldt County.

Because of the apparent risk of Aleutian Canada Geese being killed by hunters, in 1975 the California Department of Fish and Game closed 3 areas to hunting of all Canada Geese in order to protect the Aleutian Geese. These included the northwest coastal counties of Del Norte, Humboldt, and Mendocino for the entire season, part of the Sacramento Valley in Glenn and Colusa Counties during the period from the season opening in mid-October to December 15, and part of the San Joaquin Valley in San Joaquin, Stanislaus, and Merced Counties from December 15 to the close of the season in the latter part of January (Figure 2).

In the 2 subsequent hunting seasons, 12 and 14 banded birds have been recovered, mostly in agricultural lands of the Sacramento and San Joaquin Valleys and the intervening Delta area. As a result, the closed area of the Sacramento Valley has been enlarged to include parts of Butte and Sutter Counties, and the San Joaquin Valley closure now starts on November 25. Because there were no recoveries or sightings of banded wild birds in Mendocino County, this county is to be reopened to Canada Goose hunting in 1977.

Five of the recoveries during the 1975-76 hunting season, 4 of which represented a single family group, were recorded considerably farther south near the Salton Sea and along the lower Colorado River in Arizona and Sonora, Mexico. They appear to represent birds seeking suitable foraging conditions during this droughty period.

In addition to the recoveries by hunters, Aleutian Canada Geese were discovered in the spring of 1975 near Crescent City on their northward migration. Careful observations of bands, behavior and plumages during this and the following springs have revealed that essentially all the birds are Aleutians, not more than 10 being Cackling and Taverner's Canada Geese (*B.c. minima* and *B.c. taverneri*). The entire population of Aleutian Canada Geese apparently stages here during the period from late March to mid-April. Very accurate census figures have been obtained as the birds fly the 2.4 km from their roost on 5.2 ha Castle Rock to the mainland to feed in pasturelands. Peak counts from 1975-77 have totalled 790, 900, and 1,150 birds, respectively, for an average annual increase of over 22 percent.

DISCUSSION

The principal program accomplishments to date have included: learning more about the biology and ecology of the geese, determining their numbers and distribution, ridding 3 former nesting islands of foxes (a fourth island has been rendered nearly fox-free), and providing protection to the wild population on their migration and wintering areas. Surveys of all major islands and many smaller ones in the Aleutians show that the birds apparently nest only on Buldir. Most depart during September, flying to the eastern Aleutians and possibly stopping at Unimak Island. In late October, birds gather at Castle Rock, where up to several hundred birds are observed for a period of several weeks, and near Colusa in the Sacramento Valley, where most of the population gathers. The lack of definite records in British Columbia, Washington, and Oregon suggests a transoceanic flight to California. The birds leave the Sacramento Valley in the latter part of November, moving on to the Delta and subsequently to the San Joaquin Valley. By January, some birds have already returned north to Castle Rock, and most have left California by the end of April. They appear to retrace their flight to the Aleutians, with a few possibly stopping near the mouth of the Columbia River. Birds have already been present on Buldir when investigators land on the island in early May.

The encouraging increase in the population seems attributable primarily to saving birds that otherwise would have been lost to hunters. Nesting studies during the same period reveal that breeding success has remained relatively stable. Some losses result from shooting outside the closure areas, and such losses may increase if drought causes birds to seek more favorable habitat in unprotected areas. Other losses result from poaching and diseases, such as avian cholera which appears to be spreading in the state. The total loss from fall 1976 to spring 1977 was estimated to be 130 birds, or about 10 percent of the population, based on 1,280 birds seen mainly in the Colusa area in mid-November and 1,150 seen at Crescent City in April.

FUTURE PLANS

Despite the success to date in increasing the number of wild birds on Buldir, attainment of the program goal to restore the Aleutian Canada Geese to a secure status will be achieved only after breeding geese are established on other islands. Fox control will be completed on Agattu and continued on Kanaga, and in 1978, captive-reared birds will again be released on Agattu where Bald Eagles are very scarce. Radios will be placed upon the geese to help trace their movements. When geese are released again on Amchitka, some means will have to be found to minimize eagle predation on the birds until a self-sufficient breeding flock is established.

The size and distribution of the wild population will continue to be monitored to determine changes, the importance of various geographic areas, and the possible need for additional protection. In this connection, comprehensive surveys are needed to determine the current status of the populations breeding on the Commander and Kuril Islands and wintering in Japan.

Critical habitat is being proposed in the Crescent City area and will likely be proposed elsewhere as the location of key areas is established. In addition, steps will be taken through purchase or easement to safeguard the integrity of the heavily used areas near Crescent City.

A continuing problem is the difficulty in distinguishing Aleutian Canada Geese from similar subspecies. Studies are underway to determine the usefulness of morphometric, mineral composition, and electrophoretic techniques.

The recovery program is based upon a coordinated, multi-faceted approach involving all known pertinent factors. Good cooperation has been received from all concerned, and this is expected to continue in the future. With this strong support, prospects for achieving the program goal of restoring the Aleutian Canada Goose to a secure status appear promising.

LITERATURE CITED

Byrd, G.V. and P.F. Springer. 1976. Recovery program for the endangered Aleutian Canada goose, p. 65-73. *In* Cal-Neva Wildlife Trans.

Delacour, J. 1951. Preliminary note on the taxonomy of Canada geese, *Branta canadensis*. Am. Mus. Novitates No. 1537. 10p.

Grinnell, J., H.C. Bryant, and T.I. Storer. 1918. The game birds of California. Univ. of California Press, Berkeley. 642p.

Jochelson, W. 1933. History, ethnology and anthropology of the Aleut. Carnegie Inst. Wash. Publ. 432. 91p.

Jones, R.D., Jr. 1963. Buldir Island, site of a remnant breeding population of Aleutian Canada geese. Annu. Rep. Wildfowl Trust 14:80-84.

Kenyon, K.W. 1961. Birds of Amchitka Island, Alaska. Auk 78(3):305-326.

Snow, H.J. 1897. Notes on the Kuril Islands. Royal Geogr. Soc., London. 91p.

Stejneger, L. 1883. Contributions to the history of the Commander Islands. Proc. U.S. Natl. Mus. 6:58-89.

Tikhmenev, P.A. 1861. Historical review of the origin of the Russian-American Company and its activities up to the present time. Part I. Edward Weimar Printing Office, St. Petersburg (Translated from Russian by Michael Dobrynin).

Turner, L.M. 1886. Contributions to the natural history of Alaska. U.S. Government Printing Office, Washington, D.C. 226p.

38

Reintroduction of Hawaiian Geese

Andrew J. Berger

The Hawaiian Islands lie in the Pacific Ocean more than 3,218 km from the continents of North America and Asia. Because of this remoteness and isolation, few ancestral land-birds were successful in reaching and colonizing these islands. Hawaii has one endemic bird family (Drepanididae, Hawaiian honeycreepers), and 10 other families are represented by endemic genera, species, or subspecies (Berger, 1972). The Nene or Hawaiian Goose (*Branta sandvicensis*), the Koloa or Hawaiian Duck (*Anas wyvilliana*), and the Laysan Duck (*Anas laysanensis*) are the Anatidae endemic to the Hawaiian islands.

HISTORY OF THE NENE

During the early 19th century, the Nene had a wide distribution from 2,743 m to sea level. It has been said that the birds descended to the lower elevations during the winter and spring in order to feed on new vegetation, returning to the uplands to feed on berries during the summer (Henshaw, 1904). Baldwin (1945) postulated a decrease in range of the Nene from 6,410 km^2 in 1800 to 2,979 km^2 in 1940. Baldwin added that "the wild Nene population may have totalled 25,000 or more in the latter part of the 18th century. It is now reduced to about 50 birds." Smith (1952) wrote that "the population of wild Nene today can hardly exceed 30 birds."

There are several reasons for the decline in the Nene population. Henshaw (1904) noted that "it is when leading about their young that the old birds undergo the moult, and, when deprived of their wing feathers and unable to fly, they, and the young, are easily run down by the fleet-footed natives and secured." The natives ate the birds and also used the feathers for making *kahili* (Malo, 1951). Henshaw also pointed out that, during the early part of this century, most of the hunting season (15 September to 1 February) corresponded with the breeding season of the Nene. Feral pigs, dogs, cats, and mongooses preyed on eggs and young as well as on flightless adults. Feral goats, sheep, cattle, and horses also foraged unchecked over much of the range of the Nene.

The Nene is a highly specialized goose, adapted for living in a rugged habitat of lava flows far from any standing or running water, and it is unlikely that wild Nene ever swim. Among the more noticeable anatomical specializations for this terrestrial life is a reduction in the webbing between the toes (Miller, 1937). The birds spend most of the time on sparsely vegetated lava flows on Mauna Loa and Haulalai at elevations between approximately 1,525 m and 2,440 m. Here the birds build their nests, usually concealed in clumps of vegetation. The species is unique among the *Anser-Branta* group in that the breeding season begins in the fall when daylengths are growing shorter. It is noteworthy that the first nest ever seen in the wild by biologists was discovered on 9 November 1956 (Elder and Woodside, 1958). All too little is still known about nesting of wild Nene, but the egg-laying period is thought usually to extend from November to March, annual variations apparently being common.

CAPTIVE PROPAGATION IN HAWAII

1949 was a critical year for the Nene. The world's total population of captive Nene then numbered 13 birds: 11 of these were held by Herbert C. Shipman of the island of Hawaii. Shipman began with 2 pairs in 1918; the flock had increased to 42 birds by 1946. On April 1 of that year, however, a tidal wave swept over his lowland estate and killed all but 11 of the birds. Shipman then transferred these birds to an estate on higher land in what is now Hawaii Volcanoes National Park. In 1949 he loaned 2 pairs to the State, and these birds were penned at the Territorial Forestry and Fish and Game camp at Pohakuloa, located on the Saddle Road at an elevation of 1,980 m. However, one goose died before nesting was attempted; the gander of this pair was sent to the Wildfowl Trust at Slimbridge, England, in March 1951. The goose of the remaining pair laid 4 eggs in December 1949. These eggs were removed and placed in an incubator, but the eggs failed to hatch. The goose proceeded to lay a second clutch of 5 eggs; she incubated this clutch and the 5 eggs hatched; 3 of the young survived to adulthood.

The Shipman birds were so inbred that both fertility and hatchability of eggs were low even during the early years of the rearing program. Only 24 young Nene were raised during the first 7 breeding seasons (1949-1950 through 1955-1956). Only 40 percent of the eggs laid during this period were fertile, and only 53 percent of the fertile eggs hatched.

Waterfowl experts from North America and Europe visited the Pohakuloa project between 1949 and 1961. They suggested 3 potential problems for study: inadequate diet, rearing techniques, and a presumed genetic deficiency in the Shipman geese. Dietary requirements were less of a problem than the other factors, and an adequate diet that met the birds' nutritional requirements was soon developed.

Rearing Techniques

A successful technique used for other waterfowl involved removing the first clutch of eggs and placing them under a foster broodparent. In addition to electrical incubators, domestic hens (1949-1952), domestic ducks (1953-1960), and silky bantams (1960-1965) were used to incubate the first clutches of Nene eggs and to act as foster mothers to the goslings. For the most part, however, these efforts were unsatisfactory, in part, because it was difficult to induce broodiness behavior in the foster mothers during the winter months at Pohakuloa. Consequently, hatchability of fertile eggs remained low.

During the 1965-1966 breeding season, it was learned that a high percentage of Nene would lay a second clutch of eggs after incubating and hatching a first clutch of goslings. As soon as they hatched, the goslings were removed to indoor brooders, and the nest was destroyed. A majority of the Nene pairs renested within 8 weeks, and the females laid a second clutch of eggs and proceeded to incubate them. This technique, of course, made it possible to raise 2 broods from each female during a single season; later some females were induced to lay 3 clutches, thus leading to a marked increase in the number of young produced each year.

This new technique was used on the entire flock of 30 breeding pairs during the 1967-1968 nesting season, and 123 goslings were raised, bringing the production per pair to 4.1 young. Because of this striking success, 10 additional pairs were added to the breeding flock for the 1968-1969 nesting season. The 40 pairs produced 156 young birds; however, by nearly doubling the production of goslings in a 2-year period, the two-man staff at Pohakuloa found that they had created an excessive workload. Therefore, the breeding flock was reduced to 30 pairs, those birds with the best productivity records being selected for the rearing program. The captive flock at Pohakuloa was reduced further to 12 breeding pairs for the 1976-1977 nesting season.

The Genetic Strain

The Nene that were loaned to the State by Shipman in 1949 were the result of inbreeding among the offspring of 2 pairs of geese that he had maintained in captivity since 1918. It soon became evident at Pohakuloa that there was a high degree of infertility; of all eggs laid by these geese, fertility amounted to only 54.5 percent. An adult wild female was added to the flock about 1950, and a pair of adults and an immature wild bird were captured on the breeding ground on Mauna Loa and added in 1960. The result was a significant increase in the fertility of the eggs laid.

The Nene propagation program has been funded almost entirely by the Federal government. The project began in 1949 with $6,000 appropriated by the Territorial Legislature for a 2-year program. The Board of Agriculture and Forestry did not approve the ecological study, and no additional funds were provided. Woodside (1961) wrote that "it is to the credit of Mr. J. R. Woodworth of the Division of Fish and Game that the project was able to survive for almost nine years on a two-year budget!"

In 1958, Congress allocated $15,000 per year to the U. S. Fish and Wildlife Service for the Nene propagation program at Pohakuloa; in 1968 the Federal grant to the State was increased to $25,000 per year. In addition, the cost of sending 200 geese to Hawaii from England has been estimated at about 5,000 English pounds (Janet Kear, *personal communication*).

CAPTIVE PROPAGATION AT SLIMBRIDGE

In May 1950, John Yealland, Curator of the Wildfowl Trust, left Hawaii for England with two Nene (presumably a pair) obtained from Shipman. During the following March, however, both birds built nests and laid eggs. A gander was then sent to England; this bird was in full molt, and the second clutches also were infertile. Nevertheless, a successful rearing program was begun in 1952, when the 2 geese laid 19 eggs; 14 were fertilized, 9 hatched, and all of the goslings were raised successfully.

Fertility was fairly good (74 percent) during 1952, but, as the years passed, the fertility rate for first and second clutches dropped to an average of 41 percent; the rate was only 23 percent in third clutches. Again, the evidence suggested that the low fertility rate stemmed from the inbred geese of the Shipman stock. Two young wild males were sent to Slimbridge from Hawaii in 1962, and 2 additional ganders arrived in 1966. By 1970 the fertility rate had increased to more than 80 percent. More than 750 Nene had been raised at Slimbridge by 1973.

Evidence accumulated by this time revealed that inbreeding had affected the sperm production of the ganders, but it apparently had not affected the fecundity of the females.

RELEASE OF NENE ON HAWAII

In his unpublished 1958 report to the Hawaii Board of Agriculture and Forestry, William H. Elder remarked that "with so much invested in these birds (at Pohakuloa) in time, money and hope, they must not be dumped out, without experience in flying, food finding and without knowledge of the whereabouts of the present Nene breeding ground. Experience with hand-reared waterfowl in North America has shown that a gentle release method gives much superior results to a sudden release." Elder recommended, therefore, that birds be confined to large--"10 acres or more"--predator-proof enclosures for several months during their normal flightless period.

The first sanctuary for the Nene was created in 1958. This Keauhou Sanctuary encompassed the area where Elder and Woodside had found the first Nene nest in 1956. An open-topped release pen covering approximately 0.405 ha was built in the sanctuary. The first

release of Nene into the wild was made during March 1960, when 20
birds from Pohakuloa were placed in the pen. The birds were wing-
clipped; water and commercial foods were provided until the birds
began to eat natural foods in the enclosure. Poison baits were
placed around the enclosure in an effort to prevent predation on
the flightless birds by mongooses and feral pigs and dogs. After
the annual molt was completed and the birds were able to fly, they
left the enclosure and eventually mingled with wild birds.

Three other sanctuaries and release pens were established later,
one each in 1961, 1967, and 1974. By July 1976, 1,244 Nene from the
Pohakuloa rearing project were released in these 4 sanctuaries.

RELEASE OF NENE ON MAUI

Haleakala Crater on the island of Maui is a dormant volcano that
last erupted about 1790; its highest elevation is slightly over
3,050 m. The crater is about 11 km long and 3 km wide. The west
end of the crater is very dry and barren, but the eastern end is an
area of high rainfall and rich vegetation. It was here that a small
(about 0.202 ha) release pen was constructed in 1962. In June of that
year, 30 geese were flown from Slimbridge to Hawaii. Five birds from
Pohakuloa were added to the group, and the 35 birds were carried in
back packs by boy scouts for the 13.6 km hike from the crater rim to
the release site. As of July 1976, 391 Nene had been released in
Haleakala Crater. Of these, 197 were raised at Slimbridge, 187 at
Pohakuloa, and 7 at the aviaries of S. Dillon Ripley. Carriage on
the backs of boy scouts and personnel of the State Division of Fish
and Game has been replaced by mule pack-train and, during 1972, by
helicopter.

SUCCESS OF THE RELEASE PROGRAM

Despite the expenditure of some $350,000 of Federal money at
Pohakuloa and of 28 years of effort, there is no reliable information
on the size of the wild Nene population. Published estimates of the
population are admittedly "pie-in-the-sky" guesses. Such estimates
are based primarily on the numbers of captive birds that have been
released on Hawaii since 1960. Similarly, there are no meaningful
data on the annual reproductive success of the wild population.
Consequently, we still do not know if this population can be self-
sustaining without an annual release of pen-reared birds.

Two reasons for this lack of information are clear. First, no
biologist with training in waterfowl or gamebird management has been
assigned to the field studies for more than a decade, even though
Schwartz and Schwartz (1949) urged an immediate study of the life
history of the Nene in its mountain habitat. Similarly, Smith
(1952) pointed out the importance of an ecological study of the
wild Nene that would "provide a foundation upon which public service
agencies and private organizations can act swiftly and surely ...
to form a Nene conservation program basically sound and continuous

in duration and effort." As yet, however, no intensive, year-long field studies have been initiated.

Secondly, the Nene habitat, particularly on Mauna Loa, is one of the most difficult areas in the world to study. As compared with precipitous cliffs of Kauai, Maui, and parts of Hawaii, the slopes of Mauna Loa are gentle, but large areas occupied by the Nene are covered by lava. Travel by foot over the sharp, angular blocks of lava is very slow and tiring because one has to test almost every block before taking a step forward. Thin-roofed lava tubes and crevices also make hiking dangerous.

On Maui, as well, study of the Nene has been restricted to short periods of time when State personnel take time from other duties to visit the crater. The first Nene were released here in 1962; the first nests were not found until 1968; as of 1972, apparently only 2 young birds survived to enter the breeding population in Haleakala. Fish and Game personnel believe that 8 young may have survived to adulthood during the 1972-1973 breeding season, but the size of the Haleakala population remains unknown.

LITERATURE CITED

Baldwin, P.H. 1945. The Hawaiian goose, its distribution and reduction in numbers. Condor 47(1):27-37.

Berger, A.J. 1972. Hawaiian Birdlife. University Press of Hawaii, Honolulu, 270 p.

Elder, W.H., and D.H. Woodside. 1958. Biology and management of the Hawaiian goose. Trans. 23rd North American Wildlife Conference, 1958: 198-215.

Henshaw, H.W. 1904. Complete list of the birds of the Hawaiian Possessions, with notes on their habits. Thrum's Hawaiian Almanac and Annual 1904: 113-145.

Malo, David. 1951. Hawaiian Antiquities (Moolele Hawaii). (Transl. from Hawaiian) Bernice P. Bishop Museum Spec. Publ. 2.

Miller, A.H. 1937. Structural modifications in the Hawaiian goose (Nesochen sandvicensis), a study in adaptive evolution. Univ. Calif. Publ. Zool., Vol. 42, No. 1, 79 p.

Schwartz, C.W., and E.R. Schwartz. 1949. A reconnaissance of the game birds in Hawaii. Board of Commissioners of Agriculture and Forestry, Honolulu, 168 p.

Smith, J.O. 1952. The Hawaiian goose (Nene) restoration program. J. Wildl. Manage. 16(1):1-9.

Woodside, D.H. 1961. Future for a State bird. Pacific Discovery 14:24-26.

39

Reintroduction Techniques for Masked Bobwhites

David H. Ellis, Steven J. Dobrott, and John G. Goodwin, Jr.

The Masked Bobwhite (*Colinus virginianus ridgwayi*), a distinc-
tively-colored race of the Bobwhite, was once found in a large area of
central and northern Sonora, Mexico, and in south-central Arizona. By
1900 the bird was largely or completely extirpated in Arizona (Tomlinson, 1972), and now remnant populations in Sonora are decreasing
rapidly (Ellis and Serafin, 1977). Strong but circumstantial evidence
suggests that the bird was eliminated because its habitat was altered
by grazing.

The bird's plight led to several reintroduction attempts. Wild-
caught birds and captive-reared birds were released at many locations
in Arizona and New Mexico beginning in 1937. Details of each release
are included in the Masked Bobwhite Recovery Plan prepared for the
U.S. Fish and Wildlife Service (Brown and Ellis, *in press*).

Between 1937 and 1974, the reintroduction efforts consisted of
freeing either wild-trapped or captive-reared quail in covey-sized
units in the best available cover. Few of the propagated birds survived the first year in the wild; none of the reintroductions resulted
in a self-sustaining population. The early reintroductions probably
failed because: (1) some releases were made outside the historical
range, (2) many of the propagated birds were physically unsuitable for
for release, and (3) the habitat, even within historical range, was
probably unsuitable (Gallizioli et al., 1967; Tomlinson, 1972).

GENERAL APPROACH OF CURRENT REINTRODUCTION PROGRAM

In an attempt to promote survival of released birds, in 1974 we
intensified our efforts to upgrade the stock produced in captivity
(Ellis and Serafin, 1977). To reduce plumage damage in pen-held
birds, overhead nets were installed in holding pens, and pen walls

were covered with opaque materials (both tar paper and burlap proved
suitable). Remiges and rectrices still showing excessive wear were
plucked 6 to 8 weeks before the birds were placed in the pre-release
training program. Bill deformities, a chronic problem with pen-reared
birds, were largely eliminated by the use of a debeaking guard, a
metal plate with holes of varying size through which the bird's bill
is protruded against a hot debeaking plate.

In a search for the most suitable reintroduction techniques, we
considered the following methods:
1. Stocking with wild-trapped Sonoran birds,
2. Placing Masked Bobwhite eggs in the nests of other native
    quail,
3. Using bantam hen foster parents in a semi-domestic state,
4. Developing a training program to condition Masked Bobwhites
    to the wild,
5. Using wild-caught quail as foster parents.

RESTOCKING WITH WILD MASKED BOBWHITE

Perhaps the simplest method of establishing the Masked Bobwhite,
if habitat was favorable, would be to release wild-caught birds from
Sonora. Unfortunately, the remaining wild populations in Sonora are
dwindling rapidly (Ellis and Serafin, 1977), and it would be political
ly, if not biologically, unsound to further jeopardize the last-known
wild populations in an attempt to establish the bird on Arizona ranges
which are, at best, marginal.

EGG TRANSPLANTS

We located several Gambel's Quail (*Lophortyx gambelii*) and Scaled
Quail (*Callipepla squamata*) nests in 1975. We placed 15 well-incubat-
ed Masked Bobwhite eggs in the only nest--a Scaled Quail's--that did
not fail before hatching. After 5 days, the nest contents indicated
that 10 Masked Bobwhites had hatched successfully. We received reports of 2 fall observations of Masked Bobwhites in mixed coveys with
Scaled Quail. This technique shows promise of producing good wild
stock. However, the excessive amount of time required to locate nests
made it impractical.

BANTAM ADOPTIONS

Rearing young game birds with Domestic Chickens (*Gallus gallus*)
has proven successful with pheasants (*Phasianus* sp.) (Westerskov,
1953) and with Bobwhites (Stoddard, 1931; Hart, 1935; Nestler and
Bailey, 1941; Hart and Mitchell, 1947; Hunt, 1956). So in 1975 we
fostered 61 Masked Bobwhite chicks to bantam hens. Chicks were attacked by the hens, and other events caused high mortality of chicks.
Only 2 chicks were known to have been reared to independence in this
experiment, so we discontinued the adoptions with bantams.

RELEASE OF PEN-REARED JUVENILES AND ADULTS

For pen-reared birds to have the best chances for survival in the wild, it is essential that: (1) wild populations be well below their carrying capacity (Lehmann, 1946; Ligon, 1948), (2) the birds gain experience with natural cover before their release (Frye, 1942; Westerskov, 1953; Jacobs, 1955; Kosicky, 1972), and (3) the birds are in excellent physical condition. Because the best survival of pen-reared birds has been achieved with juveniles, it may also be essential that the birds are of the right age (Stoddard, 1931; Frye, 1942; Baumgartner, 1944). The final requirement for a successful release is suitable habitat. Unfortunately for the Masked Bobwhite, this requirement is the most difficult to satisfy.

In our program, we adapted the covey-box technique (also called call-trap, call-back pen, comeback pen, etc.) used by sportsmen in training dogs (Robinson, 1975; Stanford, *unpublished data*). By taking advantage of the quail's gregarious nature, one or a few confined call-birds daily lure the released birds back into their predator-proof pen by their covey calls. Hardy and McConnell (1967) were first to suggest the use of a call-bird in encouraging released game birds to remain near the release site.

In our first attempts, the covey-boxes were poorly designed and, because we released too many birds too early in training, they often left the area as a group. After modifying the program, we achieved better survival during training and better stock on release. We experimented with 2 sizes of covey-boxes. The smaller box measured 183 x 91.5 x 40.6 cm; the dimensions of the larger one are given in Figure 1.

In its final form, the covey-box training program included the following steps:

1. Birds were removed from the holding facilities and confined for 2 weeks in a net-covered (3.8 cm mesh) and well-vegetated flight pen (30 x 6.1 x 1.8 m). A strip of burlap 91.5 cm wide, positioned along the upper half of the sides of the vegetated enclosure, was effective in preventing excessive feather wear which would otherwise have resulted from birds colliding with the woven wire.

2. Groups of 20 or 24 birds (depending on covey-box size) were removed from the flight pen and confined in one side of the covey-box for 1 day.

3. One-quarter of the birds was released twice each day for 4 days; birds reentered the covey-box through one-way funnels.

4. After the fourth day of training, half of the covey was released each day.

5. From 7-10 days after training began, the birds were pursued by humans on foot after leaving the box.

6. From 11-20 days after training began, the birds were harassed by dogs or humans on alternate days.

7. About 21 or 22 days after training began, the birds were released and then harassed by a trained hawk (often both dogs and the hawk were used together).

8. On day 23, no releases were made, and the funnels were left

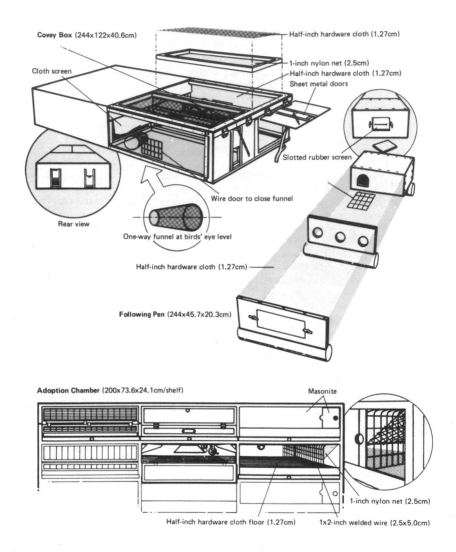

FIGURE 1. Equipment used for handling and training Masked Bobwhites
prior to release. Diagrams illustrate the construction of a
covey-box, a following pen and an adoption chamber.

open to capture stragglers.
9. On day 24, all birds in the covey-box were evaluated, and
    those found suitable were transferred to an appropriate site
    and released.

During training, the birds rapidly improved in general mobility,
in coordination within the covey, and in ability to hide and avoid
predators. Dogs proved very useful in simulating mammalian predation,
and the quail quickly learned when to hold and when to flush. The
Harris' Hawk (*Parabuteo unicinctus*) was not as useful as a training
device as the dogs because, even from the beginning, the quail responded appropriately to the hawk's presence by holding in dense cover.
However, the hawk was very useful in evaluating whether birds were
strong enough for release. When flushed by the dogs, suitable birds
were able to easily out-distance the hawk, but even some of these
were captured when they escaped into insufficient cover.

During the final days of training, the quail were evaluated for
final release. To be acceptable for final release, each bird had to:
(1) have at least 90 percent of its wing surface intact, (2) have at
least 50 percent of its tail surface present (many birds were still
in a tail molt on release), (3) have no serious deformities or injuries, (4) be able to fly strongly at least 200 m on the second flush,
and (5) be able to use cover effectively and avoid predators.

In the final analysis, the covey-box training program proved to
be a valuable technique for producing a moderate number of release-
worthy birds. The training schedule described above gives each bird
a minimum of 11 days in the wild before its final release. Figure 2
shows that a high percentage of the birds that underwent this train-

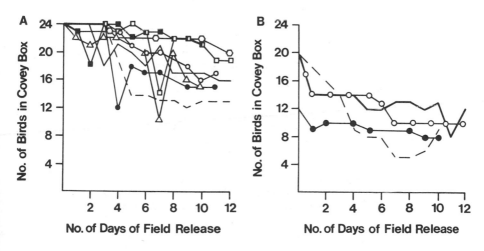

FIGURE 2. Survivorship of Masked Bobwhites during covey-box
    training. Graph A shows results from 7 coveys trained in
    large covey-boxes; graph B shows results from 4 coveys
    trained in small covey-boxes. Symbols indicate different
    coveys.

ing survived (71 percent for large covey-box; 54 percent for the
small) and satisfied criteria for final release (66 percent for the
large covey-box; 44 percent for the small). In 1976 those covey-box
trained birds that survived the 6 months from release to the breeding
season dispersed when the habitat near the release site was destroyed
by cattle. In 1977 there are birds preparing to breed at several locations, but all of these sites are still subject to grazing.

ADOPTIONS BY TEXAS BOBWHITE FOSTER PARENTS

     Stoddard (1931) and his colleagues induced about 500 wild-caught
male Eastern Bobwhites (*C.v. virginianus*) to adopt about 6,000 chicks
of the same race. They were unable to follow the releases intensively, but the fall recovery rates were from 1 to 4 percent. Stanford
(1952) experimented with various foster parent groups--males only,
pairs, and females only--and with variously-aged chicks. He reported
low adoption rates--46.7 percent of the cocks, 23.1 percent of the
hens, and 15.3 percent of the pairs adopted chicks--and very low fall
survival rates--1.1 percent for the chicks. However, he later reported that his recovery rates were low because many of the foster parents
moved away from the study area (Stanford, *personal communication*).
Stanford speculated that chick survival rates would probably have been
much higher if he had released only those broods in which the adults
had fully adopted the chicks--as determined by their aggressiveness in
defending them.
     In our program we fostered Masked Bobwhite chicks to adult Scaled
and Gambel's Quail, and covey-box trained Masked Bobwhites, but the
most suitable foster parents were wild, male Texas Bobwhites (*C.v.
texanus*) obtained from around Big Spring, Texas, an area botanically
much like historical Masked Bobwhite habitat. Males were chosen because they readily adopt chicks, and they can be easily sterilized by
vasectomy to prevent interbreeding with Masked Bobwhites.
     In 1975 we used 1- to 4-day old chicks in the adoptions, but we
achieved much better survival rates in 1976 by using 2-week old chicks
(Figure 3).
     In its final form, our program consisted of the following steps:
     1. Two-week old chicks were received from the propagation facil-
         ity at Patuxent Wildlife Research Center in Maryland and
         divided into groups of 15; each group was then placed in a
         pre-heated adoption chamber (Figure 1).
     2. A Texas Bobwhite foster parent was placed in the adoption
         chamber, and the heat was turned off.
     3. If no brooding was observed after 5 hours, the foster parent
         was exchanged for another.
     4. After 1-2 days in the adoption chamber, broods were moved to
         "following" pens (Figure 1) in dense vegetation.
     5. After 5-10 days in the "following" pen, the broods were re-
         leased.
     In 1976 we released over 700 chicks with Texas Bobwhite foster
parents. The 2-week old chicks had higher survival rates both during
training (Figure 3) and after release than did the 1- to 4-day old

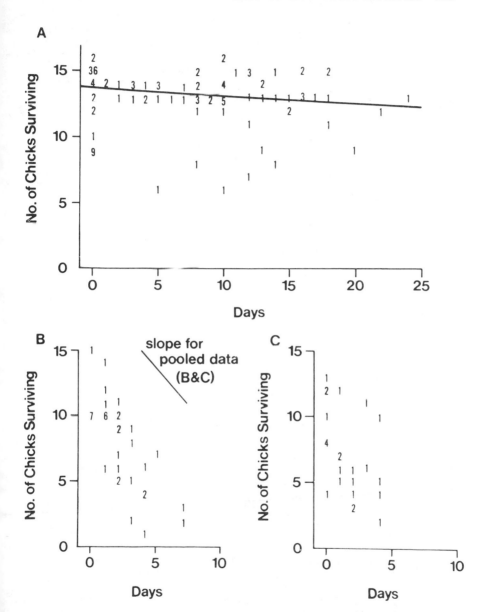

FIGURE 3.   Pre-release survivorship of Masked Bobwhite chicks fostered
   by other quail species.   Graph A shows results when 12- to 16-
   day old chicks were fostered by Texas Bobwhites; graph B shows
   results when 1- to 4-day old chicks were fostered by Gambel's
   Quails; and graph C shows results when 1- to 4-day old chicks
   were fostered by Texas Bobwhites.   Numerals represent the number of broods with indicated survivorship.

chicks.   We accumulated many observations of scores of birds more than 1 month after release, and in spite of widespread emigration from the release areas which are still excessively grazed, a small population--estimated to be 30-50 birds from the spacing of calling birds and the extent of the occupied habitat--overwintered near one 1976 release site and is preparing for the late summer breeding season.

CONCLUSIONS

In our efforts to reintroduce the endangered Masked Bobwhite to the wild, we experimented with several possible methods for restoring the bird to Arizona ranges.   The two most promising techniques are the covey-box training program and the Texas Bobwhite foster-parent adoptions for 2-week old chicks.

The adoption program has several advantages over covey-box training.   A large number of birds can be released in a 3-month period from a small training area, whereas the covey-box program requires a large area to prevent the birds from various covey-boxes from mixing.   The expense of holding birds is minimized; Texas Bobwhite foster parents were held an average of 22 weeks, and chicks were held only 4 weeks. Covey-box trained birds were held an average of 31 weeks.   Finally, the facilities for holding and training the adopted birds are simpler to construct; they are also much more compact than the covey-box training facilities.

Both programs have the same limitation: they can only be employed for part of the year.   The covey-box program must be restricted to the period from late fall to early spring when birds normally run in coveys.   Adoption releases can best be performed following the summer rains when food is available for the chicks.

The Masked Bobwhite program is not beset by many of the problems that plague restoration efforts with other species: (1) the bird is easily maintained and bred in captivity, (2) it has high fecundity,(3) our captive breeding flock is genetically very close to the wild population, (4) problems with nutrition and disease have largely been eliminated, (5) the bird is non-migratory, and (6) suitable reintroduction techniques are now operational.

The only remaining stumbling block--which is also the prime cause for the birds' original endangerment--is the lack of suitable habitat. But because the birds prefer pioneer and sub-climax plant communities which are easily created and maintained, this problem can readily be solved once a Masked Bobwhite management area is designated.   Several good sites for a management area exist in Arizona.   Even though the last wild population of the Masked Bobwhite in Mexico is dropping rapidly toward extinction, the future of the birds seems brighter now than it has for many decades.

ACKNOWLEDGMENTS

We dedicate this paper to J. Stokley Ligon who pioneered the efforts to restore the Masked Bobwhite to Arizona.   Many indi-

viduals and agencies have offered support and encouragement for our
studies. We are especially indebted to Ray C. Erickson for his persistence in arranging financial support, to C. Roger Hungerford for
arranging University of Arizona cooperation, to Herb Kothman and his
assistant, Bill DelMonte, both of the Texas Parks and Wildlife Department, for their enthusiastic support in supplying us with Texas Bobwhite foster parents, and John Nordstrom, Gary Hensler, and Earl Adams
for technical advice and logistic support. Roy Tomlinson devoted much
time and effort in arranging field station facilities. David Fischer
and Jane Dobrott prepared the figures. Cathy Ellis assisted in various aspects of preparing the manuscript.

LITERATURE CITED

Baumgartner, F.M. 1944. Dispersal and survival of game farm bobwhite
    quail in northcentral Oklahoma. J. Wildlife Manage. 8(2):112-118.
Brown, D.E. and D.H. Ellis. *In press*. Status summary and recovery plan
    for the masked bobwhite. U.S. Fish and Wildlife Service.
Ellis, D.H. and J.A. Serafin. 1977. A research program for the endan-
    gered masked bobwhite. World Pheasant Assoc. J. 2:16-33.
Frye, O.E., Jr. 1942. The comparative survival of wild and penreared
    bob-white in the field. Trans. N. Am. Wildlife Conf. 7:168-178.
Gallizioli, S., S. Levy, and J. Levy. 1967. Can the masked bobwhite be
    saved from extinction? Audubon Field Notes 21(5):571-575.
Hardy, J.W. and C.A. McConnell. 1967. Bobwhite quail: propagation,
    conditioning, and habitat management. Tennessee Game and Fish
    Commission. 54p.
Hart, D. 1935. Liberating quail chicks with bantams. Game Breeder and
    Sportsman 39(3):62-62, 76.
Hart, D. and T.R. Mitchell. 1947. Quail and pheasant propagation.
    Wildlife Management Institute, Washington. 72p.
Hunt, R.M. 1956. My experiences during 38 years of breeding and rear-
    ing game birds and wild waterfowl at the Mason State Game Farm.
    Michigan Department of Conservation. 28p.
Jacobs, K.F. 1955. Conditioning of pen-raised bobwhite quail and a
    quail hunter's bag check on the Lexington Public Shooting Area.
    Oklahoma Game and Fish Department Research Report. 12p.
Kozicky, E.L. 1972. Bobwhite quail on shooting preserves, p. 1-4. *In*
    J.A. Morrison (ed.). Proceedings of the First National Bobwhite
    Quail Symposium. Oklahoma State University Research Foundation,
    Stillwater.
Lehmann, V.W. 1946. Mobility of bobwhite quail in southwestern Texas.
    J. Wildlife Manage. 10(2):124-136.
Ligon, J.S. 1948. Unit administration for upland game birds. Oklahoma
    Game and Fish News 4:6-7.
Nestler, R.B. and W.W. Bailey. 1941. Bobwhite quail propagation. U.S.
    Fish and Wildlife Service, Conservation Bull. 10. 50p.
Robinson, J.B. 1975. How to build a call-back quail pen. Sports Afield
    173(3):110-112.
Stanford, J.A. 1952. An evaluation of the adoption method of bobwhite
    quail propagation. Trans. N. Am. Wildlife Conf. 17:330-337.

Stoddard, H.L. 1931. The bobwhite quail--its habits, preservation, and
    increase. Charles Scribner's Sons, N.Y. 559p.
Tomlinson, R.E. 1972. Current status of the endangered masked bobwhite
    quail. Trans. N. Am. Wildlife and Natural Resources Conf. 37:294-
    311.
Westerskov, K. 1953. Techniques of pheasant liberation. New Zealand
    Department of Internal Affairs, Wildlife Publication 25. 28p.

40

Reintroducing Birds of Prey to the Wild

Stanley A. Temple

Birds of prey have become the objects of many management programs during the past decade (*see* Hamerstrom et al., 1974; Chancellor, 1977). Sometimes these management programs have succeeded in preserving regional raptor populations, but in many other cases, management was insufficient or too late, and local populations were extirpated. In these cases, there has been considerable interest in the possibility of reintroducing raptors into their former geographic ranges.

Perhaps the earliest such attempt involved the reintroduction of the Eagle Owl (*Bubo bubo*) into vacant portions of its European range (Wayre, 1975; Broo, 1977). However, the most ambitious attempts are current programs to reintroduce the Peregrine Falcon (*Falco peregrinus*) into vacant portions of its North American range. In addition, several other small-scale reintroductions of raptors have occurred, and a variety of observations of wild raptors suggest the possibility of yet untried techniques.

TECHNIQUES FOR REINTRODUCING RAPTORS

There are a variety of procedures that could be used to reintroduce birds of prey into a region. The choice of technique depends on whether adults or nestling raptors are being released and on whether or not there are wild raptor populations in the area where the reintroduction is to occur. Basically, there are 4 general approaches that could be followed:
1. Release of cross-fostered nestlings,
2. Release of translocated wild birds,
3. Release of mature birds that have been held in captivity,
4. Release of fledglings by some modification of "hacking".

The first technique requires the presence of a wild population of
raptors that can serve as cross-foster parents, whereas the others
can be used to reintroduce raptors into completely vacant range.
The first and the last 2 techniques can be used for releasing birds
produced in captivity.

Release of Cross-fostered Nestlings

Cross fostering of young raptors to wild parents is a very promising technique for releasing birds when a wild population of potential foster parents exists. Fyfe et al. (Ch. 23, *this volume*) and
Meyburg (Ch. 24, *this volume*) have demonstrated that cross-fostering
is a workable technique with raptors, but, so far, this technique has
not been used extensively in actual endangered species' reintroduction
attempts. Apprehensions about maladaptive behaviors and inappropriate
sexual imprinting--problems which have still not been resolved com-
pletely--discourage some managers. Nonetheless, in 1977, three young,
captive-produced Peregrine Falcons were reintroduced to the wild by
cross-fostering in the Snake River Canyon of Idaho (Cade, 1977). A
pair of wild Prairie Falcons (*Falco mexicanus*) served as the foster
parents and successfully fledged the young in a region that has not
had wild Peregrine Falcons since 1975. Although cross-fostering
should be used with caution, it is certainly a workable procedure for
reintroducing certain raptors into areas where they have been extirpated.

Release of Translocated Wild Birds

Certainly, one of the most straight-forward reintroduction schemes
involves trapping wild birds, transporting them, and releasing them in
an area where the species no longer exists. Although this would, no
doubt, be the simplest reintroduction technique, it has not been used
extensively for a number of reasons. First, if a raptor species is
endangered, it is unlikely that there will be nearby populations from
which birds could be removed without having a disruptive effect.
Furthermore, most raptors have rather good homing abilities so that
the translocated birds would probably wander away from the reintroduction site in an attempt to relocate their home ranges. No permanent
attachment to the reintroduction site would develop.
     Nonetheless, for raptors that have relatively weak dispersal or
homing abilities, this approach could work. It has been employed successfully as part of the Eagle Owl reintroduction program in Europe;
owls captured in eastern Europe were transported and released at reintroduction sites in West Germany (Wayre, 1975). I can find no other
examples in which the translocation of wild raptors was a part of a
successful reintroduction.
     There are, however, situations where translocation of wild raptors
could be a very useful procedure. Perhaps one of the most obvious
cases involves translocating endangered island raptors. For example,
because of past persecution, the Seychelles Kestrel (*Falco araea*) has
been extirpated on a number of islands of the Seychelles archipelago
(Feare et al., 1974). With the adequate legal protection and conser-

vation education that exists in the Seychelles today, there is no reason why birds could not be translocated from the island of Mahé--where
a dense population of several hundred birds exists--to some formerly
occupied islands. This reintroduction scheme has already been proposed (Temple, 1977) and may soon be initiated.

Release of Mature Birds that Have Been Held in Captivity

A possible way to get around the lack of site tenacity in translocated wild raptors might be to keep the birds in captivity at the
intended release site. By releasing the birds from a cage in which
they had spent some period of time, it might be possible to establish
the birds in the vicinity of the cage site. This approach has been
attempted as part of the Eagle Owl reintroduction program, and it has
been demonstrated to work in a number of unintentional releases--more
correctly escapes--of captive raptors.

In the Eagle Owl reintroduction program in Sweden, a number of
modifications of the basic scheme described above have been used
(Wayre, 1975; Broo, 1977). The most promising appears to be the release of captive, adult owls while they are rearing young in their
cage. The presence of the young owls in the cage is a strong lure
that keeps the adults faithful to the site. Eventually, when the
young owls fledge, an entire family group has been reintroduced to
the wild with excellent prospects of their remaining in the vicinity
of the release site.

There seem to be several examples of unintentional releases of
captive birds--mostly falconers' birds--that have led to the establishment of birds in a region. Perhaps the most intriguing involves
the Goshawk (*Accipiter gentilis*) in Great Britain. The Goshawk population in Great Britain was greatly reduced and possibly extirpated
in recent decades. The species is now making a comeback with an estimated population in 1975 of less than 25 pairs (Prestt, 1977).
There is strong circumstantial evidence that this population may have
been derived from continental Goshawks that escaped from British
falconers and subsequently became established in the wild (Prestt,
1977; R. Kenward, *personal communication.*)

In another apparent example, a Peregrine Falcon that escaped
during the winter from a falconer near Philadelphia, Pennsylvania
returned to overwinter in that city for at least 3 subsequent years.
Presumably, the bird, which was a migrant when captured, returned to
the North American arctic during the breeding season. The escaped
bird had apparently become attached to the area of its escape and
returned there to spend the winter, despite the fact that Philadelphia
is now rarely visited by Peregrine Falcons in the winter.

Cade (1974) has proposed a way of reintroducing Peregrine Falcons
to vacant aeries by releasing falconry-trained birds. The idea is to
permit cooperating falconers to fly a pair of Peregrine Falcons in the
vicinity of a potential nesting site. Through repeated exposure to the
region while being flown in falconry, the birds would presumably develop an attachment to the area. When the pair of birds reached breeding age, they would be gradually released with the hope that they
would mate and adopt the preselected nest site. As far as I know,

this scheme has never been attempted--even with non-endangered rap-
tors--and it would be of great interest, for example, to see if it
could be accomplished with Prairie Falcons in western North America.
     There are numerous examples of single birds that have been kept
in captivity for varying periods of time and then released to the
wild by their keepers. The accounts of some of these releases should
serve to underscore the tremendous investment of time and effort that
must go into such an attempt (e.g., Hamerstrom, 1970).
     One thing is certain; birds kept in captivity rarely become suc-
cessful in the wild without proper conditioning--either through falconry or other training. Such training is an absolutely essential
aspect of any program to release raptors held in captivity.

Release of Feldglings Using Some Modification of Hacking

     The technique of hacking has, no doubt, been used by falconers
for many centuries. Fredrick II of Hohenstaufen wrote about it in
his classic *De Arte Venandi cum Avibus* in 1245. Falcons taken from
the wild as eyasses need to have early flying experience if they are
to develop their flight muscles and perfect their flying skills. To
give a young falcon this crucial early experience, the falconer em-
ploys the procedure of hacking. The basic procedure is to place the
young falcon in some sort of artificial nest site--in the falconer's
parlance, a hack house--where the young nestling can be hand-reared.
The hack house should be situated in open country because once the
young falcon reaches fledging age, it is allowed to fly free in the
surrounding countryside. Young raptors have a strong tendency to return for food to the nest site from which they fledge. Hence, young
falcons that are being hacked return to the hack house for the food
that the falconer provides. The food at the hack house keeps the
young falcon under the falconer's control during the weeks after
fledging when the bird is flying free and developing its flying abilities. After several weeks of free-flying experience, the young
falcon begins to kill wild prey and starts to become independent of
the food at the hack house. At this point, the falconer would trap
the bird and begin training it for falconry with the confidence that
the bird has already achieved expertise at flying and hunting.
     Using the hacking procedure as a reintroduction technique follows
this same sequence with the important exception that the bird is never
trapped and taken back into captivity. Rather, the hacking procedure
is extended until the young birds become completely independent of
the food provided at the hack house and no longer return in search of
food. At this point, young raptors naturally disperse and for all in-
tents and purposes become completely wild birds. Falconers have described how young birds left at hack for too long become wild and un-
trappable (Mitchell, 1900), so there was precedent for the reintroduction procedure outlined above. Cade and Temple (1977) describe reintroduction of Peregrine Falcons by hacking in greater detail.
     Hacking has now been used to return a wide variety of raptors to
the wild, and a number of these have been true reintroduction attempts.
Some of the most notable attempts have been with Eagle Owls in Europe
(Wayre, 1975; Broo, 1977), Peregrine Falcons in North America (Cade

and Temple, 1977; Fyfe, 1976), and Bald Eagles (*Haliaeetus leucocephalus*) in North America (Cade, 1977). There have also been successful programs with non-endangered species such as the Prairie Falcon (T. Smiley, *personal communication*), Barn Owl (*Tyto alba*) (Temple, *unpublished data*), and a number of other raptors.

Certainly, the current attempts to reintroduce Peregrine Falcons into vacant portions of their North American range by releasing young captive-produced birds is the most intensive hacking program to date. Cade (1974, 1975, 1976, 1977) has chronicled the development of the program in the eastern United States, and it is possible to evaluate the results of this program which is now in its fourth year. Between 1974 and 1977 a total of 101 young captive-produced Peregrine Falcons were released by hacking. The fates of these birds up to the time of their dispersal from the hacking sites are summarized in Table 1. The overall success rate to dispersal of 72 percent is quite encouraging and is almost certainly better than wild Peregrine Falcons can achieve with their broods.

Despite these encouraging results, it is instructive to examine the problems that caused 28 percent of the hacked falcons not to reach the age of normal dispersal (Table 2). Clearly predators are the greatest threat to young falcons that are being hacked. Lacking the type of protection that parents would provide, the young birds are very vulnerable, especially at night. Great Horned Owls (*Bubo virginianus*) and Raccoons (*Procyon lotor*) have been the most serious predators. The 4 birds that were retrapped also failed to disperse because of predation. They were trapped to prevent them from being killed like their siblings. Over half of the loss was, therefore, directly or indirectly caused by predators. Options for avoiding this loss include removing all potential predators from a site before releasing falcons or releasing falcons only at known predator-free sites. The first option is extremely difficult, but the second is possible,

TABLE 1. FATE OF PEREGRINE FALCONS RELEASED BY HACKING IN THE
EASTERN UNITED STATES

Year	No. of Falcons Hacked	No. That Dispersed Normally	No. Killed or Lost Prematurely[a]	Percent Success
1974	2	0	2	0
1975	16	12	4	75
1976	37	25	12	68
1977	46	35	11	76
	101	72	29	72

[a]Includes birds trapped and returned to captivity.

TABLE 2.   CAUSES FOR PEREGRINE FALCONS HACKED IN THE EASTERN UNITED
STATES NOT REACHING THE AGE OF INDEPENDENCE

Losses Apparently Due to:	No. of Birds in Indicated Year:				
	1974	1975	1976	1977	Total
Predators	0	2	5	5	12
Human Persecution	2	0	0	0	2
Accidents[a]	0	1	0	2	3
Premature Dispersal	0	0	7	1	8
Retrapping	0	1	0	3	4

[a]Includes drowning and electrocution.

especially where the release site is a hacking station built on a
man-made tower.

Premature dispersal is apparently another problem inherent in
hacking.   Young birds quite simply get lost and cannot find their
way back to the hacking station.   Almost certainly such birds starve
to death.   Although there is no way to guarantee that young falcons
will not become lost, such losses can be minimized by carefully
timing the sequence of events in the hacking procedure (see Cade
and Temple, 1977).   Birds must be allowed to fledge as soon as they
are able to; holding them back beyond this age can precipitate early
distant flights that take the birds out of sight of the hacking
station.

Post-dispersal suvivorship of birds that have been released by
hacking appears to be good.   Cade (1976,1977) and Cade and Temple
(1977) have summarized the observations of released falcons after
they become independent.   Perhaps the clearest results come from the
12 falcons that reached independence in 1975.   At least 4, and perhaps
6, of these birds are known to have overwintered within about 200 km
of their fledging sites.   The following spring, 5 of the birds were
resighted at or near the release sites where they had been hacked one
year earlier.   Young (1969) has estimated a first-year survivorship of
33 percent for wild Peregrine Falcons.   The released birds achieved
this survivorship, a further indication that they had become normal,
wild birds.

EVALUATION OF REINTRODUCTION TECHNIQUES

There are a number of desirable features that a successful reintroduction technique for birds of prey should have: (1) it should
promote good survivorship in the released birds; (2) it should have a
good potential for establishing in the birds some degree of fidelity
to the release site so that they will remain in the vicinity; (3) it
should require a relatively small investment of time and effort ex-

pended per released bird, and (4) it should be versatile so that
releases can be made wherever deemed appropriate and not limited by
many constraints.

Survivorship of Released Birds

The best possible survivorship would probably be achieved by releasing wild-caught and translocated birds; they would presumably show
survivorship typical of a wild population. Release of nestlings by
cross-fostering or some modification of hacking also seems to lead to
survivorship that is comparable to that achieved by normal, wild
birds. Release of birds held in captivity probably results in poorer
survivorship unless the birds undergo intensive conditioning prior to
release.

Potential for Site Tenacity

It is clearly desirable to have reintroduced birds of prey remain
in the general vicinity of the release site. Both cross-fostering and
hacking assure a certain fidelity to the release site by taking advantage of young birds' natural philopatry or tendency to return at breeding age to the vicinity of their fledging sites. Release of birds held
in captivity can only lead to site tenacity if the birds are given extensive exposure to the region prior to release and develop an attachment to it. Release of wild-caught and translocated raptors has a
very poor potential for establishing site tenacity in the reintroduced
birds.

Amount of Effort Required

In terms of the time and human effort expended per reintroduced
bird, the release of wild-caught and translocated birds is the easiest
procedure. Cross-fostering requires more preliminary effort, but once
the actual adoption has taken place, there is little more effort required. Release by hacking requires several weeks of fairly intensive
effort by the person who attends the hacking site. However, each person can supervise the hacking of several raptors so that the effort
per bird released is reduced. The release of birds held in captivity
requires comparatively huge investments of time and effort by skilled
handlers. Each handler can only reintroduce one or two birds at a
time this way.

Versatility of Techniques

Reintroduction of wild-caught and translocated birds is perhaps
the most versatile technique. Birds can essentially be trapped and
released anywhere at anytime. Release by hacking is also very versatile. If the young birds are hacked from man-made structures, these
structures can be erected almost anyplace where other environmental
features are desirable. However, if the birds are hacked from more
natural nest sites, such as cliffs, the possible locations for releases
are clearly limited. Release of birds that have been held in captivity

is limited by the locations where qualified handlers reside; such experienced individuals are not often found in the regions that are best for reintroduction work. Finally, cross-fostering is perhaps the most restricted type of reintroduction technique. Release sites are severely limited by the availability and location of nesting raptors that can serve as foster parents.

Overall Merits of Techniques

On the basis of the 4 criteria listed previously, it appears that the release of young raptors by some modification of the hacking procedure is the best available technique. It leads to survivorship comparable to that of natural, wild birds; it establishes in the birds an attachment to the release site; it is versatile and can be used in a wide variety of situations and with almost any species. The only drawback is that it does require an investment of time and effort by the people attending the hacking sites.

Success at reestablishing a wild population by hacking young birds is not easily achieved. Cade and Temple (1977) have made some preliminary projections of how long it will take to repopulate the eastern United States with Peregrine Falcons solely by hacking young falcons. It will take yearly releases of 250 falcons over a 15-year period to establish a wild population of 146 successfully breeding pairs in a total population of 1,180 falcons.

The obvious implication is that it is probably easier to prevent a regional extirpation of a species than to reestablish it after it is gone. If it is deemed worthwhile, and if the environment will support the birds, the reintroduction of birds of prey into vacant portions of their ranges presents a management challenge that can probably be met but one that takes years of sustained effort and dedication.

LITERATURE CITED

Broo, B. 1977. Project Eagle Owl in southwest Sweden, p.338-342. *In* R.D. Chancellor (ed.) Report of proceedings, world conference on birds of prey, Vienna, 1975. Int. Council for Bird Preservation, London. 442p.

Cade, T.J. 1974. Plans for managing the survival of the Peregrine Falcon, p. 89-104. *In* F.N. Hamerstrom Jr., B.E. Harrell and R.R. Olendorff (eds.) Management of raptors. Raptor Research Report No. 2.

Cade, T.J. (ed.) 1975. The Peregrine Fund Newsletter No.3:1-6.

Cade, T.J. (ed.) 1976. The Peregrine Fund Newsletter No.4:1-8.

Cade, T.J. (ed.) 1977. The Peregrine Fund Newsletter No.5:1-12.

Cade, T.J. and S.A. Temple. 1977. The Cornell University falcon programme, p. 353-369. *In* R.D. Chancellor (ed.) Report of Proceedings, world conference on birds of prey, Vienna, 1975. Int. Council for Bird Preservation, London. 442p.

Chancellor, R.D. (ed.) 1977. Report of proceedings, world conference on birds of prey, Vienna, 1975. Int. Council for Bird Preservation, London. 442p.

Feare, C.J., S.A. Temple and J. Proctor. 1974. The status, distribution, and ecology of the Seychelles Kestrel (*Falco araea*). Ibis 116:548-551.

Fyfe, R. 1976. Rationale and success of the Canadian Wildlife Service Peregrine breeding program. Can. Field-Nat. 90(3):308-319.

Hamerstrom, F. 1970. An Eagle to the Sky. Iowa State Univ. Press, Ames.

Hamerstrom, F.N., Jr., B.E. Harrell and R.R. Olendorff (eds.) Management of raptors. Raptor Research Report No. 2.

Mitchell, E.B. 1900. The Art and Practice of Hawking. The Holland Press, London. 291p.

Prestt, I. 1977. A review of the status of birds of prey in Great Britain, p. 114-117. *In* R.D. Chancellor (ed.) Report of proceedings, world conference on birds of prey, Vienna, 1975. Int. Council for Bird Preservation, London. 442p.

Temple, S.A. 1977. The status and conservation of endemic kestrels on Indian Ocean islands, p. 74-83. *In* R.D. Chancellor (ed.) Report of proceedings, world conference on birds of prey, Vienna, 1975. Int. Council for Bird Preservation, London. 442p.

Wayre, P. 1975. Conservation of Eagle Owls and other raptors through captive breeding and return to the wild, p. 125-132. *In* R.D. Martin (ed.) Breeding endangered species in captivity. Academic Press, London. 420p.

Young, H.F. 1969. Hypotheses on Peregrine population dynamics, p. 513-519. *In* J.J. Hickey (ed.) Peregrine Falcon populations: their biology and decline. Univ. of Wisconsin Press, Madison. 596p.

41

Interisland Transfers
of New Zealand Black Robins

J. A. Douglas Flack

In September 1976 the New Zealand Wildlife Service transferred 5 of the last 7 remaining Black Robins (*Petroica traversi*) from the only island on which they occurred to another nearby island. The transfer occurred years ahead of the planned date. The survival of this species now hangs entirely on hopes for improved breeding and survival in the new habitat. This drastic management attempt had been preceded by intensive ecological studies of both the Black Robin (Flack, *unpublished data*) and the South Island Robin (*P. australis australis*) (Flack, 1973, 1974, 1976). Experimental transplants of South Island Robins (Flack, 1975) showed that new populations could be established from the transfer of only 2 pairs of adult birds to a new island.

This paper summarizes the events that precipitated the Black Robin transfer and evaluates the use of interisland transfers as a management tool for this species. The wider application of the technique is also discussed, with special mention of applications to other New Zealand species.

AN ECOLOGICAL HISTORY OF THE BLACK ROBINS

Black Robins have been confined to one tiny, precipitous island, Tapuaenuku or Little Mangere, for over 70 years. Forest and scrub cover there has been decreasing so that now approximately 50 percent of the original area of the robin habitat remains. Most of the remaining 6 ha which still contain woody plants are in poor condition, and the litter fauna, crucial to this species, is now poor in species and numbers (Flack, *unpublished data*). The original population on the island may have numbered 20 to 30 pairs, but with the loss of habitat, especially in the last 20 years, the population was greatly reduced. It is also likely that the quality of the remaining habitat has been degraded, causing a further decline in the population size. On other small islands, South Island Robin populations achieve densities 2 to 6 times greater. By 1968, the Black Robin population probably numbered less than 20 individuals, and between 1973 and 1976, it declined to only 7.

Population size, survival rates, and productivity were monitored yearly after a banding program began in 1972. Comparisons of these data with data from several populations of South Island Robins on the mainland and inshore islands has provided a means for population analysis. There are clear indications that the recent population decline is related primarily to poor survival rates of adults during the breeding season and of immatures after autumn, and secondarily, to a low reproductive output (Flack, *unpublished data*).

These comparative studies indicate that the Black Robin has by far the smallest population of any *Petroica* robin, that its habitat is in poor condition in both its physical structure and its invertebrate fauna, that its heavy overbalance of males is related to poor habitat quality, that it is the most unstable of several populations, and that it shows indications of possible inbreeding.

Two observations may indicate recent genetic change in the robin population. The colored foot-pads, characteristic of all *Petroica* species, have been lost in the Black Robin during this century. The poor survival of juvenile birds and the absence of improvement in reproductive output in response to large increases in territory size could be indicators of deleterious inbreeding (Flack, *unpublished data*).

Histories of breeding, survival and movements indicate large differences in habitat suitability on Tapuaenuku. Successful breeding occurred in only 5 out of 10 territories. It became apparent that Black Robins could be removed from unproductive territories in poorer habitat without reducing the overall reproductive output of the population. This provided a key to a means of starting a new population without disrupting the parent population.

PRELIMINARY MANAGEMENT EXPERIMENTS

The special situation presented by the size and location of the Black Robin population precluded the use of many management practices. In particular, captive breeding, cross-fostering, and supplementary feeding could not be used. Manipulations to improve and increase the area of habitat offered some opportunities, but preliminary results from experiments with South Island Robins indicated that establishment of a new wild population on another island was the best approach (Flack, 1975). The major obstacle to this approach was a lack of another island with suitable habitat. It was soon determined that nearby Mangere Island would provide the only practical location for a new population if the island was first planted with trees (Flack, 1975). Planting began in 1973 and had covered a wide area by 1976, but development of suitable habitat requires at least 10 year's growth.

The transfer of birds to new habitats has successfully established populations of many species throughout the world, especially during the last century. Frequently, release or escape of the progeny of captive birds has started new populations, rather than the direct transfer of wild stock. Direct transfer of endangered and rare birds to new habitat is not a new technique, but it has remained an uncommon management tool except in New Zealand. Pioneering attempts in New Zealand (Oliver, 1955) to relocate Kakapo (*Strigops habroptilus*) populations were followed by early attempts with Saddlebacks (*Philesturnus carunculatus*), and today efforts are again being made with the Kakapo. The New Zealand Wildlife Service succeeded recently in establishing viable, new populations from direct transfers of wild Saddlebacks (Merton, 1966a, 1966b; 1975), and Chatham Island Snipe (*Coenocorypha aucklandica pusilla*), while failing with Stead's Bush Wrens (*Xenicus longipes variabilis*) and Shore Plovers (*Thinornis novaeseelandiae*). The successful cases involved the release of numbers of birds exceeding the size of the entire Black Robin population. There was minimal knowledge of the habitat requirements, behavior, and ecology of the various species. Transfer of the Black Robin needed to be on a firmer base of knowledge because there could be no margin for error.

Therefore, experiments were designed to determine whether closely-related, but nonendangered robins were amenable to direct transfer, how transfers could be accomplished safely, and whether success could be achieved with very small numbers of birds.

All New Zealand robins inhabit closed forests or scrub, are highly sedentary as adults, and breed as pairs in territories. I found that transferred adults and young-of-the-year will settle as close to the release point as possible when the habitat is suitable; otherwise they move about or fail to form pairs. In suitable habitat they reform pairs rapidly, either with new mates or original mates, and begin establishment of new territories within days, and possibly, hours of being released. If it is spring, typical pairing behavior quickly leads to breeding activities, and successful nesting can occur within a few weeks of release. Birds were successfully transferred in autumn, winter and early spring. No experimental transfers were made in later spring or during summer moult. The most critical factor to success was proximity of acceptable habitat at or near the release point.

Transportation methods were assessed by weight changes of birds during captivity, the visual condition of birds at release, and by survival after release. The results showed great improvement when carrying boxes were redesigned from the types successfully used for Saddlebacks (Merton, 1975).

My boxes each held a single bird on a perch in a small area which was well ventilated, darkened toward the top with light from vents falling on water and live food provided near the bottom. During the 3 to 8 hours of captivity, the North and South Island Robins withstood heat, car and boat engine noise and vibration, and the movements associated with walking and scrambling over 2 km. I found that the birds fed themselves if the boxes were put down and left quietly for a few minutes at convenient intervals. Using this method, robins often showed a slight net gain of weight instead of loss between capture and release, and they did not show the signs of dehydration that were seen in the first experiments using a box designed to the requirements of another species.

The first transplant experiments were begun before the very reduced size of the Black Robin population was known, and they involved 4 pairs of South Island Robins (Flack, 1975). When I found that the Black Robin population consisted of only 17 adults in 1973, experimental releases were reduced to 2 pairs and an extra bird which would be more like the Black Robin case. Two such releases from 2 different South Island Robin populations were made on 2 islands in 1973, and both established new populations. These two closely-studied transplanted populations grew from 4 to 36 and 16 individuals, respectively, and continue to grow. During the same period the Black Robin population declined by over 60 percent.

Comparisons of these rapidly-growing, experimentally-established populations with several other long-established robin populations show that growth in good habitat is rapid due to higher survival rates of adults and immature robins, to a longer breeding season, and to a larger clutch size than the same birds experienced in their former situation. However, in poorer habitat the rapid population growth led to an unbalanced sex ratio because the survival rate of females was lower than for màles. These results were extremely encouraging because they suggested that Black Robins transferred to new habitat would rapidly show improved survival of juvenile birds while also increasing productivity.

APPLICATION OF MANAGEMENT TO BLACK ROBINS

Results from the study of the Black Robin population and the transfer experiments gave clear indications that chances were good for establishing a new population in new habitat by transferring a few adult or independent juvenile robins from nonproductive territories. We were hopeful that inbreeding had not seriously effected the population, and that it would maintain itself for another 10 years while the habitat on the new island was developing. Economic, geographic, and other difficulties eliminated all other management options.

Within the natural range of the Black Robin, the Chatham Islands, only Mangere Island could be used. Mangere Island was still unsatisfactory because the total area of available habitat was only 1.7 ha in broken patches scattered over 4.7 ha, less than that on Tapuaenuku. The Mangere habitat does appear to be good in quality except that its topography is steep, and the exposure unfavorable for winds and winter sunshine. Thus, the reafforestation program was essential for development of a suitable transfer site.

South-East Island, where there is extensive good habitat, had to be eliminated as a choice because of its large population of Chatham Island Tits (*P. macrocephala chathamensis*). Tits and robins compete severely on islands (Flack, *unpublished data*), and in this case, the evidence indicates that the release of a small number of Black Robins into a dense, established tit population would result in the competitive exclusion of the robins.

Unfortunately, by late 1976 it was necessary to decide between transferring all remaining productive birds to nearby Mangere Island before that habitat was fully rehabilitated, or leaving the population to take its own course, most likely to extinction. Circumstances forced a choice between two unsatisfactory alternatives.

The actual transfer of the Black Robins was hampered by the remoteness of the islands, bad weather and accidents, but finally occurred on the third attempt. On the first attempt in February 1976, we attempted to move only 2 or 3 robins rather than all remaining pairs. There were 4 pairs in that breeding season, and these occupied 4 of the 5 territories where regular breeding was known to occur. Thus, at that time, the potential for breeding was 4/5 of the maximum, although the total population was down about 50 percent (Flack, *unpublished data*). The February attempt failed because we were unable to remove the tits from Mangere Island and because a serious boating accident resulted in loss of transportation. In May and June 1976, a party spent over 6 weeks planting trees on Mangere Island and waiting for a break in the weather that would allow a second transfer attempt. The weather was so bad that when we finally got onto the island, the trapping and transport of the robins was impossible. We discovered that 2 females had died during the autumn, an extremely unusual event which forced a decision to remove all remaining productive birds. The 2 pairs and an extra male were moved by a third and successful expedition in September.

The transplanted robins immediately accepted the new habitat, formed new pair bonds and began to show courtship and territorial behavior. Eight weeks after the transfer, the pair with an old and experienced female had one chick; the pair's second egg failed to hatch. The second pair either did not nest, or failed to raise any young. By February, the new bird, a female, was associated with a male while still occasionally begging from her parents.

Sometime before March 1977, the bachelor male disappeared. The two remaining males on Tapuaenuku were moved to Mangere Island. During the last visit in March 1977, 3 pairs and a solitary male had divided the Mangere habitat. I am concerned that this number of robins may be too great for the small area of habitat on the island. Conditions in the winter may not be as good as they appeared to be in the summer. In addition, I have found that productivity is severely reduced in island populations by crowding. Only 2 of the territories were in habitats of good quality.

Any further population increase will require transfer of some birds back to Tapuaenuku or to a suitable island near the New Zealand mainland. The ultimate rescue of this species depends on development of large populations in good habitat on at least 2 islands.

EVALUATION OF INTERISLAND TRANSPLANTS AS A MANAGEMENT TECHNIQUE

Each of the many techniques used for management of endangered and rare birds have limited application because of special features of the biology of particular species. Transfers of wild birds are favored by their simplicity and the relatively small impact on a species' behavior. Bird species amenable to being transferred may have several features in common. These could include either weak powers of flight or sedentary, non-exploratory behavior; adaptable or flexible habitat requirements; and relatively small territory size.

Robins illustrate these features admirably. Although powerful fliers, they are highly sedentary, lacking any tendency to migrate or wander. They are found in several habitats in a broad range of altitudes, and the minimum requirements for their territory are few. This allows large populations to develop in small areas.

The Weka (*Gallirallus australis*) has been successfully transferred in a haphazard and unorganized fashion to new habitats on numerous occasions since the beginning of this century. Although this prevented the extinction of one subspecies and greatly reduced the losses of local populations, the new populations have been very destructive to native insects and birds on islands where the Weka did not originally occur (Atkinson and Bell, 1973).

Saddlebacks show a number of features that might predispose them to being successfully transferred; these include a reluctance to disperse widely, limited flight range, adaptability to several types of forest, and small territory size. Chatham Island Snipe were successfully transferred to Mangere Island by D.V. Merton. The 23 birds caught on South-East Island rapidly increased their numbers and spread into new areas. From what little we know of their biology, they also show many of the desirable characteristics.

Bush Wrens are poorly known, but they are likely to have the characteristics that make this management technique applicable, but the tiny size of the birds greatly increases chances for stress and mortality caused by capture and confinement to carrying boxes. The single attempted transfer of this species occurred at the time of the rescue of the Saddleback from Big South Cape Island, but appears to have failed to establish a new population (B.D. Bell, *personal communication*). Unfortunate circumstances acted against success. The number of birds available was extremely limited, they suffered a lot of stress after capture, partly because they had to be held longer than planned, and they had to be released on a tiny island offering rather limited habitat choices.

Several attempts to transplant New Zealand Shore Plover have also failed, in this case because the birds would fly home soon after release. The present population of this species numbers around 80 adults and has been confined to South-East Island for over 70 years. The birds show a very strong attachment to small segments of their available habitat. This species is a powerful flier and has the ability to leave its island; former populations in New Zealand were probably somewhat migratory, but it now seems that tendencies to wander are weak. My observations also indicate that the habitat on Mangere Island into which they were experimentally introduced was lacking in some important features. Hopes for establishing this species on a second island lie in finding suitable habitat outside of the Chatham Islands and in success with my proposed experiments to see if very young Shore Plover can be moved before the development of strong site attachment.

In New Zealand, wild transfers may become widely used on relatively common species where local populations are endangered or where newly recovered or developed habitats need enrichment by introduction of birds that are slow or unable to disperse. North and South Island Robins present fine opportunities for widespread transfers of birds, and I believe that this will become a necessity for preservation of this species in the more distant future.

Nevertheless, direct transfer of endangered birds will probably not become widespread elsewhere in the world, especially in continental areas. As a group, island birds are probably predisposed for success with this technique. Most non-island birds lack the biological characteristics that might predispose a species to successful transfer. Nevertheless, more careful appraisals should be made because even traits such as a strong homing behavior might be overcome with some application of ingenuity. Morton (Ch. 43, *this volume*) has shown that the technique works on some tropical forest birds. The technique is wonderfully simple when compared to most alternatives.

ACKNOWLEDGMENTS

Field work was carried out while I worked for the New Zealand Wildlife Service for 6 years, from 1971. Support came from the World Wildlife Fund and the Royal Forest and Bird Protection Society. I am grateful for the assistance of numerous field staff who will be named in future papers dealing with specific studies. Jean R. Flack provided helpful criticisms of the manuscript. I am particularly grateful to Mamie S. Flack for making it possible to travel to Madison and participate in this symposium.

LITERATURE CITED

Atkinson, I.A.E. and B.D. Bell. 1973. Offshore and outlying islands, p. 372-392. *In* G.R. Williams (ed.). The Natural History of New Zealand. A.H. and A.W. Reed, Wellington.

Flack, J.A.D. 1973. Robin Research--A Progress Report. Wildlife--A Review 4:28-36.

Flack, J.A.D. 1974. Chatham Island Black Robin. Wildlife--A Review 5:25-31.

Flack, J.A.D. 1975. The Chatham Island Black Robin, extirction or survival? Bull. Int. Council for Bird Preservation 12:146-150.

Flack, J.A.D. 1976. The use of frontal spot and crown feathers in inter- and intraspecific display by the South Island Robin, *Petroica australis australis*. Notornis 23:90-105.

Flack, J.A.D. 1976. Hybrid parakeets on the Mangere Islands, Chatham group. Notornis 23:253-255.

Merton, D.V. 1966a. Transfer of Saddleback from Hen Island to Middle
    Chicken Island, January, 1964. Notornis 12:213-222.
Merton, D.V. 1966b. Some observations of feeding stations, food and
    behavior of the North Island saddleback on Hen Island in January.
    Notornis 13:3-6.
Merton, D.V. 1975. Success in reestablishing a threatened species:
    the Saddleback--its status and conservation. Bull. Int. Council
    for Bird Pres. XII:150-158.
Oliver, W.R.B 1955. New Zealand Birds, 2nd Edition, A.H. and A.W.
    Reed, Wellington.

42

Establishing Atlantic Puffins at a Former Breeding Site

Stephen W. Kress

Early accounts of the birds which nested on the coastal islands of Maine include frequent references to the Atlantic Puffin *(Fratercula arctica)* (e.g., Pearsall, 1879; Norton, 1923; Forbush, 1925). According to the summary by Palmer (1949), puffins nested on at least 7 Maine islands during the mid-1800's. However, by 1900, puffins had disappeared from all of these breeding stations except Machias Seal Island and Matinicus Rock (Norton, 1923). The extinction of these breeding populations is attributed largely to excessive hunting for food and feathers during the 18th and 19th centuries. With protection from hunting, the puffin populations on Machias Seal Island and Matinicus Rock have increased to approximately 1,500 pair and 170 pair respectively, though no new colonies are known (Drury, 1973).

PROJECT OBJECTIVES

The primary objective of this program is to develop procedures for reestablishing puffins at former breeding sites. The project design is based on the assumption that puffins normally return to breed at their natal colony and often assume breeding activities in the same vicinity where they were reared (Harris, 1976). Eastern Egg Rock in Muscongus Bay, Maine, was selected as the site for the experiments because of its history as a former puffin colony (Norton, 1923), the abundance of breeding places under large boulders, the absence of terrestrial mammals, and proximity to the National Audubon Society's Workshop on Hog Island, which serves as base for project operations.

BACKGROUND EXPERIMENTS TO TEST PROCEDURES

In 1973 a feasibility study demonstrated that puffin chicks at approximately 10 days of age could be transported 1,600 km from Great Island in Witless Bay, Newfoundland, to Muscongus Bay, Maine. With an estimated population of 160,000 pairs, Great Island was selected as the source for the chicks because it is the largest colony of puffins in North America (Nettleship, 1972). The feasibility study established highly successful procedures for transporting puffin chicks and concluded that the disturbance resulting from 12 hours of transportation involving boat, airplane and automobile had no apparent effect on the behavior or appetite of the chicks. The study also demonstrated that puffin chicks will pick up and eat small fish that are placed on the floor of their burrows. Puffins could, therefore, be reared with little disturbance by placing the birds in artificial burrows and providing them with ample food.

During the summer of 1974, a program was begun to reestablish the puffin to its former breeding site on Eastern Egg Rock in Muscongus Bay. A staff of 3 research assistants took turns living on the island and fed the birds a diet of frozen smelt (*Osmerus mordax*) with vitamin supplements until the birds reached fledging age. All 54 of these birds appeared to mature normally and successfully fledged from Eastern Egg Rock. Between 1973-1977, a total of 347 out of 354 transplanted puffins fledged from Eastern Egg Rock for a total fledging success of 98 percent.

TRANSPLANT PROCEDURES

Puffin chicks were selected from earthen burrows on the maritime slope habitat of Great Island. Chicks with flattened, left-wing chord measurements ranging from 30-50 mm were considered to be approximately 10-14 days old. Birds at this age are capable of thermoregulation and are no longer dependent on the adult for brooding (Sealy, 1973). Experience with birds above this range suggests that older birds adjust to new burrows with greater difficulty and are more likely to wander from their new burrows.

Selected puffin chicks were transported from Great Island to Eastern Egg Rock in specially designed carrying cases. Each carrying case contained 20 individual compartments constructed from metal juice cans. Both ends of the cans were removed and the floor of each can was covered with coarse sand held in place by silicone rubber cement. Each set of 20 cans was housed in a wooden frame with burlap back and 2 burlap-covered doors. The rough flooring and small size of the cans prevented the birds from slipping during transit, and the burlap doors and back blocked most daylight yet provided adequate ventilation. While in transit by boat, the cases were covered by a tarp to avoid sea spray and wind chill. The chicks were not fed while in transit.

After the birds were collected on Great Island, they were taken by boat to the mainland and transferred by automobile to the St. John's

airport. After a 6 hour chartered flight from St. John's, Newfoundland, to Wiscasset, Maine, the birds were transferred by car and
boat to Eastern Egg Rock. The transplant of birds from their burrows
in Newfoundland to their new burrows in Maine was completed in
approximately 19 hours.

DESIGN OF ARTIFICIAL BURROWS

Transplanted puffin chicks were reared in sod burrows consisting
of shallow L-shaped trenches approximately 20 cm wide, 5 cm deep, and
1 m in length, with walls and roof built from sod blocks dug from
the center of the island. The sod walls were approximately 20 cm
wide and 20 cm high. Where possible, adjoining burrows shared a
common wall. The walls supported 4 cm wide lath braces and green,
vinyl-coated, welded wire that functioned as a base for the sod
roofs.

The sod burrows permitted excellent drainage, as well as
moderate temperatures and humidity, while the relatively loose
nature of the sod permitted the chicks to enlarge the burrow and
nest cavity to their own preference.

FEEDING PROCEDURES

Puffin chicks were fed twice each day by a team of research
assistants who lived on Eastern Egg Rock. Each chick received 3
smelt at the morning feeding (approximately 0730) and evening feeding (approximately 1700). Each smelt was cut in half for easier
ingestion, resulting in six half-fish sections, each about 6 cm
long. The fish were individually frozen and stored in insulated
coolers for about 4 days at a time on Eastern Egg Rock.

To quantify the food intake of the puffins, 5 lots of smelt
were sampled each season, and 20 meals per lot were weighed to
the nearest gram. Each meal consisted of approximately 53 g for
a total daily feeding of approximately 106 g. This diet was
supplemented with 100 mg of vitamin B_1, 100 I.U. of Vitamin E and
a capsule of multiple vitamin mixture. The vitamins were administered once each week by placing the pills or capsules in the
mouths of the smelt. Sea minerals were added to the chicks' diet
by soaking the smelt in a bucket of salt water just prior to feeding.

BANDING OF TRANSPLANTED PUFFINS

When the birds were approximately 4 weeks old, each chick was
banded with a plastic leg-band on its left leg and a U.S. Fish and
Wildlife Service monel metal-band on the right leg. The bands were
color-coded for the different years in which puffins were transplanted: green in 1973, blue in 1974, white in 1975, black in 1976,
and yellow in 1977.

RETURNS OF TRANSPLANTED PUFFINS TO EASTERN EGG ROCK

After wintering at sea, puffins return to breeding sites in the western Atlantic about mid-April. Lighthouse keepers on Machias Seal Island and Matinicus Rock report rafts as early as 11 April off Matinicus Rock, and off Machias Seal Island by 20 April (Pettingill, 1940). These birds usually raft offshore for at least 1 week before landing on their nesting island. This arrival schedule is similar to that on Great Island in Witless Bay, Newfoundland. Nettleship (1972) observed that adult puffins arrive in the vicinity of Great Island in early April, but the first mass landings do not occur until the last third of April. Nettleship also found that immature puffins first appear in late May or early June. Most puffins do not visit land until they are at least 2 years old and breed for the first time when they are 5 years old (Petersen, 1976).

Since non-breeding puffins usually arrive after the adults have occupied the available breeding site, it is possible that the presence of adults is a factor encouraging young puffins to approach land for the first time. Following this rationale, 40 models of adult puffins were carved and painted to resemble breeding adults. These were placed in small groups atop conspicuous boulders in several locations around Eastern Egg Rock.

On 12 June 1977, a puffin circled Eastern Egg Rock several times and then landed in the water near the research team which was in the process of landing on the island. The bird was easily approached from the water, and the sighting of the conspicuous leg bands confirmed the first return of a transplanted puffin to Eastern Egg Rock. During the summer of 1977, there were a total of 19 sightings of puffins at Eastern Egg Rock. White leg-bands (identifying 2-year old birds) were observed on 9 of these occasions. The remaining birds (with the exception of one unbanded puffin) may have been banded but were not close enough for the bands to be seen. There were 7 sightings of puffins landing on Eastern Egg Rock. Five of these landings occurred on boulders with wooden models, suggesting that the models may be useful in encouraging the birds to land on the island. Some of the birds stayed in the near vicinity of the island for periods up to 2 days.

Though the 19 sightings may represent fewer than 19 birds, the sightings demonstrate that some of the transplanted chicks have homed to the release site. Since the age at first breeding is normally 5 years, it will be several more years before the first breeding can be anticipated. In the interim, it is hoped that recruits from the 1976 and 1977 age classes will increase the non-breeding population to a level sufficient to establish a new colony on this former breeding site.

ACKNOWLEDGMENTS

This study was conducted with the assistance of grants from the National Audubon Society and the Joint Scientific Staff of the National Audubon and Massachusetts Audubon Societies. Generous gifts from many private contributors have also helped to make this study possible.

I gratefully acknowledge the continued support of David N. Nettleship of the Canadian Wildlife Service, and I also appreciate the continued assistance and support of the Maine Department of Inland Fisheries and Game, U.S. Fish and Wildlife Service, and the Animal and Plant Health Inspection Service of the U.S. Department of Agriculture.

I am also very grateful to Duryea Morton, Director of the Audubon Workshop in Maine for his continued support and for use of the facilities on Hog Island.

LITERATURE CITED

Drury, W.H. 1973. Population changes in New England seabirds. Bird-Banding 44:267-313.

Forbush, E.H. 1925. Birds of Massachusetts and other New England states. Vol. 1. Massachusetts Dept. of Agr., Boston. 481 p.

Harris, M.P. 1976. Inter-colony movements of Farne Island puffins. Trans. Nat. Hist. Soc. of Northumberland 42:115-118.

Nettleship, D.N. 1972. Breeding success of the Common Puffin, *Fratercula arctica*, on different habitats at Great Island, Newfoundland. Ecological Monographs 42:239-268.

Norton, A.H. 1923. Notes on birds of the Knox County region. Maine Naturalist 3:31-35.

Palmer, R.S. 1949. Maine Birds. Mus. of Comp. Zool., Cambridge, Mass. 656 p.

Pearsall, R.F. 1879. Grand Manan notes. Field and Stream 13:529-535.

Petersen, A. 1976. Age of first breeding in Puffin, *Fratercula arctica* (L.). Astarte 9:43-50.

Pettingill, O.S. 1940. The bird life of the Grand Manan archipelago. Auk 52:359.

Sealy, S.G. 1973. Breeding biology of the Horned Puffin on St. Lawrence Island, Bering Sea, with zoogeographical notes on the North Pacific puffins. Pacific Science 27:99-119.

43

Reintroducing Recently Extirpated Birds into a Tropical Forest Preserve

Eugene S. Morton

It is unfortunate, but true, that most tropical-habitat preserves will not, in and of themselves, serve to preserve all of the avian species that might exist in them. Unless these areas are sufficiently large enough to contain refugia from local vagaries of climate, food supplies, or periodic outbreaks of predators and competitors, some species will be extirpated for "non-successional" reasons (Willis, 1974; Terborgh, 1974). The quickening pace of forest destruction by man dictates that these preserves will become islands of habitat and that potential refugia outside of preserves will be rare.

This means that we will be faced increasingly with the need to reintroduce extirpated species to preserves, a responsibility not to be taken lightly if we are to maintain the naturally evolved traits of the reintroduced species. These propagules should ideally have the ability to survive without undue alteration of the environment by man. If the conditions that caused the original extinction lasted but a short time, we should expect the reintroduced birds to live about as long as individuals of that species lived before they disappeared, and we should see some reproduction. If the conditions are chronic, then we would not expect reproduction, and the lifespan of the propagules could be used as an index of how "bad" conditions are and whether it is feasible to reintroduce the species again. Thus, the key to developing a theory of reintroduction strategies is knowledge of the demography of a population before it became extirpated, as well as the ecological and behavioral attributes that produce the demographic pattern. At one level, a reintroduction can only be said to have succeeded if reproduction takes place, but at the theoretical level, the decline of a reintroduced species--with or without reproduction--may tell us much about the "island effect" itself, if we study the causes intensively.

It was to study what I presumed would be the decline of a

propagule that I reintroduced 2 recently extirpated species of wrens (family Troglodytidae) onto Barro Colorado Island in the Canal Zone of Panama.

THE BARRO COLORADO STUDY AREA

Barro Colorado Island (BCI) comprises 15.6 km^2 of a hilltop that was surrounded by the water of Gatun Lake during the construction of the Panama Canal in 1910-1914. More details about the site may be found in Willis (1974). No hunting or clearing has been permitted legally since 1923, when the island became a biological preserve. It is administered by the Smithsonian Tropical Research Institute.

Various authors have discussed the maturity of BCI's forest. It is generally accepted that the eastern half is less mature than the western half, that the western half is "mature" but not "virgin", and that the forest is "maturing gradually." Eisenmann (1952) reported 209 breeding bird species; Willis (1974) stated that 45 of those species had disappeared from the island, and some others are declining. Thirty-two (71 percent) of the extirpated forms were second-growth species that were lost because of forest maturation and resulting loss of habitat, while 13 are presumed to be forest birds that were extirpated due to the island effect and predation.

My observations of the structure of forests on BCI since 1964 indicate that areas of then "mature" forest are now much less so. Treefalls occur with incredible frequency such that the previously "more mature" western half of BCI is becoming "less mature", while the forest of the eastern half is maturing since the treefall rate in a younger forest is lower than that in an older one. One of the extirpated species listed by Willis (1974) as a second-growth species, the Thick-billed Euphonia (*Euphonia lannirostris*), was rediscovered in May 1977 breeding along the Barbour Trail, an area that in 1964 was mature forest, but is now less mature.

METHODS

Between 23 June and 12 July 1976, I reintroduced onto BCI 2 species of wrens, the Song Wren (*Cyphorhinus arada*) and the White-breasted Wood Wren (*Henicorhina leucosticta*), both considered forest species that occupy habitat types existing on BCI. The Song Wren disappeared between 1960 and 1970 (Willis, 1974), but the wood-wren was lost before 1960. Seven individuals of each species were released at the same point on BCI on the same day they were captured. The Song Wren is nearly twice as heavy as the wood-wren, and they may have overlapping territories. Both are strictly insectivorous. The Song Wren feeds exclusively on the ground in leaf litter while the wood-wren feeds in vine tangles and deadfalls near or on the ground. Thus, little or no interaction, either ecologically or behaviorally was expected between the 2 species.

The technique used to capture birds for reintroduction was one that may be used to capture any species that defends its territory by using far-carrying vocalizations. In this case, the wren's songs were played back on a tape recorder that was placed on the ground at the apex of 2 mist nets positioned in an "L" shape. The species differed in their responsiveness. The wood-wrens responded immediately and were easily captured, but only one bird was caught at each site. Song Wrens responded as a family group to any Song Wren call I played, but they did not stay near the tape recorder. They passed by once or twice and then remained too stationary to capture in the mist nets. However, I found that I could then flush them into the net. Birds were captured in late morning to early afternoon and released at the same spot between 1700 and 1800 h. At the capture site, the birds were weighed, inspected for molt, individually color banded, then placed in small screen cages or large paper bags for transport to BCI. Data on the birds used in the experiment are presented in Table 1. The time between capture and release varied from 2 to 8 hours. Mealworms and crickets were provided and were eaten by the birds during transport and just before release.

The Song Wrens subsequently marked with red and white bands were captured together, as were the ones subsequently marked with yellow and green bands; birds marked with pink, orange, and blue bands were captured singly. This marking scheme enabled me to determine if birds released singly would survive as well as those released together with a presumed family member.

I also censused the island's populations of antwrens (*Myrmotherula axillaris, M. fulviventris* and *M. quixensis*) in an attempt to confirm my previous impression that they were more abundant on

TABLE 1. DATA ON BIRDS RELEASED ON BARRO COLORADO ISLAND, JUNE 1976

Species and Date	Weight	Molt Condition	Color Band	Location of Capture
Song Wren				
23 June	27.0 g	molting	white	Pipeline Road
23 June	24.0 g	molting	red	Pipeline Road
24 June	23.5 g	no molt	pink	Pipeline Road
25 June	29.0 g	no molt	yellow	Madden Forest
25 June	-	molting	green	Madden Forest
30 June	29.5 g	molting	blue	Madden Forest
30 June	28.4 g	worn plumage	orange	Pipeline Road
Wood Wren				
23 June	18.0 g	no molt	white	Pipeline Road
25 June	18.5 g	no molt	orange	Pipeline Road
26 June	17.5 g	no molt	red	Madden Forest
26 June	15.5 g	no molt	yellow	Madden Forest
26 June	18.5 g	no molt	blue	Madden Forest
30 June	17.5 g	no molt	pink	Madden Forest
30 June	17.0 g	no molt	green	Pipeline Road

BCI than on the mainland. Antwrens could be important competitors of the wood-wren and Song Wren, and their abundance on BCI could influence the interpretation of reintroduction experiments.

Two return trips were made to the reintroduction site from 5-12 December 1976 and 12-24 May 1977, 22 and 44 weeks after the release. I attempted to relocate the reintroduced birds and to assess their territorial size, breeding success, and pair formations.

RESULTS OF REINTRODUCTION EXPERIMENTS

White-breasted Wood-wren

In December 1976, by playing recorded songs of both species at intervals of 200 m along the trails on BCI, I was able to locate only one wood-wren (the yellow banded one) 300 m from the release point. This was in an area of young, second-growth vegetation, one of the few patches left on the island. Edwin O. Willis, who spent January and February 1977 on BCI, reported a single, white-banded wood-wren, which I later located in May, about 1000 m southeast of the release site. In May, the white-banded wood-wren was discovered when it responded to playback of its song. I could not relocate it after this initial resighting. Thus, 2 out of the 7 introduced wood-wrens survived for almost a full year and appeared to be sedentary. Both occupied either second growth or heavy treefall areas in mature forest; they did not occupy mature forest.

Song Wren

The day following the release, I obtained responses to playback from the red- and white-banded birds which were a mated pair at capture. In all respects, this was identical to their response to playback the day before, even though they were in foreign territory. In December 1976, I found the red- and yellow-banded birds feeding 2 fledged young. Willis found a second pair with 2 fledged young in January, the adults being orange- and green-banded. The red-banded bird was later captured with the white-banded bird, and the green-banded bird was recaptured with the yellow-banded bird. Thus, two released pairs had broken up and remated with new individuals, and both new pairs reproduced successfully within 5 months after release. This was totally unexpected, given the 90-96 percent nest failure rate reported by Willis (1974) for several species of forest antbirds on BCI. In May 1977, two independent young still foraged with the red- and yellow-banded pair but, in addition, so did the white-banded bird, the red-banded bird's former mate. The pink-banded bird was also seen alone near the red- and yellow-banded pair's territory. Thus, of the original 7 Song Wrens, only the blue-banded bird was unaccounted for and presumed dead. The total population on BCI is now 9; one young disappeared.

The red- and yellow-banded birds ranged over an area of 150,000 m^2, which included the original release site. The orange- and green-banded birds were located 2000 m from the release site. There was no

apparent reason for the long dispersal of one pair and short dispersal of the other. There is no obvious structural similarity in
forest structure, nor is there dissimilarity in unoccupied areas
between the 2 territories.

DISCUSSION

Reintroduction of these wrens on BCI has answered several
questions that could not have been answered in other ways. The
wood-wren's habitat choice--and choice is the key word since they
had no conspecifics to force them into marginal habitats--illus-
trates the difficulty in defining a species' habitat requirements
in tropical forests. Their choice of young second-growth shows
that they are not true forest-birds and that their extirpation
on BCI was probably due to habitat maturation beyond the second-
growth stage.

The Song Wren, in contrast, is doing well; better than expected.
A lesson from these introduced wrens is that known pairs are not
needed for a successful introduction; the introduced pairs separated
and reformed easily. However, adult birds that were paired at the
time of capture and release perhaps perform better as propagules
than single, young individuals.

Observations of Song Wren foraging behavior show that they commonly flush insects, such as cockroaches and orthopterans, from
hiding places under leaves on the ground. I was convinced that
this is why the young stay with the adults for so long and why
the white-banded bird was allowed to rejoin the other 2 adults,
the red- and yellow-banded birds. They flush insects for each
other--an escaping insect can elude the bird it runs from, but
not the bird it runs into. Thus, Song Wrens forage most efficiently in tight groups rather than as single birds.

I censused the 3 antwren species that I hypothesized might
be contributing to the extirpation of the wren species. These
species are smaller than true wrens and occur in small mixed species flocks. They forage for insects in vines below the forest
canopy and, thus, are potentially competitors for food with the
true wrens. On BCI, I encountered flocks of antwrens on the average
of once every 200 m along forest trails. On the mainland I encountered flocks of antwrens every 1000 m. The wrens may have
become extinct on BCI, but the antwrens have increased by about
500 percent.

Why have the antwrens prospered on BCI while the wrens have
become extinct? I believe that the smaller body size of the antwrens
has been the chief factor. It takes less food per individual to
support an antwren than a wren. In times of food shortage, the true
wrens are not as likely to survive. If this is true, then perhaps
we can tentatively speculate that in a tropical-forest reserve of
limited size, (i.e., the 15.6 km^2 area of BCI), the larger species
in any particular foraging guild will tend to die out faster than
smaller species. This hypothesis can be tested by artificially
maintaining the populations of the smaller species at densities

similar to those found in huge forest tracts. Perhaps we would see
that direct or diffuse competition from "super abundant" smaller
species contributes to the demise of larger ones.

Repeated reintroductions may, therefore, be necessary to maintain certain species in small habitat-island preserves. The study
of the effects of such reintroductions will provide meaningful data
on competitive forces in tropical forests. The data from the reintroductions on BCI suggest that it may be difficult to formulate broadly
applicable reintroduction theories. Rather, they show that an
autecological approach is necessary; each species may present a
unique challenge requiring special techniques.

ACKNOWLEDGMENTS

I am very grateful to the Wildlife Preservation Trust International and to the World Wildlife Fund for financial support. The
staff of the Smithsonian Tropical Research Institute were helpful
in many ways, and Bruce Groff helped capture the birds for release.

LITERATURE CITED

Eisenmann, E. 1952. Annotated list of birds of Barro Colorado Island,
    Canal Zone. Smithsonian Inst. Misc. Collect. 177:1-62.
Terborgh, J. 1974. Preservation of natural diversity: The problem
    of extinction prone species. Bioscience 24:715-722.
Willis, E. 1974. Populations and local extinctions of birds on Barro
    Colorado Island, Panama. Ecol. Monogr. 44:153-169.

Part IX
Integrated Approaches
to Management of Endangered Birds

44

Integrated Management of Endangered Birds
A Review

Richard L. Plunkett

If we attempt to look at the development of management techniques for preserving endangered species in historical perspective, it is perhaps appropriate that a member of the staff of the National Audubon Society was chosen to introduce the final paper session on integrated approaches, since for the past 70 years the National Audubon Society has been involved--and in many cases has taken a leading role--in efforts to assist endangered bird populations in North America.

Two of the most important early successes in reversing the fortunes of whole groups of birds reduced to very low numbers, to the point that entire families or even orders might well have been classified as threatened or endangered by man's activities on this continent, were the subject of National Audubon's early efforts. These were, first, the restoration of the populations of the long-legged wading birds (herons, egrets, ibises) that had been extirpated from most of their historical breeding range and reduced to extremely low numbers by the turn of this century as a result of the depredations of the plume trade, and, second, the restoration of the populations of those migratory shorebirds that nest at high latitudes, which similarly had been reduced to very low numbers by decades of market and sport hunting.

In the case of the herons, egrets and ibises, the management techniques were simple, even rudimentary by today's standards: they consisted of halting the slaughter by ending the feather trade, obtaining legal protection that was made effective by wardening, and establishing sanctuaries to protect the few remaining breeding colonies. With effective protection and a system of sanctuaries and wardens, the wader populations began a slow recovery that has seen decade by decade increases in numbers and gradual recolonization northward as one wader species after another has returned to parts of its range from which it had been extirpated (Ogden, 1978).

Similarly, the passage of the Migratory Bird Treaty Act, the ban on spring shooting in 1918, and the achievement of a completely closed season for most of the shorebirds in 1927, allowed populations of those migratory shorebirds that nest at high latitudes to recover slowly. These birds were particularly vulnerable to overhunting because of their low clutch size, their relatively low annual reproductive success which results from vagaries of weather, their inability to renest during the short arctic summer, the special hazards arising from their immensely long migrations, their flocking behavior, and their tendency to be lured to decoys.

It might be useful to note, however, that in each instance, the response to the early management programs was very slow. It has taken 5 to 6 decades for some of the herons, egrets and ibises to recolonize New York and southern New England, and some of the populations of shorebirds that nest at high latitudes have not yet recovered to anything approaching their former abundance despite a full half century of complete protection, in North America, from the hunting pressure that they were not equipped to withstand.

These two examples of rather simple management programs, drawn from the early history of the conservation movement in North America, were clearly responses to what was perceived as a relatively simple problem: excessive mortality resulting from overharvesting.   As the focus of conservation efforts shifted to other species endangered by loss of habitat and other more complex factors, it became obvious that much more sophisticated management programs would be required.   Examples of this shift in the perception of what must be included in a management prescription may be drawn from a series of research monographs commissioned by the National Audubon Society beginning in the late 1930's.   Designed to produce the essential data on a species' life history and biological requirements that even then was seen as necessary in order to plan effective management programs, these included reports on the Ivory-billed Woodpecker (*Campephilus principalis*) (Tanner, 1942), Roseate Spoonbill (*Ajaia ajaja*) (Allen, 1942), Whooping Crane (*Grus americana*) (Allen, 1952, 1956a), American Flamingo (*Phoenicopterus ruber*) (Allen, 1956b), and California Condor (*Gymnogyps californianus*) (Koford, 1953; Miller et al., 1965).   These monographs provided guidance to the National Audubon Society in developing its own conservation programs and in planning further additions to its sanctuary system, which presently comprises almost 80,900 ha of prime bird habitat in North America. In at least 2 instances, those of the Whooping Crane and California Condor, the monographs largely determined the early directions of federal management programs for these endangered species.   The information contained in these monographs clearly fulfilled what many previous speakers at this symposium have identified as a critical requirement for effective management of any endangered species and, indeed, as the starting point for any selection of a management option: a complete biological assessment that indicates the species' requirements and those factors that have led to its endangerment, as well as those factors that may limit its potential for increasing its numbers and expanding its range.

KEY ELEMENTS OF INTEGRATED MANAGEMENT

The following seven elements appear to cover the current state
of the art as to what we now believe must be included in an integrated approach to the management of endangered species.
1. Research is needed to determine the biological requirements
of the species and to identify those factors that led to the species'
endangerment and those limiting factors that retard or prevent its
recovery. Included are information on the species' life history,
its habitat (including any changes that may have made that habitat
less suitable in terms of the species' requirements), its range
(both the historically occupied range and the species' present
distribution within that range), population size, age structure,
sex ratio, age at first breeding, mortality rates, reproductive
potential, nesting requirements, feeding ecology, sociobiology,
genetic structure (including the likelihood of gene flow between
now isolated subpopulations), general health, and, particularly in
the case of species that feed at high trophic levels in long food
chains, its relative degree of susceptibility to the toxicants
that man has introduced into the environment. An additional item
that may be included under research is information on the availability and suitability of non-endangered surrogates on which any new
techniques may be tested and perfected before such techniques are
employed in an attempt to assist the endangered species. Thus,
many of the techniques used in captive propagation of the Peregrine
Falcon (*Falco peregrinus*) were first tested in experiments with the
Prairie Falcon (*F. mexicanus*); similarly, the Sandhill Crane (*Grus
canadensis*) was used to test procedures later applied to the Whooping Crane.
2. Protection of the species and its essential habitat is
necessary. This can include the establishment and effective enforcement of full legal protection that reduces man-induced mortality to
an absolute minimum, as well as the identification and protection
of sufficient portions of its essential habitat to meet its biological requirements (including its nesting sites, feeding areas, and,
in the case of highly migratory species, its wintering habitat and
any staging areas that are regularly utilized during migration).
Although we now have the means of protecting essential habitat by
establishing refuges and other specialized management areas for
threatened and endangered species in North America, the effective
protection of migratory species and their wintering habitat in
Central and South America may well require the negotiation of new
international agreements.
3. Education of both the general public and of those management agencies charged with responsibility for protecting the species
and its habitat is often required. An effective public education
program is essential in obtaining the cooperation of the public
and its long-term support for the preservation of a sufficient portion of the species' habitat and for any management program that

must be sustained over a lengthy period of time. The effectiveness
of an education program may well depend on the adequacy of the prior
research. We may be unable to enlist the support of the public unless
we can explain, in relatively simple terms, why a given species is
endangered and how the management program relates to those factors
that caused its endangerment or that restrict its recovery.

    4. Management can include any of the more traditional techniques
for managing the habitat of an endangered species or the use of any
of the various management techniques that are detalied in this volume.
The adequacy of the underlying research is extremely important in ensuring that the management option or options selected to assist an
endangered species do, in fact, address those factors that inhibit
its recovery.

    5. Population modeling, however crude for lack of precise data
on the essential parameters of a species' life history, may nevertheless serve to indicate the probable limiting factors that may inhibit
or prevent recovery of an endangered species. A population model
may also indicate the relative likelihood of success of any management technique that may be proposed to assist that species. A mathematical or computer-based model is particularly useful in the case of
K-selected species that are characterized by long lives, low rates of
reproduction, delayed onset of first breeding, and slow response to
perturbations: management programs for such long-lived species may
require many years to show positive or negative results. The population model, even though limited for lack of data, may be used to
isolate those critical variables on which additional data are required both to perfect the model and to determine the results of
our interventions in behalf of the endangered species. Richard S.
Miller (Ch. 47, *this volume*) will discuss how population modeling
may assist in the design of management programs.

    6. Population monitoring that involves counting or censusing
the population of a threatened or endangered species is, of course,
a key element in planning a management program and in determining
the effectiveness of the management effort. Examples of such monitoring efforts include the periodic censuses of the number of singing
males of the Kirtland's Warbler (*Dendroica kirtlandii*) on the Michigan breeding grounds, the attempt to monitor the numbers and distribution of California Condors from a series of observation stations
manned for a two-day period in October of each year, and the cooperative effort to survey the status of breeding populations of the
Peregrine Falcon in North America at five-year intervals (Cade and
Fyfe, 1970; Fyfe et al., 1976). Other long-term population monitoring programs for avian species in North America include the Breeding
Bird Census, Winter Bird Population Study and Christmas Bird Count
organized by the National Audubon Society, the Breeding Bird Survey
organized by the U.S. Fish and Wildlife Service, and two computer
data banks operated jointly by the Cornell Laboratory of Ornithology
and the National Audubon Society, the Colonial Bird Register and the
North American Nest Record Card Program. McCrimmon and Bart (Ch. 46,
this volume) will discuss the usefulness of such long-term population
monitoring programs for threatened and endangered species.

    7. Coordinated overall planning is the final element in an

integrated management program. This should involve all agencies
charged with responsibility for the management of an endangered
species, together with continuing scientific review and a means
of providing independent input sufficient to ensure that the political decisions of the management agencies are still responsive to
the biological requirements of the species. In North America this
has been accomplished through Recovery Plans prepared by a Recovery
Team appointed under authority of the Endangered Species Act of 1973.
Marshall (Ch. 49, *this volume*) will discuss the Recovery Plan approach
to the management of endangered species. An independent appraisal of
the strengths and weaknesses of that approach has just been published
as the Report of the American Ornithologists' Union Committee on
Conservation for 1976-77 (King, 1977).

EXAMPLES OF INTEGRATED MANAGEMENT

A review of the literature may lead one to conclude that we
are only now approaching the point where all or most of the elements enumerated above are being combined with sufficient precision--
and with sufficient feedback from one element to another--to warrant
the "integrated approach" label.

As more of the Recovery Plans for North American endangered
species are completed and approved, some of the resulting management
programs will draw on all of the elements of an integrated approach;
others, however, may focus on only a single limiting factor. Still
others that address the needs of migratory species may be flawed by
lack of information as to what is occurring on the wintering grounds.
In such cases we may be doing our best to manage the endangered
species in North America but still be unable to deal effectively
with a limiting factor on the wintering grounds.

Two outstanding examples of integrated approaches arise from
efforts to assist endangered species on island groups in the Indian
Ocean. The first of these is the Management Plan for the Cousin
Island Nature Reserve in the Seychelles (Diamond, 1976). In its
thoroughness of treatment and attention to each of the elements
enumerated above, Diamond's management plan could be used as a
model by anyone charged with preserving island endemics.

A second example, one with enormous potential but one unfortunately not being carried forward for lack of a receptive political
climate, is the program for the conservation of endemic birds and
other wildlife on Mauritius that was prepared by the organizer of
this symposium (Temple, 1976). I am sure that any reviewer would
agree that Temple's report to the International Council for Bird
Preservation and his proposal for future activities on Mauritius
constitute a remarkably complete assessment of all of the problems--
and potentials--for integrated management of the native flora and
fauna of this island group.

A third example, and again an outstanding one, is the program
developed by LaBastille (1969 and Ch. 45, *this volume*) to assist
the flightless Giant Pied-billed Grebe (*Podilymbus gigas*) endemic
to Lake Atitlán in Guatemala. A review of her dissertation indi-

cates thorough research into the life history and ecology of this species, protection of the grebe and critical portions of its habitat, establishment of a sanctuary, wardening, conservation education, and the development of a cooperative conservation and management program for this species. This is remarkable because it was accomplished in a country with little prior history of conservation activity.

Returning to North America, one may find thoroughly integrated approaches to the management of at least 4 species.

Osprey (Pandion haliaetus)

Research and management programs for the Osprey are well summarized in a review by Henny (1976). This review includes analyses of the population dynamics of this species with special attention to mortality rates, wintering distribution and migrations, age at sexual maturity, dispersal of young, and observed recruitment as compared to a recruitment standard derived from a mathematical model; an assessment of historical and current Osprey numbers and production by regions, an analysis of the role of the persistent pesticides in Osprey population declines, and an appraisal of Osprey management plans, which include the creation of management areas specifically designed for this species. The first such Osprey management area in the Deschutes National Forest was created as early as 1969 by the Oregon Wildlife Commission, the Bureau of Land Management and the U.S. Forest Service. Since then, habitat management plans for the Osprey have been developed for designated portions of several other National Forests. Olendorff and Zeedyk (Ch. 48, *this volume*) will discuss land management for endangered species by the Bureau of Land Management and U.S. Forest Service.

Peregrine Falcon

With no less than 4 Recovery Teams engaged in the preparation of separate Recovery Plans for the Eastern, Rocky Mountain/Southwestern, Pacific Coast and Arctic populations of the Peregrine Falcon in the United States, plus the highly innovative Canadian Wildlife Service program for this species, it would be surprising if the Peregrine Falcon were not being managed through an integrated approach. Each of the 7 key elements of an integrated approach is incorporated, in whole or part, in one or another of the draft Recovery Plans and the associated research and management efforts. However, despite the provisions of each of the Recovery Plans, the wealth of field observations on the status of breeding populations of the Peregrine Falcon in North America, and the highly encouraging results of the captive-breeding programs and experimental reintroductions of this species, it must be noted that no approach has yet been found to deal with what may be the crucial limiting factor inhibiting the recovery of all of the migratory populations: the continued use of organochlorine insecticides on the species' wintering grounds in Central and South America.

Whooping Crane

The development of the research and management program for this species over the past 40 years is perhaps the best available example of an integrated approach to the management of a highly endangered species. The research element is outstanding, with the reports by Allen (1952) and Novakowski (1966) providing data on the life history and population dynamics of this species based on detailed field observations on the wintering grounds and breeding grounds, respectively. Protection of both the wintering grounds at Aransas National Wildlife Refuge on the Texas coast and the breeding grounds in Wood Buffalo National Park, Northwest Territories, Canada, was achieved at an early stage. Protection of the species against losses from shooting along the migration route between these areas involved a massive and highly effective effort that also served to direct the public's attention to the crane's plight. An attempt to model the population (Miller et al., 1974) was particularly useful in showing that periodic fluctuations in the death rate may reflect discontinuities in the population's age structure which resulted from its growth from an all-time low of only 14 individuals in 1938. Support for the captive-breeding program at Patuxent Wild-Research Center was achieved by first demonstrating the techniques and the ability to maintain cranes for long periods in captivity by experiments with a non-endangered surrogate, the Sandhill Crane (*Grus canadensis*). Similarly, the decision to attempt cross-fostering of Whooping Cranes by Greater Sandhill Cranes (*G. c. tabida*) at Grays Lake, Idaho was preceded by a thorough study of the status, distribution, seasonal movements, and wintering areas of the Sandhill Cranes (Drewien and Bizeau, 1974). However, one cannot help but contrast the success of the earlier public education effort designed to ensure protection of the Whooping Crane along the migration route with the recurring controversy surrounding the captive-breeding program at Patuxent, now coming into the production stage only 10 years after its inception in 1967. This breeding program is certainly a remarkable success, but it is not so regarded by the press and the public, because the conservation community and the management agencies failed to raise a full generation of captive Whooping Cranes to sexual maturity. Identification of this failure in education is particularly significant because we may have an even more difficult task in explaining the time involved by a proposed program of captive propagation and reintroduction for the California Condor.

California Condor

This is perhaps the most extreme example we have for North America of a long-lived, *K*-selected species that we are attempting to manage. Although each of the 7 elements identified earlier in this paper has been used in the management program for this highly endangered species, we are now considering the adoption of a program of captive propagation and subsequent reintroduction of the California Condor as a true "last resort." Despite apparent success in reducing excess mortality caused directly by man to an absolute minimum and in reducing undue disturbance related to human activities near the traditional nesting and roosting sites, which were the principal limiting factors identified by earlier researchers (Koford, 1953; Miller et al., 1965), the Condor population has continued to decline. This indicates some shortcomings exist in current research and management efforts. Indeed, all available data would seem to indicate that the condor population is not responding to the management program and is continuing to decline in numbers. Annual production of fledged young has averaged less than 2 per year for the eleven-year period from 1966 through 1976, as compared to the goal of 4 young per year established by the California Condor Recovery Plan (U.S. Fish and Wildlife Service, 1975) and an estimate by Verner (1976), drawn from a series of population models utilizing the existing data, that annual production of at least 5 or 6 young per year is the minimum production necessary to sustain a population of 50 California Condors well distributed within the 1974 range.

A further review of the management program suggests that we have been attempting to manage the California Condor in the absence of essential information required to manage this species. This is in part owing to restrictions placed on research in an attempt to minimize disturbance of condors. What Verner has termed the "critical unknowns" of condor life history may have seriously handicapped any management effort. These unknowns include total population size (we don't know how many condors are extant and have no effective means of counting the population), age structure, sex ratio, age at first breeding, frequency of breeding, survival rates of adults and and subadults, movement patterns (we have no banded or color-marked individuals in the population and, thus, are unable to trace the movements of known individuals). Finally, we lack an extremely important datum for a species that feeds at a high trophic level: we have little information on the effects on the population of those toxicants that man has introduced into the condor's environment. What data we do have, based on analyses of three salvaged condor specimens over the past twelve years, suggests relatively high levels of organochlorine pesticide contamination.

The only conclusion that I can draw from reviewing these unknowns is that we lack the information required for integrated management of this species, that the first and most important of the key elements on the list of what constitutes an integrated approach has not been satisfied, so that much of the effort to manage this species may have been misdirected. Thus, I return to a point repeatedly emphasized earlier in this paper, that integrated management of an endangered species is dependent on adequate research.

LITERATURE CITED

Allen, R.P. 1942. The Roseate Spoonbill. National Audubon Society Research Report No. 2.

Allen, R.P. 1952. The Whooping Crane. National Audubon Society Research Report No. 3.

Allen, R.P. 1956a. An Report on the Whooping Crane's northern breeding grounds. Supplement to National Audubon Society Research Report No. 3.

Allen, R.P. 1956b. The flamingos: their life history and survival. National Audubon Society Research Report No. 5.

Cade, R.J. and R.W. Ryfe. 1970. The North American Peregrine Survey, 1970. Canadian Field-Naturalist 84(3):231-245.

Diamond, A.W. 1976. Management plan for Cousin Island. Nature Reserve, Seychelles. Int. Council for Bird Preserv., London.

Drewien, R.C. and E.G. Bizeau. 1974. Status and distribution of Greater Sandhill Cranes in the Rocky Mountains. Wildlife Manage. 38(4):720-742.

Fyfe, R.W., S.A. Temple and T.J. Cade. 1976. The 1975 North American Peregrine Falcon survey. Canadian Field-Naturalist 90(3):228-273.

Henny, C.J. 1976. Research, management and status of the Osprey in North America, p. 192-222. *In* R.D. Chancellor (ed.). Report of Proceedings. World Conference of Birds of Prey, Vienna, 1975, Int. Council for Bird Preserv., London.

King, W.B. 1977. Report of the A.O.U. Committee on Conservation, 1976-1977: The Recovery Team--recovery plan approach to conservation of endangered species: a status summary and appraisal. Supplement to Auk 94(4):3DD-19DD.

Koford, D.B. 1953. The California Condor. Nat. Audubon Soc. Res. Rep. No. 4.

LaBastille, A. 1969. The life history, ecology, and management of the Giant Pied-billed Grebe (*Podilymbus gigas*), Lake Atitlán, Guatemala. Unpublished Ph.D. thesis, Cornell University, Ithaca, N.Y.

Miller, A., I. McMillan, and E. McMillan. 1965. The current status and welfare of the California Condor. Nat. Audubon Soc. Res. Rep. No. 6.

Miller, R.S., D.B. Botkin and R. Mendelssohn. 1974. The Whooping Crane (*Grus americana*) population of North America. Biol. Conser. 6(2):106-111.

Novakowski, N.S. 1966. Whooping Crane population dynamics on the nesting grounds, Wood Buffalo National Park, Northwest Territories, Canada. Canadian Wildlife Service Rep. No. 1.

Ogden, J.C. 1978. Recent population trends by colonial wading birds on the Atlantic and Gulf Coastal Plains. *In* Proceedings of North American Wading Bird Conference, Charleston, S.C., 14-17 October 1976. National Audubon Society and U.S. Fish and Wildlife Service (*in press*).

Tanner, J.T. 1942. The Ivory-billed Woodpecker. Nat. Audubon Soc. Res. Rep. No. 1.

Temple, S.A. 1976. Conservation of endemic birds and other wildlife on Mauritius. Progress Report and Proposal for Future Activities (International Council for Bird Preservation, Washington, D.C.).

U.S. Fish and Wildlife Service. 1975. California Condor recovery
    plan, U.S. Fish and Wildlife Service, Washington, D.C.
Verner, J. 1976. An appraisal of the continued involvement of forest
    service research in the California Condor recovery effort.
    Report to U.S. Forest Service (U.S. Forest Service, Washington,
    D.C.).

45

Management of Giant Pied-billed Grebes on Lake Atitlán

Anne LaBastille

The Giant Pied-billed Grebe (*Podilymbus gigas* Griscom)--or as it is known by the local Mayan Indians, the *Poc*--is a flightless waterbird endemic to Lake Atitlán in the Guatemalan highlands. During the early 1960's, following introduction of Largemouth Bass (*Micropterus salmoides*), the grebe population abruptly dropped from an apparently stable population of between 200 to 300 to approximately 80 birds. The species was apparently in danger of extinction and was considered one of the rarest waterbirds in the Western Hemisphere (Bowes and Bowes, 1962; LaBastille, 1974).

In 1965, a cooperative conservation and management program, entitled "Operation Protection of the Poc", was started in collaboration with the Guatemalan Ministry of Agriculture, using various foreign grants and matching funds. The 4 aims of this program were classic wildlife management procedures: (1) to develop legal protection to guard the species; (2) to devise management techniques for preserving the grebe's habitat; (3) to introduce conservation education to local inhabitants; and (4) to establish a refuge.

In addition, we initiated short-term, innovative, crisis procedures which focused on rapid improvement of the environment, publicity, and dealing with those human elements most susceptible to positive change. Although all this was directed to a small endemic population of birds, these techniques may have broader application to other endangered species, and they help to demonstrate an imaginitive approach towards their management and preservation. The basic goals of both long- and short-term techniques were to prevent extinction and correct environmental problems.

Limiting factors found at Lake Atitlán included competition for food and probably predation upon grebe chicks by introduced

-397-

bass; decreased foraging success by adult and juvenile grebes; a naturally-limited shoreline habitat (only 26 km of vegetated shore-line out of a total of 105 km) which is further reduced through reed-cutting for home industry by local Indians; poaching, hunting, and egg-stealing; and the increasing recreational and touristic development of shoreline real estate further decreasing grebe habitat.

At the outset of Operation Protection Poc, it was determined that nothing short of heroic measures could counteract the introduced bass due to the size (130 km^2) and depth (340 m) of Lake Atitlán (Williams, 1960); the domestic use of lake water by an estimated 50,000 Mayan Indians living within the watershed; and the thriving population of bass. Therefore, management measures were concentrated on the procedures mentioned below.

LEGAL PROTECTION

A basis for the protection of the grebes was provided through a Presidential decree issued 14 January 1959 by President Miguel Ydigoras Fuentes. This decree prohibits hunting of the grebes and other waterbirds at Lake Atitlán and imposes a fine and confiscation of firearms. The first and most crucial step was placing a game warden--the first ever hired--at Lake Atitlán. The warden operated under the authority of the Division of Fauna, Ministry of Agriculture. The Government was able to supply gas and oil but could not afford a fast patrol boat which was needed to apprehend wealthy Guatemalan sportsmen who hunted waterfowl on weekends, as well as local Indians who poached birds for food with slingshots and old firearms. There-fore, I applied for and received a suitable patrol boat from the World Wildlife Fund in Switzerland. I also purchased new uniforms, arm emblems, patrol boat banners, binoculars and walkie-talkie radios in order to instill efficiency and pride in the patrol. My choice of uniforms proved to be unfortunate; the khaki-colored uniforms were also worn by insurgent guerillas. We had to rectify the mistake with colored sashes and arm emblems.

During 1965, we visited 19 villages around Lake Atitlán to explain the enforcement program to the mayors, secretaries, and chiefs of police. In the larger villages, the mayors sent out a "pregon" (town crier and drummer) to inform the populace. Most of the inhabitants do not read or write, and they have no phones, radios, or television sets. Several meetings were held with the Governor of the Department of Sololá within which Lake Atitlán lies. The governor has complete power over the department and ranks close to the President of Guatemala. It was deemed advisable that he understand this conservation program and agree with the enforcement policies. He sent telegrams to each village mayor supporting Opera-tion Protection Poc.

CONSERVATION EDUCATION

Concurrently with our enforcement program, we also met with

school teachers, children, and young men in each village. Because of the language barrier--most local Mayans speak the Cachiquel or Tzutuhil dialects--Jorge Ibarra, Director of Guatemala's Museum of Natural History, was invited to give simple conservation lectures in both Spanish and Mayan. Posters in both languages and with sketches of the grebe were also erected in the schools and municipal offices.

Justifications used to promote this conservation campaign were local economic benefits and national pride. It was completely unrealistic in this environment to speak about conservation for the sake of moral, aesthetic, scientific, or ecological reasons.

A side-light of our conservation education was to obtain as much accurate and lively news coverage as possible since this is one of the fastest, cheapest, and most effective ways to inform literate urban inhabitants of the need to protect their natural recources. Such publicity often leads to unexpected support and donations from individuals and organizations. The Giant Pied-billed Grebe and its magnificent environment served as an excellent key symbol upon which to focus public sympathy and attention.

Another important aid in the education campaign was the issue of airmail postage stamps and a commemorative conservation cover depicting the endangered grebe and Lake Atitlán. These were printed by the Guatemalan National Postal Service. As of April 1973, $123,000 worth of stamps in this issue had been sold (J. Cuyun, *personal communication*).

Miscellaneous efforts to promote public interest in the Atitlán Grebes included designing "poc" motifs for hand-loomed rugs through the Society for the Economic Development of Indians and encouraging primitive paintings of the grebes.

HABITAT PRESERVATION

Reed and cattail cutting by Indians is a fairly important part-time industry of long traditional standing. Practically every reed and cattail stand is owned or rented by a native cutter or cooperative that harvests the vegetation for sleeping mats and woven seats. Prior to Operation Protection Poc, reeds were heavily cut during most of the year, whenever rains permitted. A very conservative estimate of this industry might be between 1,000 to 1,500 mats and 500 seats produced per year by all Lake Atitlán villages. Cutting was done mainly from November into May (when the rainy season starts), and again in the short dry season (July-August). Stalks and fronds need at least 10 days drying in hot sun. The March through May harvest caused much disturbance during the grebes' nesting period. Indians clear-cut the vegetation, often smashing nests and eggs as they passed.

Based on these observations, plus my ecological study of grebe habitat, it became clear that regulations had to be set up to control the cutting. Following discussions held with a large group of Indian reed cutters and the Division of Fauna, a Presidential decree was issued by President Mendez Montenegro on 12 February 1968, prohibiting

reed and cattail cutting from 1 May to 15 August. It stipulates that
each man can cut only half of his plot one year and half the next, so
as to leave some undisturbed nesting and roosting cover for waterfowl
throughout the year. While it is unfortunate that April is not included in this moratorium, the Guatemalan authorities felt it was important
to allow Indians to cut during this month as it is the last opportunity to dry vegetation before the rainy season starts. Therefore,
only partial protection is offered to mating and early nesting Giant
Pied-billed Grebes whose territories occur in stands where cutting is
permitted.

Coincidentally with this habitat preservation practice, it was
found that the controlled cutting of shoreline vegetation resulted
generally in growth of fresher, straighter stalks; less matting and
choking of old vegetation; better seeding; and elimination of debris
which can cause a possible hazard to grebes from predators or form
tangles too thick for nesting sites.

REAL ESTATE DEVELOPMENT

Real estate development along Lake Atitlán's spectacular shoreline is increasing rapidly because of the burgeoning population,
greater ease of travel, and willingness of local Indians to sell
their corn fields and property. In 1968, it was estimated that 65
of the 92 vacation homes (71 percent) had been built since 1960.
But a greater boom was occurred more recently. In 1972 there were
110 such homes; 140 in 1973; and in 1977, well over 200. In addition,
a six-story, elegant hotel has been built on the north shore, and a
three-tower, twelve-story condominium is under construction.

Unfortunately, many property owners are cutting shoreline
vegetation to make beaches, docks, seawalls, and boathouses, or
to remove what they think is mosquito-breeding habitat. This type
of cutting has now become far more critical in destroying grebe habitat than the Indian harvesting. Of the 92 vacation homes counted in
1968, half had cleared some or all emergent aquatic vegetation from
their lakeshore. Also, sewage facilities, even of hotels, are often
inadequate or nonexistent and may gradually pollute this beautiful,
clear lake.

The impact of this type of development has grown enormously
since 1970 and seems uncontrollable at present. There are presently no land-use plans or sewage laws in effect for Lake Atitlán.
Therefore, it appears that this real estate boom is now the greatest threat to the survival of the Giant Pied-billed Grebe and the
entire aquatic ecosystem of Atitlán.

SURVEYS OF OTHER GUATEMALAN LAKES

As a crisis procedure, other lakes in Guatemala were surveyed,
with the hopes of finding new or additional suitable habitat where
some of the endangered population might be transferred and protected
in case conditions worsened at Lake Atitlán. The two critical factors

considered were the presence of sufficient shoreline cover and the absence of introduced bass and other large carnivorous fish or predators. Seven lakes were visited; however, none could provide proper cover, food, and protection sufficient to ensure the survival of introduced Atitlán grebes. Only Atitlán, the natural habitat, appeared to have the necessary ecological requirements.

REFUGE ESTABLISHMENT

A small refuge of 2 ha was established so that a few pairs of grebes could be harbored as a breeding nucleus to preserve the species; the refuge also enabled tourists, scientists, and photographers to easily observe the birds. Thus, the rationale for the refuge was moral, economic, and scientific.

Largemouth Bass and other fishes were removed from the refuge's small bay with the fish toxicant, antimycin (Powers and Bowes, 1967) This chemical, and a technician to administer same, were donated by the Wisconsin Alumni Research Foundation. Shortly after treatment, 10,000 fingerlings of small native species were stocked by the Division of Fauna. Bluegills were also introduced, and they now inhabit much of the shallow waters of Lake Atitlán (E. Bauer, *personal communication*).

An observatory and visitors' building, small office, sanitary facilities, guardian's hut, and terraces were constructed, and a permanent watchman hired to live there.

Two male and two female Atitlán grebes were captured and stocked in the refuge. Although a severe storm later tore down the gate to the refuge, the bay continued to be occupied naturally by Giant Pied-billed Grebes and other waterbirds.

An official inauguration was held on 15 June 1968, to declare the sanctuary the National Giant Grebe Refuge under jurisdiction of the Division of Fauna. At this point, full responsibility for its management and funding were turned over to the Guatemalan authorities.

As a result of all these conservation efforts, the wild population of grebes has increased from an all-time low of 80 individuals in 1965 to 233 birds in 1977. The population will probably stabilize here even though the carrying capacity is estimated at 280 grebes. The presence of predaceous bass, however, will prevent full realization of this number, as will the decrease in natural habitat.

In reality, Operation Protection Poc was a modest, cooperative wildlife conservation campaign in Guatemala. Yet, it provided a focal point for understanding the complex ecology of Lake Atitlán, identifying the serious consequences of an unwise introduction, and allowing a developing nation to become involved in basic conservation practices. Moreover, it provided insight into management techniques which apparently served to save a species from extinction.

LITERATURE CITED

Bowes, A.L., and C.V. Bowes, Jr. 1962. Recent census and observations of the giant pied-billed grebe. Auk 79(4):707-709.

LaBastille, A. 1974. Ecology and management of the Atitlán grebe, Lake Atitlán, Guatemala. Wildlife Monogr., No. 37. 66p.

Powers, J.E. and A.L. Bowes. 1967. Elimination of fish in the Giant Grebe Refuge, Lake Atitlán, Guatemala, using fish toxicant, antimycin. Trans. Amer. Fish. Soc. 96(2):210-213.

Williams, H. 1960. Volcanic collapse--basins of Lake Atitlán and Ayarza, Guatemala. Intern. Geol. Congr. (21st Copenhagen, Denmark), 21 (1960) 110, 113-116.

46

Using the North American Nest Record Card Program to Monitor Reproductive Patterns in Raptors

Donald A. McCrimmon, Jr., and Jonathan Bart

The reproductive misfortunes of Peregrine Falcons (*Falco peregrinus*), Ospreys (*Pandion haliaetus*), Brown Pelicans (*Pelecanus occidentalis*) and other large predatory birds have dramatized the need for studies that will detect avian population declines before they reach crisis proportions. Unfortunately, effective monitoring studies are difficult to carry out. To be most useful, monitoring programs should be continuing efforts which encompass broad geographic areas. Such programs should also employ standardized methods so that results from different regions and years are comparable. Estimation of the abundance and nesting success of many species depends upon time-consuming ground surveys. These often use hundreds of observers with specialized knowledge such as the ability to recognize the songs or the flight characteristics of several dozen birds.

Because of these difficulties and the growing awareness of the serious but unpredictable threats of environmental perturbations, increasing attention has been paid in recent years to monitoring programs in which the data are collected by volunteers. The principal volunteer-supported source of information on winter bird abundance is the Christmas Bird Count, conducted annually since 1900 by the National Audubon Society. Each count is made on a 24 km circle surveyed on 1 day by as many observers as possible. Currently, about 1,000 counts are made per year, and some count results have been computerized. Tramer (1974) and Bock and Lepthein (1974, 1976) provide examples of population analyses using Christmas count results.

Avian abundance during summer is monitored by the Audubon Breeding Bird Censuses, conducted since the mid-1930's and by the Breeding Bird Survey begun in the mid-1960's. In the Audubon Breeding Bird Censuses, observers make repeated counts of an area's avian density and diversity. An analysis of the vegetation on the area is also reported. Coverage is heaviest in the northeast, but reports from as many as 34 states have been received in 1 year.

The Breeding Bird Survey uses randomly distributed roadside counts taken once each year at the height of the breeding season. Each route consists of 50, 3-minute stops 0.8 km apart. Coordinated by the U.S. Fish and Wildlife Service, the survey is conducted in all Canadian provinces and in all states except Hawaii (Robbins and Van Velzen, 1967; 1969). The results for 120 species are monitored annually to detect population changes.

Avian abundance during migration has proved difficult to monitor despite thousands of observations by competent field observers reported regularly in dozens of state and local journals and in the Audubon Society's national journal, *American Birds*. The recently formed Hawk Migration Association of North America has prepared standardized record-keeping forms currently in use at many observation posts throughout the United States and southern Canada. The U.S. Fish and Wildlife Service has agreed to have the 1974-1976 data keypunched so that computer analysis and evaluation of these results will be possible.

Nesting success, the key to a species' future status and often the first life table parameter to be effected when a species' status changes, is monitored by the newly formed Colonial Bird Register and by the North American Nest Record Card Program, organized in 1966. The Colonial Bird Register is designed as a long-term program providing information useful for environmental impact statements as well as for fundamental biological research. Information on the location, species diversity, and breeding density of colonies of birds throughout the United States is collected and computerized (McCrimmon, 1977). Although only 2 years old, Register files contain more than 2,500 records of bird colonies.

The North American Nest Record Card Program (NRCP) relies on hundreds of amateur and professional field ornithologists to collect information on the nesting success of birds throughout North America. Data collection begins when an observer finds a nest and records information about it on cards supplied by the Laboratory of Ornithology at Cornell University. The cards request descriptive information about each nest's location and the number of eggs and young in the nest each time it is visited. Completed cards are returned to Cornell where they are edited by hand and coded for computer processing. NRCP files contain information on more than 200,000 nests. About 45,000 records have been stored on tape; several species' files contain more than 5,000 records. The program currently receives about 8,000 completed cards per year.

This paper is one of the first efforts to assess the NRCP's potential as a means of detecting changes in avian reproductive success. The NRCP can be an early warning system focusing attention on species which may be in trouble. However, nest record card information is suggestive rather than conclusive; once evidence is obtained that a species' nesting success is declining, intensive studies employing more careful sampling control than is possible for the NRCP must be carried out to confirm the existence of a problem. Thus, the NRCP cannot do the entire job of monitoring nesting success. Rather, at extraordinarily low cost, the NRCP can provide information about the reproductive success of dozens of species about which biologists currently receive little or no information.

METHODS

In this paper, we use NRCP data to analyse the reproductive pattern of 3 North American birds of prey: the Red-tailed Hawk (*Buteo jamaicensis*), the American Kestrel (*Falco sparvarius*) and the Osprey. Since nests recorded in NRCP files were observed for different periods of time, the first step in estimating nesting success was to standardize observation periods. We followed Mayfield (1961, 1975) who recommended the day as a convenient unit of time and suggested calculating daily survival as:

Daily Survival = 1-(number of deaths/number of exposure days)

where, 1 exposure day means 1 egg or nestling observed for 1 day.

Ideally, each egg or nestling that dies would be observed until its death, and thereafter, no additional exposure days would be recorded. When mortality occurs between visits, however, the date of death is usually not known exactly. This causes difficulty in deciding how many exposure days to record. Following Mayfield, we assumed that mortality occured halfway through the interval and calculated exposure days accordingly. For example, if a nest had 3 eggs or nestlings on the first visit and was visited 6 days later then,
1. If all 3 eggs or young were still present, 3 x 6 = 18 exposure days were recorded;
2. If all 3 were gone, 3 x (6/2) = 9 exposure days were recorded; and,
3. If 1 egg or young were gone, (2 x 6) + (1 x 3) = 15 exposure days were recorded.
The approximate probability of surviving throughout the incubation or nestling period was obtained by raising the daily survival rate to the power equalling the length of the period in days. For example, if the estimated daily survival rate during incubation was 0.98, and the length of the incubation period was 30 days, the calculated estimate of an egg's chance of surviving from laying until hatching was:

$$0.98^{30} = 0.545$$

We have found it useful to distinguish between loss of the entire nest and loss of individuals in nests with at least 1 survivor. This procedure, carried out for both eggs and nestlings, leads to the following survival rates:
1. Survival rates of all eggs laid
2. Survival rates of entire clutches
3. Survival rates of individual eggs in surviving clutches
4. Survival rates of all nestlings hatched
5. Survival rates of entire broods
6. Survival rates of individual nestlings in surviving broods.

The Mayfield method of calculating egg and nestling survival rates is subject to at least 3 biases. First, if visits tend to fall during high mortality periods, the mortality rate will be over-estimated; if visits tend to fall during periods of low mortality, the mortality rate will be under-estimated. Second, visiting the nests of some species (e.g., a ground nester) may increase the mortality rate by attracting predators. Finally, nests visited after the young have fledged are likely to be recorded as failures.

Because of these biases, survival values derived by the Mayfield approach are best viewed as indices, rather than actual survival rates. The strength of the Mayfield method is that the biases are often about the same for different groups of nests, and thus, when survival indices are compared, the biases cancel out.

In addition to calculating survival indices for each species, we estimated the average clutch-size and calculated a "non-hatching index", a measure of how frequently eggs remained in the nest throughout incubation but failed to hatch due to addling, infertility, embryo death, or some other cause. Average clutch-size was calculated using all nests first visited before any eggs hatched. Some of these were first visited well into the incubation period, and, thus, single eggs may have been lost before the visit. Consequently, our estimated clutch-size is probably slightly lower than the actual clutch-size.

To calculate the non-hatching index, we first selected all nests visited at least 8-10 days apart (depending on the species), with the first visit coming during or after hatching. An 8-10 day interval between visits insured that hatching was completed by the second visit and that any eggs remaining were not going to hatch. The index was calculated as:

$$\text{Non-hatching Index} = \frac{\text{No. of eggs on second visit}}{\text{No. of eggs \& nestlings on second visit}}$$

To investigate regional differences in nesting success, survival indices, clutch-size, and non-hatching indices were calculated for the eastern, central and western portions of the continent, the regions shown in Figure 1. Another drawback of the Mayfield estimate is that variance formulas are not available. Consequently, we have not been able to assign confidence intervals to the estimates. We plan a modification permitting variance estimation using the method of maximum likelihood.

RESULTS

Red-tailed Hawk

Survival indices for Red-tailed Hawks were calculated for four periods: 1956-65, 1966-68, 1969-71, and 1972-74 (Table 1). Total egg survival was high (0.74) initially, lower (0.53 and 0.58) during the next 2 periods and high again (0.85) in the final period. Nestling survival showed a similar trend in the first 3 periods but did not recover in the final period. The NRCP data suggests a decline in both

TABLE 1. SURVIVAL INDICES FOR EGGS AND NESTLINGS OF 3 RAPTORS WHICH BREED IN THE UNITED STATES AND CANADA AND FOR WHICH DATA IS AVAILABLE IN THE NORTH AMERICAN NEST RECORD CARD PROGRAM

Species and Years	No. of Nests (State)	Non-hatch Index	Mean Clutch Size	Survival Indices for:					
				All Eggs Laid	Entire Clutches	Egg in Clutch	All Nestlings	Entire Broods	Nestling in Brood
1. Red-tailed Hawk[a]									
1956-65	59	0.00	2.18	0.74	0.81	0.91	0.62	0.74	0.85
1966-68	58	0.02	2.29	0.53	0.70	0.76	0.38	0.51	0.74
1969-71	112	0.02	2.00	0.58	0.80	0.7?	0.40	0.51	0.79
1972-74	163	0.00	2.16	0.85	0.91	0.9?	0.36	0.50	0.71
2. American Kestrel[b]									
1966-70	74	0.06	4.54	0.59	0.71	0.83	0.28	0.42	0.66
1971-72	79	0.00	4.44	0.65	0.76	0.86	0.36	0.47	0.76
1973-74	76	0.33	4.66	0.66	0.85	0.77	0.39	0.48	0.81
3. Osprey[c]									
1958-61	68 (CT)	0.00	2.17	0.21	0.37	0.55	0.09	0.21	0.43
1970-72	28 (MA)	0.15	2.86	0.43	0.64	0.67	0.39	0.65	0.60
1970-72	61 (DE)	0.00	2.90	0.47	0.64	0.74	0.56	1.00	0.56
1973-75	74 (DE)	0.00	2.74	0.49	0.65	0.76	0.57	1.00	0.57

[a] Incubation period, 30 days; nestling period, 45 days; data from Bent (1961), Brown & Amadon (1968) and Harrison (1975).
[b] Incubation period, 30 days; nestling period, 30 days; data from Bent (1961), Brown & Amadon (1968) and Harrison (1975).
[c] Incubation period, 35 days; nestling period, 56 days; data from Bent (1961), Brown & Amadon (1968) and Harrison (1975).

FIGURE 1. Geographical partitioning of American states and Canadian
provinces into western, central and eastern regions.

egg and nestling survival during the mid-1960's, with egg survival
increasing recently but nestling survival remaining low.

Closer examination of the results indicates that they probably
were not produced by sampling error alone. If this were the case,
there would be little reason to expect similar trends to appear when
the total survival rate is broken down into its components (i.e., nest
survival and individual survival in surviving nests). Trends for nest
and individual survival, however, are quite similar to the overall
rates. This is particularly true for nestling survival where the
brood-survival trends (0.74, 0.51, 0.54, and 0.50) and the trend for
nestling survival rates within surviving broods (0.85, 0.74, 0.79, and
0.71) are strikingly similar to trends for total nestling survival.
The trends for total egg survival, clutch survival, and egg survival
in surviving clutches are also similar, though there is more variation
than in the nestling survival rates.

Some information on regional differences can be gleaned from the
data in Table 2. Egg survival was not detectably different in the
regions we studied. The low survival rate for eggs in central states
during 1966-68 is not regarded as important because of the small sample
size for this period. Nestling survival, however, was quite consistent in the East (0.48, 0.56, 0.58 and 0.50), whereas in the central
and western regions, it was substantially higher in the mid-1950's
to mid-1960's than in the later periods.

TABLE 2.   REGIONAL TABULATIONS OF SURVIVAL INDICES FOR RED-TAILED HAWKS AND AMERICAN KESTRELS[a]

Species and Year	No. of Nests:			Survival Index for All Eggs Laid:			Survival Index for All Nestlings:		
	West	Central	East	West	Central	East	West	Central	East
1. Red-tailed Hawk									
1956-65	2	43	14	-	0.77	0.45	0.65	0.68	0.48
1966-68	20	11	27	0.66	0.11	0.66	0.27	0.24	0.56
1969-71	52	14	46	0.48	0.77	0.50	0.26	0.45	0.58
1972-74	64	39	60	0.85	0.78	0.90	0.32	0.26	0.50
2. American Kestrel									
1966-70	-	39	35	-	0.64	0.48	-	0.21	0.38
1971-72	-	54	25	-	0.68	0.57	-	0.25	0.81
1973-74	-	39	37	-	0.68	0.63	-	0.39	0.37

[a]Geographic boundaries of west, central and east regions are shown in Figure 1.

American Kestrel

NRCP data for the kestrel comes primarily from the eastern and central United States and shows slight but steady improvement in 5 of 6 survival indices from 1966 to 1974. The regional breakdown (Table 2) suggests that improvements may have been most pronounced in egg survival in the East and nestling survival in central regions. However, the total nestling survival index for eastern nests during 1971-72 seems disproportionately high (0.81), indicating that sample sizes may be too small for confidence in the regional trends.

The most interesting result for kestrels is a dramatic increase in the non-hatching index (from 0.06 and 0.00 to 0.33) in the 1973-74 sample. Infertile eggs were reported by 2 observers in different states (Wisconsin and Massachusetts). For each of these observers, 50 percent of the eggs reported did not hatch. Possibly the observers were disrupting incubation, or they found unsuccessful nests simply by chance.

Osprey

In some areas, for example parts of coastal Connecticut, Osprey populations have suffered substantially from environmental contamination. Our data on total egg and total nestling survival in Connecticut reflect the decline in Osprey nesting success reported by others for essentially the same time period (e.g., Ames and Mersereau, 1964). On the other hand, our data for Delaware and Massachusetts show that Osprey populations in these states have had a greater degree of nesting success during the 1970's. Among Delaware and Massachusetts nests, components of total egg survival were similar. Interestingly, brood survival was higher in Delaware nests than in Massachusetts nests.

DISCUSSION

Red-tailed Hawks probably are less affected than many other raptors by organochlorine pesticides (e.g., Anderson and Hickey, 1972; Stickel, 1973; Haque and Freed, 1975). Seidensticker and Reynolds (1971), however, found some decrease in eggshell thickness in a study of Red-tailed Hawks in Montana. Other studies (Gates, 1972; Wiley, 1975) have compared survival rates during the incubation and nestling periods (which is difficult with NRCP data due to different biases in data from the 2 periods). However, there is little published information with which to compare the trends in Red-tailed Hawk nesting success observable in NRCP data.

The NRCP is one of the few sources of broadly based long-term field information on temporal trends about kestrel nesting success. Laboratory studies by Porter and Wiemeyer (1969), Lincer (1972), and Lincer and Sherburne (1974) have shown that kestrel productivity can be effected by organochlorine pesticides. This work supports the NRCP data which showed a slow, steady increase in most survival indices during a time when use of persistent pesticides was declining.

The strongest confirmation of NRCP data comes from studies of Osprey nesting success. Henny (1977) reported that "improvement [in production] in affected populations, mainly those along the Atlantic Coast and in the Great Lakes region, began in the late 1960's and is continuing in the 1970's..." This trend is clear in NRCP data despite rather small sample sizes. Also, Henny et al. (1977) state that in Delaware, "production was normal in 1970-75." Their data for young fledged per occupied nest show a nearly constant success rate as was shown by the NRCP analysis above.

The relatively few studies on temporal trends in raptor nesting success tend to support the trends we have described using NRCP data. Equally important, for many species, there is virtually no information available except that in NRCP files. Finally, review of the conclusions above will show that doubt over the validity of each one could be significantly reduced if more field observers contributed their data to the Program. Information that would increase the size of NRCP raptor files many-fold is currently in the possession of investigators throughout the continent. The Program would welcome contact from these observers and agrees, in advance, to preserve the confidentiality of any characteristics of the nest, including its location, which the collector of the data wishes not be made available to the public.

Contribution to the Program insures that an observer's data are integrated with those provided by many others. By compiling the data of numerous observers, the NRCP can provide a unique information resource for monitoring the nesting success of threatened or endangered birds.

ACKNOWLEDGMENTS

The World Wildlife Fund provided support for collection and analysis of data. T. Cade, S. Sherrod, and P. Spitzer gave valuable advice. C. Bart, J. Gulledge, M. Richmond, and R. Stehn reviewed the manuscript.

LITERATURE CITED

Ames, P.L. and G.S. Mersereau. 1964. Some factors in the decline of the Osprey in Connecticut. Auk 81(2):173-185.
Anderson, D.W. and J.J. Hickey. 1972. Eggshell changes in certain North American birds, p. 514-540. *In* Proc. 15th International Ornithological Congress.
Bent, A.C. 1961. Life Histories of North American Birds of Prey. Dover, New York.
Bock, C.E. and L.W. Lepthein. 1974. Winter patterns of bird species diversity and abundance in the United States and southern Canada. American Birds 28(2):556-562.
Bock, C.E. and L.W. Lepthein. 1976. Growth in the eastern House Finch population, 1962-1971. American Birds 30(4):791-792.
Brown, L. and D. Amadon. 1968. Eagles, Hawks and Falcons of the World. McGraw-Hill, New York.

Gates, J.M. 1972. Red-tailed Hawk populations in east-central Wisconsin. Wilson Bull. 84(4):421-433.

Hague, R. and V.H. Freed (eds.). 1975. Environmental Science Research Vol. 6. Environmental Dynamics of Pesticides. Plenum Press, New York. 387p.

Harrison, H.H. 1975. A Field Guide to Birds' Nests. Houghton Mifflin Co., Boston. 257p.

Henny, C.J. 1977. Research, management and status of the Osprey in North America, p. 199-222. In R.D. Chancellor (ed.) World Conf. on Birds of Prey, Vienna, Report of Proceedings. ICBP, London.

Henny, C.J., M.A. Byrd, J.A. Jacobs, P.D. McLain, M.R. Todd and B.F. Halla. 1977. Mid-Atlantic coast Osprey population: Present numbers, productivity, pollutant contamination and status. J. Wildlife Manage. 41(2):254-265.

Lincer, J.L. 1972. The effects of organochlorines on the American Kestrel (Falco sparverius Linn.) Ph.D. Thesis. Cornell Univ., Ithaca, N.Y.

Lincer, J.L. and J.A. Sherburne. 1974. Organochlorines in Kestrel prey: A north south dichotomy. J. Wildlife Manage. 38(2):427-434.

Mayfield, H.F. 1961. Nesting success calculated from exposure. Wilson Bull. 73(3):255-261.

Mayfield, H.F. 1975. Suggestions for calculating nest success. Wilson Bull. 87(4):456-466.

McCrimmon, D.A., Jr. 1977. The management and exchange of information on colonially nesting birds. In A. Sprunt, IV, J.C. Ogden, and S. Winckler (eds.). Wading Birds: Research Report No. 7 of the National Audubon Society, New York. (in press).

Porter, R.D. and S.N. Wiemeyer. 1969. Dieldrin and DDT: Effects on Sparrow Hawk egg shells and reproduction. Science 165(3889):199-200.

Robbins, C.S. and W.T. Van Velzen. 1967. The Breeding Bird Survey, 1966. Bur. Sport Fisheries and Wildlife Spec. Sci. Rep.---Wildlife 102.

Robbins, C.S. and W.T. Van Velzen. 1969. The Breeding Bird Survey, 1967 and 1968. Bur. Sport Fisheries and Wildlife Spec. Sci. Rep.---Wildlife 124.

Seidensticker, J.C. and H.V. Reynolds. 1971. The nesting, reproductive performance, and chlorinated hydrocarbon residues in the Red-tailed Hawk and Great Horned Owl in south central Montana. Wilson Bull. 83(4):408-418.

Stickel,L.F. 1973. Pesticide residues in birds and mammals, p. 254-312. In C.A. Edwards (ed.). Environmental Pollution by Pesticides. Plenum Press, New York.

Tramer, E.J. 1974. An analysis of the species density of U.S. landbirds during the winter using the 1971 Christmas Bird Count. American Birds 28(2):563-567.

Wiley, J.W. 1975. The nesting and reproductive success of Red-tailed Hawks and Red-shouldered Hawks in Orange County California, 1973. Condor 72(2):133-139.

47

Population Modeling as an Aid to Designing Management Programs

Richard S. Miller

During the past several years my students and colleagues and I have been developing computer simulation models to study the population dynamics of a variety of species, including the Sandhill Crane (*Grus canadensis*), the Whooping Crane (*Grus americana*), the Atlantic Right Whale (*Eubalaena glacialis*), and the African Elephant (*Loxodonta africana*). While this may seem to be a rather mixed bag of species, they all have a number of important properties in common which they share with many threatened or endangered species and, probably, with an even larger number of species which are now extinct. They are relatively large representatives of their class or family and at least 3, the North American cranes and the African Elephant, are survivors of a mostly extinct Pleistocene fauna. But in this discussion, it is important to note that their common biological characteristics are: (1) relatively long maximum longevities, (2) delayed maturity, (3) small clutch or litter sizes, (4) correspondingly low rates of increase, (5) relatively long generation-times and, therefore, (6) low replacement rates. Also, in each of these species, there is a considerable investment in parental care of the young, even though they have few, if any, natural predators. In other words, they allocate their reproductive energies so as to increase the probability of survival to maturity of only one or a few young (Miller, 1972). According to the theory of *r*- and *K*- selection, this strategy allows a correspondingly greater allocation of resources to competitive ability and the development of greater population stability, but there is also the inherent disadvantage that when a population suffers a severe reduction in population size, its recovery may be slow and erratic, increasing the possibility of extinction. This, in fact, is another common factor among most of these species--they have experienced severe reductions in natural habitat and/or direct exploitation by man.

Classical population theory has been based mostly on simple, deterministic models such as the Lotka-Volterra equations. These models depend upon a number of initial assumptions, including stationary age distributions, instantaneous responses in birth and death rates to density changes, and density-dependent growth at all densities (Pielou, 1969). While these models have been instructive conceptually, they are inadequate when dealing with populations of long-lived (K-selected) species with deferred and intermittent breeding, low replacement rates, and a correspondingly low capacity to respond to marked variations in environmental conditions adjusting their rate of increase.

In order to develop predictive models for species with the characteristics we have enumerated, several basic concepts will have to be re-examined. As Wilson (1975) notes, "Vertebrate populations have proved markedly more difficult to analyze than invertebrate populations. Much of the basic theory has therefore been constructed with reference to invertebrates, especially insects. The reason is evidently the greater complexity and flexibility of vertebrate systems as well as the much greater practical problems encountered in studying large, slow-breeding animals. This difficulty of vertebrate ecology has had an important impact on the study of social systems by contributing confusion to many of the most basic concepts." This confusion exists not only in the study of social systems, but also in general population theory.

It is obviously very difficult to obtain long-term data for organisms whose life span approaches or exceeds that of man, and experiments with such species are often impossible. Nevertheless, large, long-lived species comprise a considerable proportion of the biomass of an ecosystem and occupy key positions in food chains; an understanding of their population dynamics is obviously important and necessary. One possible approach to this problem is through computer simulation.

A model is merely an abstraction or simplification of a system. One of its major values is in the conceptualization of a system, allowing us to recognize and identify its important components. In other words, it helps us "see the woods for the trees" in an array of complex parts and interactions. Models can help us understand the structure and function of a system, allow us to test the validity of field measurements or assumptions derived from data, or assist in optimizing management programs. But, perhaps most importantly, they also generate hypotheses (Hall and Day, 1977).

Analytic models, such as the Lotka-Volterra models, are mathematical procedures for finding exact solutions to equations. As such, they are more precise than simulation models, but do not allow the simultaneous solution of several equations, as do simulation models, nor do they have the capability of simulation models for dealing with the non-linearity that is a property of most biological systems.

Given enough accurate information about the population characteristics of a species, such as age of reproductive maturity, clutch or litter size, breeding interval, maximum longevity, reasonable estimates of mortality rates or survival rates, and the effect of population density on breeding and survival, we can also calculate generation time and replacement rates, or annual recruitment of new individuals into the population. With this information, we can assign the parameters necessary to simulate the population growth of a species, but more importantly we can conduct a sensitivity analysis to test the relative importance of each parameter by varying the value of each parameter independently or in selected combinations during successive simulations. In this manner, we can test the probable results of different management practices, such as setting rates of annual harvest of exploited species and the probability of extinction under different management regimes. In other words, once you have decided upon a given set of parameters, have developed a model, and have entered the appropriate program into the computer, you can, in effect, manipulate the population in any way you like. This consists of forming hypotheses, asking relevent questions, and simulating the results over extended time periods far beyond the observational life of any direct observer, or any existing institution for that matter.

Obviously, some parameters are more difficult to measure than others; unfortunately, the most difficult may be the most critical. For example, many of us have struggled through the tedium of locating nests and measuring clutch size, but this is, nevertheless, an easily obtained and direct measurement. While we know this parameter is subject to geographic variation, the difference between a clutch size of 3.5 at one latitude and 4.0 at another is much less important in a population model than what would appear to be relatively small variations in an exponent such as density-dependence, yet this is perhaps the most difficult parameter to measure or obtain a reasonable estimate for.

Nevertheless, in spite of these kinds of inaccuracies, population models can be extremely useful. In their recent book on *Ecosystem Modeling in Theory and Practice*, Hall and Day (1977) give an example of "the model that failed," showing how, in spite of its inadequacies, the process of developing and testing the model led to important insights into a complex system. While I am not willing to say that the model I will describe failed, I will admit that it was in some respects inaccurate, but it seems to have, at least partially, accomplished its purpose. For many years, I had been concerned about the establishment of hunting seasons for Sandhill Cranes. Aside from the aesthetic beauty of these birds, the rather gross hunting methods I had observed, and the obvious failure of hunting as a means to achieve the original management objective of crop protection, I was particularly concerned about the fact that the U.S. Fish and Wildlife Service and the Canadian Wildlife Service had embarked upon a management program for which there was no precedent. In spite of their expertise with ducks and geese, which have relatively high rates of increase and whose populations can respond quickly to reduced bag limits or closed seasons, they had not managed the hunting of species with the population characteristics of Sandhill Cranes. In view of the fact that the closely related Whooping Crane is endangered and has a life history which is quite similar to that of the Sandhill Crane, that many of the cranes of the world are threatened or endangered, that 3 of the 6 subspecies of North American Sandhill Cranes are on the endangered list, there was good reason to be concerned about the problems that might be associated with the management of a hunted population of Sandhill

Cranes. With the best data available in the published literature, we constructed a model for an estimated population of approximately 200,000 cranes of the migratory subspecies *G.c. canadensis* and *G.c. rowani* in the Central Flyway of the United States and Canada (Miller et al., 1972; Miller and Botkin, 1974). We assumed a maximum life span of 25 years, reproductive maturity at age 4, and an annual recruitment of approximately 8 percent of the equilibrium population. Starting with an initial flock of 1,000 birds 4 years of age, the population grew to the equilibrium of just under 200,000 in approximately 120 years. We were now in a position to test various artificial perturbations of this population. For example, when we artificially raised the density from 200,000 to 300,000 to test the stability of the model, the population returned to within 5 percent of its original equilibrium in 19 years and reached equilibrium in 55 years. This very slow approach to a final equilibrium is not unexpected, but these simulations also indicate a relatively low overall rate of population growth and a relatively high stability of the population.

The reported annual harvest in 1970, for which the most complete returns were available, was over 9,800. An additional loss of 30 percent by crippling and illegal hunting would raise this total to approximately 12,770, or over 6 percent of the population. Our simulation showed that with this level of hunting, the population would become extinct in 19 years. We then experimented with different levels of hunting in order to examine the capacity of this population to sustain a continued annual harvest. These simulations showed that with an annual kill of 5,000, the population would decline gradually to extinction in 114 years; but with an annual kill of 4,000, it would decline and stabilize at a new equilibrium level of 125,800.

I said earlier that this model was inaccurate but not a failure. With new and better data, we would revise some of the parameters in the model, such as the total population size, which is now known to be 300,000 or more, rather than 200,000. But, regardless of such inaccuracies, a model of this sort can still be instructive. It demonstrates, for example, that a species with this set of population characteristics presents management problems which are far different from those of, say, a duck, which will respond relatively quickly to reduced bag limits or closed seasons. Let us assume, for example, that the annual harvest were 6,000 birds. At this rate of hunting, the population in our model would be reduced to about 120,000 in 20 years. If hunting were stopped at this point, it would take almost 60 years for the population to return to equilibrium. This raises the question of whether the annual estimates of population size are sufficiently accurate to detect this decrease or whether a population of this sort might not be dangerously near extinction before this fact is detected. This model also showed that annual recruitment is an extremely important variable which was not being measured. In an earlier model, we accepted a value of 30 percent, but subsequent research (Miller and Hatfield, 1975) showed that it might be as low as 5 percent in some years and probably averages about 7 to 10 percent. Annual recruitment is now being estimated regularly at various localities along the flyway, and we will, hopefully, have good values for this parameter in the future.

I have presented a description of this particular model to show how this approach can identify specific properties of a population and its sensitivity to particular parameters. This approach is not an exact solution to all the needs of management, but it helps frame appropriate questions and identify the research that must be done to improve our management procedures and establish policies which are appropriate to the needs of different species.

ACKNOWLEDGMENTS

This research was supported by a grant from the World Wildlife Fund and NSF Research Grant DEB76-10247.

LITERATURE CITED

Hall, C.A.S. and V.W. Day, Jr. 1977. Ecosystem modeling in theory and practice. John Wiley and Sons, N.Y. 673p.
Lack, D. 1968. Ecological adaptations for breeding in birds. Methuen and Co., Ltd., London. 409p.
Miller, R.S. 1972. The brood size of cranes. Wilson Bull. 85:436-441.
Miller, R.S., G.S. Hochbaum and D.B. Botkin. 1972. A simulation model for the management of sandhill cranes. Yale Univ. Sch. Forestry and Environmental Studies. Bull. No. 80. 49p.
Miller, R.S. and D.B. Botkin, 1974. Endangered species: models and predictions. Amer. Sci. 62:172-181.
Miller, R.S. and J.P. Hatfield. 1975. Age ratios of sandhill cranes. J. Wildlife Manage. 38:234-242.
Pielou, E.C. 1969. An introduction to mathematical ecology. Wiley-Interscience. 286p.
Wilson, E.O. 1975. Sociobiology. Belknap Press. Cambridge, Mass.

48

Land Management for the Conservation of Endangered Birds

Richard R. Olendorff and William D. Zeedyk

This symposium so far has been concerned mostly with what S.A. Temple has identified as proximate factors responsible for the endangerment of birds. We have heard about artificial nesting platforms, artificial nest boxes, and artificial nesting ledges; about supplemental feeding programs and egg or nestling manipulations; and about captive propagation followed by reintroductions to the wild. But, we have heard far less about attending to the ultimate factors that bring us together here--namely, environmental pollution and physical destruction or other alterations of both local and regional ecosystems.

We have learned that habitat loss is the cause of 65 percent of avian endangerments (W.B. King, Ch. 2, *this volume*). Recognizing that habitat encroachment by man has the greatest negative effect on wildlife populations around the world, this paper addresses one group of strategies to reduce the rapid rate of extinctions occurring today throughout the world. Admittedly, this material applies primarily to the United States, and only to a portion of the United States, but it is a start toward achieving an integrated approach to the management of endangered birds.

The Bureau of Land Management (BLM), an agency of the U.S. Department of the Interior, and the Forest Service (FS), an agency of the U.S. Department of Agriculture, are the largest land-managing agencies in the United States. Collectively, they administer over 1,630 million ha, which is nearly equivalent to the land area of all states east of the Mississippi River plus the State of California. These lands include the National Forest System and the vast "public lands," a term used at the Federal level to refer to lands administered exclusively by the BLM.

Practically all of these lands provide habitat for wildlife, including 12 species and subspecies of birds listed as endangered in the Endangered Species Act (Table 1). This paper illustrates ways in

TABLE 1.   ENDANGERED BIRDS THAT OCCUR ON PUBLIC LANDS AND ON
THE NATIONAL FOREST SYSTEM

Species	Occurs on Land Controlled by:	
	BLM	FS
Masked Bobwhite (*Colinus virginianus ridgwayi*)		X
California Condor (*Gymnogyps californianus*)	X	X
Mississippi Sandhill Crane (*Grus canadensis pulla*)		X
Mexican Duck (*Anas diazi*)	X	X
Southern Bald Eagle (*Haliaeetus l. leucocephalus*)	X	X
American Peregrine Falcon (*Falco peregrinus anatum*)	X	X
Arctic Peregrine Falcon (*Falco peregrinus tundrius*)	X	X
Brown Pelican (*Pelecanus occidentalis*)	X	X
Yuma Clapper Rail (*Rallus longirostris yumanensis*)	X	X
Bachman's Warbler (*Vermivora bachmanii*)		X
Kirtland's Warbler (*Dendroica kirtlandii*)		X
Red-cockaded Woodpecker (*Dendrocopus borealis*)		X
Puerto Rican Parrot (*Amazon vittata*)		X

which these species are being or might be conserved utilizing the
legislative mandates, executive orders, and other authorities granted
to the major land-managing agencies. The objective is to create a
better understanding outside of our agencies not only of the possible
conservation strategies but also of the opportunities for public and
interagency involvement in processes that can minimize the adverse
effects of land use on known populations of threatened or endangered
birds.

It is impossible in this paper to review all of the BLM and FS
programs that benefit endangered birds. Specifically omitted are most
aspects of programs relating to land-use planning, environmental
assessment, direct Endangered Species Act compliance guidelines, procedures for intra- and interagency cooperation (e.g., development of
recovery plans, reviews of a species' status, consultation, assistance
etc.), protection of sensitive but not yet endangered species, and the
opportunities for special land classifications to protect endangered
species' habitats (e.g., protective withdrawals, determination of
Critical Habitat, etc.). Instead, this paper focuses on activities
relating to authorities (laws), inventory, research, and habitat
management (including direct habitat protection).

AUTHORITIES PROVIDED BY LAW

Many laws authorize the FS and the BLM to become involved with
the conservation of threatened and endangered species. The following
are among the more important of these.

Endangered Species Act of 1973

Sections 2 and 7 of this law relate directly to Federal land management for the conservation of endangered species. Section 2 declares that all Federal departments and agencies shall utilize their authorities to conserve officially-listed endangered species. This national policy is repeated and expanded in Section 7 which briefly sets forth procedures to be used and requirements to be met in complying with the Act.

The mandates of Section 7 have 3 main objectives: conserving endangered species, ensuring that the continued existence of an endangered species is not jeopardized, and ensuring that the critical habitats of endangered species are not destroyed or adversely modified. In recognition of these mandates, both the BLM and the FS have accepted the responsibility for reviewing their own programs and actions to identify any that may effect an endangered species.

Sikes Act of 1960, as Amended

The Sikes Act of 1960, as amended on 18 October 1974, directs the Secretaries of the Interior and Agriculture to establish on-the-ground habitat conservation and rehabilitation programs jointly with state wildlife management agencies. These programs are to include specific habitat improvement projects for wildlife in general, although one specific mandate is for adequate protection of species considered threatened or endangered either by Federal or State agencies.

Federal Land Policy and Management Act of 1976

Although this Act of 21 October 1976 does not deal directly with threatened or endangered species, it provides the basis for most land management strategies that the Secretary of the Interior, through the BLM, is authorized to use to further the purposes of the Endangered Species Act on public lands. For example, the Secretary shall develop and maintain an inventory of all public lands and their resource and other values, giving priority to "areas of critical environmental concern." An "area of critical environmental concern" is a newly defined land-use planning category for public lands where special management attention is required to prevent irreparable damage to important historic, cultural or scenic values; to fish and wildlife resources; or to natural systems or processes. Critical habitats--and sometimes merely occupied habitats--of threatened or endangered species will be considered as "areas of critical environmental concern."

This new act also mandates that the public lands be managed under the principles of multiple use and sustained yield; sets forth procedures for land withdrawals, acquisitions, and exchanges; provides enforcement authority on the public lands; authorizes the Secretary of the Interior to conduct studies and research; and provides guidance on several specific programs, such as range management, wild horse and burro management, the granting or rights-of-way, California Desert management, a public lands wilderness study, etc. In short, the Federal Land Policy and Management Act gives the scope of possible actions that the BLM can employ in managing any resource on the public lands.

McSweeney-McNary Act of 1928, as Amended

FS research relating to wildlife and wildlife habitat is authorized by this Act. It gives the FS responsibility for "...such experiments and investigations as may be necessary in determining the life
histories and habits of forest animals, birds and wildlife, whether
injurious to forest growth or of value as supplemental resources, and
in developing the best and most effective methods for their management
and control..." This includes endangered species research. The FS
also has the Federal responsibility for wildlife habitat research on
Federal forest and rangeland ecosystems, including National Forests,
National Parks, and public lands.

*Multiple-Use and Sustained-Yield Act of 1960, Resources Planning
Act of 1974 and National ̄orest Management Act of 1976*

FS authority to manage wildlife and wildlife habitat on the
National Forests and Grasslands is set forth in the Multiple-Use and
Sustained-Yield Act of 1960 which stated it to be "...the policy of
the Congress that the National Forests are established and shall be
administered for outdoor recreation, range, timber, watershed, and
wildlife and fish purposes." The National Forest Management Act of
1976 reaffirms the principles of multiple-use and sustained-yield
management through coordination of uses and is based on the availability of lands and their suitability for resource management. It
further provides that a land-use plan be developed by interdisciplin-
ary teams for each unit of the National Forest System and, further,
that such plan contain guidelines to "...provide for diversity of
plant and animal communities based on the suitability and capability
of the specific land area in order to meet overall multiple-use objectives..." Endangered species considerations are included in these
objectives.

Cooperative Forest Management Act of 1950, as Amended

This Act provides for FS cooperation with the states in furnish-
ing technical advice and assistance to private forest owners. This
is achieved through state forestry agencies in a program known as
general forestry assistance. Being a Federal program, however, it is
also subject to the constraints of the Endangered Species Act of 1973.

INVENTORY

A good inventory of resources is essential to implementing the
legislative authorities of land managing agencies. Such agencies must
obtain and use current quantitative information to full advantage
within their respective planning and decision-making frameworks,
though in many cases such information is still unavailable for endan-

gered species. Nevertheless, the requirements for endangered species habitat inventories are increasing as a result of new legislative authorities and several court cases stemming from the National Environmental Policy Act.

The endangered species information needed for land-use planning and decision making includes the limits of occupied and suitable unoccupied habitats, population statuses and trends, and modes of habitat use--particularly the ways in which animal use is encouraged or discouraged by special habitat features (e.g., cliffs, caves, topography, etc.). Data on existing vegetation (e.g., species composition and density, plant structure and vigor, and forage and cover availability) and data on selected abiotic habitat components (e.g., temperature and precipitation regimes) are also useful for managing sites occupied by endangered species. Specific inventory procedures used by the FS and BLM will meet standards necessary for adequate protection of most threatened or endangered species.

This is not to imply that the agencies did nothing prior to the development of the new legislation, the court cases, and the inventory methods. Species and habitat inventories for endangered birds have been conducted in the past by both the BLM and FS, usually in cooperation or coordination with state fish and game agencies.

For example, the FS has invested substantially in inventories of the Red-cockaded Woodpecker, Southern Bald Eagle, Peregrine Falcon, Kirtland's Warbler, Bachman's Warbler, and such sensitive but not endangered species as the Northern Bald Eagle (*Haliaeetus leucocephalus alaskanus*), Osprey (*Pandion haliaetus*), and Spotted Owl (*Strix occidentalis*). With at least one species, the Bachman's Warbler, the inventory has resulted in thousands of hours of fruitless searching--no breeding population having been found in recent years.

Maximum FS effort has gone into inventorying the Red-cockaded Woodpecker. About 75 percent of the known populations of this species occur on National Forest System lands in 11 states. In these areas, this species' needs are almost entirely dependent upon coordination with timber management programs. Active and inactive clan sites are located, delineated on the ground, mapped, tabulated, and cross-indexed with timber management control records and land-use plans. Similar efforts are expended on Bald Eagle nesting territories and winter roosts.

The BLM is also actively inventorying endangered birds and their habitats. For example, in Alaska during the summer of 1975, the Tuxedni Bay area, 2,590 km^2 of the Iliamna Lake Region, the Noatak River Valley, and the Forty-Mile River Valley were inventoried for Peregrine Falcons and other raptors. The Bureau also assisted in the falcon survey of 1,931 km of the Colville River drainage and several other rivers proposed as national wild rivers. In 1976 and 1977, the Bureau's involvement in Peregrine Falcon inventories expanded considerably to include more of the Upper Yukon River drainage and southwestern Alaska.

Examples involving other areas include the following. In California, the BLM has contributed to inventories of Yuma Clapper Rails, Southern Bald Eagles, and Brown Pelicans. In Colorado, Peregrine Falcon surveys have been funded by BLM as part of the enormous

Piceance Basin habitat management plan.   And in New Mexico, inventories
of Mexican Ducks have been conducted by the Bureau each year for about
a decade.

Clearly, both the BLM and FS are authorized to conduct endangered
species habitat inventories on the lands they administer.   The opportunities for both public and academic involvement in these inventories
are readily available, because the surveys are not conducted solely by
agency personnel; cooperators, contractors, and volunteers are all
used under varying circumstances.   A heavy reliance upon cooperative
effort and volunteer help has long been the case in conducting annual
counts of California Condors, Kirtland's Warblers, and Yuma Clapper
Rails.   More recently, volunteers from the National Audubon Society,
National Wildlife Federation, and other non-governmental organizations
have been helpful in making counts of Bald Eagles on winter roosts and
in searching for the Bachman's Warbler on FS lands.

RESEARCH

The above are examples of inventory and not research.   These 2
terms have distinctly different meanings and are usually funded differently within a given Federal agency.   Inventory is generally considered as part of and is funded through the overall land-use or
resource planning effort, while research is usually problem-solving in
nature and funded with specially earmarked money.   The FS traditionally has had the lead role in applied habitat management research for
Federal agencies.   This is also true to an extent for endangered
species habitat research, although the BLM has accomplished several
research objectives under its own authorities as included in the following examples.

With regard to the Red-cockaded Woodpecker, research on this
species is being conducted by the FS's Southeastern Forest Experiment
Station at the Work Unit in Clemson, South Carolina.   The Unit is in
the third year of quantifying the essential habitat elements of 20
Red-cockaded Woodpecker clans on the Francis Marion National Forest.
The study includes the foraging and breeding behavior of these clans
which occur in a variety of habitat types.   A related objective of the
Unit is to develop a method to estimate distribution and habitat conditions and trends throughout the South.

FS Bald Eagle research is being done by the Rocky Mountain Forest
and Range Experiment Station at the Work Unit in Tempe, Arizona.   Using aerial photogrammetric techniques, the Unit is describing and
analyzing the physical parameters of all known occupied and historical
nest sites in Arizona and is conducting a telemetry study to establish
habitat preferences and dispersal patterns.

For the Puerto Rican Parrot, the FS's Institute of Tropical
Forestry in Puerto Rico is quantifying habitat parameters and is preparing a study plan.   Some of the past research on the management of
this species has also been partially funded by the FS.

The FS's Rocky Mountain Forest and Range Experiment Station at
Tempe, Arizona is also preparing a description and analysis of the
physical parameters of occupied and historical Peregrine Falcon aeries

in Arizona, the same as for Bald Eagle aeries. The BLM has financial-
ly supported the Peregrine Fund's captive breeding effort and has par-
ticipated in the experimental release of Peregrine Falcons into the
Snake River Birds of Prey Natural Area in Idaho. The latter was
justified partially on the basis of an earlier BLM research project
by Morlan Nelson. The FS has also funded Peregrine Falcon reintroductions on the White Mountain National Forest in New Hampshire and
the Green Mountain National Forest in Vermont. More of this sort of
effort is expected in the future, depending on the availability of
captive-bred birds. The BLM is also cooperating with the U.S. Fish
and Wildlife Service on a team that is attempting simultaneously with
an enforcement effort to analyze the effects of recreation and other
river activities on Peregrine Falcon breeding behavior along the
Yukon River.

The BLM has also funded 2 research projects on the San Simon
Cienega Mexican Duck Habitat Management Area in New Mexico. One was
a general biological analysis of the area, and the other was an
evaluation of past habitat management efforts and recommendations for
the future.

For the Kirtland's Warbler, the FS's North Central Forest Experiment Station at St. Paul, Minnesota is conducting a quantitative
analysis of vegetation in the most productive territories and is preparing a five-year study plan for the species.

The FS Southeastern Forest Experiment Station, again at the Clemson, South Carolina, Work Unit, in cooperation with Clemson University
is making a thorough review and analysis of the literature on Bachman's Warbler habitat. In addition, an intensive systematic field
search is being conducted in an attempt to determine the distribution
and status of the species in the southern United States.

HABITAT MANAGEMENT

One of the substantive mandates of section 7 of the Endangered
Species Act is for Federal agencies to carry out programs for the conservation of threatened species and endangered species. Conservation
is defined in the Act as the use of all methods and procedures which
are necessary to bring any such species to the point at which the
measures provided by the Act are no longer necessary (i.e., the species
has recovered and is no longer endangered). Endangered species conservation programs carried out by land managing agencies include--in
addition to inventory and research which are really means to ends and
not ends in themselves--the control of public access to and the degree
of use of lands occupied by endangered species, as well as direct
habitat management to benefit them.

For example, both the FS and the BLM can and do close areas to
public use, either seasonally or throughout the year, to provide
seclusion for endangered species. This is done by either FS Regional
Foresters or BLM State Directors under the authority of appropriate
regulations. These closures bear with them an obligation to enforce
and patrol the boundaries, an authority that the FS had for many
years but that the BLM has had only since passage of the Federal Land

Policy and Management Act in October of 1976.

Closures of designated endangered species areas on FS and BLM lands are currently in effect for the California Condor, Mississippi Sandhill Crane, Mexican Duck, Southern Bald Eagle, American Peregrine Falcon, Kirtland's Warbler, and Puerto Rican Parrot. In many cases, surveillance is intense with either researchers, wardens, or enforcement personnel keeping close watches. Interagency cooperation and volunteer public involvement are also important aspects of maintaining these closures.

Acquisition and protective withdrawals to preclude incompatible uses of key habitat are also effective and prudent courses of action in many cases. These strategies are clearly within the existing authorities of land-managing agencies, although neither the FS nor the BLM can purchase land solely to protect endangered species under the authority of the Endangered Species Act using Land and Water Conservation Fund monies. This is an important discrepancy, and the legal details of the entire land acquisition matter would require more space than allowed here. Thus, the following habitat management discussion is limited to several examples of direct habitat management for endangered birds that have been supported by the FS or BLM through funding, manpower, and/or cooperative agreements.

For the Mexican Duck, the BLM has an intensive management program in 2 areas of New Mexico--the San Simon Cienega and Elephant Butte Marsh. At San Simon Cienega, several dikes and small ponds have been constructed to collect water pumped from drilled wells. The area has been fenced to provide better livestock management, and vegetation planting and control are parts of the maintenance schedule provided in the overall management plan. Elephant Butte Marsh management has involved fencing and a cooperative effort on the part of the Bureau of Reclamation to maintain an adequate water level in the marsh. The FS also has a Mexican Duck program in New Mexico involving fencing and marsh revegetation.

For the Red-cockaded Woodpecker, the FS has conducted prescribed burnings and commercial and noncommercial thinnings in pine stands. The objective is to create a forest composition more suitable to the woodpecker. Similar efforts are being made by several state agencies as well as by the U.S. Marine Corps on Camp LeJeune, North Carolina.

Prescribed burning and both commercial and noncommercial forest type conversion are parts of the FS program for Kirtland's Warblers. Timber management plans have been altered to accomodate the demonstrated habitat needs of the species. For example, sites which would have been planted with Red Pine (*Pinus resinosa*) for maximum timber production have been regenerated to Jack Pine (*Pinus banksiana*) which the warbler prefers.

INDIRECT ENDANGERED SPECIES HABITAT PROTECTION

Most of the inventory, research, and habitat management discussed thus far requires direct capital investment. However, the integrated approach to habitat management and protection for the benefit of endangered species also includes the modification of other resource-management activities (e.g., livestock and timber management, oil and gas leasing, granting of rights-of-way, control of off-road vehicle use, etc.).

Such modifications are more prevalent in the land-use planning and decision-making processes of the BLM and the FS than most might imagine. For example, by maintaining long, pine-sawtimber rotations, the FS benefits Red-cockaded Woodpeckers. Colony sites of this species that might otherwise be regenerated are retained instead. Colony sites are managed under all-age rather than even-age timber management regimes, and forage or support stands are retained adjacent to known colonies. Such decisions require high level policy decisions.

Many modifications of and constraints placed on the Trans-Alaska Pipeline by the BLM to protect raptors were long-range, resource planning directives. Drilling for oil and gas is not permitted within 1.6 km of the Colville River or its major tributaries which are important nesting habitat for Arctic Peregrine Falcons. There has also been considerable effort to identify and provide buffer zones, approximately 1.6 km in diameter, around all eagle nests along the pipeline corridor south of the Yukon River. Even Rough-legged Hawk (*Buteo lagopus*) nests are given at least a 0.8 km diameter circle of undisturbed habitat. Protection of Peregrine Falcons includes establishment of buffer zones 3.2 km in diameter.

The site for one of the 12 pumping stations for the Trans-Alaska Pipeline was relocated to protect nest sites for Rough-legged Hawks, Gyrfalcons (*Falco rusticolus*), and Arctic Peregrine Falcons. In the same area, the BLM rewrote a lease to prohibit landings and takeoffs between 15 April and 15 August at an airfield too near the nest sites. This effort also included cooperation from the Federal Aviation Administration which contacted aircraft operators to advise them of the problem and to solicit their help in directing pilots to maintain altitudes at least 305 m above nesting sites and at least 1.6 km horizontal distance from them during the nesting season.

The pipeline highway was also re-routed at one point--at considerable expense to the pipeline construction company--to avoid raptor nest sites. And, because of noise and other disturbance associated with air-cushion vehicles, their use on the North Slope of Alaska is delayed until 1 August each year by BLM action.

CONCLUSION

If man's influence on wildlife is multi-factoral, a policy to protect wildlife from extinction should also be multi-directional. This must be and is the crux of integrated approaches to the management and conservation of endangered birds on our National Forest System and public lands--a goal toward which many are working both from within and from outside the agencies. But this requires close coordination between those who are doing endangered species work, those who are effective in the political arenas, and those who are in positions to advocate endangered species conservation directly within the agencies on whose programs the future of some species may depend.

APPENDIX

References to the United States Congress numbers for the various legislative acts mentioned in this chapter are as follows:

1. Endangered Species Act of 1973 (16 U.S.C. 1531 et seq.)
2. Sikes Act, as amended (16 U.S.C. 670 et seq.)
3. Federal Land Policy and Management Act (43 U.S.C. 1701 et seq.)
4. McSweeney-McNary Act of 1928, as amended (16 U.S.C. 581, 581a, 581a-1, 581b-581i)
5. Multiple-Use and Sustained-Yield Act (16 U.S.C. 528-531)
6. National Forest Management Act of 1976 (16 U.S.C. 1601 et seq.)
7. Cooperative Forest Management Act of 1950, as amended (16 U.S.C. 589c, 568d)
8. National Environmental Policy Act (42 U.S.C. 4321 et seq.)

49

The Recovery Plan Approach to Endangered Species Restoration in the United States

David B. Marshall

One of the most innovative and far-reaching pieces of conservation legislation ever enacted in the United States was the Endangered Species Act of 1973 which was signed by the President in December of that year. Two of the stated purposes of the Act are to conserve ecosystems needed by endangered and threatened species and to provide a program for the conservation of endangered and threatened species. It was specified as a policy that all federal departments and agencies shall participate in implementing the Act.

Within the Act are provisions for maintenance of a worldwide list of endangered and threatened species, the acquisition of habitat for endangered and threatened species in the U.S., provisions for state participation, including a grant-in-aid program, interagency cooperation, international cooperation, and protection against taking. The interagency cooperation provision requires that appropriate federal agencies cooperate in carrying out programs to restore endangered and threatened species. It also requires that federal agencies must take action to insure their activities do not jeopardize the continued existence of endangered species or result in destruction to habitat determined by the Fish and Wildlife Service to be critical.

This paper is concerned about 2 of the provisions: (1) that appropriate federal agencies cooperate in carrying out the program and (2) state cooperation. The Fish and Wildlife Service has been designated the lead agency for coordinating the entire effort for all but a few marine species which are handled by the National Marine Fisheries Service. This means coordinating a national program for endangered species restoration among 56 state and territorial governments and their associated agencies; numerous Federal agencies, including major landholders such as the Bureau of Land Management; U.S. Forest Service, National Park Service, and Department of Defense; local government groups; private conservation organizations; and educational and research institutions. For the restoration of even a single species, we can have up to 20 or more agencies and organizations involved. Very often these organizations have diverse goals because they were established for different purposes. Getting them to work in harmony toward restoration of an endangered or threatened species when, in fact, they often have other missions of higher priority to them is no easy task.

As a means to combine these varied resources into common goals for each endangered species and to cooperate in their restoration, the Fish and Wildlife Service devised the recovery plan approach. A recovery plan has 4 basic parts. The first section or introduction provides a sketch of the species (or group of species where more than one species occurs within a common ecosystem). The sketch includes remarks on the species' range, both present and former, its population status, habitat requirements, suspected and/or known causes of endangerment, and corrective actions needed. The introduction in essence provides sufficient background for the reader to understand the rest of the plan. The second part is the most important part of the plan. It delineates a restoration goal or prime objective, the subobjectives necessary to meet the goal, and all actions or jobs required to accomplish the objectives. The jobs, if accomplished, will result in completion of the prime objective. The jobs are assigned priorities in the third part of the plan and assigned to those agencies or other organizations that have agreed or are required by law to implement the plan. Costs are assigned to each job, and they are allotted in segments by fiscal years. This provides each agency or other organization with an annual budget for the species which delineate assignments. The fourth part of the plan comprises an appendix which includes comments from knowledgeable parties and letters from organizations indicating intent to handle the jobs assigned them.

A correctly prepared recovery plan delineates only those actions that must be taken to meet the plan's prime objective, unneeded actions fall aside. As indicated above, a typical recovery plan is built around a step-down outline, an abbreviated example of which is provided by Figure 1 for an imaginary species. Some of the terminal boxes in this figure would probably have to be broken down into sub-units to be at the job level.

The most thought-provoking aspect in the preparation of a recovery plan is delineating or stating the restoration goal or prime objective. If at all possible, this considers a population goal for the restoration, and the proportions of the species' original range in which the species is to be restored. It may be possible even to restore within all of its former range, but this is seldom feasible. The prime objective must be a reasonably obtainable goal from biological and social-economic standpoints.

Most recovery plans are being prepared by recovery teams which are groups of specialists assigned to an individual species or group of species. However, we also envision or have underway plans prepared by federal government agencies, state fish and wildlife agencies, interagency committees, private individuals, or profes-

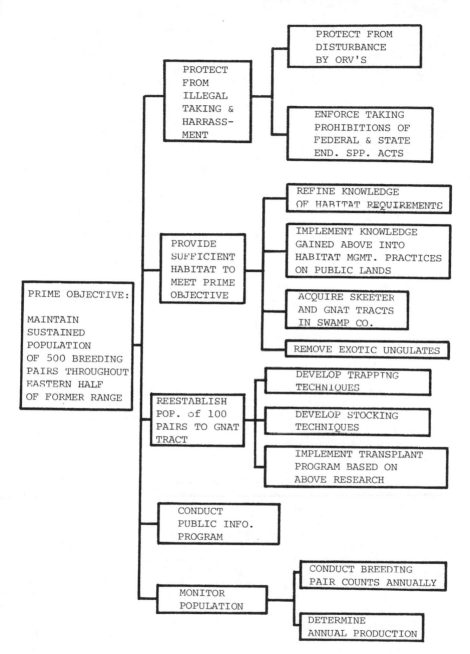

FIGURE 1. An example of a step-down outline for a hypothetical recovery plan for an endangered species.

sionals from universities or other institutions. Fish and Wildlife
Service staffs in regional offices are responsible for putting plans
into final shape, or they are assigned to a state fish and wildlife
agency which has consented to undertake the task. Final approval
of plans is the responsibility of the Fish and Wildlife Service
Director.
    Since many of the plans are being drafted by recovery teams, it
appears appropriate to discuss the composition of such groups.
Members of recovery teams are typically professional employees of
organizations expected to implement or are already implementing
recovery actions for a given species or group of species. These are
usually government agencies having legal responsibility for restoration of the subject species. In some instances, however, the teams
also include employees of private conservation organizations or
scientific institutions which have elected to undertake a portion
of the restoration effort. Team members in general are those who
are most closely involved personally with restoration of the subject
species. An ideal team is composed of about 5 professionals of
various disciplines, including habitat management, research, administration, and programing. Some, but not all members, need to be
experts on the species. They need to have a feel not only for what
must be done, but also for who can do it and for how much money.
Teams larger than 7 individuals become unwieldy, and it is difficult for them to meet at one time. Often, the expertise needed
covers more than seven individuals. Therefore, in addition to team
members, we have a consultant category. Consultants can be anyone
with special expertise needed by the team in the preparation of a
plan.
    Therefore, recovery teams are basically composed of individuals
representing agencies which will be implementing the recovery
effort. If a team does not contain all the biological or other
expertise available, it is obligated to bring in these people as
consultants. The teams, which are appointed by the Director of
the Fish and Wildlife Service, have as their primary responsibility
the drafting of recovery plans and the preparation of updates on an
annual basis. Recovery teams may also be called upon to provide
recommendations for management and research actions by various
government agencies. Recovery teams oversee and monitor the implementation of recovery plans, but they do not have authority to
implement or direct them. Recovery teams are autonomous bodies
which do not speak for any agency. They are instructed to stay
within the biological aspects of their assignment and not become
involved with social, economic, and political issues. They do not
solicit funds through political pressure for their individual species, become activist groups, or in any way divest government agencies
of their responsibilities.
    To date, the Fish and Wildlife Service has appointed 59 recovery
teams which have responsibility for 70 listed species. Thirty of
these are concerned with 41 species of birds (Table 1). The species
selected for this effort were based on complex criteria which include
degree of endangerment and the need to coordinate existing restoration efforts. Full species have higher priority than subspecies.

TABLE 1. U.S. FISH AND WILDLIFE SERVICE RECOVERY TEAMS FOR
ENDANGERED BIRDS, AS OF SEPTEMBER, 1977

Species or Group

Eastern Brown Pelican (*Pelecanus occidentalis*)
Hawaiian Goose (*Branta sandvicensis*)
Aleutian Canada Goose (*Branta canadensis leucopareia*)
Laysan Duck (*Anas laysanensis*)
Mexican Duck (*Anas diazi*)
California Condor (*Gymnogyps californianus*)
Everglades Kite (*Rostrhamus sociabilis plumbeus*)
Southern Bald Eagle (*Haliaeetus leucocephalus leucocephalus*)
    Southwest and Chesapeake Bay Populations
American Peregrine Falcon (*Falco peregrinus anatum*)
    Eastern, Rocky Mountain/Southwest, and Pacific Populations
Arctic Peregrine Falcon (*Falco peregrinus tundrius*)
Masked Bobwhite (*Colinus virginianus ridgwayi*)
Light-footed Clapper Rail (*Rallus longirostris levipes*)
Yuma Clapper Rail (*Rallus longirostris yumanensis*)
Whooping Crane (*Grus americana*)
Mississippi Sandhill Crane (*Grus canadensis pulla*)
California Least Tern (*Sterna albifrons browni*)
Puerto Rican Plain Pigeon (*Columba inornata wetmorei*)
Puerto Rican Parrot (*Amazona vittata*)
Red-cockaded Woodpecker (*Dendrocopus borealis*)
Dusky Seaside Sparrow (*Ammospiza maritima nigrescens*)
Hawaiian Crow (*Corvus tropicus*)
Palila (*Psittirostra bailleui*)
Hawaiian Waterbirds
    Hawaiian Gallinule (*Gallinula chloropus sandvicensis*)
    Hawaiian Coot (*Fulica americana alai*)
    Hawaiian Stilt (*Himantopus himantopus knudseni*)
Hawaii Forest Birds
    Hawaii Honeycreeper (*Loxops maculata maculata*)
    Hawaii Akepa (*Loxops coccinea coccinea*)
    Akiapolauu (*Hemignathus wilsoni*)
    Ou (*Psittirostra psittacea*)
Kauai Forest Birds
    Large Kauai Thrush (*Phaeornis obscurus myadestina*)
    Small Kauai Thrush (*Phaeornis palmeri*)
    Kauai Oo (*Moho braccatus*)
    Kauai Akialoa (*Hemignathus procerus*)
    Kauai Nukupuu (*Hemignathus lucidus*)
    Ou (*Psittirostra psittirostra*)
Molokai-Maui Forest Birds
    Molokai Thrush (*Phaeornis obscurus rutha*)
    Molokai Creeper (*Loxops maculata flammea*)
    Maui Nukupuu (*Hemignathus lucidus*)
    Maui Parrotbill (*Pseudonestor xanthorphrys*)
    Crested Honeycreeper (*Palmeria dolei*)

The team approach to recovery plan preparation is most appropriate for those species which are widespread and involve restoration efforts by several or more agencies or other organizations. A simple recovery effort involving land acquisition in a small area or one agency, for example, would not require a recovery team. Eight recovery plans have currently been approved, four of which are for birds. Nine recovery plans are under the Director's review, seven of these are for birds. Interim drafts of plans are present in regional offices for most other species covered by recovery teams. Funds for the implementation of portions of most approved and draft plans are being provided in fiscal year 1978.

The recovery plan approach has not been without problems. No effort of this type involving numerous agencies and individuals with varied opinions and objectives can operate with full harmony. We have been criticized because of delays in appointment of recovery teams and approval of recovery plans. However, if any of you know of a better approach, we would like to hear it. Overall, the effort has met with our satisfaction and has received widespread acceptance among government agencies which are basically responsible for accomplishing the restoration efforts.

50

Manipulating Behavioral Patterns of Endangered Birds
A Potential Management Technique

Stanley A. Temple

If we accept Hutchinson's (1957) concept of the niche as an n-dimensional hypervolume, it becomes clear that the dimensions of such a niche are subject to many limitations. Certain dimensions are set primarily by physical constraints which usually have to do with the species' morphology, physiology and sometimes, behavior. These characteristics of a species' niche are usually maintained through successive generations as genetically-fixed traits. Another important set of constraints on the dimensions of a species' niche is psychological in nature. These have to do with behavioral and competitive interactions that influence such variables as habitat selection, nest-site selection, food habits, and migration patterns. Very often these psychological components of the niche are passed on from generation to generation through the establishment of traditions. These traditions are maintained through learning processes such as imitation and imprinting; they are the types of traits that progeny learn from the previous generation.

Both genetic and traditional (i.e., resulting from learning) means of transmitting niche information to successive generations are highly efficient when environmental conditions are fairly constant from one generation to the next or when they change relatively slowly. Each insures that successive generations will receive a legacy of fitness from their ancestors. However, when environmental conditions change rapidly, both genetic and traditional inheritance of information can lead to a time-lag during which the population is essentially locked into unadaptive old ways by phenotypic or acquired traits. During this time-lag, the change in the environment reduces the fitness of individuals in the population, and often the population becomes endangered or actually goes extinct.

Natural selection will, of course, continue to favor those

individuals in an endangered population who acquire traits that
increase fitness in the new environment. Nonetheless, geneotypic
changes that establish new phenotypes usually occur slowly, over
generations of selection. For most vertebrates, acquiring new
phenotypic traits becomes a time-consuming process that usually
falls short in the race with accelerated environmental change.
Given the rate at which natural ecosystems are being changed today,
it seems clear than an endangered species would be doomed if it
could only increase its fitness through phenotypic changes resulting from genetic drift or mutation.

A different picture emerges when we look at traditions that
are passed on from generation to generation by learning. Traditions
can be initiated or altered by a single, successful individual in
the population. Wilson (1975) has noted that "tradition drift,"
unlike genetic drift, has the potential for rapidly changing the
traits--including niche dimensions--of a population. It is not
unusual to find a new spontaneously-developed tradition spreading
throughout a population in only a few generations. A species that
can adapt to a changing environment by merely altering a tradition-
ally-fixed trait has, therefore, a far greater chance of enhancing
its fitness and surviving in a new environment.

It we look at the types of problems that many endangered birds
face, it is clear that most are the result of a rapidly changing
environment with which the endangered population has failed to keep
abreast. Indeed, we have learned that habitat alteration is the
major cause of avian endangerment (W. B. King, Ch. 2, *this volume*).
One might ask why most endangered birds have failed to make the
types of behavioral changes that would increase their fitness in
an altered environment. Are endangered species locked into old,
unadaptive ways by genetically-fixed traits or by tradition? It
seems that in many cases, the problems of endangered species may be
the result of unadaptive traditions. Problems relating to habitat
selection, nest-site selection, food habits and migration patterns
are important components of the unadaptive niches of many endangered
birds. These are all strongly influenced by tradition.

As managers of endangered populations, it becomes logical for us
to ask whether we can intervene in an endangered bird's life cycle
and effect a rapid alteration of an unadaptive tradition thereby increasing the fitness of the population. The proposition of this
paper is that we can and that, in certain instances, such an approach
holds considerable promise as a management procedure.

EVIDENCE FOR TRADITION CHANGES IN AVIAN POPULATIONS

There are many examples of how avian populations have naturally
and rapidly acquired new traditions that have resulted in significant increases in population sizes and expansions of geographic
ranges. These are the stated goals of most endangered-species
conservation efforts, and it, therefore, seems wise to examine
some of these naturally occurring cases of tradition changes to
see whether they may provide models for management programs.

Habitat Selection

Habitat selection in birds has been the subject of several excellent reviews (Hildén, 1965; Klopfer and Hailman, 1965). The general conclusion is that the mechanisms of habitat selection have evolved in response to natural selection. Both innate and learned processes are involved.

Site tenacity or *ortstreue* results when birds establish a traditional attachment to a location and will return to it in spite of habitat deterioration. For example, the arena display grounds or leks of certain birds such as grouse, shorebirds and pheasants are strongly fixed by tradition. Armstrong (1947) describes how a local population of Ruffs (*Philomachus pugnax*) returned to the precise location of their ancestral lek even when a road was constructed over the site.

Although not immediately apparent, site tenacity can lead to the occupation of new environments and the establishment of new traditions. This becomes possible when site tenacity is coupled with habitat imprinting, another important component of habitat selection in birds. Basically, young birds become imprinted on the type of habitat in which their parents reared them. This habitat imprinting seems to be an example of early, rapid learning which enables the young bird to readily identify the habitat that it will ultimately use for breeding. A tradition of habitat-use is thereby passed on from generation to generation.

There are several examples of how site tenacity and imprinting, both means of maintaining traditions, can combine to lead to a rapid and dramatic change in traditional habitat-use patterns. Peitzmeier (1947) describes the case of Mistle Thrushs (*Turdus pilaris*) which originally nested only in unbroken tracts of coniferous forests. As forests were destroyed, some adults exhibited site tenacity and returned to their traditional nesting sites even though the forest had been severely altered. The progeny produced by these returning adults became imprinted on the more open types of habitat in which they were reared. This established a new tradition of nesting in open-parkland habitats, and the Mistle Thrush population rapidly increased its numbers and geographic range once the new tradition of habitat-use became established.

Similarly, Peitzmeier (1952) describes how Curlews (*Numenius arquata*) in Scandinavia made a dramatic shift from a tradition of nesting in bogs to a tradition of nesting on agricultural land. Motivated by site tenacity, old birds returned to their former bog nesting-sites even after they had been cultivated. Young Curlews imprinted on the agricultural lands where they were reared and sought out such habitats when they matured. Since bog habitat was becoming increasingly scarce, this change in tradition allowed the Curlews to expand their range through use of abundant agricultural land.

Hildén (1965) offers this process as the explanation for many birds which have become urbanized. New traditions of habitat-use added a new dimension to the birds' niche which allowed them to expand their numbers and range within habitats modified by man.

Needless to say, it is impossible through the establishment of
new traditions for a bird to occupy a habitat type that does not
supply its ultimate requirements for existence. Usually innate
behavioral characteristics or phenotypic restrictions will prevent
a species from being more than temporarily successful in unsuitable
habitats. To use an extreme example, no matter how strong site
tenacity and imprinting may be, tropical rainforest birds would
never be able to shift to a sugar-cane field habitat! We are concerned with less dramatic shifts in habitat-use which, nonetheless,
could potentially open new niche dimensions for an endangered bird.
    As a management tool, the traditional aspect of habitat selec-
tion has great potential. By artificially rearing young birds in
new never-before-used habitats that still meet the species' ultimate
requirements, we could effect changes similar to those that occurred
naturally in Mistle Thrush and Curlew populations. Often populations
have failed to naturally make changes in habitat-use because of the
random nature of "tradition shift", not because the new habitat is
unsuitable.

Nest-Site Selection

    The selection of a nesting site is a very important aspect of a
bird's breeding biology; the choice can affect fecundity and hence
population demography. Not surprisingly, natural selection has
favored the evolution of mechanisms that will maximize the likelihood of a bird making a proper choice. As with habitat selection,
the nest-site selection mechanism in birds is strongly tied to
traditions which are maintained by imprinting and social facilitation.
    Young birds clearly imprint on the type of nest site from which
they fledge. In this way a traditional preference for a certain
type of nest site is passed from generation to generation. In most
instances, this maintains fitness in subsequent generations, but
when birds persist in using a traditional type of nest site which,
due to changing environmental conditions, is no longer adaptive,
the population may suffer.
    There are many examples of birds that have made shifts in
traditional nesting sites that have added new dimensions to their
niche and allowed the species to increase its numbers and geographic
range. In some instances, the new tradition apparently became
established through "tradition drift." Initially, a few individuals may have made the shift to a new nest site and enjoyed breeding success in the new situation. Their offspring imprinted on the
new site, and the new tradition spread rapidly through the population;
sometimes completely replacing the old traditional site.
    Chimney Swifts (*Chaetura pelagica*) formerly had a tradition of
nesting in hollow trees and were no doubt severely limited by the
availability of such sites. Probably because of a tradition shift,
the swifts established a new tradition of nesting in chimneys, and
their populations benefitted from the proliferation of these new
nesting sites that accompanied man's development of North America.
Likewise, Barn Swallows (*Hirundo rustica*) traditionally nested on

cliffs and were, no doubt, limited by the availability of these widely dispersed nesting sites. After adopting a new tradition of nesting in man's buildings, Barn Swallows almost completely abandoned the tradition of cliff-nesting. Likewise, Purple Martins (*Progne subis*) have almost completely abandoned the tradition of nesting in hollow trees in favor of a tradition of nesting in artificial nesting boxes (Wade, 1966).

In an even more appropriate example of an endangered species adopting a new nest-site tradition that increased its fitness, I can relate some of my findings concerning the Mauritius Kestrel (*Falco punctatus*). This endemic, island falcon nests in natural cavities, either tree cavities or caves and crevices on cliffs. I found that one could easily determine, from museum specimens collected during or after the kestrel's breeding season, which type of nest site the bird had used. Cliff-nesters had extremely worn rectrices from abrasion with the rough basalt that forms the cliffs on Mauritius; tree-nesters showed much less wear. Up until about 1900, most specimens showed the extreme feather wear characteristic of cliff-nesters, but during this century a tradition shift apparently took place. Recent museum specimens all appear to be tree-nesters, and recent observations of the wild population confirm that tree-nesting was the established tradition in the remnant population. This tree-nesting tradition was unadaptive because of a change in the environment; exotic Macaques (*Macaca irus*) introduced onto Mauritius were so efficient at locating and destroying eggs in tree cavities that the kestrel's reproductive success was extremely reduced. The population declined accordingly and was, in 1973, reduced to only 6 individuals, 4 in the wild and 2 in captivity. In 1974, with the 4 wild birds apparently locked into a fatal tradition of tree-nesting, an unexpected tradition shift took place. One pair nested on a sheer, basalt cliff and, in what was probably the first successful nesting in many years, reared a full brood of 3 young (Temple, 1977). Being imprinted on a cliff-nesting site, two of these offspring paired and bred successfully on another cliff in 1975; meanwhile their parents also continued to breed successfully at cliff sites. In 1976, both these pairs again bred successfully on cliffs. The second wild pair that survived in 1973 persisted in nesting in tree-cavities and produced no young. Because of this tradition shift, the wild kestrel population has tripled from 4 to 12 in 4 years time.

The management potential inherent in the nest-site selection mechanism is again rather clear. By artificially rearing young birds in a new type of nest structure which is believed to be more adaptive than the old traditional one, we can introduce a new tradition into an endangered population. This type of approach clearly works; there are several examples in which man has purposefully altered the nest-site traditions of birds in just such a way. We have already learned of some of these in this symposium. Peregrine Falcons (*Falco peregrinus*) reared on towers return to establish territories on such structures (S.A. Temple, Ch. 40, *this volume*). Puffins (*Fratercula arctica*) reared on a previously abandoned nesting island return there when old enough to breed (S.W. Kress, Ch. 42,, *this volume*). Cross-fostering can cause the adopted species to use nest sites typical of the foster parent (T. Cade, Ch. 21, *this volume*). As long as we can make sensible choices for new nesting sites, the mechanisms exist that will allow managers to establish their use as a tradition in a population.

Food Habits

Aspects of the feeding behavior of many birds are acquired through imitation of parents, through social facilitation or through observational learning (Alcock, 1969). In imitative foraging, young birds simply follow their parents and learn to feed on the same items. They learn foraging behaviors by imitating their parents. Such imitative foraging leads to the establishment of traditions which are passed from parent to offspring.

Social facilitation occurs when a behavioral pattern, such as a foraging tactic, is increased in pace or frequency by the presence or actions of other animals. Facilitation may produce only temporary results, but it can lead to an individual acquiring new traits by imitating other individuals. If rewarded by using the imitated foraging tactic, the observer may adopt it permanently. This becomes another form of social tradition.

Observational learning occurs when one individual watches another individual's activities and, at a later time, imitates the actions that it had observed.

These types of imitative foraging can rapidly lead to new traditions in a population. Perhaps the best-documented example is the spread of cream-stealing by British birds (Fisher and Hinde, 1950). Probably as a result of a tradition drift, the habit of stealing cream from unprotected milk bottles appeared spontaneously in the population. Through imitative learning processes, the habit spread rapidly through England and then to Scandinavia and central Europe. Because birds were rewarded (with a meal of cream) by imitating their parents or other birds, the response was reinforced, and the tradition became established. There have been other studies that have, under more controlled conditions, demonstrated the effect of one bird watching another feed (Klopfer, 1959; Turner, 1964). In these experiments a trained bird (the "actor") was exposed to an inexperienced bird (the "observer"). As expected, the "observer" did pick up the foraging tactics of the "actor", but the opposite also occurred so that both "actor" and "observer" influenced each other's behavior. Younger birds were more impressible as "observers" than older birds.

Occasionally, imitative foraging can open new niche dimensions that increase the numbers and geographic range of a bird. By acquiring the habit of visiting winter bird-feeders to take seeds and suet, birds such as the Tufted Titmouse (*Parus bicolor*), Cardinal (*Richmondena cardinalis*) and Red-bellied Woodpecker (*Centurus carolinus*) have expanded their geographic ranges northward into regions from which they were previously excluded by winter food shortages (Beddal, 1963).

A similar change in tradition can theoretically be forced on an endangered population through careful management. It appears that the winter feeding programs for several endangered cranes (G. Archibald, Ch. 18, *this volume*) provide an example of how a tradition of feeding on a novel food at a specific location can become established in an entire population.

Migration Patterns

The stereotyped migration patterns of many birds, especially gregarious birds such as waterfowl, provide another example of a traditional aspect of a species' niche. Each year migratory flocks follow the precise traditional migration route, use the same traditional stopover places, and occupy the same overwintering sites that were used by their ancestors. Since migratory flocks are often of mixed-age composition, young birds have a clear opportunity to learn the traditional routes and sites from their elders (Hochbaum, 1955).

Experimental results show that young birds are very receptive to acquiring new migratory traditions. For example, when Perdeck (1958) trapped migrating juvenile Starlings (*Sturnus vulgaris*) and displaced them to the east of their normal fall-migration route, the displaced birds became traditionally fixed on a new wintering range to the east of the Starling's normal winter distribution. In a similar experiment, Ralph and Mewaldt (1975) demonstrated that juvenile White-crowned Sparrows (*Zonotrichia leucophrys*) trapped on their wintering grounds in California and displaced to a new winter range would return to the new locality in subsequent winters. They also showed that this receptivity to new migratory traditions was a trait only of juveniles. Birds trapped and displaced as adults or juveniles trapped and displaced after mid-December would return to the place where they were trapped and not the place where they were released.

We have already learned how one endangered species program--for the Aleutian Canada Goose (*Branta canadensis leucopareia*)--has taken advantage of experienced wild birds to guide inexperienced captive-produced stock on the traditional migration route (Springer et al., Ch 37, *this volume*). Also, Whooping Cranes (*Grus americana*) cross-fostered to Sandhill Cranes (*Grus canadensis*) adopt the migratory habits of their foster parents (Drewien and Bizeau, Ch. 25, *this volume*). In another example, Cade (1974) has proposed intercepting migrant Arctic Peregrine Falcons (*Falco peregrinus tundrius*) on their fall migration and allowing falconers to keep them at selected temperate latitude locations over the winter. The birds would be released the following spring to migrate northward. The expectation is that the short-stopping of their first migration would result in a new tradition of wintering at temperate latitudes where they would avoid the pesticide problems encountered on the normal tropical wintering areas. There are many other possibilities for establishing new nontraditional migration patterns through displacement of juveniles or through the use of "guide" birds which will lead juveniles on a novel migration to a new wintering site where the environment may favor the species.

IMPLICATIONS FOR ENDANGERED BIRDS

The first tactic for preserving an endangered bird is, of course, to preserve the ecosystem of which the bird is an integral part. This is clearly the most acceptable form of endangered species management. However, for a myriad array of social or economic reasons it is often impossible to preserve intact ecosystems. In such situations, alternative tactics must be adopted. One such alternative is to accept the conclusion that the species no longer has a future in its natural setting. In some of these cases, long-term maintenance in captivity is an acceptable way of keeping the species alive. We have already learned that such long-term commitments to captive maintenance are difficult to obtain (W. G. Conway, Ch. 26, *this volume*).

A more attractive and less demanding approach is to leave the bird in the wild but somehow change it so that it fits into an altered ecosystem. Taken to its extreme, the strategy is essentially the inverse of habitat preservation: rather than making the environment compatible with the bird's niche dimensions, we would make the bird's niche dimensions compatible with the environment. The potential for altering traditions in endangered bird populations gives us a management tool that can accomplish this goal in a comparatively short period of time.

This manipulative approach is certainly not a panacea for all the problems faced by endangered birds, but I believe it holds promise for aiding many. There will certainly be critics of such an approach. They will, no doubt, hold out for ecosystem preservation and reject--as an unacceptable substitute for the real thing-- a bird whose niche has been altered. Nonetheless, faced with the choice of either allowing a bird to become extinct or manipulating its niche, I think most would vote for the latter. Given the level of sophistication that has already been demonstrated in past interventions into the ecology of endangered birds, there is reason to be optimistic over the chances that forcing tradition shifts in endangered populations can be carried out on an ecologically sound basis.

In the end, accepting a bird that has behaviors which are quite different from its ancestors is often a matter of time. We have come to accept swallows in barns, swifts in chimneys, songbirds at bird-feeders, and other species that have naturally incorporated new dimensions into their niches. Is it that much more difficult to accept Peregrine Falcons on towers, California Condors (*Gymnogyps californianus*) at feeding stations, Whooping Cranes in Idaho, or other results of manipulations that may take place in the future?

LITERATURE CITED

Alcock, J. 1969. Observational learning in three species of birds. Ibis 111:308-321.

Armstrong, E.A. 1947. Bird display and behavior: an introduction to the study of bird psychology. Lindsay Dummond, London. 431 p.

Beddal, B.G. 1963. Range expansion of the Cardinal and other birds in the northeastern states. Wilson Bull. 75:140-158.

Cade, T.J. 1974. Plans for managing the survival of the peregrine falcon. Raptor Res. Report 2:89-104.

Fisher, J. and R.A. Hinde. 1950. The opening of milk bottles by birds. Brit. Birds 42:347-357.

Hildén, O. 1965. Habitat selection in birds. Ann. Zool. Fenn. 2: 53-75.

Hochbaum, H.A. 1955. Travels and traditions of waterfowl. Univ. of Minn. Press, Minneapolis. 301 p.

Hutchinson, G.E. 1957. Concluding remarks. Cold Spring Harbor Symposium on Quantitative Biology 22:415-427.

Klopfer, P.H. 1959. Social interactions in discrimination learning with special reference to feeding behavior in birds. Behavior 14:282-299.

Klopfer, P.H. and J.P. Hailman. 1965. Habitat selection in birds, p. 279-303. *In* D.S. Lehrman, R.A. Hinde, and E. Shaw (eds.). Advances in the study of behavior. Academic Press, Inc., New York.

Peitzmeier, J. 1947. Uber die weitere Entwicklung der Parkland schaftspopulation der Misteldrossel in Nordwest deutschland. Ornithologische Forschungen 1:31-36.

Peitzmeier, J. 1952. Oekologische Umstellung und starke Vermehrun des Grossen Brachvogels (*Numerius arquata*) in Oberen Emsgebiet. Natur und Heimat 12:1-4.

Perdeck, A.C. 1958. Two types of orientation in migrating Starlings, *Sturnus vulgaris*, and Chaffinches, *Fringilla coelebs*, as revealed by displacement experiments. Ardea 46:1-37.

Ralph, C.J. and L.R. Mewaldt. 1975. Timing of site fixation upon the wintering grounds in sparrows. Auk 92:698-705.

Temple, S.A. 1977. The status and conservation of endemic Kestrels on Indian Ocean islands, p. 74-82. *In* R.D. Chancellor (ed.). World Conf. on Birds of Prey, Vienna, 1975, Report of Proceedings, ICBP. London.

Turner, E.R.A. 1964. Social feeding in birds. Behavior 24:1-46.

Wade, J.L. 1966. What you should know about the Purple Martin. J.L. Wade, Griggsville, Ill. 218 p.

Wilson, E.O. 1975. Sociobiology: the new synthesis. Belknap Press of Harvard Univ. Press, Cambridge and London, 697 p.

Part X
Summary

51

Concluding Remarks on the Problems of Managing Endangered Birds

Ian C. T. Nisbet

In summarizing this symposium, I would like to take a hard look at the profession of managing endangered species and to discuss both its role as a sub-discipline of ecology and its larger role in human society.

When a biologist starts to explore the ecological role of a population, one of the first tasks is to examine the population and define its characteristics. If the contributors to this symposium are a representative sample, endangered species biologists appear to have some very peculiar characteristics. As has already been pointed out, the sex ratio of this population is extremely unbalanced, with a disturbingly high proportion of males. Moreover, although the females look quite promising, the males--to judge from the preponderance of grey pigmentation in their pelage--appear generally past their peak of fitness. Of still greater concern, this symposium has shown that endangered species biologists are specialized animals, dependent on very limited and localized resources which have low productivity and very long turnover times. They tend to be conservative, unadaptable, and prone to form dominance hierarchies and exclusive territories. In a word, endangered species biologists have all the characteristics of endangered species.

These remarks are not entirely facetious because one of the most important issues raised by this symposium is the way in which professional managers of endangered species approach their work and how it relates both to our scientific understanding of the world and to our responsibilities as informed citizens to help manage and preserve it.

This symposium has been primarily devoted to exchanging information about management techniques. I think we all appreciate that the techniques we have discussed are not sufficient by themselves for the long-term preservation of endangered species. Rather, they are stop-gap measures to help endangered species through a crisis. Beyond the crises, they will need long-term, multi-faceted management programs of the kind discussed in the final chapters of this book.   Several papers in the symposium have emphasized a point that we should already have appreciated: that most endangered species are endangered for more than one reason, so that we will need multiple management techniques to conserve them.

The technical papers have been so good that there is no need to do more than put them into context here.   We have heard about a re-markably wide variety of management techniques, and a number of indi-viduals deserve acclaim for some remarkable practical achievements. Some techniques which were only daydreams 5-10 years ago have now been shown to be feasible and effective.   We now know that birds of prey can be bred in captivity and reestablished as breeding birds in the wild; that some extremely improbable species can be enticed to breed in artificial nest sites; that we can control predators, manipulate breeding habitats, and increase food supplies; and that in some cir-cumstances we can even convert endangered species from carnivores to herbivores or convert migratory populations into sedentary ones.   The main thought raised by these stories of successful management is that we may be too reluctant to "interfere" with other species.   Perhaps we should be more active in manipulating species such as condors, eagles, cranes, and seabirds.

It is invidious to make comparisons, but two management programs presented here seemed particularly imaginative.   The first is the management of the interaction between the Puerto Rican Parrot (*Amazona vittata*) and the Pearly-eyed Thrasher (*Margarops fuscatus*) described by Snyder and Taapken (Ch. 14, *this volume*).   Not many biologists would have realised that the way to minimize the impact of an inter-fering species would be to attract it to nest only a few feet away from the species which needed protection from it.   The second is the management program for the Cahow (*Pterodroma cahow*) described by Win-gate (Ch. 12, *this volume*).   After achieving success in securing its nest sites against a directly-interfering competitor, most of us would have been content to leave the Cahow to recover naturally.   It requir-ed real understanding and insight to appreciate that the Cahow was actually nesting in the wrong habitat, so that long-term management required luring it to nest elsewhere.

These and other examples form the theme of this symposium--that in order to protect and restore an endangered species one must under-stand fully the natural history, ecology, and behavior of the species and its critical requirements.   Conventional biological training or wildlife management techniques are not sufficient.   An endangered species biologist needs the insight of a naturalist in the old-fashion-ed sense of the term, together with the dedication and tenacity to follow a program through many years of experiment, frustration, and practical development.

One speaker expressed regret that endangered species biology is outside the mainstream of ecology and is not fashionable or intellec-tually respected.   This is perhaps not so unfortunate because "fashion-able" ecology, with its mathematical models and its broad generaliza-tions about ill-defined concepts, has little useful information to of-fer to the managers of endangered species.   Mathematical and systems models may in the future prove to be useful in managing ecosystems, but they tell us little about the peculiarities of individual species, especially endangered species which are by definition having trouble surviving in their environments. The concept of "K-selection" tells us nothing we did not already know about slowly-breeding species with deferred maturity--and in any case, not all endangered species are "K-selected." The most relevant piece of "fashionable" ecology may be the theory of island biogeography, which has made us think about the relation of extinction probability to the area of occupiable habitat and is leading towards the definition of minimum critical habitat. Unfortunately, the current theory of island biogeography is primarily a statistical generalization. It tells us nothing whatsoever about individual species except perhaps that the species at the tail end of the frequency-distribution curves have a high probability of extinction. If this implies that endangered species biologists are wasting their time, it is better to ignore the theory and get on with the job of management.

Practical ecologists fall into three broad categories:

1. Managers of ecosystems (e.g., foresters, farmers, park managers, fisheries biologists, gardeners, etc.);
2. Managers of pest species (e.g., "economic entomologists," "weed scientists," exterminators, and some waterfowl biologists);
3. Managers of dwindling and endangered species.

Of these three types, ecosystem managers are generally successful in achieving their narrowly-defined goals, but they certainly have not become so as a result of understanding or appreciating ecological diversity. Pest controllers are even worse: we all know what a mess they have made of the world with short-sighted solutions to complex problems. This prompts some awkward questions about the degree of ecological understanding which we ourselves bring to our work.

Regrettably, the answer to these questions is "not enough." With a few notable exceptions, the papers in this symposium have been focused too narrowly upon individual species being managed and a handful of factors in the environment that appear critical. Although we all recognize that in the long-run habitat is the key to the maintenance of viable populations of endangered species, few have faced up to the fact that in the future habitats will have to be managed as intensively as the individual species are today. Too many ornithologists implicitly view the "habitat"--especially the vegetation--as static, whereas, in fact, habitats change rapidly, often in time-scales shorter than the life spans of our endangered birds.

Since endangered species management has long-term goals, we need to look ahead periodically at the future state of the environment. Most of us are uncomfortably aware that the world is in a state of dramatic and rapid change. During the next 30 years--within our own lifetimes and within the generation time of some of the species we study--we can expect to see a fundamental transition of the earth from a generally natural state to a generally disturbed and degraded state in which even semi-natural ecosystems will become sparse and fragmented. At the same time, we can expect rapid changes in social attitudes to the natural world, although these are less easy to predict.

The papers in this symposium have made reference to about 40 endangered species of birds, which is a creditable large fraction of the 400 in the *Red Data Book*. However, I submit that the list of 400 is a serious misstatement of the dimensions of the problem. One of the few ecological generalizations that is relevant to endangered species is that the frequency distribution of abundance of animals is highly skewed. Only a few species are abundant; most of the species on earth are, in a statistical sense, very rare. Looking ahead a few decades, or even a few years, we should have the insight to recognize that the number of endangered bird species is more likely to be 4,000 than 400. If we look at the entire animal and plant kingdoms on this time-scale, the number of endangered species is more like 400,000. Moreover, the 40 bird species that we are studying are mostly temperate-zone species which have already learned to live in disturbed habitats of one kind or another. The great bulk of the world's threatened species are in parts of the globe--such as the Malay Archipelago, Amazonia and Malagasy--that have not been represented here at all.

In this wider context, it is hard to avoid a feeling of futility. The "Recovery Team" approach to the management of endangered species-- which we find barely adequate to solve the problems even of the most spectacular and highly valued species--involves 5 or 6 biologists working on each species. If we accept that there will soon be hundreds of thousands of endangered species in the world, we would need several million biologists to manage them.

The concept of millions of endangered species biologists seems too absurd even to consider. However, I would like to suggest that if we are willing to redefine our goals, some of them may, in fact, be attainable. The world already has hundreds of thousands of trained biologists in the business of managing ecosystems although, for historical reasons, most of them are professionally involved in farming, forestry, extension service, soil conservation, fisheries, etc. It is not altogether inconceivable that, as natural resources dwindle, society's attitudes may change rapidly enough to mobilize comparable numbers of people into management of ecosystems for multiple uses.

There are many scenarios for the future ranging from complete catastrophe to complete utopia. Individuals may be optimistic or pessimistic, but I suspect that most participants at this symposium are basically optimists (pessimists would not be devoting their lives to long-term, altruistic projects). Somewhere near the optimistic end of the spectrum, we can envisage a world in which social attitudes to natural systems are drastically changed so that society is willing to devote as many resources to environmental maintenance as it nowadays devotes to environmental exploitation.

Let us suspend disbelief for a moment and consider what such a world might be like. To start with, it will not be possible to manage endangered species one by one, except in special cases; there will be too many species requiring management, too much overlap in critical habitats, and too many conflicts in management needs for a species-by-species approach. In any case, there will be more important things to do than to manage single species: the primary need will be to manage endangered ecosystems. The long-range goal should be to integrate exploitative activities such as agriculture and forestry into ecosystem management, but in the shorter run the urgent need will be to preserve and maintain representative natural habitat.

The most predictable change in natural habitats in the near future is fragmentation. In the next generation, we can expect to see the final fragmentation of the earth from a predominantly natural state—a mosaic of settled clearings surrounded by relatively undisturbed ecosystems—to a man-dominated state in which natural habitats will remain only as increasingly scattered islands in a sea of development. The latter state is one with which most of us are familiar in developed countries, but it is likely to become the normal state of the world very soon. If so, we will have to develop the theory of island biogeography into the basics of practical management, for we will all be working in ecological archipelagos. Even if we are able to define the minimum critical size for maintenance of each of our ecosystems, it is idle to think that we will be able to acquire and preserve areas of sufficient size. In the future (as is already the case in some fragmented habitats) the only way to maintain ecological diversity will be by continual reintroduction of species into ecological islands that are too small to maintain them indefinitely. I predict that translocation will soon become one of the most important management tools.

What I am suggesting is that the techniques we have been discussing at this symposium for guiding endangered species through population crises will soon prove insufficient. Our entire science of managing endangered species as such is heading for a crisis. If we are to guide our own profession beyond this crisis phase, we will need to change it in several ways:

1. we need to bring more ecological expertise into endangered species biology;
2. we need to develop techniques for managing entire ecosystems;
3. we need to increase greatly in numbers.

All this may be no more than a pipe dream, of course. There are many other scenarios for the future, and I fear that society is, in fact, more likely to devote its resources to exploiting dwindling resources than to managing them rationally. If society's attitudes to the environment are to change as drastically as I have postulated, this will represent a major change in values: this is unlikely to occur without strong external forces and is certainly unlikely to result from the pleadings of a small group of idealistic biologists. However, in case it should occur, we need to develop a soundly-based science of ecosystem management. At present, our work is too narrowly focused to provide assurance that endangered species biologists could fulfill such a need.

Index

Africa: endangered birds of, 11, 16

Age determination: of Amazon parrots, 270; of Whooping Cranes, 236

Agelaius xanthomus. See Blackbird, Yellow-shouldered

Aix sponsa. See Duck, Wood

Ajaia ajaja. See Spoonbill, Roseate

Akepa: status of, 12

Akialoa, Kauai: status of, 12

Albatross, Short-tailed: threat to, 77

Amazon. See also Parrots, Amazon

Amazon, Black-billed: captive breeding, 267

Amazon, Blue-cheeked: captive breeding, 267

Amazon, Cuban: captive breeding, 266-267

Amazon, Imperial: captive breeding, 266

Amazon, Orange-winged: captive breeding, 268

Amazon, Puerto Rican. See Parrot, Puerto Rican

Amazon, Red-necked: captive breeding, 266

Amazon, Red-spectacled: captive breeding, 267

Amazon, Red-tailed: captive breeding, 267

Amazon, St. Lucia: captive breeding, 266

Amazon, St. Vincent, captive breeding, 263-266

Amazon, Vinaceous: captive breeding, 267

Amazon, Yellow-billed: captive breeding, 268

Amazon, Yellow-faced: captive breeding, 267

Amazon, Yellow-headed: captive breeding, 267

Amazon, Yellow-shouldered: captive breeding, 268

Amazona amazonica. See Amazon, Orange-winged

Amazona arausiaca. See Amazon, Red-necked

Amazona barbadensis. See Amazon, Yellow-shouldered

Amazona brasiliensis. See Amazon, Red-tailed

Amazona collaria. See Amazon, Yellow-billed

Amazona dufresniana. See Amazon, Blue-cheeked

Amazona guildingii. See Amazon, St. Vincent

Amazona imperialis. See Amazon,

Imperial
Amazona leucocephala. *See* Amazon, Cuban
Amazona ochrocephala. *See* Amazon, Yellow-headed
Amazona pretrei. *See* Amazon, Red-spectacled
Amazona versicolor. *See* Amazon, St. Lucia
Amazona vinacea. *See* Amazon, Vinaceous
Amazona vittata. *See* Parrot, Puerto Rican
Amazona xanthops. *See* Amazon, Yellow-faced
American Association of Zoological Parks and Aquariums, 303, 306
Ammospiza maritima. *See* Sparrow, Dusky Seaside
Anas laysanensis. *See* Teal, Laysan
Anas wyvilliana. *See* Duck, Hawaiian
Aquila chrysaetos. *See* Eagle, Golden
Aquila heliaca adalberti. *See* Eagle, Spanish Imperial
Aquila pomarina. *See* Eagle, Lesser Spotted
Aquila verreauxi. *See* Eagle, Verreaux's
Artificial insemination: of Whooping Cranes, 238; of Peregrine Falcons, 258-259; of Puerto Rican Parrots, 264
Asia: endangered birds of, 11
Athene blewitti. *See* Owl, Blewitt's
Atlantic Ocean, islands of: endangered birds of, 11
Atrichornis clamosus. *See* Scrubbird, Noisy
Australia: endangered birds of, 11, 15, 16; rats on Christmas Island, 122.

Baltic Sea: pollution of, 151
Bard, F.E., 201,202
Bass, Large-mouthed: as threat to Giant Pied-billed Grebes, 397

Bebrornis sechellensis. *See* Warbler, Seychelles Brush
Beebe, W., 226
Behavior: nesting, manipulation of, 167-170; sibling aggression in eagles, 195-200; of Whooping Cranes, 235-239; modification of, 435-443
Berger, D., 170
Birds of Prey: reintroduction of, 355-363; monitoring breeding success, 405-406. *See also* names of individual species
Blackbird, Yellow-shouldered: critical habitat for, 20; threats to, 77
Bluebird (Eastern, Western, and Mountain): decline of, 55-56; nesting boxes for, 56-58; "bluebird trails," 58
Bobwhite, Masked: distribution of, 345; captive breeding of, 345; recovery plan for, 345; methods for reintroducing, 346; release of pen-reared birds, 347-350; covey-box training, 347-350; conditioning released birds, 349; evaluating reintroduction methods, 352; mentioned, 316, 420
Branta canadensis leucopareia. *See* Goose, Aleutian Canada
Branta sandvicensis. *See* Goose, Hawaiian
Burnham, W., 170,201
Buteo buteo. *See* Buzzard, Common
Buzzard, Common: as foster parent to eagles, 198
Byelich, J., 86,89

Cade, T., 5
Cahow. *See* Petrel, Bermuda
California Department of Fish and Game, 336
Callaeas cinerea cinerea. *See* Kokako
Campephilus principalis. *See* Woodpecker, Ivory-billed
Canadian Wildlife Service: raptor programs of, 184; involvment in Whooping Crane reintro-

ductions, 201-220 *passim*; Peregrine Falcon breeding program, 251-261 *passim*; mentioned, 169, 251, 415
Captive breeding: role in endangered bird preservation, 5, 225; of Peregrine Falcons, 7, 184, 252-261; of Whooping Cranes, 204,207, 231-241; review of, 225-230; multigeneration propagation, 226, numbers of species bred, 227; genetic problems associated with, 228-229, 305, 307-312; and longevity of captive birds, 228; role of zoos in, 229, 304; economics of, 236; of Amazon parrots, 263-271 *passim*; of waterfowl, 243-249; influence of photoperiod on, 245-246, 316-317; genetic management in, 303-313 *passim*; goals of, 305; selecting breeding stock, 316; location of facilities, 316-317; problems caused by imprinting, 317; fitness of offspring from, 317-320; of Aleutian Canada Goose, 333; of Hawaiian Goose, 340-343; of Masked Bobwhite, 345. *See also* Artificial insemination, Imprinting
Carpenter, J., 210
Central America: endangered birds of, 11, 16; Antilles, endangered birds of, 13; Cuba, endangered birds of, 13; Puerto Rico, endangered birds of, 13, 47; St. Lucia, endangered birds of, 13; Guatemala, endangered birds of, 16; Trinidad, oilbirds in, 71-72; Bahama Islands, Kirtland's Warbler on, 85,88; Bermuda Islands, Bermuda Petrels on, 93-101; Dominica, parrots on, 266; Mexico, Masked Bobwhites in, 345; Panama, reintroductions on Barro Colorado Island, 380-384; Guatemala, Giant Pied-billed Grebes in, 397-401
Coenocorypha aucklandica. See

Snipe, Chatham Island
Colinus virginianus ridgewayi.
See Bobwhite, Masked
Colorado Division of Wildlife, 169
Competition: techniques for reducing, 6; House Sparrow and Starling vs. Bluebirds, 56; House Sparrow and Starling vs. Purple Martin, 59; as a threat to endangered birds, examples, 77-78; Tropicbirds vs. Bermuda Petrel, 93-102 *passim*; and Redcockaded Woodpeckers, 103-112; Chatham Is. Tits vs. Black Robins, 368; fish vs. Giant Pied-billed Grebe, 397
Conuropsis carolinensis. See Parakeet, Carolina
Condor, California: critical habitat for, 20; nesting sites of, 27; supplemental feeding of, 133, 135-140; food shortage for, 135,138; feeding habits, 137; reproductive success of, 138; in the Sespe Condor Sanctuary, 138; integrated management for, 393-394; failings in management of, 394; mentioned, 281-282, 388, 420, 426, 442
Copsychus sechellarum. See Magpie-robin, Seychelles
Cornell Laboratory of Ornithology, 252, 390
Cowbird, Brown headed: as a threat to Kirtland's Warbler, 86-87; control of, 87
Coyotes: as predators on cranes, 208-211 *passim*
Craig, J., 170
Crandall, L.S., 226
Cranes: supplemental feeding of, 141-148
Crane, Greater Sandhill: in cross-fostering experiments, 201-222.
Crane, Hooded: response to management, 16; supplemental feeding of, 132, 143-144; population size, 143; response to supplemental feeding, 143-144
Crane, Japanese: supplemental

feeding of, 132; population
size, 143
Crane, Mississippi Sandhill:
235, 420, 426
Crane, Sandhill: population
modeling of, 415-417;
mentioned, 393
Crane, Siberian: 141, 146
Crane, Whooping: response to
management, 16; wintering
grounds of, 145; supplemental
feeding of, 145-146; population size, 231; determining
sex of, 236; integrated management of, 393; population
modeling of, 413; mentioned
19, 228, 388, 442
-captive breeding of: 231-
241 passim; handling of eggs,
231-232; rearing chicks, 232-
235; maintenance in captivity,
235; forming compatible pairs,
236-237; photoperiod manipulations, 238; artificial insemination, 238; results
achieved, 239
-cross fostered: 168, 201-
222 passim; banding of, 204-
205, 209; fate of cross-
fostered eggs, 207; survival
of cross-fostered young, 209-
211; movements and distribution of, 211-217 passim; interactions with Sandhill
Cranes, 214-215; activities
of subadults, 217-218; losses
of, 218; interactions between,
218-219; mentioned, 239
Crane, White-naped: response to
management, 16; supplemental
feeding of, 132, 141-143; population size, 143
Crax blumenbachii. See Curassow, Red-billed
Creadion carunculatus. See
Saddleback
Cross-fostering: 168-169;
risks involved in, 168;
of gulls, 168; of Whooping
Cranes, 168-169, 201-222;
of birds of prey, 183-193
passim, 198-199, 356; men-

tioned, 440
Curassow, Red-billed: population
size, 11
Cuthbert, N., 87
Cyanoramphus auriceps forbesi.
See Parakeet, Forbes'
Cyanoramphus novaeselandiae
chathamensis. See Parakeet,
Chatham Island
Cygnus atratus. See Swan, Bewick
Cygnus cygnus buccinator. See
Swan, Trumpeter
Cygnus cygnus cygnus. See Swan,
Whooper
Cyphorhinus arada. See Wren,
Song

Dendrocopus borealis. See Wood-
pecker, Red-cockaded
Dendroica kirtlandii. See Kirt-
land's Warbler
Disease: reducing incidence of,
6; as a threat to endangered
birds, examples of, 78; at feed-
ing stations, risk of, 147; in
captive waterfowl, 248; in cap-
tive parrots, 270; threat to
Aleutian Canada Geese, 337
Dodo: extinction of, 13
Dove, Cloven-feathered: threats
to, 77
Duck, Wood: recovery of, 243
Duck, Hawaiian, 319
Duck, Mexican, 420, 426
Dunston, J., 72

Eagle, Bald: protection for, 21;
use of artificial nesting plat-
forms, 40-43; as predator of
Aleutian Canada Geese, 334; men-
tioned, 27, 150, 420, 426
Eagle, Bonelli's. See Hawk-eagle,
African
Eagle, Golden, 153, 195-196
Eagle, Lesser Spotted, 195-200
passim
Eagle, Spanish Imperial: foster-
ing of, 170, 198-200
Eagle, Verreaux's, 195, 198
Eagle, White-tailed Sea: supple-
mental feeding of in Sweden,
133, 153-158; population size

in Sweden, 149-150; nesting
success in Sweden, 149-150,
156-157; threats to, 150;
conservation of, 150-151;
transfer of eggs and young,
151; winter habits, 151-153;
migration of, 152; mortality
factors, 151-153
Ecosystem: management of, 449,
451
Ectopistes migratorius. See
Pigeon, Passenger
Education: role in integrated
management, 387-396 *passim;*
role in Giant Pied-billed
Grebe conservation, 398-399
Eggs: artificial incubation
of parrot's, 115; double-
clutching, 183-185; foster-
White-tailed Sea Eagle's,
151; fostering Osprey's,
171-174; transportation of
Whooping Crane's, 201-204;
cross-fostering of Whoop-
ing Crane's, 207; manipu-
lation of, 231; hatching
Whooping Crane's, 232;
cross-fostering of Whooping
Crane's, 239
Endangerment: causes of, 3-4,
10; examples of, 9-17; geography of, 11-13; in birds of
the U.S., 20; future problems
of, 450-451
Enderson, J., 170
Erickson, R., 316
Europe: endangered birds of,
11, 15; Eagle Owl reintroduced in, 356
Extinction: of Peregrine Falcon in eastern U.S., 5; of
the Dodo, 13; causes of, 76;
of the Passenger Pigeon, 226;
of the Carolina Parakeet, 226

Falco araea. See Kestrel, Sey-
chelles
Falco mexicanus. See Falcon,
Prairie
Falco peregrinus. See Falcon,
Peregrine
Falco punctatus. See Kestrel,

Mauritius
Falco rusticolus. See Gyrfalcon
Falco sparverius. See Kestrel,
American
Falcon, Peregrine: in eastern
U.S., extinction of, 5; cap-
tive breeding of, 7, 251-262;
nesting sites of, 27, 439;
fostering of, 169, 185-186; in
Alberta, 188-192; reintroduc-
tion of, 359-360, 362; integrated management of, 392;
habitat management for, 423;
migration of, 441; mentioned,
236, 420, 423, 426
Falcon, Prairie: cross-fostering of, 185-186; as foster
parent to Peregrine Falcon,
356
Falconry: as aid to reintroduction, 357-358
Finland: White-tailed Sea
Eagles in, 151, 156
Flamingo, American, 388
Flycatcher, Black Paradise, 13
Flycatcher, Great Crested: nesting boxes for, 59-60
Food: habits of California Condor, 137; habits of Siberian
Crane, 146; habits of Japanese Crested Ibis, 161-164;
habits of Osprey, 173; habits
of Whooping Crane, 209,217;
habits, modification of, 440-
441
-supplemental feeding: as a
management technique, 6; review of, 131-134; of Trumpeter
Swan, 131-132; of Whooper Swan,
132; of Bewick Swan, 132; of
Griffon Vulture, 132-133;
risks involved, 133-134; benefits of, 134; of California
Condor, 135-140; of cranes,
141-148; of White-tailed Sea
Eagles, 153-158; of Japanese
Crested Ibis, 161-164; mentioned, 440-441
Fostering: as a management
technique, 169-170; of Ospreys,
171-174; of birds of prey, 183-
193; of Spanish Imperial Eagle,

198-200; of Masked Bobwhite, 346, 350-352
Fratercula arctica. *See* Puffin, Atlantic
Fyfe, R., 5, 169

Genetics: implications for endangered birds, review of, 275-279; genetic drift, 276, 285-286; the "genetic bottleneck," 276, 281-289; genetic load, 276-277; genetic swamping, 277-278
-genetic diversity: in small populations, 282-284; determination of, 291-292; heterozygosity as a measure of, 292-295; heterozygosity in bird populations, 293-295; genetic distance between populations, 295-300; genetic distance between taxa, 295-300; implications for reintroductions, 298; loss in captive populations, 309-310
-genetic problems: hybridization of Forbes' Parakeet, 16, 278; in captive waterfowl, 247; inbreeding, 275-276; strategies for avoiding, 278-279, 287-289, 305-307; in captive Hawaiian Geese, 319, 341-342
Geronticus eremita. *See* Ibis, Bald
Glaucis dohrnii. *See* Hermit, Hook-billed
Goats: as threat to island birds, 76
Goose, Aleutian Canada: response to management, 16; introduced foxes as threat to, 77, 331-333; recovery plan for, 331-332, 337-338; captive breeding of, 333; reintroduction of, 334, 441; legal protection for, 334-336; recoveries of reintroduced birds, 337; population size, 337; mentioned, 245, 327

Goose, Hawaiian: recovery of, 15; population size, 339-340; habitat of, 340; sanctuary for, 342
-captive breeding: inbreeding problems, 247, 319, 341-342; rearing of young, 341; history of, 340-343
-reintroduction: behavior of released birds, 318; problems encountered, 319; review of program, 339-344; need for monitoring, 344
Goshawk: recovery in Great Britain, 357
Great Britain: swans in 312; aviculturists in, 229; Capercaillie in Scotland, 325; Goshawk in, 357
Grebe, Giant Pied-billed: response to management, 16; introduced fish as a threat to, 77, 397; integrated management of, 391-392, 397-402; threats to, 397-398; legal protection for, 398; public education about, 398-399; preserving habitat of, 399-400; refuge for, 401
Grouse, Sage, 170
Grus americana. *See* Crane, Whooping
Grus canadensis. *See* Crane, Sandhill
Grus japonensis. *See* Crane, Japanese
Grus leucogeranus. *See* Crane, Siberian
Grus monacha. *See* Crane, Hooded
Grus vipio. *See* Crane, White-naped
Gymnogyps californianus. *See* Condor, California
Gyps fulvus. *See* Vulture, Griffon
Gyrfalcon: as foster parent, 188

Habitat: of endangered birds, 10; Kirtland's Warbler's, management of, 85-86, 87-89;

for endangered birds, management of 426-427. *See also* names of specific birds
Haliaeetus albicilla. *See* Eagle, White-tailed Sea
Haliaeetus leucocephalus. *See* Eagle, Bald
Hawaiian Islands: endangered birds of, 9, 12, 15, 76; Hawaiian Goose, 315-320 *passim*, 339-344 *passim*
Hawk-eagle, African, 195,196
Hawk, Ferruginous: as foster parent, 188
Hawk Migration Association of North America, 404
Hawk, Red-tailed: as foster parent, 188; monitoring nesting success of, 405-412 *passim*
Hawk, Swainson's: as foster parent, 188
Heinrich, W., 170
Hemignathus lucidus. *See* Nukupu'u
Hemignathus procorus. *See* Akialoa, Kauai
Henicorhina leucosticta. *See* Wren, White-breasted Wood
Hermit, Hook-billed, 11
Heydt, J., 199
Hieraetus fasciatus. *See* Hawk-eagle, African
Houston, S., 58
Hunting: as a cause of endangerment, 10, 71, 142-144 *passim*, 331, 387-388, 415; as a part of controlling island exotics, 121-128 *passim*; control of, as part of management, 220, 336, 415
Hybridization. *See* Genetics

Iberra, J., 399
Ibis, Bald: nesting sites of, 27, 63-64; nesting colony in Turkey, 61-62; population size, 62-66; conservation of, 63; artificial nesting ledges, 63-64, 67-68; threatened by pesticides, 65; nesting success, 67
Ibis, Japanese Crested: sup-

plemental feeding of, 133, 162-163; natural food of, 161-162; sanctuary for, 162; nesting success, 163; diet in captivity, 163-164
Imprinting: as a problem in cross-fostering, 168, 188, 220; in captive breeding programs, 226, 245, 253, 255, 258, 259, 317; as part of maintaining traditions, 435-443 *passim*
Inbreeding. *See* Genetics
Incubation: artificial, 170, 247
India: endangered birds of, 9, 146
Indian Ocean, islands of: endangered birds of, 11. *See also* names of islands
Institute of Tropical Forestry, 424
International Council for Bird Preservation, 9, 16, 391
International Crane Foundation, 204, 229, 234, 238-240
International Union for the Conservation of Nature and Natural Resources, 9, 226
Introduced animals: as a threat to bluebirds, 56-59; as a cause of endangerment, 76-78; measures for controlling, 79-80; rats as threat to Bermuda Petrel, 93; as threat to island birds, 121-126; on islands, controlling, 121-128
Islands: endangered birds on: 12-13, 76-79, 121-122; inter-island transfers as a management technique, 15, 323, 356-357, 365-372; extinction of birds on, 121; introduced animals as a threat on, 121-127; theory of island zoogeography, 379, 449, 451
Israel: Griffon Vultures in, 132

Japan: winter feeding of cranes, 132, 141-148; Japanese Crested Ibis in, 161-164; Aleutian Canada Geese wintering in, 338
Jones, R. 333

Kakapo: population size, 12; interisland transfer of, 15, 367
Kepler, C., 49
Kestrel, American: nesting success of, 405-412
Kestrel, Mauritius: population size, 12; introduced monkeys as threat to, 77, 439; "tradition shift" in nesting sites of, 439
Kestrel, Seychelles: introduced Barn Owl as threat to, 77; interisland transfers of, 356-357
Kirby, E., 266
Kite, Black: as foster parents to eagles, 198
Kite, Everglades: nesting sites of, 27-28; nest predators as threat to, 77
Kokako: status of, 12
Koloa: status of, 16
Kuyt, E., 204

Lane, J., 58
Laws: protecting endangered birds, 18-24 passim, 89, 388, 391, 421-427 passim, 429-434 passim; as part of integrated management, 489
Longevity: of Bermuda Petrels, 97; of captive birds, 228
Loxops coccinea. See Akepa

Madagascar: destruction of habitat on, 11, 12; endangered birds of, 15
Magpie-robin, Seychelles: status of, 13; introduced animals as threat to, 77
Management of endangered species: goals of, 3; "clinical ornithology," 4-5, active vs. passive, 13-15, results of, 15-17; value of, 447-451; relationship to ecology, 448-449; future of, 449-451
-integrated: key elements of, 389-391; research as part

of, 389; legal protection as part of, 389; education as part of, 389-390; habitat management as part of, 390; population modeling as part of, 390; population monitoring as part of, 390; coordinated planning as part of, 390-391; examples of, 391-394; Recovery Plan approach to, 429-434; of Giant Pied-billed Grebe, 391-392, 397-402
Margarops fuscatus. See Thrasher, Pearly-eyed
Martin, Purple: nesting boxes for, 59
Mauritius: endangered birds of, 12, 13; conservation on, 391
Merton, D., 370
Michigan Audubon Society, 86,87
Michigan Department of Natural Resources, 36, 87
Migration: of White-tailed Sea Eagles, 152; of cross-fostered Whooping Cranes, 211-216 passim; of Aleutian Canada Goose, 331-338 passim, 441; modification of, 441
Milvus migrans. See Kite, Black
Moho braccatus. See O'o, Kauai
Mongoose: as a threat to island birds, 76
Morocco: Bald Ibis populations in, 66
Mowbray, L., 94
Musselman, T., 58
Myiarchus crinitus. See Flycatcher, Great Crested

National Audubon Society: sponsor of Colonial Bird Register and North American Nest Record Program, 390; sponsor of Christmas Bird Counts, 390, 403; sponsor of Breeding Bird Census and Breeding Bird Survey, 403; publishers of American Birds, 404; mentioned, 387, 388, 424
National Parks. See Reserves
National Wildlife Federation, 424
Nene. See Goose, Hawaiian

Neophema pulchella. *See* Parakeet, Turquoise
Nesoenas mayeri. *See* Pigeon, Mauritius Pink
Nest-sites: alleviating scarcity of, 6, 30-32; scarcity for endangered birds, examples, 27-33 *passim*; competition for, 29-30, 56; of Puerto Rican Parrot, 47-53; of Bald Ibis, 63-64; of Oilbirds, 71-72; of Bermuda Petrel, 94; of Red-cockaded Woodpecker, 104-109; of captive waterfowl, 246; selection of, examples, 438-439; selection of, modifying, 439-440; of Mauritius Kestrel, 439
-artificial: providing, as a management technique, 629-630; for Ospreys, 35-40, 171; for Bald Eagles, 40-43; for Puerto Rican Parrots, 49; 115-118; for bluebirds, 56-57; for Purple Martins, 59; for Great Crested Flycatchers, 60; for Bald Ibises, 63-64, 67-68; for Oilbirds, 72; for Peregrine Falcons, 439
New Mexico Department of Game and Fish, 169, 211
New York Zoological Society, 71, 228
New Zealand: extinct and endangered birds of, 11, 12, 15, 76; controlling introduced animals in, 121-126; translocation of endangered birds in, 323, 365-371; introduced gamebirds in, 325-326
New Zealand Forest Service, 125
New Zealand Wildlife Service, 15, 16, 121-126, 365, 367
Niche: genetic aspect of, 435-436; traditional aspect of, 435-436; modification of, as a management technique, 435-443
Noegel, R., 266, 267

North America: endangered birds of, 11, 15; introduction of exotics to, 324. *See also* United States
Norway: White-tailed Sea Eagles in, 151
Notornis mantelli. *See* Takahe
Nukupu'u: status of, 12

Oilbird: scarcity of nest sites, 71-72; artificial ledges for, 72
O'o, Kauai: status of, 12
Osprey: effect of pesticides on, 171; population on the Atlantic coast, 171-182 *passim*; food availability as a limiting factor, 172; nesting success of, 173, 405-412 *passim*, feeding ecology of, 173; dispersal movements of, 175; integrated management of, 392
-transfers: egg transfers, 171-174; nestling transfers, 171-174; survival of transferred eggs and nestlings, 174-177; effect of transfers on population, 178-180
-nesting platforms: use by Ospreys, 35-40, 171; nesting success on, 37-39; value in management, 40
Owl, Barn: threat to endemic birds in Seychelles, 77-78; reintroduction by hacking, 359
Owl, Blewitt's: rediscovery of, 9
Owl, Eagle: reintroduction of, 323, 355-363 *passim*
Owl, Great Horned: threat to reintroduced Peregrine Falcons, 190, 359
Owl, Laughing: status of, 12
Owl, Seychelles: competition with introduced Barn Owl, 77

Pacific Ocean, islands of: endangered birds of, 9, 11
Parakeet, Carolina, 226
Parakeet, Chatham Island: genetic swamping of, 16, 278

Parakeet, Forbes': control of, 16

Parakeet, Turquoise: management of, 16

Parasites: as threats to endangered birds, 6, 78; Brown-headed Cowbird as brood parasite on Kirtland's Warbler, 87; of Japanese Crested Ibis, 163; in captive birds, 317

Parrot, Amazon: captive breeding of, 263-271; illegal taking of, 268; diets in captivity, 270; disease in captivity, 270. See also names of specific Amazon Parrots

Parrot, Eastern Ground: response to management, 16

Parrot, Puerto Rican: response to management, 16

Parrot, Puerto Rican: response to management, 16; nest sites of, 27; population size, 47-48; causes of decline, 48; nest-site scarcity 47-53; providing artificial nest boxes, 49-50, 115-118; nesting success, 51; competitors as a threat to, 77-78; nest predation by Pearly-eyed Thrasher, 113-114; guarding nests, 115; artificial incubation of eggs, 115; captive breeding of, 263; mentioned, 113-120 passim, 420, 426, 448

Passer domesticus. See Sparrow, House

Peregrine Fund, 169, 229, 251-261 passim

Pesticides: as threat to endangered birds, 10; as threat to Bald Ibis, 65; as threat to White-tailed Sea Eagle, 133; as threat to Japanese Crested Ibis, 161; effects on Ospreys, 171, 174; threat to Brown Pelicans, 174; mentioned, 150,202

Petroica australis. See Robin, South Island

Petroica traversi. See Robin, Black

Pelican, Brown: pesticides as threat to, 174; reintroduction of, 174; mentioned, 420

Pesoporus wallicus. See Parrot, Eastern Ground

Petrel, Bermuda: response to management, 16, 100-101; tropicbirds as threats to, 77, 93, 96-97; rats as threats to, 93; rediscovery of, 93; nesting sites of, 94; development of nest baffler, 94-96; breeding cycle of, 96-97; artificial burrows for, 98-101; expansion of nesting habitat for, 101; mentioned, 93-102 passim, 448

Phaeornis obscurus rutha. See Thrush, Molokai

Phaeton lepturus. See Tropicbird, White-tailed

Phasianus colchicus. See Pheasant, Ring-necked

Pheasant, Ring-necked: reintroduction of, 325; mentioned, 4

Phoenicopterus ruber. See Flamingo, American

Photoperiod. See captive breeding

Pigeon, Mauritius Pink: status of, 12

Pigeon, Passenger, 226

Piopio: status of, 12

Pitcher, E., 170

Plover, New Zealand Shore: interisland transfer of, 15, 367. 370; threats to, 77

Podylimbus gigas. See Grebe, Giant Pied-billed

Population dynamics: monitoring long-term fluctuations, 403-412; programs for monitoring, 403-405

Population modeling: as part of integrated management, 390; value in management of endangered birds, 390, 413-415, 417; of endangered birds, examples, 413-415, 417; analytical vs. deterministic models, 414

Pough, R., 94
Predation: as threat to endangered birds, examples of, 6, 77; threat to bluebirds, 57; threat to island birds, 76; as threat to Hawaiian birds, 319; foxes as threat to Aleutian Canada Goose, 331-334 *passim*; as threat to Puerto Rican Parrots, 113-114; Coyotes as threat to Whooping Cranes, 208-211 *passim*; threat to reintroduced Peregrine Falcons, 359; monkeys as threat to Mauritius Kestrel, 439
Preserves. *See* Reserves
Progne subis. See Martin, Purple
Protection, legal: for Bald Eagle, 21; for Aleutian Canada Goose, 334-336; birds saved by, examples of 387-388; as part of integrated management, 388; for Giant Pied-billed Grebe, 398
Pterodroma cahow. See Petrel, Bermuda
Puffin, Atlantic: status in Maine, 373; reintroduction of, 373-377; survival of reintroduced birds, 376; mentioned, 439

r- and *K*-selection: mentioned, 3, 277, 413, 449
Radabaugh, B., 87
Rail, Barred-wing: rediscovery of, 9
Rail, Lord Howe Wood: status of, 12
Rail, Yuma Clapper, 420
Raphus cucullatus. See Dodo
Rallus longirostris yumanensis. See Rail, Yuma Clapper
Rallus poecilopterus. See Rail, Barred-wing
Rallus sylvestris. See Rail, Lord Howe Wood
Rats: as threat to island birds, 76-78, 81
Recovery Plans: for California

Condor, 20, 394; for Yellow-shouldered Blackbird, 20; description of, 22, 429-430; for Kirtland's Warbler, 89; for Peregrine Falcon, 169, 392; for Aleutian Canada Goose, 331-338 *passim*; for Masked Bobwhite, 345; as an example of integrated management, 391; objectives of, 430; preparation of, 430-432; problems with, 434; value of, 434; mentioned, 429-434 *passim*
Red Data Book: mentioned, 3,9, 13, 122, 199, 450
Refuges. *See* Reserves
Reintroductions: of Brown Pelicans, 174; genetic aspects of, 298; of captive-reared Hawaiian Geese, 318-320, 323, 339-344; review of, 323-329; of Eagle Owls, 323, 355-363 *passim*; island colonists as natural examples of, 324; of exotic birds, examples of, 325-326; requirements for success, 326-328; mortality in released birds, 327; fitness of released birds, 327-328; monitoring released bird, 328; of Aleutian Canada Geese, 334, 337; of Masked Bobwhites, 345-354; of birds of prey, 355-363; of Peregrine Falcons, 358-360; of Barn Owls, 359; interisland transfers, 365-372; of Atlantic Puffins, 373-377; of tropical wrens, 379-384; into "habitat islands," 379-384; theoretical aspects of, 383-384
Reserves: Monte Vista National Wildlife Refuge, 20, 211-220 *passim*, 333; National Wildlife Refuge system, endangered species on, 22, 23; Pelican Island Refuge, 23; Luquillo Forest, Puerto Rico, 31, 47, 48, 114, 116; Huron National Forest, 87; Francis Marion National Forest, 103,424; Noxubee National Wildlife Refuge, 103-109 *passim*; Hawaii Volcanoes National Park,

125, 340; Red Rock Lakes National Wildlife Refuge, 131;
Sespe Condor Sanctuary, 135-
137; Hopper Mountain National
Wildlife Refuge, 136; Aransas
National Wildlife Refuge, 145,
201, 231, 393; Keoladeo Ghana
Bird Sanctuary, India, 146;
Wood Buffalo National Park,
201-220 *passim*, 231, 236,
238, 240, 393; Grays Lake
National Wildlife Refuge,
201-220 *passim*, 239, 240,
393; Bosque del Apache National Wildlife Refuge, 201-220
passim; Bernardo State Wildlife Management Area, 211,
217; Ouray National Wildlife
Refuge, 211-220 *passim*; Malheur National Wildlife Refuge,
220; Pohakuloa Propagation
Center, 318, 340, 343; Haleakala Crater National Park,
318, 343-344; Aleutian Islands National Wildlife Refuge, 331; San Luis National
Wildlife Refuge, 334; Snake
River Birds of Prey Natural
Area, 350, 425; Deschutes National Forest, 392; National
Giant Grebe Refuge, Guatemala,
401; U.S. National Forest System, endangered species on,
419; White Mountain National
Forest, 425; Green Mountain
National Forest, 425; San
Simeon Cienega Mexican Duck
Management Area, 425
Reunion Island: endangered
birds of, 13
Ripley, S., 261, 243
Robins, Black: status of, 12;
interisland transfer of, 15,
365-372 *passim*; population
size, 365-366; habitat manage-
ment for, 368; mentioned, 327
Robin, Scarlet-breasted: introduced ants as predators of, 77
Robin, South Island: interisland
transfer of, 365
Rodrigues Island: endangered
birds of, 13

Rostrhamus sociabilis. *See*
Kite, Everglades

Saddlebacks: reintroduction
of, 323, 367, 370
Sanctuaries. *See* Reserves
Sceloglaux albifacies. *See* Owl,
Laughing
Scott, P., 243
Scrubbird, Noisey: response to
management, 16
Seychelles: endangered birds
of, 13; translocation of en-
dangered birds, 15, 356-357;
management of Cousin Island,
16, 391
Shipman, H., 340
Sialia currocoides. *See*
Bluebird, Mountain
Sialia mexicana. *See* Blue-
bird, Western
Sialia sialis. *See* Bluebird,
Eastern
Smithsonian Tropical Research
Institute, 380
Snipe, Chatham Island: inter-
island transfer of, 15, 367,
370
Snow, D., 71
South America: endangered birds
of, 11, 15, 16; forest destruc-
tion in, 11, 269; Amazon par-
rots of, 267
Southeast Asia: endangered birds
of, 11, 16; forest destruction
in, 11, 16
Spain: Griffon Vultures in, 132;
Spanish Imperial Eagle in, 198-
200
Sparrow, Dusky Seaside, 22
Sparrow, House: as competitor
of bluebirds, 56
Spoonbill, Roseate, 388
Starling, European: as competi-
tor for nest sites, 56
Steatornis caripensis. *See* Oil-
birds
Strigops habroptilus. *See* Kakapo
Sturnus vulgaris. *See* Starling,
European
Swan, Bewick: supplemental feed-
ing of, 132

Swan, Trumpeter: recovery of, 15; supplemental feeding of, 131-132, 144

Swan, Whooper: supplemental feeding of, 132

Sweden: White-tailed Sea Eagle in, 149-159

Swedish Museum of Natural History, 149

Swedish Society for Conservation of Nature, 149, 153, 156

Takahe: response to management, 16

Teal, Laysan: recovery of, 278, 339

Temple, S., 281, 419

Terpsiphone corvina. See Flycatcher, Black Paradise

Thinornis novaeseelandiae. See Plover, New Zealand Shore

Thorsell, R., 94

Thrasher, Pearly-eyed: as nest predator on Puerto Rican Parrots, 113-114; nesting boxes for, 115-120

Thrush, Molokai: rediscovery of, 9

Tinbergen, N., 167

Tit, Chatham Island: as a competitor of Black Robin, 368

Trefry, P., 261

Trichocichla rufa. See Warbler, Long-legged

Tricholimnas sylvestris. See Rail, Lord Howe Wood

Tropicbird, White-tailed: as competitor of Bermuda Petrel, 93-102 *passim*

Turkey: Bald Ibis population of, 61-68

Turnagra capensis. See Piopio

United Kingdom Science Research Council, 247

United States: Trumpeter Swans in Alaska, 15; Ospreys in Michigan, 35-43; Ospreys in Chesapeake Bay, 36, 39; Kirtland's Warbler in Michigan, 85-89; Trumpeter Swan in Montana, 131-132; Ospreys in New England, 171-181; Aleutian Canada Goose in Aleutian Islands, 331-338

U.S. Government: Fish and Wildlife Service, 18-23 *passim;* Office of Endangered Species, 19-24 *passim,* 48; National Fish and Wildlife Health Laboratory, 218; Patuxent Wildlife Research Center, 19, 20, 31, 201-220 *passim;* 229, 231-240 *passim,* 316,317, 333, 393

-Forest Service: 48, 87, 169, 392, 419-427 *passim,* 429

-Bureau of Land Management: 169, 392, 419-427 *passim,* 429

-Department of Agriculture: 267,419

-National Park Service: 125, 429

-Federal Aviation Administration: 427

-National Marine Fisheries Service: 429

-Department of Defense: 430

-Atomic Energy Commission: 332

U.S.S.R.: Cranes in, 142, 145; White-tailed Sea Eagles in, 156

Vulture, Griffon: supplemental feeding of, 132-133

Waldrapp. *See* Ibis, Bald

Warbler, Bachman's, 420,423

Warbler, Kirtland's: response to management, 16, 88; habitat requirements of, 85-86; population size, 86-87; cowbird parasitism of, 86-87; possible threats to, 88-89; recovery plan for, 89; mentioned, 315, 420, 423, 426

Warbler, Long-legged: rediscovery of, 9

Warbler, Seychelles Brush: management of, 16

Waterfowl: captive breeding of, 243-249. *See also* names of specific birds and captive breeding

Weaver, J., 261

Weka, 370
White-eye, Seychelles:
threats to, 77
Wildfowl Trust, 229, 243,
316, 340, 342
Willis, E., 382
Wingate, D., 79
Wisconsin Alumni Research
Foundation, 401
Woodpecker, Ivory-billed,
388
Woodpecker, Red-cockaded:
competitors for cavities of,
78, 109-110; characteristics
of cavities, 104; cavity enlargement by other woodpeckers, 104-106, 108-109; use of
cavities by other animals,
106-108; cavity tree dispersion, significance of, 109;
management suggestions for,
110-111; habitat management
for, 426-427; mentioned, 420,
423, 426
World Wildlife Fund, 48, 72,
149, 162
Wren, New Zealand Bush: status
of, 12
Wren, Song: reintroduction on-

to Barro Colorado Island,
379-384 *passim*
Wren, Stead's Bush: interisland
transfer of, 367, 370
Wren, White-breasted Wood: reintroduction onto Barro Colorado Island, 379-384 *passim*

Xenicus longipes. See Wren, New
Zealand Bush and Wren, Stead's
Bush

Yealland, J., 342

Zimmerman, D., 4
Zoos: Basel Zoo, 66, 164; New
York Zoological Society, 71,
228; Melbourne Zoo, 253; role
in endangered bird management,
229, 303-313 *passim;* Jersey
Wildlife Preservation Trust,
229, 266; Houston Zoo, 265;
San Diego Zoo, 265, 268; London Zoo, 267; American Association of Zoological Parks
and Aquariums, 303, 306; International Species Inventory
System, 303, 306; Honolulu Zoo,
318

MANUFACTURED BY INTER-COLLEGIATE PRESS, INC.
SHAWNEE MISSION, KANSAS

Library of Congress Cataloging in Publication Data
Symposium on Management Techniques for Preserving En-
    dangered Birds, University of Wisconsin — Madison,
    1977.
    Endangered birds.
    Sponsored by the U. S. Fish and Wildlife Service et al.
    Includes bibliographical references and index.
    1. Rare birds — Congresses. 2. Birds, Protection
of Congresses.   I.   Temple, Stanley A., 1946–
II. United States. Fish and Wildlife Service.
III. Title.
QL676.7.S95 1977   639'.97'82   77-91060
ISBN 0-299-07520-6

British Library Cataloging in Publication Data
Symposium on Management Techniques for
    Preserving Endangered Birds, University of
    Wisconsin-Madison, 1977
    Endangered birds.
    1. Birds, Protection of — Congresses
    2. Rare birds — Congresses
    I. Title. II. Temple, Stanley A
    639'.97'82   QL676.5
    ISBN 0-85664-831-0